# FROM Emergency TO Confrontation

# FROM Emergency TO Confrontation

## The New Zealand Armed Forces in Malaya and Borneo 1949–1966

CHRISTOPHER PUGSLEY

Published in association with
the Ministry for Culture and Heritage

OXFORD
UNIVERSITY PRESS

*To the members of the New Zealand armed forces who served in South-East Asia between 1949 and 1989, and their families.*

*'I see them there in the sun, figures of our time, unhurried, carrying their guns.'*

W. J. POMEROY, *THE FOREST*[1]

*'You who know war in a romantic dream, or in the sob-stories of newspapers, might imagine that it is only the thunder of bombardment or the terrors of the charge which breaks a soldier's will and manhood; but the slow-burning acid of monotony and sterile days can be as bad or worse. You live constantly with a small fear that can never be spoken, and never become real, but can never be dispelled.'*

JOHN HEPWORTH, *THE LONG GREEN SHORE*[2]

1 W. J. Pomeroy, *The Forest*, New York, 1963, p. 14, quoted in Keith Buchanan, *Out of Asia*, Sydney University Press, Sydney, 1968, p. 56.
2 John Hepworth, *The Long Green Shore*, Picador, Sydney, 1995, pp. 116–17.

253 Normanby Road, South Melbourne, Victoria 3205, Australia

Oxford University Press is a department of the University of Oxford. It furthers the University's objective of excellence in research, scholarship, and education by publishing worldwide in

Oxford New York

Auckland Bangkok Buenos Aires Cape Town Chennai
Dar es Salaam Delhi Hong Kong Istanbul Karachi Kolkata
Kuala Lumpur Madrid Melbourne Mexico City Mumbai Nairobi
São Paulo Shanghai Taipei Tokyo Toronto

OXFORD is a trade mark of Oxford University Press in the UK and in certain other countries


First published 2003



National Library of New Zealand
Cataloguing-in-Publication data

Pugsley, Christopher.
From emergency to confrontation: the New Zealand armed forces in Malaya and Borneo 1949-1966 / Christopher Pugsley.

Includes bibliographical references and index.
ISBN 0 19 558453 8

1. Malaya—History—Malayan Emergency, 1948-1960—Participation, New Zealand. 2. New Zealand—Armed Forces—Foreign service—Malaysia—Malaya. 3. New Zealand—Armed Forces—Foreign service—Borneo. 4. Borneo—History, Military. I. Title.

959.504—dc21

Cover design by Patrick Cannon
Typeset by Cannon Typesetting
Printed in China through the Bookmaker International Ltd.

# *Contents*

## Appendices

# *Maps*

# *Preface*

This story of the eighteen eventful years between 1949 and 1966 describes New Zealand's growing military commitment to South-East Asia. It was a time when most New Zealanders believed that the communist threat was a real one that must be met by a national commitment to Western security arrangements. This commitment led to elements of all three services being stationed overseas in peacetime for the first time in New Zealand's history. In hindsight, New Zealand's involvement in South Vietnam overshadows all the other conflicts in which it played a part during the 1950s and 1960s. Yet it was New Zealand's commitment to the British Commonwealth Far East Strategic Reserve in Singapore and Malaya from 1955 that had the defining influence on the evolution of all three services in the second half of the twentieth century, shaping the role, organisation and equipping of New Zealand's armed forces until their withdrawal in 1989.

New Zealanders played a small but significant part in the Malayan Emergency, during which British and Commonwealth forces fought against the Malayan Races Liberation Army, the armed force of the Malayan Communist Party, between 1948 and 1960 on the Malay Peninsula, and also in Confrontation, an undeclared war initiated by Indonesia in an attempt to destabilise the new Federation of Malaysia between 1962 and 1966. The latter conflict involved largely British and Malaysian forces, with contributions from Australia and New Zealand, in operations on both the Malay Peninsula and along the frontier between the North Borneo territories and Indonesian Kalimantan on the island of Borneo.

New Zealand made a much greater contribution of military resources to the Malayan Emergency, and to Confrontation, than it did to South Vietnam. Yet these two conflicts have become New Zealand's forgotten military involvements of the twentieth century, so much so that, in the pamphlet on eligibility for war-related pensions issued in the 1990s by the Department of Social Welfare, Confrontation was not included in the list of conflicts in which New Zealand has participated. Measured by the numbers killed and wounded, these were not major conflicts; they are dwarfed by New Zealand's contributions in two world wars. Yet on the ground, each involved weeks or months of patrolling in extremes of climate and country which varied from fetid swamps to tortuous rainforest-clad mountain ranges. The physical and mental demands that this placed on those involved were real and long-lasting, but remain largely unappreciated by the general public. These conflicts, like all wars, left unseen, often permanent, scars on those who fought in them.

Each episode in this story is more deserving of a book rather than a chapter. Yet, even within these limitations, this volume unashamedly endeavours to capture the detail of what it was like to be a member of the New Zealand Army, RNZN or RNZAF; whether moving stealthily on foot as part of a patrol through tropical rainforest, flying above its endless green canopy, servicing aircraft on the flight lines in Singapore, or serving on an RNZN warship on station with the Far East Fleet.

On the ground there was the monotony of platoon-strength patrols for weeks on end in the vast expanse of rain-forested highlands, the rare contacts with the enemy signalled by a burst of fire over in seconds, but perhaps followed up by members of the Battalion tracking team. Balanced against this was the experience of garrison life, and seeing the sights or visiting the bars of Kuala Lumpur, Ipoh or Malacca. It is also the story of the families who accompanied their service spouses to Malaya or Singapore. All this was part of introducing a microcosm of New Zealand society to the countries and cultures of Asia.

This is a volume of official history which tells the story of these years in the context of New Zealand defence and foreign policy. But it is 'official' only in the sense that this status gave the author access to documents which would otherwise have been closed to him, as many had not yet been released to archives. It is a warts and all story that does not hesitate to pass judgement and comment on how effectively New Zealanders performed. It is also a story of personal and group endeavour and achievement against a background of ongoing government parsimony. Many people have helped and advised me during the writing of this volume, but its judgements and conclusions, errors and omissions, are my own.

This volume has been a long time in the writing, and I owe a debt of gratitude to the many individuals and institutions who have assisted me over the past ten years. The then Secretary of Defence, Denis McLean, originally suggested the project; Lieutenant-General Sir John Mace, as Chief of Defence Staff, commissioned it; and he and his successors have waited patiently for this outcome. The supervisory committee under Paul Sinclair, including Ian McGibbon and John Crawford, gave the encouragement, advice, patience and steel needed to bring it to publication. A similar debt is owed to Jock Phillips, Claudia Orange and Bronwyn Dalley of the Historical Branch of the Department of Internal Affairs (now the History Group, Ministry for Culture and Heritage) over the course of the project. I thank David Green, Alison Carew and Simon Cauchi for their editorial expertise. I am indebted to Julie Keenan for checking references, and to Clas Chamberlain for checking names. John Crawford obtained the photographs, the maps were drawn by Craig MacAlpine and Pat Sargison compiled the index.

I am grateful to Victoria University of Wellington for appointing me as Writer in Residence during 1994, which assisted in the drafting of this manuscript. I am also grateful for my time as a Senior Lecturer in the Department of Classics, History and Religion at the University of New England, Armidale, New South Wales. It was during these years that the draft was finally shaped into a story.

Listed in the bibliography are those who gave up their time to be interviewed about their experiences in those years, or who provided letters, manuscripts, diaries or photos; all have my thanks. My only regret is that so much of what they told me could not be included in the final manuscript. However, their personal accounts provided the atmosphere of and gave a context to the times which are central to the story. Master copies of the interview tapes have been deposited with the Oral History Centre within the Alexander Turnbull Library at the National Library of New Zealand.

I am grateful to the principals and staffs of the following institutions in New Zealand for their invaluable assistance: Archives New Zealand, Wellington; Oral History Centre, Alexander Turnbull Library, National Library of New Zealand; 1RNZIR Museum, Linton Camp; NZ SAS Group Archives, Hobsonville; Kippenberger Archives and Library, Queen Elizabeth II Army Memorial

Museum, Waiouru; Base Records, New Zealand Defence Force, Wellington; RNZE Museum, Linton Camp; Wellington Central Public Library; Ministry of Foreign Affairs and Trade; Auckland Institute and Museum; and the Victoria University of Wellington Library.

I am particularly indebted to: Carolyn Carr and the ever-helpful staff of the Defence Library, Wellington; Lieutenant-Commander Peter Dennerly and the staff of the RNZN Museum, Devonport, Auckland; and Thérèse Angelo, Research Officer, and Mathew O'Sullivan, Keeper of Photographs, at the RNZAF Museum, Wigram. I wish to thank the typists of Headquarters New Zealand Defence Force for transcribing the thousands of pages of interviews from cassette tape. This alone made possible the daunting task of assessing and synthesising the many interviews listed in the bibliography. I also owe special thanks to the Registrar and his ever-willing staff in the Registry, Headquarters New Zealand Defence Force, and in particular Ngaire 'Cookie' Swinton and Tony Williams, who always managed to ferret out the files that I was searching for.

I am equally grateful to the following overseas institutions: Australian Archives, Mitchell, ACT; Australian War Memorial, Canberra; Dixson Library, University of New England, Armidale, NSW; Royal United Services Institute of New South Wales, Sydney; Australian Defence Force Academy Library, Canberra; Fiji National Archives, Suva; Fiji Military Forces Archives, Queen Elizabeth Barracks, Suva; National Library of Malaysia, Kuala Lumpur; National Library of Singapore, Singapore; Public Record Office, Kew, London; Imperial War Museum, London; Ministry of Defence Library, Old Scotland Yard, London; Prince Consort's Library, Aldershot; and Royal Military Academy Library, Sandhurst. Miss Alex Ward and her team at Army Historical Branch in the Ministry of Defence, particularly John Harding, provided me with an office and made me feel at home during my research in the United Kingdom. I am indebted to the historical branches of all three services for providing access to campaign narratives and other unreleased material relating to New Zealand operations in Malaysia during Confrontation.

I am very grateful to the many people who so willingly and often painstakingly commented on the draft in its various forms. These include: Bill Barnes, Brigadier John 'Blackie' Burns, Brigadier Ian 'Buzz' Burrows, Clas Chamberlain, Peter Cooper, John Crawford, Lieutenant-Commander Peter Dennerly, David Duxbury, Denis Fairfax, Colonel Peter Fry, Major-General Ken Gordon, Jeffrey

Grey, Brigadier Bob Gurr, Lieutenant-Colonel John Hall, Colin Hanson, Squadron Leader Paul Harrison, Lieutenant-Colonel Peter Hotop, Major Ray Hurle, W. David McIntyre, Air Commodore Stuart McIntyre, Lieutenant-General Don McIvor, Graeme McKay, Lieutenant-Colonel Stan McKeon, Colonel David Maloney, Colonel Owen Mann, Robert Mann, Major Roly Manning, Lieutenant-Colonel Eru Manuera, Lieutenant-Colonel Tony Mataira, Brigadier John Mawson, Major Bill Meldrum, Julia Millen, Brigadier Kim and Mrs Anne Morrison, Helen McNaught, Noel O'Dwyer, Lieutenant-Colonel David Ogilvy, Colonel Roger Pearce, Major-General Piers Reid, Colonel Frank Rennie, Lieutenant-Colonel Max Ritchie, Jim Rolfe, Rear-Admiral Michael Saull, Brigadier Lin Smith, Lieutenant-General Sir Leonard Thornton, Brigadier Ian Thorpe, Group Captain Fred Tucker, Group Captain Geoff Wallingford, and Lieutenant-Colonel Bryan Wells.

I am also grateful for the hospitality and assistance that I have received from so many people during my research travels both within New Zealand and overseas. These include: Maurice Shadbolt and Elspeth Sandys in Auckland; Bill, Morf and Ann McGough, who provided a room with a view in London; General Sir David Fraser, Christina Goulter, Commodore John Leonard, General Sir John Mogg, Robert O'Neill, Tom O'Reilly, Mike Pugh, Viscount John Slim, Ian 'Tanky' Smith, Rex and Eileen Wait, Howard and Clare Walker, J. J. West, Mike Wicksteed, Lieutenant-Colonel John Woodhouse, and Alexander Zervoudakis in the United Kingdom; Wayne and Yoshika Anker, John Bishoprek, Michael Chilton, John Granville, Maurice Cheong, Leong Chi Who, and William Pillay in Malaysia and Singapore; Lieutenant-General John Coates, Peter Dennis, Peter Edwards, Ashley Ekins, Bill Gammage, Greg Pemberton, and Peter Stanley and his colleagues at the Australian War Memorial. I am grateful to Moreen Dee for her hospitality, for conducting research on my behalf in the Australian Archives, and for insights offered from her own work in this area.

I would like to acknowledge my debt to Laurie Barber, a pioneer in the study and teaching of military history in New Zealand, who from our first meeting in 1RNZIR in 1971 encouraged me to pursue my interest in military history, and continues to do so. I would also like to thank Maurice Shadbolt, who encouraged me to write and who, by his own example, showed me the dedication and discipline needed to become a writer.

In particular I owe an enormous debt to three people who have encouraged me and provided sound advice at critical times throughout this project: 'Buzz'

Burrows, Bill Meldrum, and my good friend Ray Grover, each of whom has my thanks.

I wish to acknowledge my debt to my family: Joanna, Susan, David and Dylan, but most especially of all to Deanna, who made sure that I finished what I started.

CHRISTOPHER PUGSLEY
ROYAL MILITARY ACADEMY, SANDHURST

# *Abbreviations*

| | |
|---|---|
| **2IC** | second in command |
| **2NZEF** | Second New Zealand Expeditionary Force |
| **AB** | Able Seaman |
| **ABRI** | Angkatan Bersenjata Republic Indonesia (Indonesian Armed Forces) |
| **AC1** | Aircraftman First Class |
| **AD** | air despatch; Army Department |
| **ADF** | automatic direction finder |
| **AGS** | Army General Staff |
| **ALO** | Air Liaison Officer |
| **AMDA** | Anglo-Malayan Defence Agreement |
| **ANZAM** | Australia, New Zealand and Malaya |
| **ANZUK** | Australian, New Zealand, United Kingdom |
| **ANZUS** | Australia, New Zealand and United States |
| **AOC** | Air Officer Commanding |
| **ASW** | anti-submarine warfare |
| **AWF** | Armed Work Force (Malayan Races Liberation Army); sometimes referred to as Armed Work Committee (AWC) |
| **AWOL** | absent without (official) leave |
| **BCM** | Branch Committee Member (Malayan Races Liberation Army) |
| **BCOF** | British Commonwealth Occupation Force |
| **BDCC(FE)** | British Defence Coordinating Committee (Far East) |
| **BDLS** | British Defence Liaison Staff |
| **BEM** | British Empire Medal |

| | |
|---|---|
| **BRIMOB** | Police Mobile Brigade, Indonesia |
| **BT** | German-built Jaguar-class fast patrol boats of the Indonesian Navy |
| **CAS** | Chief of the Air Staff |
| **CBE** | Commander of the Order of the British Empire |
| **CBF Borneo** | Commander British Forces Borneo |
| **CCO** | 'Clandestine Communist Organisation' |
| **CDS** | Chief of Defence Staff |
| **CEP** | captured enemy personnel |
| **CGS** | Chief of the General Staff |
| **CIGS** | Chief of Imperial General Staff |
| **CINCFE** | Commander in Chief Far East |
| **CMT** | compulsory military training |
| **CNS** | Chief of Naval Staff |
| **CO** | Colonial Office; Commanding Officer |
| **COMBRITBOR** | Commander British Forces Borneo |
| **Comd** | Commander |
| **COMLANDBOR** | Commander Land Forces Borneo |
| **COMWEL** | Commonwealth |
| **COS** | Chief of Staff |
| **Coy** | Company |
| **CPO** | Chief Petty Officer; Chief Police Officer |
| **CQMS** | Company Quartermaster Sergeant |
| **CRE** | Commander Royal Engineers |
| **CSM** | Company Sergeant Major |
| **CSR** | Commonwealth Strategic Reserve |
| **CT[O]** | communist terrorist [organisation] |
| **DAAG** | Deputy Assistant Adjutant-General |
| **DAQMG** | Deputy Adjutant and Quartermaster-General |
| **DCM** | Distinguished Conduct Medal; District Committee Member (Malayan Races Liberation Army) |
| **DFC** | Distinguished Flying Cross |
| **DLI** | Durham Light Infantry |
| **DSC** | Distinguished Service Cross |
| **DSM** | Distinguished Service Medal |
| **DSO** | Distinguished Service Order |
| **DWEC** | District War Executive Committee |
| **DZ** | drop zone |
| **ED** | Efficiency Decoration (New Zealand Territorial Force) |
| **ER** | Emergency Regulation |

| | |
|---|---|
| **FAC** | Forward Air Controller |
| **FARELF** | Far East Land Forces |
| **FE** | Far East |
| **FEAF** | Far East Air Force |
| **FESR** | Far East Strategic Reserve |
| **FIR** | Fiji Infantry Regiment |
| **Flt** | Flight |
| **FMF** | Fiji Military Forces |
| **FMS** | Federated Malay States |
| **FOO** | Forward Observation Officer |
| **FWC** | Federal War Council |
| **G** | General or operational aspects |
| **GLO** | Ground Liaison Officer |
| **GOC** | General Officer Commanding |
| **GSM** | General Service Medal |
| **GSO** | General Staff Officer |
| **HAAMG** | heavy anti-aircraft machine-gun |
| **HF** | High Frequency |
| **HMNZS** | His/Her Majesty's New Zealand Ship |
| **HMS** | His/Her Majesty's Ship |
| **HQ** | headquarters |
| **IBT** | 'Irregular Border Terrorists' |
| **IO** | intelligence officer |
| **J Force** | Japan Force (New Zealand's contribution to the British Commonwealth Occupation Force in Japan) |
| **JOC** | Joint Operations Centre |
| **JSO** | Joint Service Operations |
| **JTF** | Joint Task Force |
| **JWS** | Jungle Warfare School, Ulu Tiram, Johore State |
| **KAR** | King's African Rifles |
| **Kayforce/K Force** | Korea Force (New Zealand's contribution to United Nations operations in Korea) |
| **KBE** | Knight Commander of the Order of the British Empire |
| **KD** | Kepal Di Rajah (Ship of the Rajah), Malaysian Navy |
| **KKO** | Korps Komando Operasi (Marine Commandos of the Indonesian Navy) |
| **KOSB** | King's Own Scottish Borderers |
| **LAC** | leading aircraftman |
| **LMG** | light machine gun |
| **LRDG** | Long Range Desert Group |

| | |
|---|---|
| **LSG** | Logistic Support Group |
| **LST** | Landing Ship Tank |
| **Lt** | Lieutenant |
| **LZ** | landing zone |
| **MAF** | Malaysian Armed Forces |
| **MBE** | Member of the Order of the British Empire |
| **MC** | Military Cross |
| **MCP** | Malayan Communist Party |
| **MEAF** | Middle East Air Force |
| **mid** | Mentioned in Despatches |
| **Min** | Minister |
| **Mk** | Mark (of aircraft) |
| **MM** | Military Medal |
| **MOBRIG** | Police Mobile Brigade, Indonesia |
| **MOD** | Ministry of Defence |
| **MPABA** | Malayan People's Anti-British Army |
| **MPAJA** | Malayan People's Anti-Japanese Army |
| **MRLA** | Malayan Races Liberation Army |
| **MV** | motor vessel |
| **NAAFI** | Navy, Army, Air Force Institute |
| **NATO** | North Atlantic Treaty Organization |
| **NMD** | Northern Military District |
| **NS** | National Service (selective-ballot compulsory military service scheme introduced in New Zealand in 1961) |
| **NZ Regt** | New Zealand Regiment |
| **NZDLO** | New Zealand Defence Liaison Officer |
| **NZMLO** | New Zealand Military Liaison Officer |
| **NZNF** | New Zealand Naval Forces |
| **O Gp** | Orders Group |
| **OBE** | Officer of the Order of the British Empire |
| **OC** | Officer Commanding (at company equivalent level) |
| **OCPD** | Officers Commanding Police Districts |
| **OCS** | Officer Cadet School, Portsea, Australia |
| **OD** | other denominations |
| **Op/Ops** | Operation/s |
| **OR** | other ranks |
| **OSPC** | Officers Superintending Police Circles |
| **PFF** | Police Field Force |
| **PGT** | Pasukan Gerak Tjepat (Quick Reaction Force), Indonesian Air Force |

| | |
|---|---|
| PI | platoon |
| PO | Petty Officer |
| PW | psychological warfare |
| QDG | Queen's Dragoon Guards |
| QM | Quartermaster |
| R/T | radio-telephone |
| RA | Royal Artillery |
| RAAF | Royal Australian Air Force |
| RAF | Royal Air Force |
| RAN | Royal Australian Navy |
| RAP | Regimental Aid Post |
| RAR | Royal Australian Regiment |
| RASC | Royal Army Service Corps |
| RCAF | Royal Canadian Air Force |
| REME | Royal Electrical and Mechanical Engineers |
| RF | Regular Force (New Zealand Army) |
| RMAF | Royal Malaysian Air Force |
| RMC | Royal Military College, Duntroon |
| RMN | Royal Malaysian Navy |
| RMO | Regimental Medical Officer |
| RMR | Royal Malay Regiment |
| RN | Royal Navy |
| RNZA | Royal New Zealand Artillery |
| RNZAC | Royal New Zealand Armoured Corps |
| RNZAF | Royal New Zealand Air Force |
| RNZE | Royal New Zealand Engineers |
| RNZIR | Royal New Zealand Infantry Regiment |
| RNZN | Royal New Zealand Navy |
| RNZNVR | Royal New Zealand Navy Volunteer Reserve |
| RO | Routine Orders |
| RP | Regimental Police |
| RPKAD | Resimen Para Komando Angkatan Darat (Parachute Commando Regiment), Indonesian Army |
| RSM | Regimental Sergeant Major |
| RSO | Regimental Signals Officer |
| RV | rendezvous point |
| SAS | Special Air Service |
| SB | Special Branch |
| SBS | Special Boat Service |
| SCM | State Committee Member (Malayan Communist Party) |

| | |
|---|---|
| **SEA** | South-East Asia |
| **SEAC** | South East Asia Command |
| **SEACDT** | South East Asia Collective Defence Treaty |
| **SEATO** | South East Asia Treaty Organization |
| **Sect** | Section (a subdivision of an infantry platoon) |
| **SEP** | surrendered enemy personnel |
| **SLAT** | Special Logistic Aid Thailand |
| **Sqn** | Squadron |
| **SS** | steamship |
| **SSM** | squadron sergeant-major |
| **SWEC** | State War Executive Committee |
| **Tac HQ** | Tactical Headquarters |
| **TDP** | Target Director Post |
| **TF** | Territorial Force |
| **TNI** | Tentara Nasional Indonesia (Indonesian Army) |
| **TNKU** | Tentara Nasional Kalimantan Utara (National Army of North Kalimantan) |
| **Tp** | Troop (SAS equivalent of a platoon) |
| **TS** | top secret |
| **UHF** | ultra high frequency |
| **UMNO** | United Malays National Organisation |
| **USAF** | United States Air Force |
| **USO** | United Service Organization |
| **V Force** | Vietnam Force |
| **VC** | Viet Cong (US/South Vietnamese term for the National Liberation Front in South Vietnam) |
| **VD** | venereal disease |
| **VHF** | very high frequency |
| **Wasp** | Weapon Anti-Submarine Platform |
| **WO** | Warrant Officer |

# Glossary

| | |
|---|---|
| **amah** | housekeeper |
| **Anzac** | Australia and New Zealand Army Corps |
| **Asal (also 'Asli')** | Malay term for 'origin' or 'original' people; used by the MRLA to describe the 'aborigines' |
| **attap** | palm thatch |
| **basha** | jungle shelter made from local vegetation |
| **char** | tea; cook |
| **CLARET** | codeword for cross-border operations into Kalimantan during Confrontation |
| **dhobi** | washing |
| **durbar** | meeting |
| **firedog** | pre-planned bombing, strafing and rocket attack by aircraft |
| **jongkong** | small sailing vessel (Indonesia, Strait of Malacca) |
| **kampong** | Malay village |
| **kati** | 1lb $5\frac{1}{3}$ oz |
| **kumpit** | shallow-draft, wooden-hulled catamaran (Philippines, Indonesia) |
| **ladang** | jungle clearing with cultivations |
| **lallang** | long grass |
| **Min Yuen** | 'Masses Movement' |
| **Orang Asli** | 'original people'; 'aboriginals' of Malaya's Central Highlands |
| **Owen Gun** | sub-machine gun designed and manufactured in Australia |
| **panji** | sharpened bamboo stakes |
| **Pathet Lao** | 'land of the Lao'; term applied to Laotian communist movement and its military forces |

| | |
|---|---|
| **prahau** | open wooden canoe (Malaya, Indonesia) |
| **sakai** | 'slave'; term used by security forces and government authorities to denote 'aboriginal' peoples |
| **Senoi Pra'ak** | 'fighting men'; organised bodies of armed 'aboriginals' deployed in squadron-size groups by the Protector of Aborigines |
| **smash hit** | 'on-call' strike by aircraft against a target of opportunity |
| **Sten gun** | British sub-machine gun |
| **ulu** | jungle |
| **Viet Minh** | Vietnamese Independence League; communist-led national front organisation founded in Indo-China in 1941 |

# PART I

# *Malayan Emergency*

# I

# A 'SIDE ISSUE ONLY', 1949–55

> I joined in May 1959 and the reason, well the main reason, I actually joined was I was working up north and I was having a few problems in the area upsetting the locals. And we had a constable up there, a Constable Wells, and he bailed me up one day, and he said, 'Well, you know you're causing a lot of problems in this town?' And I said, 'Oh yeah?' and he said, 'There's a battalion that will be going to Malaya within the next six months or so.' He said, 'Why don't you join it?' and I said, being a young fellow and cheeky, 'Yeah, well, I might.' And his reply was, 'Well, if you don't, you're going to finish up in prison.' So this is what made me join the Army.[1]
>
> SERGEANT J. T. ('JOHNNO') JOHNSTON, RNZIR

Johnno Johnston, from the Ruawai district of North Auckland, was one of thousands of young men who served in South-East Asia with the New Zealand armed forces in the 1950s and 1960s. They joined for a variety of reasons, as their elder brothers, fathers and grandfathers had done in two world wars. But this time it was different. New Zealand was at peace, and the units they joined were not raised specially for wartime service, but were Regular units of the New Zealand military forces.

This is Johnston's story, but it is also the story of thousands of New Zealanders like him who, in looking for adventure, a chance to do something different, or simply to get away, found themselves serving in South-East Asia. You will meet them again and again in these pages—airmen like Ron Manners, who in 1949, as a flight lieutenant with Second World War experience, commanded the Dakotas of A Flight No. 41 (Transport) Squadron RNZAF, the first New Zealand Regular unit to serve in South-East Asia, and returned in 1955 as commander of No. 41 Squadron RNZAF, this time flying Bristol Freighters; and Geoff Wallingford, who flew Venom jet fighters with No. 14 Squadron RNZAF during the Emergency in 1956–57, and returned as commander of No. 14 Squadron flying Canberra jet bombers during Confrontation in 1964; sailors like John Carter, who served as a leading hand on the cruiser HMNZS *Royalist* during its first tour with the Far East Fleet in 1957, and went back again as chief boatswain's mate on HMNZS *Taranaki* during Confrontation in 1964–65; soldiers like Johnston himself, who served with Aitken's 2nd Battalion New Zealand Regiment in Malaya in 1959–61, joined the New Zealand Special Air Service (SAS) and served with them in Thailand in 1962, and then did two tours on active service with the SAS in Borneo in 1965–66, and one tour with the SAS in Vietnam.

Those serving in the Army or Air Force were usually young single men the first time they went to South-East Asia; often they went back the second time with their families. For soldiers and sailors in particular, it was not unusual to serve three or more times in South-East Asia. While a sailor could serve two or three 12-month unaccompanied tours on a New Zealand warship attached to the Far East Fleet, a soldier could see six to eight years' service with the New Zealand forces in Malaya and Singapore over a 20-year career, and on at least one of these tours be accompanied by his family.

Johnno Johnston was a Maori. Prior to the Second World War he would have had little chance of joining the permanent staff of the New Zealand military forces as this was very much an Anglo-Saxon preserve. While Maori were found in the ranks of most battalions in both wars, there were also dedicated Maori units, starting in 1915 with the New Zealand Native Contingent which in September 1917 formed the basis of the New Zealand (Maori) Pioneer Battalion; in the Second World War its successor was 28 (Maori) Battalion, which was disbanded in 1945.[2] The formation of a Maori battalion as part of the Territorial Force was approved in 1949 by F. Jones, the Minister of Defence in Peter Fraser's Labour administration, despite strong opposition from some senior officers of the Regular Army and some former officers of 28 (Maori) Battalion.[3] With the change of government later that year, nothing was done to implement the decision. When the matter was raised with the new Minister of Defence, T. L. Macdonald, it was decided that forming a Territorial Maori battalion would present too many difficulties, and that the existing integrated units were more 'in line with a strong body of opinion (represented strongly by the late Sir Peter Buck) that the future for race relations in New Zealand lies in the closest possible association of the two races with the avoidance of anything in the nature of discrimination'.[4] The question was raised again in the 1960s by former members of 28 (Maori) Battalion, and met with a similar response.[5] In the 1950s the services, and particularly the Army, provided one of the few career paths in which a lack of education was no barrier to entry, and a person could advance on merit. For Maori, the Regular forces provided a conduit to a professional military career, or stepping stones to an education or trade. They gave many the confidence to take their place in a society dominated by Pakeha values which was largely unaware of the barriers it still presented to Maori.[6]

Moreover, New Zealand's evolving commitment to South-East Asia offered young men from all sections of society an education in a much wider world. Despite periodic balance of payments crises these were years of full employment in New Zealand, and manpower was always in short supply for the armed forces. Civilian industry could offer far more money, but the services could offer the chance of an overseas trip, the possibility of some action, and an opportunity to see the world. New Zealand had little previous contact with Asia, and young people travelling overseas gravitated to Australia, Great Britain and Europe. South-East Asia was not yet part of the tourist route, but for thousands of New Zealand servicemen and their families it became their first contact with the outside world. They had to adapt to societies in which they were the outsiders, and to cultures that seemed totally alien to those used to the conservative parochialism of New Zealand in the 1950s and 1960s.

From 1955 New Zealand had an Army element, at least one Air Force squadron and a warship permanently stationed in Malaya and Singapore as part of the Commonwealth Far East Strategic Reserve. It is important to remember that New Zealand's military contact with Asia came before any diplomatic or trade contact. In this story, the sword leads the pen. Diplomatic contact, in the form of a Commissioner to South-East Asia, based in Singapore, was established only after it was agreed that New Zealand Regular forces would become part of the Commonwealth Far East Strategic Reserve. In fact New Zealand had little interest in Asia in the 1950s, and what interest there was developed out of its desire to foster and maintain its post-war security alliances. At the start of the Cold War in Europe, New Zealand military planners accepted that the country could be involved in a global war against the Soviet Union by the mid-1950s,[7] and prepared for this contingency.

Post-war Britain's defence planning identified its strategic priorities as Europe, the Middle East and Asia, in that order. 'It became increasingly evident that the United States regarded the Middle East as an area of British and Commonwealth responsibility', and Britain requested support there from Australia and New Zealand.[8] As early as September 1948, Peter Fraser's Labour government agreed to commit New Zealand's military resources to the defence of Egypt and the Suez Canal in the event of a Soviet thrust through Turkey.[9] New Zealand's contribution would be to mobilise a citizen force, as it had done in two world wars. Despite opposition from within his own party and the trade union movement, Fraser put the issue of compulsory military training to the New Zealand public in a referendum on 3 August 1949, the result being 568,427 votes in favour and 160,998 against.[10] Following this success, Fraser confirmed New Zealand's willingness to contribute to Commonwealth defence in the Middle East by providing an infantry division expanded by an armoured brigade, and also five Air Force squadrons.[11] In making this commitment, New Zealand was more forthcoming than Australia. Compulsory military training became the central focus of New Zealand's defence preparations, and the Army was restructured as a cadre of Regular officer and NCO instructors to train and administer the promised citizen force.[12]

In December 1949 the National Party under Sidney Holland became the government of New Zealand. Holland committed his administration reluctantly to compulsory military training, and even more reluctantly to the deployment of a New Zealand expeditionary ground and air force to the Middle East in the event of global war.[13] Despite having served as a second lieutenant with the New Zealand field artillery on the Western Front before being invalided home in 1917, Holland had a deep distrust of the services and servicemen. Parsimonious by nature, he resented these military obligations and their financial implications. Finding no way out, he blamed the situation on his Chief of General Staff, Major-General Keith Stewart, who as chairman of the Chiefs of Staff Committee was the leading advocate for New Zealand's post-war military preparedness.[14] It was an interesting contrast in personalities: the rotund, ebullient, bullying Holland, with the voice and manner of a small-town auctioneer, pitted against the lean, angular, bald, meticulous Stewart, with his prominent teeth and pronounced stammer.[15] There was no meeting of minds. Holland was equally unhappy with Stewart's successor as Chief of General Staff, Major-General William Gentry. Neither received a knighthood on completion of office, and it was the incoming Labour administration of Walter Nash that recognised their work by awarding them both the KBE in 1958.

Despite increased security commitments, parsimony in defence spending remained an underlying if unstated principle of defence policy under the National governments of the 1950s and 1960s. Nevertheless, in 1951 Holland's government approved £107 million in military expenditure over four years on aircraft, minesweepers, and other equipment to meet the military's post-war commitments. Indeed, during the 1952/53 financial year, 'New Zealand spent almost as much on defence as on state housing, education buildings, and hydro-electric construction combined'.[16] However, the prosperity created by the wool boom of the early 1950s was not sustained. Overseas defence commitments and equipment purchases involved a drain on precious overseas reserves. Both Holland and his successor, Keith Holyoake, distrusted their military advisers and wanted to spend as little as possible on what they saw as insurance premiums for New Zealand's security. Stretching existing resources a little further was always preferable to the expense of raising additional military units. Both men had firm views on what New Zealand's maximum defence effort should be in the uncertain world of the Cold War, and their administrations largely kept within these limits.

It was Labour, first under Peter Fraser in 1948, and then under Walter Nash from 1957 to 1960, that demonstrated a wider global view. Fraser established New Zealand's willingness to play a part in post-war Commonwealth defence arrangements, and it was Nash's government that signalled the shift away from citizen forces to totally professional Regular forces. However, economic difficulties and a lack of manpower frustrated this move, for the Army at least. The planned expansion of the services was ruthlessly pruned back by Holyoake's government in the 1961 Defence White Paper.[17] New Zealand's commitments in the 1960s were met with strictly limited Regular forces and an embryo Territorial Force, based on the reintroduction of selective compulsory National Service, which really became effective only after the likelihood of deployment to South-East Asia had long passed.

Despite British assurances that South-East Asia was a 'side issue only', the New Zealand government and its military staffs became increasingly preoccupied with security concerns in South-East Asia during the 1950s.[18] In 1951 New Zealand was a small country of some 1.9 million people, whose cultural and economic focus was on the United Kingdom. Despite New Zealand having been a base for American operations in the South Pacific during the Second World War, this focus was mirrored in its defence arrangements. Unlike Australia, whose security concerns were its northern boundaries, including the Indonesian archipelago and the Malay Peninsula, New Zealand had no such focus on South-East Asia, and apart from some Air Force elements had had no major involvement there during the Second World War.

Since 1949 New Zealand had been part of a highly secret regional defence arrangement known as 'ANZAM', an acronym for Australia, New Zealand and Malaya Area.[19] This had grown out of the stillborn Canberra Pact of 1944, and married the common defence interests of Australia, New Zealand and Britain in South-East Asia and the Southwest Pacific. Discussions began in 1946, and Australia, Britain and New Zealand agreed to co-ordinate their defence planning for the ANZAM region, which was defined as that part of the Pacific 'including Malaya, Indonesia, Borneo, Australia, and New Zealand, Fiji and certain of the islands to the north'.[20] Initially, ANZAM was seen as primarily a naval and air contingency planning arrangement for the protection of convoys through New Zealand, Australian and Malayan waters; but inevitably, ANZAM planning also covered security problems in the British territories in South-East Asia, principally Malaya. Although not directly concerned, and indeed unwilling to be dragged into Asian affairs, New Zealand unavoidably became a party to discussions on these issues.[21]

This Asian focus increased after the signing in 1951 of the ANZUS or Pacific Pact between Australia, New Zealand and the United States, which became the cornerstone of New Zealand's defence security arrangements.[22] New Zealand's membership of ANZUS highlighted the gulf between British and American security policies in Asia. New Zealand wanted both powers to be active in the region, and this forced the government to become increasingly focused on Asia as it tried to reconcile its global war commitments with the Cold War concerns facing the western powers in Asia. The principal problem New Zealand faced was that its primary security arrangement, namely ANZUS, excluded the United Kingdom, and although the pact gave New Zealand valuable access to American thinking on security issues, it lacked the administrative machinery for military contingency planning.[23] ANZAM became the agency for such planning. By 1953 its focus had been enlarged to include the defence of Malaya. ANZAM planning was co-ordinated by the ANZAM Defence Committee, later renamed the ANZAM Chiefs of Staff Committee. In theory, it comprised the Australian Defence Committee and representatives of the British and New Zealand Chiefs of Staff Committees. In practice, it met in Singapore, Canberra and Wellington, and was chaired by an Australian, with representatives of the Australian, British and New Zealand Chiefs of Staff. The convention of co-ordination through the Australian defence machinery, first established in the 1940s, continued, with the ANZAM Defence Committee issuing a formal directive to the British

Commander-in-Chief Far East which placed operational command arrangements in his hands.[24]

The United States was not included in these ANZAM arrangements, principally because it had no wish to be drawn into discussions on the security of British colonies in Asia. The resulting credibility gap was bridged temporarily by a series of discussions on security issues in Asia, involving senior military staff from Britain, France, the United States, Australia, and New Zealand; these discussions, which became known as the Five-Power Staff Agency, were conducted between 1951 and 1954, but ceased after the French withdrawal from Indo-China. They highlighted the differing approaches of Britain and the United States to security issues in South-East Asia, most starkly in Britain's unwillingness to submit to American pressure to give military support to the French in Indo-China.[25] Here again, Australia and New Zealand became the meat in the sandwich between the two major powers on whom their security arrangements depended.

The demise of the Five-Power discussions overlapped with the negotiation and signing of the South East Asia Collective Defence Treaty in Manila on 8 September 1954, which established the South East Asia Treaty Organization (SEATO).[26] This regional defence pact brought both Britain and the United States together with Australia, New Zealand, France, Pakistan, the Philippines, and Thailand. The Treaty was aimed at countering aggression in general, which to the United States meant communist aggression; but its effectiveness was undermined by the disparate nature of the grouping, and by the United States' unwillingness to declare any military commitment in advance. What the Treaty did signify, however, was the almost inexorable shift of New Zealand's defence focus towards Asia.

New Zealand's commitment of Kayforce to Korea in 1950 as part of the United Nations forces highlighted the limited extent of the country's defence resources. By 1953, Korea had absorbed all the volunteer capacity that New Zealand could sustain without affecting its defence commitments to the Middle East.[27] Should New Zealand be asked to help shore up the deteriorating French position in Indo-China, it would not be possible to respond 'without radical changes in New Zealand's defence policy'.[28] The conflict was between meeting a possible Cold War contingency in South-East Asia, and then extracting these forces and redeploying them to the Middle East in the event of global war. In October 1953, discussions were held in Melbourne between the Chiefs of Staff of Britain, Australia and New Zealand. Led by Field Marshal Sir John Harding, Chief of Imperial General Staff, the British Chiefs of Staff recommended that if a world war broke out the entire Australian ground and air commitment should be directed towards the defence of Malaya. They also recommended that New Zealand switch its Air Force undertaking from the Middle East to Malaya, but retain its Army obligation in the Middle East.[29] This split was initially seen by the New Zealand Chiefs of Staff as both militarily and politically unworkable. The Chief of Air Staff, Air Vice-Marshal D. V. Carnegie, and his successor, Air Vice-Marshal W. H. Merton, both RAF officers on secondment, had serious reservations about the viability of the level of air support that was to be available for the defence of Malaya. Unless this was increased, neither officer could 'recommend to the Government that New Zealand's major air contribution should be deployed to Malaya. As he [Carnegie] saw it under the present plans, a repetition of [the disasters of the Malayan Campaign against the Japanese in] 1942 was inevitable'.[30]

The Chiefs of Staff reluctantly recommended support for the British suggestions, but Holland was equally sceptical and no government decision was made.[31] Nonetheless, it seemed increasingly that in the event of global war, New Zealand's ground and air resources would be more sensibly deployed to the Malayan area than to the Middle East. In talks with Holland in November 1954, the British Commissioner-General in South-East Asia, Malcolm Macdonald, proposed that New Zealand ground forces be deployed to Malaya in such circumstances.[32] British authorities also raised the question of New Zealand's participation in a Commonwealth Far East Strategic Reserve, based on Regular forces stationed in Malaya. Once again, the New Zealand government gave no commitments. At the end of 1954, New Zealand's global war commitments remained as initially agreed in 1949: a mobilisation of ground and air forces to the Middle East.[33] All this was on the agenda at the Commonwealth Prime Ministers' Conference in London in February 1955. With the advance agreement of his Cabinet, Holland made commitments at the conference which ensured that New Zealand's military contributions to South-East Asia would no longer be a 'side issue only', but a matter of central concern for the next 34 years.[34]

## A Flight No. 41 Squadron RNZAF in Malaya, 1949–51

New Zealand's first military commitment to South-East Asia after the Second World War came in response to the creation of the People's Republic of China in 1949. There were fears for the security of the British colony of Hong Kong.

In response to a British request for assistance, Peter Fraser agreed to dispatch a flight of Dakota aircraft from No. 41 (Transport) Squadron RNZAF, as well as up to three RNZN frigates and four Mosquito fighter–bombers if they should be required.[35] As it turned out the frigates and bombers were never sent, but the Dakotas were deployed to the Royal Air Force base at Changi on Singapore Island to transport passengers and supplies to Hong Kong as part of the RAF's courier service. A small number of New Zealand Regular Army officers were also attached to British units in both Malaya and Hong Kong during this period.[36] This was not in response to the Hong Kong crisis, but rather followed on from the pre-Second World War policy of attaching officers to British and Indian Army units to gain regimental experience.

New Zealand's contribution, however small it may seem, was a major commitment from a country in the throes of a complete reorganisation of the three services to meet its post-war defence requirements.[37] The withdrawal of No. 14 (Fighter) Squadron RNZAF from Japan the previous year marked the end of New Zealand's residual wartime commitments.[38] No. 41 Squadron was the sole transport squadron of the Royal New Zealand Air Force. Already three of its crews, flying RAF Dakotas, were committed to Operation PLAINFARE, the Berlin airlift in response to the Soviet blockade of West Berlin that began in July 1948.[39] Indeed, between the dispatch of the Dakotas to Singapore and the return of the crews from Berlin, there was only a single trained crew remaining with the squadron in New Zealand. This, as well as the offer of the frigates and bombers, indicated how seriously Fraser viewed the situation. While the Royal New Zealand Navy had two cruisers and six frigates in service, manpower shortages meant that only three or four vessels could be fully manned at any one time. New Zealand thus offered everything it had available, short of mobilisation. It was an expression of the government's concern at the worsening situation in Asia, where the communist success in China was matched by the Viet Minh's gains under Ho Chi Minh against the French in Indo-China. As we shall see, the situation in Malaya was by now also deteriorating.

On 20 September 1949 the first of three RNZAF Dakotas (C-47Bs, or DC-3s as they were more commonly known), arrived at RAF Changi on Singapore Island to serve with the Far East Air Force. Commanded by Flight Lieutenant Ron Manners, A Flight of No. 41 (Transport) Squadron RNZAF consisted of three wartime Dakota transport aircraft, 12 officers, 11 NCO air crew, a total of four crews, as well as five senior NCOs and 34 aircraftmen.[40] In 1940 Ron Manners had been a grocery clerk; he had put himself through night school to achieve his ambition of becoming a pilot, and after training in Canada under the Empire Air Training Scheme, had served on Spitfires and Hurricanes in the United Kingdom before ending the war as a flying instructor on twin-engine aircraft. Manners had just returned from Japan with No. 14 Squadron when he took command of A Flight. Few of his pilots had seen wartime service; many of them were Pilot IIIs, a rank and designation that was soon to disappear from the RNZAF.[41] A Flight of No. 41 (Transport) Squadron RNZAF was the first New Zealand Regular unit to serve in South-East Asia in peacetime.

The New Zealanders were stationed at RAF Changi and flew from the Japanese airstrip built by Allied prisoners of war quartered in the nearby Changi jail. The New Zealand Flight lines were in cramped quarters adjacent to the strip, with accommodation in the officers' and sergeants' messes and barracks on the hills overlooking the runway. The colony of Singapore was then a separate political entity from the Federation of Malaya, which occupied the Malay Peninsula. Both countries were very different from what they are today. The city of Singapore was largely clustered around what is now the downtown central business district, centred on Parliament Buildings and the Padang. It was a raucous, stinking, teeming, largely Chinese seaport; most of the rest of the island was covered in plantations and scattered kampongs interspersed with military installations. Singapore was still the principal British military base east of Suez, accommodating both Headquarters Far East Land Forces and Headquarters Far East Air Force, while Headquarters Far East Fleet was located at the Royal Naval Base at Sembawang on the north side of the island.

The Federation of Malaya was slightly smaller than the South Island of New Zealand in area. Linked by a causeway to Singapore, it stretched 400 miles north to the Thai border; the peninsula has a maximum width of 200 miles. Flying over today's Malaysia, with its regular pattern of palm oil and rubber plantations reaching as far as the eye can see, is a vastly different experience from doing so in 1949, when 80 per cent of the country was covered in dense tropical rainforest known colloquially as 'the jungle'. The upper canopy reached heights of 150 feet, and beneath its cover the vegetation varied from open cathedral-like spaces between majestic trunks to densely tangled secondary growth, with rattan cane or bamboo thickets which cracked like rifle shots in the heat of the sun.[42] Here visibility was reduced to a few yards. Like the South Island of New Zealand, Malaya has a central spine of mountain ranges which were then entirely covered in forest, apart from scattered clearings in remote river valleys where the indigenous peoples known as 'aborigines' lived. The rest of the country consisted largely of commercial rubber and palm oil plantations on the coastal lowlands and fringing the few major inland highways. In the south of Johore State pineapples were harvested, while in the north rice padi predominated; tin was mined around Ipoh. Throughout the country the Malay population lived largely in rural kampongs, with Indian Tamil and Chinese labour working the plantations and mines, and Chinese dominating the economic life of the many small towns. Malaya's population in 1947 was 4,908,086, of whom 2,427,834 were Malays, 1,884,534 were Chinese (three-quarters of whom had no citizenship rights), and 530,638 came from the Indian subcontinent or Ceylon.[43] The bulk of the population lived on the western lowlands, but the ravages of war and the Japanese occupation had seen some 500,000 Chinese squatters escape Japanese pogroms and move to the jungle fringes, where they hacked out small gardens to raise food for their families, selling the surplus in the local markets.[44]

There were also an estimated 100,000 aborigines, or 'Orang Asli'. Looked down on by the Malays, they were the guardians of the rainforest and its secrets.[45] During the war the mountains had been the base of the Malayan People's Anti-Japanese Army, which was largely Chinese and communist; this group was in contact with members of the British Force 136, whose aim was to encourage guerrilla activity in Japanese-occupied territories.[46] The long-term aim of the Malayan Communist Party (MCP) was to overthrow the colonial administration and establish a communist state, but in the short term it participated in the Allied war effort against the Japanese and received support and supplies from the British. After the war, members of the People's Army paraded through the towns as heroes, handing in weapons and receiving medals and small gratuities before returning to their towns and villages.

Post-war Malaya was one of the few profitable colonies of a financially destitute Britain. Malayan rubber and tin were in demand, but in many other respects it was an unhappy country.[47] The Japanese occupation had pitted Malays against Chinese, and the administration was a shambles, with many experienced officials either dead or recovering from years in prison. Those who had fled the Japanese now found themselves seen as deserters by those who had stayed.[48] In 1946 the British tried to impose the Malayan Union, which would have given citizenship to immigrant Chinese and Indians; the Malays opposed the move, seeing it as an insult to the sultans who were the titular rulers of each state. In the face of this opposition, the British backed away from the Union concept and instead formed the Federation of Malaya, which restored traditional Malay dominance, in February 1948.[49] The Federation consisted of the nine Malay states and the two British settlements of Penang and Malacca; Singapore remained a separate Crown Colony, because its Chinese population would have overturned the Malay majority in the Federation.[50]

These developments took place against a backdrop of constant economic and political strife. The MCP worked to gain power within the existing political framework, while the trade unions heightened public dissatisfaction and unrest through a series of increasingly violent protests and strikes. By 1948 the MCP, under its dynamic young general secretary, Chin Peng, had realised that government prohibitions were limiting the effectiveness of the party's approach. In March 1948 a meeting of the central executive committee, chaired by Chin Peng, decided on a policy of armed struggle. Increasingly frequent strikes were countered by police raids and arrests. Veterans of the restyled Malayan People's Anti-British Army—soon renamed the Malayan Races Liberation Army (MRLA)—moved back into their forest camps.[51] Caches of arms hidden since the war were distributed, and Chin Peng's forces embarked on a three-stage strategy to wrest control of the government from the British colonial authorities. Chin Peng anticipated that each stage would take about six months. An initial period of assassination and sabotage in rural areas would undermine public confidence and the power of the police and the authorities; these areas would then come under communist control. The same process would then take place in the towns, leading to the total collapse of the administration and the establishment of a communist government. On 16 June 1948 the beginning of the first stage was signalled by the killing of three European planters at Sungei Siput in Perak State.[52] Two days later the federal government declared a State of Emergency. At the time this response was deemed too little, too late, but in hindsight it forestalled the MCP's plans. The MCP's activities were poorly coordinated, and the government's pre-emptive action forced it to begin an armed struggle before its forces were positioned and ready, which fatally handicapped its chances of success.[53] The Emergency declaration marked the beginning of a 12-year campaign (which actually continued at a much lower level until 1989) that pitted the MCP and its fighting arm, the MRLA, against the Malayan government and security forces formed from the Malay police and the British, Malay and Commonwealth military.[54]

The original eight regiments of the Malayan People's Anti-Japanese Army had grown into ten regiments of the MRLA, each containing 200–500 guerrillas divided into four or five companies and ten or 12 platoons. This structure was

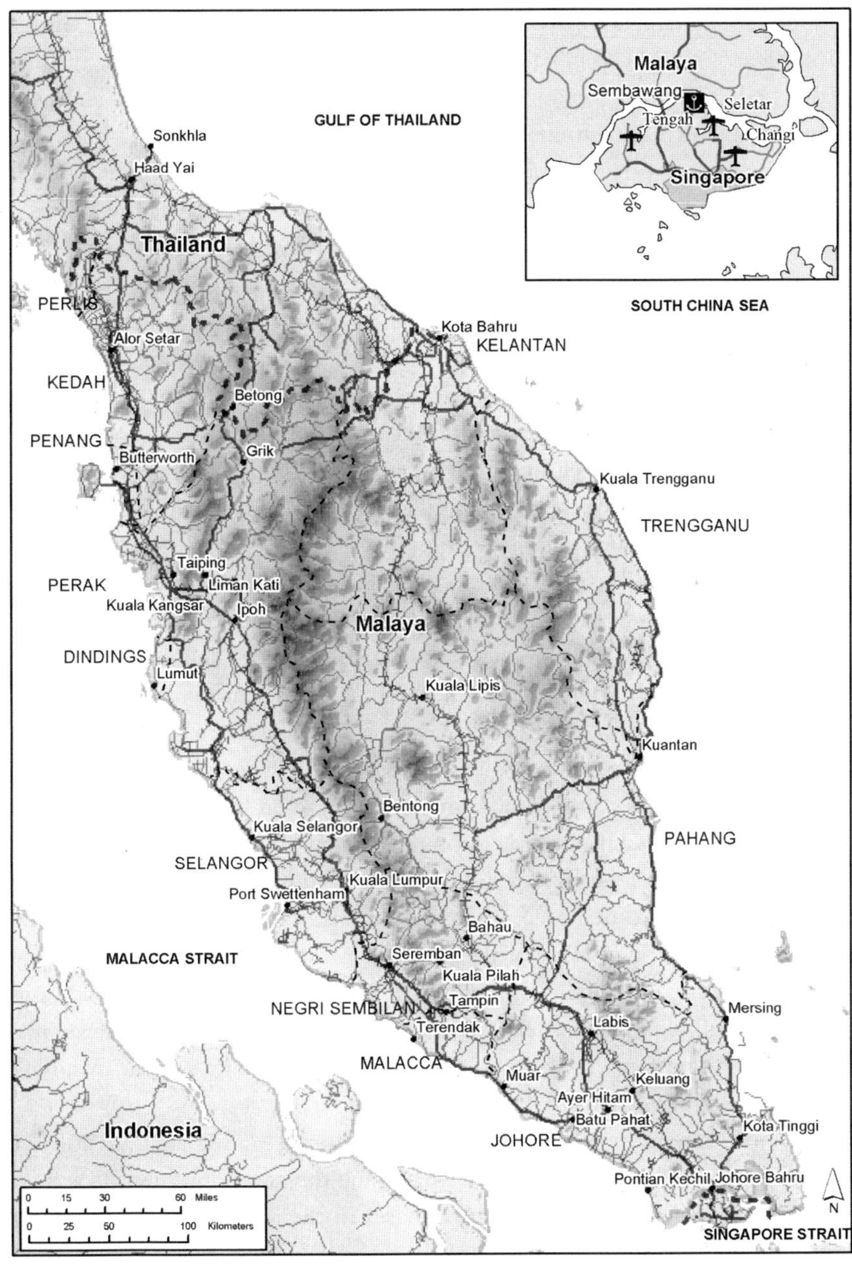


**Map 1** Malaya in 1949
Inset: Singapore showing principal military bases

supported by a large network of people known as Min Yuen (literally, 'Masses Movement'), who lived in squatter smallholdings on the jungle fringe, along main roads and in the predominantly Chinese towns, and provided supplies, money and information to the guerrillas.[55] By late 1949, Chin Peng's hopes for a swift popular uprising had ended, and his regiments retreated into well-guarded and camouflaged camps in the jungle. Although cut off from external sources of arms, ammunition and supplies, the MRLA waged an effective war against police posts in small towns and villages as they sought control of the rural areas. Also spurring them on was the triumph of communism in China; Britain's recognition of the new regime was taken as a sign that 'the imperialists were weakening'.[56] At the start of the Emergency the MRLA was estimated to number about 3,100; its strength would reach 8,000 in 1951.[57]

When A Flight of No. 41 Squadron arrived in Singapore in September 1949, the battle for control of the rural villages was about to reach its peak, with large companies of guerrillas besieging village and police posts. The security forces, consisting of British, Gurkha and Malay battalions, were operating in a conventional manner, attempting to surround and eliminate the guerrillas in large-scale operations. This strategy saw ill-trained British National Servicemen floundering through an alien jungle, searching for an elusive foe who easily avoided their porous security nets and was able to raid police posts and mount ambushes on roads and railway lines almost at will. The mistakes committed because of this approach included the use of coercion by police and security forces to make the Chinese population break their links with the MRLA. The security forces found themselves conducting operations with the very 'frightfulness' the British had deplored when the perpetrators were the Dutch in the Dutch East Indies (Indonesia) or the French in Indo-China.[58] This was ruefully acknowledged by the High Commissioner, Sir Henry Gurney: 'the police and army are breaking the law every day'.[59] The first New Zealand air crews thus found themselves supporting ground forces who were losing the war by failing 'either to kill guerrillas or to prevent terrorism'.[60]

The most important role played by the RAF during the Malayan Emergency was air transport support, as roads were few and threatened by guerrilla action. Mounting operations against guerrilla bases in the jungle was possible only with supply from the air.[61] There were never enough aircraft available, so New Zealand's three aircraft were a small but valuable contribution. The primary task of A Flight, No. 41 Squadron RNZAF was to help run the regular RAF courier services both within Malaya and on a regular thrice-weekly schedule to

Saigon and Hong Kong; as well, it assisted with the weekly services to Butterworth Air Base on the mainland opposite Penang Island, and then on to the island of Car Nicobar, an RAF refuelling station in the Indian Ocean. In addition, special flights were constantly needed both within Malaya and to airfields as far apart as Ceylon, Hong Kong, Saigon, Iwakuni in Japan, Rangoon, Clark Field in the Philippines, Kuching in Borneo, and Australia.[62]

After familiarisation flights on RAF aircraft, the first duty flight by a New Zealand aircraft took off from Changi for Butterworth on 7 October; three days later Flying Officer Johnny Trolove flew to Kai Tak Airport (Hong Kong) via Saigon to undertake interception exercises with RAF Spitfire squadrons based in the colony. By December 1949 the New Zealanders had settled into the RAF courier routine. Car Nicobar, with its golden beaches, was a favourite destination. The Hong Kong run was always made to a tight deadline.

> You would take off from Singapore at 4 o'clock in the morning ... Arrive at Saigon at 8 o'clock. And you had to get airborne from Saigon by 11 o'clock otherwise you wouldn't be able to land at Kai Tak in Hong Kong. Kai Tak had two runways and one of them you had to fly down the face of a hill and land towards the sea. The other one you had to creep over great tall buildings and land towards the hills. It wasn't the most pleasant place to land and you didn't want to miss your approach because they were evacuating Canton and there was a continual stream of aircraft going into Hong Kong with refugees. And if you missed your approach there was an hour and a half before you got in again and of course you didn't have enough petrol to do that. And there was nowhere else to go. You couldn't go into China. So you didn't miss your approach, no matter what happened on the way down.[63]

On 2 December 1949 one aircraft was detached to the wartime airfield at Kuala Lumpur to support the Dakotas of No. 52 Squadron RAF in dropping supplies to the security forces operating in the jungle against the communist 'bandits'.[64] This usually involved an aircraft and two crews for a month at a time. Flying Officer Johnny Trolove and Pilot Officer Reginald Plane were the first of the New Zealand crews to make these drops, which involved flying over jungle-covered ridges and peaks rising steeply from the populated valleys to heights of up to 5,000 feet. 'Often aircraft have to be taken deep into narrow valleys to locate prearranged dropping places, and most flying must be done in the mornings, to avoid the afternoon mist that fills the valleys and makes flying at low altitudes impossible.'[65] Each sortie followed a similar pattern. Requests for an air supply were radioed from Army or police jungle patrols to their district headquarters, who relayed them to the Joint Operations Centre at

Kuala Lumpur. Details were passed on to No. 55 Air Despatch Company, Royal Army Service Corps (RASC), who packed the supplies, attached the parachutes, and provided the air dispatchers to each aircraft. Supplies were normally prepared in 200-lb packs containing essential rations, ammunition, replacement clothing and medical supplies, as well as items such as beer and cigarettes that were ordered and paid for by individual soldiers.[66]

Kuala Lumpur looked like any wartime airstrip in the Pacific or South-East Asia, with ground crews 'swarming over Beaufighters, Spitfires, Tempests and a couple of Harvards'. The early morning monsoon storms turned the dispersal area where the New Zealand Dakota was parked into a 'sea of red sticky mud. Stripped to the waist, the ground crew are giving the Dakota a final check, while the four RASC dispatchers are putting the final lashes on the load'.[67] Flying Officer Johnny Trolove was the aircraft captain.

> Through the pools of liquid mud the Dakota lumbers and slides out onto the strip and soon is airborne and climbing away to the first DZ [drop zone] miles to the north. Below the country is typical Malayan jungle. Mountains of 4000 to 5000 ft enclose valleys cloaked in a thick mat of dense vegetation, with here and there the grey scar of a tin mine or the neat rows of a rubber plantation.
>
> The pilot and navigator have decided that the easiest way to 'Z' is to go to a certain landmark and then fly in from there. After the ranges have been crossed the Dakota drops down into a valley, picks up the river and follows it down.
>
> Meanwhile the signaller is busy calling the DZ on R/T [radio-telephone]. It is five minutes to dropping time and about a mile ahead the pilot sees a plume of white smoke rising above the jungle. He heads straight for this and is soon over the DZ. The smoke candle gives the wind direction, but, as usual, it is light and variable. In any case it makes no difference as most DZs are in very difficult country, and as a rule the drops can only be made in one direction regardless of wind.
>
> After crossing the clearing and checking that the letter 'Z' is displayed—occasionally the bandits have been supplied due to not carrying out this check—the pilot reduces speed to 100 knots, places the mixture in Auto Rich pitch to 2300 revs, booster pump on, lowers a flap and comes around on a 'dummy run'. The approach to this DZ is steep, so the Dakota comes in with throttle off, [stall-warning] horn blowing [indicating dangerously low air-speed] and the speed slowly building up, then immediately the clearing is crossed she climbs around for the first run in.
>
> As this is a Malay Unit the R/T is not very successful so the signaller is down the fuselage on Inter-Com. On instructions from the pilot he orders the despatchers to move the first pack down to the door.
>
> Meanwhile the Dakota is staggering over the treetops, climbing hard at 95–100 knots at full throttle. Then, on the turn in, the pilot gives the despatchers three

> short warning bells—30 seconds to go. Throttles off; horn blowing; can't get low enough and keep the speed down too; darn the speed, these chutes will stand 200 mph: careful now, watch those wingtips, you didn't miss those trees by much; hope those cylinder head temps don't drop too much; here she comes; 120 knots, not too bad; good, that's about 300 ft. NOW!!! Drop the bell button, slight lurch as the pack leaves, then full throttle, stick back, and hope you can clear the wall of jungle immediately ahead. 48°, 2300 revs, 95–100 knots and the tree-covered ridge passes a few feet below.
>
> There are ten packs to be dropped here, and as all are 'awkward loads' they must be dealt with one at a time, with the result that the performance is repeated 10 times. One slip here and the Air Force is out of a Dakota and crew, and the Security Forces out of rations.
>
> After the last pack goes the Dakota climbs and circles the DZ to confirm that all the packs are on. They are, so off goes a green Very and the course is set for the next DZ.[68]

This type of mission was flown many times. The Dakota, the air supply workhorse of the Second World War, had been critical to the success of the Burma and Pacific campaigns; it proved its worth once again in the critical first years of the Emergency. The narrow, steep-sided, jungle-clad valleys of Malaya demanded great piloting skill, as the Dakota's low angle of climb made getting in and out difficult and dangerous, and the pilot's poor forward and downward visibility made accurate supply-dropping difficult. There was no prospect of a crash landing in an open field if something went wrong. When the New Zealanders arrived there were only 17 airfields in the whole country that could take a Dakota-sized aircraft.[69] After taking off from the airfield, the planes flew low over an impenetrable jungle canopy that would swallow up wreckage as if the aircraft had never existed. Despite the obligatory half-hourly radio schedules giving the aircraft's position and the pilot's intentions, it might take days for a ground party to get into a crash site, assuming it was located. This knowledge was a gnawing, suppressed constant in the back of each air crew's minds. They just had to get on with the job, and trust that the pilot knew what he was doing, and was as keen to get back as everyone else.[70] Manners recalled that after a morning's flying pilots would return exhausted and wringing wet with sweat.

> I wouldn't wear many clothes on a supply drop. It might be underclothes and a flying suit. But it was very, very hot work, because it's sheer concentration all the time. You don't want to lose your parcels in the back. You don't want to drop

> them in the wrong place. You want to be going at the right speed and at the right height. You want to be watching how to get out ... And this might take a couple of dummy runs ... I found it hard work.[71]

The tempo increased during the New Zealanders' tour, as a pattern was established of regular air supply to police posts as well as major drops to the largely unsuccessful operations mounted against the guerrillas in those early years. By 1951 the New Zealanders and their three aircraft had carried out 211 sorties, parachuting in some 625,000 lb of supplies. These ranged from 'routine pack-ups of food and ammunition to such unusual items as collapsible boats and outboard engines, explosives, barbed wire, metal sheeting, and sacks of rice to feed isolated Sakai [aboriginal] tribesfolk'.[72] In 1950 a total of 3,500,000 lb of supplies was dropped over Malaya by parachute, nearly twice as much as in the previous year.[73] Initially the New Zealanders were the only Commonwealth personnel assisting the RAF, but in June 1950 they were joined by four Dakotas of No. 38 (Transport) Squadron Royal Australian Air Force (RAAF) in working alongside Nos 48, 52, and 110 Squadrons RAF, who rotated tours of duty at Kuala Lumpur.[74]

New Zealand crews were rotated at regular intervals. The air crews were relieved after three months' service, the married men among the ground crews after six months, and the single ground staff after a year.[75] Maintaining the Flight in Singapore placed strains on an undermanned RNZAF, which finally received its first post-war aircraft, De Havilland Vampire jet fighters, in 1951. It was planned to replace the Dakotas both with twin-engine Bristol Freighters (B170 Mk 31(NZ) M) for medium-range transport, and with four Handley Page four-engine Hastings (HP.95 C3) aircraft, the latter giving the RNZAF its first true long-range transport capability.[76]

In 1951, while New Zealand aircraft dropped supplies to jungle patrols in Malaya, the Holland government declared a state of National Emergency in New Zealand as a result of the waterfront dispute, and the three services (including compulsory military trainees) were mobilised to work the wharves. This affected support to A Flight, as most No. 41 Squadron personnel were employed first on the Auckland wharves and later in Wellington, with no crews available for the monthly courier run to Singapore.[77]

In April 1951 a No. 41 Squadron Dakota left Whenuapai for the United Kingdom, carrying two crews who would take delivery of the first two Bristol Freighters. There had been continuing doubts about A Flight remaining in

Malaya, and the British authorities were quick to head off talk of any possible withdrawal. In April 1950 the Marshal of the Royal Air Force, Sir John Slessor, wrote to the New Zealand Chief of Air Staff, Air Vice-Marshal A. de T. Nevill, on the need to retain the Dakota Flight in Malaya. After expressing satisfaction that it would not be withdrawn immediately, he added:

> I am most grateful for your statement that the matter will be referred to us again before any action is taken to withdraw it. I am wondering if the recently agreed move of the Gurkha Brigade from Hong Kong and the possible move of a Spitfire Squadron from there to Malaya may perhaps have given the impression that we regard the threat to Hong Kong being less serious and in consequence the New Zealand Government may have thought your Dakota flight could be released ... The threat to Hong Kong is, however, by no means over and if we are to have that essential flexibility enabling us to move units back there from Malaya, we must of course hold as many transport aircraft as we can in the Singapore area ... I very much hope, therefore, that you will be able to allow your Flight to remain for some little time in Malaya, not only to help meet the Transport requirements, but to provide a Commonwealth element in the active prosecution of the Cold War. The latter I think is very important.[78]

The British also hoped that the arrival of the Dakotas of No. 38 (Transport) Squadron RAAF would cement the New Zealand presence as part of an Anzac commitment, but instead the imminent arrival of the RNZAF's replacement aircraft provided the opportunity for the New Zealanders to depart.[79] This was decided in June 1951, and in September the Minister of Defence, Thomas Macdonald, announced the withdrawal of A Flight by the end of the year.

> Withdrawal of the flight becomes necessary as No. 41 Squadron will shortly be re-equipped with Bristol Freighter and Hastings aircraft and the personnel now in Malaya will be required to do conversion training on them ... In addition a number of crews from the Squadron are needed to ferry these new aircraft from the United Kingdom to New Zealand. However, once the squadron members have converted to these aircraft and have the necessary operational training, the flight will be available for service in Malaya if the Malayan Government wishes it to return.[80]

In December 1951, A Flight No. 41 Squadron returned to New Zealand.

Although the prospect of a renewed commitment to Malaya was also expressed by the new Chief of Air Staff, Air Vice-Marshal D. V. Carnegie, the RNZAF wished to be involved in the priority area of interest, the Middle East. On 8 April 1952, in response to a request from the British government, the

New Zealand Cabinet reluctantly approved the stationing of No. 14 (Fighter) Squadron RNZAF in Cyprus from September 1952. This decision necessitated leasing 16 De Havilland Vampire jet aircraft from the RAF. To the RNZAF, the Cyprus opportunity was far more important than returning the transport flight to Singapore.

> The value to New Zealand of the operation is immense. An operational squadron, ready for war, is training and flying with the Commonwealth Squadrons with which it will fight. This enables the whole fighter force to be welded into one, with an increase in efficiency and operational effectiveness which can only be achieved in an active theatre. The prestige of New Zealand and the Commonwealth is enhanced, and the morale of the squadron and in fact of the whole of the R.N.Z.A.F., is correspondingly raised.[81]

The Middle East, after all, would be New Zealand's theatre of operations in the event of a global war—and flying new Vampires over the Mediterranean was far more attractive than flying aged Dakotas over Malaya. However, in 1955 New Zealand RNZAF transport aircraft would return to the skies over Malaya to build on the small but significant part played by the Dakotas and crews of A Flight No. 41 Squadron during the most critical phase of the Emergency.

## New Zealanders with the First Battalion, Fiji Infantry Regiment in Malaya, 1952–56

New Zealand soldiers first went to fight in South-East Asia with the Fiji Infantry Regiment. This unexpected and, as it turned out, important role was announced in October 1951 when the British government accepted an offer from the Fiji Legislative Council of a battalion of the Fiji Infantry Regiment for service 'against the communist terrorists in Malaya'.[82] New Zealand contributed the commanding officer, other officers and NCOs, who acquired experience that would underpin subsequent army contributions in the region.

The New Zealand Army, as it was constituted in 1950, had no Regular units; rather, its role was to provide a cadre of officers and NCOs for the augmented division that would form the basis of a 'Third New Zealand Expeditionary Force' when the citizen soldiers trained under the compulsory military training (CMT) scheme were mobilised.[83] The headquarters of the New Zealand Division, manned by both Regular and Territorial Force personnel, was established at Linton Camp on 1 May 1951. This assumed command of the units of the

Division on 1 June 1951 as part of 'the policy of having a New Zealand Army organized and trained in peace so that it can efficiently take over its tasks and responsibilities in time of war'.[84] Since 1949 a number of Regular officers had served with British units in Malaya to gain regimental experience, just as New Zealand Staff Corps officers had been sent to India in the 1920s. The deployment of 16 Field Regiment Royal New Zealand Artillery to Korea as part of Kayforce provided further opportunities for a limited number of Regular Force officers and NCOs attached to this specially raised unit.[85]

In 1948 New Zealand had 'accepted the responsibility for defence coordination and for providing, through the New Zealand Chiefs of Staff, advice and assistance to the Governor of Fiji on the reorganisation, administration and training of Fiji's defence Forces'.[86] Brigadier C. L. Pleasants became Commander Fiji Military Forces, and he was supported by a small team of New Zealand officers and NCOs whose role was to raise, train and administer Territorial units.[87] On the shoulders of this small group fell the responsibility for raising the First Battalion, Fiji Infantry Regiment (1FIR) for service in Malaya. Major R. A. Tinker, Chief of Staff, Headquarters Fiji Military Forces, was selected as the Commanding Officer. This proved to be an inspired choice. Tinker had risen through the ranks with the Long Range Desert Group in North Africa, winning the Military Medal, and had commanded in the Aegean and the Balkans, where he won the Military Cross. His strength was practical soldiering in difficult situations. Raising 1FIR from scratch also suited his talents. As his adjutant, Captain Val Brown, noted, the 'unconventional was normal for Ron Tinker'.[88] He also had the necessary strength of character.

> The Fijians really thought he was everything. He had had a hard life particularly in the Long Range Desert Group. The New Zealand Army didn't help him very much by not promoting him because he was still a substantive captain, temporary major, acting and never paid lieutenant-colonel, and that was bad in the eyes of the British Army who insisted on examining very carefully the pedigree of every CO in Malaya. He loved his drink, was a great raconteur ... a man's man. He was soft in many, many ways but when he wanted to be hard, by God, he was hard.[89]

Tinker's impact on the Fijians was comparable to that exerted by Lieutenant-Colonel George Dittmer on 28 (Maori) Battalion during the Second World War. Both men established standards of performance that became the yardstick for the rest of the unit's existence. Tinker's skills were complemented by those of his second-in-command, Ratu Edward Cakobau, a paramount chief who had been awarded a Military Cross as a company commander with 3FIR in the Solomon Islands during the Second World War. Cakobau's urbanity and charm were complemented by his implacable determination to succeed. He was the battalion disciplinarian, and 'as far as the Fijians were concerned, he was God and there were no arguments'.[90]

New Zealand saw the raising of the battalion as an agreement between Fiji, the United Kingdom and Malaya, with 'New Zealand's only commitment being the provision of a few officers and NCOs'.[91] As with all things Fijian, it was never that simple. Four Regular New Zealand officers and a handful of Regular NCOs already in Fiji were earmarked for the battalion, and it was intended that Fijian officers with experience in the units that had served so successfully in the Pacific during the Second World War would make up the company leadership cadre.[92] However, until Fijian officers could be trained in New Zealand, there would be a critical lack of both junior officers and experienced NCOs. Volunteer New Zealand officers and NCOs with Second World War or Territorial experience were sought to fill the gap. The New Zealand Army was reluctant to release more Regular officers and NCOs, and finding volunteers for 1FIR was not high on its list of priorities in 1951: the needs of CMT came first, and then Kayforce. It was considered 'a matter of luck if any capable of acting as Coy Comds or Coy 2ICs can be found'.[93] Eventually New Zealand provided four Regular officers (including Tinker as Commanding Officer), seven Regular warrant officers and NCOs, six volunteer officers and seven other volunteers from the limited selection available. Many of the latter were to be sacked by Tinker and returned abruptly to New Zealand.[94]

Only with great reluctance did the New Zealand Army post Regular junior NCOs to 1FIR. Army General Staff wanted them as CMT instructors in New Zealand, and was loath to send them either to Korea with Kayforce or to Malaya with 1FIR. Only when some junior NCOs threatened to resign from the Regular Force in order to volunteer for active service did the Army back down: 'It has therefore been decided that it is better to lose their services for a short period than permanently.'[95] The first of these men to arrive in Suva was Corporal R. A. ('Roly') Manning, who became an institution in the New Zealand Army of the 1970s because of his skills as an instructor in infantry tactical and small arms training. Having joined up at the age of 18, he was trained on one of the first courses run by Army Schools to establish the cadre of Regular instructors needed for the CMT scheme. One week after arriving in Fiji as a corporal, Manning was an acting sergeant, and company sergeant-major of B Company.

1FIR was raised from scratch in barely three months with everything having to be improvised and its administration a shambles. Most of the battalion had never worn boots before; the few trained New Zealand instructors needed interpreters to teach their totally inexperienced Fijian NCOs, who in turn had to instruct their soldiers without fully understanding much of the material. 'So what the soldier got was about 20 per cent of what he must know, and the fact that we killed about eleven buggers [in the battalion] before we got out of training and went on operations was probably proof of that.'[96] Nevertheless, on 8 January 1952 the 831 officers and men of the First Battalion Fiji Infantry Regiment embarked on the *Asturias* for Singapore with an emotional send-off.[97]

The teething problems continued in Malaya. In June 1952, despite the reservations of British training staff at the Jungle Warfare School at Ulu Tiram in Johore State, the still-green battalion was committed to operations in Negri Sembilan as part of 63 Gurkha Brigade, commanded by Brigadier H. C. Henniker. Many mistakes were made, and it was very much a case of learning on the job. Fortunately, the Fijian company commanders and many of the Fijian NCOs had seen war service in the Solomons and they, together with the best of the New Zealand cadre, gradually increased the battalion's operational efficiency. This process caused friction. Not all the New Zealanders adapted to commanding Fijian soldiers, and the actions of one New Zealand officer in A Company led to a mutiny which was solved only by removing the officer.[98] Weak officers, both Fijians and New Zealanders, were weeded out. The situation began to improve when Fijian officers started arriving from commissioning courses being run in New Zealand, and increasingly New Zealanders were appointed to staff and administrative appointments where there was a lack of Fijian expertise.

Tinker himself was 'quite bloody ruthless' at this time. 'On reflection that was the only thing that got us through. I think if we'd had weak leadership allied to bad training it could have been bloody disastrous.'[99] 1FIR made a slow start in operations in its first battalion area around Bahau in Negri Sembilan. Initially, experienced officers and NCOs from the Commanding Officer down accompanied every patrol, teaching such basic military skills as making the seven days' rations issued to each soldier actually last for seven days.[100] Second Lieutenant Jim Barker had served as a platoon commander in Malaya with the Devonshire Regiment in 1951, and on his return to New Zealand volunteered for a tour as a platoon commander in 1FIR. He found that while the Fijians 'had a lot to learn in terms of military things ... they were much more at home in the jungle than the average British soldier [and] consequently working with them was almost a pleasure'.[101] By trial and error the Fijian soldiers of 1FIR improved, and in a series of successful contacts in August and September 1952 they showed they had the ability to find and kill guerrillas.

The arrival of 1FIR in Malaya coincided with the appointment of General Sir Gerald Templer as both British High Commissioner and Director of Operations, four months after his predecessor as High Commissioner, Sir Henry Gurney, had been assassinated, and after the retirement of the previous Director of Operations, Lieutenant-General Sir Harold Briggs. With Templer's appointment, 'the prosecution of the war and the running of the country became a single process under a single head'.[102] Under his forceful leadership, the war that the Federation was in danger of losing was turned around. It was not all Templer's doing, however; Briggs had bequeathed him the strategy for success in Malaya, and indeed in counter-insurgency operations anywhere in the world.

The Briggs Plan acknowledged that the Emergency was a competition between the Malayan authorities and the Malayan Communist Party and its fighting force, the MRLA. The struggle was for the 'hearts and minds' of the half-million mostly Chinese squatters who occupied land on the jungle fringes adjacent to roads, rivers, kampongs and towns, and grew vegetables for subsistence and the local markets. The fact that they were illegal squatters put them outside the compass of government administration. During the war they had been willing suppliers of foodstuffs to the Malayan People's Anti-Japanese Army; now, willingly or otherwise, they were the source of supplies on which the guerrillas depended.[103] The key was to both deny the MRLA access to this support base, and give the squatters a standard of administration, a degree of prosperity and a sense of security that would earn their allegiance to the Malayan government. This separation process was achieved by resettling squatters from the jungle fringes in protected New Villages—a massive programme that required the government to harness and co-ordinate all its resources. Each New Village, surrounded by barbed wire and security posts, was sited on open ground with road access adjacent to agricultural land, and had housing, schools, health facilities and a police post.[104]

Equally important was gaining good intelligence on who and where the guerrillas were, and what they intended to do. To achieve this, the Police Special Branch was reorganised and its numbers were boosted. Briggs also recognised that at every level of authority there had to be total co-operation between the civil administration, the police and the military. A War Council was established at the Federal level, presided over by the Director of Operations and including administrative, police and military leaders. This structure was replicated at state and district level. Each State War Executive Committee (SWEC) consisted of the state's prime minister, information officer, chief of police, head of Special Branch, military intelligence representative, senior military commander, and Home Guard officer, and each District War Executive Committee (DWEC) comprised the district officer, information officer, police commander, Special Branch officer, military intelligence officer, battalion commander, and Home Guard officer. These committees pooled information, decided on priorities, and 'ran the war' in their areas.[105]

Briggs had developed the plan, but lacked the authority and the support to put it into action. Templer not only accepted the Briggs Plan as the framework for success but had the drive to push it through, and to insist that the disparate elements of government work together to defeat the guerrilla threat. He jolted government officials out of their complacent belief that somehow fighting the Emergency was different from running the country. 'Any idea that the business of normal civil Government and the business of the Emergency are two separate entities must be killed for good and all. The two activities are completely and utterly interrelated.'[106] Templer's initial priorities were the reorganisation and training of the police, the improvement and expansion of public information services, and the continuation of the resettlement programme. Combining improved administration and information with enhanced security paid dividends. The number of guerrilla incidents declined markedly, the monthly average falling from 507 in 1951 to 311 in 1952.[107] By the latter year, 423,000 squatters had been resettled in 410 New Villages.[108]

While this was a campaign fought according to the laws of the land, the powers conferred by the Emergency Act were draconian. It was the task of the police to protect the population and prevent the Min Yuen working among them. The military's role was to dominate the jungle fringe and, using intelligence provided by both its own sources and Special Branch, deny the guerrillas contact with their sources of information and support.[109] The integration of the police, military and civil administration was the key to the success of counter-insurgency in Malaya. This demanded an administration with authority and drive that was not corrupted by the power it wielded. Achieving such unity of purpose is difficult, particularly when the very nature of counter-insurgency operations breeds distrust between civil, police and military branches, encourages empire-building among competing intelligence agencies, and allows the police and military to descend to the level of the guerrillas by using unlawful methods of terror and violence. This is how things went terribly wrong in South Vietnam. That they did not in Malaya is a tribute to Templer.

The Briggs Plan had been to clear Malaya by 'rolling them up from the south',[110] but Templer decided instead that the security forces would work out from the centre around Kuala Lumpur to clear both north and south. In each area, all the resources available would be concentrated on what were known as federal priority operations. Squatters would be resettled and foodstuffs controlled so as to limit the supplies reaching the guerrillas; then, through Special Branch intelligence, police and military efforts would be co-ordinated to separate the MRLA from the Min Yuen and eliminate both. Once this was achieved, the area would be declared 'White' or free from insurgents (as opposed to 'Black' and still subject to guerrilla incidents), and the occupants would enjoy a relaxation of Emergency restrictions, particularly the hated food control measures.[111]

Of critical concern to Templer was the district around Yong Peng in northern Johore, the 'most troublesome area' in Malaya.[112] There were guerrilla hideouts in the fetid, leech-ridden jungle swamps on either side of the 12-mile-long road between the Chinese-populated towns of Yong Peng and Ayer Hitam, both of which strongly supported the MCP. This section of highway was under constant threat from the outstanding insurgent leader (and former schoolteacher) Goh Peng Tuan and his 7th Independent Platoon MRLA. Designated a 'Black' road, it could be travelled only in convoys escorted by armed vehicles.

1FIR's success around Bahau led to the battalion taking over from 2/6th Gurkhas at 'Bloody Yong Peng' in late October 1952 as part of 26 Gurkha Brigade.[113] The Fijians' increasing skill at small-group patrolling coincided with Templer's decision to abandon the large-scale multi-battalion sweeps that had hitherto dominated the thinking of Headquarters Malaya Command. Templer placed his trust in platoons and sections working from company bases, and insisted that each battalion have an operational reserve ready to respond at short notice whenever intelligence indicated a suitable target.[114] Two of 1FIR's companies were based around Yong Peng, the third at Muar, and the battalion's headquarters at Batu Pahat. Each company commander was a member of the local DWEC. Their experience in operations around Bahau had taught them the importance of knowing what was happening in the company's area, and of using police and Special Branch information effectively. Templer's faith in the Fijians was immediately rewarded: five guerrillas were killed in two contacts in the first five days, and Templer showed his pleasure by visiting A Company 1FIR in Yong Peng on 11 November.[115] Templer so admired 1FIR's performance that he goaded other battalion commanders who were not producing results in their areas with the scarcely veiled threat that he would send in the Fijians instead.

Within 1FIR, each company fought its own war in its own area. These wars were waged on the fringes of the jungle, often within sight and sound of villages. They were fought at section level, with the section commanders leading small patrols into the rubber plantations on the edge of the jungle, and around the swamps bordering the main road. The MRLA had also abandoned large-scale operations, and the war was waged between small groups that patrolled and ambushed along the tracks and red-laterite roads through the rubber and palm oil plantations, or in the now-overgrown squatters' clearings along the jungle fringe. Much of the Fijians' work around Yong Peng was in the swamps, where they waded slowly through waist-deep black water among contorted roots, pestered by mosquitoes and leeches and watching warily for water-snakes as they searched for the small islands where the guerrillas had their camps.

Most successful contacts depended on getting good intelligence. This meant that 1FIR had to gain the trust of the police and Special Branch, and convince them that information would be used effectively and not wasted through poor tactics. Both organisations had seen too much hard-won intelligence squandered by British battalions whose young National Servicemen found the jungle claustrophobic and occupied by nameless terrors. 1FIR gained its first successes by intense blanket patrolling along the jungle fringes, initially without useful Special Branch or police information. These successes increased the flow of intelligence, and over the next four years the Fijians were to provide good returns on the information they were offered. On 31 May 1953, Tinker relinquished command of the battalion to his second-in-command, Lieutenant-Colonel Cakobau. By the time he left, 1FIR had been on operations for 12 months, achieving 37 'kills', and had become one of the most effective units in Malaya.

The battalion's growing tactical efficiency was not matched by that of its administration. Postings such as 1FIR Regimental Quartermaster Sergeant or

Quartermaster were not to be envied. The battalion's administrative shambles ruined the reputations of the succession of New Zealand officers and warrant officers who were overwhelmed by the task of applying British Army accounting procedures to the chaotic practices of 1FIR. The battalion had 'never really taken to stores accounting in a big way', and auditors blanched at the confusion they found in the administration of pay, stores, rations and equipment.[116] It had been a hard struggle too for Tinker, not only to raise the battalion from scratch and get it released on operations, but also with Malaya Command to have it recognised as a Fijian unit responsive to the wishes of the Fijian people, not just another colonial battalion.[117] Tinker's willingness to stand up for his battalion had not endeared him to Malaya Command, and while he received an OBE for his period with the battalion, his officers and men believed he deserved a DSO. Tinker personified 1FIR; its existence and performance reflected his tenacity.

Lieutenant-Colonel Cakobau commanded 1FIR for only a few months before he was recalled to resume his position as a district officer in the Fijian Administrative Service. Cakobau continued the pattern established by Tinker and maintained the battalion's operational efficiency, despite difficulties dealing with the rotation of personnel and the absorption of reinforcements. By the end of his tour 1FIR had recorded 87 'kills', a measure both of the unit's growing professionalism[118] and the success of Templer's implementation of the Briggs Plan. There was no question now that the war against the MRLA was slowly being won, and that the increasingly skilled and confident soldiers of the British, Gurkha, Malayan and Commonwealth forces were playing a leading role in this turnaround.

By 1953 most officers of 1FIR were Fijians, although the battalion continued to include Regular officers and NCOs from New Zealand receiving regimental experience in an operational environment. The first was Lieutenant Tony Mataira, who arrived during the battalion's period in Bahau and proved an outstanding platoon commander in Major George Mate's D Company.[119] Another was Lieutenant R. Ian Thorpe, who had graduated from the Royal Military College at Duntroon in 1951. After being warned out for service he was told to expect to be attached to an Australian battalion in Korea, but found himself being sent to 1FIR in Malaya instead. As Thorpe recalled, Army General Staff believed Malaya was more suitable for giving young infantry officers operational experience; Korea had proved too expensive, with Lieutenant Robert Unsworth killed and Lieutenant John Brooke badly wounded.[120]

Once the Armistice was signed in Korea in July 1953, 1FIR became the only unit in which New Zealanders could gain operational experience.

The swamps and rubber plantations around Yong Peng and Batu Pahat became the testing ground for the infantry tactics developed by the first generation of New Zealand officers and NCOs to serve in South-East Asia. What they learned there became the foundation of New Zealand's jungle expertise, the techniques of which were passed on to generations of New Zealand infantrymen who served in Malaya, Borneo and Vietnam. This was certainly the experience of Sergeant C. G. ('Shorty') O'Brien, who arrived at 1FIR in July 1953 and became perhaps the outstanding New Zealand patrol commander in the battalion. 'I worked in the same format ... we have been teaching ever since ... I always had two lead scouts, plus a commander within the section and then I had a gun group and a rifle group, and they were switched in accordance with how I wanted things.' But when they made contact with the enemy, O'Brien found, the Fijians' shooting skills were rarely effective:

> Once that first shot was fired, all hell would break loose. They liked the sound of shooting, and I think they had the impression that the sound was sufficient so long as the weapon was pointed in the general direction ... I thought, 'Well if we can't shoot them at 20 yards, let's get them at one yard.' My method of assaulting was straight up the guts with me in the lead or as close as I could [get] ... Our method of responding to an ambush was an immediate assault regardless ... there were no exceptions, even if the enemy ambush was sprung from 75 yards away. Take your chances. If we all run [at him], we confuse him, and those tactics worked 99 times out of 100.[121]

The platoon had a series of successes, with O'Brien killing five guerrillas in separate encounters despite being seriously wounded. This aggressive approach typified Fijian tactics in Malaya. As Brigadier Henniker, Commander 63 Gurkha Brigade, succinctly put it, 'A Fijian with a Bren gun can run faster than a Chinaman for his life'.[122] It was in this environment that the New Zealanders learned their trade.

> If you had a chance encounter, there was no feeling that you would have a reconnaissance, make a plan, and develop it into an attack. Fijian-style tactics [were] just 'there's the fox' and they're off, and of course through the jungle they were fast. Time after time an incident report would show the Fijians running down these fellows and taking them with a close-range shot right at the end, almost as an afterthought. And once they got the feeling of success and ... knew they were doing it right ... they just went from strength to strength.[123]

On 30 September 1953 Cakobau was succeeded by another New Zealand officer, the battalion's second-in-command, Major H. J. G. Low. Harry Low was a very different personality from either Tinker or Cakobau. A clerk before the war, he had joined 2NZEF as a private in 1940 and served with 26 and 23 Battalions, rising to major and winning the Military Cross as a company commander in Italy in 1945. He was invited to join the post-war Interim Army in 1947, and came to 1FIR from the United Kingdom, where he had spent a year as a student at the British Army Staff College at Camberley and a further year as an Acting Lieutenant-Colonel in the New Zealand Army Liaison Office in London. The highly ambitious Low worked his battalion hard. He got to grips with its chaotic administration, sending in a British quartermaster to finally sort things out.[124] He was equally determined to maintain the battalion's operational record and uphold the standards set by Tinker and Cakobau. For Low, getting the 'kills' was all important:

> he was not inclined to be generous with leave ... even leave to Battalion Headquarters [at Batu Pahat], their local provincial town, was stopped. And so soldiers could look forward to almost nothing except two-thirds of their time on operations and one-third in the company base, which still had its guards, sentries, patrols, and was no more than a tent line in the rubber trees with wire around it ... that was the pattern of operations in the Battalion.[125]

Low 'wanted action and he got it'.[126] The first goal was 100 'kills', which was achieved in November 1953 and celebrated with a fireworks display of 'tracers, 2" Mortar flares and HE [high-explosive] bombs'.[127] Intense patrolling in the battalion area was maintained into 1954. From headquarters, the area stretched nearly 40 miles to the north and east, with A Company at Muar, B Company with Battalion Headquarters and the Headquarters Company at Batu Pahat, C Company at the Craigie Lea Estate, and D Company at Yong Peng.

In July 1954 Batu Pahat was declared a White area. While this demonstrated the Fijians' success, Goh Peng Tuan's 7th Independent Platoon still sheltered in the swamps around Yong Peng, and the battalion area as a whole was still one of the most active MRLA areas. As the number of guerrillas dwindled, Fijian rifle companies were lent to other battalions for operations. This reflected both their effectiveness and Low's determination to kill the 'elusive 150th Bandit'.[128] This goal was achieved in August 1954; further celebrations followed, and the target became 200 'kills'.

Goh Peng Tuan remained the key opponent, and he was always capable of striking back. On 15 November 1954 his platoon carried out a carefully planned ambush of a truckload of B Company soldiers on the Yong Peng River Estate road; five Fijians were killed and six wounded. Goh Peng Tuan had noted that the vehicle always came down the road at the same time each day, and acted accordingly. The Fijians paid the price for being predictable. There was another incident in February 1955, when an unescorted vehicle carrying a Fijian officer, Major R. Genge (commander of A Company), one of his platoon commanders, Lieutenant Toganivalu, a driver and a Bren gunner, was ambushed. Genge was killed and Toganivalu wounded. He and the two soldiers were captured, but they were released unharmed after having their wounds dressed and being denounced as 'British lackeys'. The guerrillas' haul included weapons and the company payroll of M$2,520.10.[129]

This was a difficult time for the battalion. There was uncertainty about its future in Malaya, and there were no contacts and therefore no 'kills' in the seven weeks to 30 June 1955.[130] Low stopped all leave within the battalion in an effort to increase its 'elimination rate'. He wanted results, and showed little regard for the impact his continual demands were having on his soldiers' morale. Thorpe recalled: 'It seemed to some of us that the men were probably stale, although they showed no real signs of it.'[131] However, Major George Mate of D Company, the outstanding company commander in 1FIR, put the interests of his men ahead of those of Battalion Headquarters. 'Even when it was forbidden, he used to sneak leave parties down to Batu Pahat.'[132] Lieutenant John Webster, the sole New Zealand platoon commander in C Company, also worked out with his platoon sergeant ways of keeping up morale when, after coming in from patrolling, the men were ordered to go back out on patrol the next day. They enlisted the services of two prostitutes who, having negotiated a mutually satisfactory price, were established in tents just outside the wire marking the platoon perimeter. 'I don't know how many they serviced, but it saved the situation ... we were due to go out the next morning so there was not much time, and all the guys were lined up.'[133]

Low never had the same rapport with the men as his two predecessors had enjoyed. His determination to achieve results blinded him to the demands he was making on his soldiers, and the fact that he might be exhausting his most precious resource at a time when the target itself was becoming increasingly scarce. Low was not with the battalion when it achieved its 200th 'kill'. On 1 October 1955 he handed over to his second-in-command, Ratu Penaia Ganilau, who served as Commanding Officer until the battalion was withdrawn from operations on 20 April 1956 and returned to Fiji. Low was awarded the DSO, the last ever received by a New Zealander because of the change to the awards system.[134] Given the battalion's performance during his years in command the award was appropriate, but it is regrettable that Tinker was not equally honoured.

By the time Templer returned to the United Kingdom in 1955, the MRLA had gone on the defensive and withdrawn deep into the jungle. The strategy and tactics needed to defeat it were clear, but the continuing slog of putting these into effect in the vast Malayan rainforests would occupy another five years. The Fijians had played a critical role in this victory, creating a benchmark by which the success of other battalions in Malaya was measured. This achievement had been hard-won; from 1953 it was built on the initial training of reinforcements in Fiji and their careful assimilation into the battalion through the training cell at Battalion Headquarters. New Zealand NCOs such as Manning and O'Brien played a pivotal role in establishing this training system, and from 1954 this was New Zealand's major contribution to 1FIR's performance.

By 1956 only a handful of New Zealanders remained with 1FIR.[135] In 1955 the battalion was joined in Malaya by the New Zealand Special Air Service Squadron, which became part of 22 SAS Regiment. The Fijians' 200th 'kill' on 21 January 1956 seemed less significant than their 57–0 rugby victory over 22 SAS Regiment in the Malaya Cup final, which greatly embarrassed the recently arrived New Zealanders. This third successive Malaya Cup win for 1FIR qualified them for the finals of the FARELF Cup which they also won for the third successive time. In the same year their old adversary Goh Peng Tuan and most of his 7th Independent Platoon were killed when their camp was bombed in a co-ordinated strike by Lincolns of No. 1 Squadron RAAF, Canberras of No. 12 Squadron RAF, and Venoms of No. 14 Squadron RNZAF. This was one of the few successful bombing missions conducted during the Emergency. Two companies of 1FIR formed part of the outer cordon when the aerial attack went in, and it was perhaps appropriate that their principal and most effective opponent was killed in these last months of Fijian operations in Malaya.[136]

In Templer's opinion, 1FIR was the best battalion to serve in the Emergency.[137] It was never a battalion in the sense of participating in co-ordinated conventional operations; it never had to do so. It always comprised four isolated company bases, each running its own separate war, often with little overall co-ordination from Battalion Headquarters in Batu Pahat. Its success was based on the closeness of the relationships between the company commander, the district officer, the police commander and Special Branch. While Fijian soldiers already possessed bushcraft skills, their ability as soldiers had resulted from effective training, and they performed best under the command of Fijian officers and NCOs. A New Zealander coming into the battalion, whether Maori or Pakeha, officer or NCO, had to prove his worth, because Fijian soldiers took nothing on trust. This parallels the experience of British officers joining the Gurkhas that has been described brilliantly in John Masters' autobiography, *Bugles and a Tiger*.[138] Indeed, calculated distancing from a newcomer until he has proved himself is characteristic of all military elites. Certainly, 1FIR fully tested the leadership skills of the approximately 40 New Zealand officers, warrant officers and NCOs who served in its ranks.[139] When the battalion returned to Fiji in 1956, Lieutenant Ian Thorpe was its adjutant, Major Stan McKeon commanded Headquarters Company, Major 'Mac' MacDonald A Company, Major Lete Petersen B Company, and Lieutenant Gerry Brown the Mortar Platoon; there was also a New Zealand sergeant in the Training Platoon.

Two of the 27 servicemen who died in Malaya while serving with 1FIR were New Zealanders. Both had prominent fathers. Second Lieutenant Peter Hargest, son of the wartime brigadier, was killed in a road accident, while Sergeant G. Nepia, son of the All Black fullback of the 1920s, died in a shooting accident. Some of the New Zealanders who served with the battalion failed, but those who succeeded drew on their experiences in the years to come.

> Somebody once asked me after I had commanded a company of our own people in Borneo and on operations on the Malayan Peninsula, who were the better soldiers; Fijians or New Zealanders. I can only say that they were different. Equally rewarding to command, but different. Different characteristics, horses for courses. For some tasks you would prefer your Kiwis, and for some, the Fijians, but both were very domineering soldiers ... in that they take it for granted that they can see off at least as many of the enemy, whoever they may be.[140]

# 2

# FINDING THEIR WAY

## *Naval Duties, 1949–62*

> When I was [with the Royal Navy] in Bermuda my parents immigrated to New Zealand, and when I got back [to England] in 1955 … I was toying with the idea of getting married with my fiancee at the time and if I had got married in England she would have become my next-of-kin and then I couldn't have switched navies to the New Zealand Navy. So we decided not to get married and my next-of-kin remained my parents in New Zealand, and so I switched navies from the Royal Navy to the [Royal] New Zealand Navy. You signed off one day in the Royal Navy and you signed on for the New Zealand Navy the next day.[1]
>
> Chief Petty Officer Fire Control 1st Class
> J. L. C. Carter, RNZN

The stationing of New Zealand naval vessels in South-East Asia was first prompted by the same crisis that led to the deployment of the Dakotas. In response to the British request in 1949 to assist with the defence of Hong Kong, Prime Minister Peter Fraser offered three frigates. In the event these were not required, but the crisis raised expectations that New Zealand ships would join the British Far East Fleet, and contributed to the debate about the shape and role of a peacetime navy.

The New Zealand Naval Forces had been established in 1914 and the New Zealand Naval Board in 1921; since 1 October 1941 the Royal New Zealand Navy (RNZN) had existed under that title. Its reputation in the Second World War was built largely on the deeds of its two cruisers, *Achilles* and *Leander*, both lent by the Royal Navy. *Leander* was torpedoed and badly damaged in

1943, and replaced by the larger Fiji-class cruiser *Gambia*. At the end of the war the *Achilles* was 13 years old and obsolete, while the *Gambia*, which required a ship's crew of 1,000, was too large for New Zealand's needs. In planning its post-war Navy, the New Zealand Naval Board sought to retain this cruiser capability. It even dreamed of acquiring a light fleet carrier, which could make up a self-contained portion of a naval task force in combination with either one cruiser and four destroyers, or two cruisers and two destroyers.[2] This dream was never realised. The Royal New Zealand Navy had been born in war, and its traditions were those of the Royal Navy; in 1946, however, it was a small navy with ambitions far greater than either its funding or its available manpower could sustain. The Admiralty agreed that the existing cruisers would be replaced by two modified Dido-class anti-aircraft cruisers, *Bellona* and *Black Prince*. On its commissioning in 1946, HMNZS *Bellona* joined HMNZS *Arbutus*, *Tui* and *Kiwi* and, for a time, *Hautapu* as the operational fleet of the Royal New Zealand Navy.

In 1948 these ships were joined by six war-surplus Loch-class anti-submarine frigates, whose purchase allowed the re-establishment of a New Zealand Squadron. The first four frigates were handed over in 1948, and named after New Zealand lakes. HMNZS *Hawea*, *Kaniere*, *Pukaki* and *Taupo* formed the 11th Frigate Flotilla in 1949, and were joined by *Rotoiti* and *Tutira* the same year.[3] 'Getting the ships to New Zealand was as much as we could manage with 250 of the ships' crews being Royal Navy ratings on short-service engagements.'[4] Manned by a crew of 120, with a displacement of 2,260 tons, a Loch-class vessel had a maximum speed of 20 knots; it was armed with one 4-inch gun, two Squid anti-submarine mortars, and four 40-mm Bofor anti-aircraft guns and two pom-pom; the last-named were later replaced by two 40-mm Bofors. The frigates were roomy for their type, and when purchased were still effective in their anti-submarine role. In hindsight they were perfect for New Zealand's requirements: 'they had long range, they were easy to maintain and our dockyard facilities were such that we could look after them. If we had gone into something more complicated [especially] as we already had two Cruisers on station ... we wouldn't have been able to cope.'[5] For the next 12 years the Lochs were the Navy's workhorses, and the last two were paid off in 1965 after 17 years' sterling service. 'I think [buying the frigates] was the best thing that happened to the New Zealand Navy. The CNS [Chief of Naval Staff] of the day did us a great service and got us off the Cruiser level and down to ships we could understand, in which we could get a fleet together.'[6]

Although it was Naval Board policy to man the RNZN 'entirely with New Zealand officers and men', the newly acquired ships depended on personnel on loan or recruited from the Royal Navy.[7] Indeed, Royal Navy personnel filled most of the principal appointments in the RNZN. All three professional members of the Naval Board were British officers on loan, and it would be 1957 before a New Zealand-born RNZN officer became a Board member.[8] Half the non-specialist officers in the ranks of lieutenant-commander and above (28 per cent of the total officers on establishment) were British officers on loan or exchange. It was similar below decks; in 1950 some 17 per cent of the ratings were either on loan from the Royal Navy or former Royal Navy personnel recruited in Britain. In 1950, officers and ratings with Royal Navy connections comprised just over 25 per cent of RNZN personnel, the level set by the Naval Board in 1948 as an appropriate ceiling for recruiting from the Royal Navy. RNZN pay and conditions of service were so poor that a series of incidents in 1947 culminated in mutinies. Recruiting was difficult, and the RNZN remained undermanned in both officers and men throughout the 1950s and 1960s.[9]

John Carter had joined the Royal Navy in 1950 as a boy seaman and served on a Battle-class destroyer in the Mediterranean and then on the cruiser HMS *Superb* in the West Indies. After his parents migrated to New Zealand he transferred to the RNZN in 1955 as a 19-year-old leading seaman. He found the New Zealand Navy something of a shock.

> I felt it was not as disciplined as the Royal Navy and generally speaking very 'slack'. A lot of people spoke to officers [which] you never did in the Royal Navy ... The person you would speak to was the person immediately above you, Petty Officer or maybe a Chief. I mean if an officer addressed you, you would obviously reply to him, but you would never talk to one. Here it seemed to be quite all right to talk to virtually anybody.[10]

As Carter discovered, things were different in New Zealand; but given the size of the Navy, they had to be. Although not necessarily as 'slack' as the young man imagined, the RNZN was still in the process of finding its way and forming its own identity.

Under the ANZAM arrangement, the RNZN's role was to co-operate closely with the Royal Australian Navy in the protection of sea-lanes within the designated ANZAM area. The Radford–Collins understanding of 1951 divided the responsibility for naval operations in the Pacific between the Royal, Australian and New Zealand navies in the ANZAM area and the United States Pacific

Area of Command. The agreement covered the escort of shipping, the control and routing of convoys, reconnaissance, anti-submarine warfare, and search and rescue.[11] Any ships not needed for ANZAM duties would support Commonwealth naval forces in the Middle East.[12] Unlike the Army and Air Force, the RNZN's focus was always the defence of home waters and the ANZAM region, which included 'Malaya, Indonesia, Borneo, Australia and New Zealand, Fiji and certain of the islands to the north'.[13]

New Zealand's cruisers had been designed to fulfil their most important role: protecting Australia's aircraft carriers in the planned ANZAM naval task force. The Navy's immediate commitment to ANZAM duties in the event of global war would comprise one cruiser and three frigates.[14] On 18 August 1949, Prime Minister Peter Fraser announced the New Zealand government's agreement to provide a Dakota transport flight to assist the British forces in Hong Kong. He went on: 'Discussions have also taken place with the United Kingdom authorities regarding other forms of cooperation and assistance, and arrangements are being made to send three of the Navy frigates to Hong Kong if they should be required there.'[15] *Taupo*, *Pukaki* and *Tutira* were placed on one month's notice to sail for the Far East from 15 September 1949. The flotilla was due to do a tour of Australian ports, but the ships were now loaded with stores and charts in anticipation of their diversion to Hong Kong. The New Zealand Naval Board expected that they would join the Far East Station and be based at Singapore with the Royal Navy, rather than stationed permanently in Hong Kong.

This potential commitment to Hong Kong forced the RNZN to decide what it really was: Royal Navy or Royal New Zealand Navy. One decision that taxed the Naval Board was whether 'New Zealand' shoulder flashes should be worn, as had been the custom in 1944–45 before it was forbidden. The Board was worried that 'the initiative of [ship's] Canteen Managers etc. may lead to an assortment of flashes appearing'.[16] In typical New Zealand fashion, it was decided that shoulder flashes would not be worn; once again, it was a case of 'if in doubt, remain anonymous'. In the event, the New Zealand ships remained on standby and were not deployed. *Taupo* and *Hawea* sailed for the Mediterranean in April 1950, on exchange with two Royal Navy frigates which, it was agreed, might have to form part of New Zealand's Hong Kong commitment. However, the North Korean invasion of South Korea pushed Hong Kong into the background. On 3 July 1950 *Tutira* and *Pukaki* sailed for Korea, where they served under United Nations command. With one ship always in dock being refitted, any possible New Zealand assistance to Hong Kong was reduced to a single frigate.[17] Two frigates were maintained in Korean waters for the next four years. The role of the RNZN in the Korean War has been described in detail by Ian McGibbon, and will only be outlined here.

The Korean War involved all six frigates and half the total Navy in the course of eight completed tours of duty, with 1,350 personnel on deployments of 12 to 14 months at a time. By the time the ceasefire was agreed, New Zealand ships had steamed 339,584 miles and fired 71,625 rounds of ammunition. Two seamen were killed, one during *Rotoiti*'s first tour and one from *Tutira*. Naval personnel were awarded eight DSCs, one OBE, two DSMs, and 18 Mentioned in Despatches (one posthumous). New Zealand ships intercepted attacks on shipping, mounted commando raids, and patrolled the coastline bombarding shore targets.[18] This commitment was sustained only by keeping three frigates on the active list and three in reserve. In 1952 the First Naval Member, Commodore F. A. Ballance, proposed that the two New Zealand frigates be transferred from United Nations command to that of the Far East Station for up to eighteen months.

> Some of the time would naturally be spent in Korea but not all. From our point of view it would be infinitely preferable as the ships could be attached to one of your Frigate Squadrons permanently instead of chopping and changing when you change round in Korea. The Captains and Ships' Companies would feel that they really belonged to somebody and I am sure it would make the administration easier.[19]

This arrangement was acceptable to the Royal Navy but not to New Zealand, where the Chiefs of Staff advised the government that it would be inappropriate for the country to be seen to be reducing its contribution to United Nations operations in Korea.[20]

It was not until after the Korean armistice that New Zealand's commitment to Korea was reduced to one ship on station and one held in readiness in New Zealand. *Pukaki*, under Lieutenant-Commander A. V. Kempthorne, became the first New Zealand ship to be attached to the Royal Navy on the Far East Station when it transferred from United Nations command in 1954. *Pukaki* joined the Third Frigate Squadron and took part in exercises with both its other three ships and with Indian, Australian and Dutch warships. The professional benefits gained by the ship's company validated Commodore Ballance's recommendation made two years earlier. Simple things were instituted, such as annual ship inspections, which 'had been few and far between on the Far East Station since the Korean War commenced'. Kempthorne commented: 'The opportunity of working with other ships of near similar type has proved invaluable in assessing our own abilities and of producing a standard from which to work. It has also helped to create a spirit of competition amongst the ship's company, in an effort to prove that a New Zealand ship can be as good as and even better than her R.N. counterparts.'[21] The constant critical evaluation resulting from working alongside comparable ships of other navies was to be of major ongoing benefit to the New Zealand Navy for the next 20 years.

Sailing in Malayan waters formed part of each attachment. In July 1954 *Pukaki* and HMS *Possum* bombarded a coastal jungle area in Negri Sembilan in the first of a number of bombardments carried out by New Zealand ships during the Emergency. Each was directed by a Forward Air Controller in an Auster aircraft. On this occasion, *Pukaki* gave leaders of the local Chinese and Malay communities a demonstration of naval gunfire. While the bombardment was spectacular, there was very little feedback to the crews on its effectiveness. These naval bombardments, like most indirect artillery fire missions and air strikes into jungle areas, had little military effect beyond impressing local villagers and providing training exercises for the gun crews.

*Pukaki* carried out a range of operational activities, most of which had little real connection with the Emergency operations on the Malay Peninsula. A pattern of exercises and visits was part of every ship's twelve-month tour with the Far East Fleet. For example, *Pukaki* and a British destroyer escorted a British merchant ship through the Formosa (now Taiwan) Strait after it was stopped by a Chinese Nationalist warship. Lieutenant-Commander E. C. Thorne, who commanded *Pukaki* on its next tour in 1955, recalled:

> We all took turns doing the Formosa Strait patrol. You patrolled off, and you would sit off Swatow outside the twelve mile limits providing a presence while these [merchant] ships went in. We were told if they were attacked we would go and try and protect them. Some of these China coasters flew the red ensign. They were a tough bunch of skippers. We would tell them they weren't to go in at night. They would go roaring in, and we had a lot of problems looking after them. I had one incident where a coaster was chased by a Chinese Patrol Craft. Fortunately the ship was fairly fast and we went in and got in between them ... There was constant firing going on across the Formosa Strait at the Island of Quemoy ... which the National Chinese held. Sometimes there would be a lot of firing there and you were never quite sure what it was.[22]

At that time patrols in Korean waters were still important; in fact they were insisted upon by the New Zealand government, which was keen to demonstrate ongoing support for the United Nations.[23] As Thorne related:

> We went as a Squadron from Hong Kong and did a Formosa Strait patrol and then we went on to Japan to Kure ... the main base for Commonwealth ships. In those days in the Kure Dockyard, you could get the whole of the quarter deck re-teaked for a dozen 4-inch [brass shell case] canisters. K Force, the New Zealand Army was there. It became a bit of New Zealand territory ... We went over and did two patrols off Korea, one down off Pusan and one around on the other side. I remember we really learnt what it had been like in the winter up there. The Loch Class Frigates were lovely little ships. In the winter time and even at slow speed the spray coming over the focsle was icicles by the time it hit the bridge. You were standing up there in a sou'wester and oil skins and a towel around your neck. You would have to duck as you could get badly stung by the ice. Ice all over the 4-inch and over the Squid up forwards. You were watching that you weren't getting top heavy. The ship would be sweating down below, cold as charity. We had heaters in the ship, but trying to keep any warmth in the ship was difficult ... It was pretty miserable.[24]

The cold on the Korean patrol was in stark contrast to the heat and humidity in Malayan waters. Here living conditions were hot as well as crowded; metal wind-scoops over the portholes provided the only means of circulating air. Ratings slept in hammocks, with the regulation 18 inches of space allowing a gap of two or three inches between them as they swung in unison. There was an art to getting out of a hammock during the night watch without upsetting the sailor sleeping alongside. Messing conditions were primitive; the cooks had to carry food from the galley to the mess decks. With no laundries on board, each man was responsible for doing his washing in the traditional bucket.

The frigates carried the New Zealand flag to Asian ports, where visits ashore invariably involved the odd 'incident'. As Lieutenant-Commander Kempthorne reported after *Pukaki*'s first tour on the Far East Station:

> 90% of the Medical Officer's time was taken up by the treatment of Venereal Diseases which were extremely prevalent in the civilian population in Hong Kong and Japan ... Almost daily the dismal tale came out, giving a history of exposure from three to five days previously, usually under the influence of alcohol with no prophylactic measures having been taken, and the lady in question usually a prostitute.[25]

During its 12-month tour in Asian waters *Pukaki* reported 148 cases of sexually transmitted disease, with 14 men appearing twice, eight men three times, eight men four times, and two men five times! Repeat offending was 'particularly prevalent among the Cooks and Stewards Branch, involving considerable loss of man-hours, as they were not allowed to prepare or serve food while under treatment'. Kempthorne recommended that 'more care be given to selection of ratings for this branch'.[26] The easy availability of both alcohol and prostitutes, and the resulting high incidence of venereal disease, were to pose continuing problems for New Zealand commanders of all three services.

In August 1954 *Pukaki* was relieved by HMNZS *Kaniere,* captained by Lieutenant-Commander Sam Mercer; the First Lieutenant was Peter Trent, and the watch-keeping officers were Lieutenants Keith Cadman, Denis O'Donoghue and Cedric Steward. Trent, Cadman and O'Donoghue were New Zealanders who had risen from lower ranks, while Steward had been a New Zealand Cadet entrant. Their presence signalled the RNZN's transition from almost total dependence on Royal Navy officers to increasing manning by New Zealanders. *Kaniere* was in the Far East for 14 months, 'which was quite a long time [away] from New Zealand. We did the whole period with only three Watch-keeping Officers ... That meant we were one in three at sea continuously and one in three watch-keeping in harbour ... We did our patrols up to my old grounds again, the west coast of Korea, and we did patrols on the 38th Parallel.'[27] The Formosa Strait patrols also continued.

> On one patrol I think near Foochow ... we actually had a call from a British merchant ship that she was being raided by pirates. This was in the middle of the night, and in darkness we steamed very carefully into Chinese territorial waters to see if we could be of assistance ... We picked up on radar ... a fast frigate coming out of the port in Foochow. We were all on the bridge not really knowing what was going on because of the darkness ... The next thing we saw was a huge search light beamed out to us and we received the international code for 'heave to or we will open fire' ... We were in territorial waters and so we had no legal right to be where we were ... We managed to get a message through to [HMS] *Newcastle* who was further off the coast, and I recall we received instructions to return to international waters immediately. We didn't need any second ordering. I can recall now the Captain's anxiety in ordering 'starboard thirty'—we increased revolutions and were out of there like a shot.[28]

*Kaniere* also spent an extended period hunting pirates off north-east Borneo, in the vicinity of Sandakan.

> We had to go in there and intercept these very shallow draft, wooden-hulled catamaran vessels called 'Kumpits'. The Kumpits were driven by twin American Mercury outboards, very highly powered; they could virtually skim over the coral reefs, perhaps drawing about a foot of water ... [at] up to thirty-five knots ... They were [operated by] Filipinos who came down from the Philippines into that part

> of Borneo and raided the coastal villages, raped the women and caused havoc. There was a great need to at least show some resistance to this by putting ships into the area.[29]

Intense competitiveness was (and remains) a New Zealand trait. 'Sport ... became a very important part of our existence. In a ship's company of about 120 we had four Rugby Fifteens that played regularly.'[30] Competition was not confined to rugby; ship's teams competed in many sporting codes against other ships, other services, and local teams. Each ship also had its own haka and concert party, as Maori were a significant proportion of crews from the beginning; on the cruiser HMNZS *Royalist,* for example, 106 of the complement of 600 were Maori.[31] This was a feature of the lower decks only; the RNZN (like the RNZAF) had very few Maori commissioned officers.

*Kaniere* was relieved by *Pukaki* in July 1955, and returned to New Zealand. It was to go back to South-East Asia in 1956, when it spent most of a 12-month tour on anti-piracy patrols around north Borneo, with frequent visits to Singapore and Hong Kong.

> I don't think anyone ever got better at separating from [their] family. Twelve months away was almost standard in those days to go up to the Far East. The time away was determined by the amount of time, after the work up and deployment and transit, that one could usefully employ as a fully worked up member of the Strategic Reserve. As we relieved on station, twelve months couldn't be argued with, but it did create very extensive welfare problems. I don't think any of the wives ever got used to it. I think probably it was about that point in time that the welfare side of the Navy started to really develop into the kind of organisation that we have today. In those days the Navy was first and the wife and family was second ... it created some quite large problems in terms of the morale and well-being of members of the ship's company and the Navy as a whole.[32]

Lack of concern for family welfare was not solely a naval problem. Both the Air Force and Army were headed by men who had spent six years away from their families during the Second World War, and saw extended absences as part of the job. It was not until 1954 that married men were allowed to live ashore, after the barracks in HMNZS *Philomel* at Devonport were refurbished and bunks installed to replace the hammocks. Prior to that, married men had leave from Saturday afternoon to Monday morning, except when 'long weekend leave' was granted from Friday night.[33] Only gradually was it appreciated that the provision of welfare and housing for families was essential if ratings were to be retained in a seriously undermanned service. A policy of recruiting actively in the Royal Navy would not make up the shortfalls unless the seamen stayed. Pay, housing, conditions of service and family welfare forced their way onto Naval Board agendas as seamen were increasingly attracted into a civilian economy that was critically short of labour.[34]

By 1954 New Zealand had committed itself to providing two cruisers and two or three frigates to the ANZAM region, where they would be used for anti-submarine and anti-raider convoy escort if a world war broke out. The remaining frigates and four minesweepers were reserved for the defence of home waters. One cruiser, two frigates and two minesweepers would be immediately available, but it would take six months to prepare the rest of the fleet, apart from the second cruiser which would require eight months to commission. The Navy was still committed to providing up to three frigates for the defence of Hong Kong in the event of a Cold War emergency, or to assist anti-infiltration and anti-'bandit' operations in Malaya. The frigate under the operational control of the British Naval Commander-in-Chief, Far East Station, was 'available for the above duties or for operations with the United Nations forces in Korean waters'. By now the New Zealand ships were over 11 years old. Both cruisers, *Black Prince* and *Bellona*, were obsolescent and in need of upgraded air defence capabilities. Thanks to advances in submarine technology, the Loch-class anti-submarine frigates were now too slow, and their equipment was obsolete. The government baulked at the cost of replacing ships, and delayed making any decisions.[35] Recruiting remained a serious problem, with manpower fluctuating between 800 and 1,000 below the approved naval rating ceiling of 3,500.

Following the recommendation of the 1953 Melbourne Chiefs of Staff conference that New Zealand's defence commitment shift to South-East Asia, it was decided in 1955 that units of all three services would become part of the Commonwealth Strategic Reserve. New Zealand's Chiefs of Staff warned that 'the Services in their present state are not capable of fully meeting the commitments imposed by our defence policy'.[36] The forces committed to the Strategic Reserve were controlled by the British Defence Coordinating Committee (Far East)—known as BDCC(FE)—in Singapore, an 'integrated political–military committee chaired by the British Commissioner-General for South-East Asia and with the three British service Commanders-in-Chief as members'.[37] On purely British matters, the BDCC(FE) answered to the United Kingdom Chiefs of Staff in London; but on ANZAM matters it reported to the ANZAM Defence Committee in Melbourne, which was primarily Australian-staffed but included liaison cells from the United Kingdom and New Zealand.[38] The RNZN was to provide one frigate, and occasionally two, on station as part of New Zealand's contribution, and the Royal Australian Navy two destroyers or frigates, plus an annual visit by the carrier HMAS *Melbourne*. The Royal Navy would provide four destroyers or frigates.[39] Given this commitment, the New Zealand Naval Board believed it was time to move to a 'six-frigate navy'. This stance had been forced on the Board by the Cabinet's decision not to replace *Bellona*, and its recommendation that two modern frigates be purchased instead as part of the Loch-class replacement programme.[40] However, during his visit to London in February 1955 for the Commonwealth Prime Ministers' Conference, Sidney Holland was persuaded by the Admiralty that Commonwealth interests would best be served by New Zealand retaining cruisers rather than purchasing two frigates. New Zealand was offered the cruiser HMS *Royalist*, which was being modernised by the Royal Navy. Always on the lookout for a bargain and assured that *Royalist* would not be an orphan, Holland agreed to lease the cruiser, with New Zealand meeting the costs of its modernisation. As it turned out, *Royalist* was indeed an orphan, the only one of its class to be modernised.[41]

*Royalist*, a modified Dido-class cruiser displacing 5,900 tons, was armed with eight rapid-fire, dual-purpose, 5.25-inch guns in four twin turrets. Four turbines produced a top speed of 30 knots; the ship's company numbered 39 officers and 508 crew. The last Dido-class cruiser to be built, in 1942, *Royalist*'s modernisation cost £4.5 million. The upgrade provided the communications and facilities of a headquarters control ship, which increased the crew to almost 600 but reduced the space available to them. *Royalist* was commissioned in the Royal New Zealand Navy on 17 April 1956.[42] Captain Peter Phipps, RNZN, who oversaw the commissioning process, regarded the purchase as 'an unmitigated disaster which will affect us all for the next ten to fifteen years'.[43] His fears were realised. The first two Loch-class replacements were not ordered until 1956, and a balance of payments crisis delayed the ordering of a further replacement ship until 1963. The 'six-frigate' fleet the RNZN wanted was thus rendered impossible; even a 'four-frigate' fleet was unlikely. In fact, the *Royalist*'s purchase was still influencing the shape of the RNZN in the 1990s, when the number of frigates required to meet New Zealand's needs under the Anzac frigate replacement programme continued to be debated.

Following *Royalist*'s arrival in December 1956, the Naval Board explored the implications of attaching it to the Far East Fleet. The Navy could now provide a cruiser to defend sea lanes as part of its ANZAM role if a global war broke out. The Naval Board acknowledged that it was beyond New Zealand's resources to modernise the second cruiser, *Black Prince*, which would remain in reserve.[44] After much debate, the Chiefs of Staff recommended to the government the attachment of *Royalist* to the Far East Fleet in early 1957. Both the Chief of General Staff, Major-General C. E. Weir, and the Chief of Air Staff, Air Vice-Marshal C. E. Kay, believed that New Zealand's most effective contribution would be to provide ground and air resources, 'as at present there were insufficient troops and air forces to meet the needs of the cold war, let alone the requirements of limited war'. Providing *Royalist* as the RNZN's contribution to the Commonwealth Strategic Reserve would mean doubling or even trebling the naval commitment. The Army and Air Force staffs feared that the government would then trim back the commitments of the other two services. The Navy believed (correctly) that *Royalist* could operate efficiently only as part of a larger naval force; this had already been proved with the frigate attachments. Cabinet agreed that *Royalist* would replace *Kaniere*, joining the Fleet in July 1957.[45] The ANZAM Defence Committee was told that New Zealand's naval contribution to the Commonwealth Strategic Reserve would change from 'One (occasionally two) frigates(s)' to 'One cruiser *or* one (occasionally two) frigate(s)'.[46]

*Royalist*, commanded by Captain G. D. Pound (a Royal Navy officer on secondment), was welcomed into Singapore on 18 July 1957 by an escort of Bristol Freighters of No. 41 Squadron RNZAF and Venom fighters of No. 14 Squadron RNZAF. It joined HMS *Newcastle* and HMS *Newfoundland* in the 5th Cruiser Squadron. Pound was very conscious that this was the first long-term deployment of a New Zealand cruiser in peacetime. Indeed, attaching *Royalist* to the Far East Fleet was the New Zealand Navy's first major peacetime test. Some two-fifths of the Navy's personnel were needed to man the cruiser, 'with more or less the same proportion of Navy wives also having to face a separation of some twelve months or so'.

> This was something they were hardly likely to welcome, and their reaction undoubtedly had an unsettling effect on the ship during the early months. For instance, no sooner had the ship commissioned than I was informed by my P.O. [Petty Officer] Steward that he expected to leave the ship very shortly on medical grounds. Many others tried to follow his example and for a long time various ways were tried ... one offender [came] up before me on a serious charge towards the end of the work up, and he obviously expected the punishment ... would get him

> back to New Zealand. The expression on his face was quite something when I gave him punishment which didn't do that, and ... he promptly hit the Master at Arms to make quite sure that the next charge did ensure his return. We had this sort of trouble in the early days and it was only when the Navy Board agreed that any man sent back from the ship to New Zealand for whatever reason will always be returned to the ship and not left in New Zealand, that things settled down.[47]

The stresses Pound referred to had not been thought through by the RNZN. The *Royalist*'s crew was the equivalent of five frigates' crews. Manning *Royalist* and the frigates that were not in reserve meant that every available seaman was put on seagoing duties. There were also strains on the RNZN's administration, with another cause of discontent during the work-up period being 'the unsatisfactory state of the mail, and also what was coming in the mail when it did arrive'—complaints from home.[48]

Pound reported to the Naval Board on the state of discipline in the New Zealand Navy in highly critical terms. While deficiencies were less apparent on short-term deployments to the Pacific, the demands of maintaining a large ship on operations highlighted lax basic training and 'too easy routines ashore in Auckland'. While the ship was in Australian waters, the combination of an intensive work-up period and the attractions of Australian beer and bar opening hours was too much for the ship's crew.

> It became very apparent that their outlook was that they had joined *Royalist* for a jolly [time] and that work very definitely took second place. They were slow and surly, leave-breaking and drunkenness assumed alarming proportions, and the tarts of Sydney had far more control over them than we did. Most alarming of all was that they didn't seem to understand the error of their ways ... nor did they have any real conception of what a taut routine in an operational ship entailed. Their manners, small courtesies of standing up and so on, weren't there because they didn't know. There was friction among themselves on the mess deck, and all in all they were not a happy ship. Above all they had no idea of their purpose in life, as a sailor in the Navy. They had a forty-hour-week complex with some limited travel and gay lights thrown in.[49]

In Singapore, *Royalist*'s New Zealand naval stewards were replaced by locally employed Chinese stewards. Pound's only regret was that he could not also replace his New Zealand cooks, 'the junior rates of which are of a deplorably low professional standard mainly due to a lack of interest'. The ship also took on board 'Unofficial Chinese', local tradesmen employed for the duration of the tour, who 're-started the Ship's laundry and set up shop in the

Forward Capstan Flat with their tailoring and Bootmaking business'. As a result, a 'reliable twenty-four hour laundry service is in operation and the quality of the work done is good'. The employment of Chinese ratings and laundry staff remained a feature of New Zealand naval deployments to South-East Asia into the 1990s. Like the crews of the Loch-class frigates, *Royalist*'s complement experienced the difficulties of shipboard life in the tropics—although the frigates were roomy by comparison. The heat and cramped conditions in the mess-decks affected the crew's health and morale, leading to 'isolated and entirely unconnected crimes of temper'. While these were dealt with firmly, working conditions were not so easily improved. 'Many Engine Room ratings are suffering from boils ... Heat exhaustion among men working in Boiler Rooms and Engine Rooms is quite common at present.'[50]

Pound's success in drilling and cajoling the *Royalist*'s crew into shape was evident during the ship's tour with the Far East Fleet. Leading Seaman John Carter, a Fire Controller 2nd Class in the forward Transmitting Station or Fire Control Director for the two forward 5.25-inch turrets, had a far more positive view of his crewmates than did his Captain:

> Quite a few of the crew were Maori, most of them were New Zealanders, a few like myself were Poms, but we all got on famously together. It was a very, very good competitive crew. We excelled at everything we did and we were the smallest cruiser on the Singapore station, and we became Cock of the Fleet for all our regatta pulling races with boats. I think we did very well at the rugby games. In fact anything we participated in we did well at.[51]

The fire control and gunnery system on *Royalist* was state of the art for its time, and very accurate. Indeed, so accurate were the ship's guns that on fleet firing exercises, where the ships steamed in line and fired in turn at an aircraft-towed drogue target, *Royalist* was always positioned last in line because 'invariably once it came past us we would shoot and hit it', thus stopping the shoot until the drogue was replaced. The ship was equally successful against remotely piloted aircraft (drones), which 'they said could never be hit because the guy controlling it can actually see where the shells were bursting and move the plane away, but that didn't allow for the first shot, and we invariably knocked it out of the sky'. Carter recorded *Royalist*'s success on the door of the transmitting station. 'I had five complete drones painted on the door, and two half ones which didn't mean that we only hit half of it, it means that both systems forward and aft were firing at the same time when we got it, and so we both claimed half.'[52]

On 25 July 1957 *Royalist* bombarded an area of jungle inland from Tanjong Lampat in south-east Johore that was thought to contain guerrilla camps. The operation was directed from an Auster aircraft by a Royal Artillery officer, who reported that all 86 rounds 'fell in the target area'. As always, 'no positive results could be determined until Police patrols went through on foot and inspected the damage'.[53] After visits to Hong Kong, Japan and Korea, interspersed with exercises and training, the ship returned for a refit in Singapore in December 1957. On 20 February 1958, *Royalist* again carried out a coastal bombardment in south-east Johore, at Tanjong Punggai. Directed from a spotter aircraft, the gunners fired 152 rounds in two-gun salvos over two hours at suspected communist positions. Once again, no immediate confirmation of damage was possible.[54] These two bombardments were *Royalist*'s contribution to the Emergency. For the crew they were simply more tasks, and perhaps less satisfying than shooting a drone out of the sky because there was nothing to see and no feedback on the results, just good exercise for the gun crews over an extended period.

*Royalist* took part in a number of major exercises, including the SEATO exercise OCEANLINK with ships of the Royal, Australian, United States and Pakistan navies. *Royalist* proved to be a highly efficient ship, with by far the best gunnery in the 5th Cruiser Squadron, and with her communication and command equipment was a great asset to the British Far East Fleet. When *Rotoiti* replaced it in June 1958, *Royalist* was farewelled from Hong Kong with a 'salute of firecrackers from the "Sampan Marys"'.[55] Pound had achieved his aim. 'To operate alongside these ships was a real challenge to New Zealand's Cruiser ... I can only say that throughout our eleven months on the Station we very frequently led the field and we were always hard to beat.'[56] The RNZN was fortunate in the calibre of *Royalist*'s captain. Lieutenant-Commander Michael Saull, the Second Gunnery Officer, remembers Pound as 'probably one of the finest naval officers I have ever met in my life. He seemed to imbue in the ship's company an enormous spirit.'[57] *Royalist*'s first tour with the Far East Fleet came at an important time in the Navy's development, and was part of its growing up.

In 1956, two Type 12 Whitby-class frigates were ordered to replace the ageing Loch-class ships. As it turned out, the continuing development of the Whitby class resulted in the RNZN receiving two modified Type 12 Rothesay-class frigates. The Whitbys and Rothesays were the latest design in anti-submarine frigates, being fast with a good range, as well as having 'sufficient armament to provide good protection from aerial attack and a useful surface gunnery role'.[58] The keel of HMNZS *Otago*—originally intended for the Royal Navy—was laid in 1957. The ship was launched in 1958 and commissioned in 1960, with HMNZS *Taranaki* following in 1961. Though replacement thus took five years, the next vessel was not ordered until 1963. The cost of maintaining a New Zealand cruiser standard had already ended any chance of maintaining a 'six-frigate' navy. In hindsight, a modern four-frigate navy with accompanying smaller vessels was what the RNZN should have planned for after its post-war reformation. The size of the reserve fleet in the 1950s disguised its inability to ever man more than four frigates simultaneously.

*Otago* and *Taranaki* were innovative in that they differed from the Royal Navy's standard design. The RNZN had to fight to have changes made, but the outcome was the development of a 'New Zealand' frigate concept, the Otago class.[59] Completed in June 1960, *Otago* displaced some 2,500 tons, and was 370 feet long and 41 feet in breadth. Twin steam-turbine engines produced 30,000 horsepower and gave a maximum speed of 30 knots. *Otago* was armed with two 4.5-inch guns in a twin turret forward, two 40-mm Bofors, and two Limbo three-barrelled depth-charge mortars and eight 21-inch torpedo tubes for anti-submarine work. It had the latest in medium-range radar as well as sonar for submarine detection.[60] In 1963 the RNZN entered the missile age when a quadruple Seacat missile launcher for air defence was added to both *Otago* and *Taranaki*. While *Royalist* had marked a significant step forward in gunnery and fire control systems, the new frigates introduced the RNZN to advances in a comprehensive range of operational equipment in anti-submarine warfare, gunnery and communications, all of which presented a significant challenge to its professional standards. 'For the first time the operational capabilities of the RNZN could be measured against the standards of the RN, the RAN and the US Navy who generally had similar equipments.'[61] The RNZN rose to the occasion, establishing a reputation for efficiency that was evident in the reports of the Flag Officer Sea Training Staff at the Portland work-up facility of the Royal Navy.[62]

The Naval Board insisted that *Otago* have centralised cafeteria-style messing from a single galley, bunks rather than hammocks for all crew, and a ship's laundry. Unlike their Loch-class predecessors, both *Otago* and *Taranaki* had enclosed bridges with a below-decks operations room from which the Captain fought the ship.[63] Commander E. C. Thorne, who took command of *Otago* in 1963, recalled that 'The change from a Loch-class frigate was noticeable right from the start. The CO's cabins ... were extremely comfortable because they had been designed so that we could take Governor-Generals and various VIPs around the islands ... Also it was a joy to get on board a ship with proper air-conditioning.'[64] The crew were also positive:

> They had dining halls on the ship, one for the ship's company, one for senior ranks, and the wardroom for officers. All the food was cooked in the one galley and the chefs were really top-line chefs, the food was absolutely marvellous. In fact you can virtually judge a ship by the food they serve. If a ship goes into harbour and everybody goes ashore at 4 o'clock when they are entitled to, it is because it is not worth staying on board for the evening meal. In the *Otago* nobody ever went ashore until after they had eaten their evening meal.[65]

*Taranaki* was completed in March 1961 and became the first of the new frigates to join the Far East Fleet in Singapore, relieving *Pukaki* in 1962. This ended 12 years of service in Asian waters by New Zealand's Loch-class frigates, a sequence which had begun with *Pukaki*.[66] Initially the Chief of Naval Staff, Rear-Admiral Peter Phipps, wanted to order two more Type 12 frigates, but he recognised that this goal was unrealistic given the government's unwillingness to commit itself to major increases in defence expenditure. Nonetheless, Phipps fought for and won approval for the purchase of a third frigate; the Leander-class HMNZS *Waikato* was ordered in 1963. Whereas *Otago* and *Taranaki* had taken the RNZN into the missile age, *Waikato* gave it a small ship-aviation capability thanks to the inclusion of Wasp (Weapon Anti-Submarine Platform) helicopters.[67]

The Royal New Zealand Navy played only a minor role in the Malayan Emergency. During the early 1950s it was committed to the Korean War. A broadening of focus to include South-East Asia in 1954 saw it meeting its Commonwealth Strategic Reserve commitment to SEATO planning from 1955. Through its contribution to the Far East Fleet, the RNZN showed the New Zealand flag in ports throughout Asia, including the Indian subcontinent. For many of the New Zealanders who served on the ships for 12–14 months, this was their first extended contact with Asia. It was also the RNZN's first experience of meeting sequential 12-month deployments involving an ongoing rotation of ships in peacetime.[68] Strains on personnel and their families were compounded by the deficiencies of the RNZN's administration and welfare services. Such problems were not at first appreciated by the Naval Board, whose members had served overseas for a number of years at a time, and saw an absence of one to three years as a normal condition of service. The RNZN found itself trying to recruit and retain a generation who would no longer accept such privations.[69] The Navy had to improve its administration to match the demands it placed on its personnel. The pressures on its financial and manpower resources raised doubts as to its ability to meet its obligations under the ANZAM arrangements. The government's decision that the RNZN remain on the cruiser standard had long-term implications for the size of its fleet, implications which still reverberate to this day. The end of the Emergency in 1960 made no difference to the Navy's commitment to the Commonwealth Strategic Reserve and the demands this placed on an increasingly obsolete fleet. However, the arrival of the Otago-class frigates in the 1960s, even though these were far too few, signalled the evolution of an increasingly distinctive New Zealand Navy, officered and manned by New Zealanders, which would find an important role for itself in South-East Asia.

# 3

# FLYING THE SILVER FERN

## *Air Force Operations, 1955–62*

> It has become increasingly clear that the security of South-East Asia, and as part of it the security of Malaya, are of special significance to New Zealand ... I was able to announce at a meeting that our Cabinet had authorised me to agree to the transfer to Malaya of No. 14 Fighter-Bomber Squadron at present stationed on Cyprus and of the 41st Half Transport Squadron. This latter had been brought back to New Zealand from Malaya in 1952 for re-equipment.[1]
>
> RT HON. SIDNEY HOLLAND,
> PRIME MINISTER OF NEW ZEALAND

At the Commonwealth Prime Ministers' Conference in London in February 1955, New Zealand's Prime Minister, Sidney Holland, committed Regular Force units of the Army, Navy and Air Force to Malaya as part of the newly instituted Commonwealth Far East Strategic Reserve. This ended New Zealand's commitment to the Middle East as part of defence planning for global war. It was a major step for New Zealand to take with its minuscule Regular forces, one raising important questions about their existing organisation and structure; it also highlighted the need for Regular units that could be deployed immediately to dampen down a brushfire before it became a major conflagration. New Zealand's military forces were not organised to meet such a 'cold war' contingency, having been structured to respond to a 'hot war' situation by providing an expeditionary force. The one exception was the Royal New Zealand Navy; the New Zealand Army had no Regular units at all, while the Royal New Zealand Air Force had a limited number of Regular squadrons backed up by the five squadrons of the Territorial Air Force.[2] It was becoming increasingly obvious that the government could not afford to equip and man the Territorial Air Force to meet the challenge of a modern air war.[3]

In the early 1950s the RNZAF was re-equipped with Vampire jet fighters, Hastings long-range transport aircraft, and Bristol Freighters.[4] At the time of Holland's announcement the No. 5 (Flying Boat) Squadron was stationed at Lauthala Bay in Fiji, while No. 14 Squadron, flying leased Vampire jets, was in Cyprus as part of the Middle East Command of the Royal Air Force.[5] Now New Zealand was committing both 14 and 41 Squadrons to the Commonwealth Strategic Reserve in Malaya; Holland also announced that No. 5 (Flying Boat) Squadron would conduct regular deployments to Malaya, and that the Hastings transport aircraft of No. 40 Squadron would provide support. Consequently, from 1955 onwards, the RNZAF deployed almost everything it had as part of the Commonwealth Strategic Reserve. For the next 11 years, the RNZAF was to be overstretched by its commitment to South-East Asia.

## The Ubiquitous Bristol Freighter, 1955–62

> The Kiwis seem to be really infiltrating into this part of the world.[6]
>
> No. 41 Squadron RNZAF Unit History

As he farewelled No. 41 Squadron RNZAF on its departure for Singapore in May 1955, Sidney Holland declared that Malaya was now 'the front-line of New Zealand's very defence system'.[7] New Zealand was 'not going to allow Malaya to fall under Communist influence. It can and will definitely be defended ... Your task will be helping to root out the terrorists who have been driven back into the hills.'[8] Once again, the Squadron became an integral part of the Far East Air Force (FEAF), this time as part of the newly formed Commonwealth Strategic Reserve. Its primary role was to 'train and operate in a medium range transport role' for operations in South-East Asia; it was also available to be used 'in operations against the Communist terrorists', although this was a secondary consideration.[9]

Thanks to the Briggs Plan, the security forces were winning the war. By the time General Templer left Malaya in mid-1954 the guerrillas' numbers had fallen to around 3,000 from their peak strength of some 8,000 in 1951.[10] After Templer's departure his responsibilities were once again split; his civilian deputy, Sir Donald MacGillivray, became High Commissioner, and Lieutenant-General

Sir Geoffrey Bourne became Director of Operations.[11] The MRLA, now on the defensive, was reduced to a total of 30–40 platoons, many comprising only 10 to 12 men. This hard core, skilled at survival and adept at jungle craft, had been driven back into the fastness of the central highlands. In June 1955, Chin Peng, the general secretary of the MCP, offered to negotiate a settlement, but this was rejected by the Malayan authorities. The following month the Alliance Party under Tunku Abdul Rahman won Malaya's first Federal elections.

During the last six months of 1955 hostilities between the guerrillas and the security forces subsided. In September the guerrillas were offered an amnesty. Chin Peng and the Chief Ministers of the Federation of Malaya and Singapore met at Baling, in Kedah State near the Thai border, on 28–29 December. The talks reached stalemate, and on 8 February 1956 a full-scale shooting war resumed.[12] The first New Zealand components of the Commonwealth Strategic Reserve thus arrived just in time for the final act: the lengthy process of mopping up the MRLA, which was now intent on surviving until Malayan independence was declared. If their organisation remained intact, Chin Peng and the MCP believed they could play a significant role in the new state's political life.

No. 41 Squadron's wartime Dakota aircraft had been replaced by twin-engine Bristol B170 Freighters.[13] With its distinctive nose-opening cargo doors and fixed undercarriage, the B170 was designed as a freight or passenger aircraft capable of transporting a large payload over comparatively short distances.[14] At the time the Dakotas' replacements were selected, the RNZAF was involved in aerial top-dressing experiments, and the Freighter was seen as suitable for a dual role of transport and top-dressing.[15] New Zealand eventually purchased twelve Freighters, and for the next 22 years this ugly, bulbous-nosed machine was to symbolise its defence effort in South-East Asia.[16]

On 12 May 1955 the first two Bristol Freighters took off from Whenuapai for Singapore, with Squadron Leader Ron Manners once again going first. 'I was determined to arrive right on time, which we did, and over the next three days the other aircraft arrived with all the ground staff.' Initially they were accommodated in one building and several marquee tents at the end of an old runway at RAF Changi. 'Pretty poor generally but that didn't last forever because they slowly built us our own dispersal area.'[17] Squadron officers were accommodated in the Temple Hill Mess, and airmen in the large multi-storey pre-war concrete barracks. It was an unsettled time, made worse by all personnel being confined to base because of riots in the city during the election of Singapore's first representative government.[18]

Ron Manners was surprised to discover that the RAF had no Bristol Freighters. 'They were astonished to see these darn things too. They were not a pretty aeroplane. Not as pretty as a Dakota, [but] nevertheless very functional.' The New Zealanders practised dropping supplies over the airfield and almost immediately started flying the courier routes, 'the best way to find out what the area was like'. Manners found Malaya and Singapore to be little changed. 'The terrorists were still active and we did the same sort of jobs except this time going to Hong Kong on the courier runs we would always go through Saigon or alternatively we'd go through Labuan which is an island off the north coast of Borneo, then Clark Field in the Philippines, stay overnight, then on to Hong Kong.' No. 41 Squadron were keen to show the RAF what they and their aircraft could do, particularly its short take-off and landing capability. 'We'd get right down to about 65–70 knots and really hang it on its propellers, [then] at the end of the runway [we'd] land, stop, put on the brakes, stop quickly and have all the RAF people with their mouths open, then we'd open up and take off. You could do that two or three times along the runway length.'[19]

The RAF was particularly short of transport aircraft, at a time when the MRLA's retreat into the jungle meant that the security forces needed to be supplied by air to mount patrols lasting up to three months. Helicopters had been introduced and were to prove invaluable, but they were limited in number and extremely limited in what they could carry. The responsibility for resupplying patrols continued to rest mainly on the short- and medium-range transport aircraft, and it was here that No. 41 Squadron came into its own. The Dakotas of the RAF squadrons had been replaced by British-designed, twin-engine Valetta transport aircraft.[20] The Valettas were initially plagued by mechanical delays and servicing problems, and their limited capacity and layout made them difficult aircraft for Army air dispatchers to work with. By contrast,

> we could carry about twice as much as their aircraft could. We could stay out longer and cover more dropping zones. The dispatchers enjoyed going in Bristol Freighters because it was a flat floor. The Valetta aircraft that the RAF used had a spar down the middle and they had to hump the supply packs across it to get to the door. In fact they doubled up on the number of dispatchers in our aircraft to what the RAF had because we carried so much.[21]

A Bristol Freighter could carry 9,000 lb, compared to the Valetta's 3,000 lb. The RAF Movements staff were 'overjoyed to see the Bristol Freighter arrive' because of its ease of loading and unloading.[22]

Operational supply-dropping began in June 1955, when a Bristol Freighter was stationed at Kuala Lumpur to make supply and propaganda leaflet drops over the jungle, the latter encouraging guerrillas to surrender.[23] The first drops caused concern when dents were found on the aircraft's fuselage opposite the rear door exit. Getting the dispatchers to cut the bindings on the leaflet bundles so that they blew apart when released, rather than bouncing their way along the fuselage as a solid bundle, solved the problem.[24] There were mixed reactions on the ground to both the amnesty and the leaflets. John Cross, a company commander in 1/7th Gurkha Rifles, recalled:

> These surrender leaflets were of interest and had photographs of contented men, the theme being, 'You too can lead an easy life if you give up.' Some of them had little scenes depicting, in strip cartoon fashion, the return of the prodigal son. Father rushes out and falls on the neck of his returning and once-errant offspring who shakes father's hand and they all live happily ever after. It was clear that this was the work of a European ill-versed in the Chinese etiquette. No such parental joy would be expressed in public nor [would] such carefree filial bad manners be entertained. These leaflets must have nullified much patient good work by those who knew what they were doing but could not advertise it.[25]

None of this was known to the sweating air and despatch crews as they covered the forest canopy with fluttering streams of paper.

In early 1956 problems with servicing the Valettas saw three Freighters sent to Kuala Lumpur to carry out all the supply drops for a period of six weeks, including on 'days when ... visibility [was] down to a matter of a few feet and the jungle DZs were almost hidden from view'.[26] A typical mission from Kuala Lumpur would begin with the crew being briefed while the Army despatchers loaded the aircraft with supplies to be dropped. Ron Manners remembered that the pilot would check the weather,

> and then you'd go to the aircraft. The Army despatchers would all be waiting there. You would take the door off the aircraft, because there was no way you could open it from the inside. Well you could but you would lose it, so you flew with no door on. You would have worked out with your navigator how to get to the various dropping zones. He would have marked them all on his map and then you'd head off. As soon as you were getting close you would start calling the DZ and establish contact. A lot depended on the type of drop, and whether you were dropping into a jungle DZ as opposed to a fort. A fort you can see but a jungle DZ is a small hole or chimney in the trees, and these trees can be anything up to 250 feet high. So you are flying not very high up over the trees when you drop, usually 300 feet. They

were supposed to put up smoke to mark the DZ, some of them would put up a balloon. If there was smoke then it could drift out through the trees and you could be led real and truly up the garden path. Once you locate it you can look down as you go over for a dummy run, and see all these faces looking at you. You go round and hopefully pick it up again. Hopefully the smoke's still there, and then you come in again.

[The supplies] are normally packed in 200 lb lots with the parachute attached to a wire inside the aircraft and the supply is loaded onto a hinged tray with a couple of handles and a guy on each side. As you are getting closer to the DZ, you're warning them '10 seconds', '5 seconds', and then 'Drop!' You also push a button and a light comes on and a bell goes off, and the despatchers tip it out the door. Then they load up the next one and you go round and go on and on until you have dropped all the supplies. Then you go on to the next DZ. Your navigator tells you where to go. So you either dodge around the hills or go over them. [It was not difficult flying] providing you didn't get into clouds. If you went into cloud then it was very difficult because we weren't altogether sure of the height of some of the hills.[27]

Supporting ground operations in the central highlands of Malaya called for a great deal of skill.

[The terrain] was extremely hilly, lots of cloud hanging around ... Most of our dropping zones were in rather tricky places. Fort Brooke was one of these. It was a little area with a little airstrip with hills all around. You had to go in, drop and pour on the power and climb out. This made it extremely difficult. But nevertheless it was all gratifying particularly when you hit the target and they got their food, clothing, medical supplies, ammunition and whatever they needed ... In the actual dropping the Bristol Freighter was magnificent. You drop a bit of flap and it's got tremendous power, so you can get the speed right down. On a supply drop I used to aim at about 95–100 knots, dropping one package at a time.

A simple drop might be completed in an hour and 20 minutes, but three to four hours was usual, and a mission could take up to six. It was demanding work that tested the pilots and their crews. Flying so low 'in intense heat, turbulent conditions and often in bad weather', aircrew could lose several pounds in body weight through sweating in a single mission.[28]

Members of Nos 14 and 41 Squadrons RNZAF were joined by their families in Singapore, where the first small party of five wives and 11 children arrived by RNZAF Hastings in late June 1955. Soon there were 42 families on the island, living in local civilian accommodation or RAF quarters on the bases. For married couples there were many attractions, the *New Zealand Herald* reported. '"Housie", dances and parties are popular forms of entertainment and ... life for Air Force wives seems to be one long siesta. Malaya certainly sounds like a serviceman's paradise. A sergeant just back from Changi reports nylon stockings at 3s 6d a pair, wrist watches of the finest quality for £4 and cameras for a third of the New Zealand price.' Allowances gave the families money to spend, and the New Zealand wives found that it was normal to hire local women as amahs to clean the house, cook the meals, and mind the children. All this took some getting used to. Many women found it very difficult having someone else in their house, doing the work they had always done, especially as skill in housekeeping and cooking was proof of a New Zealand woman's status as a wife in the 1950s. Now their lives revolved around the local RAF swimming club, ladies' golf days, learning the intricacies of mah-jong, and shopping at Robinsons Department Store or Cold Storage. There was also the opportunity for families to purchase a car, such as 'a 1948 custom-built Packard for £240. Another New Zealander paid £100 for a 1949 Hudson and several others have bought late model American cars for prices ranging from £90 to £140. Second-hand English cars are dirt cheap.'[29] New Zealanders at home could purchase a new car only if they had overseas funds, and paid more for a second-hand car than the list price of a new car.

Life for the families was never as easy as it seemed, even in the RAF housing enclaves around Changi and Tengah air bases. Downtown Singapore was a strange, dirty, largely Chinese city, very different from anything they had experienced in New Zealand. The heat and humidity; the resulting lassitude and the nagging colds that came with it; the strange vegetation; the smells of the markets and the drains; the many different peoples and languages; the sheer bedlam of an Asian city; the impossibility of getting the men at the garage to listen to what the European memsahib thought was wrong with the car, or the grocer's boy to bring the brand the family was used to at home; the slow-turning ceiling fans, the flying foxes and bats at twilight; the quarrelling 'chit-chats' (house-lizards) on the ceilings; the need for large tent-like mosquito nets over the beds at night; the likelihood of snakes in the garden—all these things caused considerable stress and made bouts of homesickness inevitable. Families gradually learned to cope, and in most cases enjoy these new experiences; but most were happy to go home after two years.[30]

Single airmen had more to complain about. They felt excluded from the social activities available to married personnel living in rented housing around the bases. Instead they went sightseeing 'at places like "Change Alley", the

"Tiger Balm Gardens", or window shopping in magnificent Orchard Road. The Indian quarter had silversmiths, goldsmiths and shoemakers and were a revelation to us in quality and price. A sightseeing tour to Raffles Hotel was almost obligatory, but only once—colonials were definitely not welcome.'[31] They rarely had the opportunity to visit private homes, and like their counterparts in the RNZN and Army usually had contact with local civilians only in bars. The RNZAF, like the other services, attempted to reduce the disturbingly high rate of venereal disease among its personnel, with little success.[32]

Conditions for single servicemen on base were also unsatisfactory. Everyone complained about the quantity and quality of the food served in the airmen's messes. It was a gripe they shared with the New Zealand SAS Squadron in Kuala Lumpur when they too tasted British services cooking. 'Poor food wrecks morale'; moreover, the disgruntled airmen found no compensation in their pay packets for their inadequate conditions of service.[33] Malcolm McNaught, who had joined the RNZAF on leaving school in 1950 as an airman cadet, arrived at No. 14 Squadron in Tengah in November 1955 as 'part of a group of replacement ground staff for personnel whose tours had expired when the squadron arrived from Cyprus'.[34] At 21 he was an experienced Leading Aircraftman, having worked on Mustangs and Vampires, and on Sunderland flying boats for the last 15 months at Lauthala Bay with No. 5 Maritime Squadron. He remembered that dissatisfaction about the food built up for some time, especially with the dehydrated potatoes served at midday: 'Always mashed, they were pale grey in appearance, with a consistency of thick, gluey rubber'. The response of the RNZAF and Australian airmen was to have lunchtime competitions to see who could make 'balls of this stuff stick to the slow revolving ceiling fans'. This activity led to a heated confrontation one lunchtime between the New Zealand airmen and the messing staff. When the senior RAF Flight Lieutenant responsible for catering intervened, he was shown the empty cans, labelled 'Dehydrated Potato–Mashed–1944', which had been rescued from the rubbish tins as proof. He promised a better standard of food in the future. This protest action had a sequel some weeks later when the New Zealand airmen boycotted a visit by their Defence Minister to a midday meal in the airmen's mess. The result was a special squadron parade at 7.30 the next morning, at which the commander 'read the Riot Act'.[35]

A policy that airmen's allowances were reduced with each pay increase led to a decrease in the real pay of single airmen in Singapore. A major cut in allowances in early 1957 added to the growing dissatisfaction with conditions of service.[36] While some improvements were made, the 'on-pay and off-allowances' policy remained a source of complaint for single servicemen for the duration of New Zealand's presence in Malaya and Singapore.

On 1 November 1956 Ron Manners was succeeded by Squadron Leader A. S. ('Stu') Tie. British transport squadrons had been relocated from South-East Asia to the Middle East in response to the Suez crisis, and supply-dropping was now the responsibility of No. 41 Squadron. Three of its four Freighters based at Kuala Lumpur, together with a single RAF Valetta under New Zealand operational command, carried out all the supply drops to the security forces patrolling in the jungle.[37] Although Stu Tie lacked experience flying Bristol Freighters in these conditions, on 10 December he captained a mission that was being filmed by a Malayan film unit. This sortie was originally allocated to Flight Lieutenant Graeme Bayliss, DFC, the most experienced supply-dropping pilot in the squadron. Instead, it became Tie's first experience of captaining an aircraft over central Malaya, and ended in disaster. Tie flew under the cloud ceiling up a narrow valley towards the mountains. When he found the valley narrowing, instead of turning around as an experienced pilot would have done, he climbed into the cloud and flew into the mountainside at a height of about 4,200 feet, killing himself, his three crew, three Army air despatchers and the two members of the film unit. Incredibly one despatcher survived, being thrown out of the open doorway just as the plane crashed, and having his fall cushioned by the jungle canopy. Although the wreckage was spotted by an RAF light aircraft, it was two days before ground parties could reach the site. The sole survivor walked out, and was found in an exhausted state 12 days later.[38] This 'most unfortunate and tragic incident' could have been avoided by a more experienced captain.[39]

The tragedy highlighted the dangers of flying over the mountains of central Malaya, dangers the aircrews lived with and their families dreaded. The difficult flying conditions, with constant low cloud shrouding jungle-covered hills, meant that the 'casualty rate amongst supply-drop aircrews was about four times that of the infantry'.[40] Between March and December 1956, four transport aircraft were lost over Malaya. The gradual construction of airstrips alongside the jungle forts or police posts in the mountain valleys, and the increasing number of helicopters, helped alleviate the pressure on transport aircraft. The number of troops deployed in the Malayan jungle had reached its peak in 1955, when 4,000 tons of supplies—and more than 140 million leaflets—were dropped.[41]

After the Freighter crash, it became RNZAF policy to send 'only the most experienced aircrews to No. 41 Squadron'.[42] Tie was replaced as

Squadron Leader by 31-year-old Gordon Tosland, who had been born and educated in Hawera and worked on his parents' farm before joining the RNZAF in 1943. After training as a pilot in New Zealand and Canada, he served as a Sergeant Flight Engineer on Lancaster bombers over Europe in the closing stages of the war. In 1945 he was discharged from the RNZAF and returned to the family farm. Two years later he re-enlisted as a Leading Aircraftman Mechanic and in 1948 he was re-mustered as a pilot, flying Sunderland flying boats with No. 5 Squadron at Lauthala Bay before being commissioned in 1949. Tosland served as a captain on four-engine Hastings aircraft with No. 24 (Commonwealth) Squadron RAF, and with Nos 41 and 42 Squadrons RNZAF in New Zealand. From 1955 he commanded the Transport Support Unit at Whenuapai, which operated the RNZAF's Bristol Freighters that were based in New Zealand. He was thus the obvious choice to pull the squadron together after Tie's death.

The Freighters were back in business in March 1957, reinforcing their RAF counterparts of Nos 48, 52 and 101 Squadrons.[43] Flying Officer Merle Preece made a series of drops into Fort Chabai of bulldozer parts and railway track needed for the construction of a new airstrip. Chabai was north of Kuala Lumpur in the central mountain ranges, 'tucked in a narrow valley, and even from hundreds of feet up there is no sign of civilisation in any direction'. It was one of many difficult drop zones that necessitated 'a dog's-leg approach up the valley'.[44] Preece made 20 runs over the fort on his first sortie, and 25 the next day. This was the country in which the New Zealanders of the Special Air Service Squadron had operated throughout 1956, and the infantry of the First and Second Battalions New Zealand Regiment were to operate between 1957 and 1960.[45] Lieutenant Ken Gordon, a platoon commander in 1 New Zealand Regiment, received a New Zealand supply drop in 1958.

> [It] was fabulous because up until then all our airdrops in our platoon had been by RAF Valettas and this was the first time we had an RNZAF Bristol Freighter. It was a very impressive sight. It stood on its wing literally going around in circles, round the little DZ, and I said to it at the time, 'Why don't you do straight runs?' He said, 'You obviously can't see the hills that are behind you.' And so it just stood on its wing and went round and round, almost at no miles an hour. We had everything dropped right onto the DZ, just like that.[46]

The Kiwi transport crews flying courier routes regarded themselves as the 'kings of aviation' in Malaya.[47] The Bristol Freighters of No. 41 Squadron were the aerial equivalent of tramp steamers, flying the regular RAF schedules to Hong Kong via the Philippines, Negombo (an RAF airfield in Ceylon), Butterworth, Labuan and Kuala Lumpur, as well as any special tasks to Australia or elsewhere in Asia. They carried anything—and anybody—anywhere. In 1958 the squadron's duties became more varied when it took over from No. 48 (Transport) Squadron RAF, which was redeployed to the Middle East. One task was taking a team of detectives from Singapore to Christmas Island for a murder investigation, then on to Cocos Island after some anxious moments as the crew 'waited for the Freighter to unstick itself from the mud of the short (3000') hump-backed runway built on the side of a hill that is Xmas Island'.[48] Others were a run to the Maldives, 'uplifting Pakistani labourers held up by a wharf strike and regulations in Ceylon'; and flying the Far East Air Force Band to Jesselton (Kota Kinabalu) in British North Borneo to celebrate the centenary of the town of Beaufort. The latter was a great success, 'as are most shows where the men drink their brandy neat and by the tumbler'.[49] Other duties included surveying the Maldives, ferrying New Zealand Army wives and families to Ipoh, supporting SEATO exercises in Thailand, carrying supplies for the construction of the new British Embassy at Vientiane in Laos, and supply-dropping operations from Kuala Lumpur. All were done in a single month by the Bristol Freighters of No. 41 Squadron.[50]

In November 1958 one of the Freighters took part in Exercise PROTAIN, ferrying the radio communications equipment and signallers of a Gurkha Signals Regiment from Singapore to Nepal to assist in the running of the first elections to be held there. Two crews under Gordon Tosland were deployed to Calcutta to fly into airfields at Kathmandu, Pokhara, Biratnagar and Siara. 'All these strips are less than 4000 ft in length and that at Kathmandu [is] 4400 ft above sea level. The last three named are just grass paddocks with rough markings defining the landing strips ... A good short landing had to be carried out each time and brakes worked overtime.'[51] The new year began with a casualty evacuation flight into Cocos Island.

> An appendicitis case ... would appear to be routine but a Chinese patient complicated proceedings with Peritonitis, Ulcerated intestines, and Pneumonia. Recovering from these with a collapsed lung from the pneumonia, he contracted an abscess of the spine and was given four days to live unless an immediate operation could be performed ... a Bristol Freighter was dispatched to the rescue. After a 2 hour stop to rectify a small unserviceability and refuel, the freighter, with the patient aboard, was airborne for Singapore and the benefits of modern medical knowledge. Surprisingly he appears to have survived.[52]

The grounding of the Valettas of No. 52 Squadron RAF in March 1959 saw the Freighters take over the Malayan supply-dropping and air ambulance schedules for the month, but flying the courier routes was their more normal routine. In these years, detachments of No. 41 Squadron were also deployed to regular exercises in Thailand as preparation for their SEATO role as part of the Commonwealth Strategic Reserve. On one such exercise in 1959, a Bristol Freighter was part of the bomber force used to test the SEATO force's air defences. It was the only plane to get through; the pilot, Flight Lieutenant Craigie, eluded detection 'by flying down the cloud tops'. On the next phase, Craigie flew his Freighter into Khorat in central Thailand with a jeep mounting, a 75-mm recoilless rifle and two jeep crews, and 'earned a clap from the onlookers when it landed, unloaded, and took off again in 6 minutes'. Craigie capped the performance with a demonstration of precision supply-dropping, landing 'three packs of 400 lbs on a white sheet about 20 feet square ... "Just Routine" said Flt Lt Craigie uncrossing his fingers.'[53]

In September 1959, Squadron Leader O. D. Staple succeeded Gordon Tosland in command of No. 41 Squadron.[54] May 1960 saw the start of Operation SCHOOLROOM, the delivery of 56,000 lb of school supplies to Laos as a gift from New Zealand under the Colombo Plan. The job took 12 days, with the Freighters flying continuous return shuttles using slip (relief) crews from Singapore to Vientiane via Butterworth and Bangkok. The Freighters also delivered these supplies to the Laotian airfields of Pakse, Seno, Luang Prabang, and Xieng Khouang. They were on their way back to Singapore, the job done, when Vientiane airport closed with the arrival of the monsoon.[55]

The Malayan Emergency officially ended on 1 August 1960, and by October the last New Zealand Freighter crew was on supply-dropping detachment in Kuala Lumpur. Flying Officers D. G. McAllister and B. G. Anderson and Sergeant I. G. Ball dropped 160,000 lb of the total of 360,000 lb of supplies dropped that month—a record for the weight dropped in a month by one crew. Flying Officer Anderson completed 177 operational sorties as the navigator on missions that dropped over one million pounds of supplies, 'a record in the Squadron's history'.[56] The year ended with a Freighter flying into Udon Thani in northern Thailand with medical supplies for Laos, and evacuating British Embassy staff and their families to Bangkok as the Laotian situation worsened.[57]

Such tasks remained typical until May 1962, when the Laotian crisis led to a build-up of SEATO forces, based on the town and airfield at Khorat. No. 41 Squadron (Detachment) Korat, as it was officially known, part of New Zealand's contribution to Operation SCORPION, worked closely with American forces in Joint Task Force 116. The detachment, now under the command of Squadron Leader B. A. Wood, carried out a daily courier run between the bases occupied by the task force, completing 'its one millionth pound of freight and 3,600 passengers' in five months of constant operations until October 1962.[58] Having more than proved their worth, the Freighters returned to Singapore in December, before again being deployed to Thailand in 1963.[59]

The Bristol Freighters of No. 41 Squadron earned a reputation for New Zealand and the RNZAF throughout South-East Asia that was out of all proportion to the number of aircraft involved. Ironically, the RNZAF had not really wanted to perform a short- to medium-range transport role. In 1956 the Chief of Air Staff, Air Vice-Marshal C. E. Kay, informed Foss Shanahan, the New Zealand Commissioner for South-East Asia, of his plans to rationalise the Air Force to achieve economies in both manpower and finance. 'What we have in mind is to standardise on the Canberra in Nos 14, 41, and 75 Squadrons. This change of role in the Theatre is known to be favoured by the Air Ministry and, if approved, would solve many of our aircraft replacement problems. The Bristol Freighter for instance is now out of production and its type of replacement would be most costly.'[60] In reply, Shanahan stressed that No. 41 Squadron had done 'an exceptionally good job in the transport role and it seems to me that this is the one role in which we can continue'.[61] Kay accepted that the RNZAF should not abandon this role entirely, but wanted to concentrate on providing long-range transport through a commercial carrier such as Tasman Empire Airways, with the RNZAF only 'retaining one aircraft and having a charter arrangement for emergency'.[62] But while the RNZAF wished to concentrate on its strike role, theatre realities made it impossible to do away with the Bristol Freighters. They were not withdrawn from South-East Asia until 1977, long after the strike squadrons had returned to New Zealand.[63] These ugly aircraft with a Silver Fern on their roundels that brought emergency supplies to isolated airstrips few transport planes could land on were the only contact many people in the region had with New Zealand and New Zealanders.

## Jets over the jungle: No. 14 Squadron RNZAF in Malaya, 1955–58

> We would shoot out there to the target, call for 'Marker John',[64] who would be lurking down there just above the treetops, often in and out of cloud, and when we found him we'd have a chat to him and he'd say: 'Right I've got the target.' He'd say which way he was going in and then: 'Marking, marking now.' We

> would see the smoke marker and if necessary he would give us a correction like 'target 100 yards west of the smoke'. So, often without seeing anything other than just the smoke, we would go in. We normally went in individually ... the leader when he was ready would say: 'OK going in.' He'd dive in and then the others would go in after him. The other pilots would see his rockets or his bombs go off and make a correction on them if they could. Then afterwards the Marker [aircraft] would go back and have a look at it and see what we had done.[65]
>
> AIR COMMODORE STUART MCINTYRE, FLIGHT COMMANDER
> NO. 14 SQUADRON RNZAF, 1955–57

On 1 May 1955, five Vampire aircraft of No. 14 Squadron RNZAF, led by Flight Lieutenant Stuart McIntyre, took off from Tengah airfield, Singapore, on the Royal New Zealand Air Force's first operational strike mission since the Second World War, and the first ever conducted by New Zealanders in jet aircraft. Like many such missions in the Emergency, it was against a suspected guerrilla camp in the jungle, in the Pulai area of Johore.[66] Except for the smoke from explosions, nothing was ever seen from the air, and rarely was anything reported from the ground. That did not matter to the pilots in their early twenties who made up most of No. 14 Squadron RNZAF. They were fulfilling many a young man's ultimate dream: overseas on active service, flying jet fighters over the jungles of Malaya.

Flight Lieutenant Stuart McIntyre had joined the RNZAF straight from Wellington College in 1949, and completed his flying training in the fifth course run in New Zealand after the war. This course was interrupted when the RNZAF was mobilised to work on the wharves during the 1951 waterside dispute, but McIntyre graduated as a sergeant pilot at the age of 19. After a six-week commissioning course he was posted to No. 14 Squadron at Ohakea, which flew the newly acquired Vampire jets. On the day the young pilots went solo for the first time, Ohakea shut down and everyone turned out to watch. 'I guess it must have been like this in the Colosseum ... You had a rough idea what they were there for and it wasn't to watch you doing good things.' But the joy of going solo quickly replaced any apprehension. 'Oh it was tremendous. It was a beautiful aircraft, so light and easy to handle. By our standards it went awfully quickly ... and it was really quite an adventure for a young guy.'[67]

By 1955 McIntyre was a 23-year-old veteran jet pilot. He had completed a tour with No. 14 Squadron in Cyprus, flying Vampires as part of New Zealand's contribution to the Middle East Air Force (MEAF). Being 'the right seniority and single', he was Acting Squadron Commander of the advance party sent up to establish the squadron in its new home at Tengah, where it became a unit of the Far East Air Force. Meanwhile, Squadron Leader N. H. Bright was re-deploying the rest of the squadron from Cyprus to Tengah.

The squadron had been part of MEAF from September 1952, earning a reputation as one of the best squadrons in the Middle East. In Cyprus the New Zealanders had flown Vampire aircraft leased from the RAF, and this arrangement continued in Malaya.[68] The squadron was New Zealand's strike contribution to the Commonwealth Strategic Reserve. Its primary role was the air defence of Singapore, but like the Bristol Freighters of No. 41 Squadron it also undertook 'anti-bandit' operations as a secondary role.[69] Squadron Leader Nelson Bright had flown Lancaster bombers with No. 75 (New Zealand) Squadron RAF during the war, and Corsairs in Japan with No. 14 Squadron.[70] He and his senior flight commander, Flight Lieutenant Clarrie Berryman, both in their early thirties, were the old men of the squadron, and the only two pilots with wartime flying experience; for most of the pilots and ground crew, ten years their junior, this was their first time overseas.

At Tengah the New Zealanders found themselves working with three other Commonwealth air forces as part of the Far East Air Force: No. 60 (Fighter) Squadron RAF, operating Venom fighter-bombers; a detachment of No. 1 (Bomber) Squadron RAAF, operating Lincoln bombers; and a Malayan Auxiliary Air Force Squadron. All flew 'anti-bandit' strikes against guerrilla targets in the Malayan jungle from Tengah's single 6,000 ft runway. These fell into two categories: 'firedogs', 'pre-planned bombing, strafing and rocket attacks' against suspected 'communist terrorist' (CT) targets; and 'smash hits', immediate 'on call' strikes against targets of opportunity in response to a guerrilla raid or 'hot' information.[71]

The New Zealanders arrived at Tengah during an ongoing debate in air and army circles on the value of offensive air operations against guerrilla ground targets. This debate intensified as the guerrillas withdrew further into the jungle and dispersed into smaller groups. The re-equipping of RAF squadrons with Venoms in 1955, and the replacement of Lincoln bombers by Canberras, saw a reduction in the amount of offensive air support being given to the ground forces.[72] Both Venom jet fighter-bombers and Canberra jet bombers lacked the endurance of their piston-engine predecessors. In Canberras and Vampires—and their Venom replacements—the air conditioning did not function where it was most needed, on the tarmac. While heat and humidity had a major impact on their crews, the maintenance needs of high-performance jet aircraft reduced their serviceability.[73] The two fighter squadrons spent increasing time training for their air defence role. The shift was rarely recognised by the pilots, who simply did their job as a 'day fighter/ground attack squadron, we didn't look any further than that'.[74]

At Tengah each squadron in turn was on standby for 24 hours, with their aircraft ready to go. As McIntyre recalled:

> What would happen was that the army would have a contact on the ground with the terrorists, and would call Group. Group would alert Tengah Ops. Tengah Ops would phone the mess, the duty pilot would pick up his other three blokes and at the same time Operations would have rung the duty ground crew. We would race down, be briefed, told what the target was, what the problem was, who the marker aircraft was, where it was all happening, pick up revolvers, and go out to the aeroplanes. By that time the ground crew would have bombed up the aircraft or fitted the rockets or whatever. We normally carried 150 rounds of ammunition per gun and either two 1000 lb bombs or eight rockets, and away we'd go.
>
> Initially we probably didn't do very well. The aeroplanes were new to us, we didn't have enough people. I remember one of the first strikes we went on, suddenly you're in a situation where the dispersal area is littered with bombs and people towing them around and pushing them under aircraft and carrying live rockets and all sorts of things. I recall we didn't put up warning signs saying live rockets and guns. We were overwhelmed by the event. So we had to learn the business ... As a pilot I didn't want to fail. You had to find this little aeroplane in the middle of the jungle somewhere and at times the blood pressure would really start to rise when you went out there and here was this jungle stretching as far as you could see and where's the marker? And you are running out of fuel. So there was a lot of pressure on you to do the job well.[75]

When they arrived in Singapore the New Zealanders were provided with Vampires, but they soon received the Vampire's successor, the De Havilland Venom FB1. This single-seat day fighter/fighter-bomber was a 'straightforward development of the Vampire' designed to take advantage of the more powerful De Havilland Ghost engine.[76] A 'good aeroplane', it came to the New Zealanders with a reputation for being temperamental which they found was largely undeserved.[77] McIntyre made his first solo flight in a Venom on 4 May 1955. When he flew it again the next day on a 'firedog' operation, this was believed to be 'the first time a Venom has been used on active service operations anywhere in the world'.[78] This 'first' had sparked fierce competition between the New Zealanders and No. 60 (Fighter) Squadron RAF, the veteran squadron at Tengah who were very much 'cock of the walk'. After this squadron carried out the first operational Vampire strike, the aircraft's manufacturers had presented them with a silver Vampire which had pride of place in the officers' mess. The New Zealanders hoped for a similar presentation, and after McIntyre's sortie believed they were 'home and hosed ... 60 Squadron were absolutely livid'.[79] But although De Havilland replied, noting the record, there was no mention of a trophy to mark the occasion.

The Venoms' primary role was defending Singapore. No. 14 Squadron practised high-level interception and air-to-air cannon firing, and participated in air defence exercises.[80] Code-named JOSS STICK, these pitted No. 14 Squadron RNZAF and No. 60 Squadron RAF against No. 1 (Bomber) Squadron RAAF (the Lincolns based at Butterworth) and some USAF B29s from the Philippines.[81] 'The American B29s would come down from Clark Air Force Base ... and we would try to intercept them.'[82]

For the young pilots, life in Singapore was 'a lot of fun'. Everyone worked hard and played equally hard.[83]

> The bar at night was divided into three camps. On one side was the Aussies and the other side was the New Zealanders and in the middle were the Poms ... a great deal of nonsense went on. But we got on pretty well with the Aussies. They were great. The thing that impressed me was to see the Aussie armourers who had bombed up a Lincoln and then been told that the bomb-load had changed. Some fellow would climb up in the bomb bay and just trip the Mickey Mouse and all the bombs would just fall on the tarmac. That was pretty impressive—that casual Australian nonchalance ... The officers' mess was parallel to the runway in those days, and in the middle of the night (because they were always operating at night) you'd hear these Lincolns burning off down the runway. [We usually] slept through until the odd occasion when someone would have a problem and he'd chop everything and just stop, and the sudden hush would wake everyone up.[84]

Flying jets in the tropics was always an uncomfortable business, and flying the Venom was no exception.

> The air conditioning only worked when you didn't need it. You couldn't run it on the ground, that's when you were hot, so you had to wait until you were airborne before you could turn the air conditioning on, then you had to turn it off when you came back into the circuit because it would overheat at low speed and the turbine would burn out. In the cockpit ... you actually sat on a water bottle [shaped to form part of the ejection seat] ... If the aeroplane was in the sun without a sunshade on, it heated up, and as we flew in just underpants and a flying suit with a Mae West on over the top, I have on more than one occasion leapt into an

> aeroplane onto a red-hot water bottle and been really burnt. The cockpit temperature would get up to 130/140 degrees Fahrenheit and you would be soaked through. There weren't too many fat pilots around the place. You lost a lot of weight.[85]

Flying a Venom was 'hard physical labour. But that's the same with any aeroplane. It didn't have powered controls but it flew very nicely.' One thing you couldn't do with a Venom, though, was spin it.

> It simply did not come out of a spin. It was just the design of the aeroplane. You could take it up to .86 Mach and it would go out of control. So you would go up to 45,000 feet, roll on your back, and go for it and eventually there was nothing you could do. The aircraft would just roll and you would throttle off and put the speed brakes out and when you fell below the critical mach about .86 you would get control again. So we used to do these 'mach' runs every now and then, just to keep people alert to what happened if you got too interested in going too fast, and aware that you could lose it.[86]

In June 1955 the New Zealanders converted to Venoms, and the squadron's Vampires carried out 20 'firedog' strikes and one 'smash hit' in the Kulai, Keluang and Kota Tinggi areas of Johore. Both Vampires and Venoms were often unserviceable in the first months in Singapore, and at one point in November 1955 the squadron was reduced to two serviceable Venoms. The keen rivalry with No. 60 Squadron was heightened when the RAF willingly helped out with 'smash hits', to the discomfort of the New Zealanders.[87] On 3 December 1955 only four New Zealand Venoms were available for a 'firedog', and 'we had to borrow four of 60 Squadron's Venoms. They were very jubilant about this and notices such as "Aircraft For Hire" began appearing round the station.'[88]

Such embarrassment was temporary; No. 14 Squadron's growing effectiveness was based on the ability of its ground crew to keep the planes operational. Among them was Joe Keegan, who arrived at Changi in 1956 as an Aircraftman First Class.

> I was 20 when I went to Singapore ... Well even before the door opened at Changi, you could see this tropical countryside, banana trees, palms and all that sort of thing ... It had been wet and raining and we sploshed down this runway and got out, and the first thing that hit you was the heat and smell which you can only appreciate if you've been there ... You hopped off the aeroplane, grabbed your kitbag and threw it on the back of a truck and it was all eyes, all the way, because you virtually went from one end of the island to the other. It was only 11 years

> after the war, and its immediate past history was all too vivid. We got to Tengah and were shown our billets. There were these barracks, large, open-aired concrete buildings, three storeys high, and you had a narrow iron bed, it had a horse-hair mattress about three inches thick. You had one small cupboard and you had one wardrobe and there was about two feet between your bed and the next one. I think in that particular room which was just one long dormitory, there was probably 50 people.[89]

The ground crews used the RAF operational system, with each pilot allotted an aircraft and a permanent ground crew consisting of a fitter (engine), rigger (airframes) and armourer.

> One day this new aeroplane flew in ... it had the number ... WE438 and my Warrant Officer said, 'Joe Keegan that's gonna be your aeroplane.'... Me, and an engine mechanic by the name of Barney Gibbons, got that aeroplane ... They had a life of 750 hours and under my care you might say it flew its entire life out and was retired while I was on No. 14 Squadron. It was a good aeroplane. When a pilot used to come back he used to report what was wrong with the aeroplane. If there was nothing wrong with it, he used to just write 'satis' [for 'satisfactory'] in the remarks column [on the aircraft maintenance form] and I can remember that was the only aeroplane that did a complete page and the page had 30 lines on it with no complaints.[90]

The squadron flight line, at one end of a disused runway, at its full complement had 14 Venom FB1s and two Vampire T11 twin-seater trainers. These were parked day and night on a hard standing area beside the squadron's offices and equipment huts.[91] LAC Malcolm McNaught remembered that the early morning routine included

> removing cockpit covers and air intake blanks and checking around wheels and chocks for snakes. Checks were made on fuel tanks for leaks. There were checks for hydraulic leaks, and checks on tyres. We cleaned windscreens and canopies and drew starter cartridges from the explosives store. Then we made a thorough check right around all control surfaces, wings and tail booms, and before anyone stepped into the cockpit we had to ensure the safety pin was correctly fitted to the ejection seat.
>
> A dud start could cause our pilot to miss a sortie, so we soon learned to load the starter with one shot while he was doing his pre-flight check prior to strapping in. We always assisted pilots to strap in as it was a very snug fit in a very confined cockpit. Once you had the thumbs up from the pilot, the [ejection seat] safety pin was pulled and shown to the pilot and you then stepped clear for start up ... Wet [i.e. false] starts were usually caused by mishandling throttle settings and were a

pain to everybody. Spare bodies would launch themselves onto the tail booms to lift the nose and drain any excess fuel from the tail pipe, while another cartridge was fitted to the starter, and (fingers crossed) away he would go, all in about two minutes flat.[92]

It was a three-way relationship between aircraft, pilot and ground crew. Joe Keegan recalled:

> Every time your pilot came back, you'd listen to what he would say about his aeroplane before he went and signed in. You could get a feel as to how things were ... Sometimes just on some sort of intuition of the pilot you might just go in and have a look to see what was going on. I think that worked fairly well, because even years after, I met Geoff Wallingford, who had been my pilot, when he was the CO at Woodbourne and he looked at me and said 'WE438' and it was our aeroplane—just like that.
>
> [On the flight line] days were never predictable ... if there was nothing special on like a strike, you'd probably be at work at 7.30 in the morning. You might have to have your aeroplane ready ... to go by 8.30. You might fly two or three sorties and the object then would be to have your aeroplane serviceable for the next day. Now if your aeroplane was good, you could refuel it, wrap it up and put it back to bed, and you might knock off at 4.30–5 o'clock. But if there is an extended day on you might start at 6 o'clock in the morning, you might finish at 7 o'clock at night ... We were out in the sun, it was very hot, you were continually bathed in sweat. The aeroplane would get so hot you could hardly touch it. All you'd be running around in was a pair of sandals and a pair of shorts. You're either flat out [or] you're flat out waiting; but I don't remember ever sitting round with nothing to do for too long. You were always involved.[93]

An increase in guerrilla activity in Johore in December 1955 broke the countrywide lull and led to a resumption of offensive air strikes. The RAAF Lincolns and RAF Canberras were committed to Operation SATURATION against the suspected camp of the Johore State Secretariat in Negri Sembilan. This involved a systematic and intensive bombardment of the target area, during which 752 1,000-lb bombs were dropped over a ten-day period with no significant results.[94] The first 'firedog' for 1956 was flown by a section of four Venoms led by Squadron Leader Bright, each armed with two 1,000-lb bombs and 600 rounds of 20-mm cannon. This got the year off to an interesting start, especially when Flying Officer Pere, the only Maori officer in the squadron, had both his bombs 'hang up'. Unable to drop either bomb on the target, he flew out to sea to the jettison area at the China Rock range and managed to release one. After throwing his aircraft about to ensure the remaining bomb was secure, he landed at Paya Lebar, Singapore.[95] When McIntyre flew over with a couple of armourers to make the bomb safe, 'there was a little ... policeman standing there holding a fire extinguisher and looking at the bomb [hanging from the aircraft]. I always wondered ... what he thought he was going to do if it had gone off.'[96]

In February 1956, with the number of air strikes declining, the Director of Operations gave priority to making air attacks against all identified guerrilla camps for an experimental period of two months. This culminated in the mounting of Operation KINGLY PILE against the base of Goh Peng Tuan, 'the notorious commander of the 7th Independent Platoon MRLA', near Keluang in central Johore. The strike followed careful work by Special Branch in pinpointing the camp's location and confirming Goh Peng Tuan's presence. Originally planned for 20 February 1956, the attack was delayed until the following day because of bad weather. It was carried out by seven Lincolns of No. 1 (Bomber) Squadron RAAF, who were directed onto their target 'on a time and distance to run basis from a ground marker, [and] followed by four Canberras of No. 12 Squadron [RAF] bombing on a smoke marker dropped by an Auster'.[97] The Lincolns made a second attack after returning to Tengah to bomb-up. At three o'clock Bright led seven Venoms of No. 14 Squadron onto the same target.[98] KINGLY PILE was the only successful attack of its type ever conducted by the air forces in Malaya; Goh Peng Tuan and 13 others were killed by two 1,000-lb bombs.[99] The outstanding guerrilla leader and tactician had been long sought by the First Battalion Fijian Regiment, who had lost a number of soldiers in ambushes by his platoon. During KINGLY PILE the Fijians formed part of the cordon around the camp and witnessed the 'great carpet of destruction' created by the bombing. 'It was our people who went in and discovered the destroyed camp, but we would have loved to have attacked it ourselves.'[100]

KINGLY PILE's success was followed by further air attacks on known guerrilla camps, but such targets were few and the number of strikes continued to decline. Most were mounted against Grade Four Targets, 'areas of 1,000–2,000 yards square which were believed to contain ... terrorists'.[101] It was extremely unlikely that this needle-in-a-haystack approach would be effective. With the exception of KINGLY PILE, no kills were confirmed as a direct result of aerial bombing, despite the increasing sophistication of target-marking methods, delayed-action ground marker flares, and radar target-location devices.

June 1956 was a busy month, with ten 'firedogs' and three 'smash hits' flown. Targets up to 140 nautical miles from Tengah were attacked in tasks complicated by generally poor weather, which necessitated low-level flying. Fuel consumption had to be calculated to extremely fine margins to allow aircraft ten minutes on their targets. Any further delay would threaten the aircraft's ability to return to base. On 18 June, Operation CANTERBURY was mounted against a target in the Keluang area. The pilot briefing was at 6.15 a.m., and ground crews worked from very early in the morning to bomb and arm the Venoms. At 7.45 the New Zealanders in 'eight chequered Venoms led by Flt Lt McIntyre took off behind eight 60 Squadron [RAF] Venoms'—16 aircraft in bombing formation laden with 14,545 kg of bombs. As the Venoms arrived at the target, six Lincolns of No. 1 (B) Squadron RAAF called: 'Bombing in ten minutes'. On the first run the Australian aircraft pulled out of their bombing run as they did not see the target-marking flare until too late. By now 22 Venom pilots (including six from No. 45 (Fighter) Squadron RAF) and eight Canberra pilots (from Butterworth) were anxiously monitoring their fuel gauges. Seventeen minutes after their first attempt, No. 1 (Bomber) Squadron RAAF successfully bombed the area. The Venoms immediately began their bombing run. No. 14 Squadron was just 45 seconds behind No. 60 Squadron, and 'a most impressive sight it was to see the bombs exploding with a visible shock wave going through the jungle. The Venoms completed their bombing run with one minute to go before the Canberras bombed.'[102] There was no margin for error and no time to loiter on target; little fuel was left in the tanks when the aircraft arrived back at base.

Frequent thunderstorms during the monsoon were another hazard; it was quite common to fly at 42,000 feet and still be below the top of the cumulonimbus clouds. In these conditions canopies misted over and there was 'very limited forward visibility'.[103] With only a few airfields able to take jet aircraft, there could be problems if the weather changed rapidly. McIntyre was in one of four Venoms returning from Butterworth after practising interceptions.

> [W]e had two new people, John Scrimshaw and Barry Flavell, and they were very young, about 19. We were miles up the coast when suddenly the controller said: 'It's all turning to custard, Changi is out, Butterworth is looking dodgy, Seletar's out, you've got to get home in the next fifteen minutes before Tengah becomes unusable because of bad weather.' I remember hearing this instruction and doing a bit of mental arithmetic and saying to the other senior pilot, Fred Kinvig, 'Well if we do 600 knots we'll make it.' This was well beyond our capability [but] we let these two young guys, John and Barry, take the lead for the experience. Anyway we finally got back, and as we landed we couldn't have covered more than a couple

of hundred metres when we ran into thick rain coming over the runway, and no visibility ... It was real from the point of view that you were expected to deal with these situations. You were no longer pussy-footing around. There was no, 'It's too wet, we won't go out today'. You had to do the job.[104]

If a downpour occurred while the aircraft were away from base, 'they would have to land with water two or three inches deep across the runway. This resulted in some spectacular landings, with aircraft disappearing in a shower of spray and sometimes aquaplaning with the brakes quite ineffective. The Mk 1 Venom did not have anti-skid brakes which would have reduced such ... risks.'[105]

In September 1956 Bright was succeeded by Squadron Leader Fred Tucker, who had served with the RNZAF in the Pacific. One of his first memories of No. 14 Squadron was of '21st birthday parties among the pilots. I was the "old man"'. Tucker was conscious that in his squadron the 'experience level was lower than RAF squadrons at that time. There was nothing wrong with our basic training. It was simply ... that our young officers coming straight from New Zealand had not the experience of the RAF people.'[106] Like his predecessor, Tucker was determined to have the best squadron on the base. The rivalry with No. 60 Squadron RAF was intense, and 'there was pride in other things than just flying. We always had a bloody good scrum, our serviceability improved, we gained our place in the sun. It was a bloody good Squadron.'[107] This was also the view from below. LAC Malcolm McNaught remembered that relations between ranks were 'the best I had experienced'.

[This] seemed to be related to the distance between the Squadron and Bullshit Castle in Wellington. The 'Ockers' used to joke about the Kiwis all being related and that the country was so darn small everyone knew everyone else anyway. It certainly worked for us as there was none of the friction that we observed in other units. Indeed coloured RAF airmen preferred to spend their off-duty time with us rather than their own people because of the absence of prejudice.[108]

Rugby was important for the New Zealand squadrons, and No. 14 Squadron prided itself on having the best team. 'We used to play in the local competition and ... do very well ... our biggest rival on the island was No. 41 Squadron who were over at Changi ... when we used to meet, that used to be real tough and a lot of needle because we weren't going to let those fellows beat us at all.' It was hard New Zealand-style rugby, with no quarter asked or given. 'We knew their players from home ... their fullback, Bruce Menzies, was an excellent fullback but if you could get in there in the first five minutes and knock him over and give him a punch or two, he'd be mad for the rest of the game and he'd be useless. Then you'd know you could beat them.'[109] In January 1956 No. 14 Squadron won the Sanderson Cup by beating RAF Butterworth at Changi.

> At five o'clock our team in bright red jerseys and Butterworth in light and dark blue trotted onto the field amidst wild cheering from the spectators. Despite the wet ground, a fast and exciting game was played with neither team really having the upper hand. Butterworth were in the lead 6 points to 3 when we scored a penalty right in front of the posts. The score at full time was still 6 all. The referee decided to play 10 minutes extra each way and ... due to greater fitness, our team had the best of the play and scored three tries making the final score 15 points to 6.

The cup was presented to 14 Squadron's captain, LAC 'Choo Choo' Makutu, by the Commander in Chief Far East, Air Marshal Fressanges, who called the win 'a splendid example of guts and tenacity'.[110]

As captain of the squadron team the following season, McIntyre had to deal with a wing three-quarter 'who was a bit of a character and would always be in trouble'.

> There was a standard rule in those days that anyone found downtown in an out-of-bounds area was charged. So this chap was found wandering round down that area and was punished. I think at that time it was seven days in the base slammer and that would be Monday morning. Wednesday I would go down in my Land Rover and spring him because I wanted him for rugby practice. So we'd get him out of the cells, go play rugby, I'd take him back again and say 'see you Saturday'. Get him out on Saturday again and we'd play rugby. Minor misdemeanours were all very well but we had to win the rugby.[111]

In February 1956, armed 'with Sten guns and pistols', the squadron team ventured north into Malaya to play the First Fiji Infantry Battalion.

> We were all armed to the teeth and off we went up to Kuala Pilah. We arrived there in the afternoon. Their RSM was the captain of the rugby team, a big guy, he was also the Fijian heavyweight boxing champion. So he said, 'We're all going to have a beer.' I said, 'We can't really, we're playing rugby.' He said, 'No, no, it's only a friendly game.' So we were all having a few pints when the RSM said he was going to referee. There was a prize for the first team to score which was a couple of dozen beer, which was put on the half-way line. We kicked off, they caught the ball. The RSM said it was a knock-on, we had a scrum. He penalised them, we had a free kick in front of the post, over it went and we had to drink the beer. But at the end

> I cannot imagine what the final score was. 100–nil to the Fijians wouldn't have surprised me.[112]

In between the strikes, both Venom squadrons continually practised air-to-air combat and high- and low-level battle formation flying. They also regularly participated in SEATO exercises. In 1956, for example, five Venoms from No. 14 Squadron went to Bangkok to take part in Exercise FIRMLINK with forces from the United States, United Kingdom, Australia, the Philippines, Thailand and Pakistan. New Zealand's contribution included the frigate *Pukaki* and part of the SAS Squadron serving in Malaya, who were transported by Bristol Freighters of No. 41 Squadron. Participation in SEATO exercises became an annual event for detachments from No. 14 Squadron. The Americans referred to the Venoms as 'little toy aeroplanes'; on one deployment Tucker put things in perspective by parking his Venom under the wing of a United States Air Force F-100 (Super Sabre).[113]

In tropical conditions accidents were sometimes inevitable. In April 1957 Flight Lieutenant Mike Palmer, who had replaced McIntyre as senior Flight Commander, had a flame-out over the Johore Strait within sight of Tengah.

> I looked for a suitable beach area for ditching but the jungle appeared to come right down to the edge of the water. Remembering 'Pilot Notes' concerning the ditching properties of Venoms I decided to abandon the aircraft and turned to head down the middle of the Straits ... Height was now about 1,000 feet, speed 150–160 knots. I unsealed, wound back the canopy one turn, and pulled the hood jettison lever; the hood came away cleanly. I had a last look at the altimeter which showed approximately 800 feet ... I reached up, grasped the ejector seat blind handle in the approved fashion and pulled up and down. The blind moved what seemed to be a long way, then stopped, but the seat did not fire. I did a quick manual check and recalled that I had been told that considerable force was required to operate the firing mechanism. I pulled harder still and the seat fired ... I blew clear, the blind came away, and the seat drogue developed with a snap. It appeared that the seat was spinning and I was completely disorientated until the pilot parachute developed ... I was then tipped clear of the seat, the main canopy opened, and I stabilised and was able to get my bearing again. I had just sufficient time to register that I was coming down in water and to turn and hit my parachute harness release before I plunged in.[114]

Palmer was picked up by a police launch which had to take evasive action as the aircraft hit the water. This was the first time an ejection seat had been successfully used in an RNZAF aircraft; apparently it was also the first successful ejection in the Far East Air Force.[115]

During 1957 offensive air support strikes continued to diminish as information on worthwhile air targets became increasingly rare. Harassing tasks accounted for 55 per cent of air activity that year, compared to 28.5 per cent in 1956. This expensive misuse of air resources continued because of the determination of Tunku Abdul Rahman, the Malayan Prime Minister, to use 'all available methods' to end the Emergency by the first anniversary of Malayan independence in August 1958. In May 1957 No. 14 Squadron made a number of strafing and rocket attacks on jungle targets in Johore. Suspected camp sites of No. 3 Platoon MRLA, led by Teng Fook Loong, had already received some 545,000 lb of bombs in late 1956 and early 1957, with no apparent results. On 7 May the suspected camp was again attacked by five Lincolns of No. 1 Squadron RAAF and 12 Venoms from No. 60 Squadron RAF and No. 14 Squadron RNZAF. Tucker led four New Zealand Venoms, each carrying two 1,000-lb bombs, in the co-ordinated dawn strike. Ground reconnaissance reported that with the target area 'completely devastated', it was impossible to see whether there was anything under the 'mass of tangled trees'.[116] It was later established that the strike had missed the camp by about 200 metres. Later that month RAAF Lincolns dropped 70,000 lb of bombs during a night raid in the Jelebu district of Negri Sembilan, killing four guerrillas, including Teng Fook Loong and his wife.[117] In July the New Zealand squadron attacked a camp believed to contain the remnants of Teng Fook Loong's platoon with 16,000 lb of bombs, 75 rockets and several hundred rounds of 20-mm cannon, but it had been evacuated three hours earlier.[118]

The squadron's level of activity fluctuated during 1957, reaching a peak in July just before the Federation of Malaya became independent. There were no operations in August, and on 1 September 1957 six Venom aircraft took part in a fly-past over Kuala Lumpur as part of the 'Merdeka' celebrations. Malaya's independence saw a change in the Far East Air Force's structure. Air Headquarters Malaya was renamed Headquarters 224 Group, and both the conduct of operations and the maintenance of law and order became the exclusive responsibility of the governments of Malaya and Singapore.[119] At Malaya's request the three governments contributing to the Commonwealth Strategic Reserve agreed to continue to provide whatever military assistance towards ending the Emergency was practicable. From 1 September 1957 the Commander-in-Chief Far East Air Force and the Air Officer Commanding 224 Group took their directions on anti-guerrilla operations from the Federation of Malaya's Director of Emergency Operations.[120]

Operationally things remained quiet until January 1958, when a series of harassing strikes were made in the Kota Tinggi area of south Johore in response to a guerrilla raid on a village in October 1957 in which a large quantity of food and some arms had been taken. Intensive follow-up operations by the security forces included harassing air strikes on suspected food dumps and resting places to keep the guerrillas on the move. Tucker and his pilots continued the strikes throughout the month, and on 24 January the Unit History noted that 'Any C.T.'s in the Penggarang area must certainly be harassed by now.'[121]

In March 1958 eight Venoms led by Tucker were detached to Butterworth to participate in Operation BINTANG in Perak State in support of 28 Commonwealth Infantry Brigade. Harassing strikes were made in the Ipoh/Chemor area and the Parit Forest Reserve. 'Lincolns from Tengah carry out night harassing and during the day Canberras and Venoms as well as Artillery take part.' On 18 March the squadron did two strikes, each with seven aircraft armed with rockets and cannon. 'The targets are in valleys and along jungle covered slopes and today was the first time most pilots had ever rocketed up hill.'[122] After each strike the Venoms flew 'flag-waving' exercises over the villages along the Perak River valley before returning to RAF Butterworth. In the second week of operations the Venoms bombed targets to which they were led by Canberra bombers of No. 45 Squadron RAF. The 99 hours of flying in March was one-third of the squadron's operational work for the past year: 'the frequency of strikes was not very high. I suppose we would do four or five a month. It certainly wasn't the major part of our flying. It was good to go on a strike. You felt you were really doing something, even though you were probably only killing monkeys or chopping firewood.'[123] Between April 1955 and March 1958 the squadron flew 488 operational hours in completing 585 sorties on 115 strike missions. This involved dropping 439 1,000-lb and 226 500-lb bombs, and firing 1,523 rocket projectiles and 156,052 rounds of 20-mm cannon.[124]

By 1958 the New Zealanders were the last squadron in the Far East Air Force operating Venoms. As each aircraft reached its 'life' of 750 hours, replacements (also 'fairly old') came from No. 45 Squadron RAF, which had changed to Canberras, or from No. 28 Squadron RAF. During its last twelve months of service, the squadron 'lifed' or wrote off 19 aircraft and gained 15 replacements. It maintained an average strength of 14 aircraft rather than its establishment of 16. Spares were available, 'but frequently considerable servicing ingenuity and the judicious cannibalising of lifed aircraft has had to be resorted to, to maintain a high state of airworthiness and serviceability'.[125]

On 1 July 1958, No. 14 Squadron was replaced at Tengah by No. 75 Squadron RNZAF, operating Canberra bombers. The RNZAF's shift from a day fighter/ground attack role to a light bomber/interdictor role followed the British Far East Air Force adopting a more offensive emphasis in support of SEATO contingency planning. In the event of a war with China, US carrier-based aircraft and RAF 'V' bomber units would strike at targets in China, while light bombers of the Far East Air Force would bomb likely routes and bridges between the Chinese border and the Mekong River. To enable this, some RAF squadrons were re-equipped with Canberra bombers and others with night fighters; the daytime air defence of Malaya was now the responsibility of Australian Sabre fighter squadrons based at Butterworth.[126] New Zealand re-equipped its No. 14 and No. 75 Squadrons with Canberra aircraft. Those for No. 75 Squadron were hired from the RAF, while those for No. 14 Squadron (now to be based in New Zealand) would be purchased from the United Kingdom.[127]

After gaining experience with bombers during the Second World War, the RNZAF had wanted to equip itself with a bomber squadron since the early 1950s. It believed that an 'Air Force without bombers could not be considered as a complete tool in the maintenance and exploitation of all the advantages accruing from air power'.[128] The original intention had been to re-equip No. 14 Squadron with Canberras in theatre, but this was changed to replacing it with No. 75 Squadron. In order to have enough trained Canberra crews, some personnel from No. 14 Squadron were posted to No. 75 Squadron and went to the United Kingdom on courses during the squadron's final months in Singapore.

On 30 April 1958 the Commander-in-Chief, Air Marshal the Earl of Bandon, officially farewelled No. 14 (Fighter) Squadron RNZAF from his Command. A parade, presentation, and fly-past took place in Kuala Lumpur on 15 May, during which the Federation Minister of Defence, Dato Abdul Razak, presented Squadron Leader Tucker with a kris (ceremonial Malay knife) in gratitude for the part No. 14 Squadron had played in the Emergency. The following day, 16 May 1958, was a 'sad day for 14 Squadron—its last as a fighter squadron and its last day flying Venoms. At 1000 hours the squadron taxied out for a final flypast over Tengah, Seletar, Changi, and F.E.A.F. Headquarters and the Singapore waterfront. Ten Venoms and three T.11's formed the figure 14 formation with Sqn. Ldr. Tucker leading in a T.11.'[129] For three exciting years, No. 14 Squadron had been involved in all aspects of the fighter role, from ground attack strikes against suspected camps to the air defence of Singapore. As Flight Lieutenant Geoff Wallingford, who had graduated with the Sword of Honour from Cranwell in December 1954 and flown with No. 14 Squadron since late 1956, summed up: 'We felt we had a worthwhile role and we certainly enjoyed what we were doing.'[130]

## Canberras in Malaya with No. 75 Squadron RNZAF, 1958–62

> We love a bit of competition. Wherever I've been overseas with a New Zealand squadron we've shone. For one thing we have got some amazing engineers in our Air Force, and that is reflected in our serviceability rate, whether it is bombers, transports or fighters ... As for flying we are always very competitive and when there are weapons involved we can hold our own with anyone ... We have got nothing to be ashamed of, even though some of our equipment may be a little bit older and not quite up to date at times.[131]
>
> AIR COMMODORE HAROLD MOSS, SQUADRON LEADER, NO. 75 SQUADRON RNZAF

In 1958 the RNZAF's presence in South-East Asia expanded with the arrival of a Canberra bomber squadron. No. 75 Squadron RNZAF was formed on 1 July 1958 at RAF Coningsby in England under Squadron Leader Geoff Highet. The New Zealanders had a frustrating time in England; their Canberra B2s and T4 trainer aircraft were delivered unmodified and had to be returned to the factory. The resulting delays dampened morale. Like the Venoms of No. 14 Squadron, No. 75 Squadron's nine Canberra B2s and one Canberra T4 were leased from the RAF. Leasing arrangements suited the New Zealand government, which was very conscious of the drain on the country's overseas funds imposed by defence commitments.[132]

On 14 July 1958 the first five Canberras and their RNZAF crews landed at Tengah, where they were welcomed by Air Vice-Marshal Hancock, commanding 224 Group, and B. S. Lendrum, the Acting New Zealand High Commissioner to Singapore. There were further frustrations in Singapore as the B2s, having been modified to Bomber Command standard in England, now had to be modified to FEAF standards. Equipped for the European theatre, they lacked the advanced navigation aids needed in South-East Asia. On operational missions it was found that both the British and New Zealand Canberra squadrons had to rely on No. 2 Squadron RAAF, whose Canberras had more advanced navigational equipment, to lead them to the target.[133]

The Canberra B2s were designed to be flown at 30 to 40 thousand feet and drop 500- and 1,000-lb bombs. By the time No. 75 Squadron arrived in Singapore, the skills learned from RAF Bomber Command during the Second World War had been lost, and the RNZAF had to develop medium-level bombing skills from scratch.[134] The squadron's primary role in the Commonwealth Strategic Reserve was to form part of a bombing force in support of SEATO contingency planning, carrying out predominantly medium-level bombing, 70 per cent of it at night.

By 1958 developments in surface-to-air missile systems were causing the RAF growing concern about the viability of operations using the bomber stream tactics of the Second World War.[135] These tactics were seen as out of date, and the Canberras as obsolete. However, this was not initially a worry for the New Zealanders, who were more concerned with solving the inevitable teething troubles.[136] As the aircraft's serviceability improved, the air crews were keen to fly at every opportunity. The B2 Canberra had a crew of two; the navigator sat behind the pilot, and both had ejector seats. Flight Lieutenant Ian Gillard was the Senior Flight Commander with No. 75 Squadron.

> It was a good crew aircraft and you became bonded with your navigator, because you experienced a lot together which you wouldn't have believed could have happened to you or you couldn't believe you could have survived ... You would fly with another navigator reluctantly. The navigators, of course, had their own opinions about who were good pilots, and were equally reluctant to go off with another pilot, because so much of what you did was team-work.[137]

The first operational strike took place on 30 September 1958.

> Crews crowded at the dispersal area in the early hours of the morning. The aircraft were ready. All pre-flight preparations had been completed, and at 0710 hours the three Canberras, led by the squadron commander, took off for the target area in North Malaya. Method of bombing was TDP [Target Director Post], and at 0830 hours ... the New Zealand crews came under TDP control. Apart from one hang-up in the leading aircraft ... all the bombs were dropped successfully [and] ... this bomb was subsequently released on target in the course of a second attack. In all, eighteen 1,000 pounders were dropped.

Army units who went in to examine the site reported a direct hit on the target, a 'most gratifying result for the Squadron's first operation'.[138]

> Bombing by TDP involved the Canberras being directed along a radar beam to the target by an Army radar controller. Gillard's Canberra would take off from

> Singapore, and fly out into Malaya at perhaps 20,000 feet. You would make contact with the operator and he would take control, and come down to bombing height, normally 10,000 feet. He would vector you onto his screen and then you rode along the beam. He would give you distance to target, tell you to open bomb doors. We would resettle the aeroplane again because when the doors opened all the trim would change. We would get the aeroplane settled down and then just do exactly as we were told ... and eventually he would say 'drop now' and once we pressed the button, the old aeroplane would leap in the air, and away the bombs would go.[139]

One of the senior navigators with No. 75 Squadron was Flight Lieutenant Pat Neville, who had transferred from the RAF to the RCAF and then the RNZAF, and was posted to No. 75 Squadron after navigating on Sunderland MR5 flying boats with No. 5 Squadron at Lauthala Bay. This had involved a number of flying-boat deployments to Singapore, which included night-time harassing bombing missions over the jungles of Johore from the moorings at Seletar.[140] As a Canberra navigator with No. 75 Squadron, Neville had a major role to play on a bombing mission. During the bomb run, the navigator would move forward from his seat behind the pilot bulkhead into the nose of the aircraft and take control of the release of bombs.

> You would ... call out as the bombs were falling, because you could see them falling away from the aircraft. And you would stay there and see the impact. With 1,000 pounders up to 20,000 feet you could feel the impact of the blast against the aircraft ... You had a very good idea of where they were going to impact by the angle on your bomb sight ... the moment the bombs hit you could actually see the shockwave of the bomb radiate from the point of impact. There would be a deep orangey-red colouring under the jungle canopy, so you could actually see even by daylight the impact point, and then you would see the second, third, fourth, fifth, sixth, and each of them, the blast area extending a surprisingly long way.[141]

When the New Zealand Canberras arrived, offensive air strikes had been drastically cut back. The Canberras were important assets for a conventional bombing and interdiction role in a limited war situation, but they were 'too elaborate' for offensive air strikes in counter-insurgency operations. They had half the payload of a Lincoln bomber, and like all jet aircraft in the tropics suffered from 'a serious limitation in their endurance at low level'. The rate of abortive air strikes increased from 1958, and there were none in the first seven months of 1959. Then Auster reconnaissance aircraft located several guerrilla camps near Bentong in northern Pahang, and on 13 August two targets were bombed by Canberras of Nos 2 RAAF, 45 RAF and 75 RNZAF Squadrons.

'Four days later, on 17 August 1959, a target on the northern slopes of Bukit Tapah in Perak was attacked by Canberras and the offensive air support provided during the Malayan campaign came to an end, even though the Emergency continued for a further eleven months.'[142]

Although strikes against guerrilla targets had stopped, No. 75 Squadron continued training for its primary night-bombing role alongside Canberras of No. 45 Squadron RAF and the Canberras of No. 2 Squadron RAAF at Butterworth. Given the natural competitiveness of the New Zealand ground and air crews, completing the monthly schedule of tasks was a matter of unit pride.

> New Zealanders everywhere tend to do very well and when you put two squadrons together on an airfield like Tengah ... I think the Kiwis probably do 110 per cent even if the others are doing 100 per cent. It was always our intention to do better than anyone else and I think that's still a fact today. On those grounds I do think that we were as good [as] and possibly better than our equivalent British squadron.[143]

Back in New Zealand, No. 14 Squadron was reformed and re-equipped with B(1)12 Canberra bombers purchased by the New Zealand government. Compared to the B2s being flown by No. 75 Squadron on lease from Britain, New Zealand's B12 was a high-performance model.

> It was a totally different type of aeroplane, with a fighter cockpit where the pilot sat with a view all round, and the navigator in the body of the aircraft below him. It was a much more rugged and faster aeroplane, and its role in Europe was that of an interdictor, designed to go across Europe at low level, go up the valleys and dodge Soviet radar. By comparison the B2 was a straight strategic bomber. It would fly in and drop bombs from 30,000 or 40,000 feet.[144]

No. 75 Squadron continued to practise this strategic bombing role over Malaya until 1962, when the squadron returned to New Zealand following the 1961 Defence Review. The decision was triggered by the balance of payments crisis facing Holyoake's National government. All three services were pared to the bone—to 'keep defence expenditure within reasonable bounds, certain measures of retrenchment and deferment of certain proposals for re-equipment have proved necessary'.[145] The end of the Emergency in 1960, and the fact that the now-obsolete B2 Canberras were to be replaced by a later version costing five times as much to rent, forced a reassessment of the squadron's future.[146] The government initially approved sending the B12s of No. 14 Squadron to Singapore. However, Air Staff, perhaps gambling on a change of heart by the politicians, pointed out that this would be just as expensive as the hiring option—as the only B12s in Singapore, they would require their own maintenance arrangements. Faced with this scenario, the government instead decided to withdraw and disband No. 75 Squadron, and meet its SEATO and ANZAM commitments through the regular deployment of No. 14 Squadron from New Zealand, and by leaving the transport aircraft of No. 41 Squadron in theatre.[147]

In January 1961, Squadron Leader Harold Moss succeeded the recently promoted Wing Commander Geoff Highet. By this stage 'we were doing just bomber training. On looking back it was rather unrealistic. We were still doing the old tactical things like twin bomber streams up to places like Bangkok.' No. 75 Squadron's withdrawal was announced in September 1961. It was a tough time: 'we knew six months ahead that we were a dying Squadron and it's very difficult for morale when you know that this is happening'. The blow was softened when Moss negotiated that his crews would return the leased Canberra B2s to the United Kingdom, and arranged short-term secondments for personnel who had bought cars and needed to own them for 12 months before they could bring them duty-free into New Zealand. 'It wasn't a nice period but we continued to fly and do our job, that's all you could do.'[148] Some of the local populace were equally affected, 'in particular the grocers, who proclaim loudly, in broken English, to all who will listen, that they will be bankrupted by 75's withdrawal'.[149]

The news of the withdrawal was overshadowed by the loss of one of the squadron's Canberras, flown by Flight Lieutenant P. G. Bevan and Navigator Flying Officer D. L. Finn. When the plane (WF915) went overdue on the night of 26 October, one of the largest search operations ever conducted in the theatre was mounted. Over the next five days, 'Army Austers, single and twin Pioneers and almost all the small service aircraft in Malaya took part in the search, along with Shackletons, Bristol Freighters, and Hastings. Canberras from 81 PR Squadron photographed all of the area of probability so that more time could be spent studying the ground rather than having a fleeting glimpse from an aircraft.'[150] On the 30th, Flight Lieutenant Bevan walked out of the jungle near Bahau. After ejecting from the aircraft, he had been unable to activate his 'Sarah' (search and rescue beacon) because both it and his Mae West had been torn off by the top of the tree in which he had landed. Trapped by one leg and hanging upside down, he had cut himself free with his knife after his harness failed to release. The pyrotechnics in his survival kit did not work and his matches got wet in the rain. In shock and injured in both wrists, he walked out onto a logging track where Malay timber workers found him and took him to the Bahau police station. Next day the wreckage of the Canberra and the body of Flying Officer Finn were found. Finn had been in the nose of the aircraft and unable to get into his ejection seat before the aircraft crashed.[151]

The government seriously considered pulling out No. 41 Squadron as well, but decided against this after being advised that 'the withdrawal of the Bristol Freighters would leave a serious gap in the capability of the air transport forces required in SEATO or ANZAM operations'.[152] The Freighters would continue to show the 'Silver Fern' throughout Asia. When No. 75 Squadron was withdrawn, New Zealand for the first time in ten years did not have a combat squadron deployed overseas. While the cost-effectiveness of providing offensive air support during the Emergency can be questioned, the RNZAF gained valuable operational experience by having Nos 14 and 75 Squadrons in Singapore. The Sunderland MR5 flying boats of No. 5 Squadron at Lauthala Bay were also regularly deployed to South-East Asia, and the Handley Page Hastings long-range transports of No. 40 Squadron provided ongoing support. Experience was gained first in the fighter/ground attack role, and then in the light bomber/interdictor role. The competitive environment in which the New Zealanders matched their skills against those of similar squadrons from the Commonwealth and the United States honed their capabilities to a high level of efficiency—a level that could not be sustained by the single New Zealand-based Canberra squadron after economic constraints led to its withdrawal from South-East Asia. It would take the crisis of Confrontation with Indonesia for New Zealand to once again commit a combat squadron to Malaysia.

# 4

# SETTING THE STANDARD

## *The Special Air Service Squadron Malaya, 1955–57*

On the 7th day of June we departed
To that military camp in Wai-ou-ru
Major Rennie is our master,
He will save us from disaster,
We are out to show the world what we can do.

NZ SAS Squadron song (Tune: 'Red River Valley')[1]

When Prime Minister Sidney Holland made the initial New Zealand commitment to the Commonwealth Far East Strategic Reserve in 1955, the army component was to be a Special Air Service (SAS) Squadron. On 1 May 1955, after Cabinet had given its approval, the New Zealand Special Air Service formally came into existence.[2] The Squadron's 90 personnel were to be supplemented by another 25 headquarters, signals and administrative staff, and six reinforcements. These 121 New Zealand Army soldiers were to form part of the British 22 Special Air Service Regiment in Malaya. From its formation the New Zealand Special Air Service Squadron was made up of one-third Regulars and two-thirds specially selected volunteers.[3] It would be the first Regular unit of the New Zealand Army to be deployed overseas in peacetime.[4]

It existed thanks to Holland's realisation that committing a 121-strong squadron would be cheaper than—and therefore preferable to—sending a 1,000-strong infantry battalion. The decision was made almost off-the-cuff at the Prime Ministers' Conference in London in February 1955, in response to the United Kingdom's request that New Zealand send an infantry battalion to Malaya as part of the newly agreed Commonwealth Strategic Reserve.

Holland refused, saying that New Zealand's Korean commitment 'necessarily limited our ability';[5] instead he offered an independent New Zealand Special Air Service Squadron.[6] The United Kingdom wanted both, but accepted the SAS contribution as part of a larger parcel of New Zealand commitments that included Nos 14 and 41 Squadrons RNZAF and a RNZN frigate. The promise of an SAS squadron was a watershed in the formation of a professional peacetime New Zealand Army.[7] New Zealand's defence focus had been on the Middle East, to which the Army would commit an infantry division and an armoured brigade in the event of a global war. These forces would be mobilised from the citizen soldiers of the Territorial Force; the Compulsory Military Training (CMT) scheme ensured that trained manpower would be available to meet this contingency. Everything now changed. While a territorially raised division was earmarked for service in South-East Asia in a world war, the use of 'forces in being' in Malaya and Singapore became the focus of the New Zealand Army's commitment to the continent until the withdrawal of 1RNZIR from Singapore in 1989.[8]

By 1955, changes in the way the Emergency was being fought in Malaya had underlined the need for a specialist force such as the Special Air Service. There was no question that the Commonwealth and Federation of Malaya forces were winning the war against the communist insurgency. Thirty per cent of the population was living in 'White Areas', the districts declared to be free of communist influence.[9] The Malayan Communist Party had withdrawn its fighting force, the MRLA, from the 'inhabited areas of the jungle fringe into the deep jungle'.[10] Its role now was to survive as a fighting organisation until Malaya became independent, concentrating on avoiding contact with the security forces while protecting its leaders and foraging for food and supplies.[11]

The role of 22 SAS Regiment was to follow the guerrillas into the deep jungle and destroy them.[12] Specially raised for service in Malaya, the regiment comprised regular British troops trained to 'remain in the deep jungle for months on end ... dominating wide areas and forcing the Communist Terrorist organisations out of their comfortable bases'.[13] But in 1955 there were only three SAS squadrons (A, B and D Squadrons) available to meet this expanding role, and the United Kingdom looked to the Commonwealth for assistance. The outstanding First Battalion Fiji Infantry Regiment was returning to Fiji in 1956, and the infantry battalion Australia was committing to the Commonwealth Strategic Reserve had yet to arrive. Of the forces already in Malaya, the Gurkhas, while outstanding in jungle fighting, were 'apt to be confused by the

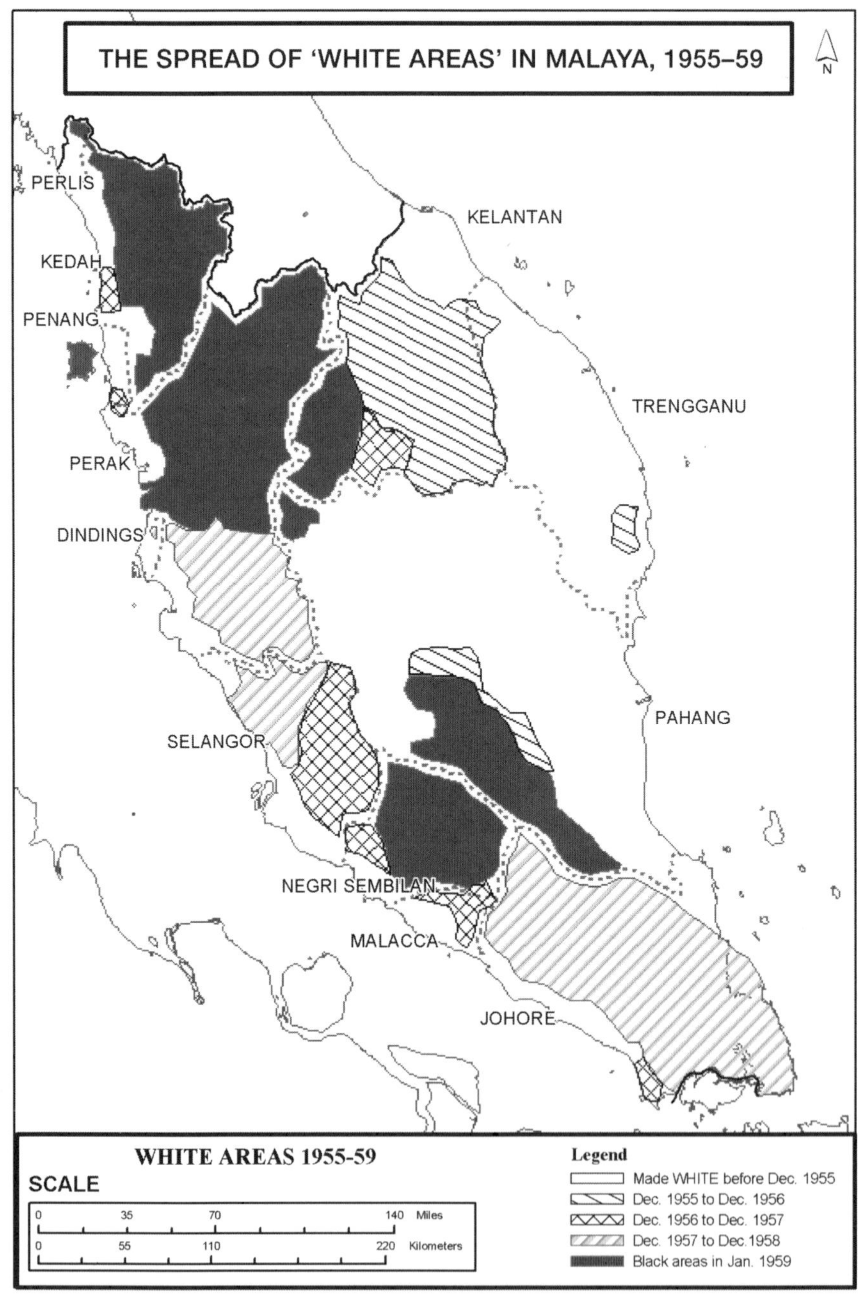


**Map 2** The spread of 'White Areas' in Malaya, 1955–59

aborigines with Chinese Communist Terrorists and find it harder to win their confidence'; and for a number of reasons the 'normal British battalion' made up of national servicemen was 'definitely not suited to deep jungle operations'.[14]

Malaya Command was so desperate for troops able to operate deep in the jungle that it was prepared to give up a British battalion in exchange for another SAS or parachute unit. But the first priority was to add a fourth squadron to 22 SAS Regiment, and it was this gap that New Zealand's contribution now filled. When Holland made his offer, New Zealand had nothing akin to special forces. While special operations had been undertaken by the Long Range Desert Group in the Second World War, the promised component had to be raised from scratch. Raising a sub-unit of squadron or company size to form an integral part of a larger British unit was the antithesis of everything the New Zealand military had striven for since the Gallipoli experience of 1915. The contribution was initially announced as an 'Independent Squadron', but the Chiefs of Staff were worried about whether it would be 'truly independent or ... operating as an additional Squadron to 22 SAS Regiment and under command of that Regiment for all normal purposes'.[15] There was a strong belief that if the squadron became part of a British regiment it would lose its identity, and lack the proper administration that was best achieved under national arrangements. That had been New Zealand's bitter experience in two world wars, and the Chief of General Staff, Major-General William Gentry, was not going to surrender his position lightly. But while Gentry wanted independence 'from a national viewpoint', Far East Land Forces preferred that the New Zealand squadron 'come under command of the 22nd SAS Regiment as an additional squadron'. Reluctantly, the New Zealand Chiefs of Staff agreed to this subordination and integration.[16]

The Malayan Constitutional Conference held in London in January–February 1956 determined that Malaya would become independent in 1957, and decided the nature of continuing Commonwealth military support.[17] Directives were agreed to which satisfied New Zealand's desire that its contribution to the Strategic Reserve be more than a quasi-police force. Unlike the United Kingdom, which was primarily concerned with the internal stability of Malaya, New Zealand saw its contribution as part of a commitment to forward defence in South-East Asia. While New Zealand accepted that there was a valid role for its forces in counter-guerrilla operations, it believed this should be separate from the 'law and order' functions of the Malayan police and security forces.[18]

Major Frank Rennie, who was selected to command the new squadron, had joined the Regular Force in 1937 and served in the Pacific, Italy and Japan. At the time of his appointment he was the chief instructor at the School of Infantry. His background and his ability as an organiser and trainer gave him an unrivalled knowledge of New Zealand Army personnel, and he was allowed to select his officers and NCOs. Of the four troop commanders, his first choice was Ian ('Buzz') Burrows: 'It had to be because he was outstanding, and [John] Mace, and then of course "Rusty" Vail. I selected him because he was full of great spirit.' Directed to include a Territorial officer, Rennie chose Earle Yandall, whom he had observed on Territorial training courses. Captain Graham Boswell, the squadron's second-in-command, had already served in Malaya; Rennie 'didn't know him particularly well but he had a great reputation'. Noel O'Dwyer was chosen as the squadron sergeant-major and Peter Quilliam as the quartermaster sergeant. 'I knew O'Dwyer particularly well because he had done a number of courses with me, and Quilliam ... had served with the Parachute Regiment.'[19]

By this time, rumours about the new unit were flying around the New Zealand Army. Few had any idea what a Special Air Service Squadron was or did, but that did not matter; every Regular soldier saw it as a chance to serve overseas. Corporal John Dixon, an instructor at Burnham Camp, recalled that 'everyone wanted a trip overseas. Korea was winding down ... They said it was going to be a Special Air Service Squadron and that it would be attached to a British unit but apart from that there wasn't a lot of information.'[20] As the only overseas trip on offer, when the opportunity came to apply, 'it was just the obvious thing to do'.[21]

Brigadier W. H. B. Bull, the Director-General of Medical Services, established the enlistment criteria. He recommended that personnel should be between 62 and 70 inches in height (tall men had been found to be 'more subject to fractures'), weigh between 140 and 168 lb, and be aged between 22 and 29. Bull concluded that those 'who had months, if not a few years of soldier training' made the best parachutists. He was not looking for 'escapists', 'glamour boys' or 'those who have flitted from job to job'; 'the good, slightly above average man, preferably with soldier training', was the type to be desired.[22] Some 615 civilians applied.[23] Ross Cameron, a Marton foundry worker, was one of them.

> I got so fed up with the repetitive work in a foundry, I went home for my lunch one day and I said to my family, 'I'm going across to Wanganui and I'm joining the Army

> and I'm going to Korea.' Of course, when I got across there, they said, 'Well, Korea's finished but we've got an outfit going to Malaya, an airborne outfit', and quite frankly I said to myself: 'Bugger it, I'll meet that when it comes and I'll have a go.'[24]

On 7 June 1955, 182 men entered Waiouru Camp for training and final selection in a squadron that was to be the 'most highly trained unit ever to leave the country'.[25] Rennie's Regulars had already 'set up the training programmes and the barracks and organised ourselves into Troops ... and on that famous day ... we picked those drunken louts off the train and brought them in'.[26] Six weeks of basic training was followed by 14 weeks of specialist training to develop the skills needed for long patrols in deep jungle. From the start, excellence was the aim. Major-General Gentry stressed that the squadron must be the best troops ever to leave New Zealand. At the beginning, the 200-strong squadron was told that in five months' time only 120 of them would be required. 'Each troop was told that only so many were wanted. We worked as a team but [were] always conscious of competition. People sorted themselves out.'[27] Some were culled on medical grounds, others as being 'a bit wet'.[28]

Training was conducted within the four troops: 1 Troop was commanded by Lieutenant 'Rusty' Vail, 2 Troop by Lieutenant John Mace, 3 Troop by Lieutenant Ian ('Buzz') Burrows, and 4 Troop by Second Lieutenant Earle ('Duke') Yandall. Each troop soon reflected the personality of its commander. Yandall's 4 Troop was 'not lax but more free and easy as against at the other end [of the scale] 2 Troop commanded by John Mace, who was a regimental Regular Force officer'.[29] Rennie, who knew precisely what he wanted, guided the whole process. 'It was all training and he had it clearly in his mind and on paper, every minute, every hour, every day, every week, every month, exactly. He was focused and he knew what to do ... I admired him as a soldier, but he was a bloody slave-driver.'[30] Fitness was paramount. There was 'lots of physical training, lots of route marching, unarmed combat, to try to give some elite feel to the unit and try to build up that you're something special, and different from the others'.[31] This started on the first day.

> We got out of bed in the morning, lined up outside and marched quietly across the road to breakfast. Went back to the barracks after breakfast, lined up again and the Troop sergeants introduced themselves and said, 'Right, we're going to pick up gear', and it was a case of 'Left turn and by the Left, Quick March!' ... and after about 100 yards, the order came 'Break into double march', and we never stopped doubling for the next six months ... It was tough.[32]

Competition was the cornerstone in building esprit de corps. Sergeant Brian ('Ugly') Martin, Troop Sergeant 1 Troop, recalled: 'Everybody knew that about half a dozen of the group were going to miss out ... so the competition was pretty intense. It wasn't as if you were out to destroy the person next to you. It was just that you were out to be a little bit better.'[33] It was the same between the four troops. Graham Brighouse, Troop Sergeant 2 Troop, remembered that 'There was competition in everything. Everyone was trying to outdo each other. Be more smartly turned out, have better barracks ... better on the drill square, better shooting ... better this, better that.'[34]

General Templer visited Waiouru in late July. 'He told the [troops] to be kind to the local inhabitants of Malaya; to maintain NZ's proud fighting name; and not to relax on [operations] in Malaya—his slogan was "If you are bloody slack you'll buy it."'[35] The word 'slack' was not in Rennie's vocabulary, and he ensured that the fundamentals were thoroughly instilled in his men. Buzz Burrows found Rennie to be 'very, very good in that area ... we had to accept that there were lots of things we didn't know, and could only guess at; but that if we were really well grounded we could handle anything'.[36] Numbers were gradually whittled down, but at the final count there were still five troopers too many. When the squadron sergeant-major, Noel O'Dwyer, marched the selected five into Rennie's office, they knew why. 'It was really terrible and I think that Frank felt [this] too ... they were crying when they came outside.'[37] The initial training was over, and Major-General Gentry's hopes were fulfilled. In O'Dwyer's judgement, the men had 'great spirit' and were 'the best trained of any soldiers I have ever been with'. Rennie had 'stamped his personality on every man ... I don't know any other officer [who] would have got them together like he did.'[38]

In November 1955 the bulk of the squadron flew to Singapore. Two groups had already gone, an administrative advance party with Captain Graham Boswell and a training advance party with Lieutenant Rusty Vail. Before they left, Gentry stressed to Rennie that the squadron was 'New Zealand's initial contribution to the Commonwealth Strategic Reserve in SE Asia and hunting terrorists is only a secondary and incidental role.' Rennie was to ensure that the men understood this, and it was 'important that New Zealand's attitude in this matter should be made quite clear when dealing with civilians, officials, or the Press in Malaya'.[39] While this was Gentry's view as Chief of General Staff, in reality the squadron's single preoccupation for the next two years was to be 'hunting terrorists'.

The first hurdle faced by the New Zealanders after arriving in Singapore was a parachute course. Between 24 October and 4 February they completed their jumps at the Far East Training Centre at RAF Changi.[40] Doug Mackintosh's feelings were typical: 'Virtually nobody said so but I certainly was scared jumping out of planes ... and I know on the day of a parachute jump you would wake up at four in the morning and you could see 20 cigarettes going.'[41] The New Zealanders then joined 22 SAS Regiment at Coronation Park in Kuala Lumpur. The regiment had been formed in 1950 by 'Mad' Mike Calvert, who had won fame with the unconventional Chindit units that operated behind Japanese lines in Burma during the Second World War. The aim was to produce small parties of specially trained men able to infiltrate into the Malayan jungle and live there for long periods of time in order to 'win the hearts and minds' of the indigenous Sakai people and isolate them from the communist guerrillas.

Originally known as the Malayan Scouts (Special Air Service), the unit evolved into 22 SAS Regiment, receiving this as its official title in May 1952. The unit had been hastily raised, with no selection criteria and dependent on recruitment from existing Far East Land Forces units. Many British units had made use of this opportunity to get rid of men they did not want, and the Malayan Scouts became a mixture of the good, the bad and the mediocre. A and D Squadrons were recruited in this manner. By contrast, B Squadron, a 'well disciplined, close-knit body of men',[42] was drawn from the Territorial Reserve 21 Special Air Service Regiment.[43] C Squadron, from Rhodesia, had not been successful in an SAS role; the Rhodesians had won a reputation for brutality and made little effort to win 'hearts and minds'. By 1955 they had returned to Rhodesia, and their place was taken by the New Zealanders.[44]

When the New Zealand squadron arrived, the regiment was still shrugging off the 'very bad impression' it had made among those with influence.[45] Lieutenant-Colonel George Lea had become its commander the previous year, and was still in the process of sorting it out. He, 'perhaps more than any other officer, put 22 SAS into proper shape'.[46] Lea did not have an SAS background, and concentrated on building up a strong team of officers and sacking those who did not meet his standards. By the time the New Zealanders joined the regiment, it was better than other British units in Malaya in a deep jungle role—but that was not saying much. The tactics of the British squadrons were inappropriate; patrols went too fast and made too much noise.[47] Moreover, squadron numbers were low, the quality of personnel was mediocre, and regimental administration was poor. On their arrival, the New Zealanders immediately encountered two graphic illustrations of the problems faced by the regiment. The first was the poor standard of the food from the regimental cookhouse, which the New Zealanders ate until their own squadron kitchen was ready. The second was the standard of regimental transport, which, as Captain Graham Boswell noted, 'is always a good indicator of the quality of any unit'. He found that 'both the vehicles and their drivers needed a lot of attention'.[48]

When the New Zealanders arrived, D Squadron, commanded by Major John Woodhouse, was the exception, and it was through his influence that the mistakes made in absorbing the Rhodesian squadron into the regiment were not repeated.[49] He believed the Rhodesians had been pitchforked into operations before they were ready and had never recovered from this bad start. Rennie spent ten days with Woodhouse before the New Zealanders began operations, and benefited from having 'a pretty good look' at a good squadron and a good command in operation. A strong rapport was established between the two men, and Rennie understood the need for a 'common starting point in the form of Standing Orders for Operations, and then to drill everyone through them'.[50] These standard procedures were roughed out and discussed before the New Zealanders' first operation, and evaluated and revised after each subsequent operation. This process ensured that Rennie's troops all followed the same drills and procedures in the jungle, and allowed them to benefit from one another's experience. In hindsight, it was the basis of the New Zealanders' success in jungle operations (see appendices 5 and 6).

The New Zealanders were not initially aware of the undercurrents within the regiment. As new boys, they were conscious only of its mystique, and of the need to fit into a working organisation without making any fuss. When they arrived at the regimental camp, all the other squadrons were out on operations. The New Zealanders, who had never been in the jungle, 'were told that the next day we were going into the jungle on a two-week training operation. "Here's your rations. Be ready 7 o'clock in the morning." We took the lot and got on the trucks. Got off the trucks at the far end and the British sergeant said: "Follow me." And that was the instruction. He said to me, "You're last man", and we learnt very quickly indeed.'[51] They were plunged straight into the strangeness, the heat, the humidity and the constant dampness of the tropics. Under the burning glare of the sun, the patrols struggled through head-high lallang grasses on the jungle fringe into lowland swamps full of tree-roots, vines, mud, leaves and waist-high water, the home of snakes, mosquitoes and leeches. The tangled maze of cut-over secondary jungle contrasted starkly with the high-altitude primary rainforest, its tree canopy some 150 feet overhead, where it could be 'cool by day' and 'cold at night'.[52]

The New Zealand squadron met all these conditions on their two training operations, which although carried out in 'live' terrorist areas gave them the chance to learn from their mistakes—of which there were many. During Operation BUKIT TAPEH, conducted in Pahang from 23 January to 27 February 1956, Rennie recalled, 'We all got lost. That was good for us. Hopelessly lost. I was sending a grid reference and I was on the wrong bloody map. When we called up the aircraft to give us a fix, it replied: "I can't fucking see you."'[53] Map-reading and navigation were skills 'you've got to learn the hard way'.[54] But the lessons were well learned. The regiment's training officer, Captain Donald Hobbs, reported that 'the training in New Zealand had been of such a standard that it was possible to spend the minimum time on elementary instruction and concentrate on the type of operations peculiar to the SAS'. In navigation, immediate action drills and physical fitness, 'all ranks had reached an outstanding level of efficiency prior to arrival in Malaya'.[55] British Army course reports did not bestow such accolades lightly; they reflect how much Rennie had achieved in New Zealand.

Captain Graham Boswell had the temperament and the tact to deal with the many administrative problems that inevitably accompanied the process of settling-in at Coronation Park. These were mainly due to differences in national characteristics, reflected in the application of discipline, standards of provisioning and welfare, hygiene and sanitation, and the handling of personal problems.[56] All were tackled and eventually solved in Boswell's quiet but effective manner. At a personal level, the New Zealanders were part of the unit 'right from the very first day'; it was 'extraordinary that they accepted these new boys, and anything we wanted we were treated like any other squadron'.[57]

Housing problems were less easily solved, as no provision had been made for the New Zealanders' families. After complaints were laid, a house was made available for Major Rennie's family, but Graham Boswell and the married NCOs, whose families were soon to join them from New Zealand, were left to fend for themselves. The shambles over their housing arrangements still rankles with squadron veterans. The newly arrived families, many with young children, faced the nightmare of being dumped in a brand-new house with 'no water and no power' in an unfinished estate in Petaling Jaya, just outside Kuala Lumpur. In Fran Martin's case, the house leaked and the recently landscaped red clay around it became a sea of mud in the monsoon rains. After her husband departed on operations she found a furnished house which fell outside the guidelines for the hiring of married quarters. The Martins had to pay the rent themselves: 'all our money was disappearing and we had to borrow money to live'.[58] It seemed that nothing could penetrate the labyrinthine bureaucracy of Malaya Command, and matters only improved after Boswell bypassed regimental headquarters and worked directly with a sympathetic Australian officer in the housing section.[59] But this was of no initial comfort to women with small children who found themselves in unsatisfactory makeshift accommodation while their husbands were on operations.

The families also faced the strangeness of living in a mainly Chinese suburb, coping with an amah (housekeeper), and adapting to different food. Often it was easier to stick to what you knew: 'Watties frozen peas were just the Godsend ... local food would have been much cheaper but we weren't very adventuresome.' But the women coped. 'I was an Army wife. I'd married into the Army so you just accepted it ... we were the first Army wives who'd been out there and you had to accept it.'[60]

Despite these peripheral problems, the squadron quickly achieved an effective operational integration with 22 SAS Regiment that was to be maintained throughout its tour. Finding that the troops in the three British squadrons were smaller than those in his squadron, Rennie decided to convert his four troops into five.[61] No New Zealand officer was immediately available as a troop commander, so Rennie placed Sergeant B. P. Martin in command of 5 Troop. He soon became increasingly unhappy with 5 Troop's performance and blamed Martin's leadership. Martin did not like the arrangement either. 'I didn't have the opportunity of mixing with the officer troop commanders and chewing over post-operational matters. I always felt that I was a bit on the hind tit as a troop sergeant trying to operate as a troop commander.'[62] When Martin fell ill, WO2 Noel O'Dwyer, the squadron sergeant-major, took over command until a replacement officer, Lieutenant Lindsay Williams, arrived from New Zealand in November 1956.[63]

On 2 April 1956 the New Zealanders became fully operational and were committed on Operation GABES SOUTH in the Fort Brooke area.[64] Fort Brooke was a small police field-post, 'a primitive type of construction set in a clearing on a ridge, with a bamboo palisade'; alongside it was a helicopter landing zone, and a clearing used as a dropping zone for aerial re-supply by parachute.[65] It was one of a number of forts built to dominate areas inhabited by the Orang Asli, the 'aborigines' of the Malayan jungle.[66] Fort Brooke was near the Ber and Perolak rivers in the central mountains of the Malay Peninsula.

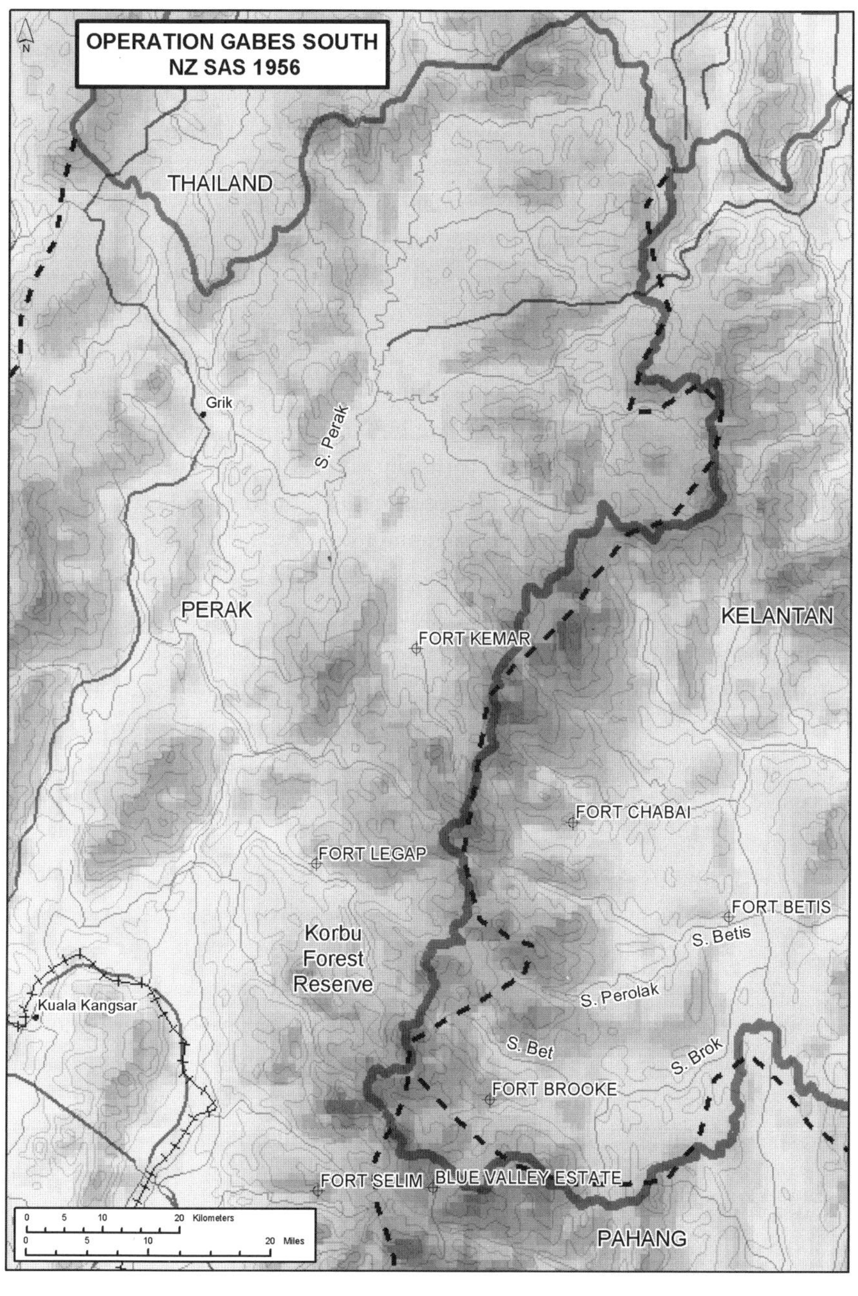


**Map 3** Operation GABES SOUTH, 1956

This high country around the junction of the states of Perak, Kelantan and Pahang was the guerrillas' fastness, protected by high mountains and deep valleys densely covered in virgin jungle. The area was inhabited by indigenous peoples with different languages and ethnic backgrounds. Around Fort Brooke were the Senoi and the Negritos. The Senoi, a semi-nomadic people, practised shifting agriculture and hunted animals in the jungle. They comprised two main tribal groups: the Semai in the low-lying southern areas of the central range, and the Temiar in the north.[67] The Negritos did not practise any form of cultivation but moved from 'valley to valley, living on jungle roots and tubers and shooting small game'.[68] Their welfare was the responsibility of the Department of Aborigines, which with police support was trying to resettle them around the police forts in order to both protect and control them.[69]

The guerrilla bases in the deep jungle that had been important during the war against the Japanese continued to be used during the Emergency. The guerrillas dominated the indigenous communities, recruiting people as 'guides and porters ... food cultivators and messengers', and to serve 'as "eyes and ears" reporting any security force activity'. The MRLA formed a small Asal Group of experienced hard-core soldiers, who by a combination of threats and intermarriage gained control of the indigenous peoples.[70] This group exercised an influence far beyond its actual numbers, establishing an invisible yet impenetrable 'Aborigine Screen' around their jungle bases through which the offensive patrols of the security forces could not pass without the guerrillas being alerted.[71]

The security forces were determined to break this domination. Every member of the New Zealand squadron was told that their 'basic task was to get deep into the jungle and win the confidence of the aborigine. If they supported the terrorist then obviously the terrorist got fed and had a good life. If they supported us, they would stop feeding the terrorist and give us information.'[72] This was easier said than done, as the squadron was to find out. The operation began with the squadron, except for 3 Troop, being trucked up the winding road to the Blue Valley Tea Estate in the Cameron Highlands. Then, with 14 days' rations on their backs, the troop patrols set off on foot on a 25-mile incursion into the Fort Brooke area. This steep and rugged country, rising to 6,000 feet, had remained largely unknown to both Malays and Europeans until the 1930s. The Protector of Aborigines, Richard Noone, described it as

> a strange unbelievable world [the higher peaks of which] are almost always shrouded in mist ... Up here the trees are stunted and misshapen like weird spectres

> draped with tangles of moss that hang in decorative festoons ... Warming sunlight leaks through the low roof of this moss forest, but ghosts of white mist stalking about will touch you as you pass with clammy, spine-chilling fingers.[73]

The New Zealanders prided themselves on their fitness, but for John Dixon this high country was 'as steep as I've seen ... First time I've seen soldiers nearly sobbing with exhaustion with the heavy packs. I remember looking back down a very steep and muddy hill and I was absolutely clapped out, and I looked back and there were these guys who I knew smoked and I thought, "If I'm just about clapped out and I don't smoke, how the hell are you making it?", and so you went on.'[74]

Rennie established his headquarters inside the police post at Fort Brooke, while his four troops searched the surrounding river systems in a pattern of operations that would continue for the next two years. A troop moved into an area and set up a base that might be occupied for the entire three months of the patrol, or moved a number of times. Patrols were sent out; if a troop was at full strength it might send two patrols out and keep two at the base. Patrols were about five strong, with either the officer, sergeant, troop corporal, or occasionally a lance-corporal in command. They would go out for three or four nights, travelling light with about 40 lb in their packs.

> Movement was quite slow. The theory was that you shouldn't move on tracks as you could be ambushed and you could see more sign off ... You were just usually hunting for anything you could find. Operating on information was very rare indeed. I think our Troop worked perhaps three or four times on information; the rest was simply checking over areas, looking for camps ... checking every stream for movement to and from water. You could go for three or four months and find nothing. The search pattern was dictated by the type of ground ... we usually had a big area to cover in a reasonably short time.[75]

The slightest sound would alert the birds and animals in the jungle canopy above. A patrol might take an hour to travel 200 yards, with every man's senses attuned, knowing that the next bush or stream might reveal signs of the enemy—or the enemy themselves. Men struggled up the sides of steep, jungle-clad mountains, bathed in constant sweat in the near-100 per cent humidity. Some patrols never came closer to the guerrillas in two years than finding deserted camp sites or food dumps. Yet the tension was unremitting, because until the operation was over men never knew if they would come face to face with an enemy around the next clump of bamboo.

While there were tactical variations between the troops, patrols always moved in single file.

> Distance between men about 5–8 metres. Usually always the one or possibly two men as scouts. Second person the patrol commander who acted as support to the scout, and then three men behind, the Bren LMG [light machine gun] behind the patrol commander. One of our scouts, Grey Otene, carried a pump action shotgun so that he could fire his five rounds very quickly. The idea was that if you were contacted to get into them very fast indeed ... You expected the enemy to be in small groups with weapons that weren't much cop.[76]

During this careful, painstaking patrolling, the visibility through thick foliage could be as little as two to five yards. This placed enormous pressure on the lead scouts. Instinct and immediate reaction made the difference between success and failure, life and death. On 9 April 1956 a patrol led by Sergeant David Ogilvy fired the squadron's first shot in anger.[77] The lead scout caught a fleeting glimpse of a nude male figure at a river; there was a scream, three quick shotgun blasts, a frantic dropping of packs by the rest of the patrol, a hurried follow-up, and then nothing—their quarry had gone.[78]

The principal target in the Fort Brooke area was the Asal group on the upper Brok, where the ruthless and capable Ah Ming commanded a small number of Chinese and aboriginals. Ah Ming became the particular target of Burrows' 3 Troop. This was an extremely difficult assignment for any troop on its first major operation, and reflected Rennie's faith in Burrows' ability. The operation was to be kept secret from the indigenous population around Fort Brooke. Burrows would work with an aboriginal named Uda and his followers, who had once been part of Ah Ming's group. Uda had absented himself from the group when one of his children died, and deserted Ah Ming after being made to dig up his child's body to confirm his story—an act of desecration that led Uda to give himself up to the Department of Aborigines.[79] The members of 3 Troop were flown by helicopter into a jungle rendezvous with Uda's 12-strong party, and with some qualms on Burrows' part presented the aboriginals with shotguns and ammunition. The inducement for Uda to eliminate Ah Ming included a reward of $4,000, with $1,500 or more 'for any other CT' according to rank; the party would also be allowed to keep the shotguns and ammunition. However, it soon became obvious to Burrows that Uda was a reluctant ally who was afraid of Ah Ming.

These two groups from vastly different cultures struggled to come to terms with each other. But gradually links were forged. It was a humbling lesson for the New Zealanders, who 'were absorbing their ability and their skills, and gradually improving communication between us as well'.[80] The experience also highlighted a universal characteristic of New Zealand service personnel: their ability to get on with people, whatever their background. This was attributed to the mix of Maori and Pakeha within the troops, and the natural linguistic skills of the Maori.[81] Working with Uda's group also brought a major improvement in their tracking skills. Burrows' lead scout, Steve Watene, a man with a warm outgoing personality, had an affinity with the aboriginals. Burrows believed that this close association 'refined [Watene's] own personal tracking and scouting skills to a degree none of us would have believed possible'.[82] Watene became the outstanding scout in the squadron, and would be awarded the British Empire Medal for his achievements.[83]

> On Burrows' advice, the group moved into the main area of indigenous occupation on the Sungei Chelapong, with members of Uda's party accompanying each patrol as scouts. On 24 April, Uda and his scouts travelling with Burrows' patrol found that two of Ah Ming's group and two aboriginals had been at a ladang (cultivated clearing in the jungle) that morning.
>
> It was fascinating on a real hot scent like that to watch Uda and his team operate. They had the sort of expertise that Huia Woods was to develop later in his tracking techniques.[84] One would be principal tracker and he would be moving very slowly but if he were cautious or hesitant about something ... his assistant would just go on one side in a cast and the other would go the other side. They satisfied themselves as to which direction to follow and then progressed on without a word.[85]

During a two-day follow-up of this discovery, 'we did no chopping and made no noise'. On 27 April, Burrows started his patrol through the jungle at first light 'to try and catch the CT having breakfast. We followed the tracks for an hour and then sensed that they must be very close. We took off our packs which we left with the Abos and crawled along the track until we heard the murmur of voices, smelt smoke, and a little bit later saw the "top" of a basha roof.' The Bren group inched their way through the jungle to a small ridge 40 feet from the palm-frond shelter, while Burrows and the rest of his patrol crawled on their stomachs to about 20 feet from the hut, roughly at right angles to where the Bren gunners were concealed.

> I suppose it might have been half an hour or so to get into position. We lay quite close, and we could see a head moving here and there and it was reasonably open jungle, so there wasn't all that much cover and they were very alert. You could see

> a head bobbing up and looking, and they were obviously CTs but we didn't know what the size of the camp was ... The Bren group opened up and we just went through. We were very lucky that the ground was so perfect for it ... The Bren group dropped one of them in the first burst and I don't know whether they hit the other fellow or not but he shot off and then I sent two of the group off after him ... and within a short time Trooper Fred Parkes came back with this CT across his shoulders like a deer, and just threw him down on the ground and said, 'well there's the other one boss'.[86]

Uda identified one of the dead men as the Asal leader, Ah Ming. The bodies were stretchered to a landing zone and flown out to Fort Brooke for identification by Special Branch.[87] It was an outstanding start to the New Zealanders' operational role in Malaya, and Rennie noted that Lea 'seemed pleased'.[88]

This success was tempered by the first and, as it proved, only New Zealand operational fatality. John Mace's 2 Troop, working on the Sungei Perolak, sent out a five-man patrol under Corporal McCulloch. Ross Cameron was one of the patrol.

> We had received information that a group of CTs were moving from the Ber across to the Perolak and we were sent out to set up an ambush. Nothing came of it and we started moving back. [On 2 May] we were moving down the hill back into the Perolak Valley... we stopped and we had a spell on the side of the track and somebody thought that they heard a metallic clink like the clink of a mess tin. So we decided to investigate which meant [the patrol] going off the track, down into this gully, across the stream at the bottom and then up the other side ... I was 'Tail-end Charlie' [the last man] ... Charlie [Thomas] was the Lead Scout ... we went down, across the stream and were going up the other side and then all of a sudden there was a bang from up front ... and then all hell broke. I dived off the track and I thought I saw something move in the bush to my right so I fired off a couple of rounds and carried on and there was Charlie lying on the track. He'd walked right into it and taken a bullet in the gut. Mac [McCulloch] decided to detach a couple of guys back to camp about an hour's walk away and get help.[89]

It was already late afternoon when the news reached camp. Mace sent a party under Sergeant Brighouse to carry Thomas out to the nearest landing zone for evacuation by helicopter. Meanwhile Cameron, the patrol's medic, could do little. 'He'd been shot in the guts. It was just a case of putting a dressing on the wound. Other than that there was nothing. At that stage we didn't have saline injections or anything like that. It was fairly basic ... he was conscious and I think he realised that he was on the way out. He lasted about an hour or so and he just quietly went downhill until that was it.'[90]

Personnel of No. 41 Squadron in Malaya, 1949.
*RNZAF Museum, Mus 01024*

Servicing the port engine of one of the Dakotas of A Flight, No. 41 Squadron, December 1950.
*Archives New Zealand, Air 165/3*

A Dakota of A Flight taxis on the runway at Kuala Lumpur.
*RNZAF Museum, Hist 495*

Dispatchers at work in an A Flight Dakota over Malaya, 1951.
*RNZAF Museum, Hist 1786*

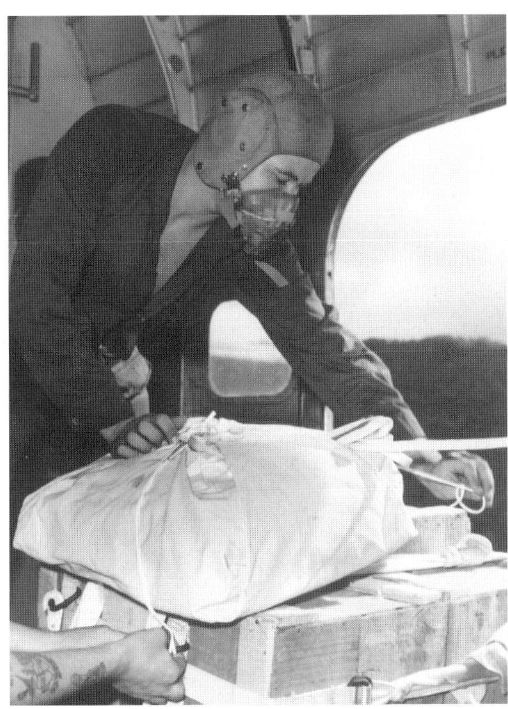

Preparing supplies to be dropped to security forces exercising in the Malayan jungle, 21 October 1960.
*RNZAF Museum, DPR SEA 69*

A Bristol Freighter of No. 41 Squadron drops supplies to security forces exercising in the Malayan jungle, 21 October 1960.
*RNZAF Museum, DPR SEA 70*

HMNZS *Royalist* at Singapore.
*Naval Museum, AAN 0047*

HMNZS *Rotoiti* arrives in Auckland in 1961 from South-East Asia.
*Naval Museum, GN 4531*

‘Hands to bathe’ was always a welcome pipe on the *Royalist* – even if a small boat had to circle the swimmers to deter sharks. This photo was taken after a SEATO exercise in the Philippines.
*Naval Museum, AAN 0204*

Beer issue on board *Taranaki*. Left to right: Able Seamen G. R. Jones, ‘Sadie’ Cameron, and ‘Scoops’ Cunningham.
*Naval Museum, AAV 0804*

Flight Sergeant Parry with his wife and children, Malaya, October 1961.
*RNZAF Museum, PR 3419~61*

A Bristol Freighter of No. 41 Squadron is unloaded and refuelled at Gan Island in the Maldives, March 1962.
*RNZAF Museum, DPR SEA G326*

Local people help to free a Bristol Freighter of No. 41 Squadron bogged down on a grass airstrip in Thailand, June 1961.
*RNZAF Museum, DPR SEA G480*

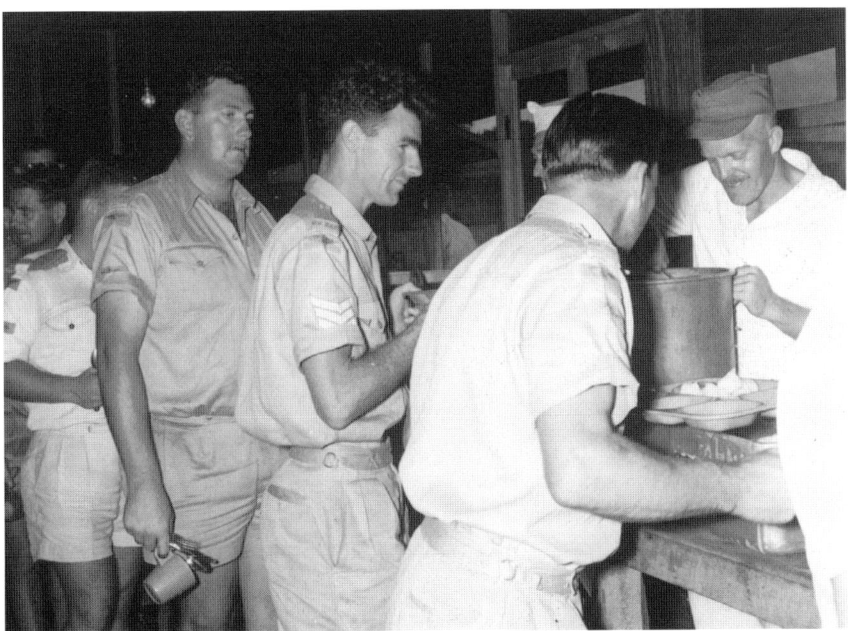
No. 41 Squadron personnel involved in Operation SCORPION line up in their mess at Khorat, Thailand.
*RNZAF Museum, DPR SEA G433*

Pilot Officer John Scrimshaw poses in his Venom at Tengah, Singapore, 1956.
*RNZAF Museum, DPR 195*

Refuelling No. 14 Squadron Venoms at Tengah, November 1956.
*RNZAF Museum, Teng 142*

Flooded barracks at Tengah, November 1956.
*RNZAF Museum, Teng 188*

A rocket-armed Venom of No. 14 Squadron flies over Changi in 1957.
*RNZAF Museum, Teng 366*

RNZAF personnel at the Kiwi Bar, Tengah, December 1956.
*RNZAF Museum, Teng 217*

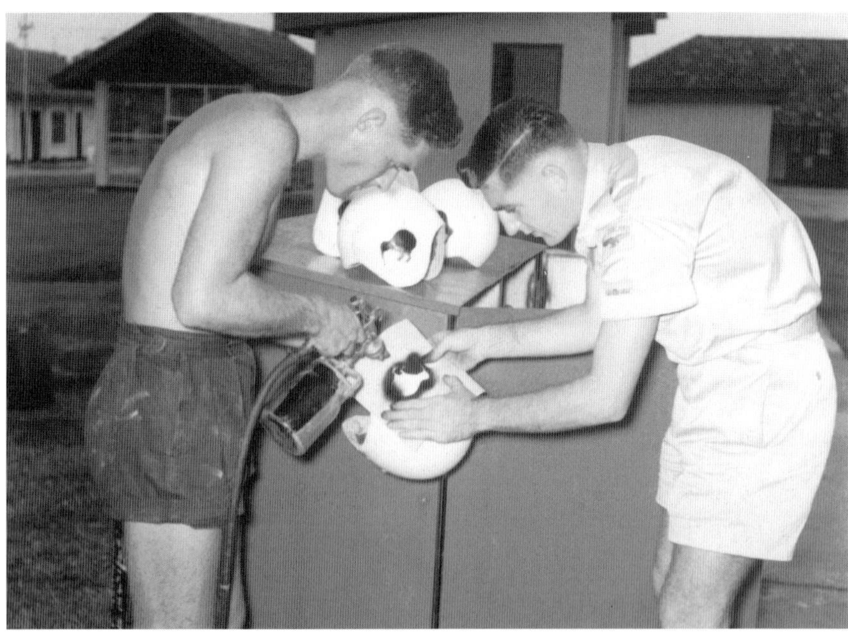

Spray-painting kiwis on flying helmets at Tengah, September 1957.
*RNZAF Museum, Teng 373*

No. 14 Squadron Venoms and personnel at Tengah, 14 April 1958.
*RNZAF Museum, Teng 500*

A Canberra drops bombs during the first operational strike in Malaya by No. 75 Squadron, 30 September 1958.
*RNZAF Museum, DPR SEA 228*

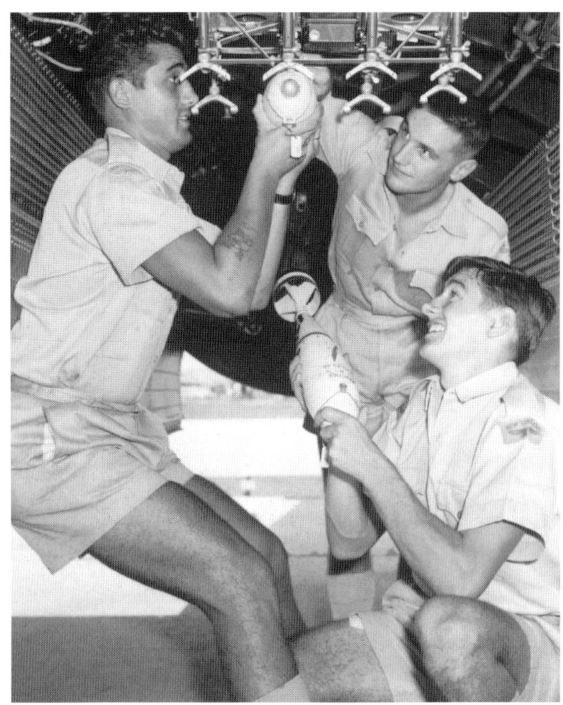

Armourers load 25-lb bombs into a No. 75 Squadron Canberra, July 1960.
*RNZAF Museum, DPR SEA 171*

Volunteers outside the SAS barracks at Waiouru on their first day in camp, June 1955.
*War History Collection, ATL, M-0011*

Local people and New Zealand troops watch a Bristol Sycamore helicopter in the Malayan jungle, 2 December 1955.
*War History Collection, ATL, PA1-q-318-M428*

Major Frank Rennie (left) with a radio operator in the SAS Squadron's operations room at Kuala Pilah.
*James E. Fraser Collection*

Trooper Bill Edwards rests after being helicoptered into Fort Brooke in 1956.
*War History Collection, ATL, M-0771*

Major Frank Rennie and Second Lieutenant Earle Randall oversee the allocation of aboriginal porters to SAS troops, c. 1956. These men carried the heavy wirelesses and batteries.
*War History Collection, ATL, M-0663*

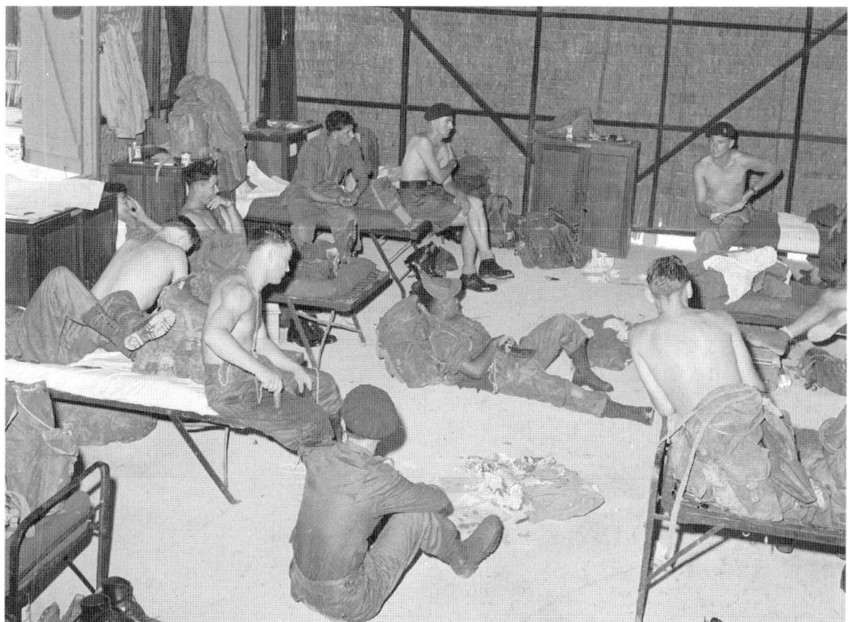

Lieutenant John Mace briefs his troop on a forthcoming operation, c. 1956.
*War History Collection, ATL, M-0635*

Corporal Huia Woods briefs a 4 Troop patrol. Malaya, April 1957.
*War History Collection, ATL, M-2114*

Members of an SAS patrol carrying packs containing two weeks' rations board a canoe at the beginning of a five-week patrol, c. 1956.
*War History Collection, ATL, M-0671*

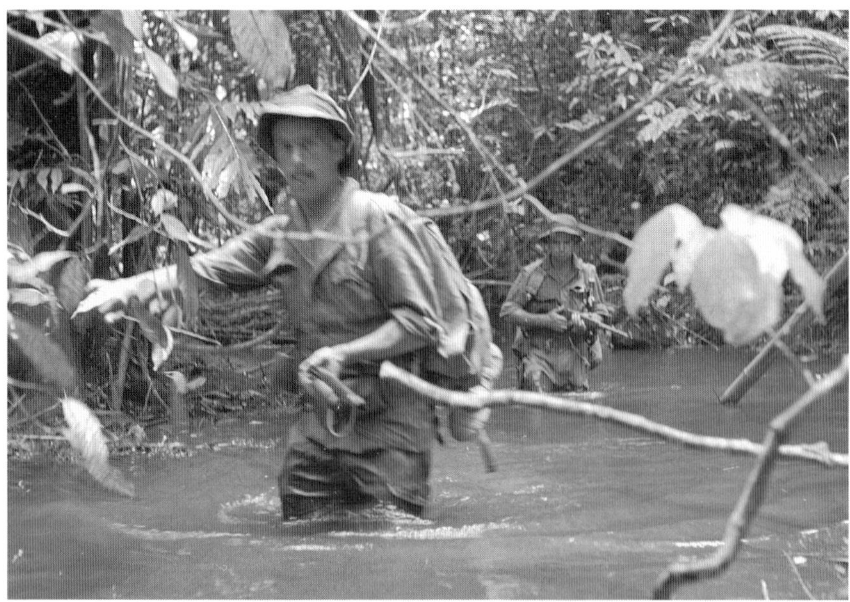

Two troopers in the Malayan jungle, c. 1956. P. F. Wildermoth, the leading scout, is followed by Grey Otene.
*War History Collection, ATL, M-0584*

The patrol hurriedly stretchered Thomas to the helicopter rendezvous, but it was dark before they got there and he died during the night.[91] A post-mortem showed 'that little could have been done for him'.[92] His death hit the troop and the squadron hard, and brought home to everyone once again that the difference between success and failure was a split second. 'It was our first casualty ... Well, I suppose we were starting to get a bit cocky, squadron-wise, and it took the cockiness out, there's no two ways about that.'[93] In the days that followed, Mace kept his men busy: 'really he flogged us from one end of our troop area to the other and it was probably the best thing that he did because it got our minds off the thing'.[94] Thomas's death highlighted the importance of helicopter support in country where a helicopter could traverse three days' march in 20 minutes. The pilot's efforts were not lost on the New Zealanders; his willingness to fly into the 'craziest of LZs was a wonderful morale booster', and confirmed the flexibility that helicopter support gave to operations deep in the rain forest.[95]

Meanwhile, Rennie at Fort Brooke evaluated the pattern of guerrilla activity and movement his troops had uncovered. 'From a study of CT techniques since the NZ Sqn has been here, [it is] obvious that they move from prearranged abo base to abo base. Camps have all been in striking distance of deserted [ladangs] in which there is plenty of food.' Rennie got Lea's approval to reduce security force activity in the area to a minimum, 'and so give the impression that troops have left'. Ambushes were prepared at the ladangs that were being used by the guerrillas. Rennie's men stopped 'looking for the CT' and allowed the CT to come to them.[96] The New Zealanders received a massive airdrop of 28 days' worth of supplies, and went to ground.

This strategy led to 'Another Big Day' on 20 May 1956,[97] when Buzz Burrows and his eight-man patrol found the tracks of a four-man group on a ridge above the Sungei Setog. These tracks were followed for the rest of the day. Burrows recalled:

> [It] was getting very late in the afternoon—about half past five ... with dark coming down at seven like an instantaneous blanket. I took Steve Watene, my lead scout, because there were signs around the place ... So I went off with Watene and we saw this CT come down diagonally towards us and we shot him. The rest of the patrol came across very, very quickly and we could smell from a little bit of smoke that a camp was just across the ridge. We put a Bren group out and went forward into the camp ... We just started to move and fire burst out from the other side. It's very difficult to tell where firing comes from unless you actually see the weapon smoke, and you're usually going for cover so damn quickly you don't get the chance to

> have a look. We heard them going up the bank on the other side of the river and we lost them. It was getting dark and a follow-up wasn't possible. We got all the packs they left and they just got away with their webbing and weapons. Uda was with me and established that there were two aborigines, and three or four Chinese.[98]

Uda identified the dead man—'a big, well-built Chinese fellow'—as Kum Chin, Ah Ming's second-in-command and scribe. After destroying what they could not carry out, the patrol brought out the body. It was 'a hell of a trip ... because we had to go back over the top of one of the big ranges to get back down to where our camp was'.[99]

The New Zealanders had hit the Asal organisation hard, but the area was too important for the communists to abandon. The MRLA tried to minimise the impact of Ah Ming's death by giving his name to his replacement. While relations between the security forces and the indigenous inhabitants improved after these successes, the latter remained reluctant to provide information. Rennie saw the importance of keeping the SAS in the area.[100] He recommended to Lea that the aboriginals continue to be resettled closer to Fort Brooke, where they could be both protected and controlled, and that selected ladangs be used for ambushes and the remainder destroyed.[101]

The New Zealanders were replaced by A Squadron on 11–12 June 1956. They had made an impressive start with an operation that was described by Lea as 'an outstanding success'. He assessed Rennie's squadron as being 'a mature and experienced Unit and all ranks have complete confidence in themselves and in each other'. The squadron had absorbed and made full use of the experience in the regiment, and was now giving something back by 'evolving techniques of its own and ... contributing to the general "know how" of the Regiment'.[102] As the New Zealanders headed back to Kuala Lumpur, Burrows recalled, 'We were pretty tired after coming to terms with the jungle which was a very solid apprenticeship.'[103] Ten weeks on operations had pushed the men to their limits.

> The 14-day ration for each man was a four-gallon kerosene tin and it had in it things like rice, oatmeal, sugar, seven tins of bully beef, seven tins of cheese, vitamin tablets—all basic stuff. It was OK to keep you going but you did some peculiar things ... towards the end of the operation. You would sit down and eat all the sugar as a meal ... We didn't realise it at the time but from the photos taken at the end of an operation we looked similar to people out of Belsen Camp ... Walking six to seven hours a day, even though it was fairly slow walking, was physically fairly tough.[104]

A rest camp was established on Pangkor Island to keep Rennie's men out of Kuala Lumpur's bars. 'It was a combination of getting them away from the military policemen, getting them into fresh air and salt sea for skin and humidity reasons and feeding them back up again.' Steak was in good supply, and 'you could almost see them growing like asparagus'.[105] As well as enjoying sun, sand and beer, there were detailed operation reports to complete, and an exhaustive debriefing. 'Every Troop Commander and every Sergeant and every Patrol Commander had their say as to: Did a drill work? ... Why didn't it? ... There were all kinds of diagrams in the sand. Then we would decide ... whether it was a good idea to change [how we did things]. Everybody had a say.'[106] Rennie summarised this debriefing process for Lea, who insisted that the lessons were passed on to the other squadrons, including by having the New Zealanders demonstrate how SAS patrol tactics could be improved.[107]

Rennie was always planning ahead. 'I spent a lot of time with the CO thinking [through] the next operation ... if I wasn't going back to the same place, I would then go off and establish contact with whoever was the commander of the organisation under which we were placed. Talk to them and be briefed. In addition to that George [Lea] would, after I had written my report, sit down and talk about things.' This close relationship was important to the New Zealanders' growing confidence. 'I think that [Lea] regarded us [a little bit] like a boxer ... What he wanted ... was to give us one or two easy contests, just to see what we could do.' Once the New Zealanders delivered results, they were tested again. 'We really couldn't have had a better commander.'[108] This careful 'blooding' of the New Zealand squadron was also influenced by Woodhouse, who considered that the patrolling and jungle skills of the British squadrons were not what they should be.[109] Spurred on by Rennie's unceasing quest for excellence, the New Zealand squadron became a benchmark for the regiment's performance, with Lea goading his other squadrons to match the success of the newcomers. That success was also important for the regiment, the continued existence of which as a unit of the Regular Army was under scrutiny in London. A successful unit was always harder to get rid of.[110]

During their break, the New Zealanders went on courses as 'part of the plan, carried out when possible ... to train members of the SAS for their normal role in war'.[111] This plan had been stressed to Rennie before he left New Zealand, but despite its participation in a series of exercises the squadron's primary role in the Commonwealth Strategic Reserve remained subordinate in practice to the full-time commitment of 22 SAS Regiment to counter-insurgency operations.[112]

These operations were ongoing, and during the rest period four New Zealanders, including Sergeant Ray Delves, were selected for a scratch group of parachutists to be commanded by Captain John Slim and known as SLIMFORCE. This was the first operational jump by the New Zealanders, and the first operational tree-descent for 22 SAS Regiment. SLIMFORCE parachuted into the Sungei Betis area at last light on 18 July as part of an A Squadron operation to flush out a group of 20 guerrillas that was believed to be in the area. This ill-conceived affair ended in disaster. The parachute drop onto the jungle canopy left each parachutist dangling 100–150 feet above the jungle floor. Each man had to release himself from his harness and abseil to the ground. Both sergeants were injured in the jump; Delves broke his ankle, while the British sergeant suffered serious back and chest injuries. SLIMFORCE played no meaningful role in the operation, instead spending two days using explosives to create a helicopter pad in the jungle so its casualties could be evacuated.[113]

On 27 July the New Zealanders farewelled the bars of Kuala Lumpur, and after midnight boarded trucks for the Cameron Highlands. The next morning they were flown into landing zones around Fort Brooke to relieve A Squadron. Without helicopter support, deep jungle operations would have been impossible. While the capacity of the machines was severely limited by both the altitude and the tropical climate, their presence did wonders for morale; soldiers knew that if they became casualties it would be possible to get them out. Rennie grouped his troops near the indigenous population centres. One and 3 Troops worked together on the Sungei Ber, as did 2 and 4 Troops on the Sungei Perolak, while 5 Troop operated to the south, between Fort Brooke and the Cameron Highlands. The New Zealanders' task was to provide a protective shield for the aboriginal groups that were being concentrated around Fort Brooke.[114]

The return of 2 and 4 Troops to the Perolak brought immediate success. As soon as the British squadron left, one of the large group of tribespeople nearby told the New Zealanders of guerrillas in the area.[115] The informant, Busu, who had given reliable information before, said that seven guerrillas had been camped some distance away for three or four days. Busu and his people had provided food that the leader, Lung Sang, had demanded.[116]

Both troop commanders wanted to pursue this group. As Mace ruefully recalled, although he was the senior 'we tossed [a coin] for it and [Yandall] won'. They had ruled out a combined operation. 'Duke's style was very different to mine and to put together two troops to go off and do that type of job, I didn't want a bar of it.'[117] Instead, four or five soldiers from 2 Troop were attached to 4 Troop to provide additional firepower. Yandall set out at 8 a.m. on 28 July, and reached the area in mid-afternoon. Orders were given quickly, and the patrol divided into assault, fire support and cut-off groups. Progress was slow in the thick jungle, and it was not until 5.30 p.m. that Busu indicated the camp's location, in a small stream re-entrant which could only be approached down a steep bamboo-covered slope. As Doug Mackintosh, who commanded the fire support group, remembered, 'I think Earle Yandall must have decided that it would be too risky to wait until morning because they may have left at first light ... He gathered the NCOs together and gave out the plan and it was fairly straightforward. He would lead the assault group straight down to where the camp should be ... John Dixon was given the task of a cut-off group on the downstream side.'[118] Mackintosh's group would give fire support; both he and Dixon would move into position 30 minutes before the assault. At 6 p.m., with dusk falling, Yandall's assault group crawled forward.

> I think there were five of us in it, we went down quite slowly and got pretty close to the camp and there was one stage [when] we were lying there and one of the CTs came out towards us to cut some firewood and pissed there. I thought, 'Do we fire or do we wait?' because if we fired we would have screwed the whole thing up ... So anyhow when he was a couple of metres away, he turned round and walked back again.[119]

Mackintosh had a powerful fire group comprising four Bren guns and his own Owen sub-machine gun. But getting into position at right angles to the assault group was difficult, and they ran out of time.

> We had to move very fast. We made a lot of noise, and eventually one of the enemy down in the valley decided to fire a shot at us. Well he must have got a big surprise when four Brens and an Owen opened back ... we fired at the lights of the fires, one magazine each. And as it turned out we fired directly at our own assault group ... Luckily we did not hit any of our own group, I doubt if we hit any of the enemy. We certainly chewed up the jungle 20 feet above the enemy camp to bits.[120]

Only 15 yards from the camp Yandall could see Mackintosh's tracer coming straight at him, 'so I buried my head fairly deeply and then it stopped and ... we got up and went in. Two guys ran out of the camp and Grey Otene and I opened fire and they both went down. We both had to change magazines. By the time we'd done that, one guy got up and he'd gone and by the time we'd got organised again, it was too dark.'[121] Yandall's group had killed four men and wounded the one who escaped. Two others must have been away from the camp at the time of the attack, as seven packs were found.[122] John Dixon recalled: 'It was just a little camp. There was a little fire, and they just slept on the ground with their little groundsheets and they were actually cooking some snake [when we attacked]'. The group camped overnight near the four bodies. 'We had quite a lot of Maori boys ... and no one would sleep and they had the fires going and that's when I first became aware I suppose of how they thought that these people's spirits could still be around.' The next morning 'we wrapped them up in our hammocks on bamboo poles and ... carried them out'.[123]

Congratulations flowed in. Boswell, standing in for Rennie at Fort Brooke after the latter broke his wrist, noted: 'Morale v high at 62/64 [2 and 4 Troop] except for Mace who is like a Bear with a sore head and difficult to discuss or reason with.'[124] One can sympathise with Mace, who had lost an opportunity on the toss of a coin. Success depended on good information, which the New Zealanders were now getting. Despite the authorities' 'hearts and minds' policy, the SAS squadrons could be less than gentle in their dealings with indigenous people. Like the police and much of the military, they used the stick more frequently than the carrot.[125] The fact that A Squadron had not been told about the guerrillas' presence reflected its poor relationship with the local people, most of whom distrusted and feared them.[126] The New Zealanders' success resulted in a reward of $7,639.18 for Busu, who promptly went bush.[127] There was to be no more guerrilla activity on the Perolak, but at first the local people feared reprisals.[128] Gradually realising that the guerrillas' strength had been broken, they began to accompany patrols again. In September 1956 they led 2 Troop into the Sungei Betis area, where local people had reported the presence of Abelum, a 'hostile aborigine', in a nearby longhouse. This was to be 2 Troop's only success. As Mace recalled: 'There was no fuss ... The guy was there and we just picked him up, and the bloke then led us to a tree some distance away where his weapon was, so we recovered that and he was choppered out.'[129]

During this operation both Mace's and Burrows' patrols destroyed apparently deserted longhouses that had been used by the guerrillas, as part of Rennie's plan to limit the areas from which the terrorists could draw supplies. This was a serious mistake, and showed how little the security forces understood the Orang Asli way of life. It also emphasised the impossible situation they were in, caught between two powerful competing forces.[130] The aboriginals' complaints about the burnings led to an investigation by the police and the Protector of Aborigines.[131] Although no further action was taken, the incident was a setback. In hindsight, Burrows believed, 'we lost a lot more ground with the aborigines doing that than we gained and it [certainly] didn't help our image'.[132]

Despite this setback, the New Zealanders' successes saw them receiving more information. On 17 October a tribesman ran into Burrows' camp 'to say that he'd been sent down to get food by two CTs who had kept another one or two aborigines with them as hostages'. It was late afternoon, and Burrows set off immediately. 'I grabbed up a mixture of Rusty's troop and mine, the rest being out on patrol somewhere.' Burrows established that the hostages were being held on a ridge about half a mile above the New Zealand camp:

> rightly or wrongly I thought it would be better to try and get there that night. We left about 10.30 p.m. We took three or four of the more reliable aborigines and we divided them among the patrol so at every couple of people there was an aborigine with a bamboo torch. It gave out an awkward sort of light. You got smoke in your eyes and hot ash down your chest, and by this light we struggled through the night. It was a sterling effort by the blokes. We had no idea how close we were and just as the first signs of dawn came up I said, 'We've just got to sit down' ... the abos were saying, 'It's close, they're close', but they'd been saying this for a couple of hours ... We sat down and had a smoke ... and then we moved on. We started to move off the ridge track and got about 20 metres and there clearly ahead of us was a basha [shelter] with a fire. We couldn't see too much. We could see a little bit of movement so we just moved very slowly forward. The next thing one of the CTs came out. I think he was going out to have a pee. He came straight out on us, and gave us no option and we shot him. I just said, 'Go for it!'[133]

The basha was hidden by a large fallen log, with only its top visible to the patrol. When the firing started the hostages ran screaming through Burrows' group. 'It really was a balls-up. We just didn't have time to do anything and we didn't really have a drill. The whole thing was just Bang! Crash! and in a couple of split-seconds it was over and the bloke's [dead]. I think we might have wounded the other fellow, I can't remember but we never did get him.'[134] Despite Burrows' reservations, the long approach march and immediate attack was an exceptional effort. Burrows was very aware that the operation would have been impossible without aboriginal support. Both parties took credit for the outcome, and the tribespeople became 'quite keen' to assist the security forces.[135] Burrows was now emerging as the outstanding young officer in 22

SAS Regiment. His achievement led to much discussion and some envy in the other troops. As Doug Mackintosh, a member of 4 Troop, recalled: 'Buzz Burrows rightly or wrongly had the reputation of being an excellent mind—he could think like the CT could, but we used to reckon he would lie in his hammock for weeks and then suddenly say "I think they will be at that river crossing tomorrow morning" and the bugger was right!'[136]

Burrows' contact was a high note on which to end the second Fort Brooke operation. George Lea reported that the New Zealand squadron had been 'outstandingly successful'. Noting that gaining the confidence of aboriginals was 'a long and laborious business', he observed that 'the current satisfactory situation in the FORT BROOKE area is very largely due to the NZ Sqn's efforts and, in particular, to the tactical skill and jungle craft of [Troop Commanders] and patrols ... All three contacts achieved during the op were due to good soldiering and forceful and skilful leadership.'[137]

This last operation by the New Zealanders in the Fort Brooke area[138] marked their transition from amateurs to professionals. The squadron had moved approximately 1,200 tribespeople into two main areas; more importantly, it had destroyed the 11-strong Asal Group, killing eight (including both the leader and his second-in-command), wounding two, and capturing one.[139] Its single combat fatality was the death of Trooper Thomas.[140] By the end of 1956 the New Zealanders reached peak performance. In 1957 their professionalism would continue to develop, but the intensity of operations would affect the squadron's health and morale. By the end of the year they would be a spent force with nothing left to give.

The future of the New Zealand element in 22 SAS Regiment was already being examined. In August 1956 Foss Shanahan, the Commissioner for New Zealand in South-East Asia, questioned whether this was the type of military unit New Zealand should maintain in the Federation once the Emergency was over. 'Although the Special Air Service Squadron is theoretically a part of the Strategic Reserve, it is not a functional part of that Force. It is a part of a United Kingdom Special Air Service Regiment which will presumably be withdrawn from the Federation if, in the post-independence period, United Kingdom forces have no substantial role in operations against the terrorists.'[141] New Zealand had withdrawn its forces from Korea, and was coming under pressure from the United Kingdom to commit a battalion to the Commonwealth Strategic Reserve in Malaya. If the government agreed, as seemed increasingly likely, it was unlikely to also keep an SAS squadron in the Federation.

In late November 1956 the New Zealanders were warned out for Operation LATIMER SOUTH in the 'Mountainous' area of Negri Sembilan, the guerrillas' name for their jungle sanctuary enclosed by the roads linking the towns of Seremban, Kuala Pilah, and Tampin. This was a very different environment from the isolation of Fort Brooke. A triangle of jungle-covered ranges rising steeply to 3,000 feet, with rubber estates and kampong gardens on its fringes, 'Mountainous' was a secure haven for high-ranking members of the MCP. It was also an important bridge on the guerrillas' communication network linking the central highlands with communist groups and supporters in north Johore. The New Zealanders were to work under the operational control of 26 Gurkha Infantry Brigade, whose battalions, the 2nd Battalion Royal Welch Fusiliers and the 2/2 and 2/6 Gurkha Rifles, had so far achieved very little against the guerrillas.[142]

Unlike the Fort Brooke operations, which depended entirely on aboriginal intelligence, the SAS effort in 'Mountainous' was just one piece in a broader operational jigsaw that also involved the Police and Special Branch, and was co-ordinated through the State War Executive Committee and the local District War Executive Committees.[143] The target was a high-powered MCP/MRLA group of 24, consisting of the state secretary, Ah Sum, a state committee member, Yeung Tin, their bodyguards, and two Armed Work Forces, each commanded by a district committee member. The more notorious of the latter, Li Hak Chi—a former Tampin schoolteacher—was a 'first class soldier and ... stern disciplinarian' whose deeds created terror among the local population. He was to the kampongs around 'Mountainous' what Ah Ming had been to the long-houses around Fort Brooke. He and his fighters received much support from the large Chinese population of the kampongs and towns surrounding 'Mountainous', including excellent intelligence and early warning of security force movements. Despite some recent setbacks, the guerrillas' morale was high.[144]

On 19 December the squadron slogged its way up forested rocky slopes into 'Mountainous', the men swearing and sweating after the pleasures of Kuala Lumpur. Rennie, who was with them, wrote: 'All rather tired—14 days rations very heavy!!' The pattern of operations was familiar; troop bases for patrols were established first. On the second day in, Rennie ruefully noted that it was bad luck that 4 Troop did not repeat its success of 21 December when one of its patrols walked into a camp occupied by four terrorists who fled, leaving two packs behind.[145] Conditions were very dry, making tracking difficult. With fallen bamboo and palm fronds covering the jungle floor, silent movement was almost impossible. The most likely campsites on the stream re-entrants were surrounded by thick bamboo and palm, and given cover by distinctive rocky outcrops. The guerrillas worked in small groups which avoided contact even with other groups. They were highly professional, moving 'particularly well' through the jungle and practising 'first class' tactical drill. Their camps were sited carefully, with sentries posted during the first few hours of darkness and early in the morning. Cooking was done before first light and the camp evacuated before daylight. The same procedure was followed with temporary overnight camps: the site was watched for hours before being occupied, and hammocks and ponchos were erected without any preparation of the ground. 'Camps were left very clean and tidy and in fact apart from the usual track to the water [supply] and the hammock marks on the trees they were most difficult to locate.'[146]

The first weeks of hard patrolling were rewarded only by tantalising signs and frustrating near misses. Appropriately, a patrol from Rennie's headquarters had the first New Zealand success. By 20 January 1957, Lance-Corporal Ray Hurle's five-man patrol had waited for ten days in ambush at a track junction. At 2 p.m. Hurle and Trooper Fred Parkes were on sentry when Hurle felt a tap on his shoulder. He looked up,

> and here was this guy, or as it turned out a girl, with the traditional khaki uniform and red star coming down the track.[147] Fred had a Bren gun and I had a M2 carbine and I said quietly, 'Fire when you're ready'. So we waited until another person came into view ... which was only about 10 or 15 metres in front of us. Fred and I fired. One [person] immediately shot out of sight straight into the bush but the other one ran back up the track.[148]

Hurle's patrol soon found a dead man behind a log 50 yards down the track. Identified as Leong Chuen, a courier, he was found to be carrying many important documents.[149] A patrol from headquarters followed a trail of blood from the second person for half a mile before it petered out.

Five days later, one of Burrows' patrols waiting in ambush under Corporal Sun shot a lone figure coming down a track at a range of two yards.[150] The terrorists started to crack under the pressure. Like many surrendered guerrillas, Li Yau, who had surrendered on 17 January 1957, was soon back in the jungle working with the New Zealand patrols.[151] On 8 February district committee member Rompah, one of the few Malay guerrillas and head of the state propaganda and press organisation, also surrendered.[152] On 12 February

Lance-Corporal Mitchell's patrol from 5 Troop had been tracking some distinctive hockey-boot prints for 24 hours when they glimpsed and immediately attacked a group of men dressed in khaki, killing all four. Unfortunately they proved to be a group of Tamils from local estates who were hunting in a prohibited area.[153] Rennie wrote that this was 'very unfortunate but have protested about hunters being in area before'.[154] The guerrillas in 'Mountainous' went to ground. Rennie now planned to simulate the withdrawal of the squadron and then ambush known tracks. Special Branch in Kuala Pilah deliberately leaked the news that the New Zealanders were coming out on 4/5 March 1957, and 1 Troop actually moved out. The other troops moved into ambush positions for a long-drawn-out ten days which saw no sightings by any of the 20 patrols.[155]

On 15 March the New Zealanders returned to Kuala Lumpur, having severely disrupted the guerrillas' supply and communication links. 'There was evidence that [the MRLA] were becoming increasingly hungry. There were signs that ubi gadong [a jungle fruit] was being eaten without being processed for 2/3 days in water ... a dangerous practice ... likely to cause food poisoning.'[156] Li Hak Chi and his group were being forced to forage for food while SAS patrols were in the area. Rennie, determined to maintain the pressure, suggested to Lea and to Headquarters 26 Gurkha Infantry Brigade that his squadron's headquarters and a fire brigade action force be based at the police headquarters at Kuala Pilah. Lea agreed, believing that 'it would be a waste of know-how and past effort to deploy a different SAS Sqn on this task—even during an interim period'. However, Lea attempted to ensure that the New Zealanders had 'an adequate break'—once 'staleness sets in it is extremely hard to eradicate'.[157] He was right to be concerned; the New Zealanders were getting stale.

Rennie's unit diary maps his contest with the enemy in this period. At the centre of a web being spun by his five troops, he positioned his patrols in anticipation of where the guerrillas might be. He drew on what little intelligence Headquarters 26 Gurkha Infantry Brigade had to offer, but during the first 'Mountainous' operation the need for closer liaison with Special Branch became increasingly clear. For the second 'Mountainous' operation, Rennie set up his headquarters next to the Kuala Pilah police station. This move, and the increasing tiredness of the squadron, affected the relationship between Rennie and his officers and men. Even when the squadron was being raised, Rennie rarely got involved with the physical training; now, as its second year of operations approached, he became even more remote in his new headquarters, rarely if ever visiting troops in the field. The patrols sweating through 'Mountainous' saw him as an increasingly distant figure, and even his troop officers thought he should at least have roadhead rendezvous with his patrols. As the year progressed and the strains on the exhausted New Zealanders increased, the gap grew wider.

It is unlikely that Rennie was ever aware of the problem, immersed as he was in his battle of tactics with Li Hak Chi. Rennie's strength was his ability to read his enemy's mind, anticipating where he would be and what he would do. Yet the unit diary reveals that he monitored his soldiers as carefully as he assessed the enemy. Everyone who visited his headquarters was interrogated on patrol conditions. Rennie therefore knew when there was tension in one of the troops, and would send in the squadron sergeant-major, Noel O'Dwyer, with the reinforcements to investigate and if necessary resolve the problem. Rennie knew which of his NCOs had found it difficult to adapt to commanding patrols after being CMT instructors. He also knew which men were not pulling their weight. He believed such problems were best left to troop members themselves. When they remained unresolved, he would sound out O'Dwyer and Boswell before intervening. While he thus knew his squadron far more intimately than his troopers imagined, the fact that this was a side of Rennie his men rarely saw was detrimental to morale in its second year of operations.

On Lea's recommendation, the security forces stayed away from 'Mountainous' for the second half of March 1957. In April, at Rennie's suggestion, the New Zealanders began a series of small short-term operations which did not involve any man in more than one seven-day patrol. The intention was to ease the pressure on the squadron until it was 'ready to re-enter the area in strength'.[158] The guerrillas were also feeling the pressure, and on 12 April another Malay terrorist, Kadir, surrendered. Li Yau had led the New Zealanders to a series of dumps during the first 'Mountainous' operation, working with Lieutenant Lindsay Williams of 5 Troop.[159] On 19 April, Li Yau was with Bob Withers' patrol when he identified footprints leading to a banana patch on the edge of the jungle.

> It was just outside a kampong and there were obviously civilians in the area, and I wasn't even sure ... we were following CT footprints because we were that close to civilisation. But we could hear a bit of talking and a bit of chopping and we got closer and closer ... Everything underfoot was cracking. The heart was in the mouth and we just moved up very, very quietly on these guys and Li Yau said, 'Yeah, yeah. There they are! There they are! CTs!' I wasn't convinced. I didn't want

> to be responsible for killing somebody who didn't deserve to be killed. We got closer and I could see the guy chopping was actually in uniform and we opened fire. Hit absolutely nothing. My Bren gunner emptied about a full magazine into this group of three people and they vanished. Missed by a country mile ... we could see one of the CTs floundering around in the open, and we had a bit of a shooting gallery for a while and he eventually fell over. I thought this guy was absolutely impervious and again maybe we weren't hitting him very often.[160]

Two rifles were recovered, and the dead man was identified as Wong Kwai, a group leader and Li Hak Chi's assistant.[161] 'He had heaps of paper on him and a nice big bundle of money too which we never told Frank [Rennie] or anybody about ... I think there was 700 Singapore dollars if I remember rightly, which we shared.'[162]

The whole squadron went back into 'Mountainous' on 29 April 1957, and with Kadir's assistance located two unoccupied camps.[163] On 12 July Grey Otene in Earle Yandall's patrol 'came across these guys crossing the river'; as Yandall recalled, 'Grey opened up and he knocked one fellow over and we just did our normal immediate action drill and got the other guy half-way across the river so that was pretty good.' The patrol had followed signs for eight days. 'We knew someone was there. You can feel it and [so] we just kept going and going.'[164] Li Yau identified the dead men as Ah Kiu and Cheung Tong. Documents found on them confirmed that the terrorists were operating in three groups.[165] State secretary Ah Sum, state committee member Tsang San and their bodyguards were in one group. State committee member Yeung Tin was in the second group, and the third included Li Hak Chi. Li Hak Chi and Yeung Tin were visiting local kampongs to obtain food and supplies, which they delivered to Ah Sum's party. The captured documents included Li Hak Chi's fairly accurate assessment of the New Zealand troops' areas of operation. Rennie therefore changed the pattern, ordering a series of six ten-day operations with breaks of three or four days between them. He assessed that by 'using a number of suitable entry points and exploiting the advantages of roads on three sides, patrols could reach any area within the Sqn boundary within 24 hrs'.[166] The first operation concentrated on locating Ah Sum's group in the Gunong Pasir–Bukit Payong area. All likely camp sites were investigated, but despite signs of movement no contacts were made.[167] Short operations continued until the end of October, Rennie judging that his men could not cope with another long operation. In hindsight, however, this series of short operations only 'increased the mental and physical strain' on his troopers.[168]

The squadron's achievements were now receiving official recognition. In May it was announced that Buzz Burrows had been awarded the Military Cross and Earle Yandall Mentioned in Despatches.[169] Burrows' MC was the first awarded to an officer of 22 SAS Regiment in Malaya. It is some indication of his outstanding performance, which was still to be capped by his ambush of Li Hak Chi. Burrows was only one of several outstanding junior officers and NCOs in the squadron; Earle Yandall must be considered unlucky not to have been similarly recognised. Appropriately enough, Rennie would also be awarded the Military Cross later in the year. In June, the squadron heard that it would not be replaced in 22 SAS Regiment by another New Zealand squadron. Instead, Lieutenant-Colonel Kim Morrison would command an infantry battalion that was to be raised for service in Malaya.[170]

In late July, Special Branch learned that Li Hak Chi's group was to carry out a major food lift. On 15 August word came that the food had been lifted and that the group had evaded a net of ambushes laid by 26 Gurkha Infantry Brigade and was on its way back into 'Mountainous'. A New Zealand tracker team under Corporal Huia Woods set out in pursuit. Burrows, who was on leave in Kuala Lumpur, was given the task of intercepting and ambushing Li Hak Chi's party. By touring Kuala Lumpur's bars he supplemented his 3 Troop men with other available New Zealanders. From his knowledge of the ground and the myriad of jungle trails, Burrows assessed that Li Hak Chi had only two possible routes to return to his safe area. He decided to ambush the more likely of these with his six men, leaving Noel O'Dwyer's ad hoc patrol to cover the second. Bill Edwards, who was with Burrows, recalled that 'Buzz looked at the map and ... said, "I think they'll hit here."'[171] Burrows had previously operated over this ground with his troop, and by late on 16 August his group was in position at the crossing point on the river. There they stayed in ambush, taking turns on sentry duty, two at a time.

At 4.15 p.m. on the 19th, Burrows and Ron Pearson were the sentries. 'Although I guessed the CT were about due, it was still a surprise to see a heavily laden CT materialise from the jungle on the other side of the river. He was closely followed by another. The two stood talking while they very carefully scanned our side of the river.' They seemed to suspect something, and 'for no apparent reason turned and moved back slowly the way they had come'.[172] Before they vanished into the trees, Burrows opened fire. Figures fell and shots were returned from the suspected direction of the rest of the guerrilla group.[173] A sweep by the patrol found a dying man in the ambush area, whom Burrows identified as Li Hak Chi. The patrol also recovered two rifles and five packs containing 100 kg of food supplies; this was too much to carry out, and was burnt on the spot. As it got dark, several well-known guerrilla contact calls were heard. Burrows believed that the guerrilla party had split up and was now trying to reunite. He and Bill Edwards, armed with the Bren gun, 'shot back to the ambush position'. By the dying light of the fire in which the supplies were burning, Edwards could see that 'a huge team' had gathered.

> 'Buzz', I said, 'what do you think?' He said, 'I believe this is a counter-attack. They know there's only a few of us and they know that we've got Li Hak Chi.' I was on the Bren and they gathered around the flames and we could see them from the knees downwards, and when I had about eight people [that I could fire at] I said, 'Buzz, I want to have a go.' He said, 'Well just hold it.' He had his mouth next to my ear and he was really gripping my wrist. In the meantime I had slipped it onto automatic and I said, 'Look, I'll take out half a dozen of them and let's high-tail it.' He said, 'Hold it! For Christ's sake, hold it!' I'd taken first pressure, and Buzz was really talking to me and the adrenalin was pumping and I really wanted to let go. And suddenly they just disappeared, they slipped away ... In the morning we high-tailed it out.[174]

Later, at the debriefing, it was established that this had been Huia Woods' tracking team who, having started some 36 hours behind Li Hak Chi's group, after five days were less than two hours behind and still on the scent. They had found the ambush site and realised what had happened, but had no inkling of how close they had come to disaster. Woods' follow-up of Li Hak Chi had been a tracking performance without peer in the whole of the Emergency, but only Burrows' instinct had prevented his party becoming the target of a potentially tragic second ambush.[175]

Li Hak Chi's death excised the heart from the terrorists in 'Mountainous'. Ah Sang, his bodyguard, had also been mortally wounded in the ambush and the group was reduced to three. It was learned that they were trying to join up with the other groups but were 'completely lost'.[176] Rennie considered this contact to be the squadron's greatest achievement. 'It epitomised the whole thing. It showed just how bloody good and how professional they were ... I was absolutely chuffed, because everything that I'd wanted to achieve was ... there ... the fine discipline, the techniques, the reporting.'[177]

The New Zealanders continued to harry the surviving members of Li Hak Chi's group. Patrols from squadron headquarters under Captain Graham Boswell had a contact on 27 August, when a tracking team was fired on by a sole guerrilla armed with a pistol. Other patrols converged on the scene; Lance-Corporal Ray Hurle's patrol challenged and fired on someone moving through the bush towards them, but the person got away and eluded a tracker dog.[178] On 12 September Bill Edwards' patrol tracked two terrorists in heavy rain. At a fork in the track the sign went in both directions. The patrol split, with two troopers going right and lead scout Steve Watene, covered by Edwards, going left. The last man and an aboriginal porter remained on the track to cover the way they had come. The two on the right fork saw two people about 30 yards away, moving slowly towards them; they 'lined [them] up and were waiting until they came closer'.[179] Meanwhile, 'tail-end Charlie', woken abruptly from a snooze by urgent tapping on his shoulder, saw a guerrilla taking aim at him from only five yards away. Fortunately the rifle misfired and the trooper rolled over, firing as he did so. Everyone now fired, but the guerrillas had vanished. Watene summed it up: 'You're wasting your time mate. They're ten seconds gone.'[180] This was the squadron's last contact. Three days later, Li Hak Chi's wife, Ah Ying, and another guerrilla surrendered at a police post. After surviving the contacts of 19 and 27 August and 12 September, they had had enough.[181]

There were three more ten-day operations. By now most of the squadron had spent nearly 14 months of a two-year tour on jungle operations, and this had taken its toll. The situation in 1 Troop was typical, with the physical condition of the men so low, and so many sick, that it was 'only possible to maintain a patrol of six'.[182] Like their quarry, the remnants of Li Hak Chi's group, the New Zealanders were burnt out. On 21 October the squadron went into 'Mountainous' for the last time, taking with it the advance party of 1 NZ Regiment.[183] Appropriately enough, it was Edwards' patrol from Burrows' 3 Troop that ended the operation in style by hijacking a logging truck into Kuala Pilah for a beer. 'A couple of Tigers [a popular local brand of beer] and it really, really got out of control.'[184] Edwards' armed and drunken crew performed haka to a gathering crowd of onlookers and increasingly nervous police in downtown Kuala Pilah. Rennie's arrival ended the performance, and Edwards ended his Malayan tour in detention. The New Zealanders finished in style, but not the style for which Rennie wanted them to be remembered.

The New Zealand squadron had mortally wounded the 'Mountainous' group by killing eight guerrillas, injuring two, and inducing nine to surrender.[185] The remnant was 'now poorly armed and short of other ranks'. State secretary Ah Sum, while strong in character, was physically weak; not a 'jungle man', he 'must be guided everywhere'. The other state committee member, Yeung Tin, was suffering recurring attacks of dysentery. Li Hak Chi's group was down to one man. Of those remaining in Ah Sum's group, only two were regarded as physically strong and only one knew his way around 'Mountainous'. Further pressure would see this group become 'even more vulnerable'.[186] Soon after this assessment, Ah Sum and his party surrendered. The New Zealand achievement was acknowledged by Headquarters 1 Federation Infantry Brigade, which had replaced 26 Brigade: 'There is no doubt that it was their effort which secured these last eliminations.'[187] Lea reported to Wellington: 'It is sufficient to say that the Sqn has followed up its highly successful 1956 operation in the FORT BROOKE area of PERAK and KELANTAN by achieving the complete and lasting disruption of the Communist Organisation in the "MOUNTAINOUS" District of NEGRI SEMBILAN.'[188] This success reflected the situation around the country. By the time Malaya became independent on 31 August 1957, one third of the estimated 1,830 active members of the MRLA had withdrawn across the border into Thailand, and the Emergency was entering its final phase.[189]

During its two-year tour, the New Zealand SAS Squadron was involved in 14 separate contacts, in four of which the guerrillas fired first. In these contacts, 15 guerrillas were killed, one was captured, and nine surrendered; a further four were known to have been wounded. This achievement came at the cost of one New Zealand combat fatality.[190] Lea saw the New Zealanders' performance as one of the 'highlights in a vital phase in the early history and development of the [SAS] Regiment'.[191] Woodhouse agreed: 'I personally feel you did a great deal not only in showing again that N.Z. soldiers are second to none, but in helping the S.A.S. as a Corps to reach its present high prestige and status in the British Army.'[192] The New Zealanders set the standard for the other squadrons of 22 SAS Regiment. Yet the many accounts of the regiment during these years have ignored the vital importance of their contribution to its very survival. Not only have the squadron's achievements been overlooked, but its performance has been dismissed in the same terms as that of the Rhodesians.

The basis of the New Zealand Squadron's outstanding record was the strong foundation laid by Rennie in New Zealand and consolidated in Malaya. Rennie was always thinking ahead. His close liaison with Special Branch provided the intelligence that the increasingly professional New Zealand troops capitalised on. Thanks to both the calibre of individual soldiers and the quality of leadership at patrol and troop level, they proved to be outstanding jungle soldiers with the temperament to withstand the stresses of long operations. With its Maori–Pakeha mix, the squadron also displayed the New Zealand flair for getting on with the locals, a quality that was essential in the Fort Brooke operations. While Rennie's strength was good intelligence and sound planning, he was also an ideal frontman and able to put on a show. Although in late 1957 he appeared to lose contact with his troops in the jungle, his tactical control and superb planning remained the basis of their operational success. In many ways his squadron outgrew him, but their success remained his achievement.

Rennie identified two main differences between the techniques of the New Zealand and British squadrons: 'we probably patrolled more slowly', and carried a Bren gun on 'each patrol, regardless of size'. The New Zealand squadron also benefited from the aptitude for tracking of its Maori personnel.[193] The procedures the squadron developed were recorded by Lieutenant Burrows in a paper on jungle techniques (see appendix 5), and then absorbed into the New Zealand Army's tactical doctrine when he was posted to the School of Infantry in Waiouru as an instructor on his return to New Zealand.[194] The squadron's standing orders, tactical notes and aides-memoires were passed on to the advance party of 1 NZ Regiment. This ensured that the professional experience of the best SAS squadron to serve in the Emergency was not wasted. They laid an essential foundation for 34 years' service by New Zealand Army Regular units in South-East Asia, and established a reputation that their compatriots were determined to maintain.

By late 1957, Rennie's troops were spent. This was, as Noel O'Dwyer said, 'the only time there was any problem of morale ... It was a difficult time for a lot of the boys. A difficult time for Frank, and being in my position [as squadron sergeant-major] I could hear both sides and it was definitely time to go. Two years was enough. It was time to come home.'[195] Sadly, while New Zealand's Chief of General Staff, Major-General Stephen Weir, acknowledged the squadron's 'very fine record', there was no place as yet for the Special Air Service in the New Zealand Army. The tired troopers returned to an uncomprehending Army which was in the throes of reorganisation and not interested in what they had done. Posted as barracks orderlies and storemen to see out their time, most of Rennie's men had left the service in disgust by the time the Army began to understand what it had lost.[196]

# 5

# FIGHTING A JUNGLE WAR

## *Infantry Operations, 1957–59*

> [These were New Zealanders] who'd seen their brothers go to the war ... who were busting to get into some sort of similar action and so when the call for volunteers came for the battalion, they trooped forward in droves. And you know, in a way, they were the 'crème de la crème' ... They were the deerstalkers, the deer cullers ... freezing workers, shepherds, not just rural people but people associated with the rural industry and ... townspeople associated with hard living ... most of these blokes were as hard as nails and they could live hard, play hard ... I don't imagine any of them had criminal records but I think a lot of them had been sailing close to the wind ... but they made for a wonderful battalion.[1]
>
> MAJOR-GENERAL K. M. GORDON,
> FORMER PLATOON COMMANDER 1 NZ REGIMENT

In 1957, New Zealand's contribution to the Commonwealth Far East Strategic Reserve was enlarged. The SAS squadron was replaced by a full infantry battalion which became part of the Commonwealth Brigade. On 19 June, members of the New Zealand SAS squadron on operations in Malaya heard over the radio that Lieutenant-Colonel W. R. K. (Kim) Morrison had been appointed to command a New Zealand infantry battalion which would relieve them in November. The commitment of the battalion had been announced in the New Zealand Parliament by the Prime Minister, Sidney Holland, on 12 June.[2] Morrison was equally surprised at his appointment, having thought he was out of contention because of his age (43).[3] Commissioned in 1933 as a Territorial second lieutenant in the 1st Canterbury Regiment, he had risen to captain before being accepted into the Royal Military College at Duntroon in Australia, from which he graduated into the New Zealand Staff Corps in 1939. Posted for active service with 2NZEF, he served with 24 and 25 Battalions, and was awarded an immediate DSO for conspicuous gallantry as a rifle company commander in North Africa on 21 March 1943. He was lucky to survive after being badly wounded six days later; the severity of his injuries threatened to end his military career. After the war he was New Zealand instructor at Duntroon, and later Commandant Army Schools in Waiouru. A short, dapper, bristly man with a wicked sense of humour, Morrison's sayings and pranks became legendary throughout the Army.

His battalion, the 1st Battalion, New Zealand Regiment, was the first Regular unit formed in the New Zealand Army. It was to form part of 28 Commonwealth Infantry Brigade, the land component of the Commonwealth Strategic Reserve. With the arrival of the New Zealanders, the brigade would consist of three infantry battalions, an artillery regiment, and supporting units drawn from Britain, Australia and New Zealand. Originally formed in Korea on 25 April 1951 as part of the 1st Commonwealth Infantry Division, the brigade was re-formed in Malaya on 16 September 1955, with its primary role being to train 'for major operations against an enemy of similar capabilities to Communist China'.[4] It was intended to provide a sense of security in South-East Asia against the perceived threat from the People's Republic of China. However, until the Emergency ended, the brigade remained committed to its secondary role of assisting the Malayan government in operations against the MRLA.

Malaya's independence on 31 August 1957 was followed by the Anglo-Malayan Defence Agreement, under which the British government undertook to provide Malaya with such assistance as it might 'require for the external defence of its territory'.[5] In return, Malaya granted Britain the right to station forces on its territory. When New Zealand formally associated itself with these arrangements in 1959, in essence this simply confirmed its pre-existing participation in the Commonwealth Strategic Reserve.[6]

New Zealand's move to deploy Regular forces overseas was consolidated by the Labour Party's election victory on 30 November 1957.[7] Walter Nash's new government took the bold initiative of establishing a Regular brigade group in New Zealand, based on two yet-to-be-raised battalions in addition to 1 New Zealand Regiment (1 NZ Regt) in Malaya. The 2nd Battalion, New Zealand Regiment (2 NZ Regt), was raised to eventually replace 1 NZ Regt in Malaya; the 3rd Battalion, New Zealand Regiment (3 NZ Regt), together with 16th Field Regiment RNZA and the other elements of what would be known as 4th

Infantry Brigade, were to be manned by Regular personnel. Labour's abolition of compulsory military training saw the strength of the now-volunteer Territorial Force decimated. Overnight, the New Zealand Army lost the ability to commit a division based on its citizen forces to South-East Asia if a global war broke out.

The commitment to provide an 18,000-strong New Zealand division now existed only on paper. Acceptance of the concept of a Regular brigade marked a realisation that any war in South-East Asia should be fought by professional forces. The Regular Force was to be transformed from a professional cadre of instructors and administrators whose task was to train the Territorial Force to a self-contained formation capable of fighting as an entity in South-East Asia. It would take a major shift in the Army's thinking to match the government's far-sighted and realistic assessment of what was needed if New Zealand was to meet its alliance commitments. As it turned out, a strong recruiting campaign failed to attract sufficient men for the Regular brigade, as the labour market remained buoyant despite the economic difficulties facing New Zealand in 1958. Nonetheless, Labour's initiatives broke away from the expeditionary force concept which had dominated defence thinking since 1909, and began the 40-year process of creating the small professional Regular Army that was one of the cornerstones of the defence of New Zealand at the end of the twentieth century.

The dominant military figure during this period of radical change was the Chief of the General Staff, Major-General Stephen Weir. When he took over from Gentry as CGS in 1955 Weir was 50 years old, and he would hold the position until 1960. For his successor, Lieutenant-General Sir Leonard Thornton, Weir was probably the best military leader New Zealand produced during the Second World War. The 'most dynamic' of Freyberg's field commanders, Weir had an 'extraordinary capacity to inspire people around him in battle conditions'.[8] Tall, robust, good-humoured, with a strong physical presence and an instinctive understanding of his men, he was the only Commonwealth soldier to command a British division during the war (the 46th, in Italy). In 1955 his strong public profile and reputation contrasted sharply with the image of his predecessors, Stewart and Gentry. Weir saw a role for all three services in the Commonwealth Strategic Reserve, but believed that the priority had to be the Army's contribution to 28th Commonwealth Brigade. Throughout his time as CGS and later as military adviser to the Holyoake government in 1960–61, Weir sought to increase the military resources committed to South-East Asia so that they could better match New Zealand's defence commitments. This paralleled a general public consensus on the need to contribute to the stand against communism in South-East Asia. It was an issue that did not need to be debated; to most New Zealanders, the post-war turmoil in Europe and Asia was proof enough of communist intentions, and it was accepted that New Zealand had to play its part in meeting this threat.[9]

Thornton believed that Weir had a 'great vision' of the role New Zealand should play on the international stage. 'He was a man who was very much committed to South-East Asia and towards the end of his service that became more and more expressed.'[10] Indeed, this commitment continued after his retirement from the military with his appointment as Ambassador to Thailand and the Republic of Vietnam. With his support, Nash's government did more than any other administration to establish sufficient Regular forces to allow New Zealand to meet its treaty obligations. This occurred despite Labour's attitude of 'loyal dissent' towards United States' policies in South-East Asia, and Laos in particular.[11]

Morrison established his headquarters at Waiouru Military Camp on 1 August 1957, and this date became the regimental birthday.[12] He had a say in all the key appointments, and was able to choose his adjutant and RSM. For these positions he selected two men with whom he had worked at Army Schools: Captain Ian ('Shorty') Launder as his adjutant, and WO1 'Bunny' Forsythe as his RSM. Forsythe claimed that 'the only person who knew [Morrison] better than I did was his wife because she slept with him'.[13] Morrison's second-in-command was Major Russell Ainge, an Army Service Corps officer who 'was strong on administration. I could handle the "G" ['general', i.e. operational] side by my upbringing, but I was not renowned for being a "pots and pans" man and interested in weights of rations and things like that and I knew Ainge could do it.'[14] Morrison's company commanders were Major 'Alf' Voss MC, DCM (A Company), Major 'Ash' King (B Company), Major Jack Harvey (C Company), Captain Tony Mataira (D Company), and Major Bryan Boyd (Headquarters Company). All were Second World War veterans except for the 28-year-old Mataira, who was also both the only Maori and the only senior officer with experience in the Emergency. Matiara had been awarded an MID during his service as a platoon commander in Major George Mate's D Company 1FIR.[15]

The battalion was raised both from serving Regular personnel and by enlisting recruits for terms of either three or five years. Applicants had to be New Zealand citizens 'of European or Maori ancestry'; be medically and dentally fit;

have passed Standard Six in their education; and be aged between 21 and 35, with preference given to those under 30. With parental consent, 20-year-olds could also apply. Single men were preferred; married men could apply, but those with more than two children were unlikely to be accepted. With the Territorial Force still the cornerstone of New Zealand's military capacity, Territorial officers below the rank of major and NCOs below the rank of WO2 could also apply. The recruiting offices opened on 19 June, and closed in late July as each Military District filled its quota.[16] The recruits flocking in were motivated less by a desire to fight the communist menace in Asia than by the opportunity to get overseas. Peter Rutledge had another incentive: 'It was the first of the battalions and the reason that I joined, well I had a bet with a guy for five pounds that I'd pass the test and I did and I was accepted and that was that, I was in the Army.'[17] The four rifle companies were recruited geographically. A Company was drawn from Auckland and North Auckland; B Company from the Bay of Plenty, Rotorua and the King Country; C Company from Wellington, Manawatu and Wairarapa; and D Company from the South Island. There was an ethnic mix, with 163 (22 per cent) of the 739-strong battalion declaring themselves as Maori on their enlistment forms. Their allocation to companies according to tribal affiliation was a deliberate reflection of the tribal distribution used in 28 (Maori) Battalion during the Second World War—'Ngapuhi to "A", Ngati Porou to "B", Arawa to "C" and all the others to "D" Company'.[18] Inevitably A and B Companies, being drawn from the major areas of Maori population, had the most Maori recruits (42 and 55 respectively), while Mataira's D Company, drawn from the South Island, had the fewest (12).[19]

In 1956, only 6.3 per cent of the total population identified themselves as Maori.[20] The provincial basis of recruiting was one factor encouraging Maori to enlist. They were drawn into the Army for the same reasons as their Pakeha counterparts: to escape from the shearing shed and the farm; to see the world; to follow in the footsteps of their fathers, uncles and older brothers. Maori were especially conscious of the tradition of their elders, many of whom had served in the world wars. Soldiering was a profession at which Maori excelled, and for which limited formal education was no barrier to enlistment, although it did prevent rising to commissioned officer rank. Maori adapted easily to service life, in which their skill and pride in drill, discipline and dress were matched by ability at bushcraft. Many stayed on after the tour to Malaya and became career soldiers, rising through the non-commissioned ranks and providing examples for other Maori of the opportunities the Army offered. In 1961, 304 (11.9 per cent) of the 2,559 servicemen listed by the census as serving overseas identified themselves as Maori.[21] It is likely that most of these men were serving with the battalion in Malaya, and that this over-representation of Maori in the Army continued.[22]

Basic training for the new recruits was conducted in Burnham and Papakura military camps, and on 3 September 1957 the 1st Battalion, New Zealand Regiment concentrated as a unit for the first time at Waiouru. Peter Rutledge recalled:

> [We] arrived there in the middle of the night off the Auckland to Wellington express and had a rude awakening. We were all marched into the gymnasium and screamed at from all directions and we found ourselves posted to B Company, and ... the platoon I was posted to was going to be commanded by Bill Meldrum. He was from the West Coast and he had been given two junior non-commissioned officers for his three sections and he wanted one more and he said: 'Which of you bastards comes from the West Coast?', and I said, 'Well I've been working over there.' 'You'll bloody do, get over there' ... I was given the job as section commander and I even managed to keep the job, even though I got into the crap that many times it was amazing.[23]

Entries in the battalion's war diary for its period in Waiouru invariably begin: 'Once again the weather was wet and cold.'[24] The battalion spent September under canvas in the satellite camp at 'Helwan', which was a quagmire. 'All tracks and roads were deep in mud and numerous lakes had formed in low-lying ground. All troops were wet and clothing and bedding very damp.'[25] These were not the best conditions for preparing a battalion for service in South-East Asia. 'It snowed and we were preparing to go out into the tropics ... but, you know, it was all a bit of fun and games I suppose ... We were all just looking forward to the time when we could get the hell out of there and get into what we had been trained to do.'[26]

Nor was it all plain sailing for the officers. Army General Staff policies regarding the calibre of recruits, length of tour for Regular personnel, and rates of pay all created problems that would haunt the battalion throughout its time in Malaya. Morrison's first problem was his inability to remove men he considered unsatisfactory. He did not have the luxury of being able to thin his numbers down, as Rennie had done. Instead, he was told: 'You've got to keep every man you've got and you've got to turn him into a first-class soldier.' Some 'rat bags' Morrison would rather have got rid of were kept on.[27]

Secondly, Army General Staff wanted as many of the younger Regular officers and soldiers as possible to serve with the battalion. It was intended that 'long service Regulars serving with the force will not necessarily complete a full tour of 2–2½ yrs, but may be replaced earlier'.[28] The married men had assumed that their families would accompany them, but on 'Black Friday' Morrison dropped the bombshell that most married Regular personnel would be going for just 12 months, and were therefore ineligible to take their families at the government's expense. This decision affected two of the five company commanders, three of the company 2ICs, and all the subaltern officers. It also struck a quarter of the warrant officers and senior NCOs, half the platoon sergeants, and three-quarters of the junior NCOs.[29] In some cases the families involved had already moved out of Army accommodation; they now found they could not move back again. Morrison had no illusions about the impact of this ruling: 'They have destroyed my battalion.'[30]

By contrast, Territorial officers and NCOs who enlisted specifically for two years' service were able to take their families. This created enormous resentment and an inevitable rift between Territorials and Regulars which remained for the life of the battalion. Two Regular Force wives, Florence Hall and Betty Paget, went to Wellington to ask the Minister of Defence, Dean Eyre, to allow the wives and families to accompany their husbands. Eyre indicated that he was prepared to consider their individual cases, but not those of other families. Both refused this offer and remained in New Zealand.[31] When some Regular officers took their wives and families at their own expense, Army General Staff was almost vindictive in the lengths it went to to ensure that these dependants received no assistance. The wife of Captain Graeme McKay was told by Air Staff that if Army General Staff agreed, she could get a flight for a nominal sum on an RNZAF aircraft to Malaya. Army General Staff not only refused, but asked the Ministry of External Affairs not to issue a passport to Mrs McKay, as she 'will almost certainly be unable to support herself and would become a charge on the NZ Government to get her back to NZ'.[32] Sensibly, External Affairs told the Army to mind its own business, and Mrs McKay travelled independently to Singapore by ship. Most wives swallowed their anger and stayed in New Zealand, but the slight rankled.[33] 'It was really hurtful, the fact that they brought in all these other people with families and took them and left us behind.'[34]

Army General Staff belonged to the generation that had accepted separation from their families for up to six years during the Second World War as a normal condition of service. The policy, while dictated by financial constraints, was justified as getting the best return for the Army by rotating the maximum number of Regular officers and NCOs through operational command appointments. The longer-term impact on personnel management and Regular Force morale was never considered, and when they were questioned Army General Staff closed ranks and interpreted any criticism as disloyalty.[35]

On 16 October 1957 the advance party, led by the battalion's second-in-command, Major R. W. K. Ainge, flew by No. 40 Squadron RNZAF Hastings to Malaya. The rest of the battalion enjoyed their final leave before taking a troop train to Wellington and marching through the streets on a cold, wet, blustery day (28 November) to embark on the passenger ship SS *Captain Cook*. The ship berthed in Singapore on Sunday 15 December as the band of the 2/2 Gurkha Rifles played military marches. A haka party from HMNZS *Royalist* gave a challenge, and Captain Mataira responded for the battalion. The next fortnight was spent in open corrugated-iron transit barracks at Nee Soon Camp, with local leave to Nee Soon village and one evening's leave in Singapore city. On 28 December the battalion moved to the Far East Land Force's training centre at Kota Tinggi in Johore. They occupied Nyasa Camp, which WO2 Wally White described as being 'on one slope of a broad green valley. The men are housed in corrugated iron tents with hinged sides which ensure a flow of air. Jungle bounds the main camp area on all sides and there is real atmosphere at this centre ... which already is giving the battalion an incentive to get on with their jungle training.'[36] To almost everyone the Malayan jungle was strange and new, but during hard weeks of training they adapted.

> Our 'bashas' are better, and take less time to erect. You've only got to sleep wet once, and you do better next time ... The insect noises are unbelievable, especially at night. As soon as it gets dark, every imaginable species of grasshopper, cicada, and tree frog tunes in. Some quite tuneful, others something awful. One makes a noise like an alarm clock ringing, others like bicycle bells, one like the brakes on Joe's car. If you can imagine a band made up of cymbals, road drills, bicycle bells, those clickers the boys play with, a few hunting horns, some bees in a box, and a fishing reel winding in with a clicker on, all played by mad musicians in a sawmill going full blast, you might get the idea.[37]

By early February 1958, Morrison's company commanders believed the men were ready and 'need now to get out on intensive operational work'.[38] The one 'dark grey cloud' was the pay. On arriving in Singapore the battalion found that single and unaccompanied men would have 4s 8d per day deducted from their pay to cover the cost of local rations eaten in the messes. What that actually meant for each man's paybook took some time to sort out, as the unit war diary bitterly noted: 'Evidently the complex nature of the mathematics involved is rather more than the Pay Staff at Force HQ bargained for. So on this New Year's Eve the vast majority of the battalion do not know how much money they possess—if any. It is a situation which calls for urgent remedy for nothing could be worse for the morale of the battalion.'[39] Unaccompanied married men were hit particularly hard. Alan Polaschek, a headquarters clerk, recalled:

> In my case and in a number of other cases, this influenced our entire period in Malaya. We were leaving our wives and families behind so we worked out our finances fairly carefully indeed so that I would have had two [shillings] and six [pence] a day to buy presents, or the little things that happen. As it happened [because allowances were halved] I was right dead square and if anything happened, I had no money, so what this meant was that throughout my period in Malaya, whenever I could, I went bush because we used to get paid cash to compensate for the fact that we were getting English dried rations.[40]

Pay was but one of many problems. While Battalion Headquarters and its administrative staff faced all the usual difficulties in settling into 28th Commonwealth Infantry Brigade, Colonel George Cade's Headquarters New Zealand Army Far East Land Forces (FARELF) also had to establish its own internal procedures. The adjutant, Ian Launder, remembered that the battalion 'really bogged down with administrative problems ... we had to answer to a British system which was the Brigade Headquarters ... and in addition to that we had to answer to our own Force Headquarters administrative system.' It was a bedding-in period for both the battalion and Force Headquarters, and things were in a 'bugger's muddle'.[41] Major Russell ('Fish Eyes') Ainge, the second-in-command, established the administrative systems of this 'pioneering' unit. Ainge was 'almost pedantic in his correctness ... He demanded it to be exactly right. Near enough was never good enough for him ... He was a hell of a hard man to get on with.'[42] Probably the worst feature of the administration was 'the accounting for and administration of unit personnel who are injured and or hospitalised'.[43] The battalion had three medical officers (RMOs) between November 1957 and April 1958; but this area, along with pay, housing, civilian contracts and everything else, was eventually put in order. In his gruff and peremptory way, Ainge laid the administrative foundation for 1 NZ Regt and for all the battalions that followed; nothing would ever be as difficult again.

Colonel George Cade, who commanded all New Zealand Army personnel in theatre, took his orders from the Commander-in-Chief FARELF. Cade was responsible for monitoring whether New Zealand troops were being employed in accordance with the ANZAM Directive, but as the battalion was under the operational control of 28th Commonwealth Brigade he had no real day-to-day function.[44] He also kept New Zealand's Commissioner in Singapore and High Commissioner in Kuala Lumpur informed 'on matters affecting the national interests of New Zealand in the employment, well being and administration of the New Zealand Army Force'. Cade was also responsible to (and communicated directly with) Army General Staff in New Zealand with respect to the 'safety, well being and domestic arrangements' of the Force and its dependants.[45] The Singapore-based Cade and his staff were often seen by the battalion as interfering and unco-operative during this difficult bedding-in period.[46]

On 5 February 1958, Morrison and his intelligence staff flew to Ipoh, the centre of the north Malayan tin-mining area, to establish his command post. The New Zealanders took over from the 1st Battalion, The Royal Lincolnshire Regiment, in 28th Commonwealth Infantry Brigade, which also comprised the 3rd Battalion, Royal Australian Regiment (3RAR), which had replaced 2RAR in September 1957, and the 1st Battalion, The Loyal Regiment.[47] The brigade commander was Brigadier P. N. M. Moore, a Royal Engineers officer who had commanded the Commonwealth Division's Field Engineer Regiment in Korea. He had an outstanding combat record, having won a DSO and a Military Cross in North Africa, another DSO in Yugoslavia, and a third in Korea. An intense, dedicated man, totally lacking in humour, Moore had a tendency to interfere and was unwilling to listen to his commanding officers, who wanted some freedom to get on with their jobs.[48] Morrison's relationship with Moore was to be a prickly one, exacerbated by their very different personalities and by the New Zealander's willingness to voice his views on how operations should be conducted. This made for interesting times for the new battalion.[49]

On 20 February 1958 the battalion's advance parties moved to Ipoh and Taiping, and groups were attached to brigade units on operations. Three days later the New Zealanders faced the reality that they were on active service when they learned of the death of Private Tui Kawha of the Signals Platoon, who had been attached to the First Battalion, Royal Lincolns, in the 'Jungle

Island' area.[50] Kawha had been 'cutting & clearing a landing zone for helicopters. He and another bloke were felling a big tree. But the trunk was rotten half way up, and as it fell it snapped in the middle, the lower half kicked back and drove him right into the deck. The Royal Lincolns lost a bloke exactly the same way a month ago.'[51] This made for a subdued prelude to the arrival of the main body of the battalion by train on 3 March. 'We thought that was quite an adventure, because we had this big armoured engine out in front of the train and another one at the back. There were machine-guns poking out in all directions. It looked like a porcupine.'[52] On their arrival the next day, the companies were driven in armed convoys to the operational camps set among the patchwork of cultivations, tin tailings and villages on the Ipoh valley floor. On each side was the sobering sight of the sheer jungle-clad mountains harbouring the enemy they would soon be fighting. Voss's A Company and Harvey's C Company were located together in a tented camp at Sungei Kuang, 16 miles from Ipoh and six miles off the main road to Taiping. King's B Company occupied a semi-permanent hutted camp at Tanjong Rambutan, nine miles from Ipoh and seven miles off the main road. Mataira's D Company and the battalion's tracker team (led first by Lieutenant Tad Hatherley and later by Lieutenant Huia Woods) were based in a semi-permanent wooden camp just outside the 'New Village' of Tanah Hitam, 12 miles from Ipoh and four miles off the Taiping road. All the company camps were on 'Black' roads, where there was a risk of ambush and vehicles were required to travel in pairs with armed escorts. 'Even going to the swimming hole a couple of miles down the road, we have to take an armoured car and a couple of Bren guns. Not that anything ever happens. It doesn't, for months. Then all of a sudden there's a road ambush. It has yet to happen to us, but it doesn't pay to get careless. This all sounds very warlike, but it's not, really. Very monotonous.'[53]

Ainge ran the main headquarters, which was grouped with Headquarters Company and the Quartermaster's elements at Sobraon Camp in Taiping. This was a permanent wooden camp with enough accommodation for a rifle company as well. Morrison's tactical headquarters, located in the compound of the police district headquarters in Ipoh, 50 miles to the south, was staffed by the intelligence officer, Lieutenant Neville Wallace, his intelligence section, and a signals detachment providing communications with Taiping and the rifle company bases. Moore's tactical headquarters for 28th Commonwealth Brigade was just across the road in the Ipoh Railway Station Hotel, and his main headquarters was also in Taiping.

At one minute to midnight on 8 March 1958 the battalion formally took over the 1st Royal Lincolns' area and became fully operational, seven months after the first of its personnel had marched into Waiouru Camp.

> We are finally on operations, as from last night, and our first patrol went out today ... There is a big operation on here at present, in which we are joining. It has been going on for the last three weeks, and although we have yet to open the Battalion score, the tally for all units engaged is so far 9 killed, 3 wounded, 2 captured and one surrendered. There are about 30,000 security forces engaged, so it will give you an idea how scarce the CTs are. They try to avoid contact if possible and are very hard to find. The country is very rugged, hills up to 6000 ft, heavy jungle, lots of swamps, and the terrific heat to cap it off. We will be going in for as long as 6 weeks at a time, by helicopter.[54]

This was one of two concurrent operations comprising the last large-scale (Federal Priority) operation of the Emergency. Operation BINTANG covered a large section of the Kinta district. Operation GINGER covered the Sungei Siput area, including parts of the Kangsar and Kinta districts. It had begun in January 1958, and involved 28th Commonwealth Brigade, 2nd Federal Infantry Brigade, the 1st Royal Lincolns, the King's Dragoon Guards, Police, and Home Guards, supported by a psychological warfare operation involving broadcasting from aircraft and the strict denial of food. The aim was to destroy the MRLA units and organisations operating in the 7th, 9th and 10th MCP districts, which encompassed Ipoh, north and central Perak. The estimated 170 guerrillas included the 20-strong 13/15 Platoon MRLA, the last operational platoon in the Ipoh area.[55]

The New Zealanders became responsible for the Ipoh police district east of the Ipoh–Taiping road. Their first operations were familiarisation patrols and an intensive programme of ambushes around the New Villages of Gunong Rapat and Bercham, and on possible supply routes east of Tanjong Rambutan.[56] While three companies were committed to Operation GINGER, Mataira's D Company operated in the 'Jungle Island', a D-shaped area of mountainous, jungle-covered country in the Keledang Sayong Forest Reserve. This 'island' separated the Kinta valley from the valley of the Sungei Perak and Kuala Kangsar, the capital of Perak state, and gave the guerrillas access to the surrounding population centres.

Operation GINGER followed well-practised procedures. The aim was to subject the guerrillas in a given area to the greatest possible pressure and cause their organisation to crack.

> Intelligence is first gathered through Special Branch regarding the distribution of terrorists in the area and their civilian contacts and sources of supply. Food denial measures are then instituted, after which the maximum military pressure is applied by patrols, bombardment and aerial attack. In this way the terrorists are harassed and their morale weakened. The intelligence available to them is restricted as much as possible. Voice aircraft and leaflets are used to exploit the declining morale and induce surrenders. Active patrolling in the jungle fringes combined with deep jungle patrols also causes small but regular losses of personnel.[57]

The key was effective intelligence, and the Malayan Police Special Branch played the primary role in obtaining this.[58] By 1958 the MRLA had been reduced to a hard core of dedicated and experienced personnel possessing few resources beyond superb bushcraft skills and finely-honed survival instincts. Many of the Min Yuen, the civilian support group organised among the Chinese population in surrounding towns and villages, were now giving 'only casual and often unwilling support'.[59] In Perak state the hard core of the MCP was in the north, 'in the tin mines, around Ipoh, and in the tapioca fields and rubber estates in the Sungei Siput District, which had been Chin Peng's stamping ground in the Japanese occupation, and where the Emergency had begun in 1948'.[60] The city of Ipoh had a population of 150,000, but it was the Chinese population of some 125,000 in the towns and villages of the river valleys that provided the MCP/MRLA with its main support. An elaborate intelligence system which made it impossible for security forces to move without the guerrillas being informed was particularly effective in tapioca-growing areas. As the crop stood roughly chest-high, it was easy for farmers 'to watch unobserved, and then when necessary, to stand up and "adjust" their highly coloured head-scarves with a flourish, as a signal to the guerrillas overlooking the fields from the jungle covered hillsides'.[61]

Morrison's headquarters and company bases were linked through No. 62 HF wireless sets. The battalion net remained open 24 hours a day, and communications were interrupted only by late-afternoon thunderstorms. Each company headquarters used the Australian-manufactured A510 HF wireless to communicate with its platoons. Communications were always difficult in the steep hill country surrounding the Ipoh plain, and a good platoon signaller was an asset to be prized. Each company was allocated an area of operations to patrol. This was a platoon and section commanders' war, with the company commander rarely going bush but playing a co-ordinating role from his headquarters at the company's base.

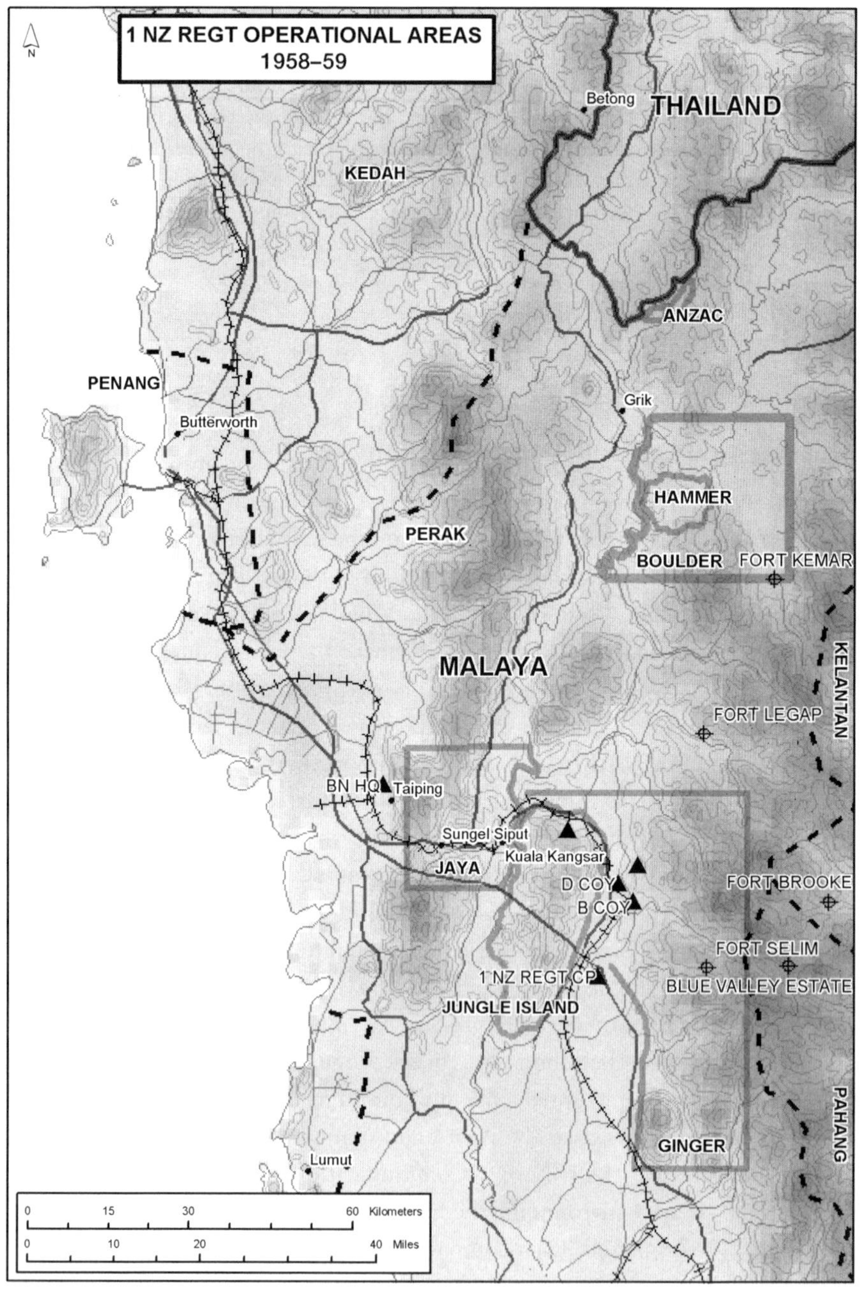


**Map 4** Operational areas of 1 NZ Regt 1958–59

Each man went out on patrol dressed in a jungle-green shirt, trousers, jungle boots, and jungle hat with an identifying coloured band around the rim. He wore a web belt holding a water bottle and a machete, and carried a Bergen pack and a compass. Each section of eight to ten men carried a Bren light machine gun; in many cases patrols carried two or more Brens to increase their firepower. Riflemen had a range of weapons, including shotguns, American M1 jungle carbines, Australian Owen sub-machine guns, and the newly introduced 7.62 mm FN self-loading rifles. Lead scouts often carried smooth-bore 12-gauge Remington pump-action shotguns, which proved to be ideal weapons at up to 40–50 feet when loaded with small-game ammunition.[62] The men carried six magazines per Bren, 50 rounds for each self-loading rifle, and 20 rounds per shotgun.

Going out into the 'ulu', as the tropical rainforest was known, the patrols suffered from the intense heat and humidity as they pushed through the thick belt of lallang grass to the jungle fringe and then faced a steep climb into the mountains. Buster Hornbrook, a corporal with C Company, recalled: '[It was] strange because it was almost as though you were walking around in the bush country in New Zealand except for the fact it was so bloody hot. You tended to say, I know that I can get from A to B without too much trouble, but you never took the heat into consideration. The jungle wasn't a problem, it was the heat.'[63] Patrols invariably faced a three- or four-day walk at the beginning of operations, as helicopters were used only for urgent evacuations or to get bodies out for identification. 'Everything was by compass and map, and regimental as button sticks ... and that was a good way to start ... The jungle wasn't an enemy and I think once you got over that, the jungle really was beautiful.'[64] Platoons went out for from three to six weeks, and were resupplied from the air every seven to ten days. Each platoon gradually found its own pattern of operating.

> The thing that the Kiwis had over everybody else was that they were more adaptable to bush life ... We had blokes carrying gunny sacks, old sugar bags tied top and bottom, and that was it. And that's how they operated ... about 4 o'clock when you were on patrol you started to look for somewhere to settle. You made sure you were on good ground, that you could get to the water easily, but you were concealed enough to be comfortable ... You'd cut little lanes that you could see and you'd put the vine around. Cooked your kai and as soon as it got dark you'd climb into your pit and kept quiet ... The Kiwi was good in the bush.[65]

The first patrols found clear indications of guerrillas in the area, but the first month of operations was one of intense frustration and missed opportunities.

This was a reflection of the New Zealanders' inexperience. On 15 March Lieutenant J. B. Prince's 2 Platoon was patrolling the Sungei Beremban, east of the Kinta valley. A sentry armed with a shotgun was guarding a water point outside the platoon base camp when, glancing to his left, he saw a khaki-coloured figure and fired, but the person dropped from sight. After some initial suspicion that the tracks were made by wild pig, a jungle-boot trail was found.[66] This was the battalion's first contact. There was another on 21 March, when a four-man patrol from 7 Platoon, C Company, fired at two figures above them on a ridge track while searching for a suspected enemy camp.[67] The camp itself was found by 9 Platoon the following day. It was well defended, could accommodate ten people, and had been hurriedly evacuated two to three weeks earlier. Patrols in the 'Jungle Island' area found numerous signs of camps, resting places and tracks, which indicated that the food-denial operations were forcing guerrillas to seek food from local villages. On 18 April a four-man patrol from A Company waiting in night ambush on the edge of the Tanjong Rambutan rubber estate opened fire at an approaching figure, who escaped without apparent injury.[68] The following day the battalion was credited with its first success when Wong Chan, a member of 31 Independent Platoon MRLA, surrendered to Major Alf Voss as he was driving along the road from his company base in his armoured car.

Lieutenant Neville Wallace, the battalion's intelligence officer (IO), saw the Special Branch as the key to getting good intelligence in the Ipoh area and deliberately set out to win their trust. The battalion's tactical headquarters was located in the police district headquarters.

> In the operations room sat the IO of the Battalion and the police operations officer ... and in the next office I had the Commanding Officer of the Battalion. Every morning [there] was 'Morning Prayers' attended by Special Branch, military, police, and civil representatives ... The aim of these conferences was to review the previous day's activities, and, consistent with security, announce daily intentions ... A fellow called Peter Coster ran Special Branch. He had several Chinese Police Special Branch Inspectors and I quite deliberately went about cultivating them, because they were the doers. I had them in my house, I used to eat breakfast with them, I'd go drinking with them, I'd do all those things. And in the end one of the Special Branch Inspectors and I would go ambushing on our own ... but the bonus was that he would tell me anything that was going on anywhere.[69]

In April the New Zealanders sent out a number of patrols with surrendered enemy personnel (SEPs) or in response to Special Branch intelligence, but without success.[70] The New Zealanders were on trial, being closely assessed by Headquarters 28th Commonwealth Infantry Brigade, Special Branch and the SEPs themselves, who risked their lives by accompanying patrols. In May it all started to pay dividends. A patrol acting on information located a food dump containing 400 lb of rice, and on 29 May came the first successful contact, involving 6 Platoon, B Company, on the jungle ridges above Ampang Baharu New Village. The platoon had taken great pains to enter the jungle and establish a platoon base without alerting the village.[71] Corporal Peter Rutledge was leading a five-man patrol,

> and as I came out to where the main track was, I couldn't believe my eyes because I saw this guy walking towards me in a khaki uniform and he had a khaki hat on and [I thought] 'Good God! This must be what one of them looks like!' I just stood there, put my rifle up and looked down the sight straight at him and he wasn't actually looking at me. He hadn't heard me, and he had no idea the other guys were behind me. Nobody had made any noise. Anyway when he was about five yards away ... I said 'Halt!' Straight away he dived to one side and he had a really big pistol and he tried to drag that out and I let him have it ... Tubby [Phillips], my Bren gunner, came right up beside me ... [and] opened up on automatic ... and there was tracer flying in all directions, and the other guys came up on either side of me ... It was quite fun for a few seconds. I found out then that it's very hard in those sort of situations to regain control immediately because there's such a hell of a din going on, and nobody really listening.[72]

Leaving a guard with the wounded man, Rutledge searched the area. A helicopter was requested but the man died before it arrived. Special Branch identified him as Man Ko, a central member of the Pulai Armed Work Committee of the 7th MCP district, who was apparently on his way from Ampang Baharu to meet up with his group, not realising that security forces were in the area.[73] It was an important kill. Man Ko, the son of a shopkeeper, had been in the jungle since 1950, and led one of the three groups that brought supplies and messages to the MCP state committee in its jungle fastness in the Cameron Highlands.[74]

In late May 1958, Mataira's D Company assumed responsibility for deep jungle operations on the Sungei Ber and Perolak in Kelantan, over the range east of the Ipoh valley, to the north of Fort Brooke. This was the area in which the New Zealand SAS Squadron had been so successful in 1956. Efforts by the security forces to win the support of the indigenous tribespeople were continuing; too many operations had promised much, but delivered little. The treatment of aborigines was often harsh, with demands for information sometimes accompanied by bashings.[75] Patrols could have a positive influence on the local people only while they were in the field; the guerrillas regained the upper hand on their withdrawal.

Sergeant Bruce Jamieson, the battalion's intelligence sergeant, who had served in the Malayan police and spoke colloquial Malay, initiated the battalion's first contact with the aborigines. He established a base in the Kinta Hills above Fort Selim, and employed a network of aborigines on daily patrols to gather information.

> I am sitting in the middle of a huge spider's web stretching from KARAMAT PULAI to Fort SELIM and several thousand yards NORTH and SOUTH, I am told everything, [including] what the OC at Fort SELIM has on the walls of his room, his personal habits and what Sgt DIN has for his meal. They have a fantastic knowledge and they love to sit in my basha and pass it on, thus by paying 3 men we have the service of 90 ... So long as we are here these people will [co-operate] fully but, as the headman says frankly, if armed CT come to the village and we are NOT here what can they do? They have NO shotguns at all and their blowpipe poison is NOT strong enough to kill a man quickly.[76]

The companies rostered platoons in rotation to ensure an ongoing presence in the area. This strategy paid dividends in June 1958, with the elimination of six terrorists—five were killed and one surrendered. On the morning of 3 June, Jamieson and a mixed patrol of 12 Platoon, D Company, and police under the command of Inspector Leong Chi Woh of Ipoh Special Branch, ambushed three armed aborigines in an area reserved for Special Branch operations, near an aboriginal settlement north of the Kinta waterworks.[77] 'The first [man] carrying a long-barrelled shot gun was allowed to pass through, the second and third were carrying Sten guns.' Something caught the eye of the last man, who cocked his Sten and moved towards the ambush. A policeman shot at him and everyone started firing. Private Cannon shot and killed the second man, while the other two, apparently both wounded, fled.[78] The dead man was identified as Itam Bin Pandak, a member of the Asal organisation. A Sten gun, three magazines, 104 rounds, food, and nine pairs of boots and shoes were recovered. Twelve Platoon, D Company, tracked a blood trail intermittently for two days until it was lost.[79]

Special Branch intelligence also led to the battalion's next success on 22 June, when a six-man patrol from D Company Headquarters under Staff Sergeant Lawrence shot and killed Bah Payang, one of the men who had been wounded in the ambush of 3 June.[80] The next day, the lead scout from a 12 Platoon, D Company, patrol saw two armed men crossing a clearing about 50 feet in front of him. After giving an 'immediate ambush' signal the scout opened fire. He killed the first man with a shotgun blast, while the Bren gunner killed the second man; neither had had time to react.[81] They were identified as Kwong Ming, a courier of 31 Independent Platoon, and Anjang Bin Pandak, the brother of the man killed in the D Company contact on 3 June.[82] On the same day, a soldier in C Company on patrol near Bekor was squatting over a hole answering nature's call when he was surprised by the approach of an armed, uniformed figure. Fortunately the guerrilla, Phang Kee Sang, a member of the Central MCP Printing Press, had come to surrender. The official report put this incident in a better light, but it was another success.[83] Within a month, the Ipoh Asal organisation had been broken by a combination of good intelligence from Special Branch and effective battle craft by the New Zealand patrols.[84]

These successes marked the start of a close association with Special Branch. Neville Wallace and his section mounted a number of ambushes in association with Leong Chi Woh, culminating in the capture of Kit Seong, a member of the Pulai Armed Work Committee, in September.[85] The association with Special Branch flourished to the extent that the New Zealanders were 'on occasions provided with information on enemy activity not in our area of operations'. Wallace once had to 'apologise to the Commanding Officer of the Australian Battalion because I mounted ambushes in an area which was not ours'.[86] As Buster Hornbrook recalled:

> [Leong Chi Woh] was a fantastic man. Very small of stature, a very slightly built fellow, but he was able to glean information from so many sources ... Leong would suddenly disappear and he'd be off for days and weeks at a time. And then he would reappear and all of a sudden you would find that Special Branch would put a freeze on a particular piece of real estate ... you knew damned well that Leong Chi Woh had been in there, or had pretty good information ... and they would go in and carry out their own operations.[87]

Special Branch patrols often took New Zealanders with them as signallers and to provide additional firepower. They preferred Maori soldiers; Willie Nathan, Sergeant Noel ('Shorty') Jamieson's radio operator, 'was the bloke that was always used and he went almost loopy in the end because he spent a lot more time in the jungle on operations than the actual platoon did, because he looked like a Malay'.[88]

The New Zealanders' varied skills were utilised in the information-gathering process. Having been a communicator in the RNZN, Hornbrook was attached to the Intelligence Section at Ipoh—and broke the police code. 'John O'Brien who was the Signals Sergeant in those days used to listen to the police net, and we would get all their information and we would break it down. Let the Colonel know what we were doing ... We were only interested in what was affecting us. We could then pre-empt what was going to happen and be there waiting.'[89]

Already, particular individuals and platoons stood out. Sergeant Jamieson's 12 Platoon, D Company, was by far the most successful platoon in the battalion. Jamieson, who would be awarded the Military Medal for his achievements in Malaya, had enlisted straight from school as a 16-year-old Regular Force Cadet in 1950, and despite wanting to be an infantryman had been allocated to the Armoured Corps. Now, after years of instructing, he was serving overseas for the first time as a platoon sergeant with D Company. Although this was officially a South Island company, 'in fact in my platoon over two-thirds of them were North Islanders [who had been] working down in Bluff in the freezing works'. On arrival at Kota Tinggi the platoon commander, Lieutenant Paul Hayes, had been promoted to company second-in-command; Jamieson took over as platoon commander for the rest of the battalion's tour. He attributed his platoon's success to 'practice, practice, practice ... before we ... went out on any operation we went right through our IA [immediate action] drills. We did our range shooting ... and we used to check everybody before they went out, until it was just automatic.' This preparation was matched by the platoon's bushcraft skills; on patrol, each man became part of the jungle.

> Scented soap could be smelt quite a long way away, cigarette smoke, rum was the worst, you could smell rum for a hell of a long distance. So all these things went by the board. So what you did, you washed down in the creek, hung the gear that you had been wearing during the day ... and climbed back into that gear the following morning, cold, wet, and smelly. But by then you got to the stage where you could smell people coming before you could hear them.

You had to be always on the alert, Jamieson recalled, 'because you didn't know what you were getting into ... Once we ran into a Gurkha platoon who were in our area by accident, the lead scout heard a noise up front, gave the warning signal, "Immediate ambush right", and the whole platoon just melted into the bush and the Gurkha platoon went through and didn't even know that we were there.'[90]

Good battle craft and patrolling did not guarantee success, but they did minimise the risk when the MRLA occasionally fought back. On 12 June 1958, 5 Platoon, B Company, under Sergeant I. G. Ross found fresh footprints leading up a steep jungle-covered ridge. Ross split the platoon into two patrols, and ten men under Corporal Dick Scadden moved up the ridge track, led by dog-handler Private Paea. A concealed sentry opened fire, missed, and ran back along the narrow ridge as Scadden's patrol 'pepper-potted' forward, firing. Nothing could be seen because a large tree completely blocked the way ahead. The patrol found themselves on the fringe of an 'extremely well sited' jungle camp. Documents, equipment, baby clothing and baby food were found in the camp, but a 'follow-up failed to make any further contact'.[91]

In late June, Major Ash King's B Company carried out one of only two company-scale operations undertaken by the battalion during its two years in Malaya. An indigenous SEP reported a camp in deep jungle east of Fort Selim, towards the Cameron Highlands, at which senior members of the MCP state committee were believed to be meeting. After flying to Fort Selim, King left at first light on 29 June with 4 Platoon and a section of 5 Platoon, B Company, together with the fort's commander, Inspector Chapman, a party of aboriginal Home Guards and the SEP, 'who became less helpful as the patrol neared the area'.[92] The plan was to place a series of stop groups below the camp, which was sited on a steep spur. King and the assault group, above the camp, would place a radio beacon to direct an aircraft strike which they hoped would flush the occupants out into the ambush positions.[93] On 30 June, after a cold wet night during which smoking and cooking were impossible, five stop groups were placed in position, with some 'close enough to hear sounds of chopping and talking'. As King's group moved forward to place the beacon, they heard firing; one of the stop groups had been seen. The camp was evacuated, with one man shot dead when he ran into one of the stop groups. By the time King's assault group scrambled down the jungle slope, across a creek and up into the camp, it was deserted. The guerrillas 'were well drilled as very little was left behind'.[94]

A follow-up was mounted by a seven-man patrol under Lance-Corporal Pat Dillon, with Private B. J. Tuxworth and his black Labrador 'Tammy' leading. Thirty minutes from camp, the patrol was ambushed. Tuxworth was killed instantly, and a light machine gun and automatic weapons opened up on the rest of the patrol. When Dillon counter-attacked, the ambushers broke contact. A thorough search failed to pick up their tracks. The ambush had been 'skilfully placed and it appeared to have been well rehearsed'.[95] Later it was found that there had been two State Committee Members in the camp, and the man killed was identified as Ah Yoong, personal bodyguard to Chan Hong, the senior State Committee member in Perak.[96] Among the documents in his pack was a military appreciation of the MCP/MRLA organisation in Perak. After it was deciphered, Special Branch assessed this as the 'most important find of that year'.[97]

Tuxworth's death underlined the enormous strain on the lead scout. This was the hardest job, given to the best man in each patrol. Lead scouts were a special breed who could read signs and get inside the mind of the person they were tracking. They had an instinct for sensing the presence of others. Lieutenant Roy Taylor of A Company used Danny Wilson as his lead scout. 'He was very good. I used to feel safe with that guy in front. He had eyes like a hawk and reactions to match.'[98] It was not a position in which men were rotated: too much was at stake. The same could be said for trackers and dog-handlers. Private Paea had been lucky in the contact of 12 June, but this time being in the lead position cost Tuxworth his life.

The battalion's tracking team, and five company tracking teams, had been formed at Kota Tinggi in January 1958 under Lieutenant Tad Hatherley, who was succeeded by Lieutenant Huia Woods. Having served as a scout with the New Zealand SAS Squadron in Malaya, Woods had 'an unrivalled knowledge of the bandits' habits, tactics and deceptions'.[99] A schoolteacher in civilian life, Woods was accepted for a short-service Regular commission after finishing his tour with the SAS, and was posted to 1 NZ Regt in 1957. He stayed a further year with 2 NZ Regt in 1960, thus spending five consecutive years on operations in Malaya. His tracking skills and exploits were legendary, and he was the only Commonwealth serviceman to gain an 'A' pass for tracking at the Jungle Warfare School. The battalion team initially comprised 22 New Zealanders, 29 Iban trackers from the Sarawak Rangers, three SEPs, nine civilian liaison officers, and a Royal Army Veterinary Corps sergeant. The New Zealanders in the team became the dog-handlers; they were 'hand-picked for fitness and experience with dogs ... the handler and his dog were inseparable, and when the hunt is [sic] on they worked to a strict code of discipline understood as much by the animal as his master'.[100] The 16 dogs with the battalion were golden or black Labradors and Alsatians. Some were trackers and followed the scent on the ground; others were patrol dogs, and worked in the same way as sporting pointers.

Each of the company tracking teams included Iban trackers, cover men, dogs and handlers. The battalion tracking team, which followed up immediately after any contact or incident and was always on standby, comprised the best personnel. The company teams were used to search less promising targets, such as unidentified tracks, and would follow up an immediate contact only if the battalion team was not available.[101] Woods respected the skills of his enemy. He also considered the aborigines and some of the New Zealanders to be better than the Ibans at tracking human prey. He taught his teams to combine their skills. 'First you must learn to recognise the jungle in its natural state; then you must learn to look for things that are unnatural. Broken sticks, squashed sticks, skid marks or the more obvious impression of a foot in dry powdered earth are all signs to be sought. A broken spider's web, the blurring of raindrops or dew on leaves can also indicate the direction taken by a hunted man.'[102]

The Iban trackers, and to a lesser degree the SEPs, became an integral part of the platoons to which they were attached. Shorty Jamieson's 12 Platoon, D Company, had two Iban trackers, Sang and Ukit.

> [They] were absolutely excellent. Sang was an elderly gentleman. You could guess he was about 55 to 65 ... Ukit was married to his daughter and he was about 25. They were excellent trackers. Saved us a lot of problems with navigation ... You didn't need a compass, they'd take you straight back. They carried weapons. Couldn't hit anything but at least it gave them confidence ... We had them for the full time and it was a sad day when they went home.[103]

The New Zealanders' successes in June were followed by a series of contacts in July. For a patrol from Lieutenant John Hall's 1 Platoon, A Company, 1 July was its third day in ambush at a guerrilla camp. As fate would have it, the four-man ambush party was changing over just as four guerrillas entered the camp. Seeing the ambush group, they immediately fled; the ambush party opened fire, to no effect. A follow-up was mounted but heavy rain washed out the tracks. Medium artillery was called in on likely escape routes, and 1 Platoon continued to ambush trails along the Sungei Chenka for the next week, with no success. The only excitement came when Privates G. Pratt and G. McCoshery, a two-man stop group, opened fire on an elephant that charged them.[104] On 10 July a patrol from Voss's A Company headquarters, led by Voss himself, who always wanted to be involved, encountered five guerrillas, who fled, leaving behind two rifles and equipment. Voss grabbed one aborigine but he got away, leaving his rifle behind.[105] The next day another of Voss's patrols located a cache of 175 lb of tapioca in the Sungei Siput area. They were fired at by two men, both of whom were wounded by return fire but escaped.[106]

On 28 July Lieutenant Peter Anaru's 8 Platoon, C Company, ambushed a food-dump site near a cemetery on the edge of a rubber estate on 'Jungle Island'. Special Branch had reported that a Malay rubber-tapper had been approached by four armed guerrillas and told to leave food in a cache at the base of a distinctive tree near the cemetery, from which it would be collected on that day. With four trees to choose from, Anaru 'decided to select the most likely tree ... and sight my killer [group] to cover it and place my stop [groups] in a [position] to cover the other three trees and at the same time cover the likely approaches and exits to the area'. At first light next morning four men, three of them carrying weapons, walked into the ambush and were fired on at a range of five yards. One man fell, then got up and ran off towards the east; the other three, one of whom may also have been hit, fled towards the north-east. Anaru called in a tracker team, and organised members of his own platoon into an eight-strong tracking party, with the remainder under his platoon sergeant following up. 'After tracking for 150/200 yds we discovered a blood trail which thickened as we moved further into the jungle ... Pools of blood collected in leaves and blood stains on logs showed he had frequently rested.' After tracking for about 500 yards, the dog left the blood trail and followed a ground scent until it stopped and pointed. Anaru halted his tracker team and swept the area with his platoon, but found nothing. 'I ... decided to retrace my steps and take the Tracking Team back to a log where we had last seen the blood trail. I ... put the Iban on to [follow] the trail. The Iban [followed] the blood trail over a log and he sighted the wounded CT lying under another log approximately 10 yds away.'[107] Despite being critically wounded he attempted to draw his pistol, and the New Zealanders shot him. He was identified as Yeung Cheong, the central figure in the Bekok Min Yuen and C Company's target for the past ten weeks. A second set of tracks, now over five hours old, was followed up without success.[108] The three remaining members of Yeung Cheong's group surrendered to police in August.[109]

On 1 August 1958, 1 New Zealand Regiment was a year old. WO2 Wally White, CSM A Company, noted: 'As at 28 Jul 58, this company has been operational for one hundred and forty-four days ... In this time a grand total of 6754 man/days has been logged. The average number of days per man is 54.03. The highest individual figure is 94 days. (Pte COOK, R.) The average number of men on operations on any day is 46.9.'[110] It had been a busy and productive period for the battalion. The padre noted that while morale among the soldiers was very good, there was 'a noticeable look of strain in the faces of many troops and some are very tired'.[111]

It had also been a busy—and instructive—period for the 61 families (including 100 children) who had joined the battalion in Malaya. Forty-three families were in Ipoh, including the families of four officers who had come at their own expense, and 18 in Taiping. The families trickled in on flights from New Zealand as accommodation became available, moving into hired houses in the town or the married quarters which were constructed around the permanent camps.[112] Many of the rented houses were built by developers keen to capitalise on the growing demand for housing as the British army changed from a National Service army to professional Regular battalions with large numbers of married personnel. WO2 Wally White and his family lived in Ipoh.

> The house is very nice, all concrete, including the floors. The living room floor is polished red flagstones. It's supplied fully furnished down to cutlery and linen. Only the stove supplied is a rather primitive kerosene job, which I've promptly kicked out, & hired an electric one from the local power board for 5 dollars a month. I'm also having the telephone installed this week, which is a big help because I'll be getting home once a week or so if I'm lucky ... The house has three bedrooms and three bathrooms. The windows are the louvred type, all around the house. A car port across the front door and tiled roof.[113]

Some families found it difficult to adjust to the different climate and lifestyle. New Zealand wives had never had to contemplate dealing with a housekeeper.

> We are also supplied with an Amah, who does all the housework except the cooking, which Beet does herself. The Amah lives out, although there is a room provided for her, and works from 9 am to 5 pm, and for a few dollars will look after the kids if we want to go out ... It's a bit awkward though. Her English is very limited and what there is is almost unintelligible.[114]

Nothing had prepared the families for garrison life, because there was no equivalent in New Zealand, even in the married quarters of military camps. Anne Morrison, who lived in Ipoh for the first year, recalled that one of the British officers' wives asked her:

> 'Don't you look after the New Zealand wives?' I said, 'No ... I think they are all right.' Of course this got to the New Zealand wives' ears and they decided that they

> would like someone to come and look at all the things that were wrong ... so that involved me in a lot of travel. Up and down finding where the houses were ... But they were all good houses, nothing really wrong; but a lot of children seemed to have bites, colds and sores ... they needed a bit of advice [about hygiene] ... You could get a cold very easily over there. Every time anyone sneezed you would say 'Redoxin' [sic]... which is ascorbic acid, absolutely solid vitamin C.[115]

Anxiety was ever-present when husbands were in the bush on operations. 'When a soldier was killed they were very tense and upset about it.'[116] The same worries were experienced in New Zealand by the wives and families of servicemen. Most were not living in military housing, and little thought was given to their welfare and the need to keep them informed. Owen Mann caught leptospirosis in Malaya and was in the British Military Hospital in Taiping. 'All my wife got, even though I was on the dangerously ill list, was a telegram to say "Regret to inform you ...", no contacts, no nothing ... Nobody [from the Army] went near her, nobody.'[117] This was not an isolated case. If dependants were living in a camp housing area they were looked after, but the New Zealand Army had yet to learn how to cope with other families.

The families of officers on 12-month unaccompanied postings who decided to bring them anyway also had a hard time. Neville Wallace discussed this with his wife Augusta, and said: 'OK. If it costs us everything, you're going.'

> Graeme McKay did the same. Roger Pearce did the same, Bill Meldrum. We took our wives and we got absolutely no assistance whatsoever ... We found our own accommodation ... No furniture, no nothing. No RAP [Regimental Aid Post], things like that. We did not have access [to facilities other families took for granted]. You could go to the NAAFI [shop] and buy your groceries. I managed to get a cot out of the Garrison Quartermaster, and that was the only bit of Army furniture that we had ... Augusta went out and bought a Pedigree pram from Mrs Titter, Harold's wife ... the day the Pedigree pram arrived [the Amah] disappeared for hours and she went out every day and we suddenly realised that we had invested our Amah with some status. And up until then I think she had been rather ashamed of us.[118]

Garrison life exposed a wide cross-section of New Zealanders to South-East Asia and its cultures for the first time. '[We had] no knowledge of the East or of how people there lived. We did some terribly insensitive things simply because we knew no better, like thinking we were wearing a hat when in fact it was a meat-cover. We thought we were frightfully smart in what looked like a coolie hat ... we were laughed at quite a lot by the locals.'[119] In Ipoh and

Taiping the New Zealanders were the outsiders, surrounded by different peoples and having to fit in with different cultures, often without the support of other New Zealanders living nearby. 'It was like an adventure almost. I think some of [the wives] had difficulty with their children. Some of them had never had a servant before. They treated them [as one of the family, and would] sit down and have tea together, do everything together.'[120]

The New Zealanders found that cars were cheaper in Malaya. 'All going well we hope to get a car in a few weeks time. The big American cars are pretty cheap. '49 Buick £140, '52 Chev £180. '51 Rover 75 about £240. The smaller English cars are much dearer, because of their M.P.G. [miles per gallon] Petrol [is] about 5/4 a gallon.'[121] In the barracks, cars, like everything else, became common property, which led to headaches for headquarters staff when road accidents occurred. Despite a number of potentially serious accidents, only one New Zealand soldier was killed in a car crash during the battalion's tour.[122] Another incident resulted in Private K. B. Chesterfield being awarded the State of Perak Distinguished Conduct Medal for his bravery in rescuing personnel trapped in an armoured car that was upside down and leaking petrol.

When soldiers came out of the bush they went on leave to Ipoh or Taiping. Married personnel with families were granted at least two full leave days each fortnight, while single and unaccompanied married personnel could apply for overnight leave. Day leave was granted to off-duty personnel until 10.30 p.m., provided they had a leave pass and were properly dressed. Each soldier received £10 worth of clothing, enough to purchase 'two respectable shirts and trousers'. These were essential; everyone going on leave after 7 p.m. 'must wear long-sleeved shirts, trousers and TIES.'[123]

Out-of-bounds areas were promulgated, and though everyone went 'out of bounds' at some time out of curiosity, the permitted areas provided more than enough entertainment. Each battalion adopted its own bars. In Taiping the Springtide Night Club was popular, while in Ipoh the Boston Milk Bar in Cockman Street, near the Lido Cinema, was one of a number of bars where New Zealanders let off steam. Its rival across the road, the Sydney Bar, was an Australian haunt. The bars became homes away from home for some. Like the FMS Bar on Brewster Road, by the Ipoh Padang, most had rooms upstairs in which bar girls provided other services. Cheam Yeom Toon's family owned both the Boston and the FMS Bar. 'Thursday night was pay night for the Kiwi boys. Anchor Beer was 65 cents a big bottle, and there was broken glass on the floor that thick, and ... guitars and ... singing. Wild men but happy times.'[124]

Rugby, cricket and athletics also provided opportunities for contact with the civilian population. M. Dattaya, a surveyor who played in the second row of the Perak State rugby team, believed that a number of good young local players developed as a result of the New Zealand influence. Geoffrey Cheam, who ran the Boston Bar and was also the hooker for the Perak State team, captained the Boston rugby team, a social side consisting mainly of New Zealand soldiers. After a game everyone went back to the bar; out came the guitars, 'then there would be a session until morning and that's when I learnt "Hoki Mai".'[125]

Regular customers could record their purchases in the bar 'book', and in many cases most of the soldier's pay packet was already spoken for by pay day.[126] Each company also had its own 'char wallah' who could produce milky coffee and egg banjos at the drop of a hat; a tailor and dhobi wallah who laundered issue clothing on contract, charging the soldier only for doing his civilian clothes; a platoon boot boy who cleaned boots, polished brass, made beds and tidied bedspaces for $2 a week per soldier. The char and dhobi wallahs were sources of credit for the soldiers, and would 'come bleating to the CSM when they can't get their money'.[127]

The battalion's venereal disease rate was very high, despite every attempt to reduce it. In July 1958 Morrison reported that the 'incidence of Venereal Disease is still high but the weekly rate is slowly falling', an improvement he attributed to 'the talks given by the OC's, Padre and the RMO'.[128] This was a false hope: VD would preoccupy every New Zealand battalion commander in South-East Asia, as well as their RNZN and RNZAF counterparts. Threats of disciplinary action only encouraged the men to seek treatment from local civilian practitioners. The problem was as old as armies themselves, and not easily solved. Soldiers would come out of the bush, get drunk, go upstairs with a girl and become infected. Companies worked hard to convince their men to use the condoms which were given to each soldier as he went on leave. In B Company, the system when the men came off operations, usually late in the afternoon, was as follows:

> You'd get back into base, the chaps would clean up, we'd give them ten dollars, take them into our own little company canteen and let them drink themselves stupid ... Guys would let their hair down, get all the steam out of them, and the next day they would clean up, get rid of their hangover, get themselves dressed up, get all their money [and] they'd go on leave. I believe that that was a great system for cutting down the amount of VD ... If you'd let them go straight out it would have been disastrous. I think we had a VD rate of well over 100% anyway.[129]

Platoons were rostered through a leave centre established on Pangkor Island when they came out of operations. Soldiers enjoyed a week at the beach with plenty of beer; their char wallahs fed them steaks, and the sun cleared up jungle sores and leech bites. They were also kept away from Ipoh's fleshpots.

During the battalion's tour of duty a number of marriages were made by proxy between soldiers and women in New Zealand, some of whom then came to Malaya. In March 1959 Private Dawson married an English nurse from the British Military Hospital in Taiping; this was the first wedding between a New Zealand serviceman in this battalion and a resident of Malaya.[130] No marriages to local Chinese or Malay women are mentioned in the Padre's reports. These were to become an issue for later battalions.

Morrison was regarded by some of his officers as being 'too soft on the guys. He loved his troops. He was really too nice to them.'[131] Morrison himself was well aware of this.

> Soldiers said the only difference between Russell Ainge and myself was 28 days [stoppage of leave]. Russell had no sense of humour and he did hit hard in his orderly room whereas I knew that I would frighten hell out of the accused, his escort, and everybody else in the room by blasting them and cursing them in every way, and calling on the gods to send them to hell when they died, and then would let them off on the charge.[132]

In 1959 Army General Staff finally granted approval to return soldiers whose conduct had been unsatisfactory. This affected 16 personnel, of whom three were returned to New Zealand in February and another five in March. This broke up the hard core of battalion offenders. A further ten courts-martial were held in 1 NZ Regt during April and May. Colonel Cade reported that this represented 'a determined effort by the Unit Commander to stamp out the incidence of absence without leave and associated offences, but does not indicate any decline in the general standard of discipline within the unit'.[133]

This purge was what 1 NZ Regt needed. 'Wild Man' Morrison was deliberately larger than life, both to his own soldiers and within 28th Commonwealth Brigade. He was determined that his battalion would be the best, and had a clear view of what battalion life in Malaya should be like. While the battalion was still in Waiouru he made all his subalterns read John Masters' *Bugles and a Tiger*; 'that gives you the best idea of the type of Battalion he wanted'.[134] During the tour in Malaya, Morrison worked hard to establish both a tradition and a sense of style for his battalion. His pursuit of this goal was not always recognised or appreciated by his subordinates, but it has continued to influence 1RNZIR.

In late July 1958 Brigadier Moore was succeeded by Brigadier H. J. Mogg, CBE, DSO, a former light-infantryman. Mogg was very different from his predecessor, and Morrison enjoyed the change. '[He had] a grand sense of humour and he endeared himself to all the soldiers.'[135] Operationally, Mogg allowed his battalion commanders more latitude, as his brigade major, Colin East, recalled: 'John Mogg's approach to the operations of the brigade was to make the plan, delegate the tasks to unit commanders and then let them get on with it until he considered it necessary to step in.'[136] There were also changes within 1 NZ Regt as some 70 long-service Regulars, including 12 officers and 21 sergeants on 12-month unaccompanied tours, began to return to New Zealand.[137] Morrison saw this an opportunity to strengthen command of the platoons, particularly as most of the 'minor disciplinary and administrative problems that are arising are directly caused by poor leadership at platoon commanders level'.[138] A number of his Territorial officers were on two-year accompanied tours, and could not be returned to New Zealand despite unsatisfactory performance. Instead, Morrison removed them from command and found them positions in Taiping. At the other end of the scale were Territorial officers such as Lieutenant P. H. Anaru, who was so successful in C Company, and Second Lieutenant P. K. Power of D Company, who despite achieving no contacts was regarded by his company commander as being one of his most effective platoon patrol commanders.[139]

The newly arrived Regular officers found themselves having to fit in to what were now very experienced platoons. Lieutenant Bryan Wells, who was posted to 5 Platoon, B Company, remembered:

> I was 22 years of age and I was given a platoon of some fairly hardened soldiers ... it was the best education I ever had ... I found it difficult for a while but I was fortunate in that I had a very good platoon sergeant, Dick Scadden ... he'd been with the battalion from the beginning, so he had about a year and a half's jungle warfare experience over and above mine, and so he was able to take me under his wing ... I was the outsider and it took me something like three or four months ... Not that the jungle was friendly or neutral; the real problem for me was to become established as a leader of that group of 30 or 32 young men. It was very hard physical work for the young officer. I found it was also a very lonely existence to maintain discipline throughout that period of time ... you needed to have that individual drive to be able to constantly motivate people to carry out their function

in that environment because it was only too easy to just sit back, put up your hammock and lay there for three days and send in a patrol report that said you'd carried out these enormous activities.[140]

Section commanders experienced similar pressures. Peter Rutledge recalled: 'One of the most important things was to feel that your guys knew what was going on all the time ... I always made sure they knew everything that I knew ... [and] that they didn't feel that they were just wandering around the bush ... I think it's important to lead by example. It's no good telling a guy ... you've got to toe the line all the time and not do it yourself.' The battalion's experience highlighted the fact that while the New Zealand Army turned out Regular Force instructors superbly equipped to meet the needs of a Territorial Army, many lacked man-management and leadership skills. 'They had to rely on their abilities as opposed to being the "boss" ... a number of people ... never made the grade ... we appreciated that there's more to the Army than being an instructor.'[141] Experience also underlined the importance of the professional infantry rifleman and the need to train him in the skills of his trade in the same way that the Army trained instructors, with pay matched to qualifications as an incentive. While Morrison's battalion identified this issue, its operational commitments gave it little time to address it. It would be 2 NZ Regt, commanded by Lieutenant-Colonel D. J. Aitken, that introduced a systematic programme of training riflemen.

The personnel changeover did not affect the New Zealanders' run of success. On 8 August, Shorty Jamieson's 12 Platoon, D Company, contacted three men and killed Lim Kim, a courier of the Tanjong Rambutan Armed Working Force. On 16 August, A Company and A Squadron Senoi Pra'ak captured Wai Ming and his wife in the Korbu Forest Reserve in the high country north-east of the Kinta valley. The Senoi Pra'ak ('fighting men') were groups of scouts raised and organised by Richard Noone, the Protector of Aborigines, in three squadrons for operations deep in the jungle.[142] As a result of information given to Special Branch by Wai Ming, a series of ambushes was mounted by 1 Platoon, A Company. This led to the capture of Ah Fuk on 21 August by a combined 1 Platoon/Senoi Pra'ak patrol commanded by Corporal W. K. Brown. That night, the patrol heard a baby crying and a dog barking. The next day, while Ah Fuk was evacuated to a landing zone, the rest of the patrol under Lance-Corporal Percy Brown moved forward to ambush the area around a basha which was believed to be a potential guerrilla rendezvous. As they approached, the lead scout, Private Davis, saw two figures coming towards them. Brown thought they were Senoi Pra'ak, and did not open fire. The pair suddenly split up and disappeared behind a bamboo clump. Brown and Davis moved forward in short bounds, covering each other. Suddenly a green-clad figure ran out, dropped, ran and dropped again. Everyone started firing and the two figures retreated the way they had come, leaving Brown mortally wounded. The patrol followed up, firing into any likely ambush positions until their Bren jammed; they then returned to the contact area. Brown was the battalion's second and last fatality resulting from guerrilla action. His death illustrated yet again that in jungle fighting a split-second hesitation could mean the difference between success and failure.[143]

Brown's death was the only interruption to a run of successful contacts. Just after midnight on 21 August, a six-man patrol under WO2 Ken Carrington, CSM D Company, ambushed four people on a track through fishponds near Tanah Hitam. Two men and a woman were killed, while the fourth guerrilla was hauled out of a fishpond and taken prisoner.[144] Mataira's D Company had its tenth success on 11 September, when 11 Platoon ambushed and killed Sui Lin, the wife of Low Ming, a member of the Ipoh Asal district committee. Mataira demonstrated the same skills as George Mate, his mentor in 1FIR, in using Special Branch information to good effect in deploying his patrols; he was Morrison's outstanding company commander. Woods' tracking team was flown in to follow up the contact, but by the time they arrived it was late afternoon. Heavy rain then delayed them for three days. Finally, on the Saturday: 'Started first light—track easy to follow first 500 yds then became extremely difficult. CT practised deception—splitting up into ones for up to 50 yds. CT travelled west for 100 yds then swung round to the north and varied between north and north-east ... 5–6 CTs. No packs and very lightly laden.' The tracking party found that the group had split up at the river, and after spending the rest of the day casting for tracks, finally decided that they had gone back the way they had come. Next day, the team followed the track to an overnight camp where their five prey had slept 'under the stars, I would say had a very wet night'. They had been eating green durian. The tracks were then lost. The team split up in heavy rain and made 'extensive casts but with negative results'. Monday was spent looking for signs, and on Tuesday the follow-up was called off. Despite the lack of success this was an impressive effort which highlighted the skills of Woods and his team. Woods was convinced that, given tracks that were no more than three days old and 'where the CT did not know they were being followed, I could almost guarantee a contact'.[145]

In October the New Zealanders were directed increasingly into operations deep in the jungle. On 29 October a second squadron of Senoi Pra'ak was placed under the battalion's command. There were no contacts, but two terrorist groups surrendered to B Company in the Korbu Forest Reserve. Until now, the tribespeople had seen the SAS come in, 'do the operation for a month and then go'. But the New Zealanders replaced platoon after platoon, making it clear that they were staying. It was a combination of patrolling and 'winning hearts and minds'. Lieutenant Roy Taylor's 'very competent medic', Corporal G. J. Braybrooke, ran a sick parade in the village.

> [The queue] stretched right into the bloody jungle ... One old guy came in complaining about a sore back. The medic laid him out on his bamboo slatted table that he had. You could see this guy's spine come down and then jump sideways, and then carried on. At some stage he had either dislocated or broken his back. [Braybrooke] got some gentian violet and wrote 'VERY SORE' right down this guy's back. 'There's your treatment mate.'[146]

The power of gentian violet paid off. On 3 October the village elder told Sergeant Len Hepi's patrol from 4 Platoon, B Company, that one of the guerrillas wanted to surrender. Hepi, alone and armed with a sub-machine gun, walked down the track and was met by a barefooted man in a faded uniform holding a Japanese rifle above his head. He was Chan Sau Po, a member of the 10th North District Asal Organisation. Suspecting that he was being watched, Hepi took the rifle and escorted the man back to his patrol base. On 12 October Hepi was told that more guerrillas wished to surrender. He returned to the track and was met by an Indian, four Chinese (including two women) and two aborigines —the rest of the 10th North District Asal Organisation. Some had been in the jungle since the beginning of the Emergency in 1948. They told Hepi they were starving and could no longer attract recruits. Constant ambushing by security forces had cut their contacts with other groups, and 'they had had enough'.[147] This was the largest surrender so far during Operation GINGER.[148] On 23 October five members (including one woman) of 25/29 Section of 31 Independent Platoon surrendered to 6 Platoon, B Company, commanded by Sergeant Bruce Hill. Corporal Rutledge was part of the patrol. They 'sent in one of the abos and told us they'd like to come in and surrender to us ... We set up an ambush straight away ... and they came in with their hands up, and this particular guy [Tsei Ko Yin] was the one in charge ... he was quite a large guy for a Chinese person and very fit-looking. He surrendered to us and said he wanted to call it off. He had his wife with him and a small child.' The group showed the strain of years of jungle warfare. They were all 'rather worn out. Their clothing was still clean but it was very much worn ... They didn't have very much food left ... the chief had a revolver, the others had rifles and these were well looked after ... but they were just about at the end of their tether ... They had definitely had enough.'[149]

In October 1958, 13 guerrillas surrendered and one was killed in the Operation GINGER area. This brought to 80 the total number eliminated since the start of the operation: 40 had surrendered, with 35 killed and 5 captured. The New Zealanders accounted for 23 of these: nine surrenders, 12 kills and two captures.[150] The battalion had no contacts in November, and at the end of the month it was redeployed to the Sungei Siput Police District, once again taking over responsibility for the 'Jungle Island' area. December saw the lifting of the Emergency Regulations in a large area of the state, including what had been the New Zealand operational area south of Ipoh. A, B and C Companies closed their camps at Sungei Kuang and Tanjong Rambutan and moved into Sobraon Camp at Taiping. For the first time since their initial jungle warfare training at Kota Tinggi, most of the battalion was concentrated together. Mataira's D Company remained at Tanah Hitam Camp. Many soldiers shared Corporal Rutledge's view of the shift. 'I didn't really enjoy the second year terribly much because we were transferred up to Taiping ... and I did feel that there was too much bullshit that went on there.'[151]

In early 1959 there was a last flurry on Operation GINGER after an SEP was murdered in the Gunong Rapat area. D Company was placed under the command of 1 Loyals; then B and C Companies worked with 1 Loyals, 2/6 Gurkha Rifles and 1/10 Gurkha Rifles in a major effort to destroy the last MRLA elements in southern Perak. GINGER ended on 20 April 1959, having largely destroyed the Malayan Communist Party's organisation in the Ipoh area. This was also the end of the battalion's first year of operations. Morrison noted:

> The past year has not been an easy one and the continuous strain on the administrative personnel has been as great as on those soldiers required to operate in the jungle. Despite the apparent fatigue now showing, the morale of the unit remains remarkably high. The influx of good junior officers replacing those who, after one year's hard work, have lost their sting has been an immense help.[152]

The New Zealanders now shifted their attention to the Grik area of northern Perak as part of Operation BOULDER. This area was 90 miles from the battalion's camp at Taiping; patrols operated to within 30 miles of the Thai border. The task was to destroy the MRLA's influence among the tribespeople in the jungles of northern Perak. At the end of December, 1 NZ Regt moved its tactical headquarters to Grik, where it took over from B Squadron, 22 (SAS) Regiment. There was also a changeover of intelligence officers, with Tad Hatherley replacing Neville Wallace, who returned to New Zealand. At Grik the New Zealanders found that their information was increasingly what they discovered themselves, as Special Branch lacked adequate intelligence sources in the deeper jungle. Local information was often suspect—'the sources appear to be eager to help by passing on all info collected in the past 10 years, and claiming that it is up to date'. The New Zealanders were critical of B Squadron's tactics, which appeared 'to have been too harsh'. Their experience was that once 'an Abo befriends you, he will offer you information—you will not need to ask for it, but use a mailed fist and he will become stubborn and will not co-operate under any circumstances'.[153]

The battalion spent its remaining 11 months on hard patrolling in deep jungle for very little reward. It was responsible for an operational area of some 600 square miles. The operations during 1958 had broken the back of the MRLA, and 1959 was a very lean year. Lieutenant Don McIver commanded the Mortar Platoon, which was used as a rifle platoon. 'We spent most of our time chasing limited trails which quickly became cold and in fact during my whole period there, I didn't see a live CT in the jungle.'[154] Like the SAS before them, Morrison's men acquired a reputation for the duration of their patrols. 'Normally the average stay in the bush ... was probably about six weeks. Sometimes four weeks. We regarded four weeks as a short patrol. My longest period in that 14 months with the Battalion was just a week under three months in the deep jungle away from any other contact.' Commanders differed on the optimum length of an operation.

> I formed the opinion that about four weeks was a maximum time that I could maintain my own drive and enthusiasm. You peaked at about ten days and your patrol was really going well. You kept at that level for another 10 days and then after that you certainly started to come downwards. I used to worry about our alertness, certainly towards the end of that six-week period. For the last week I believe we were not particularly effective.[155]

The pulse of the platoon had to be constantly monitored. When a group of 35 men spend six weeks together in the jungle, 'you can get on each other's nerves very easily and if you're putting out ambushes you had to look very carefully and make sure that you separated [someone] who wasn't seeing eye to eye with somebody else ... in case it blew up, and it would never be anything serious, but would be over where they'd slung their hammock, [or] who got the best trees.'[156]

Patrols lived from 'airdrop to airdrop'; that became the measure of their days. They carried in ten days' supplies on their backs, and after seven days the platoon sergeant would compile a list of what was needed in the first airdrop. This included each soldier's NAAFI requirements, 'things that the guys bought on credit and then paid [for] when we got out, from their pay books'. Next day the order was signalled to the company base. These were 'very long laborious transmissions ... sometimes three to four hours to just send your airdrop request in'. Day 9 was spent looking for a suitable drop zone. 'Sometimes if you were lucky enough you stumbled on an area where a storm had gone through and big trees had fallen down so you could actually clear that away and you had a drop zone.' The other option was to cut a drop zone, 'an enormous undertaking'. Day 10 was the day of the drop.

> You'd put up your balloon at the appointed time, and you had your coded letter that you stuck in the middle of the drop zone, and you got your drop of between 12 and 15 chutes ... Now we always loved to get the New Zealanders dropping to us because they dropped from Bristol Freighters and the Bristol Freighter was slow, could fly low, very manoeuvrable, and you could be assured that at least 90 per cent or more, sometimes 100 per cent, would drop in the drop zone. If it was a Valetta or Hastings doing the drop it was not unusual that you got three or four chutes in the clearing and the rest were hung up in the trees all over the place.[157]

In January 1959, 10 Platoon, D Company, was lifted out from Fort Chabai after completing two months in the Sungei Betis area. It was replaced by the battalion's pipes and drums, and then by its regimental band, which was given a taste of jungle operations protecting friendly tribespeople around Fort Chabai.[158] One night a tiger pulled Private F. Burdett from his hammock and dragged him through the camp, its curved eye-tooth biting through Burdett's hand, which was over his face, and piercing his cheek. Fortunately Burdett was sleeping in a parachute, and the cords became tangled in the undergrowth. Burdett's cries woke a corporal who fired his sub-machine gun, causing the tiger to release his prey and vanish into the night. The seriously injured Burdett was evacuated to the British Military Hospital in Taiping by helicopter the next day.[159]

During this second year the New Zealanders were also committed to Operation JAYA, which took place around the new village of Liman Kati, situated on cultivated plains overlooked by jungle-covered limestone crags between Grik and Kuala Kangsar. They undertook 'framework operations', manning observation posts and identity-card checkpoints, mounting night ambushes, and occasionally checking that searches by police and the Home Guard at the main gate of the village were being done properly.[160] The New Zealanders disliked the 'direct policing' nature of such operations. Lieutenant Peter Hotop recalled: 'You could always feel a little bit of resentment [from the villagers] ... they had to check out in the morning and check back in at night ... when they came in with their carts from the field they were searched ... and when they went out they were searched. Our troops didn't like working around the villages for that reason.'[161] The New Zealanders always preferred to 'go bush'.

In late April, 1 NZ Regt conducted its second and last company-sized operation, Operation PITCHIT NINE. The combined company group known as ANZAC Force comprised 2 and 9 Platoon from 1 NZ Regt, and 8 Platoon and the Assault Pioneer Platoon from 3RAR. It was led by Captain Tony Mataira, who took over the position at short notice when the designated company commander became sick. Its task was to support a major Police Field Force operation by providing cut-offs and ambush positions on the Malayan side of the border to prevent guerrillas escaping from a large terrorist camp in the so-called Betong Salient inside Thailand. After a five-day march, Mataira's platoons set up a series of ambushes along the likely crossing points on the border ridges. Shooting was heard when the Police Field Force attacked the camp, and later that day a patrol of 8 Platoon 3RAR ambushed and killed an armed man just south of the border. This was the only contact. A difficult operation was followed by an equally difficult march out, during which Mataira almost drowned in the flooded Grik River. Tragedy was averted by the quick intervention of Privates P. Morehu and H. K. Hingston, who pulled the struggling Mataira out as he was in danger of being swept away.[162] Morrison met the force when they came out of the jungle, 'tired and worn ... One of the dog handlers was actually carrying his dog because it had cut its paws on sharp bamboo stakes ... I wrote out a citation for a Military Cross for Mataira ... [but] it was converted to an MBE.'[163]

The wind-down in counter-insurgency operations enabled 28th Commonwealth Infantry Brigade to give some attention to training for its primary role in conventional warfare as part of 17th Gurkha Division.[164] Conventional training was carried out by half the battalion at a time. In August 1959, A and B Company completed their training and were replaced by C and D Company. A Company then replaced C Company on operations in the Sungei Belum area, while B Company took over on Operation JAYA. Elements of D Company continued the liaison duties at Fort Chabai, and then patrolled out to Fort Kemar before returning to Chabai at the end of the month. A party of 24 Territorial officers and NCOs was attached for three months' training, and at the end of August the first elements of 2 NZ Regt's advance party arrived.[165] Planning for the location and training of the battalion once counter-guerrilla operations ceased was also under way. In June 1958, Morrison attended the laying of the foundation stone at the site of the proposed 28 Commonwealth Brigade 'Malacca Cantonment', north of Malacca; it was anticipated that the brigade would move to Bukit Terendak in late 1961.

In October 1959 the battalion was committed to Operation BAMBOO in the jungle east of Grik. Its last incident occurred on 27 October, when Corporal Peter Rutledge's patrol fired on an approaching figure, only to find to their horror that they had killed their Iban tracker, Private Kumpang Anak Tinngi, who had left the perimeter without their knowledge.[166] In a cruel irony, Rutledge now had the battalion's first and last kills.

On 31 October the battalion, apart from a small training element working with 2 NZ Regt's advance party, was withdrawn from operations in preparation for its departure from Malaya. On 9 November, at a farewell parade on the Taiping Padang, the Acting Prime Minister of Malaya, Tun Abdul Razak, presented the battalion with a kris in appreciation of its efforts. Major-General J. A. R. Robertson, GOC 17th Gurkha Division, recorded that 1 New Zealand Regiment had

> operated against the terrorists in the jungles of Perak continuously since you joined the Commonwealth Brigade, and in doing so have directly eliminated 14 terrorists. In addition you have made a speciality of patrols of long duration which were most successful in the fight to release the aborigines from terrorist domination, and not only led to the surrender of 11 terrorists in the Fort Legap area last year, but gained the respect and confidence of the aborigines themselves.[167]

1 NZ Regt had made a small but significant contribution during 1958, at the tail end of the Emergency. It then shared the frustrations of most 28 Commonwealth Brigade units during 1959, mounting countless patrols against a vanished

enemy after the MRLA withdrew across the Thai border. Nonetheless, it had maintained the professionalism developed during its busy first year of operations. Most platoons conducted patrol after patrol without seeing a guerrilla. but those who did showed a high standard of junior leadership and tactical skill. Their performance confirmed New Zealanders' aptitude for this mode of warfare. In many ways Morrison's battalion was never a battalion at all, but rather a collection of platoons that rarely saw each other during two years of active service. What made it a battalion was the personality of Morrison himself.

It was also a 'pioneering' battalion in that it was New Zealand's first Regular unit. This inexperience showed in its administration, and the battalions that followed learned from its mistakes. For the New Zealand Army it marked a transition from an army consisting of cadre instructors for the Territorial Force to one made up of increasingly professional Regular soldiers. Lieutenant Owen Mann reflected: 'when you look back on it, [1 NZ Regt] did a damn good job, but it was the first one up, and most of us only remember the good things, and there's some awful bad things about it ... but having said all that, it was something I would never have missed.'[168] The battalion's two-year tour in Malaya also marked New Zealand's acceptance of a long-term commitment to South-East Asia following the Nash government's formal association with the Anglo-Malayan Defence Agreement.[169]

The battalion sailed from Penang on the SS *Captain Cook* on 28 November 1959. Lieutenant 'Scotty' Gordon remembered: 'it was late in the afternoon and the sun was going down and I was standing by the CO, Colonel Morrison, and he started to quote a bit of Kipling about the troopships on the tide, and it really was as if we were part of the old trooping days of the British Army, though indeed it was the very end.'[170] But it was not the end. For New Zealand, it was merely the end of the beginning.

# 6

# INTERLUDE: SEATO COMMITMENTS, 1960–64

> The emphasis is now changing to making the formation fit for larger operations anywhere in South East Asia, where we are the Strategic Reserve for the Commonwealth.[1]
>
> BRIGADIER H. J. MOGG,
> COMMANDER 28TH COMMONWEALTH BRIGADE

Although most of the Army's activities within the Commonwealth Strategic Reserve were responses to the Malayan Emergency, the government never forgot that the original intention of the Reserve was to back up SEATO and deter any expansion by communist China. The reorganisation of the Army in New Zealand was geared to forming a Regular brigade group able to meet Cold War commitments in South-East Asia. As the Malayan Emergency wound down, some New Zealanders also found themselves deployed in Thailand.

## Aitken's Second Battalion, New Zealand Regiment, 1959–61

The 2nd Battalion, New Zealand Regiment (2 NZ Regt), commanded by Lieutenant-Colonel D. J. Aitken, was formed in Waiouru Military Camp at the end of 1958 to prepare to replace 1 NZ Regt in Malaya in November 1959. Jock Aitken had a distinguished Second World War record, serving with the Long Range Desert Group in North Africa, Yugoslavia and Albania. His posting to Japan with J Force after the war as second-in-command of 27 Battalion had shown him the difficulties faced by garrison battalions.

> [In Japan] the platoon commanders and some others were not facing up to the needs of an occupation force to have a tight control of people and to do it in a sensible way. So I knew that you had to take steps to see that you didn't have that. Some of the chaps would say to me from time to time perhaps I went a little much the other way but I did it deliberately, and then after the sharp period, people settled down and knew the form ... We had very few disciplinary problems.[2]

Like its predecessor, 2 NZ Regt was recruited throughout New Zealand. The South Island companies trained at Burnham, the North Island companies at Papakura, and the Headquarters Company, Support Company and Battalion Headquarters at Waiouru. The battalion was concentrated in Burnham in July 1959, and 'started corps training followed by sub-unit and unit training and it culminated in a major exercise before sailing for Malaya'.[3]

As with Morrison's battalion, men joined for a wide range of reasons and competed keenly to get away to Malaya. Rex Harris was a qualified butcher from Pokeno and a staff sergeant in the Territorial Force. He had always wanted to join the Army, but his father had refused to consent to him serving in Korea. Now Harris 'was one of the lucky ones that got selected to go because, if I remember the numbers, there was something like 1,400 men to be selected for this battalion. And every Saturday when we had a battalion parade guys were taken off the parade ground and you never saw them again. They just handed their gear in and left.'[4] Like Morrison before him, Aitken was allowed to pick his adjutant, Captain R. G. Williams, his quartermaster, Captain N. M. Laing, and his RSM, WO1 J. Allan.

> I knew exactly who I wanted ... We got a few territorial officers, some very good ones. Bob Burt was one of them. Lots of young officers who were just out of Duntroon and Portsea. They of course leapt at the opportunity to get a platoon. I think we had 1,100 soldiers; we were oversupplied, and one of the difficult jobs that had to be done then was to sort them out. I think we were allowed 750 in those days, and we had to leave the rest in a big company called 'E' Company behind—'Evil' Company.[5]

Aitken set high standards. His adjutant, Captain Rob Williams, who had served in Malaya with 1FIR, recalled that 'he was a very tough CO on his company commanders and I heard one or two of them say over the years, "Very little of the carrot and a lot of the stick"; and he was quite clear about what he wanted in terms of discipline ... when people failed, they were fired ... he was quite ruthless.'[6] Because of the surplus of men, Aitken had the necessary latitude during selection and training to build up the battalion with officers and soldiers who met his criteria and understood the standards he expected.

The formation of 2 NZ Regt followed the election in 1957 of the third Labour government and the ending of compulsory military training, which saw the Territorials' strength plummet from 28,000 to some 7,000 volunteers. Under the ANZAM agreement, New Zealand remained committed to sending an 18,000-strong division to South-East Asia in the event of global war, but the organisation needed to achieve and maintain this commitment no longer existed.[7] The 1958 Defence Review led to a reorganisation of the Army; a Regular Brigade Group was formed as a 'force in being' to meet both limited and Cold War commitments to South-East Asia. This operational brigade would be supported by a static Regular Force and a reduced volunteer Territorial Force. The Regular Brigade was to be constantly available for service; one of its battalion would be deployed overseas at all times as part of the Commonwealth Strategic Reserve. The static Regular Force was to 'command, administer and equip the Army as a whole, and ... mobilise such portions of it as and when circumstances may require'. Individuals would play roles in both aspects of the Regular Force.[8]

The 4th Infantry Brigade Group, as it was named, was organised along the lines of a standard British infantry brigade group plus an SAS squadron, which brought its total strength to 5,619 personnel. In peacetime it was to be deployed as four regimental 'combat teams' located at Papakura, Waiouru, Linton, and Burnham.[9] To place the Army on a war footing, Territorials would provide reserves of trained officers and NCOs, and additional formations if the conflict escalated. With Kim Morrison as its nominated commander, 4th Infantry Brigade Group was to be at one-third strength by 1 April 1960, two-thirds strength by 1 April 1961, and full strength by 1 April 1962.[10] 1 NZ Regt would return to Burnham, and a cadre for 3 NZ Regt was established at Waiouru. The Chief of General Staff, Major-General Stephen Weir, anticipated that the brigade's formation would see New Zealand's contribution to the Commonwealth Strategic Reserve expanded to include an artillery battery and an engineer troop.

The 1958 Defence Review was a radical step for the New Zealand Army. It accepted that while the Territorial division still existed on paper, New Zealand's military contribution to future conflicts in South-East Asia was likely to be no larger than a brigade based on Regular forces. This would inevitably serve within a Commonwealth division, surrendering the concept of a national force of at least divisional size which had been the sine qua non for New Zealand expeditionary force planning since the First World War. In its structure, 4th Infantry Brigade Group anticipated the shape of the New Zealand Army at the end of the twentieth century. It also resurrected the SAS, which was re-formed in Papakura Camp under the command of Captain John Mace, with the newly commissioned Second Lieutenant David Ogilvy instrumental in raising and training its first troop.[11]

Despite a major recruiting effort, a Regular brigade was never raised. 1 NZ Regt returned to Burnham and the first company of 3 NZ Regt was raised in Waiouru, but sufficient recruits were not attracted. New Zealand's balance of payments crisis caused growing doubts about increasing defence expenditure. Initially, all that could be provided was the battalion in Malaya, plus the first-line reinforcement needed to bring it up to war strength. The Territorial Force was now so reduced as to be ineffective, with barely enough volunteers in the first 12 months to replace those soldiers who were leaving. However, there was time to solve this problem: the 4th Infantry Brigade Group was not intended to be at full strength and able to meet New Zealand's ANZAM commitments until 1962.[12]

This was the backdrop when 2 NZ Regt sailed from New Zealand on SS *Captain Cook* on 27 October 1959. The battalion disembarked at Penang and travelled to Taiping by train; as they got out, Morrison's battalion entered the carriages from the other side—'we never saw them'.[13] Rather than disperse the unit in company-size camps, as had been the policy with 1 NZ Regt, Aitken concentrated his battalion in Sobraon Camp in Taiping. 'When we got there the Emergency was on its very last legs. I didn't like to see a battalion, especially a new battalion, outside my direct control. So one of the first things I did was to bring all the companies back into Sobraon Camp where the machinery of control could be exercised as I wanted it to be.'[14] The battalion's initial training in the hills around Taiping was supervised by Lieutenant Huia Woods, who had stayed on from 1 NZ Regt. 'We did immediate ambush drills, contact front, contact rear, contact side or the flanks. All sorts of things ... I believe [it] was probably the most intense and best training that I have ever done.'[15] There were the usual administrative hiccups; 17th Gurkha Division had to issue an instruction that Bergen packs and large-size boots be withdrawn from all units in Malaya for issue to 2 NZ Regt personnel.[16]

In his directive for 1960, Brigadier John Mogg stated that 28th Commonwealth Brigade would continue to be employed in Emergency operations until accommodation in the new camp at Bukit Terendak was ready for occupation. There was to be no relaxation of the pressure on the MRLA.[17] After Ipoh District was declared a White Area on 14 January 1960, operations shifted north into the inaccessible reaches of the upper Perak River. This was the home of the 12th Regiment Asal, which had been reduced to an estimated 50 guerrillas and was now the target of 28th Commonwealth Brigade during Operation BAMBOO. The operational area of 2 NZ Regt was around Fort Chabai on the border between Perak and Kelantan. Here the battalion had under its command the garrisons of Fort Kemar and Fort Chabai, including two platoons of 7 Police Field Force at Fort Chabai. Battalion Headquarters remained in Taiping, and each company was given its own area of operations: Major W. L. Brown's A Company was centred on Fort Chabai, Major Brian Poananga's B Company on the mouth of the Kuala Ringat, Major Joe Manning's C Company on the mouth of the Kuala Lanap, and Major John Morris's D Company on Fort Kemar. Each company initially deployed with two platoons after Aitken directed that two-thirds of each company's strength should be in the jungle at all times. Platoons were rotated in to maintain contact with local tribespeople. In contrast to Morrison's battalion, company headquarters also deployed into the jungle, each accompanied by both a field assistant from the Department of Aborigines and a section of the Senoi Pra'ak.[18]

The New Zealanders were given the tasks of winning over the indigenous population and eliminating the remaining groups of 12th Regiment Asal. One of the key targets was Kerinching,[19] the headman of the Ulu Sungei Temenggor since 1954, whose daughter was married to Ah Soo Chye, the leader of the 12th Regiment Asal. Kerinching's experience epitomised the position of the Orang Asli during the Emergency as a people used and threatened by two opposing sides. Labelled a guerrilla supporter since 1948, Kerinching had twice tried to defect to the security forces. On the first occasion he was treated roughly and escaped back into the jungle. On the second occasion, in 1955, he was flown to Ipoh, interrogated and given a reward of $3,000. On his return to Fort Kemar, the Chinese inspector in charge demanded $1,000 to protect him from Special Branch at Ipoh, who he claimed were likely to hang him at any time. Inevitably, when the Ipoh Director of Special Branch next asked Kerinching to come in for interrogation, he fled back to the guerrillas.[20] Although both Special Branch and the Protector of Aborigines were convinced that Kerinching would not surrender, the New Zealanders were directed to take him alive if possible.[21]

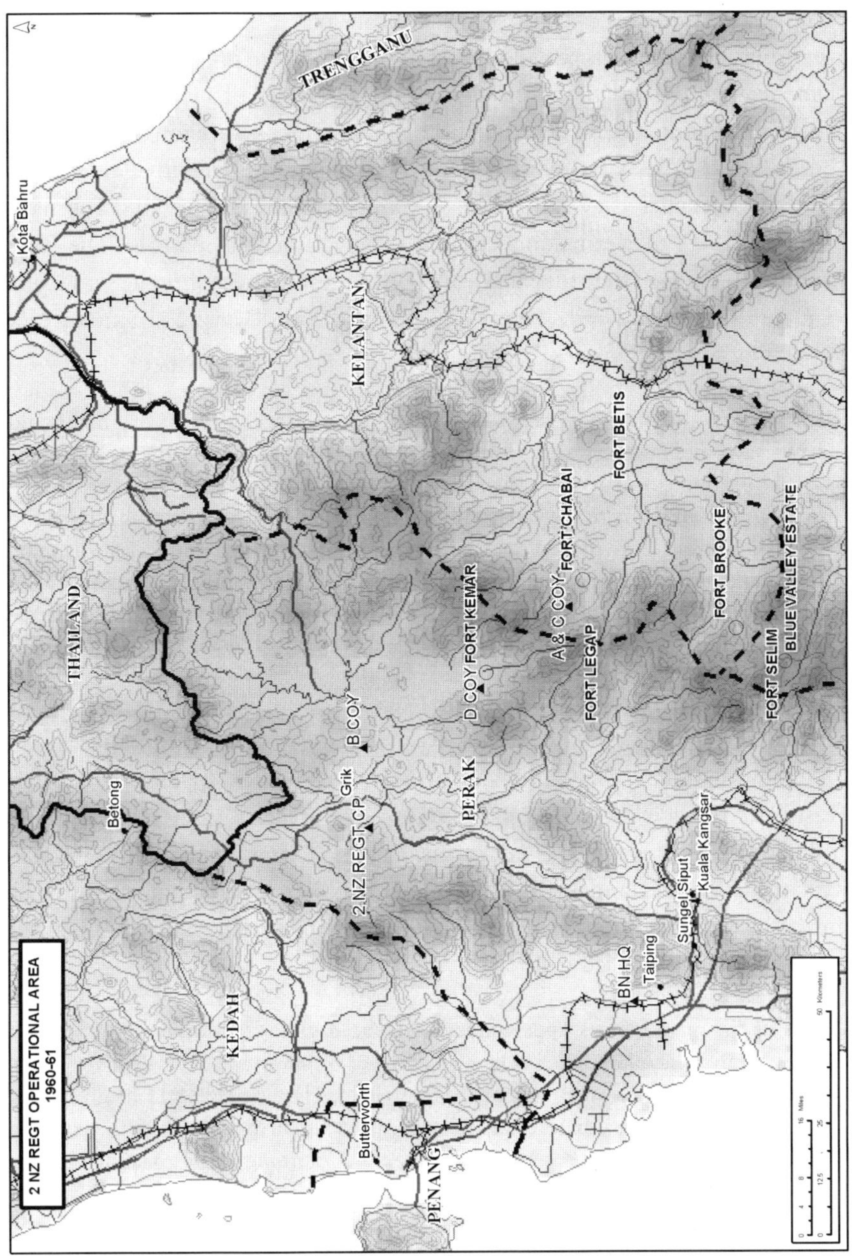


**Map 5** Operational area of 2 NZ Regt 1960–61

As with the New Zealand SAS Squadron and 1 NZ Regt before them, everything depended on gaining the trust and goodwill of the tribespeople. B Company established that Kerinching and about six of his followers were living on the Sungei Krim near 'Awai's Ladang'. Tracks were found in the area and then lost. The battalion's first success came when Angah Chai, a listed guerrilla, surrendered to 2 Platoon, A Company.[22] In January and February 1960, members of Kerinching's family met D Company patrols. The New Zealanders assessed that they had come out to test the reception he was likely to get if he surrendered. Second Lieutenant Rod Dearing's platoon met Kerinching's brother, Regek:

> we eventually managed to get an undertaking from Regek that his brother would be at such and such a spot and if we sent a party over there to meet him ... he would negotiate his surrender. Well this was splendid news. Here we were on the first operation and here we were with the first smell of success, it was almost too good to be true ... we moved out at the crack of dawn with the mists overhanging the jungle, up to the appointed rendezvous point and of course no one was there. There [were] signs of a camp, and the fire had been lit the previous night. We realised that we were being watched and that there was no way that Regek's brother was going to give himself up if there was any thought or any hint that he may have been in any danger.[23]

At the end of the month, Dearing's platoon was replaced by Lieutenant Alan Fraser's 11 Platoon. No restraints were placed on Regek's group, who were fed and allowed to move in and out of the area, and established a close rapport with the New Zealanders. Fraser's experience confirmed that of Burrows during his time with Uda in 1956, and also what Sergeant Noel Jamieson of 1 NZ Regt had practised in 1958.

> One of the main factors appreciated by the aborigine is, in my mind, a basis of being treated as equals and NOT as a backward or inferior race. They love to take part in anything for a laugh and are eager to help. They should NOT be given gifts as a reward for doing things, or assisting us. They will help soldiers for the pleasure of being useful, and appreciate cigarettes, food, clothing etc if given at random times, and NO special significance attached to the giving. They will quickly retire into their shell if spoken to harshly, and maximum and constant care should be taken at all times when conversing with them NOT to hurt their feelings.[24]

Finally, at 3 p.m. on 25 February 1960, Kerinching and eight others walked into Fraser's camp. 'Alan Fraser was lying on his bunk in his parachute hammock and this individual came in and sort of saluted the communist salute and they sat down and had a cup of tea and that was that.'[25] Special Branch assessed that as Kerinching had at last sought government protection the local MRLA groups might well have moved north across the border into Thailand.[26] This was confirmed when Kerinching told Special Branch that he had been waiting for an opportunity to surrender but could not do so while Ah Soo Chye was living with him. Once this group had withdrawn to Thailand, he had come in.[27] Kerinching's surrender was a major success, and the New Zealand achievement was praised by all.[28] Aitken was more matter-of-fact. 'The newspaper reports and sometimes the service reports tend to make a drama out of what is just a very ordinary and almost casual occasion ... It had significance of a local political nature ... but it was of very, very little military significance.'[29]

It was to be battalion's only success in two years of jungle operations because of the scarcity of their target. The enemy had moved north, and while they would occasionally move back or through the area, there was little for the New Zealanders to find.

> We arrived at a time when all the action was over, there wasn't a soul there, and the CTs that we were meant to be finding and destroying were, in fact, ghosts of the past. They were long gone and we were, I suppose, an insurance policy that was being put into effect after the event ... But of course we were doing our job in isolating the deep jungle away from the townships, and that sort of thing, but it did make [it difficult] after a while when we realised that there were no more Kerinchings ... and there were no CTs around at all.[30]

On 4 August 1960, A Company, 2 NZ Regt, took part in the victory parade in Kuala Lumpur marking the end of the Emergency. Nonetheless, it was operations as usual for 28th Commonwealth Brigade, and these were 'no less arduous than during the Emergency; all the more credit therefore to those who continue to shoulder it without much publicity or visible results'.[31]

The end of the Emergency on 31 July 1960 raised serious questions about the ongoing involvement of Commonwealth forces. Military circles saw this as very much a political decision, a change from '"emergency operations" into what will probably be termed "border operations"'.[32] A border security area was set up, extending from coast to coast across the northern parts of Perlis, Kedah, Perak and Kelantan. This area became the responsibility of the Border Security Council, chaired by the Prime Minister and comprising principal Cabinet ministers, the Commissioner of Police and the service heads, with the

Chief of the Armed Forces Staff as Director of Border Security. The Commonwealth representatives were the General Officer Commanding 17th Gurkha Division in his capacity as Commander Overseas Commonwealth Land Forces, and the Air Officer Commanding No. 224 Group RAF, plus naval representation as required.[33] A Border Security Executive Committee was established to supervise the general direction of the campaign, with an operations subcommittee providing day-to-day co-ordination.[34] Steps were also taken to improve co-operation with the Thai authorities, who had been preoccupied with events in their northern provinces and had paid little attention to the situation on the Malay border. This continued to be the case, despite an agreement between Thailand and Malaya to co-ordinate anti-terrorist operations on the border.[35] The Malayan Police Field Force and the Thai Border Police Task Force were established for this purpose, as were joint operations centres at Alor Setar in Malaya and Sonkhla in Thailand.[36]

During 1960, 28th Commonwealth Brigade's involvement in Operation BAMBOO continued.[37] The key to success had been effective intelligence, but this was now lacking. A hard core of some 600 guerrillas was known to be encamped across the Thai border, and it was feared that if operations were ended prematurely there would be a complete intelligence 'blackout'.[38] Mountains and jungle made the Thai sanctuary areas impossible to close off, and so border surveillance was needed to prevent MRLA forces moving south into Malaya.[39]

For 2 NZ Regt it was business as usual as patrols sweated their way through the 'ulu' of northern Perak. Captain Rob Williams, who now commanded C Company, believed that on 'an operational basis it had all become a bit pointless'.[40] In the platoons the patrolling routine continued. Although there were no contacts, soldiers' awareness that these could occur at any time created stresses. Rex Harris, now a platoon sergeant, remembered that:

> [We] came across a number of old enemy camps and stuff like that which were always reported. Occasionally your sixth sense would tell you that things were a little bit different. I can recall once where a sentry told me that he thought someone was out in front of the position. We never saw anybody but you certainly had that feeling that there was something strange out there ... It might have been a twig, a bit of movement, that you couldn't define but it was there.[41]

Keeping men up to the mark when it seemed the enemy had gone placed great demands on the junior NCOs. 'I was a private in the same platoon that

I was a platoon sergeant [in] and it was very hard to [cross] the gap ... You had to be a bastard at times.'[42] Guerrilla contacts or not, the jungle took its toll. On 10 December 1960, Private Toma Solia, a Territorial signaller from Wellington attached to the battalion, was drowned when the raft he was travelling on with two other soldiers went out of control in the fast-running Perak River, hit a tree and capsized. Solia's body was recovered on 13 December, and buried in the Taiping Cemetery next day.[43]

When soldiers came out of the bush they went on leave in either Taiping or Ipoh.[44] As with their predecessors, venereal disease was a major concern.[45] Aitken saw this as a disciplinary problem which he took several steps to combat. He pulled his company commanders out of the bush and insisted that they base themselves in Taiping, where, he believed, control had slipped. 'This was evidenced by the increasing VD rate, and incidence of AWOL and general air of looseness becoming apparent.'[46] The platoons with the highest VD rates were identified on a notice board outside Battalion Headquarters, and the platoon commanders were interviewed by the CO to establish the reasons. However, the publication of VD statistics was stopped after proving counterproductive; in some circles topping the list was considered an achievement![47]

VD was an ongoing problem countered by education and the issuing of prophylactics to soldiers going on leave. In June 1960, Aitken's unit had its first case of primary syphilis, and the medical officer reported that 40 per cent of those reporting with venereal disease 'have had one or more previous infections since being in MALAYA'. It also appeared that many soldiers were seeking treatment from local civilian practitioners. 'In all cases where disease occurs proper preventative measures have not been taken. The main reasons for not taking preventative measures seem to be drunkenness and stupidity.'[48] While the problem was not confined to New Zealand soldiers, it was a major concern for all three services in Malaya.[49]

The chaplains attached to the battalion played an important role in informing the CO about morale among soldiers and their families. The six-monthly visits to Singapore by chaplains from New Zealand provided similar feedback to the RNZAF. The RNZN relied on occasional tours by New Zealand chaplains serving in Malaya with the New Zealand battalions, or RNZN chaplains based in New Zealand.[50] Aitken's battalion experienced the first marriages between soldiers and local women. It became New Zealand policy to require at least six months to elapse between the application to marry and permission being granted; meanwhile, the bride-to-be was subjected to health and security checks. The system was designed to ensure a 'cooling period' by deliberately imposing as much bureaucratic red tape as possible. Often approval would be delayed until the soldier had returned to New Zealand, so he would have to make his own arrangements to return to Malaya to marry.[51] Fourteen marriages were reported, all of them just before 2 NZ Regt returned to New Zealand.[52]

The formal end of the Emergency brought an end to the awarding of the Malaya Clasp with the General Service Medal (1918). There was no longer any tangible recognition for reinforcements joining the battalion, even though operations continued and soldiers posted to the unit were still classed as being on active service. This was not an issue for 2 NZ Regt, but became a major concern for Pearce's 1 NZ Regt, which replaced it at the end of 1961.[53]

Throughout 1961 2 NZ Regt continued its commitment to Operation BAMBOO by building a jeep road along the valley of the Sungei Perak between Grik and Kampong Temengor. This was a major engineering effort involving the construction of some 60 timber bridges, culverts and fords along 40 miles of track. Although intended to support operations, this proved to be of greater value to the rural development programme in the area. For the New Zealanders, their second year became a time of transition from full-time jungle operations to peacetime garrison duties and a cycle of operations and training. From 1961, more time was spent training 'to fight a limited war with a nuclear threat against a first class ASIAN Enemy'.[54]

## ANZAM and SEATO

On 1 September 1960, after finishing his appointment as Chief of General Staff, Major-General Sir Stephen Weir was appointed chief military adviser to the Labour government. This was New Zealand's first tentative step towards establishing an integrated defence headquarters. The government was aware that important decisions needed to be made on the divisional concept, the maintenance of the cruiser standard, and the replacement of aircraft. Weir became responsible for advising 'on military matters having external implications'.[55] Growing doubts among SEATO's Asian members about the commitment of the United States and the United Kingdom to the Treaty had led to the opening of a SEATO Military Planning Office in Bangkok in March 1957, with Brigadier L. W. Thornton as its first Chief of Military Planning. By the early 1960s, contingency planning had reached the stage that member countries were asked to declare the forces they would make available under specific plans. Despite continuing British and American reservations, the designated elements eventually included the Commonwealth Strategic Reserve, the United States Task Force 116 stationed in Okinawa, and the First Philippine Combat Battalion. SEATO members were also asked how these bodies would be reinforced if the situation deteriorated.[56]

The New Zealand government regarded the SEATO alliance as the main channel through which it could contribute to South-East Asia in both war and peace. The ANZAM agreement became the vehicle for making that contribution, and it was through ANZAM that New Zealand made its specific commitments to the defence of South-East Asia. Both Australia and New Zealand were well aware that the United Kingdom was unhappy about both its exclusion from ANZUS and the wider commitment to South-East Asia envisaged under SEATO.[57] Despite the running down of British forces, and the fact that its interests differed from those of Australia and New Zealand, the United Kingdom continued to be the principal partner in Commonwealth defence planning for South-East Asia. 'Both economically and politically, Malaya ... overshadows in the United Kingdom view the broader security problem which concerns Australia and New Zealand.'[58] The United Kingdom saw ANZAM as important because of its Malayan focus, but it also recognised that this was a convenient way of fulfilling a limited SEATO commitment, particularly as it was on the latter grounds that Australasian involvement in ANZAM was predicated.[59] The vital importance of the United States to New Zealand's security was recognised; this country deliberately strengthened its links with the superpower both within SEATO and through ANZUS. It also sought 'special arrangements with the United States to meet the problems with which New Zealand will be faced in re-equipping her forces on the basis of compatibility in SEATO';[60] however, the potential for this was limited by the reality that 28th Commonwealth Brigade was organised on British lines with British equipment. Australia and New Zealand continued to walk a tightrope between the differing security perceptions of the United States and the United Kingdom.

New Zealand desperately wanted both ANZAM and ANZUS to work. On the military side,

> ANZUS has tended to be overshadowed by the wider based and more detailed planning now taking place under SEATO. The real importance of ANZUS, however, remains in the ability of the three members to discuss privately problems

> which they could not introduce in an eight-power body such as SEATO. This does not mean that ANZUS is any sort of 'inner circle' group controlling the policies of SEATO—indeed this is a development that the Americans have hitherto refused to envisage—but it does mean that New Zealand is able through ANZUS to obtain an insight into American defence thinking to a degree not possible through SEATO or other channels.[61]

New Zealand's position was that there was 'no question of making any sort of "choice" between associations with the United Kingdom or the United States. It is our belief that within the broad framework of SEATO, supplemented by the special relationships of ANZAM and ANZUS, the interests of the four countries in the security of the South East Asian area can be properly met.'[62]

The New Zealand battalion's transition from counter-insurgency operations to garrison duties and training for its SEATO role took place against the background of a series of crises in Laos between 1958 and 1962. The increasing success of the North Vietnamese-backed Pathet Lao against right-wing governments supported by the United States and SEATO raised the possibility of intervention in Laos. In 1959 the New Zealand Prime Minister, Walter Nash, spoke out strongly against committing forces to Laos.[63] There was another critically important issue. As Malaya was not a member of SEATO, its government would not allow the Commonwealth Reserve to deploy directly from its bases in Malaya to Laos or Thailand. Tunku Abdul Rahman was conscious that elements within his ruling Alliance Party opposed the presence of foreign troops in Malaya. With an election approaching, he was also concerned at press reports about a 'fire brigade' of Commonwealth forces poised to deal with 'hot spots such as Laos'.[64] Serious doubts about the Reserve's stationing in Malaya now arose. As a compromise, Rahman agreed to the deployment of elements of the Commonwealth Strategic Reserve, providing this occurred via a third country such as Singapore.[65] This face-saving solution allowed the Malayan government to 'meet our position in substance while preserving the appearance of non-involvement in SEATO military activities'.[66]

These events highlighted the 'fundamental fact that whole position of Strategic Reserve in Federation depends ultimately on Malayan goodwill, regardless of provisions of 1957 Defence Agreement'.[67] While this had little immediate impact on the New Zealand battalion, there were longer-term implications. In 1960 the National Party led by Keith Holyoake was returned to power in the face of a balance of payments crisis involving a lack of overseas funds. The new Prime Minister, despite being Minister of External Affairs, was not much interested in foreign policy and had a deep-seated distrust of the military. New Zealand's defence spending thus came under intense scrutiny at the same time as political factors in Malaya brought into question the stationing of Commonwealth forces there after 1964.[68]

In 1961 a new crisis erupted in Laos, and the Pathet Lao seemed likely to gain complete control of the country. Many South-East Asian countries saw this as a test for SEATO.[69] The United Kingdom's position was that it would support a United States commitment of military forces if no ceasefire was agreed to. The Secretary of State for the Colonies reported that, if it were necessary, Rahman would 'make no objection to the dispatch of British or Commonwealth troops from Malaya direct to the scene of hostilities provided that his country and in particular his airfields were not used as a base for active military operations'.[70] New Zealand sought a political solution to the crisis but was prepared to carry out its military obligations under SEATO Plan 5, the basis of planning for intervention in Laos.[71] In 1959 it had been agreed that the initial Commonwealth response would be a British battalion with a New Zealand rifle company and an Australian element attached. With Holyoake's agreement, this remained the basis for planning in 1961.[72]

The 28th Commonwealth Brigade was now commanded by an Australian, Brigadier F. G. Hassett, who had succeeded Mogg in November 1960.[73] The brigade had been designated Task Force BRAVO of the SEATO Strategic Reserve, and ANZAM Plan No. 1 (BUCKRAM) had been drafted for its operational deployment by air and sea to central and southern Laos, after staging through Singapore.[74] When the Laotian crisis erupted, units were mobilised on Exercise ALMOND, which concentrated the brigade as a preliminary to deploying it on BUCKRAM. As a precautionary measure the 1/3 East Anglians were moved to Singapore, and the Australian and New Zealand battalions concentrated at the unfinished Commonwealth Camp at Bukit Terendak. This occurred just as the Australasian battalions were involved in a changeover in northern Perak, where they were replaced on operations by Malayan forces. Neither the GOC Federation Armed Forces, Lieutenant-General Sir Rodney Moore, or Rahman had been informed in advance, and Rahman was understandably annoyed.[75] The New Zealand High Commissioners in Singapore and Kuala Lumpur had also not been informed and were equally annoyed.[76] The situation within the battalions was chaotic: 'at that stage, we really hadn't got started [on] the planning system ... We were sort of organising it as we ran.' To the New Zealanders' disappointment, nothing eventuated. The British government halted the redeployment of the East Anglians, and after a period the brigade stood down. It was obvious to Aitken by the time his battalion deployed to Terendak that no operational deployment was likely. This was 'a great disappointment, because the battalion [in an operational sense] really was a good machine by that time'.[77]

The Laotian scare resulted in a series of battalion and brigade exercises during 1961 to prepare the brigade for its SEATO role. Exercises BLUE ANGEL in April and TRINITY ANGEL in July and August practised air deployment. The lack of transport aircraft was ingeniously compensated for.

> Full-scale outlines of aircraft were laid in white tape on sports fields; the stripped-down vehicles—or requisite number of passengers—were driven into the taped 'aircraft' and loading and lashing drills were performed. Once completed to the satisfaction of the Unit Emplanement Officer, the 'load' (or 'chalk') then travelled by road to the designated 'landing field' where another taped outline had been prepared. The arriving vehicles drew into the taped 'aircraft' and the time of 'landing' was noted; the vehicles were unlashed, unloaded and driven away.[78]

The start of brigade-level training saw battalions working more closely with each other than before. 'The Australians had invited us over a couple of times but I guess one has to say we didn't turn ourselves inside out to see a lot of the other battalions ... It was only when we started to function at the formation level that we started to get together.'[79]

On 31 October 1961, 2 NZ Regt was withdrawn from operations. Over two years it had moved from jungle counter-insurgency operations to garrison duties and training for a SEATO contingency role. The latter roles were taken on under Lieutenant-Colonel L. A. Pearce by its successor, 1 NZ Regt, which moved into Terendak Cantonment together with the rest of 28th Commonwealth Brigade. Aitken's 2 NZ Regt was to be the only battalion to serve under that title in Malaya. On coming to power, the new National government had accepted the need for 'forces in being', as expressed in the 1958 Defence Review and implemented by the Labour administration; however, it decided that a full Regular brigade was too expensive, given New Zealand's parlous financial situation.[80] The cuts announced in the 1961 Defence Review were shared among all three services. They were the subject of bitter debate in the Chiefs of Staff Committee, where there was strong disagreement about priorities. The Chief of Air Staff, Air Vice-Marshal Calder, claimed there was too great an emphasis on the Army at the expense of the other two services.

No. 75 (Canberra) Squadron had given up its leased Canberras and returned to New Zealand, reducing the RNZAF to one Canberra squadron; and the frigate replacement programme had again been deferred.[81]

The far-sighted experiment with an all-Regular Army brigade ended; the Regular Force was reduced to the battalion in Malaya and its replacement battalion in New Zealand. A selective National Service scheme was introduced to provide the balance of a brigade plus logistic support group that could be deployed to meet New Zealand's SEATO commitments. The brigade's Regular Force component would be built up over five years to a strength of 3,000. In the same period, the Territorial Force would grow to an effective strength of 10,000 through the National Service scheme, which required every male to register in his twentieth year for an annual ballot.

> Those selected will then undergo medical examination, and allowing for a system of appeals and deferments, the balance (approximately 2,000 per year) will be inducted into the Army for 14 weeks of whole-time training during the first year, then posted to the Territorial Force for a period of three years part-time service and a further three years on the Reserve, with no liability for training.[82]

New Zealand also withdrew its commitment to provide a division of 23,000 men for South-East Asia, a move that simply reflected the reality the New Zealand Army had faced since 1958.[83] Just as the end of compulsory military training destroyed the divisional foundation built during the 1950s, the changes wrought by the 1961 Defence Review ensured that New Zealand would have a Regular battalion—but little else—with which to meet its ground commitments in South-East Asia during the 1960s.[84]

Nevertheless, the battalion's tour in Malaya had seen the emergence of a professional infantry soldier skilled in the techniques of jungle warfare. The basis of this expertise was the growing pool of experienced NCOs and warrant officers. Selected soldiers and junior NCOs returning to New Zealand with 2 NZ Regt were earmarked to return to Malaya with the regiment on its next scheduled tour in 1963. The Army General Staff was determined to rotate as many NCOs as possible through the battalion in Malaya to build up the breadth of experience in the Army. Similarly, the emphasis changed from recruiting personnel for a tour of duty in Malaya to recruiting career soldiers for three-, four- or five-year engagements in the Regular Force. The depth of talent this provided was seen for the first time in Pearce's 1 NZ Regt in 1961, and reflected widely by the warrant officers and NCOs of Gurr's 1 NZ Regt in

1963. One example was Rangi ('Sam') Christie, who served with D Company in Morrison's battalion, then with Pearce's battalion, and returned in Brooke's battalion in 1967–69. He served in Vietnam with V3 Company, and returned to Vietnam as a staff sergeant with the New Zealand Army Training Team in 1972. Prominent in battalion rugby and tug-of-war teams and the Maori concert party, Christie spent much of his Army career rotating between the battalion's depot at Burnham and South-East Asia in a pattern common to many of the Regular soldiers of his generation.[85]

This period also saw changes in counter-insurgency training in both Malaya and New Zealand. From 1961, this emphasised the New Zealand Army fighting an irregular war in South Vietnam, Thailand or Laos against an enemy patterned on the Viet Cong. During the tour of Pearce's 1 NZ Regt in Malaya, a highly sophisticated defended village was built using Viet Minh methods in the training area within Terendak Camp. One man who strongly influenced this change in New Zealand was Lieutenant-Colonel John ('Blackie') Burns, Commandant Army Schools in Waiouru from 1960 to 1964. Under his leadership, war in Indo-China became a subject for study in Army Schools. Ian Thorpe remembered Burns as 'a man of great vision who knew better than all others how to get the best out of his people'.[86] Burns was supported by a talented team of chief instructors at the various schools, including Major John Morris at Tactical School, Major Ian Thorpe at the School of Infantry, and Major Alf Voss at Recruit Training Depot. The changes he introduced had an impact throughout the Army, and while some units were slow to adapt or even actively resisted them, most accepted the challenge. 'The Army at large was moving through the schools and everyone was being indoctrinated in the system.'[87] This approach was paralleled by the training in Malaya, which anticipated the commitment of a New Zealand battalion to operations against a Vietnamese enemy in Indo-China. This became the primary focus for New Zealand battalion commanders throughout the 1960s.

## Pearce's First Battalion, New Zealand Regiment, 1961–63

1 NZ Regt, commanded by Lieutenant-Colonel Les Pearce, was the first unit to occupy Wellington Lines in Terendak Camp. This was 'a really swept-up sort of place, very well appointed, well laid out, all the facilities. We had our families with us and we were able to develop the lifestyle that fitted that particular camp.'[88] In 1961 Terendak comprised 1,500 acres of developed

accommodation and a further 3,500 acres of jungle training area, including two rifle ranges and a grenade range. A 600-yard long airstrip capable of taking Beaver and Pioneer aircraft was located immediately to the north of the camp. There was a helicopter pad inside the camp, and landing craft from Singapore maintained a twice-monthly service, delivering stores to a ramp near the Senior Ranks Club. The nearest railhead was at Tampin, 35 miles to the north.[89] For the first time, 28th Commonwealth Brigade was concentrated in one location, with the New Zealanders in Wellington Lines, the British battalion in Imjin Lines, and the Australians in Canberra Lines. The artillery regiment was located in Solma-Ri Lines, the Royal Engineers squadron in Kohima Lines, the Royal Army Ordnance Corps and the Royal Electrical and Mechanical Engineers in Arakan Lines, the hospital and field ambulance in Mandalay Lines, and Brigade Headquarters in Maryang-San Lines. Once the project was completed, the Pioneer and Civil Labour unit occupied Baldwin Lines. Much of the married accommodation was inside the camp.

New Zealand's financial contribution to the development of Terendak Camp was an unavoidable element of its forward defence policy. It was a commitment New Zealand had struggled to avoid: '[The] crux of the problem is, of course, that of security of tenure. While at this stage the presence of overseas Commonwealth forces is accepted—and indeed welcomed—by the Federation Government, it is difficult to state that the position will remain the same over ... the next five years, let alone the next ten.'[90] However, the New Zealand government was also conscious that 'one of the basic concepts of ANZAM is the equality of the three partners and, if we wish to speak with an equal voice in ANZAM, we should be prepared to pay a reasonable share of the capital cost of maintaining our forces in Malaya'.[91] Stringency in defence spending was always in conflict with New Zealand's SEATO commitment and the associated cost of maintaining a standing force in South-East Asia.

It had been agreed in 1955 that Malacca would become the base for the Commonwealth Strategic Reserve brigade.[92] The Bukit Terendak site was selected because it was relatively remote from major population centres.[93] Both Australia and New Zealand wanted to pay rent for their use of the camp, but this was unacceptable to the United Kingdom, which wished to reach a cost-sharing arrangement before beginning construction. After much discussion and an Australian gift of £400,000 towards New Zealand's contribution, the three countries agreed to share the total capital cost (estimated at £7.5 million) in the proportions United Kingdom 54.1 per cent, Australia 27.7 per cent, New

Zealand 18.2 per cent.[94] On 20 July 1959, Cabinet finally approved in principle the payment of New Zealand's share, less the Australian £400,000. It also agreed to the revised accommodation plan for 1,026 houses, of which New Zealand would be allocated 187 as married quarters.[95] Construction had begun in June 1958, and the camp was officially opened on 5 August 1960. It was estimated that the capital cost of Terendak Camp to June 1967 was A$19.4 million, of which New Zealand's share was A$3.5 million.[96] Naming the camp also caused some controversy. In August 1960 the British High Commissioner announced that the official name for the new Malacca cantonment would be 'Fort George', which had been the name of the Commonwealth Divisional Command Post in Korea. Both the New Zealand High Commissioner, Charles Bennett, and his Australian counterpart told the British that this was 'politically a most unfortunate choice as it tended to preserve an association with colonialism which the opponents of the Defence Agreement would not be slow to grasp'.[97] Despite British claims to the contrary there had been no consultation, and Tunku Abdul Rahman also indicated his dislike for the name. After much discussion, it became 'Terendak Camp, Malacca' instead.[98]

Les Pearce had joined the New Zealand Army as a Regular soldier at Trentham in 1938, and by 1945 he was in command of 26 Battalion in Italy. He was Commandant Army Schools at Waiouru in 1961, when he was appointed to head 1 NZ Regt.

> I thought I might have run out of time. I was 42, but I was a nut about fitness. I played rugby ... squash and basketball and tennis. I kept active and woe betide any chap that thought he could beat me on the squash court. It was a challenge to me at that age physically, [but] I had no problems with regard to my ability to command the battalion, none whatsoever. In fact I enjoyed the challenge, it was tremendous ... In 1940 I was a sergeant major in starting 24 Battalion, and the rules and the principles that were developed in getting that battalion ready to go to war I found of great value to me when 21 years later I had the same job only in a different position, this time as a CO.[99]

Pearce's golden rule was to keep all his soldiers aware of what was going on. His briefings to all ranks before exercises and at the beginning of a training cycle became a feature of his unit. 'I used to gather them all together, the entire battalion, and go through what I was going to do with them over the next three months. I always thought that if you could talk to the lowest private soldier as though you were speaking to an equal he would react remarkably well towards that sort of treatment.'[100]

1 NZ Regt also benefited from the valuable experience of the officers, NCOs and soldiers who had been in Morrison's 1 NZ Regt. They provided 'a degree of professionalism that we hadn't seen before. You had it in the form of a Commanding Officer [Les Pearce], an experienced commander who did all the right things in terms of officer development, and RSM [WO1 C. M. ("Doc") Schwass] who did the same in terms of NCO development. The unit melded itself into a very fine group.'[101]

The benefits of the ten months spent in training by Pearce's 1 NZ Regt were demonstrated on its arrival in Malaya in November 1961. This, the first battalion changeover carried out completely by RNZAF air transport, involved moving 1,800 personnel on 21 flights by DC-6 aircraft of No. 40 Squadron RNZAF.[102] As soon as it arrived in Terendak Camp the battalion was put on its mettle by being located alongside the rest of the brigade. The highly competitive Pearce was determined that his battalion would be best on operations, best at drill, best at sports, best at everything it attempted. His was the dominant personality. 'I was concerned for a while that New Zealand soldiers wouldn't be very good base soldiers, that we were in a garrison environment and the general feeling was that this was not the New Zealand soldier's forte. So what you did was, you worked them hard, and you put them out in the jungle at every opportunity you had.'[103]

The 21-year-old Sergeant Jim Brown, who had joined the Army as a Regular Force cadet in January 1957, commanded the anti-tank section in A Company. For him, there was no doubt about the grip the commanding officer had over his unit. The soldiers of 1 NZ Regt went on leave to Malacca wearing grey trousers, white shirt, and regimental tie. The curfew at night was enforced by a bed check of the barracks—'and these were all grown men you were talking about'.[104] Those who had enlisted in the battalion

> were out for a scrap and if there were a few hiccups along the way, no problem ... Today's soldiers are angels compared to those guys ... In the 1960s the soldiers didn't get far past pay day and by that time most of the money went into the bar and to the brothels down the road ... Basically you lived it up while you had money in your pocket and when you ran out you simply stayed in camp and waited for the next pay day to come around.[105]

Those who stepped out of line were dealt with severely. 'There were midday pack drills on the parade ground for those on Confinement to Barracks. The Brits thought that we were barbarians in the way and manner we treated the troops, but the discipline problems were just fixed like that.'[106]

Wives were very much part of Pearce's battalion in Malaya. 'Our husbands knew what Les expected and so it was passed on down the line.'[107] Settling in at Terendak was difficult for the families. While the battalion went straight into training, wives were confronted by bare expanses of red earth around their houses, and an initial lack of facilities such as swimming pools. There was a drought in 1962 and a series of high tides contaminated Malacca's water supply, so for almost a year water had to be delivered to kitchens and housing. At the same time, a very serious cholera epidemic swept throughout much of Malaya. Those who had experienced family life at Taiping made unfavourable comparisons at first.[108] But for Pru Meldrum, who had paid her own way to join her husband in Morrison's battalion, it was

> great to be back there and have a house, and having four children we were entitled to a cook and an amah. So that was heaven to me ... You were never quite sure whether you walked into your own house or the person's down the road, because the furnishings were all the same, but no it was wonderful. No washing, no cooking, to get up and walk away from the table was heaven. We were able to buy a car ... An Austin station wagon—the joy of our lives. The first car we had, and we had been married five or six years by then.[109]

In Terendak, unlike Taiping or Ipoh, the New Zealand families were able to live a somewhat isolated existence. While they mixed with Australian and British families, there was little social contact with the local community. In many ways it was an unreal existence for those who had money and free time but did not always know what to do with it. 'The days did get a bit empty so you had to put your mind to doing things and occupying the time. There were some wives who didn't like that very much and I wouldn't have liked it for too long. Two years was just great.'[110]

28th Commonwealth Brigade had an annual cycle of unit and formation training, supplemented by periodic deployments on operational tours to the border. The primary focus was on the brigade's role if it was committed into Laos under SEATO Plan 5. The 1962 training year began with Exercise RED ANGEL, a brigade study of the tactical doctrine should the brigade be deployed into the Savannakhet area of central Laos. This was followed by two exacting field exercises, HOPE ANGEL and CHARITY ANGEL.[111] The battalion developed mobilisation drills which it 'could really do in its sleep'.[112] 'We did a lot of night marching in the jungle and river crossings at night.' They were resupplied at night, and everyone was committed: 'Those truckies who never did anything ... the cooks and everybody else. We used to work their arses off and turn them into jungle people so that everybody could perform.'[113] The battalion made a major contribution to the development of the brigade's tactical doctrine for SEATO operations, and tested these drills and procedures against the full-size fortified village in the Terendak training area.[114]

The battalion's commitment to border security operations had been agreed to by the Holyoake government on the understanding that 'it would not prejudice the readiness of the battalion to perform its primary role' and that each deployment would be approved in advance by the Prime Minister.[115] Pearce compensated for the lack of current intelligence, a common feature of border operations, by keenly studying Vietnamese tactics and honing his battalion's mobilisation skills. This also reflected the changed emphasis of brigade training. The crises of 1958 and 1960 had led to increasing control of Laos by the Pathet Lao, and made the insertion into the country of a limited SEATO force (including elements of 28th Commonwealth Brigade) under SEATO Plan 5 highly unlikely. Emphasis now shifted to SEATO Plan 4, the defence of Thailand against attacks across the Mekong River from Laos by Viet Minh and Chinese forces. The Commonwealth Strategic Reserve would be deployed first, followed by national formations that would establish an ANZUK Division in Thailand alongside United States and Thai forces.[116] The plan was practised by 28th Commonwealth Brigade units, and in 1963 Pearce deployed his headquarters and Major Ian Bennett's C Company to Ubon in Thailand on a SEATO exercise which culminated with a parade before the King of Thailand.[117]

1 NZ Regt was first deployed on border operations from 12 October to 2 December 1962, under the operational control of 2 Federal Infantry Brigade, commanded by Brigadier Hamid. This was the first time a New Zealand battalion had come under the control of a Malayan brigade. Pearce's headquarters were established at Kepala Batas, with the four rifle companies deployed near the border in Perlis and Kedah.[118] No contacts were made, although tracks, dumps, and a number of empty camps were found. Despite the frustrating lack of up-to-date intelligence, this was still valuable training for platoons and sections. On operations the soldiers, like those of previous battalions, walked in and out of the 'ulu', and were supplied by airdrops. 'Whilst we had helicopters at the time they simply weren't used for troop movement. They were really for emergency evacuation ... [or] to move the rugby team out. That always got priority.'[119] Like his predecessors, Pearce also wanted his battalion to 'win all the metal', and placed great emphasis on the band and Maori concert party, and

success in sports contests. 'You see, when you weren't fighting you had to have something people could concentrate on, quite apart from training which was always as hard as I could make it, but the band and the concert party were two showpieces of my battalion.'[120]

Battalion Headquarters and two rifle companies were again deployed under 2 Federal Infantry Brigade in the Betong Salient area from 1 July to 26 August 1963.[121] During this period, 'approximately 40 miles of jungle clad, mountainous country was searched along the Border to a depth of approximately 3[000]–5000 yds'. Once again little intelligence of any value was available to the unit, which 'meant that companies carried out operations with little chance of obtaining a contact'.[122]

Pearce's 1 NZ Regt was the last battalion to move to Malaya as a formed unit before a further Army reorganisation again changed the system for reinforcing and replacing the battalion. Pearce's adjutant, Bill Meldrum, remembered 'standing with the CO watching them come on for one of the final rehearsals for their final parade, and he said then: "What a fit bunch of men." And they were. They looked seasoned professional troops at that stage. Of course they hadn't gone anywhere and that was the pity. If one can say it's a pity. It's a great shame that [the battalion] was never tried and tested.'[123] That frustration can still be sensed at battalion reunions.

When the situation in Laos deteriorated again in May 1962, it was not 1 NZ Regt that was deployed to Thailand, but 1 Ranger (SAS) Squadron from New Zealand. The battalion experienced similar frustration when British elements of 28th Commonwealth Brigade were deployed to Brunei to quell a revolt at the end of 1962, and remained in Borneo as the threat of Indonesian-inspired incursions grew. Two officers, Lieutenant Peter Browne and Captain Jack Spiers, were unofficially attached to Major-General Walker's COMBRITBOR Headquarters at Labuan in 1963. This and the equally unofficial attachment of two pilot-trained RNZA officers, Lieutenants Christopher Brown and Raymond Andrews, who flew Austers with 656 Detachment Army Air Corps in Brunei, was the total New Zealand contribution—and one of which the New Zealand government remained unaware.[124]

Despite these disappointments, 1 NZ Regt was a highly professional unit that—as its members still attest—breathed the spirit of its commanding officer.

> There was no battalion that could have equalled Les Pearce's battalion. He ruled it, ran it with a rod of iron, but with a complete understanding of every man in the battalion. His professional knowledge was unbeatable. He knew the job of every

man in that battalion. He was the pre-war instructor type like Rennie and Taylor. Then there was Les Pearce the man. The great bloody soldier, the disciplinarian, the leader. You knew where you stood with him. You'd get your arse kicked or you would get a pat on the back. Then the next day it was all straight as a die again.[125]

## Operation SCORPION: New Zealanders on the Thai/Laos Border, May–September 1962

The trained and professional Regular New Zealand battalion based in South-East Asia in the 1960s was never committed in its SEATO role, much to the chagrin of Pearce and his men. When another Laotian crisis erupted in May 1962, the United States committed Joint Task Force 116 from Okinawa to north-east Thailand under the command of Lieutenant-General Richardson. Some 6,000 personnel were deployed on what was named Operation SCORPION. The British committed No. 20 (Fighter) Squadron RAF, which flew Hawker Hunter jets, from Singapore, and the Australians committed the RAAF Sabre squadron from Butterworth. New Zealand contributed three Bristol Freighters of No. 41 Squadron RNZAF from Changi, and a headquarters and two troops, totalling 30 SAS personnel, from 1 Ranger (SAS) Squadron at Papakura.[126] Sending this token force was a political gesture of solidarity, and it lacked tactical cohesion. Its command arrangements were equally untidy and confusing. Richardson, the Task Force commander, co-ordinated the various national components except for the Royal Thai forces. New Zealand did not want its contributions to become a long-term deployment to Thailand as part of a SEATO force, and this was also the position of both Australia and the United Kingdom.[127]

The Bristol Freighters of No. 41 Squadron played a significant role by flying a daily courier run for passengers and supplies from Udorn to Bangkok and Khorat, a round trip involving some five and half hours in the air. 'Apart from a few initial difficulties teaching the ration people that when 41 Squadron has a schedule it keeps it, the service is running very smoothly.'[128] The Freighters' commitments continued to increase; in July these included carrying perishable rations from Bangkok to Udorn. Until the United States Marines were withdrawn from Udorn at the end of the month, they were flown some 7,000 lb of bread, milk, eggs, fresh fruit and vegetables daily, in addition to the normal courier tasks. There were few places in Thailand that the Freighters did not fly into, carrying RAF photographers, United Service Organization entertainers, New Zealand SAS and US service personnel. They also delivered perishable

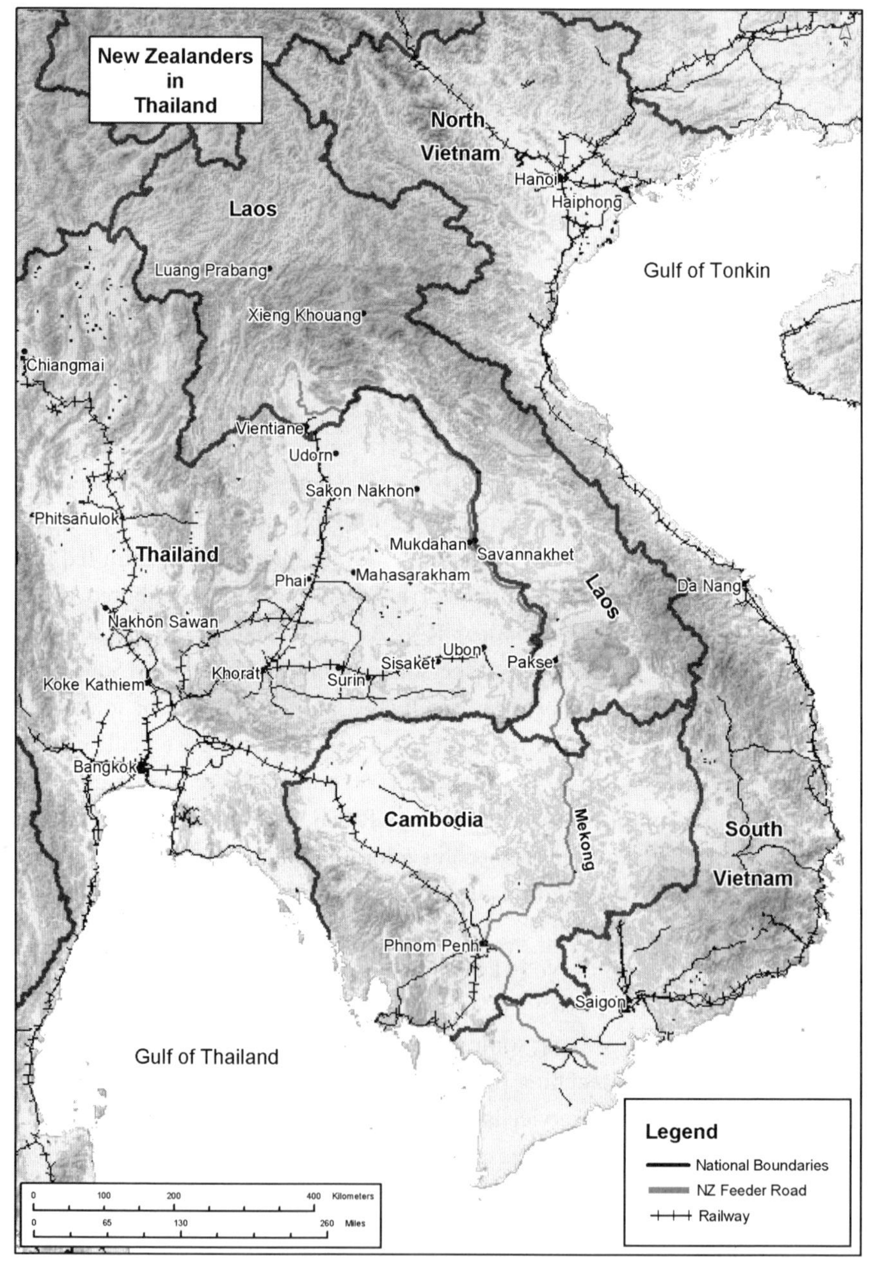


**Map 6** Thailand and Laos

rations to the Joint US Military Assistance Group teams that were training Thai forces in 'off the beaten track' locations; the schedule included Khorat, Bangkok, Koke Kathiem, Nakhon Sawan, Phitsanulok, Sakon Nakhon, Bangkok again, and back to Khorat. The Freighters stayed on while the elements of Joint Task Force 116 were withdrawn. By the end of October 1962, they had carried a million pounds of freight and 3,600 passengers since being deployed to Thailand, a daily average of nearly 7,000 lb and 24 passengers over five months.[129]

On 2 June 1962, No. 41 Squadron was joined by a 30-strong SAS detachment under Major M. N. Velvin, which flew in by Hastings aircraft of No. 40 Squadron, RNZAF.[130] Mel Velvin had been mentioned in despatches during service in Korea, and would later command 1 Field Squadron RNZE. Here he faced the difficult problem of finding gainful employment for his men. The SAS presence was a political gesture on what was hoped would be a limited timescale, but what were they to do? Initial attempts to attach them to Thai units to provide training in unconventional warfare were unsuccessful, and they remained in limbo at Khorat. A conference in Geneva was discussing arrangements for a ceasefire in Laos, and everyone was marking time. Velvin's two troops acclimatised and undertook some familiarisation training with 1 Battle Group 27 US Infantry. They began learning Thai from their liaison officer, who spoke English. Everything was done on a shoestring basis. Velvin lacked training stores, and had sufficient vehicles for only one of his troops. It was 'fortunate that the Det[achment] was serving with generous allies'.[131] There was not enough ammunition for range practices, and extra supplies got no further than Whenuapai.

Finally, 1 Troop was attached to No. 1 Marine Battalion at Udorn, and conducted reconnaissance patrols as far as the Mekong River to familiarise themselves with the ground and in anticipation of likely contingency tasking. The less-experienced 3 Troop linked up with a reconnaissance troop of 1 Battle Group 27 US Infantry and reconnoitred the main roads throughout north-east Thailand. These attachments were followed by others to United States infantry and Special Force teams, during which the New Zealanders learned Special Force techniques, and in turn gave jungle warfare demonstrations and helped to train Thai army and border patrol police. The Geneva Agreement on Laos signed in August 1962 imposed a deadline for the withdrawal of foreign troops from Laos. The Agreement also involved the withdrawal of the US Marines from Thailand; the New Zealand government was able to withdraw the SAS on 16 September.[132] The deployment of this small contingent had gained wide press coverage as well as being valuable in terms of familiarisation with the area, and enabling the first close contact with United States infantry and Special Force units. There had been many frustrations as well. Signal communications with Headquarters New Zealand FARELF in Singapore had worked only fitfully, to the 'mutual dissatisfaction' of both parties; and the administrative difficulties that plagued the deployment proved 'that an ounce of first hand local knowledge is worth more than a pound of theory and remote guesswork'.[133] On balance, it was a valuable experience for the SAS. While many of the detachment had previously served in Malaya, it underlined the lesson that not all tropical warfare would necessarily be fought in the jungle.

Operation SCORPION had highlighted the inability of the existing infrastructure in Thailand to cope with a major mobilisation. 'The terrain, climate, lack of suitable airfields and ... serious deficiencies of the internal communications systems all add up to the fact that the deployment of a SEATO force in Thailand would be a grave military risk unless steps are taken to improve the means of logistically supporting that force.'[134] In September 1962 the United States announced a major programme for the development of logistic facilities in Thailand; the aim was to improve road and rail systems, airfields, fuel distribution and communications. This Special Logistic Aid Thailand (SLAT) programme was designed to support United States operations in Thailand, and did not extend into the areas where ANZAM forces were likely to be deployed. However, the United States was keen to seek support from SEATO members. On 18 December 1962 the New Zealand Cabinet approved the detachment of up to three Freighters from Singapore to Khorat as a contribution to the SLAT programme.[135] To meet the equally serious logistic needs of ANZAM, 2 Plant Troop, 2 Construction Squadron RNZE was deployed, along with Australian and British engineers, to build a new airfield. Located at Leong Nok Tha, some 50 miles south of Mukdahan in eastern Thailand, the airfield was to be 'the corner stone in the logistic support system of 28 Commonwealth Brigade and the New Zealand Brigade Group'.[136] This commitment was followed by that of a New Zealand Army Engineers unit to a joint Thai–New Zealand road construction project in the north-east. In combination with New Zealand's involvement in the Confrontation with Indonesia over Borneo, and its commitment to South Vietnam, these projects would absorb much of New Zealand's limited military engineering resources into the 1970s.[137]

Military aid to Thailand placed further demands on New Zealand's overstretched defence resources. The establishment of the Federation of Malaysia in September 1963 was followed by growing confrontation with Indonesia over the Borneo territories; this and the commitment of New Zealand forces to South Vietnam would exacerbate the strains which were already showing. By 1963 28th Commonwealth Brigade, now commanded by a New Zealander, Brigadier R. B. Dawson, could be deployed to Thailand under Plans 4 and 6 if a limited war broke out, and under Plan 8 in the event of insurgency. Plan 7 allowed for a commitment to counter an insurgency in South Vietnam. Under Plan 4, New Zealand was to make a combat brigade group and a logistic support group available to SEATO by 1966; until then, it would provide 'an independent infantry brigade group held in reserve outside theatre'.[138]

Despite the introduction of National Service, this commitment was beyond New Zealand's capabilities and would remain so until the late 1960s. By 1963 between half and two-thirds of the equipment had been purchased for the infantry brigade, and the build-up in Territorial strength was on target. Nevertheless, the Chiefs of Staff expressed concern about the decline in the capacity of the Armed Forces since the 1961 Defence Review. Major-General L. W. Thornton, the Chief of General Staff from 1960 to 1965, reported that it would take eight months to prepare the brigade for active operations; at the current rate of purchase it would not be fully equipped until 1968—by which time much of the earmarked equipment would be obsolete.[139] New Zealand also had to provide its share of logistic support to any SEATO force, and the organisation and training of the Logistic Support Group, comprising specially tailored units made up of a mixture of Regular and Territorial personnel, became the Army's 'major pre-occupation'.[140]

## Gurr's First Battalion, Royal New Zealand Infantry Regiment, 1963–65

In November 1963, 2 NZ Regt flew to Malaysia in DC-6 aircraft of No. 40 Squadron, RNZAF, after training hard for ten months at Burnham under its commanding officer, Lieutenant-Colonel R. M. Gurr. On arrival it took over from Pearce's battalion, and in turn took on the name 1 NZ Regt. On 1 April 1964 it again changed its identity, becoming 1st Battalion, Royal New Zealand Infantry Regiment (1RNZIR). The 'Royal' in the title could not disguise the implications of this reorganisation of the New Zealand Infantry, under which the provincial regiments were amalgamated into the RNZIR. 1 NZ Regt and 2 NZ Regt were reduced in strength and merged into 1RNZIR, which remained part of the Commonwealth Strategic Reserve; meanwhile, a 402-strong battalion depot was formed in Burnham to bring the battalion up to full strength, and provide its first-line reinforcements—a total of 402. Under a new system of 'continuous relief', the equivalent of a platoon (33 or 34 men) would join the battalion each month, but this system would not be fully effective until February 1965.[141] The arrival of Gurr's battalion in Terendak also marked the final transition to a garrison role. All New Zealand Army personnel in Malaysia ceased to be on active service at midnight on 15 November 1963.[142]

Lieutenant-Colonel Bob Gurr had graduated from the Royal Military College, Duntroon, in 1942 and served with both the Third New Zealand Division in the Pacific and the Second New Zealand Division in Italy. After serving with J Force in Japan, his positions included Chief Instructor, Tactical School, and Commanding Officer, 1st Northland Regiment (1957–59). Gurr was a very different personality from Pearce: he stood back and assessed people's performance before giving them assignments, and delegated more. Those who did not measure up were sacked or reassigned to duties which they could perform. He was conscious of the range of talent and experience in his battalion, which he conducted like a professional orchestra. Most of his company commanders, warrant officers and NCOs had seen active service in Malaya. Of his rifle company commanders, Major Ian ('Buzz') Burrows, MC, had been the outstanding troop commander in 1 New Zealand SAS Squadron in 1956–57, while Major Ian Thorpe had served as a platoon commander and adjutant in 1FIR. Both men would prove to be outstanding company commanders. Together with warrant officers of the calibre of Howard James, Brian Martin and Barry Pepper, they provided the bedrock of experience required for the jungle training of the battalion's soldiers, most of whom had come straight from basic recruit courses. Major Stan McKeon had Second World War experience and had served with 1FIR in Malaya, as had Gurr's RSM, WO1 W. L. Pearless. The only other officer of Second World War vintage was the RMO, Major Jim Moodie, who had been in the 4th Armoured Brigade in Italy. Moodie served for a year in both Pearce's and Gurr's battalions.[143] In a sense, Gurr's 1RNZIR was the peak of the New Zealand Army's cumulative experience in South-East Asia. While its members hoped they would be tested and see some action, they could not foresee that they would be the only New Zealand battalion to see combat during Confrontation, and the last New Zealand battalion to do so as a unit.

The battalion's acclimatisation training was followed by a series of exercises at company and battalion level, building up to Exercises RAFFIA I and FLYING

KIWI. The latter was a SEATO mobilisation exercise under 28th Commonwealth Brigade control, in which the battalion was deployed by road to Singapore and staged through Nee Soon Camp before being flown into Kuantan, in Pahang State. After securing the airfield, it conducted operations against an enemy base in the jungle. Meanwhile, the situation in Borneo worsened.

In January 1964 the Commander-in-Chief FARELF, Lieutenant-General Sir Nigel Poet, requested authority from the New Zealand Chief of Defence Staff, Rear-Admiral Sir Peter Phipps, to deploy 1 NZ Regt on the Thai/Malaysian border in order to release a Malaysian battalion for service in Borneo.[144] A similar request was made to Australia in relation to the Australian battalion. Phipps told his Minister of Defence that while this would restrict New Zealand's capacity 'to meet the most urgent SEATO appeal', it simply reflected the situation facing 28th Commonwealth Brigade. Its field engineer squadron, including the Australian component, was already committed to the Mukdahan airfield project, and its British battalion was already rostered for a tour in Borneo. 'We have resisted pressing British suggestions regarding the use of the New Zealand Battalion in East Malaysia, and the employment in the North will go some distance towards helping the Malaysians and the British with their difficulties. Its use will not preclude a later request for its operational employment in East Malaysia.'[145]

# PART II

# *Confrontation*

# 7

# CONFRONTING INTRUDERS

## *Infantry Operations, Malay Peninsula, 1964*

We had all hoped that it would not be necessary to commit New Zealand forces against Indonesians with whom of course we are still anxious to have friendly relations. However, the Government has now come to the conclusion ... that we can no longer stand aside and should respond affirmatively to the Malaysian request, with which Admiral Begg, the Commander in Chief Far East has joined. I have therefore today authorised the use of the New Zealand Battalion from the Commonwealth Brigade in Terendak Camp to assist the Malaysians in dealing with the Indonesian infiltrators. The Battalion is now taking up its position for operations alongside the Malaysians.[1]

R. Hunter Wade, New Zealand High Commissioner to Malaysia, 4 September 1964

The presence of New Zealand forces in South-East Asia from the mid-1950s was designed primarily to fulfil the strategic role of contributing to the Commonwealth Reserve for SEATO. After the end of the Malayan Emergency, New Zealand's contributions reached a peak in the mid-1960s during Confrontation, when New Zealanders undertook arduous combat roles in both Malaya and Borneo.

The principal trigger for the Confrontation between the Republic of Indonesia and the United Kingdom and the Federation of Malaya was the outbreak of a rebellion in Brunei. The Sultanate of Brunei was one of three British colonies on Borneo, the world's third largest island, three-quarters of which is part of the Republic of Indonesia. Malaya had announced its intention to form a greater Malaysia, incorporating Singapore, Brunei, Sabah and Sarawak, by

September 1963. While the Philippines, and less openly Indonesia, already opposed this, it was the attempted coup d'état in Brunei by Inche A. A. Azahari Mahmud and his Partai Ra'ayat on 8 December 1962 which prompted the Indonesian action against Malaysia's formation that was known as Konfrontasi ('Confrontation'). This continued the tactics of 'coercive diplomacy' which President Sukarno had used against the Dutch part of New Guinea before its cession to Indonesia in 1962.[2] Sukarno saw the establishment of Malaysia as a direct threat to Indonesia's position as the leading emerging power in South-East Asia.

The Brunei rebellion was quickly put down, but low-scale insurgency continued thanks to raids and small-scale armed infiltration across the border from Indonesian Kalimantan. The United Kingdom and Malaysia, believing that this infiltration could be frustrated only by a strong defence of Brunei, Sarawak and Sabah, built up their forces in the territories. The United States, the primary influence on the ceding of Dutch New Guinea to Indonesia, was prepared to follow a similar policy over the Borneo territories, but Britain and Malaysia would not agree to this. Both believed that Indonesia did not want to escalate the confrontation into a limited war.[3]

After the inauguration of Malaysia on 20 September 1963, both the Federation and the United Kingdom sought Australian and New Zealand support. This was refused, although New Zealand allowed its Bristol Freighters to transport troops and supplies from Singapore. Both countries considered that military operations in Borneo were primarily the responsibility of the United Kingdom and Malaysia, and that the existing situation did not warrant the deployment of Australian or New Zealand ground forces to Sabah or Sarawak.[4] New Zealand saw its SEATO commitment as its principal concern, and lacked the resources to meet both that and a commitment to Borneo. In December 1963 the British Prime Minister, Sir Alec Douglas-Home, sent both Australia and New Zealand a list of what was needed to defend the Borneo territories. In reply, New Zealand agreed to the 'continued use, ferrying to and within Borneo' of the Bristol Freighters, and to the use of the RNZN frigate on station with the Far East Fleet in an anti-piracy role, although it did not want any publicity on 'our readiness to do this'. For the present, this was as far as New Zealand was prepared to go. Holyoake was concerned about

> the foreseeable political repercussions in South-East Asia to the introduction of New Zealand ground forces into Borneo just at this moment. We are by no means

> persuaded that this would be wise ... We do agree that, should the situation in Borneo deteriorate seriously as a result of Indonesian pressure, the New Zealand battalion would be made available for operations in support of Malaysian and British forces there.[5]

The British approach was followed in January 1964 by a Malaysian request for logistic and training assistance for the rapidly expanding Malaysian armed forces, for signal and anti-aircraft elements to be stationed on the Malay Peninsula, and for non-combatant forces—in particular, a field ambulance element—to be attached to the Malaysian brigade in Borneo. When talks in Bangkok in early March failed to reach a settlement, Australia supplied Malaysia with £3 million worth of military stores and equipment; it also provided training for Malaysian officers and servicemen in both Australia and Malaysia. In April, Australia also offered two minesweepers to patrol the coast of Malaysian Borneo, and a field engineer squadron to construct roads and airfields in the territories. Air support was also provided, including four RAAF Iroquois helicopters to operate on the Malaysian–Thai border. New Zealand was seen to be lagging well behind Australia. The New Zealand Chiefs of Staff examined the possibility of sending a field ambulance element to Borneo, but all that eventuated was Holyoake's offer, during a visit to Kuala Lumpur, of £550,000 worth of military aid to Malaysia, half in the form of equipment and half as the estimated cost of training Malaysian servicemen in New Zealand over a period of two years.[6]

New Zealand was doing its best not to become involved in Confrontation. The National government wanted to retain good relations with Indonesia, and also had its doubts about the nature of the conflict, suspecting its origins were as much internal as caused by Indonesian aggression. As far as Holyoake was concerned, it was a problem for the Malaysians and the British to solve.[7] He was also very conscious of New Zealand's limited defence resources. The 1961 defence cuts meant that almost everything New Zealand had in the way of deployable defence assets was already in Malaysia as part of the SEATO commitment. There was nothing more to send, and any commitment to Borneo would simply reduce New Zealand's ability to fulfil SEATO undertakings. Holyoake also feared that if New Zealand committed troops and resources to Borneo, this could develop into a long-term involvement similar to the 12-year Malayan Emergency, tying down scarce assets at a time when the situation in Thailand and South Vietnam seemed to be of more pressing concern. Holyoake personally saw any military commitment as a last resort. Unlike many of his parliamentary colleagues, he had not seen military service in the Second World War. He distrusted the military option and ignored advice from his Chiefs of Staff recommending commitment. New Zealand was to prove equally stubborn initially in resisting United States pressure to commit combat units to South Vietnam.

However, open Indonesian aggression in the form of landings on the Malay Peninsula convinced Holyoake that force had to be met with force and that New Zealand had to play its part. In January 1964, as the British and Malaysian commitment in Borneo grew, New Zealand agreed to the New Zealand battalion playing a greater role in security operations on the Thai border so as to release British and Malaysian infantry units for service in Borneo.[8] New Zealand's approval was conditional on the Australian government agreeing to a similar commitment of its battalion in 28th Commonwealth Brigade. Cabinet accepted that this would 'restrict our capacity to meet the most urgent SEATO appeal', but saw this as inevitable, and as causing similar problems for its partners in the Commonwealth Strategic Reserve.[9] As Rear-Admiral Phipps explained to his Minister of Defence, New Zealand had 'resisted pressing British suggestions regarding the use of the New Zealand Battalion in East Malaysia, and the employment in the North will go some distance towards helping the Malaysians and the British with their difficulties'.[10] This gave the New Zealand government a breathing space; if the situation in Borneo worsened, a commitment could be made then.

New Zealand's reluctance to commit even non-combatant troops to Borneo was becoming increasingly difficult for the Malaysians to understand, particularly as on 25 May the New Zealand government approved offering military assistance to Vietnam in the form of a 25-strong Army engineer unit. After informing the Malaysian Prime Minister, Tunku Abdul Rahman, of this decision, the New Zealand High Commissioner to Malaysia, Hunter Wade, reported: 'The Malaysians have always understood our political reluctance to get involved in shooting Indonesians before the situation absolutely demands it but they are, I think, beginning to wonder why we deny them the moral support of a token unit such as they now see we are prepared to send bearing our flag in Thailand and Vietnam.' This lack of support was made worse in Malaysian eyes by Australia's willingness to 'stand up and be counted in Borneo'. Wade recommended that the field ambulance elements be offered for service in Borneo. Otherwise, he warned, 'we are having to be increasingly on the alert against the danger of being relegated to the position of a second-class outer circle of the Commonwealth defence grouping here. This would accord neither with our record of military and financial assistance nor with our present and future political and defence interests in this part of the world.'[11] Despite this pressure, Holyoake would not agree to commit medical support.

On 6 May 1964, 1RNZIR under Lieutenant-Colonel Bob Gurr relieved 3rd Battalion, Royal Australian Regiment (3RAR) on Operation MAGNUS, and came under the operational control of 2 Federation Infantry Brigade for security operations on the Thai border. The six-week deployment followed a similar pattern to the border operations conducted by previous New Zealand battalions since the end of the Emergency in 1960. Battalion Headquarters was established at Sik Camp in Kedah State, and three of the New Zealand rifle companies operated in company areas immediately south of the border.[12] Platoons searched their areas and mounted ambushes on suspected cross-border courier routes, without result. The twelve Timor ponies attached to the battalion to resupply patrols became known as the 'Sik Pony Trail' or 'Pony Express'. The name was more romantic than the reality of unskilled New Zealand drovers, co-opted from the ranks, coaxing unwilling ponies along jungle tracks too narrow for the width of their loads.[13] The ponies, the hot dry conditions, and the lack of water became the lasting memories of this operation for those involved. There were two deaths in the battalion at this time. Private O. T. Dawson died on 31 March after an accident in the unit lines at Terendak, and Private A. W. Monk was accidentally shot while on border operations on 15 April. Both deaths cast a pall.[14] Nonetheless, Operation MAGNUS provided a valuable workout for 1RNZIR; although 'no contacts were made all ranks worked with enthusiasm and gained a considerable amount of experience in jungle operations'.[15] It was planned that the New Zealanders would again relieve 3RAR on Operation MAGNUS on 15 October 1964 for another two-month tour.[16]

In April 1964, although New Zealand remained unwilling to make a military commitment to Borneo, the High Commissioner in Kuala Lumpur confirmed to the Malaysian authorities that New Zealand agreed to its battalion being made available on the Malay Peninsula, 'if the need should arise', for operations in support of the police against armed infiltrators from Indonesia.[17] Such a need seemed increasingly likely as more incidents of sabotage and terrorism were carried out by Indonesian-trained dissidents on both the peninsula and the island of Singapore.

By early July 1964 it was clear that 'the scope and intent of Indonesian aggression had grown wider and more serious'. Confrontation was 'no longer a campaign of scattered infiltration and harassment in the border areas of the Borneo States', but had developed into a broad effort to revive and foment insurrection on the peninsula. Intelligence reports indicated that Indonesians had contacted guerrillas on the Thai border, and that large numbers of infiltrators were being trained in Indonesia with the intention of initiating a large-scale military insurrection in West Malaysia by September 1964. This threat was compounded by politically-inspired riots in Singapore during July and August. The Malaysian government responded by declaring a ban on barter trade with Indonesia, and by establishing security zones along the coasts of the Malay Peninsula and Singapore which were monitored by air, sea and land patrols.

The Malaysian armed forces were fully stretched in meeting these new security demands on top of their commitments in Borneo. Their operations were controlled by a National Operations Committee chaired jointly by Malaysia's Chief of Armed Forces Staff, Lieutenant-General Tunku Osman, and Inspector-General of Police, Dato Claude Fenner. The Commander-in-Chief Far East was a member of this committee, which issued 'the necessary instructions and direction to the Director of Borneo Operations and subordinate Security Executive Committees', including the Border Operations Committee.[18]

## New Zealand Operations in West Malaysia

On 17 August 1964, Indonesia's Confrontation policy escalated to a level that made direct New Zealand involvement inevitable. That night, Indonesian military forces landed on the west coast of West Malaysia in the Pontian area of Johore State. Between 50 and 100 Indonesians were reported to have come ashore at five different locations, and Malaysian Army and Police units were hurriedly deployed. The only units immediately available to help the Malaysian forces, should Commonwealth assistance be sought, were the Australian and New Zealand battalions at Terendak.[19] Despite intelligence reports, the United Kingdom was caught off-guard by the Indonesian landings; it had not yet decided on the role British troops would play against any incursions on the Malay Peninsula. On the day after the landings, Lieutenant-Colonel Robin Holloway, the New Zealand Defence Liaison Officer attached to the New Zealand High Commission in Singapore, was told by Admiral Sir Varyl Begg,

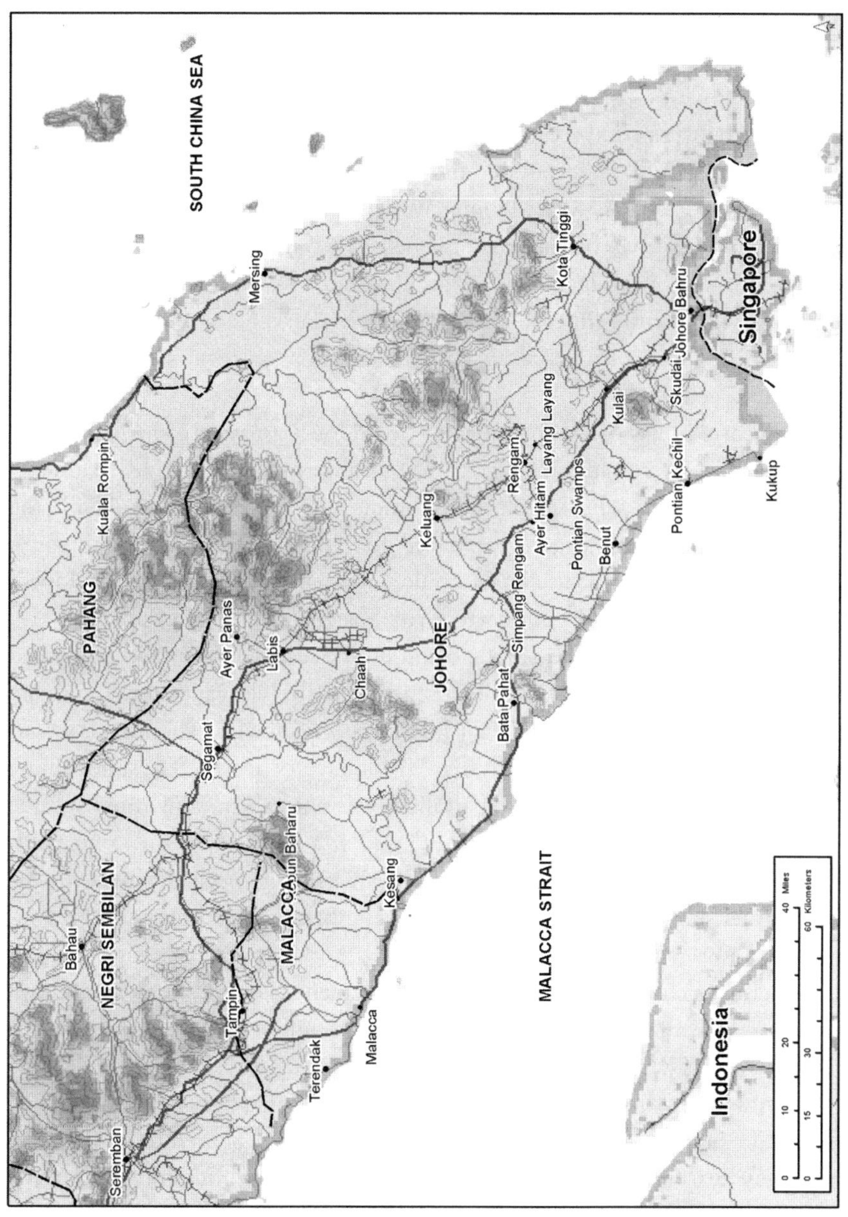


**Map 7** 1RNZIR Operations in West Malaysia, September–October 1964

the Commander-in-Chief Far East, that the New Zealand battalion 'would not be deployed if no authority was forthcoming from London for the use of British troops'.[20] However, concerns that further landings were likely before Malaysia Day (31 August) prompted the Malaysian government to ask if Commonwealth forces could undertake counter-infiltration duties in Malacca. New Zealand's High Commissioner, Hunter Wade, gained approval from Wellington that the battalion 'may be used over the next few days against infiltrators from Indonesia if, in your judgement, the circumstances warrant this. Such circumstances would include either a landing in the Malacca State or a landing elsewhere which—for example because it was one of a series—found Malaysian forces stretched.'[21]

In the early hours of 2 September 1964, Indonesian paratroopers dropped from transport aircraft into the Labis area of northern Johore. 1RNZIR, already on standby in Terendak, was placed on immediate notice to move. While the New Zealand soldiers eagerly prepared for what they hoped would be a shooting war, the diplomatic battle to deploy them on operations developed. Hunter Wade informed Headquarters Far East Land Force at Phoenix Park, Singapore, that if for any reason he could not be reached, 'they could proceed on the assumption that he would be prepared to give clearance for employing the Battalion ... but he would then like to be informed as soon as practicable'.[22] Holloway recorded that the Headquarters instructed subordinate commands that the New Zealand battalion 'was not to be used without specific clearance'.[23] It seems that the New Zealand battalion was the only one available in 28th Commonwealth Brigade. 3RAR had just been deployed to the Thai border on Operation MAGNUS, and the British battalion in 28th Commonwealth Brigade, 1st Battalion King's Own Yorkshire Light Infantry, was in the process of changing over with its replacement. The only other battalion immediately available was 1/10th Gurkha Rifles, and it could only be used for a few days as it was due for duty in Borneo.[24]

The situation worsened when racially inspired rioting between Chinese and Malays in Singapore intensified on the evening of 3 September. Next day Holloway was informed by Headquarters Far East Land Forces that the Malaysians were about to request the deployment of 1RNZIR to Labis to replace two battalions which were needed in Singapore to control the rioting. New Zealand's commitment to South-East Asia had always required walking a fine line between assisting in the defeat of communist insurgency and avoiding being involved in putting down civil disturbances. The directive on the use of New Zealand forces in the Commonwealth Strategic Reserve prohibited their involvement in policing civil unrest, and it was concern about this that now delayed the High Commissioner's agreement to despatch Gurr's battalion. After receiving the warning order, Holloway contacted Hunter Wade by late morning. The High Commissioner immediately sought clearance from Wellington.

> Guarded telephone call from Singapore conveys early warning that today's serious trouble in Singapore requires urgent troop reinforcement which for political and timing reasons can best come from the Malaysian Battalion hunting paratroopers around Labis. Phoenix Park are trying to get Begg who is in Kuala Lumpur to recommend deploying New Zealand Battalion to Labis to release Malaysians for Singapore. This would be a clear-cut military action ... Because of the indirect Popo [Preservation of Public Order] connotations I would particularly like your views before formal request is received. Battalion which has been on four hours standby has now been put on one hours standby which it will reach within half an hour.[25]

Admiral Begg personally made a formal request to the High Commissioner on the afternoon of 4 September that 1RNZIR take over operations in the Labis area by last light the same day. Hunter Wade again sought confirmation from Wellington. In the meantime, the increasingly urgent need to commit forces to Labis forced Begg's headquarters to act, and 1/10th Gurkhas were deployed. Begg would have preferred to use the New Zealanders and allow the Gurkhas to prepare for Borneo, but the need to get troops to Labis quickly was paramount, much to the frustration of the New Zealand battalion waiting in their vehicles on the parade ground at Terendak. By the time approval came through from Wellington that afternoon, Begg had already left Kuala Lumpur for Singapore. By the time Hunter Wade authorised the Director of Plans and Operations at Begg's headquarters to deploy 1RNZIR (less one company for camp security and rear details), 1/10th Gurkhas were already moving to Labis, so Gurr was instructed to move his battalion to the Pontian area.

Four days later, on 8 September, Holyoake outlined the background to New Zealand's involvement in the House of Representatives. He emphasised that a commitment to West Malaysia did not necessarily mean that New Zealand troops would fight in Borneo, which, he stressed, remained the responsibility of Britain and Malaysia. However, if there was 'a further serious deterioration in the security situation as a result of Indonesian armed activity, the New Zealand Battalion would be available for operations alongside their forces'.

He explained that New Zealand's decision was made in response to 'a most significant and serious development', the extension of Confrontation to Malaysia and Singapore. While responsibility for dealing with this situation lay primarily with the Malaysian government and its military forces, New Zealand had agreed to a Malaysian request for assistance. This decision was 'fully in accord with the objectives under which the Strategic Reserve is stationed in Malaysia, with the provisions of the United Nations Charter, and with long-standing Government policy'.[26] Clearly, Holyoake had agonised long and hard over this decision, which he had finally taken only when convinced there was no other option. New Zealand opinion was firmly in favour of this action, with the media asking why it had not been taken sooner. Holyoake would not have been unhappy with this response. He preferred appearing to be pushed by public opinion into making an operational commitment, rather than taking the initiative prior to such support.

For the third time since the Second World War, New Zealand troops were to see combat. But this time they were not a traditional citizen force, hastily raised and specially mobilised for overseas service. The days of New Zealand Expeditionary Forces were over. Confrontation in 1964 marked the first deployment into combat of a Regular New Zealand battalion from an overseas peacetime base. The professionalism of 1RNZIR was unmatched by any New Zealand unit before it, except perhaps Pearce's battalion. Its training in New Zealand and Malaysia and its commitment to border operations had finely honed the battalion's skills for the task it was about to undertake. Most important of all, it had a level of leadership and experience unmatched by any previous New Zealand unit being committed to combat for the first time. Lieutenant-Colonel Bob Gurr's service in the Pacific and Italy was complemented by that of many of his officers and NCOs, and some of his soldiers had served during the Malayan Emergency with 1FIR, the New Zealand SAS Squadron, or New Zealand battalions. For many, this was their second or third tour, and a few had also served in the Second World War and Korean War. Pearce's equally professional battalion had had a similar background, but fate had decreed that it would not be tested.

The days of committing amateur citizen soldiers to war were over.[27] New Zealand sent the best available men from its Regular forces to Vietnam and the peacekeeping operations that followed. Their effectiveness reflected the professionalism of their preparation, training, and leadership. The principle is an important one for a small isolated country with minuscule armed forces. The

Territorial Force on which New Zealand's citizen army response was based continued to be important in planning for mobilisation, and in giving some bulk to New Zealand's small Army. But the deployment of 1RNZIR on operations on 4 September 1964 signalled the inevitability of the marginalisation of the Territorial Force.

The mood within 1RNZIR while it waited at Terendak was one of intense frustration. After learning of the initial landings at Pontian, Gurr had suspended applications for leave and put the battalion on four hours' notice for active operations. It remained at this state of readiness for the next two weeks. Gurr received regular updates from High Commission staff on the likelihood of his battalion's involvement, and discussed the implications with Hunter Wade, Colonel L. Kermode, Commander, Headquarters New Zealand Army South East Asia in Singapore, and Brigadier R. B. Dawson, the New Zealander commanding 28th Commonwealth Brigade. At midday on 4 September the battalion was placed at one hour's notice to move to the Labis area. Every man had his personal kit and equipment packed, and battalion vehicles were drawn up on the parade ground in front of Wellington Lines. Ammunition had been distributed and the battalion was ready and eager to go. To everyone's dismay no word came through, thanks (as Gurr put it) 'to delay and intransigence in higher echelons'.[28] The reaction of his battalion was equally blunt: 'We sat on that bloody parade ground for hours and hours and hours waiting for our High Commission ... to give the diplomatic OK ... consequently we didn't go to Labis where all the bloody Indonesians were; we went down for the other landing at Pontian.'[29]

There was certainly delay, but not 'intransigence'; the caution of Hunter Wade and his staff in seeking clearance from New Zealand to commit 1RNZIR was sensible. War is a political act, and because of New Zealand's size the commitment of its forces will always have greater political than military significance. New Zealand's commitment to both Borneo and Vietnam was also to be marked by appropriate caution and careful decision-making on the part of Holyoake's government. Major-General L. W. Thornton, the New Zealand Chief of General Staff, later wrote that he thought the High Commissioner's hesitation was justified, 'in view of the Malaysian intention to use the released [Malaysian] units to suppress the Singapore riots'.[30] Indeed, any other course of action by Hunter Wade would have gone against the guidelines laid down by his government. New Zealand's national interests were always the High Commissioner's primary concern.

## Operation LIVER, 5–12 September 1964

At 5 p.m. on 4 September, Gurr's advance party left Terendak Camp for Majeedi Barracks on the northern outskirts of Johore Bahru, the capital of Johore State. 'We were given a very broad sort of indication that we were to take over from the Malayan Brigade down there and that we were to go and find the Pontian group of infiltrators and so off we went ... down the road at pretty high speed.'[31] Gurr was followed by three of his four rifle companies, with D Company under Major Stan McKeon remaining in Terendak as garrison security. At 10 a.m. next day the battalion established itself at Majeedi Barracks, where it came under the command of 4 Federal Infantry Brigade, which was responsible for the external security of southern Johore and internal security within Singapore. The latter responsibility preoccupied the brigade; the rioting in Singapore was stretching its resources 'beyond the limit'. In response, the 5th and 6th Battalions Royal Malay Regiment were sent to Singapore from Labis and Pontian respectively. Labis now became the responsibility of 1 Federal Infantry Brigade, using 1/10th Gurkha Rifles; and although 4 Federal Infantry Brigade remained nominally responsible for Pontian, its defence was in fact delegated to Gurr's battalion.[32]

Gurr set up his headquarters in the Police Control Centre in Johore Bahru and established what information was available. It was known that groups had come ashore at Kukup, Pontian Besar and Benut on the west coast of southern Johore on 17 August, the nineteenth anniversary of the declaration of Indonesian independence.[33] Each group numbered between 30 and 40 men, and comprised Indonesian Regular Air Force paratroopers of the PGT (Pasukan Gerak Tjepat, or Quick Reaction Force) and Marine commandos of the KKO (Korps Komando Operasi); they also included Malaysian Chinese and some pro-communist Malays who had been recruited in Malaysia before undergoing training in Indonesia.[34] The groups' role was to establish a secure operational base which would be used to train local supporters to conduct acts of sabotage and terrorism. The Malaysians within each party were to obtain food and other necessities from local supporters. However, all the arms and ammunition dumps established by sympathisers in the Pontian area had been located and emptied by Police Special Branch before the landings. By the end of August the Kukup and Pontian Besar groups had been split up and 'virtually eliminated' by Malaysian Army and Police action.[35] The Benut group proved more elusive. After two contacts, in which one Indonesian was killed and one Indonesian and two Malaysian Chinese captured, there were no further sightings. By the time 1RNZIR moved into the Pontian area, there was some doubt as to whether the group actually existed. Despite the initial contacts, Headquarters 4 Federal Infantry Brigade tended to believe that the group did not exist, or that if they had landed, they had since returned to Indonesia.[36] Police Special Branch, on the other hand, believed they were real enough and still hiding in the Pontian swamps. But with no sightings since the initial contacts on 17 August, intelligence efforts were now focused on Labis and Singapore.

Gurr's task was to find and destroy the Benut group. With little to go on, he had to start from scratch. 'I said to myself, "Well, the first thing I've got to do is get some information" ... In the meantime I deployed a couple of the companies to patrol in areas adjacent to the road and railway line. I assessed that if these people were intent on causing any damage, then these areas of communication would probably be the most vulnerable.'[37] Thorpe's A Company, Burrows' B Company, and the Reconnaissance Platoon commanded by Lieutenant 'Albie' Kiwi were deployed into the operational area. Both Burrows and Kiwi were fluent Malay speakers, and Gurr relied on them to establish whether there were still infiltrators in the area. The area was a rectangle, with one side formed by the west coast road linking Benut to Pontian Kechil. It was completed by secondary roads running north from Benut to just south of Simpang Rengam on the Muar road, then south-east through Ayer Bemban and Senai to Skudai, and south-west to Pontian Kechil. Kampongs and smallholdings bordered the coast, while large rubber and pineapple plantations straddled both the coast and inland roads. The centre was dominated by the Pontian swamps, a tortuous mass of mangrove jungle growing in waist-deep mud and stinking water. In the south-east was the forested high ground of Gunong Pulai, where two reservoirs provided a significant proportion of Singapore's water.

On his arrival at Pontian, Burrows found that there was 'considerable confusion ... rumours were rife'. He assembled the local authorities at his headquarters to assess the situation. 'Nobody was taking the initiative ... so I got this District officer and the local policeman and I think there was a Malaysian army bloke ... and we just sat down and said, "Well, what do we know?" and "Where do we go from here?"' This was an ad hoc resurrection of the District War Executive Committee system that had been so successful during the Emergency; now, chaired—'probably inappropriately'—by Burrows, 'it worked for those critical few days'.[38]

The manager of the Pontian pineapple plantation had noticed unusual activity in the area, and this became the focus of the company's operations.[39] At the same time Captain Owen Mann, the battalion's intelligence officer, was sent to 'contact every possible source of information from Special Branch, the Police Field Force, and from 4 Malaysian Brigade now in Singapore'.[40] Mann found that neither Special Branch nor 6RMR had any useful information on the Benut group. Indeed, when the Commander Far East Land Forces visited 1/10th Gurkha Rifles and 1RNZIR on 6 September, his staff officer noted that there was 'no positive information on likely enemy positions. Both Battalion commanders were working on little more than a hunch.'[41]

Thorpe's A Company was assigned to search the area south of the Pontian swamps. C Company under Major Bob Straight was initially held in reserve in Majeedi Barracks, but on 11 September it was deployed into the Gunong Pulai area after Police Field Force interrogations revealed it was probable that the Kukup and Pontian groups had been told to move there. Straight's company's patrols criss-crossed the jungle-covered high ground without finding any 'signs of an Indonesian presence'.[42]

## Operation LILAC, 12–27 September 1964

The Benut group had proved just as illusory for the New Zealanders as they had for the Malaysians before them, and on 11 September Gurr was told to expect a move north to Labis. There he would come under the operational control of 1 Federal Infantry Brigade on Operation LILAC, and assist in operations against survivors of the Indonesian parachute landings of 1–2 September. Three Indonesian C130 Hercules transport aircraft had been involved: one had apparently crashed into the Straits of Malacca, while the other two had successfully dropped 96 personnel around Labis.[43] The first aircraft had flown from Jakarta via Medan in Sumatra, and dropped its party of 33 Indonesians and 15 Malaysian Chinese around the newly established settlement at Pekan Ayer Panas. This was a Federal Land Development Area where the jungle had been cleared for planting rubber trees, and the parachutists landed on open ground dotted with newly erected houses. The infiltrators were commanded by Second Lieutenant Soetikno, who became the senior Indonesian officer by default when his superior was apparently killed in the aircraft that crashed. Their reception was not what they expected. Instead of welcoming them, the local villagers raised the alarm. Police rushed to the scene and by 4.30 a.m., still in darkness, had captured the group's supply containers, which had been dropped separately. Police Field Force reinforcements came quickly from Segamat and by dawn a search had started. The first Indonesians were contacted by 7.00 a.m., after which 'it was merely a matter of rounding up survivors'.[44] In the first two days, 5RMR and the Police Field Force killed or captured 11 of Soetikno's party. Interrogation revealed that supply containers with food for 18 days, ammunition, stores and medical supplies had been dropped first, followed by the 48 parachutists jumping one after the other in a straight line. Once on the ground, they were expected to join up at their supply drop and then move towards a rendezvous on Gunong Besar, a prominent hill north-east of the drop zone. Labis may have been chosen because it had been a communist stronghold during the Emergency, but times had changed. The villagers gave no support to either the Indonesians or the Malaysian Chinese with them, who were not locals but came from Taiping to the north and Pontian to the south. Confused and disoriented, lacking supplies and harried by police and Army patrols, the scattered Indonesians became the target of 1/10th Gurkha Rifles.[45]

Intelligence at the time was not aware that a second aircraft had parachuted 41 Indonesians and seven Malaysian Chinese into the Lesong Forest, north of Labis. In an impressive feat, the men dropped at night onto the jungle canopy, found themselves suspended 100 to 150 feet above the ground, and abseiled down to the forest floor. They too were dropped in a single stick over a distance of some five miles. Their commander, Sergeant-Major Wagimin, managed to gather in many but not all of his team. It was only when a lone Indonesian, exhausted and disoriented, walked out on the east coast of the Peninsula that it was thought a further drop might have occurred in the hilly jungle area on the east coast, inland from Kuala Rompin. This solitary arrival caused great concern in Kuala Lumpur; it was what led to the redeployment of 1RNZIR from Pontian.

Gurr flew north to Segamat by helicopter to meet Brigadier Abas Manan, Commander of 1 Federal Infantry Brigade, who told him to deploy to Kuala Rompin and search the Lesong Forest Reserve. Gurr's instincts told him that this had all the hallmarks of a wild goose chase which would remove his battalion so far from the most likely operational area that it could play no further meaningful role. This he was determined to prevent.

> I must have looked, and certainly felt, very startled … I knew the Lesong Forest was a vast area of tropical rain forest. Between Kuala Rompin and Labis there was 50 miles of real tiger country. Furthermore, Kuala Rompin was 125 miles up the East Coast road, then dependent on ancient vehicular ferries across two major rivers.

> Each ferry had the capacity for four cars or two trucks. When I asked Brigadier Manan who had made the decision to send us up the East Coast he informed me the instruction had come from Lieutenant-General Hamid Bidin, the Malaysian Chief of General Staff. I persuaded the Brigadier I was very unhappy with the proposal and that we should both go and see the Malaysian CGS as a matter of urgency.[46]

Gurr warned his battalion about the move—leaving its destination to be confirmed—and then flew to Kuala Lumpur with Brigadier Manan and the 1RNZIR intelligence officer, Captain Owen Mann. On the journey, Gurr analysed the problem confronting him. He believed his battalion could only move to Kuala Rompin by road, which would require a significant engineering effort to get across the two rivers. Apart from the logistic and administrative difficulties this would cause, his battalion would be isolated from the likely areas of infiltration and unable to respond to any further landings or air drops on the west coast. Indeed, helicopter resources were already fully stretched to meet the requirements of 1/10th Gurkha Rifles. Flying into the Lesong Forest from Kuala Rompin would take longer than from a battalion position somewhere in the Labis area. Gurr proposed to argue that with judicious use of helicopter support, the deployment of his battalion into the Labis area would also allow him to meet the east coast contingency.[47]

On 12 September, Gurr met with Lieutenant-General Hamid Bidin, the Malaysian Chief of General Staff.

> He was courteous and listened to the reasons which had prompted the sudden arrival in his office of a New Zealand battalion commander. One of my companies [Burrows' B Company] was already operating at Labis under the temporary command of 1/10th Gurkhas. If 1RNZIR was going to make a useful contribution it needed to be from a base close to Labis. General Hamid Bidin asked me where I thought the battalion should deploy. I suggested Segamat initially, and that I would co-ordinate areas of search with Colonel Burnett. The CGS agreed and 1RNZIR was in Segamat the following day.[48]

Once this was agreed, Mann rang the police station at Keluang, the junction of the East Coast Road and the road to Labis. Here an advance party under the commander of Headquarters Company, Major Des Smith, awaited his call.

> The Battalion rolled out of Majeedi Barracks ... not knowing whether they were going to the east coast or staying on the west coast ... so I rang to tell them that we were going up to Segamat as the Battalion was trundling up the road. When they got to the Kluang crossroads, the Battalion Regimental Police just directed them

straight ahead until they ran into some more RPs, and by that stage Des Smith had gone up there ... commandeered a school ... sorted out where the Battalion would be, [and] were going to bivvy up for the night and it was as simple as that.[49]

One has to imagine the long line of Land Rovers and trucks, loaded with armed men, their supplies and ammunition, seamlessly leaving one location and driving into the unknown, the men knowing from past training and long experience that somewhere along the road a New Zealand vehicle carrying a handful of soldiers wearing the white and red 'RP' brassards would give them directions.

Thanks to the fortunes of war—and the usual Burrows luck—B Company had already joined 1/10th Gurkha Rifles at Labis. After eight days of hard work and fruitless searching in the waist-deep, snake-ridden Pontian swamps, the company had been sent back to Terendak to replace McKeon's D Company on garrison duty. Burrows' soldiers had been in Terendak some 24 hours when, with Gurr's approval, they were called south to assist 1/10th Gurkhas at Labis, and temporarily placed under Gurkha command. The commanding officer, Lieutenant-Colonel 'Bunny' Burnett, deployed Burrows into the area of the original parachute drop, which by then had been searched exhaustively. 'They didn't give me the good pickings at all which annoyed me greatly, but then I couldn't do anything about it.' Indeed, Burrows was lucky to be in an area where something was happening, even if it was the Gurkha companies that were having most of the excitement. Burnett, determined to keep the Indonesian infiltrators off-balance, ran his battalion as if it were a rifle company and he the company commander. He gave orders directly to the rifle platoons, using Royal Navy Wessex helicopters to move them from point to point in the jungle. 'There was hardly a moment of the day when at least one platoon was not airborne ... The CO's reserve at any time was the platoon on the coldest scent.'[50]

Burnett's policy of deploying whoever was available resulted in a small Gurkha company headquarters group running into and being wiped out by some of the Indonesians. All were killed, including the company commander. The operation then became a personal matter for Burnett's battalion, and the Gurkhas ruthlessly hunted the Indonesians down. Burrows recalled Burnett's anger at the death of his men, and his determination to find those responsible. 'He had two Indonesians there that he wanted some information from about where the group [was, and] I saw him whack both of them and knock them down with his fist ... I thought it was a bit unnecessary ... [but] if he was knocking them over that's not half what the Gurkhas were doing to them.'

Outside Burnett's Battalion Headquarters at the Labis police station 'there would be eight or nine bodies lying out on the lawn and a big group of very impressed locals with their eyes glued to the wire, looking at these, and the jeeps would come in with a couple of bodies across the bonnet [and] it was pretty obvious who was winning.'[51]

After the long line of 1RNZIR vehicles rolled into Segamat on 12 September, the battalion's tactical headquarters was established in the Police District Headquarters by 5 p.m. The rest of the battalion was grouped around the Segamat airstrip, alongside the Wessex helicopters of HMS *Bulwark*. With the Gurkhas having more than a vested interest in this operation, Gurr's battalion was second in line, and the New Zealanders had to do the best they could with the areas allotted to them. Gurr commented: '[Burnett] had a strong proprietary interest in the Labis operation. Initially the recommendation he made for an inter-unit boundary between 1RNZIR and his Gurkhas fell somewhere out in the Gulf of Siam.'[52] Eventually the two strong-willed commanding officers agreed to a more equitable arrangement.

On 14 September, C Company was lifted by helicopter deep into the Lesong Forest in case the Indonesians had moved to the north of their original drop zone. Six days of intensive patrolling in virgin jungle brought no sightings, but a grudging admiration for the audacity of the Indonesian drop developed. Flying over the jungle canopy where the first drops had been made was unforgettable. 'Below were over a hundred parachutes suspended on the roof of the jungle. I could not feel other than impressed.' Gurr and his company commanders were well aware of the skill and professionalism 'needed to get to the ground during the night from a parachute suspended a hundred feet above the jungle floor'.[53] C Company was withdrawn and replaced on the 22nd by D Company from Terendak, which joined A Company in searching south of Labis. Gurr's Battalion Headquarters and administrative elements also shifted south, establishing themselves around the airstrip of the Johore Labis Palm Oil Estate near Chaah.[54] While both companies took prisoners, Burnett's 1/10th Gurkhas had an ongoing series of contacts. On 15 September a Gurkha patrol contacted a group of 18, killing six and capturing two, and on the 24th another patrol killed six Indonesians.[55]

Burrows' B Company was searching the area of Soetikno's original drop, north of Labis near Ayer Panas, and remained there when 1RNZIR arrived. On the evening of the 21st, Burrows was told by a local that two armed Indonesians had come to his house asking for food. The family invited them in, but at the same time sent a message to alert the New Zealanders camped half a mile away. Burrows placed a platoon cordon around the house, then with Private Williams as escort went forward and took their surrender.[56] One of the men was Second Lieutenant Soetikno, the senior surviving Indonesian officer. Next morning the battalion's intelligence officer, Captain Mann, took a patrol back to the area where Soetikno had landed and found the hide in the roots of a large tree in which he and his companion, a private, had lived for three weeks. After finishing their rations, they had buried their equipment and come out to seek food. Mann found that Soetikno was using a Shell road map of Malaya. It was obvious that the Indonesian party had no idea what to expect, and in some cases did not know where they were.[57] It was a brave enterprise, boldly launched but with no hope of success.

Soetikno's surrender was one of the few New Zealand successes at Labis. By 26 September all the companies were concentrated around the airfield, awaiting orders. B Company moved out late that day to investigate a possible sighting at Kebun Baharu, south-west of Segamat, but the following day 1RNZIR returned to Terendak, where it remained on standby. The New Zealanders had played very much a secondary role on Operation LILAC, but Gurr was more than satisfied with his battalion's performance.

> [We] didn't get too much involved and we didn't have too many direct contacts but it was a good experience ... I thought that one of the great things we got out of that was that we had a facility to move and deploy from one place to another at pretty high speed ... and the fellows just loved it. They thought it was Christmas and even though they weren't getting a lot of contacts, they had an objective and if there was nothing there, it was like going out fishing and if you're not catching anything, you've then got to go somewhere else.[58]

The battalion's willingness and the skill it displayed on difficult operations in the least likely areas were matched by their commanding officer's determination to see his battalion properly used. It took a strong man to challenge a Malaysian brigade commander and then the Malaysian Chief of General Staff about what he saw as his battalion's misemployment, but Gurr did it successfully with reason and tact. This was no small achievement in an operational situation involving different national forces, with the opponent's position and strength uncertain. Although minor in nature and thin in results, the battalion's performance was highly professional at all levels of command, and one in which the unit and its CO could take pride.

## Operation LIVER II, 29 September – 29 October 1964

On 29 September, 1RNZIR was redeployed into the Pontian area of southern Johore to search for the elusive Benut group.[59] There was some indication that they may have crossed the inland highway and moved into the jungle hills in the centre of the Peninsula, although Police Special Branch thought that they were probably still in the stinking maze of mangrove swamp between the coast and the main road. There was some scepticism among the New Zealanders as to how much searching had actually taken place before they arrived. Lieutenant Max Ritchie, a platoon commander in Burrows' B Company, recalled a conversation with a Malay platoon commander: '[He] was telling me just how difficult this country was. "It was absolutely frightful stuff," he said, and his boots and trousers were clean. At the time that didn't sink in quite as much as 10 minutes later when I found that you couldn't step out of your vehicle without sinking into the mud, and he obviously hadn't stepped out of his vehicle.'[60] After Gurr conducted a detailed helicopter reconnaissance of the area, he described it as 'the most gloomy tract of stunted jungle I had seen'.[61]

Gurr established his headquarters at the Police Field Force barracks at Rengam. Straight's C Company moved south to Layang Layang to search the jungle east of the main road, while McKeon's D Company searched west of the road, in the eastern edge of the Pontian swamp. Thorpe's A Company, and elements of the Support Company, were initially held in reserve. Captain Mann went out once again in search of information, and on 2 October was told by the European manager of the South Malaya Pineapple Growers Estate that over the previous ten days his workers had seen people moving into the western edge of the swamp from the pineapple plantations. 'These sightings had been reported to the Police but no action had apparently been taken on it.'[62] This had originally been B Company's area, and Gurr sent them in again with Albie Kiwi's Reconnaissance Platoon to see what they could find. D Company was positioned as a blocking force on the swamp's eastern edge, and the Mortar Platoon established a firing position on the road nearby. On the 3rd, Burrows' patrols found a camp that had been abandoned approximately 10 to 12 days previously in the swamp near the pineapple plantation, and over the next two days patrols found a number of fresh tracks leading into the swamp. 'Since the whole swamp extended over some fifty square miles we alerted the Police Field Force to mount further road blocks. It was a useful precaution as they picked up five Malaysian Chinese who had ... got rid of their weapons and were trying to board a civilian bus to Seremban.'[63]

On the basis of local intelligence, it seemed that in the swamp there was 'one strong group of 40 under an Indonesian officer called Suparmin. He was a large bearded man and in no time his exploits, real or imagined, were the talk of the locals. Unexplained flares went off regularly each night and generally the public were pretty scared.'[64] Villagers told of mangrove-covered islands in the swamps where Chinese refugees had hid from the Japanese during the Second World War. On 6 October Gurr, having withdrawn his patrols, attempted to flush the group out. 'The mortar platoon then fired 200 rounds on an area target which they also marked with coloured smoke. The target area was then rocketed and strafed by eight Hunter fighters of No. 20 Squadron, RAF. A voice aircraft followed, calling on the Indonesians to surrender and avoid further bloodshed.'[65] It was later established from prisoners' accounts that many of the RAF rockets landed near the Indonesians' hideout.

B, C, and D Companies went into ambush around the swamp, and Police Special Branch provided a local man who led B Company to the spot at the edge of the swamp where he had cached food for the Indonesians. On the 7th, Burrows had Lieutenant Max Ritchie's 6 Platoon 'move around just inside the swamp adjacent to the plantation hoping to identify any signs of movement into the jungle. The going through the mangrove was very difficult, but the more difficult the going, the easier signs are identified. Within about three hours Ritchie reported that he was onto very definite tracks leading into the jungle swamp and was following up.'[66]

As Ritchie recalled, it was 'absolutely terrible country. The deeper you got into it the deeper it became. There were all sorts of root systems of trees through which you'd fall, and be dragged down by your pack, extra ammunition and batteries. And then you would have to drag yourself up and try and walk on the roots, and then down you would go again.' In mid-afternoon, the leading section was following a promising track into the swamps. Burrows came forward to assess the track. He and Ritchie were talking,

> and then 'Bang! Bang! Bang! Bang! Bang!' ... So along I went and met up with the section commander who was frozen into inactivity ... He and his section had run into a sentry who had opened fire. They had returned fire and then stopped, not knowing quite what to do. The sentry had obviously buggered off back to the Indonesian camp, and they just took off, left all their kit, thinking they were about to be attacked.[67]

It should be remembered that these soldiers were standing waist-deep in mud and water in single file, facing a concealed sentry covering the only possible approach. There was no option but to go in, and as the platoon moved forward it found a well-established camp, almost completely concealed by foliage.[68] Suparmin's party had fled, leaving most of their supplies and equipment behind. This included 270 lb of rice, a hundredweight of oatmeal, assorted tins of food, civilian clothing, 24 sets of packs and webbing, 12 grenades and some 6,000 rounds of ammunition. No one had been hit in the exchange of fire, but the group's effectiveness had now been destroyed.[69]

Ritchie continued to pursue the Indonesians through the mangroves. 'I do recall smelling this very distinctive Indonesian tobacco and just a short time after that all hell broke loose ... They had these West German automatic carbines, and they let rip with these. Most extraordinary amount of fire and I was grovelling behind a tree trying to make myself as small as possible.' After a hectic exchange of fire the Indonesians withdrew. 'I got command of the situation and we started the follow-up again. Well we found the body of a fellow we had killed in the exchange of fire, and shortly after that a whole lot of ammunition and packs that they had dropped, and off we went.' The Indonesian killed by the platoon's lead scout, Private R. Burnaby, was one of a small party left behind to delay any follow-up while Suparmin's main group made their escape. 'We went until last light through the swamp and then camped out in the swamp ... we had a dreadful night. Then the following morning the trackers floundered around and announced that they couldn't find the track.' It didn't matter. The Indonesians twice exchanged fire with Albie Kiwi's Reconnaissance Platoon, first at 8.30 a.m. and then at 10.00 a.m. Ritchie was briefing Kiwi by radio on the likely direction of Indonesian movement when the first contact occurred.

> Albert was talking to me and then over the radio I heard, 'bang, bang, bang', and then Albert talking to his Platoon Sergeant, Windy McGee:
>
> 'Windy, what's going on?'
>
> 'We've been attacked, boss.'
>
> 'Bang, bang, bang, bang, bang.'
>
> Albert comes back over the radio to me and says, 'We are under fire, wait, wait out!' ... and a little while later he came back and said, 'We're in contact.'

Kiwi's pack was hit by an Indonesian bullet during the exchange, but as Ritchie noted he carried out a 'perfect radio voice procedure' despite being under fire.[70]

In each of these contacts the Indonesians fired first, but Kiwi's men remained unscathed while their prey continued to discard food, ammunition, weapons and packs in their efforts to elude their pursuers. After their contacts with B Company and the Reconnaissance Platoon, the Indonesians split into smaller groups and were tracked by 1RNZIR patrols out of the swamps and towards the coast. Burrows positioned the Mortar Platoon in ambush in the area of the Indonesian camp, 'to catch any stray Indonesians who had missed the day's excitement, and wandered back unsuspectingly. Sure enough they got one the following morning.'[71] On 9 October a lone Indonesian who had been separated from the group during the earlier contacts walked into the ambush and was fatally wounded. He died before he could be evacuated. Most of Gurr's battalion waited in ambush on likely routes out of the swamp, taking cover among the pineapples or in the swamp itself, without ever seeing an Indonesian. Rex Harris recalled: 'We started in the jungle and ended up on the tidal mudflats ambushing creeks ... We literally lay in the mud, and when the tide came in we moved onto slightly higher ground. Fifty per cent of the platoon on watch, and 50 per cent off. Pins half-way out of the grenades and changing over the watch in the middle of the night.'[72]

After being flushed from their hideout, Suparmin's group quickly disintegrated. On 10 October the Malaysian Marine Police captured nine Indonesians in a fishing vessel a mile off the coast as they attempted to return to Indonesia. In the following week 8RMR, covering the area between the coast road and the sea, killed one Indonesian and captured two. The police captured two more, and a group of five surrendered to a local headman. Suparmin managed to keep a 12-strong party together and moved north in search of food. 1RNZIR continued to search and lay ambushes, and got close to him at least once, but the chase now shifted to 8RMR's area on the coast.[73] On 24 October, 8RMR killed one Indonesian and captured another; both had been left behind by Suparmin because they were sick or injured and unable to keep up. That night a police roadblock fired at a party attempting to cross the coast road towards the sea. The following day an 8RMR patrol surrounded a house where four Indonesians had been reported. Three were shot and killed as they slept; the fourth escaped wounded, but surrendered the next day. One of the dead was Suparmin. With his death, any remaining threat from the Benut group ended.

1RNZIR was now concentrated in order to return to Terendak. B Company went back first on 26 October, followed by C Company and the anti-tank platoon the next day. There was one last flurry when A Company received a report that four Indonesians were in their area on the night of the 28th. A sweep next morning caught one Indonesian and the local man who had sheltered him.

The tracks of another four men were followed by a tracker dog until torrential rain destroyed the trail. Any thought of further pursuit ended when the battalion was ordered to move to Kesang, a small kampong on a river of the same name ten miles north of Muar in north-western Johore, where another Indonesian landing had been reported.

## Operation FLOWER, 29–30 October 1964

The Kesang landing was another in a series of Indonesian incursions into West Malaysia during Confrontation, and once again Burrows' B Company found themselves in the right place at the right time.[74] They had been the first New Zealanders into Labis, they had the contacts at Pontian, and now they were first to Kesang. The company had been back in Terendak for 24 hours when it was called out at 6 a.m. on 29 October. Brigadier T. D. H. McMeekin, the newly arrived commander of 28th Commonwealth Brigade, briefed Burrows at brigade headquarters on Operation FLOWER. 'He briefed me and instructed me to handle a group of Indonesians who had landed on the south side of the river. 3 Royal Australian Regiment was to deal with those on the northern side. The Brigadier was to coordinate and control the operation.'[75]

McMeekin first cleared the use of Burrows' company with Gurr. The Australian government had released the Australian battalion for operations against the infiltrators, and Gurr was asked if he would place Burrows under the command of 3RAR for this operation.[76] 1RNZIR and 1/10th Gurkhas would mount an outer cordon around Kesang while the Australians closed in and mopped up the Indonesians.

> [Gurr] was not happy at the prospect of placing B Company under 3RAR command and said so, particularly as we were already en route to Kesang. Brigadier McMeekin then asked to put B Company under his direct personal command until we arrived on the scene. On the understanding B Company would revert to my command once we were deployed in our new location, I agreed.[77]

B Company arrived at Kesang by 10 a.m., and with two platoons side by side and the third held in reserve, swept towards the coast south of the river, closing in on the apex of the triangle formed by the river and the mangrove-covered shoreline.

> By late afternoon we had captured ten Indonesians and believed our area to be clear. The Indonesians had been violently sea sick all the previous night during

> their crossing and were wet, cold and thoroughly demoralised. By a strange coincidence one of them was the son of Soetikno the Indonesian para leader we had captured at Labis, so I was able to update him on his father's health and assure him they would be re-united shortly.[78]

By last light on 29 October, all but four of the infiltrators who had landed south of the river had been picked up, with B Company capturing eight and the others surrendering to local residents, the Police Field Force or D Company 3RAR.

Initially it was thought that up to 100 Indonesians had come ashore, but under interrogation the prisoners revealed that there had been 52 in the party—29 Air Force paratroopers of the PGT, 21 members of the IBT ('Irregular Border Terrorists') and two Malaysians (one Malay and one Chinese). The group had crossed from Sumatra in five Malaysian fishing boats after coercing the fishermen into taking them. Their task was to distract attention from the Benut group by landing near Kuala Pilah and carrying out terrorist attacks. Their landing was delayed by bad weather, and one of the boats may have been lost at sea. The Indonesians landed in two groups on either side of the Sungei Kesang, north of where they intended, and foolishly declared their presence by firing on a local fisherman. Police Field Force units from Malacca and Johore responded immediately, and contained the landing until elements of 28th Commonwealth Brigade arrived.[79]

Meanwhile 1RNZIR drove north, commandeering the vehicle ferry at Muar to move its transport across the river, and receiving further instructions from McMeekin on the way. 1RNZIR was to link up with 1/10th Gurkhas and form a cordon about two miles from the mouth of the Kesang River to prevent any breakout by the Indonesians. While Gurr established his tactical headquarters in the Chinese School at Sungai Mati, his men quickly moved into position and awaited developments. 3RAR showed its relative inexperience in this operation. After establishing a cordon half a mile from the mouth of the Kesang River, they had not moved towards the coast by nightfall. At the brigade orders group that evening McMeekin, clearly irked by this lack of progress, goaded the Australians to act. Burrows remembered that night as

> spectacular to say the least. I was on the radio net to Brigade HQ, 3 RAR and 1RNZIR, which had moved up from Pontian. A battery of field artillery began firing into the area just to the north of us in conjunction with the [81 mm] mortars of 3RAR. Of greater concern to us was the small arms fire from the inner cordon of 3RAR, reportedly 'repelling breakout attempts'. Fortunately my company had

> the protection of some flood bunds [stopbanks] but we found it necessary to move back some distance from our side of the river.[80]

Gurr noted that it 'sounded like a prelude to World War 3'.[81] Ritchie's 6 Platoon was part of the B Company cordon on the river bank.

> It was just like the fire plan at Alamein. The films you see of the night sky being lit up as this gallant band of Indonesians took on the might of the Australian Army. I monitored the Australian command [radio] net. These Indonesians spent the whole night attempting to break out through this Australian cordon and there were enormous fire fights and battles and gallant actions throughout the night. We spent the whole night crouching down into drains and little hollows in the ground as all this fire was coming over our heads. It was actually quite funny and we thought it was funny at the time ... As it turned out, the following morning we found 25 Indonesians sheltering on the north bank of the river, most of whom were unarmed, one of whom was captured wearing only his underpants and with a nail clipper his only weapon ... The Australians had spent the whole night firing at shadows or at themselves, and the Indonesians hadn't moved the whole time.[82]

Shortly after first light, McMeekin ordered 3RAR forward to round up the Indonesians. Burrows returned to his company and was called forward by the platoon at the river mouth. 'On the other side of the river was a bunch of frightened and very muddy Indonesians, clinging to the mangroves where they had been since the day before. I tried to persuade them into coming across the river and surrendering to us, but in their petrified state they could not be persuaded. After another barrage the Australians arrived and led them away.'[83] By midday on the 30th, all but five of the 52 Indonesians who had landed had been accounted for. In a final sweep, B Company picked up another three who were attempting to cross the river from north to south. At 6 p.m., 1RNZIR and the remainder of 28th Commonwealth Brigade returned to Terendak, leaving the mopping up to the Police Field Force.

Between the Pontian landings of 17 August 1964 and 30 September 1965, Indonesia sent at least 855 infiltrators—'regular soldiers, airmen, marines, and policemen, local volunteers, conscripted boatmen and Malaysian exfiltrators'—against West Malaysia.[84] Perhaps a hundred or so were turned back by bad weather or for some other reason. Only 436 managed to land; of these, 102 were killed and 301 captured.[85] Some escaped and tried again. The Indonesians' lack of success resulted from the lack of sympathy of the local population, prompt action by police and security forces, and active naval patrolling. By

1966 Indonesian operations against West Malaysia and Singapore were restricted to selective intelligence gathering. There was no successful sabotage, although a number of incidents occurred in the Malacca and Singapore Straits. All this came to an end with the signing of the Bangkok Agreement between Indonesia and Malaysia on 11 August 1966.

Gurr's battalion was the only one to take part in all three operations on the Malay Peninsula involving Commonwealth forces. As a result, its members were awarded the General Service Medal (GSM) 1962 with the 'Malay Peninsula' clasp. 1RNZIR demonstrated a level of professionalism and skill that would be shown again during its deployment to Borneo in 1965. Its role was small but significant, and Gurr was proud of what his battalion had achieved. It had stood up to the demands of hard patrolling in very difficult country, and had suffered no battle casualties in a number of contacts initiated by the Indonesians. Morale was high, and the battalion was keen to have another go.

> The next few months were really a bit of an anticlimax because we were doing a little bit of coast watching, and we were hanging about doing odd exercises, keeping very fit. But really we were pretty sharp at that stage and so when we finally got news through Colonel Leo Kermode [Commander New Zealand Army FARELF] that we were to do a six-month tour in Borneo, it was great news.[86]

# 8

# 'A REAL JOB TO DO'

## *Air and Naval Operations, 1962–66*

### No. 41 Squadron RNZAF, 1962–66

> Operating the Freighter away from the Changi circuit is often frustrating for the crew. Cockpit lighting is poor and we are not allowed to improve it; the VHF set is unduplicated and too often fails; the ADFs are old and have caused a lot of trouble recently; the HF is outdated and ... good R/T contact during route flight is seldom achieved ... Approaching terminal areas always creates curses in the cockpit because very few people these days only have ADF as aids ... and it still surprises controllers when we tell them that all we have is ADF ... The Freighter still plays a very useful role in this area but lack of aids is professionally frustrating for the crew.[1]
>
> SQUADRON-LEADER I. A. HUTCHINS,
> NO. 41 SQUADRON RNZAF

The Bristol Freighters of No. 41 Squadron RNZAF were the first New Zealand elements to be committed to Borneo after an armed revolt broke out in Brunei on 8 December 1962. Along with every available RAF aircraft, they were soon busy flying in troops and supplies. Between 11 and 17 December the Freighters flew non-stop, day and night. By the time the last sortie was completed on 27 December, No. 41 Squadron had carried 145,305 lb of freight and 89 passengers in 223 hours of flying.

The New Zealand government was only prepared to allow its aircraft to be used in a transport capacity between Singapore and Brunei. It would not permit the Freighters to drop supplies to the British forces on jungle operations in Brunei. What Cabinet did not know, however, was that the two New Zealand

Army pilots on attachment to No. 656 Squadron Army Air Corps in Malaya were flying Auster fixed-wing aircraft in Borneo. Captains Ray Andrews and Chris Brown RNZA were both deployed for two three-month tours in 1963 without their government's knowledge. Their replacements in No. 656 Squadron, Captains Roger Pearce and Walter Steward, both members of the newly formed New Zealand Army Air Corps, unofficially flew Austers in Sarawak for three months in 1964. The Auster was a small, fixed-wing, single-engine aircraft suited both to liaison and reconnaissance tasks, and to 'light' airdrops for which the plane was flown with the right door removed. This required a high degree of skill—while the pilot controlled the plane with his left hand, 'with your right hand you would pick up the board that the parachute was on and lift it up sharply so the whole lot slid out the door. There was a static line on it which deployed the chute and it would float down into the clearing.'[2] Weather, as always, was the crucial factor in flying over the mountainous, jungle-covered terrain.

> A calm morning with the inland [air]strips under ground mist or low cloud is followed by a morning build-up of cumulus and cumulonimbus clouds with isolated storms becoming more widespread and sometimes general. Pilots fly over, between, or under the build-up, depending on what stage it has reached. One eye is always firmly over the shoulder watching that a way out remains open or, at least, the way to a diversion strip.[3]

Both Pearce, based at Sibu, and Steward, at Kuching, removed the New Zealand flashes from their flying suits so as not to be identified as New Zealanders, 'because at this stage we were not involved in the Borneo campaign'. Both pilots carried out two tours in Borneo, returning to officially fly Sioux observation and reconnaissance helicopters in 1965.[4]

Such opportunities were not available for No. 41 Squadron. However, as the Brunei rebellion evolved into an uneasy confrontation with Indonesia, Kuching and Labuan were added to a busy courier schedule. This was but one addition to the growing list of commitments for the Bristol Freighters, which now operated from Korat in support of the United States' Special Logistic Aid Thailand programme, and from Singapore to Kuching, as well as along the normal courier routes to Hong Kong. Manning was a critical problem for No. 41 Squadron in the 1960s. Two pilots were offered extensions of their commissions to take them to 20 years' service, but refused because the pay and conditions were inferior to what was available outside the RNZAF. By April 1966 the squadron was short of an aircraft captain, a navigator and two signallers; by September the shortage of navigators had become critical.[5]

Aircraft were worked to the limit, and while it was a matter of squadron pride that schedules were kept to and jobs done, the unit was feeling the strains of keeping ageing aircraft serviceable with limited manpower. In September 1964, No. 14 Squadron RNZAF and its Canberra bombers were deployed to Singapore, and a national headquarters for both squadrons was established under Wing Commander Ewan Jamieson. After his first visit to No. 41 Squadron, Jamieson reported that it was in 'a satisfactory enough state. However the chronic drag of Korat and the consequent splintering of the unit has had a bad effect. The Squadron no longer has the old feeling of unity and pride.'[6] The rundown of the Thailand commitment eased the pressure and allowed the squadron to again base all its aircraft at RAF Changi. However, this slack was soon taken up, as Headquarters Far East Air Force assigned the New Zealanders to a large number of unscheduled flights at short notice, making it difficult to arrange aircraft servicing, leave, and duty and training rosters.[7] During a routine courier run on 18 June 1965, a Freighter piloted by Flying Officer P. G. Bevin was almost hit by Indonesian anti-aircraft gunfire. Bevin was returning at night from Kuching to Changi, and was just abreast of the Rhio (now Riau) Islands when anti-aircraft fire exploded behind and below the aircraft. He managed to confuse the Indonesian gunners by switching off the navigation lights. No holes were found on landing, but the Rhio Islands were avoided thereafter.[8]

The commitment of New Zealand combat forces to Borneo in February 1965 which is discussed in the following chapters saw the Freighters assigned to supply-dropping operations. The New Zealanders discovered that the station commander at Kuching preferred to have RAF Argosy aircraft do the job. However, as the RAF Valettas had been withdrawn in June 1965 and he had a shortage of aircraft, he was prepared to see what these curious aircraft could do.[9] On 2 August 1965 a Freighter flew to RAF Kuching and convincingly demonstrated its superiority over the Valetta, 'dropping on DZs that were as small as 5 yards diameter and as close as 400 yards from the border'.[10]

The sceptical RAF commanding officer was won over, telling Jamieson on his first visit that the aircraft 'has already shown itself thoroughly reliable and more effective'. As a result, 'the Bristols are very welcome. Both the [Forward Air Commander] and CO Kuching are now lobbying for two on detachment.'[11] The first crew, comprising Squadron-Leader R. I. F. Garrett, commanding No. 41 Squadron,[12] Flight Lieutenants Tremayne and Dillon, and Flight Sergeant

Stone, backed by seven ground crew under Sergeant Piper, made seven operational drops to eight bases along the Sarawak–Kalimantan border, totalling nearly 11,000 lb of supplies. The load was mainly ammunition or stores packed in ammunition boxes, and by the end of the first week the Freighter's floor had been deeply scored in places by boxes being dragged to the door. Sergeant Piper's ground crew fixed the problem by screwing a line of hardwood planks down the fuselage between the tie-down points.[13]

The Freighters' success in Borneo depended on the devotion of 'groundies' such as Leading Aircraftman V. P. Smith, who in an after-flight inspection noticed what seemed to be hairline cracks in the Freighter's fuel-line couplings. Smith worked by torchlight to change the fuel line. By the time he finished at midnight he had been on duty for 20 hours.[14] 'Groundies' were masters of improvisation. From adapting a canvas curtain to fit over the door opening while the Freighter was loaded during the frequent Kuching downpours, to converting their area of the 'long house' dormitory at RAF Kuching into a 'Little New Zealand', they always made the best of primitive conditions.[15]

Supply-dropping in Borneo demanded the best from the crews. The drop zones were all close to an ill-defined border. Map-reading was difficult because of the hilly terrain, the lack of roads or towns, and the ground fog that lingered in valleys and around hilltops each morning. There were enough Indonesian anti-aircraft guns just across the border to make errors in navigation potentially hazardous. All this added spice to the operations. As Jamieson reported, the Freighter crews were 'very happy to get back to supply dropping ... The flying is interesting and of obvious importance. In fact, I envy the aircrew to some extent.'[16]

Each crew did an initial four-week detachment in Kuching to learn the ropes, followed by subsequent three-week detachments. The Freighters were employed exclusively on supply-dropping, averaging two drops every day of the week. The aircrews were issued with flack vests and small arms by the RAF, and parachutes became part of the Freighters' permanent equipment in theatre. The smallness of the drop zones presented problems, but the first crews devised a sight for the navigator, who 'controls the drop lying prone in the bomb aimer's position in the nose doors of the Bristol Freighter ... [using] a suitably marked sheet of acrylic ... with the edges reinforced with aluminium strips. This sheet is shaped to fit over the lower portion of the clear plastic window in the starboard nose door.'[17]

In just over seven weeks of operations, the detachment dropped 500,000 lb of supplies. They had a good working relationship with both the RAF and the

Royal Army Service Corps air despatch crews who did the hard work, 'humping packs down the aircraft'.[18] Freighter crews schooled each new despatch team before allowing them to do an operational drop, the New Zealanders' record being too important to let an inexperienced despatch team ruin it. In 1965 a Freighter captained by Flight Lieutenant Frank Roach, with Flight Lieutenant Neil Barr as navigator and Flight Sergeant Magill as signaller, won the Bennett Trophy for the best performance in low-level supply-dropping among the transport squadrons in the Far East Air Force. Another Freighter, crewed by Squadron-Leader Ian Hutchins, Flight Lieutenant Michael Dillon and Sergeant Stagg, was placed fifth. The Freighters won the trophy again in 1966.[19] When detachments changed over, the Freighters returned to Changi looking and smelling 'like a butcher's shop', food having been dropped in 'locally made crates and fresh meat in canvas bags packed with ice and sawdust'.[20] Live chickens were dropped to Gurkha battalions, and it was not unusual to see a crate burst open in mid-air, 'leaving a flock of surprised domestic birds planing over the jungle in their first, and probably last, high level solo'.[21] The only source of annoyance was that whereas RAF Kuching allowed the carriage of 'live ammunition and combustibles such as kerosene and petrol', at RAF Changi peacetime restrictions applied and it was 'difficult to load a gallon of paint'.[22]

The intensive flying schedule placed enormous pressure on the crews. On 10 September 1965 operations had to be reduced for two days because of crew fatigue. It was assessed that the four-week tour was too long; no crew could 'take this load for a sustained period'.[23] It was the same for the ground crews; from then on, Kuching tours were limited to 14 days.[24] In late September the north-east monsoon strengthened over Borneo 'with a vengeance'.[25] This caused a welcome lull in operations, but there was still enough happening to remind the crews that they were in an operational zone. On 13 October, a Freighter captained by Flight Lieutenant N. J. S. Rodger strayed into Kalimantan while dropping supplies to a border post and was holed by small-arms fire. Three bullets hit the fuselage, with two going into the toilet area; from the angle of impact 'it was fortunate that there was no one in the toilet at the time'.[26] Nonetheless, Freighter crews revelled in the good weeks when there was 'plenty of flying, adequate time for recreation and good weather. No sorties delayed for any reason.'[27]

Alongside their commitment to Borneo, the Freighters continued flying courier routes. The start of a regular courier service for the New Zealand V Force in South Vietnam gave the crews a taste of another war zone. On the night of 12 April 1966 a Freighter was on the tarmac at Tan Son Nhut Airport in Saigon when Viet Cong attacked. A mortar shell landed nearby, covering the aircraft with debris but doing no damage. Squadron-Leader Hutchins and his crew had considered sleeping in the aircraft but were pleased that they had changed their minds. A fragment of mortar shrapnel was later found to have pierced the aircraft's rudder.[28]

By the end of the year, the weather pattern over Borneo meant that most sorties were carried out in the early morning, when there was low cloud but good visibility below the cloud base. This cloud would slowly lift and break up; mid-afternoon showers often turned into several hours of heavy rain that flooded the Kuching runway and stopped all flying.[29] The pattern of courier runs and supply-dropping continued into 1966; by February the Freighters had dropped 2 million lb of supplies. However, the New Year also saw a decrease in the intensity of operations, and when there was no work Kuching palled for Freighter crews and their morale fell. On 18 February the detachment was temporarily withdrawn to Changi.[30] It returned to Kuching in March but the work never regained its former intensity, with the Freighters now being stationed in rotation with Hastings of No. 48 Squadron RAF, and operating three weeks out of every four.[31]

By the beginning of July 1966 the New Zealanders had dropped over 3 million lb of freight.[32] But the forces were being run down, and in August a single Freighter was the only air-dropping aircraft left at Kuching. The last official drop by a Freighter in Borneo was to 1RNZIR at Balai Ringin, who were also about to leave. On 12 September 1966 the detachment again withdrew to Changi.[33] The Bristol Freighters of No. 41 Squadron RNZAF, despite their outdated avionics and crew shortages, had worked miracles in Borneo. These remarkable aircraft continued to do so elsewhere until they were withdrawn from RNZAF service in South-East Asia in 1977.

## No. 14 Squadron RNZAF, 1964–66

> We formed up in battle formation and hit Jakarta at maximum speed at zero feet and in the process managed to include Halim Airfield in the turn.[34]
>
> SQUADRON-LEADER PAT NEVILLE,
> NO. 14 SQUADRON RNZAF 1966–69

On 16 September 1964, four Canberra B(I)12 bombers of No. 14 Squadron RNZAF took off from Ohakea for Singapore accompanied by two Hastings transport aircraft of No. 40 Squadron. They were followed the next day by two Canberras and a single Hastings. These aircraft flew via Cocos Island in the Indian Ocean and avoided Indonesian airspace. Squadron-Leader Geoff Wallingford, commanding the squadron, led the first four aircraft. On landing at RAF Tengah the New Zealanders found themselves immersed in tense preparations for war.

> Aircraft, including Vulcan bombers, were dispersed as best they could be, vital points on the airfield were sandbagged and guarded and anti-aircraft gun regiments were deployed around the perimeter. The all-weather Javelin interceptor fighters stood at quick alert at the end of the runway ... in case the Indonesians should dare to attack this vital strike base using their Russian-built Badger bombers or older wartime Mitchell bombers. Our aircraft were armed immediately. Within the past week the Far East Air Force (FEAF) had bolstered its strike force to 96 aircraft with the arrival of the Vulcan V-Bomber detachment, three Canberra (strike) squadrons, one Canberra (Photo Reconnaissance) squadron, and a Javelin (all weather) squadron to counter the Indonesian threat.[35]

Nine New Zealand crews and ground staff were deployed to man the aircraft. As soon as the planes landed, ground crews armed the Canberras for operations while the aircrews were shepherded into underground bunkers and issued with target details. Their primary target was Halim Air Base, 12 miles south-west of Jakarta, while their secondary target was Jakarta International Airport. The Badger bombers which presented the main threat to Singapore were based at Halim. The New Zealanders were to be part of a co-ordinated strike in which their role 'was to go in with our 72 rocket pack at low level and hope to pick up Badgers or whatever other aircraft were sitting on the tarmac'.[36]

Wallingford, who had flown Venoms with No. 14 Squadron, was one of the few pilots to have seen previous operational service in Malaya. Some of his crews had deployed on VANGUARD exercises, but for many this was their first time in the tropics. The immediate refuelling and arming of the aircraft on arrival made the seriousness of the situation obvious. Del de Lorenzo, who had joined the RNZAF in 1961 straight from high school and trained as a navigator at Wigram, remembered that things were 'pretty fraught and the tension was very real in the Squadron because we just knew that we could have actually flown that day against Indonesia and we were all pretty keyed up about it'.[37] His pilot, John Hosie, had joined as a boy entrant in January 1959 and done his Wings Course 18 months later. A career in the Air Force was what both men had dreamed of, and now they faced the prospect of war. Hosie had been on three VANGUARDs, but for the first-timers it was 'totally foreign. Just the whole thing. The heat, humidity, the [crowded] airspace, everything.' In addition, 'the weather was atrocious because in September you get a very bad haze right down the Malay Peninsula, and the Straits of Malacca'.[38]

The strain on the New Zealand ground crews was equally great. Eric McPherson, who had joined the Air Force as an aircraftman and motor mechanic in 1962, was attached to No. 14 Squadron as ground crew for the deployment. He found a situation of 'utter chaos'.

> There was a massive build-up ... We became virtually operational straight away. There was no time for any settling in. As I recall it the [RAF] aircraft were going off at intervals every two hours throughout the night on patrols ... There was nowhere near enough accommodation for everybody. When we arrived the only accommodation for us was the gymnasium. They had double bunks stacked in there about two feet apart. If you were over-enthusiastic getting out of bed in the morning you would end up in the bed of the guy alongside of you. There were about two showers and two toilets for about 100 people stacked into this gymnasium, so it was interesting to say the least for the first month before we moved into other accommodation.[39]

On the day the Canberras left New Zealand, a press release from Wellington announced that 'the squadron will take part in a routine exercise with Britain's Far East Air Force'.[40] VANGUARD VI was depicted as just another in the series of exercises in which the New Zealand-based Canberra squadron had taken part since the withdrawal from Singapore of No. 75 Squadron in February 1962.[41] No. 14 Squadron was now New Zealand's sole operational bomber squadron, held in readiness as part of the country's contribution to the Commonwealth Strategic Reserve. To meet its SEATO role, it was required to be able to deploy at 48 hours' notice and be ready for operations immediately upon arrival. The public were unaware that New Zealand was committing its bomber force to Singapore to prepare for a pre-emptive strike against military airfields in Indonesia. Only the airmen knew that something was in the wind. The 'crash programme' at Ohakea of camouflaging aircraft and fitting UHF communications, and the boosting of the squadron's numbers with additional ground crew to speed up the rearming and turnaround of aircraft, made it obvious that this would not be a routine exercise.

The landings by Indonesian paratroopers at Labis on 2 September 1964 had seen the release of 1RNZIR for operations against infiltrators on the Peninsula. The belief that these landings would be followed by further major Indonesian strikes led the previously reluctant New Zealand Cabinet to agree to the despatch of No. 14 Squadron under the convenient cover of Exercise VANGUARD VI.[42] As Grey so effectively outlines in the official history of Australia's involvement in Confrontation, ANZAM planners had evolved a series of contingency plans that incorporated elements of the New Zealand Strategic Reserve. The Labis landings had considerably increased the threat of limited war, and in response to this threat Admiral Sir Varyl Begg, Commander in Chief Far East, had requested the initiation of the mobilisation stages of Plan ALTHORPE, which required British, Australian and New Zealand air resources to mobilise to air bases in Malaysia.[43] ALTHORPE involved the neutralisation of the Indonesian Air Force and Navy by pre-emptive strikes on Indonesia. For Holyoake, committing the Canberras was a difficult decision, reluctantly made. In the months ahead, this commitment would highlight the fact that New Zealand's defence resources were now stretched to breaking point in South-East Asia.

The New Zealand pilots and navigators spent many hours poring over maps and aerial photographs, checking distances and calculating fuel expenditure, in the highly protected and guarded underground target-planning vaults at Tengah Air Base.[44] Initial planning on the New Zealand squadron's behalf was done by No. 73 (Canberra) Squadron RAF, but when the New Zealand navigators 'actually analysed the flight plans that they'd done for us, we all found we would have run out of fuel about 100 miles short of Singapore on the way home'. Del de Lorenzo, one of the navigators, 'had to spend days actually rewriting, replanning, reorganising the trips so that we would have survived the return trip even if nobody had shot at us'.[45] Target assessment continued, and as aerial photos of the targets were updated from intelligence received, the New Zealand navigators repeatedly re-examined the available information until they knew the airfield layout 'like the back of their hands'.[46]

All the air resources available to the RAF and Commonwealth air forces were co-ordinated in the strike planning.

> It was to be a fully integrated strike plan with our RAF Canberra B15 counterparts [No. 45 Squadron RAF] making a simultaneous attack on military aircraft at Jakarta International airfield. At the same time the RAF and RAAF squadrons would be striking at airfields in North Sumatra. Vulcan bomber raids would then follow with electronic jamming of the poorly operated Indonesian radars to allow us to make our escape from Indonesian fighters as we climbed back to conserve fuel for the critical 460 mile journey back to Tengah. After that it was really every aircraft for itself.[47]

The Canberras would operate in a markedly different way from the high-altitude bombing runs made by No. 75 Squadron RNZAF towards the end of the Emergency. Anti-aircraft defences had been strengthened by the deployment of surface-to-air missiles which were effective against bombers on medium- and high-altitude runs, as the United States Air Force was to learn at great cost over North Vietnam. To survive in this new environment, medium bombers had to achieve 'fast low-level weapons release with complete surprise', and it was for this very role that the B(I)12 version of the Canberra had been developed.[48] It was a very different aircraft from the leased Canberra B2s flown by No. 75 Squadron in Malaya, which had been designed for medium- and high-altitude bombing. The New Zealand B(I)12 was a variant of the Canberra B(I)8, designed as a nuclear-capable bomber for the RAF. To counter the increasingly sophisticated Soviet anti-aircraft missile defences, it was designed to fly at low levels across the European plains against targets in Russia. Using a technique known as 'loft-bombing', the plane was able to make a low-level approach before, some two miles short of the target, climbing in a 45-degree trajectory and 'lofting' or tossing the bomb. The plane then looped over and returned the way it had come, thus avoiding flying over the target and being caught in the nuclear explosion. The New Zealand B(I)12 variant was not nuclear-capable, but it too was designed to fly at low levels. Conditioned by the medium-level bombing stream tactics it had employed in Malaya, the RNZAF continued to practise medium- and high-altitude bombing in New Zealand. However, between 1962 and 1964, by trial and error, and from experience gained on the VANGUARD deployments to Singapore and Thailand, No. 14 Squadron adapted to the low-level approach, first with bombs and then with rockets.[49]

The different roles of the B2 and B(I)12 Canberras were reflected in their design. The B2 version had a bubble canopy, with the navigator sitting behind the pilot in the cockpit. There was room for a second person in the seat beside the pilot; all three had ejection seats.[50] The B(I)12 version had a fixed, fighter-type canopy, offset on top of the fuselage, with the navigator sitting below and to the right of the pilot, in the body of the aircraft. While there was a sit-down navigating position with a small desk, the navigator spent most of his time lying prone on a cushion in the nose of the aircraft, operating the bomb-aiming equipment and navigating visually. In the New Zealand B(I)12s, only the pilot had an ejection seat; in an emergency, the navigator exited from the door in the side of the fuselage after donning his parachute, which was stored on a rack above the door.

The New Zealand planning for ALTHORPE envisaged an initial high-level approach to Indonesia that would conserve fuel. The squadron would take off from Tengah and climb to 20,000 feet, crossing the Strait of Malacca and flying down the eastern coast of Sumatra. On reaching the island of Java, the Canberras would turn inland and fly at low levels along the central mountain range south of Jakarta. Masked from Indonesian radar by the hills surrounding the target, No. 14 Squadron would move into attack formation—three pairs in line astern, with 1,000 yards between each pair—while flying at 360 knots just 50 feet above the ground. 'Our aircraft were camouflaged on the top and so for anything flying above us it was very difficult to see us because the dark green and grey colours would merge pretty effectively with the countryside below.'[51]

The target was Halim Air Base. 'We had good pictures of Halim. We had refined our attack so that each aircraft approaching in pairs in stream [box formation] was directed to a particular part of the airfield—a technique which the Cyprus squadron [No. 73 Squadron RAF] had taught us, and which we practised at every opportunity.' This formation was quite different to those they had used previously. Wallingford, in the lead aircraft, had his Number Two a 'thousand yards to my right and then a thousand yards behind me would be the next pair, and then another thousand yards behind that would be another pair ... I could ... see any fighter that came in on my Number Two and the back people could watch us and each other.'[52]

Each Canberra carried 72 high-velocity 2-inch rockets in twin pods below the wings. These were fired in a single explosive burst which, because of the spread, would have a similar effect to a shotgun blast, spraying out at ground level to destroy lines of parked aircraft and ground installations. The approach to Halim was at '50 feet which is low ... We would probably pop up to about 250 feet to get a better sighting of what was on the ground and in a very shallow attack we would actually be firing our rockets at about a thousand yards ... then break left or right depending where we were in formation so that we could clear the debris.' If Halim was empty, 'we had an alternate [target] as with just a 20 degree turn after crossing Halim we could aim for Jakarta International'.[53] The attacking run over, the Canberras would climb or break sharply, accelerate to maximum speed, and fly low across the coast. After that, it was every man for himself for the flight back to Singapore.

During September 1964, tension 'built to crisis point' as the aircraft carrier HMS *Victorious* and its escorts passed through the narrow Sunda Strait between Java and Sumatra en route to Singapore from Perth.[54] The New Zealanders remained at 'cockpit readiness' in case ALTHORPE was initiated. The squadron

An SAS patrol. Malaya, April 1957.
*War History Collection, ATL, M-2061*

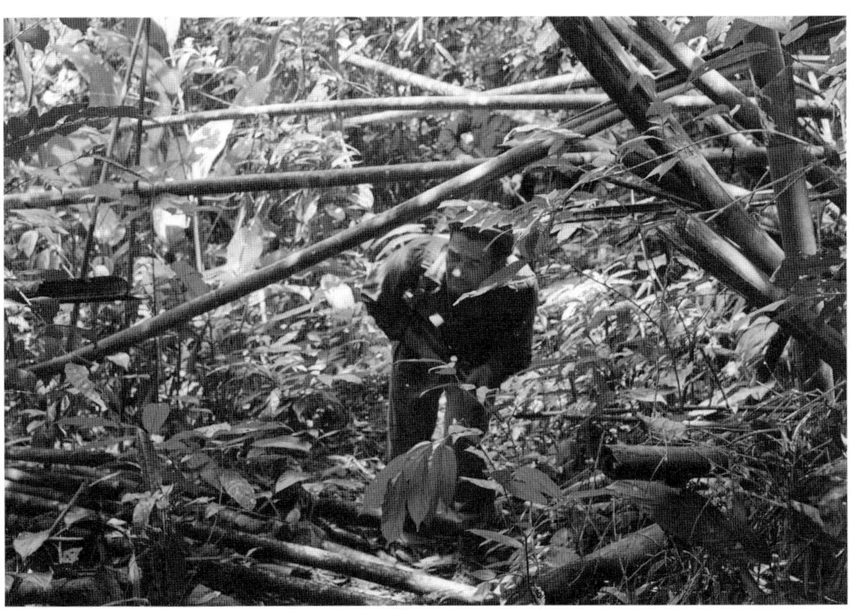

A trooper picks his way through fallen secondary growth in the Malayan jungle, April 1957.
*War History Collection, ATL, M-2096*

Troopers N. Pepene, G. Otene, A. J. Allen, P. N. Hurst, S. C. Watene and T. A. Stevens relax at a patrol base after their evening meal. Malaya, c. 1956.
*War History Collection, ATL, M-2080*

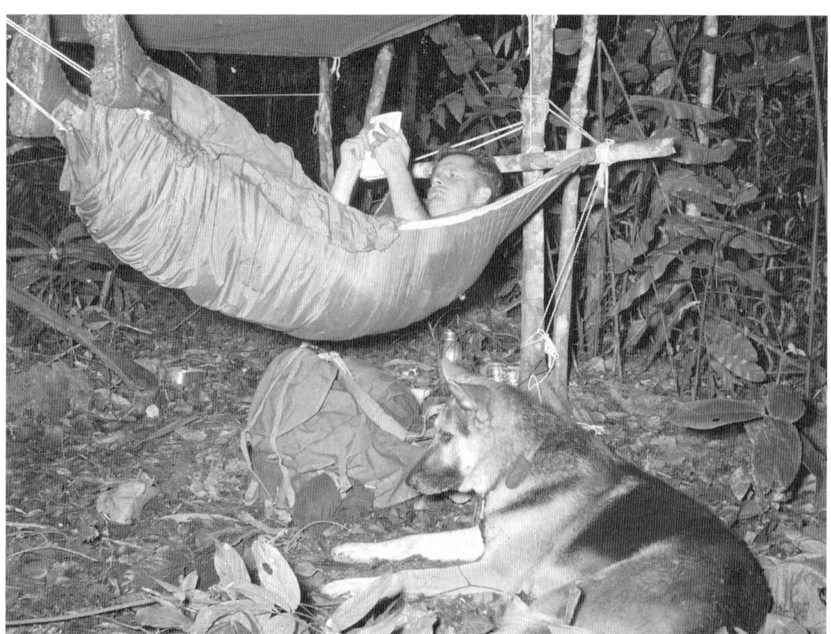

Trooper J. J. Crotty and his tracker dog 'Sin'. Malaya, April 1957.
*War History Collection, ATL, M-2094*

Two Aboriginal headmen visit a New Zealand camp in Malaya, c. 1956. Trooper Tom MacLeod faces the camera, while Corporal David Ogilvy of Pokeno (with pack) has just returned from a two-day patrol.
*War History Collection, ATL, M-0514*

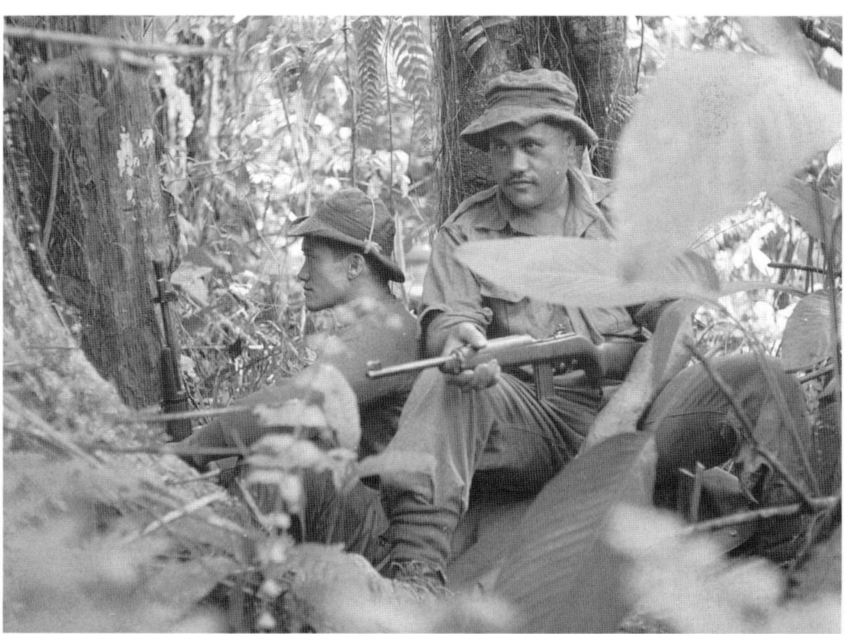

Troopers Koa and Hemopo, Malaya, c. 1956.
*War History Collection, ATL, M-0731*

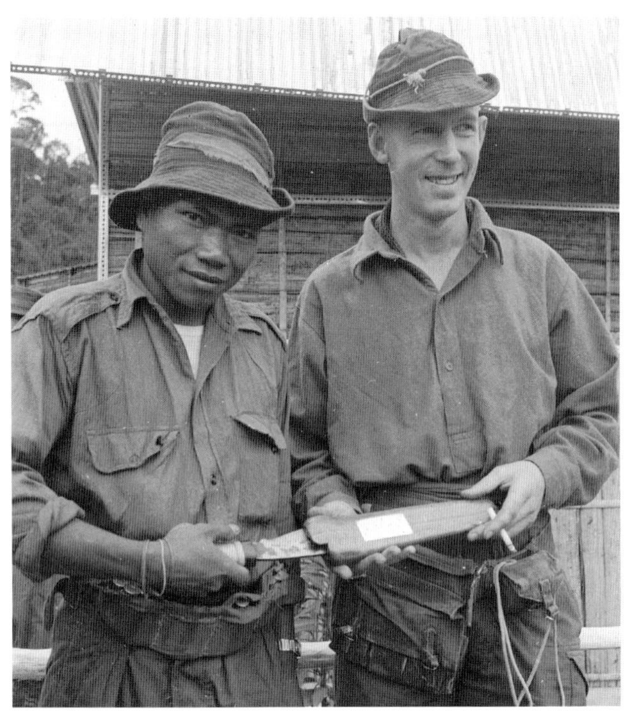

Uda and Lieutenant Burrows, Malaya, 1956.
*War History Collection, ATL, M-0766*

Lieutenant 'Buzz' Burrows relaxes in casual dress at 3 Troop's patrol base after the killing of Ah Ming.
*James E. Fraser Collection*

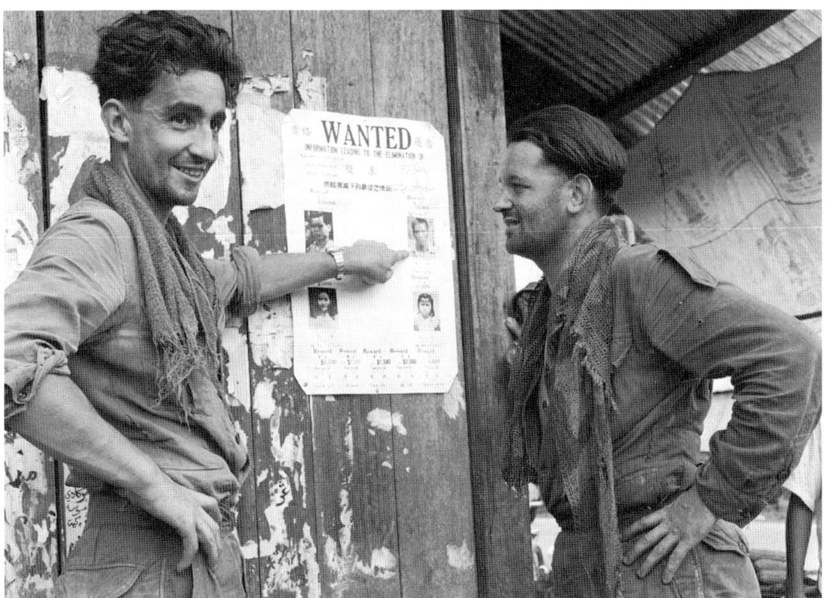


Lance-Corporal Bob Withers and Trooper Graham Nash with a reward notice for a man they have killed. Malaya, April 1957.
*War History Collection, ATL, M-2049*

SAS families picnic on a beach near Kuala Lumpur, April 1957.
*War History Collection, ATL, M-1909*

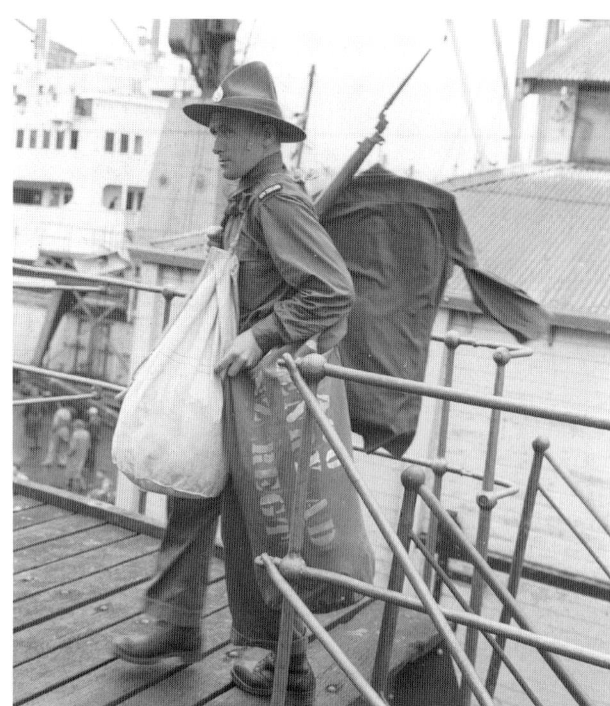

A New Zealand soldier ready to sail on the *Captain Cook*. Wellington, 28 November 1957.
*War History Collection, ATL, M-2402*

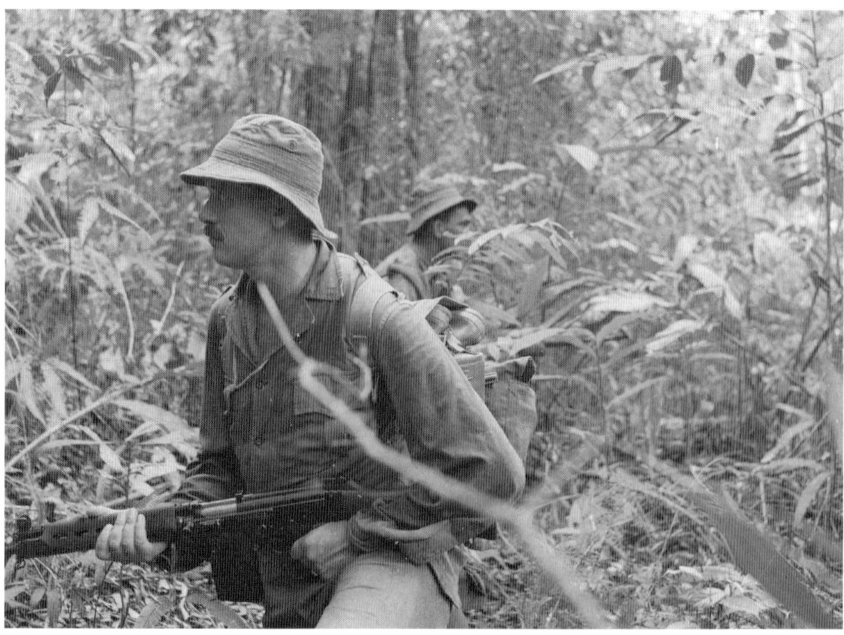

Major A. N. King on a training exercise in the Malayan jungle, January 1958.
*War History Collection, ATL, M-2651*

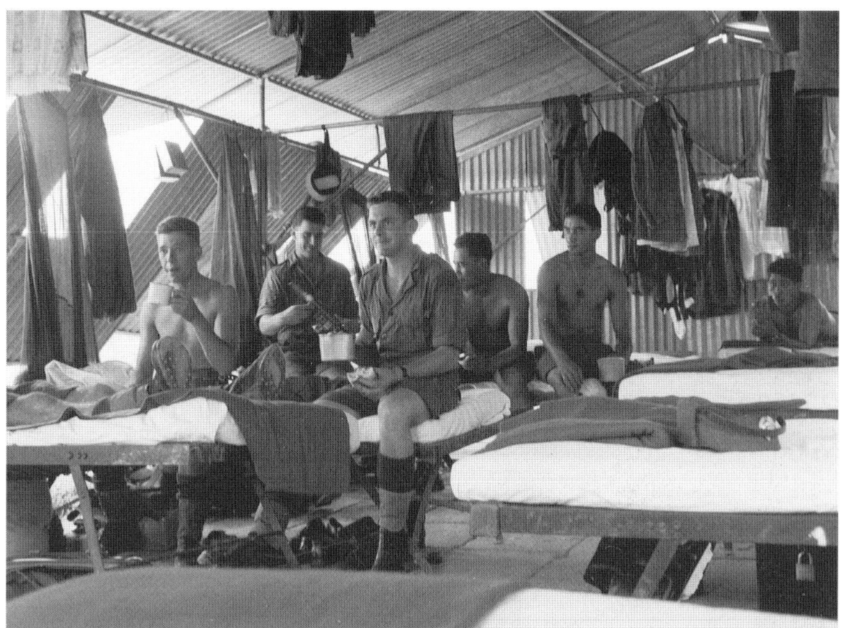

Barracks at Nyasa Camp, Kota Tinggi, Johore, January 1958.
*War History Collection, ATL, M-2628*

Families of New Zealand soldiers arrive in Malaya on an aircraft of No. 41 Squadron RNZAF, c. 1958.
*War History Collection, ATL, M-2731*

Men of B Company enjoy a hangi the night before they move out to take over jungle bases from A Company, c. 1958. From left: Privates E. A. Dawson (Wellington), S. J. Wharehoka (Taranaki), R. Kamau (Hastings), P. Harris (Kaikohe), D. Ruhi (Rotorua), R. J. Caldwell (Dunedin).

*War History Collection, ATL, M-3092*

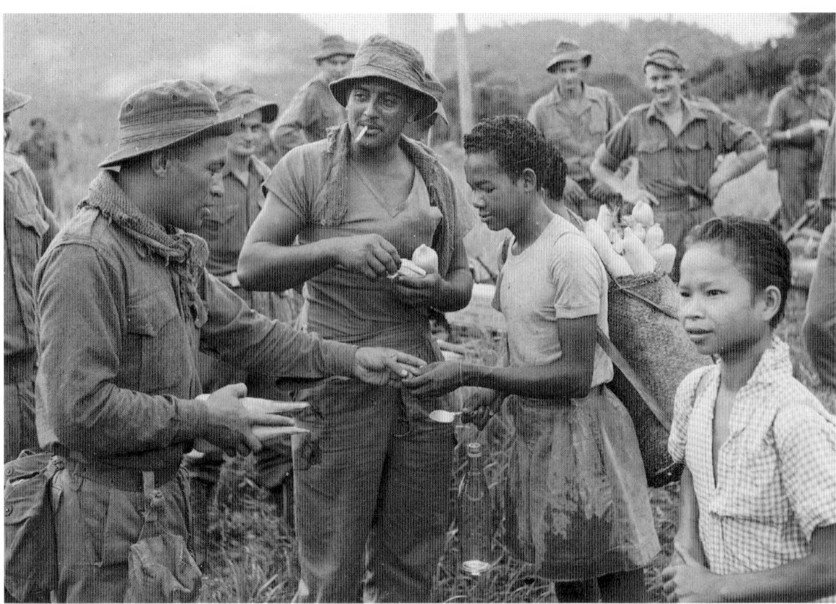

Privates S. Cribb and G. A. Horsefall buy corn to take into the jungle. Malaya, c. 1958.

*War History Collection, ATL, M-3101*

A patrol prepares to leave on the six-day walk to another village. Malaya, July 1958.
*War History Collection, ATL, M-2884*

New Zealand soldiers carry supplies after an airdrop, July 1958.
*War History Collection, ATL, M-2882*

Private W. J. Rodgers rests in the Malayan jungle, July 1958.
*War History Collection, ATL, M-2887*

New Zealand soldiers in Malaya, possibly on the Perak River, c. 1958. The two men sitting on the raft are Lance-Corporal A. E. Steele (front) and Private D. E. Beacham, both of Auckland.
*War History Collection, ATL, PA1-q-319-M3104*

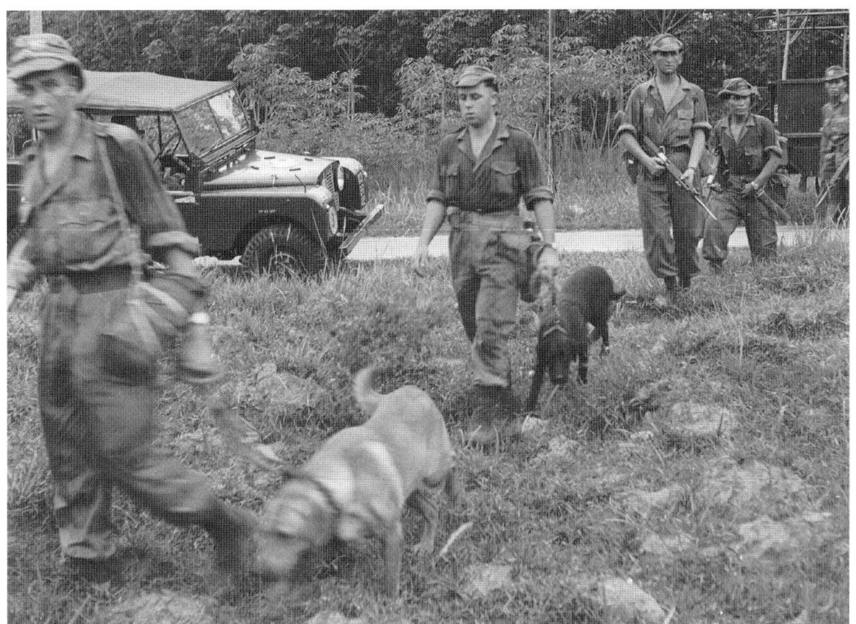

Dog teams and Iban trackers. Malaya, July 1958.
*War History Collection, ATL, M-2924*

New Zealanders man a checkpoint at the entrance to a New Village. Malaya, July 1958.
*War History Collection, ATL, M-2918*

On patrol. From front: Private E. Johnsen, Second Lieutenant Pat Power, a Chinese interpreter, Private D. Maqueat. Malaya, July 1958.
*War History Collection, ATL, M-2893*

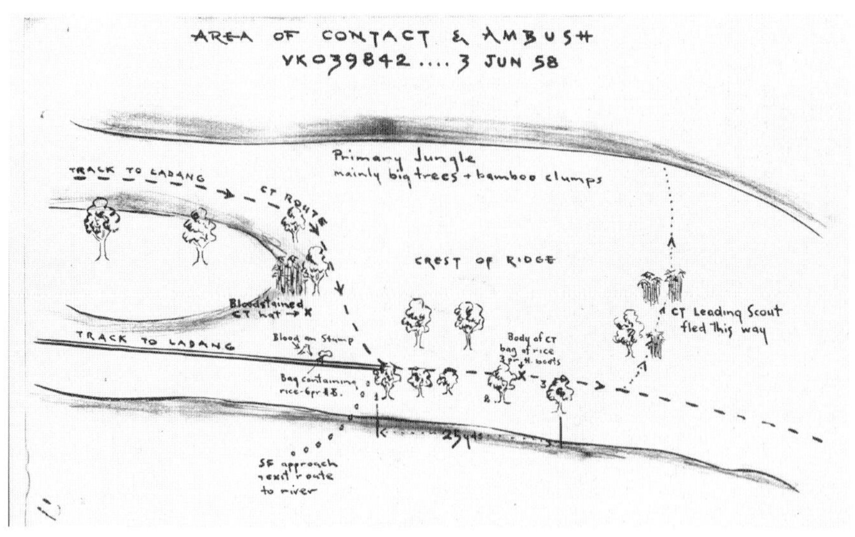


Sketch map of D Company's contact, 3 June 1958.
*Archives New Zealand, WA–M 2/1/4*

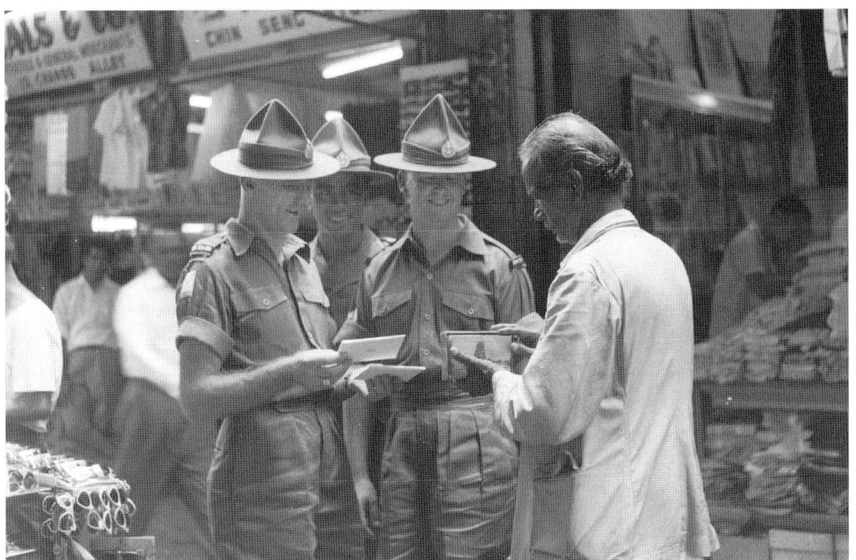

New Zealand soldiers on leave look at postcards being sold by a pedlar. From left: Private Myles (Wellington), Corporals P. Reihana (Kaikohe) and B. Drummond (Upper Hutt). Singapore, c. 1958.
*War History Collection, ATL, M-3125*

New Zealand soldiers marching through central Wellington in late 1959 just before their departure for Malaya round Stewart Dawson's corner.
*War History Collection, ATL, PA1-f-119-01-3*

Soldiers arrive by boat to construct a road. Malaya, c. 1960.
*War History Collection, ATL, PA1-f-119-17-4*

Sergeant D. Ashby watches vendors weigh vegetables for the battalion at Taiping market, c. 1960.
*War History Collection, ATL, PA1-f-119-18-2*

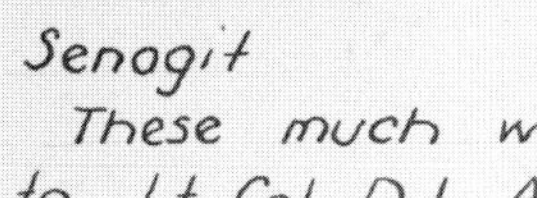

Senogit
Kerinching
Regek
These much wanted hostile abos surrendered to Lt Col DJ Aitken personally in Feb 60.


From left: Senogit, Kerinching and Regek, photographed after they surrendered in northern Malaya on 25 February 1960.
*War History Collection, ATL, PA1-f-119-20-5*

New Zealand Army engineers working on the feeder road in southern Thailand.
*RNZ Engineers Museum*

A 1RNZIR patrol on the Malaya/Thailand border, 1964.
*Chamberlain collection, A*

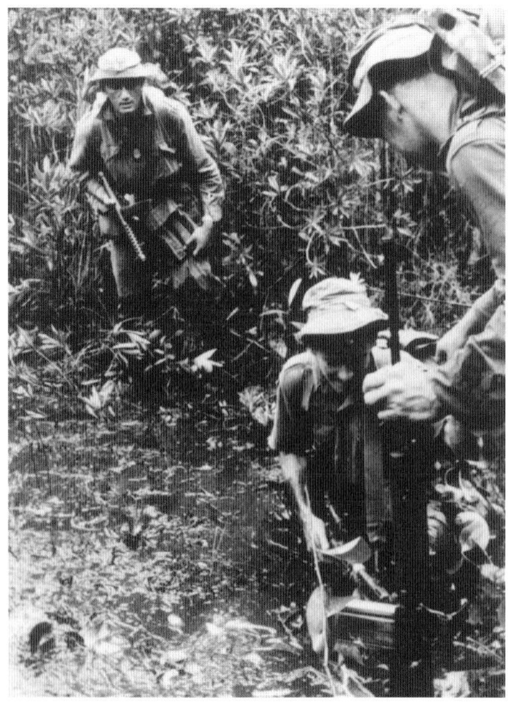

Soldiers of 1RNZIR on patrol in the Pontian swamps, Malaya, 1964.
*QEII Army Memorial Museum*

was in a state of readiness for 17 hours of each 24, flying four sorties a day during which rockets were fired from a height of 50 feet, and formations of pairs and fours flew at the same height. 'All our training was geared to that attack, so we picked parts of Malaysia and little islands off the coast, wherever we could, and even inland at small airfields where we practised exactly the same profile and ... set up the same turning bearings. Everything was matched and every time we flew low level it was as if we were coming in on Halim Air Base.'[55]

The B(I)12's fixed cockpit canopy made it a very uncomfortable aircraft in tropical conditions. The air-conditioning relied on the engine, and did not function effectively when the plane was on standby on the tarmac. Once the crew were in the plane, 'you had to get airborne in 20 minutes otherwise there was a serious risk of the pilot suffering from heat exhaustion, sitting exposed to the sun in a completely sealed glasshouse ... he just got exceptionally hot. It was no more comfortable in the navigator's position either, because in the early days our flying suit was lined with nylon and you just got hotter and hotter.' Once airborne it was a different story, with 'the pilot sitting in the glasshouse and the navigator sitting in a fridge, particularly when you reached maximum altitudes approaching 50,000 feet.'[56] Flying in the tropics was extremely demanding, and at the end of a sortie the pilot would be soaked with sweat and 'physically and mentally exhausted'. The navigator was a 'little more comfortable. He's out of the sun, his air-conditioning system is a little bit better, but he's either sitting in an uncomfortable chair or he is lying on his stomach.'[57]

The frequency of bird strikes during the low-flying exercises forced several changes. Speed was reduced to 250 knots, and the transparent nose-cones protecting the rocket pods were replaced by solid cones that did not shatter when struck by a bird. This caused some speculation among other squadrons and station staff about the nature of the new missiles being carried by the RNZAF.[58] The ground crews kept the Canberras ready to fly at two hours' notice while fixing the large number of electrical and communication faults that plagued the New Zealand aircraft during the first month in Singapore as a result of the humid conditions.

On its arrival in Singapore, No. 14 Squadron at Tengah joined No. 41 Squadron at Changi under the command of Wing Commander D. E. ('Ewan') Jamieson and formed a 'small RNZAF Task Force'.[59] Jamieson's appointment as commander of the two squadrons initially caused confusion and concern in the minds of Headquarters Far East Air Force. It was wrongly assumed that Jamieson had an operational command responsibility, interposed between each squadron and its RAF operational headquarters.[60] Far East Air Force made it quite clear that Jamieson was not wanted in this role, and initially tried to 'freeze me out if possible and minimise such role as I had'.[61] After much consultation and some acrimony, Jamieson's position was established as being similar to that of the Commander New Zealand Army FARELF in his relationship with 1RNZIR, 28th Commonwealth Brigade and Headquarters FARELF. It was stressed that Jamieson was not in the operational chain of command, but was responsible for the purely national matters that had previously been reserved for the squadron commanders.[62] This was gradually accepted by Headquarters Far East Air Force, and an effective working relationship developed.[63]

Just as importantly, as far as the RNZAF was concerned, Jamieson was in Singapore because the Chief of Air Staff, Air Vice-Marshal Ian G. Morrison, saw the commitment of No. 14 Squadron as an excellent opportunity to re-establish a New Zealand strike squadron there on a permanent basis. There was a strong belief in RNZAF circles that Air Staff had mishandled the circumstances leading to the withdrawal and disbanding of No. 75 Squadron in 1962. Confrontation offered a chance to remedy this mistake. Morrison stressed to Jamieson that he wanted No. 14 Squadron to be stationed permanently at Tengah. He had briefed the Chiefs of Staff and the Minister of Defence on his intentions, and aimed to achieve this in April 1965. It was important, therefore, that No. 14 Squadron was seen to be used in an operational role. Morrison wanted as much publicity on the squadron's efforts in Malaysia as possible, as there had been 'no press here since departure and no press space [was] likely' if the media thought its activities were purely an exercise. The New Zealanders had to be employed on operations to give Morrison the publicity he wanted.[64]

Morrison's term as Chief of Air Staff, from 1962 to 1965, saw the revitalisation of the RNZAF. Its administration was refined into an Operations and Support Group. Morrison overcame the cutbacks resulting from the 1961 Defence Review with the purchase of C-130H Hercules long-range transport aircraft, Lockheed P-3B Orion maritime patrol aircraft, Bell 47G-3B1 Sioux reconnaissance helicopters, and UH-1D Iroquois helicopters, all of which came into service in 1965 and 1966. These aircraft transformed the RNZAF into a modern and effective air force, and were still in service at the end of the century. The RNZAF's historian Matthew Wright has described his contribution:

> [Morrison] lobbied ceaselessly in the corridors of power to bring [his] vision to reality, focussing initially on a maritime and transport replacement programme, later on renewal of the strike aircraft. His frankness did not endear him to politicians, but he was effective, and indeed remains one of the RNZAF's most accomplished

> administrators, a man whose work had far-reaching effects both within the service and outside it, one of the half dozen movers-and-shakers whose personal influence and character can be said to have fundamentally shaped the service.[65]

There was a distinct lessening of tension in late September; if the New Zealanders were only in Singapore for a VANGUARD exercise, it was time for them to return home. Admiral Sir Varyl Begg, Commander in Chief Far East, and his Air Commander made it quite clear that they wanted the Canberras to stay. The New Zealand government agreed to this on 9 October; it also agreed that Begg would be consulted on any decision to withdraw the squadron. However, Morrison's keenness to see No. 14 Squadron actively and publicly employed ran counter to his government's reluctance to have it used in anything but an ALTHORPE role. While Morrison worked to keep the squadron in Singapore on a permanent basis, Holyoake was equally keen to withdraw it as soon as it was diplomatically acceptable to do so.[66] Morrison's ambition was also frustrated by Headquarters Far East Air Force's awareness that New Zealand wanted the Canberras to be involved only on a 'last resort' basis. Although the New Zealand government gave tacit approval to their use against infiltrators into Malaysian or Singaporean territorial waters or airspace, the Canberras were never called upon because Far East Air Force feared this would hasten their recall to New Zealand.[67]

Morrison's ambitions for the squadron suffered a major setback over the 'Labuan difficulty'. RAF Labuan was the principal air base on Labuan Island, which on the formation of Malaysia became part of Sabah.[68] While the New Zealand government had authorised the use of its forces in operations against infiltration of the Malay Peninsula by Indonesia, it had still not agreed to commit them to Borneo. On 2 October Jamieson informed Wellington that a 'hint has been dropped to Wallingford that squadron may be detached to Labuan within five days' for a ten-day deployment. Jamieson requested confirmation that a temporary deployment of this nature would be acceptable to the New Zealand government.[69] There was no reply, and on 27 October the New Zealand High Commission in Singapore informed the Ministry of External Affairs in Wellington that No. 14 Squadron was deploying to Labuan for three weeks the following day.[70] There was nothing sinister in this; Far East Air Force needed space at Tengah for a Canberra B8 Squadron of the RAF that was arriving from Germany. To relieve congestion, it was decided that the New Zealanders would hone their operational and mobilisation skills by deploying to RAF Labuan and familiarising themselves with conditions in Borneo.[71] The

New Zealanders were being treated as if they were just another RAF squadron. They were permitted to fly no nearer than 25 miles to the Indonesian border unless under radar direction, which allowed aircraft to approach to within 15 miles. During their first two days in Labuan the New Zealanders familiarised themselves with the approaches to Brunei and Jesselton, the designated diversion airfields. Wallingford noted that the 'unfamiliar jungle terrain which is in parts rugged and mountainous and incompletely mapped, has been the best test of navigation that the Squadron has yet experienced'.[72]

At this stage, however, both Far East Air Force and New Zealand realised the possible implications of the Labuan deployment. Headquarters Far East Air Force immediately stopped the New Zealanders flying over Borneo, switching them to high-level tactical formation flying over the sea, practising interceptions to test RAF Labuan's radar, and low-level tactical flying off Labuan. The Commander in Chief, Sir Varyl Begg, who was very conscious of New Zealand's concerns, had not been aware of the deployment; once notified, he issued instructions forbidding the aircraft to fly over north Borneo. In Wellington, Morrison set out to repair the damage. He asked the Minister of Defence, Dean Eyre, to seek Holyoake's permission to keep the squadron in Labuan, on condition that the aircraft did not fly within 15 miles of the border. If this was unacceptable, he asked that the squadron continue to train in Labuan, 'provided that training exercises are routed to "targets" in Malaya'.[73]

A reluctant Holyoake agreed to leave the decision on how long the squadron should remain in Labuan to Begg, but stipulated that no New Zealand aircraft should fly over mainland Borneo.[74] This message was passed to Begg, along with the New Zealand government's appreciation of his 'co-operation and readiness at all times to recognise the limitations imposed by political considerations'.[75] Begg could read between the lines. His own priority was to keep No. 14 Squadron in theatre, and he saw no value in risking any further strain on the relationship with New Zealand. On 2 November the squadron was ordered back to Tengah, to Morrison's disgust and the 'general disappointment' of all personnel, who believed that 'the Squadron could be put to real purpose in this area'.[76] Jamieson, attempting to salvage something from the deployment, asked that two of his staff who had been attached to the headquarters of the Commander Air Borneo be allowed to remain there.[77] This request was initially refused, but in December it was reviewed and prime ministerial approval given.[78]

After the Labuan misunderstanding, Holyoake, Secretary of Defence Jack Hunn and Secretary of External Affairs Alister McIntosh all wanted the squadron to return to New Zealand. Morrison signalled Jamieson that the

'Labuan difficulty' and 'the fiasco of latest landings [on the Malay Peninsula] leads to feeling here that very little more is likely to be attempted [by Indonesia] in near future and accordingly 14 Squadron should come home'.[79] This was the very thing Begg wanted to avoid. He spoke to both Acting High Commissioner Lendrum in Singapore and High Commissioner Wade in Kuala Lumpur and gained their support. Wade informed Wellington that:

> [The] withdrawal of our Canberras at this juncture would not be understood by our allies and might be misunderstood by Indonesia. I do not think we should let ourselves be deluded by the ease with which the Sungei Kesang landing was eliminated. For at least the next two weeks, it would be a mistake to consider the situation here as anything other than potentially critical, even if in the upshot nothing serious should eventuate.[80]

No. 14 Squadron continued to train for ALTHORPE long after it became obvious that the planned strikes against Indonesian airfields would never happen. Begg's position on retaining the New Zealanders in Singapore became more difficult to sustain when an RAF squadron was withdrawn in mid-November.[81] Nonetheless, Holyoake agreed to the recommendation of the Chief of Defence Staff, Rear-Admiral Phipps, that the squadron remain until 15 March 1965.[82] McIntosh now supported this extension, believing that it would be both prudent and possibly more economical to leave the squadron in Singapore, 'particularly as the situation had not improved and the latest press reports indicated that Sukarno had instructed that Confrontation be intensified'.[83]

Lack of manpower now became the critical issue. There were insufficient experienced Canberra aircrew and tradesmen to support the squadron indefinitely without bringing back married men, who were half of the available trained strength, for a second unaccompanied six-month tour of duty.[84] Morrison's solution was to recommend the extension of the squadron on a permanent basis, which would allow married personnel to be accompanied by their families.[85] This was not initially acceptable, but Morrison's persistence finally wore down his government's opposition.[86] On 16 March 1965 the Minister of Defence announced that No. 14 Squadron would remain in Malaysia indefinitely. 'Some families of key personnel would be enabled to join their husbands in Singapore as accommodation becomes available.' Those who were not accompanied by dependants would serve on a six-month rotational basis.[87]

Holyoake's concerns about No. 14 Squadron's deployment increased when New Zealand ground forces were committed to South Vietnam in May 1965. He expected a request from the Vietnamese or United States government that the Canberras serve in Vietnam. In June 1965 the Minister of Defence, Dean Eyre, attempted to allay the Prime Minister's concerns by reminding him that:

> The United States are saving Australia and New Zealand in South Vietnam. We have given them the political support they deserve, and will give material assistance. But we must be prepared to do more in a situation that is explosive, both to the North and South of Malaysia. The most effective contribution we could make in the event of a sudden serious deterioration in the situation would be the commitment of our Canberra Strike Squadron. It is there now in the Commonwealth Strategic Reserve as part of a visible effective deterrent and is declared to SEATO. It would be most undesirable to withdraw it. Such an action would be misinterpreted throughout the world.

Eyre then addressed the root of Holyoake's concern. 'We are unlikely to be asked by the South Vietnam government to use our Canberras offensively in Vietnam. They want their own aircraft [to be used] rather than a contribution from us.'[88] McIntosh reinforced Eyre's recommendation that the squadron remain in Singapore, arguing that it was playing a 'key part in the defence of Malaysia against aggression'. He also reminded the Prime Minister that when the government made its decision to send an artillery battery to South Vietnam, 'it was stated publicly that this would not diminish our ability to maintain existing forces in Malaysia ... Action at this point to reduce our forces in Malaysia would almost certainly be construed as a failure to honour that assurance.'[89]

In December 1964, one of the squadron's B(I)12 Canberras crashed with the loss of both crew while practising low-level rocket attacks over the sea at the China Rock range. This reduced the number of B(I)12 Canberras in the RNZAF to nine, and highlighted a dangerous shortage of aircraft.[90] Morrison assessed that the RNZAF's combat effectiveness was 'at bedrock or less'. Attempts to hire a replacement aircraft from the RAF, RAAF or USAF were unsuccessful.[91] All three services were short of manpower and equipment. In a briefing paper to the Prime Minister, McIntosh noted that:

> [In] many respects we are less well prepared to meet a war situation today than we were in 1939 ... it is certainly not lost on our allies that the proportion of national resources devoted to defence in New Zealand is among the lowest in the Western World ... [A] decision to increase our defence effort would be regarded by our allies as an indication of our intention to assume in future a fairer share of the collective defence burden.[92]

Sufficient funding to meet New Zealand's increased overseas defence commitments was never granted. Base facilities in New Zealand were allowed to run down and major equipment purchases were deferred in order to maintain the South-East Asian commitment. Conserving New Zealand's overseas funds remained Holyoake's primary concern, and he carefully juggled his limited defence assets while avoiding any major increase in defence spending. Doing more with less was the unwritten motto of his National administration, and it was apparent that New Zealand would not be in a position to 'honour completely [its] treaty obligations and commitments' until 1966 or even 1967.[93]

In February 1965, Holyoake announced the commitment of New Zealand troops to Borneo. At last No. 14 Squadron could deploy its Canberras. In April the first pair flew a sortie to Labuan for training and familiarisation. An RAF Canberra was permanently stationed at Labuan, and Wallingford reported that his squadron 'would welcome the opportunity to have similar tasking for the very valuable experience and morale boost which would be gained'.[94] Regular three-day detachments by pairs of Canberras to Labuan became part of the squadron's normal training cycle, with crews gaining 'valuable experience in operating over unfamiliar terrain'.[95] Despite the lessening of tension, the squadron maintained its operational edge through a series of mobility exercises which included deploying to and operating from unprepared airstrips throughout the Malay Peninsula, a major deployment to Hong Kong, and ongoing exercises with the RAF, RAAF and USAF. This level of activity was possible only through the efforts of the engineers and ground staff in keeping six Canberras operational.[96]

In March 1966 Air Vice-Marshal Morrison recommended that the squadron remain in Singapore until 1 April 1969, and that the number of married accompanied posts be increased.[97] This proposal went to Cabinet in August 1966 with the support of the Chiefs of Staff and the Defence Council. However, both Lieutenant-General L. W. Thornton, the Chief of Defence Staff, and W. Hutchings, the Secretary of Defence, told Morrison that they doubted Cabinet would approve anything requiring increased expenditure of overseas funds.[98] With Confrontation now over, their fears were justified, and the squadron was ordered home on financial grounds in November 1966. While some RNZAF pilots would serve with the USAF in Vietnam in the late 1960s, No. 14 Squadron was to be the last RNZAF combat squadron committed to active service as a squadron. This role was already well beyond New Zealand's capabilities to sustain; the years from 1964 to 1966 were a frustrating climax to the post-war evolution of Regular combat squadrons in the RNZAF.

There was to be a fitting sequel. Squadron-Leader Pat Neville commanded No. 14 Squadron on Exercise VANGUARD 10 in 1969, the year the Canberras were withdrawn from service. After returning to New Zealand the squadron was assigned to fly Air Commodore Frank Gill, the Air Officer Commanding Operations Group RNZAF, to Jakarta. This would be the first formal visit by an air force of any of the nations that had been involved in Confrontation. Neville decided that his squadron would arrive in the formation it had practised for ALTHORPE.

> I carried Air Commodore Gill in the lead aircraft so that we would arrive as a fighting unit of the RNZAF ... We transited down at medium altitude and I then descended the squadron a few miles back from Jakarta where we were going to land at the International Airport. We formed up in battle formation and hit Jakarta at maximum speed at zero feet and in the process managed to include Halim Airfield in the turn.[99]

## The Royal New Zealand Navy during Confrontation, 1963–66

> It was pretty much a ring of grey all around Malacca and Singapore and there wasn't much chance of any infiltration getting through without being detected.[100]
>
> LIEUTENANT C. J. CARL, RNZN, ON SECONDMENT TO THE ROYAL MALAYSIAN NAVY, 1963–65

New Zealand was as cautious in committing its naval resources during Confrontation as it was in committing the resources of its other two services. In December 1963 the government agreed that HMNZS *Otago*, which was on station with the Far East Fleet, could be used in an 'anti-piracy role' against Indonesian infiltration, although Holyoake emphasised that he did not want any publicity about 'our readiness to do this'.[101] The government had already tacitly agreed that the New Zealand naval officer, Lieutenant George Cole RNZN, could remain in command of the Royal Malaysian Navy patrol boat KD *Sri Kedah* when the vessel was assigned to preventing infiltration from Indonesia, which had begun in January 1963 with Indonesia's declaration of a policy of confrontation against the proposed formation of Malaysia. Smuggling from Indonesia across the Strait of Malacca was endemic, and the infiltration of trained dissidents became another facet of this nocturnal traffic.[102] New

Zealand recognised that to do otherwise 'would largely incapacitate the Malaysian Navy which has about seven British, three Australian and one New Zealand ship commanders'. It agreed on the understanding that there would be 'no operations outside Malaysian territorial waters'.[103] In May 1963 Lieutenant C. J. Carl RNZN, who replaced Cole, found himself at sea only 24 hours after arriving with his wife and two children for a two-year secondment to the Malaysian Navy. He was appointed commander of KD *Sri Jahor*, a British-built inshore minesweeper with its minesweeping gear removed which had a manually operated 40 mm Bofors gun at the bow and a couple of Bren guns.

> I really didn't know whether I was Arthur or Martha at that stage. I was in command of this inshore minesweeper, which had been sitting alongside with a crew, but no officers. I got on board and found I was the only officer. The next senior person was a Petty Officer, who was a Malay. There was a Chief Petty Officer Engineer and then about twenty ratings from a couple of Leading Seamen down through ABs. A mix of Chinese and Malay and Indian. I suppose about two-thirds Malay and the rest evenly [divided] between Chinese and Indian.[104]

Carl was at sea for three weeks while his wife and family, aided by other families, settled as best they could into rented accommodation in Johore Bahru. 'They were just so short, they couldn't afford to let you get too soft by giving you a week off. Ships generally were on patrol for 10–11 days and then a two-day stand down (three nights). On average, some 4,000 nautical miles were steamed in a month ... [over about] 23–26 days'.[105]

Carl's seven-month command of KD *Sri Jahor* was spent 'patrolling the Singapore Straits and up the Malacca Straits'. The task was to prevent infiltration into Singapore or the Malay Peninsula by Indonesian sabotage parties using the many small craft that plied the straits.

> The means to do this [was] to steal fishing boats. In fact much of the income for Indonesian naval personnel was stealing the boats, throwing the Malaysians into a life-raft or something or other and sending them back to Malaya. Then they would tow the boats and their catch back to Indonesia and sell them on their market, and of course make an enormous amount of money. This enabled any infiltrator to use one of the same boats and to mix in with the fishing fleet at night and come in and land with them.[106]

Meeting this threat was mostly a boring and exhausting routine, with the *Sri Jahor* at action stations each night. As the only officer on board, Carl alternated watches with his Petty Officer.

> That became quite a strain really because I slept in the chart house which in itself was unpleasant because it was very hot ... There were no showers or anything, there was a bog, one, and you had to wash out of a bucket ... Whenever the Captain took his bucket onto the sweep deck aft, everybody disappeared. It was not done to be watching the Commander have his ablutions. It was extremely lonely.[107]

The routine was broken by the occasional interception. In Carl's case, an Indonesian gunboat had rounded up some two dozen fishing boats, ejected their crews, and was towing the boats towards Indonesian waters. 'It was just on the horizon, and on the assumption that it wouldn't be able to tow them at thirty knots, I set off after it at eleven and a half knots. I actually fired a couple of 40 mm Bofors in their direction, but I never saw the fall of shot ... The result of the gunfire however was that the [Indonesian] BT boat cast off the fishing boats and set off to Indonesia at a rate of knots.'[108]

Carl worked under the direction of the Naval Officer-in-charge West Malaysia, a Royal Navy Captain seconded to the Royal Malaysian Navy. This officer co-ordinated anti-infiltration patrolling for all the Commonwealth naval forces involved. The Royal Malaysian Navy's contribution of some 25 ships included four coastal minesweepers, ten Vosper patrol craft, four inshore minesweepers, and a number of smaller craft. 'It was pretty much a ring of grey all around Malacca and Singapore and there wasn't much chance of any infiltration getting through without being detected.'[109]

After the formation of Malaysia, Carl was sent to Borneo to command a British-designed Ton-class coastal minesweeper, KD *Mahamiru*. Its patrols focused on Tawau Harbour, which separated Kalimantan and Sabah. A maze of mangrove swamps was criss-crossed by river channels that were big enough for the *Mahamiru* to navigate. 'Once you got to know where the channels were you didn't have to worry about turning around which could be quite difficult if you got your screws into the mangroves. You went in and out by day and then at night you would anchor on the border on the dotted line and use your radar to give some protection from the likely incursion by water across the border.' They were in open view from Indonesian territory. 'There was a large Indonesian Army camp just across there, which you could see from the sea. Every now and again if they got out of bed the wrong side they would lob a few artillery shells in our direction. Whether by design or bad luck they never hit anything and they never got close to any of the ships that they could have seen.'

Carl remained on the *Mahamiru* for the rest of his two-year tour, which involved two tours to the waters of East Malaysia, each of two and a half months, broken by six-month tours around Malacca and Singapore. 'I was the only European on board. My life was much more pleasant ... we had a proper wardroom which had a little air-conditioner in it which made a slight difference ... There was a shower and a proper bog which I commandeered for myself.' Nonetheless, it was a demanding tour in which cultural considerations, particularly the need to maintain 'face' with an inexperienced multi-racial crew, required a high degree of leadership and tact.

While individual officers on secondment to the Malaysian Navy served in East Malaysian waters, the New Zealand frigate on station with the Far East Fleet was initially permitted only 'to help patrol territorial waters off the Borneo coast or on the high seas ... [and undertake] troop, lift and escort duties'. Begg's request that the New Zealand ship be stationed in rotation off Tawau as a guard ship—a function always performed by a ship of frigate size—was turned down by the New Zealand government. Tawau's economy depended on bartering copra for products from Kalimantan and the Celebes, and initially it was the only place where such trade with Indonesia was allowed to continue under the watchful eye of Commonwealth naval patrols.[110] Here the Indonesian bases and Commonwealth and Malaysian garrisons on Sebatik Island were separated by only a complex of mangrove islands. The resulting potential for involvement on Borneo itself concerned the New Zealand government, especially as the Tawau Bay guard ship sometimes had to put ashore patrols to explore the estuaries and swamps around Wallace Bay. Begg's request was therefore initially refused, just as those to commit Nos 14 and 41 Squadrons RNZAF to Borneo had been.[111]

The New Zealand government relaxed its embargo on Tawau guard ship duties in September 1964, when the responsibility for land patrolling was passed to the local infantry garrison. RNZN frigates were now allowed to act as guard ships or undertake offshore patrols, 'provided they are not used against Indonesian territory or in Indonesian territorial waters unless prior national consent has been obtained'.[112] *Otago* was assigned to anti-infiltration patrols on the east coast of the Malay Peninsula, and then became the Tawau guard ship in early December. This involved co-ordinating patrolling by coastal minesweepers and other small craft, providing radar cover and naval gunfire support if required. Most nights were spent patrolling the waterways and searching trading craft.[113] Both *Otago* and *Taranaki* spent time at Tawau. HMNZS *Taranaki* fired its guns a number of times in support of operations; in September 1966, together with HMS *Devonshire* and HMAS *Derwent*, *Taranaki* bombarded the Indonesian part of Sebatik Island to impress the garrisons.[114] Ships of frigate size were ill-suited to the close inshore work required to play an anti-infiltration role during Confrontation. They were vulnerable to Indonesian artillery fire, and initially lacked the close protection necessary to deal with the fast motor boats that could speed alongside unexpectedly. Grenades thrown on board caused casualties to crew members on both Royal Navy and Malaysian Navy vessels.[115]

> Torpedo tubes, sonar and 4.5 inch guns really had little or no place in this type of threat and in fact the most important things were the Bofors and the machine guns that were fitted for the task [and] were the most valuable weapons we had. It was interesting to me and I guess to others that the most dangerous thing that we could have was some active terrorist cruising past us in a very, very fast boat, and there were plenty of them, hurling grenades at us, and there wasn't a thing we could do about it in terms of responding unless we got on deck with rifles.[116]

Fortunately, the Indonesians never attacked RNZN ships in this way. On the few occasions that land-based Indonesian artillery fired on New Zealand patrol ships, no hits were scored.[117]

Anti-infiltration night patrols in the Strait of Singapore were part of the routine for both *Otago* and *Taranaki*, which took turns deploying with the Far East Fleet between 1963 and 1966 (with the exception of HMNZS *Royalist*'s deployment between June and October 1965). Captain E. C. Thorne RNZN, *Otago*'s commanding officer in 1964, recalled that:

> There was always a frigate or destroyer on the Singapore Strait patrol. You went up and down Singapore Strait from Horsburgh Light ... and up into the Malacca Strait ... You patrolled backwards and forwards with quite often two ships, some coastal minesweepers and small craft. It was a bit terrifying for command and for the bridge. The big tankers were starting to appear on the scene and you had this constant stream of large ships steaming down the Malacca Straits. We were darkened and they couldn't see [us].[118]

*Taranaki*, under Commander K. Michael Saull RNZN, had similar experiences on its operational tour, which began in November 1965.

> We were charging around with no lights on, trying to find small boats and ... what they were there for. I guess that sharpened the mind quite significantly as the officer of the watch and myself had a pretty torrid time ... On one occasion we did catch a small boat that was half way across the strait. We were suspicious over what it

> was doing ... The Malaysian policeman talked to them and he told me they were fishermen from Indonesia, although one appeared to be in a sort of uniform. They were told to return home, but an hour later we found them again making their way to Malaysia. We decided that the time had come for decisive action. We told the Operational Headquarters that we had taken over the boat, that we had the occupants on board and we intended to land them the following day and we proposed to dispose of the ship.[119]

What followed was a frustrating comedy of errors as *Taranaki* tried to sink the craft, first with explosives and then by gunfire. When they left the scene at daylight, it was still afloat. 'Hopefully it finally sank but I doubt it. We landed the miscreants and received an over-effusive signal from the staff saying how wonderfully we had done ... I suspect the real reason was that so little happened in Confrontation on the water that they were delighted to have one incident.'[120]

While there were no major incidents with the Indonesian Navy, it still had the capacity to be a threat, comprising as it did in 1964 a Sverdlov-class cruiser, seven Skory-class and two Suraparti-class frigates, two Pattimura-class sloops, six Whisky-class submarines, 60 patrol craft and a large number of auxiliary patrol vessels. In the critical month of September 1964 there was always the threat that a spark would set off Plan ALTHORPE. If this happened, the Indonesian Navy would be a target. Because the possibility of a naval engagement had to be planned for, the RNZN ships were always on the alert as part of the Far East Fleet. Preparing to meet such an eventuality underlay their ongoing planning and exercising. The daily routine may have been humdrum anti-infiltration patrols, but the overt presence of the Far East Fleet was also intended to forestall any Indonesian attempt to strike at naval or merchant shipping. Fleet exercises, such as that involving *Royalist* in August 1965, included simulated attacks by ships representing Skory-class frigates. As Captain J. P. S. Vallant noted, the *Royalist* was frequently used during exercises to represent the Sverdlov-class cruiser.[121]

Each ship was also involved in escort duties. For example, in June 1965 the *Royalist* escorted the commando carriers, HMS *Albion* and *Bulwark*, off the coast of Borneo during a routine changeover of their helicopter squadrons at Sibu. As Captain Vallant reported, '*Royalist* was there in case the Indonesians took it into their heads to try some sort of attack on the commando carriers, which together made a very tempting target.'[122] During their respective deployments both *Otago* and *Taranaki* acted as carrier escorts and practised to meet any Indonesian threat.[123] Ships were also rostered as the anti-sabotage guard ship while at Singapore. The duties involved 'providing boat patrols around the Naval Base area, searchlight crews ashore and onboard, and manning the Ops Room overnight to maintain communications with the various patrols'.[124]

In 1964 John Rees was an 18-year-old Sonarman making his first foreign tour on *Taranaki*. 'Singapore City was just like you see in the old movies, it really was decrepit, old, beat up and a sailor's delight in all respects.' Depending on the ship's routine, sailors had shore leave in the afternoon or evening, and after a meal and a beer at the Brit Club or the Union Jack Club and Ensign Club, they moved on. Bugis Street 'was a night time playground which catered for all tastes. If you had midnight leave you had to be on the last bus out. They used to run buses to the Base for the young sailors, who had midnight leave or Cinderella leave. The ship's company used to be seen tottering back about half an hour prior to turn to in the morning.'[125]

Small ships came into their own during Confrontation. In February 1965 New Zealand agreed to man two British Ton-class wooden-hulled coastal minesweepers, *Hickleton* and *Santon*, as part of its increased commitment to Borneo.[126] Both were first-generation coastal minesweepers with Napier 'Deltic' engines capable of producing 15 knots;[127] they were 'fairly basic', with open bridges and no air-conditioning.[128] With a distinctive kiwi painted on their funnels, they were commissioned as RNZN ships and patrolled Malaysian and Bornean waters as part of 11th Minesweeping Squadron until they were returned to the Royal Navy at the end of 1966. Armed with one 40 mm Bofor and 20 mm Oerlikon, and a variety of Vickers and Bren machine guns, they patrolled the Strait of Malacca and the waters off Borneo. Initially the crews for both vessels came from HMNZS *Pukaki*, which was finishing its tour in the southern oceans, operating at 60° south on weather patrol duties in support of Operation DEEP FREEZE, and was being withdrawn to be surveyed.[129] Four RNZNVR officers were among the 11 officers and 71 ratings manning the two ships and a base support party; it was intended that the crews would change every nine months. The 13-member base support party provided to assist with the supply, pay and administration of the two minesweepers was integrated into the RN and RAN base support party operating from HMS *Mull of Kintyre*. Both the setting up of a New Zealand administrative office and the process of commissioning the two ships out of reserve struck difficulties which were overcome through a combination of local initiative and goodwill on the part of the Royal Navy in Singapore.[130]

Lieutenant-Commander M. N. Waymouth RNZN was the first New Zealander to command HMNZS *Hickleton*. 'The patrolling business was fairly routine and occasionally there was a bit of excitement.'[131] Lieutenant Gerry Wright RNZNVR, who had been accepted into the RNZN for a nine-month temporary engagement, was appointed Navigator to HMNZS *Santon* in October 1965.[132]

> The ship had a Commanding Officer which was either a Lieutenant or Lieutenant-Commander and in our case it was a Lieutenant [Commander Lin] Tempero RNZN ... There was a crew of 30 with two Chinese chefs and two Chinese stewards ... The ships were allowed one refrigerator and one water-cooler each to deal with these 35 people. Well, *Santon* somehow or other achieved seven refrigerators and deep freezes.[133]

When Tempero took over the ship he had it at sea within five days, which was 'not bad going'. By the time Wright arrived, the ship had been commissioned for six months. 'The administrative organisation was pretty vague. If you wanted a letter you had to remember when it was written. If it was written two months ago then that would be about 18 inches down the pile and that was how the filing system worked. It was a bit shambolic. But as far as keeping those ships going the crews were magic.'[134]

*Santon* was designed to go to sea for five days at a time in European waters, but like *Hickleton* was

> actually being operated at sea for ten days with two days in [harbour] ... They had a 40 mm Bofor up forward with a twin 20 mm Oerlikon down aft. To that was added a twin .303 inch Vickers machine gun, World War One vintage, right up in the bow ... secured to the ship on a piece of wire about a metre long, so when they ceased using it they could throw it over the side and it wouldn't be an obstruction for the Bofor. Behind that was a mortar for firing flares at night.[135]

Directing the fire of the ship's armament was a relatively simple exercise.

> Under each bridge wing was another twin Vickers. Down aft there was a Bren gun and on the bridge there was a Bren gun. The process ... would be that the Captain ... would direct the Bren gun on the bridge with tracer to the target and all the rest of the weapons would just follow. It was a very simple system ... If you made a mistake, and you fired a round ... accidentally, there was no argument about it, there was an automatic 28 days stoppage of leave, it didn't matter if you were an officer or a rating or whatever.[136]

*Santon* and *Hickleton* patrolled the straits, investigating the motorised kumpits and small sailing jongkongs that traded along the myriad waterways, and whose skippers might, if the opportunity arose, smuggle goods and possibly arms and men across the Strait of Malacca to West Malaysia or Singapore. The minesweepers on night patrol would pick up a darkened vessel on the radar and direct it back into Indonesian waters. Some persisted; if they were contacted again, both crew and vessel would be arrested handed over to the Malaysian police. Others would be intercepted the following night, having turned back temporarily, then reached Malaysia and unloaded their cargo. They too would be arrested for questioning.[137]

Gerry Wright, who used to take the middle watch on the *Santon,* remembered that there was a navigation buoy about ten miles off Port Swettenham,

> where I knew there would always be an Indonesian smuggler at 3 o'clock in the morning. I could always guarantee there would be one there. From time to time I would call the Captain [Lin Tempero] to tell him that something was happening; either there was a punch-up going on down the coast or there was an aircraft dropping flares. He would invariably roll over and say 'piss off, give me a call when you have something really good to tell me'. In the area of Port Swettenham I would tootle off down to 'my buoy' and arrive at 3 o'clock in the morning and catch my Indonesian and bring him alongside while going to action stations. The First Lieutenant [Trevor Jones] would lead the search team to sort them out. That would take 45 minutes, which meant that the whole operation would be finished by quarter to four. This meant that it was a waste of time for the First Lieutenant to go back to bed as he was due on watch at 4 a.m. I got relieved 10 minutes early; it was magic, well worth it as far as I was concerned, because we were very, very tired, as we worked very long hours.[138]

The minesweepers patrolled for between ten and 14 days, followed by two or three days in harbour for maintenance before the next patrol. The New Zealanders always got the Christmas tours because the Royal Navy crews had their families in Singapore. Everyone worked long hours with broken sleep in conditions of 'poor ventilation, very high humidity, and high temperatures'.[139] On the *Santon*,

> Lin Tempero wasn't all that keen about going back to the Naval Base too often because some of the hangmen in our ship's company would disappear ... We worked our way north and once you got up into the Malacca Straits there was usually some sort of mother ship anchored up there. I think we had [HMS] *Manxman* ... we could go alongside her during the day and get a few stores off

> there, you could always wangle a couple of cartons of beer when we had none left at all on board.[140]

The monotony of checking curfew-breaking fishermen and barter traders taking cargoes of batik to Singapore, where it fetched high prices, was broken occasionally by sightings of Indonesian patrol craft safely inside their territorial waters. Patrolling the approaches to Tawau in Borneo was part of the cycle; here Indonesian trading craft were inspected at random, with 'passes and licences scrutinised and the boat thoroughly searched. As nothing suspicious was ever found, gifts were made to the Indonesian crew of food and cigarettes.'[141]

The Borneo tour often gave the crews a chance for some much-needed rest, as well as qualifying some for the 'Borneo' clasp to the General Service Medal.[142] 'Barge' Bruce, the coxswain on the *Santon*, recalled that:

> They had about two patrol areas outside Tawau for the minesweepers and then the rest of it was on the river. We used to do about a week where we would come down to the Tawau wharf during the day and about 4 o'clock we would head off up the river and ... anchor right on the Indonesian border ... the river had a junction and we were just down from the junction and we could watch the Indonesian Army base which was on this side of the junction, everything coming and going there during the night and what was happening ... If they tried to come down this way then they would be reported and picked up by the smaller police boats ... We also used to take the odd SAS team up with us in their little black blow-up boats and drop them off in the middle of the night and then pick them up three or four days later. They would come out of the bush all stinking and horrible, looking for a shower.[143]

The only major incident involving any of the New Zealand ships occurred on 28 June 1966, when HMNZS *Hickleton* under Lieutenant-Commander P. N. Wright RNZN intercepted a fishing sampan off Horsburgh Light in the Strait of Singapore. The *Hickleton* was returning to the Naval Base for a formal inspection, in anticipation of which everything warlike, including the ready-to-use ammunition at the guns, had been stowed away. With Confrontation seemingly on its last legs, the last thing anyone expected to see in broad daylight, in the middle of a fleet of fishing boats, was a sampan with a civilian boatman and three armed and uniformed Indonesians on board. Despite being outgunned, the sampan ignored all instructions to stop, and rifle shots fired across its bow. After a mad dash to break out the ammunition, the *Hickleton*'s crew fired rifle shots at the boat's outboard motor. The Indonesians returned fire with a machine gun at a range of 30 yards. The *Hickleton* responded, killing both the Indonesians manning the machine gun and wounding the third Indonesian and the civilian boatman. While the *Hickleton* had not been expecting action, the prompt response saw her commander, Peter Wright, awarded the Distinguished Service Cross. Able Seaman C. K. Taylor received the Distinguished Service Medal for his immediate and accurate return of fire, which had silenced the Indonesian machine gun before it could inflict serious casualties.[144]

Every night during Confrontation, between 1963 and 1966, some 50 ships and naval craft of the Far East Fleet and Malaysian Navy were deployed on patrols and escorts. The judgement—with the benefit of hindsight—that little happened overlooks the classic role played by the Commonwealth naval forces in countering the real threat presented by the Indonesian Navy. The latter was effectively denied the use of the sea, giving Commonwealth resources freedom of movement to East Malaysia. The actions that the Commonwealth naval forces could undertake were limited by political decisions, and were designed mainly 'with the object of avoiding escalation into a hotter war'. As it turned out, the Indonesians proved to be 'inept at sea'. The Indonesian Navy 'operated at a low level of intensity and often at a low level of efficiency', confronting Commonwealth ships only with occasional patrols.[145] The 'ring of grey' formed by those ships is best appreciated in terms of what did *not* happen. As S. D. Waters commented in his summation of naval operations in Korea:

> There had been none of the headline brilliance of great naval battles. Nor was there the satisfaction of bringing important convoys safely through enemy attacks. It had been essential work, not far removed from the Navy's traditional 'watch and ward' role of the Napoleonic wars. It had been monotonous then; it was monotonous still. But its importance—that of denying the sea to the enemy while making the most of it yourself—was as great as ever.[146]

The RNZN's limited resources were committed to this task, and it played an important if unheralded role. Manning the two coastal minesweepers and maintaining a frigate—and for one tour the cruiser *Royalist*—on station was a major commitment, especially as the frigates *Otago* and *Taranaki* were the only two modern vessels available, and crewing the *Royalist* stretched the Navy's manpower to its limits. Like the RNZAF, the RNZN found that its commitment to Confrontation was at the extreme limit of what it could sustain. This service too was bearing the brunt of the forward defence policy of a government unwilling or unable to authorise the financial outlays that would make it achievable. The continual over-stretching of scarce resources has masked the reality of New Zealand's defence needs to this day. It has also fuelled the on-going debate on the minimum number of frigates appropriate to New Zealand's naval situation. The RNZN wanted to keep the concept of a six-frigate navy alive. Manning shortages, financial limitations and common sense all made this increasingly unrealistic. As Chief of Naval Staff, Rear-Admiral Phipps had fought to maintain the six-frigate concept; but on becoming the first Chief of Defence Staff in the now-integrated Defence Headquarters in June 1965, he accepted the inevitable: 'on sheer grounds of expense, I tried to talk first Admiral Washbourn and then Admiral Ross into stopping at four frigates ... By that time I did not believe that any more were attainable, not because New Zealand did not need them, but because the country could not afford them. Besides, the Navy also needed a new survey ship, a new training ship, and so on.'[147]

In November 1965, HMNZS *Royalist* broke down in the Solomon Islands on the way home from Singapore because of severe salt-water contamination in its boilers. *Royalist*'s sudden and unexpected withdrawal from service was a humiliating end to the New Zealand Navy's cruiser era.[148] With HMNZS *Waikato* still under construction, New Zealand was reduced to only two front-line ships, *Otago* and *Taranaki*. The Whitby-class frigate HMS *Blackpool* was borrowed from the Royal Navy for five years, during which a fourth frigate would be tendered for and built.[149] The commissioning in September 1966 of the Leander-class *Waikato*, with its 'Westland Wasp anti-submarine helicopter equipped with two homing torpedoes', was another major advance in capability for the Navy.[150] While a four-frigate navy had evolved by default, over the next 30 years this proved to be a sensible minimum size for the RNZN.

# 9

# 'THE CODEWORD IS "CLARET"'

## *The SAS, Borneo, 1965–66*

> It may be as well in future telegrams to avoid, so far as possible, use of the word 'retaliation'. Our friends undertake defensive operations. In certain circumstances these defensive operations may not be limited to their own territory. But they do not undertake offensive operations and even their operations in reply to an attack are in pure self-defence rather than in spite or as a form of punishment which is the impression left by the word 'retaliation'.[1]
>
> ALISTER McINTOSH,
> SECRETARY OF EXTERNAL AFFAIRS 1943–66

The deployment of the New Zealand SAS in Borneo during Confrontation raised important dilemmas for the government. 'Defensive' operations conducted inside Kalimantan might not be 'retaliation', and by some stretch of imagination might be construed as not 'offensive' in the sense of taking the fight to the Indonesians. Yet this 'aggressive defence' by the Commonwealth Forces in Borneo, however secret and limited in nature, was the major obstacle to Holyoake's government agreeing to commit New Zealand Army combat elements there. By contrast, the release of the New Zealand battalion for operations against Indonesian infiltrators on the Malay Peninsula in September 1964 was a simple decision. The Indonesians were invading what was unequivocally Malaysia, and New Zealand assistance to resist this aggression was easy to justify. As the above extract from a cable to Hunter Wade, the High Commissioner in Kuala Lumpur, shows, the government found it difficult to decide to deploy its forces on combat operations in Borneo when it knew these involved clandestine patrols and raids into Indonesian territory.

These covert cross-border operations, codenamed CLARET, grew out of the nature of the forces available to Major-General Walter Walker, the first Director of Operations in Borneo, to meet the threat of infiltration from Indonesian Kalimantan after the Brunei revolt in December 1962.[2] One squadron of 22 Special Air Service Regiment was initially deployed to Singapore in January 1963 as a reserve to be dropped by parachute to recapture landing strips in the Borneo territories if these were seized by the Indonesians. However, once Walker appreciated their capabilities in reconnaissance, communication and the Malay language, four-man SAS patrols became his eyes and ears among the tribespeople living in isolated kampongs near the border in the hilly jungle-clad Fourth and Fifth Divisions of Sarawak, through which incursions were made into Brunei.

Initially, these incursions were small-scale, ill-planned raids by groups of Indonesian-trained 'Irregular Border Terrorists' (IBTs). These comprised members of the mainly Chinese Sarawak 'Clandestine Communist Organisation' (CCO) who had fled into Kalimantan following the failure of the Brunei revolt, and irregulars of the National Army of North Kalimantan (TNKU). Following the Malayan Prime Minister's formal announcement on 29 August 1963 that the Federation of Malaysia would come into being on 16 September 1963, the raids increased in size and intensity. In the first six months of 1964, all pretence that the Indonesian Army (TNI) was not directly involved vanished. Raids were conducted by trained and heavily armed groups led by regulars from picked units of the Indonesian armed forces: Marine commandos (Korps Komando Operasi, or KKO), Army paratroops (RPKAD), and Air Force paratroops (PGT).[3] All highly trained, the regulars were extremely tough, skilled and tenacious opponents if operating in their own units. By contrast, the irregulars of the IBT and TNKU were a mix of races and military backgrounds, and lacked both administrative support and training. Many had fired their weapons only once before being sent across the border. However, being of hardy peasant stock, they were accustomed to jungle living and capable of 'surviving on the minimum of rations'.[4] Backing these groups, but rarely used in cross-border incursions, were the regular soldiers of the TNI who garrisoned the many bases along the Kalimantan border. Their quality reflected that of their company commanders and commanding officers. The best were effective, while others lapsed into the slipshod habits of remote garrisons and drew false security from the jungle depths that surrounded them.

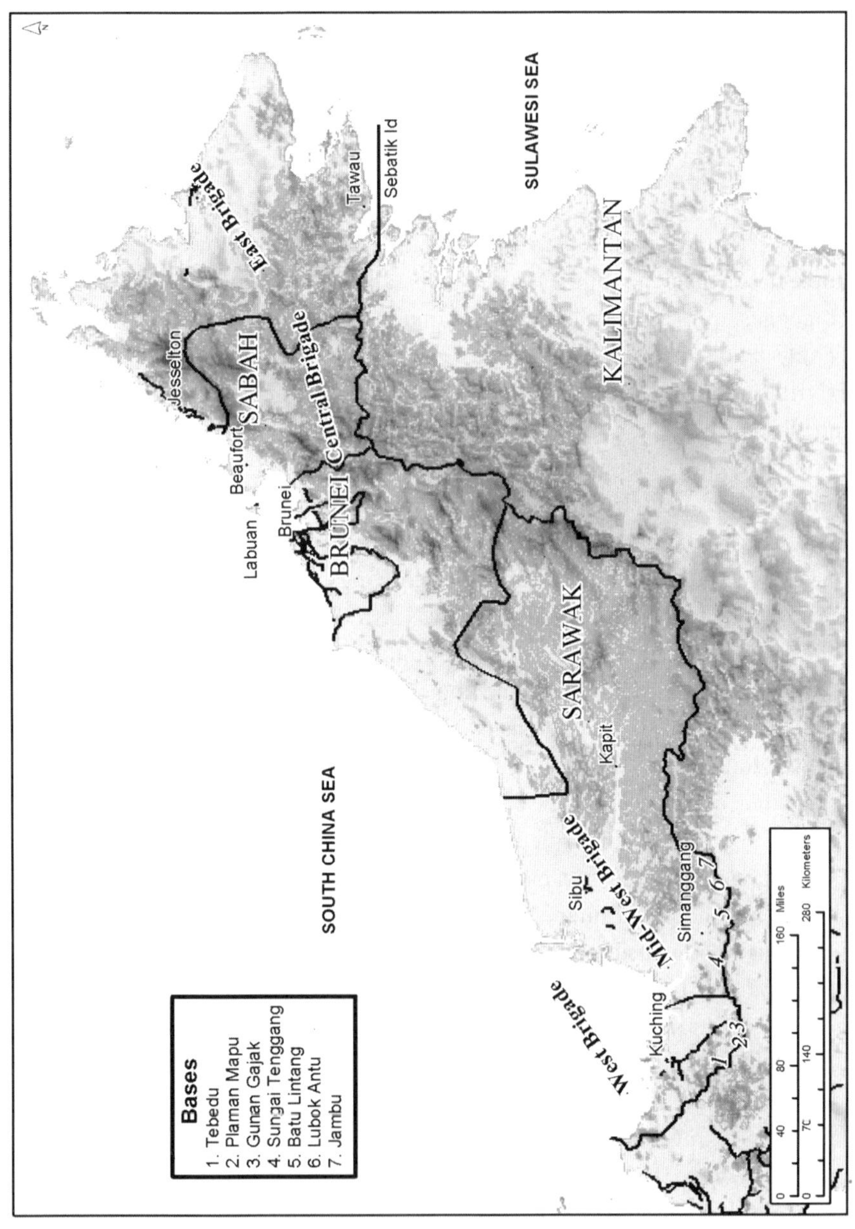


**Map 8** East Malaysia, 1965

The strategy behind the Indonesian operations paralleled the one that had been so effective against the Dutch in New Guinea. It was a combined political and military approach. At the political level, the Indonesians courted Afro-Asian support at the United Nations, where they accused Malaysia of being a neo-colonialist fabrication aimed at retaining British power in the region. At the military level, Indonesia did not want to provoke a limited war with Britain, but rather to maintain a level of operations sufficient to draw in large numbers of British and Malaysian forces for an indefinite period, with the aim of fracturing Malaysian morale and forcing Britain to question the validity of its defence commitment to the Federation.

The growing involvement of Indonesian regulars in cross-border raids into East Malaysia led to the approval of the British government on 1 May 1964 for 'hot pursuit' CLARET operations to be conducted to a depth of 3,000 yards inside Kalimantan. These operations were to be 'deniable', at least in terms of the 'uncertain demarcation of the border'.[5] Walker agitated for this policy of 'hot pursuit' to be expanded into an aggressive policy of ambushing cross-border routes up to 3,000 yards inside Kalimantan, thereby intercepting Indonesian incursions before they crossed the border. This was approved on 1 July 1964, and by December 'aggressive defence' had resulted in British and Commonwealth forces gaining the initiative by creating a no-man's land 3,000 yards deep inside Kalimantan.[6]

In December 1964 the one available British squadron was redeployed into the First Division of Sarawak, the area now under greatest threat, to undertake CLARET tasks into Kalimantan. All CLARET operations carried out by the SAS were sanctioned by Walker as Director of Operations Borneo, and co-ordinated by a Headquarters SAS Far East, established in Borneo by 22 SAS Regiment and headed by either its commanding officer or his second-in-command. Whilst patrols came under the operational control of the brigade within whose area they were operating, command was retained by SAS Headquarters.[7] CLARET operations were carried out in accordance with Walker's 'Golden Rules'.[8] It was never acknowledged that cross-border operations were taking place, and participants were sworn to secrecy. Each patrol was on its own once it entered Indonesian territory. Should a patrol or individuals be captured, they were 'to deny having deliberately crossed the border'.[9] Their presence would be explained as an accidental incursion due to faulty navigation or some such cause, and their actions would be officially disowned. The same approach was applied to public relations. Journalists were not allowed to visit forward units when cross-border operations were being carried out, and 'nothing should be volunteered to the Press or other information media' about specific operations. 'Indeed, it is of the highest importance that maximum security be adhered to throughout by all concerned.'[10]

Since September 1963 the SAS had functioned as an early-warning 'screen' by patrolling up to 3,000 yards inside Kalimantan. This sanctioned covert reconnaissance was very successful: all major incursions were identified by the SAS and subsequently intercepted by the infantry battalions stationed in company bases along the Sabah and Sarawak borders. Walker's demands on this reconnaissance shield soon expanded beyond the capacity of the two-squadron-strong 22 SAS Regiment. Borneo was but one of the SAS's many commitments world-wide, and to meet this undertaking the regiment began raising a third squadron and training a new patrol company. A Guards Independent Parachute Company was also raised from 16 Parachute Brigade.[11] British requests to both Australia and New Zealand for additional SAS support became increasingly insistent.

In January 1965, in response to a build-up of Indonesian regular forces across the border, the limit for incursion into Kalimantan was increased to 10,000 yards. Disruptive attacks against forward Indonesian bases, training camps and supply routes were also agreed to, and carried out either by the SAS or by infantry companies led to their target by SAS patrols.[12] Admiral Sir Varyl Begg, the Commander-in-Chief Far East, accepted that such operations were undeniable if Indonesia chose to protest—but they were worth the risk. Intelligence indicated that the Indonesian headquarters in Kalimantan had 'minimised the impact of our operations' over the last six months, and expected this state of affairs to continue. CLARET was an attractive alternative to mounting air operations, which 'with their greater emotional reaction in world opinion, carry a greater risk of escalation than small-scale land and or sea operations'.[13]

The New Zealand Chiefs of Staff and Cabinet were briefed on the unusual nature of the war in Borneo, where British and Malaysian forces walked a fine line in frustrating Indonesian military incursions without sparking a general war. The decision-makers in Wellington knew that if the New Zealand SAS was deployed on CLARET operations, it would be of value only if 'available for reconnaissance and patrols' inside Indonesia. Whatever the reservations of the New Zealand government, it had to either make the SAS available for these tasks or not offer its services at all. While it was not initially intended to employ the New Zealand SAS on offensive operations such as attacking bases and camps in Indonesian territory, 'there would obviously be a possibility of clashes with Indonesians, including clashes initiated by SAS'.[14]

In January 1965 the New Zealand government agreed in principle to offer additional military assistance to the defence of Malaysia against Indonesian Confrontation. This included an SAS detachment of 40 men which 'should be available for service in Borneo, including operations across the border such as reconnaissance and patrols', on the understanding that detailed limitations on the employment of the detachment would be discussed with the British and Australian authorities. The New Zealand High Commission in Kuala Lumpur was told that it could inform the Malaysian government that New Zealand was able to provide a detachment, which 'should be available for patrol and other cross-border duties on the same basis as the current British SAS squadron'. The New Zealand government was 'anxious to have a clear understanding of what we are committing ourselves to and of the safeguards on the employment of our forces across the border'; but provided no problems arose in the discussions, the SAS detachment would be sent soon.[15]

The British and Malaysian governments, Admiral Begg, Major-General H. A. Lascelles, the Commander-in-Chief Far East Land Forces, and Major-General Walker all wanted New Zealand involved in Borneo, and were prepared to accept limitations on the employment of its SAS in order to get them there. Lascelles made it clear to Colonel L. A. Kermode, the Commander New Zealand Army Far East Land Forces, that they were needed primarily in a reconnaissance role. He would 'welcome the deployment of Commonwealth SAS into BORNEO limited to purely reconnaissance tasks should this solution be more acceptable to Commonwealth Governments'.[16] Kermode's own view was that the New Zealand SAS could make an 'honourable and worthwhile contribution' in Borneo only if they had the authority to perform the same tasks as their British counterparts. Kermode considered that this was also the unstated opinion of Headquarters Far East Land Forces.[17]

The New Zealand government agreed that the commitment should be on the same terms as that of the British SAS squadrons if it was to be made at all. On 5 February 1965, on his return from London, Holyoake announced that the New Zealand battalion of the Commonwealth Strategic Reserve had been made available for service in Borneo, in rotation with Malaysian and British units. An SAS detachment of 40 men had been offered; crews to man two Royal Navy coastal minesweepers would be made available; and two Bristol Freighters currently in north-east Thailand would rejoin No. 41 Squadron in Singapore for duties in Malaysia. Holyoake emphasised that the decision to offer more aid had been made in response to 'a recent Malaysian request'.[18] On 16 February, New Zealand agreed that the SAS detachment and the infantry battalion would be 'available for operations in Borneo in the same roles and on the same basis as now apply to British units'. The New Zealand government's understanding was that the 'current authority extends to reconnaissance, ambushes and attacks on "Indonesian bivouacs and staging camps within an area up to 10,000 yards over the border"'. It expected to be kept generally informed of the 'cross-border employment of our units', on which it reserved the right to comment, but did not require specific national clearance for each operation. It was stressed that this arrangement applied only to the current situation; if the 'British Government were to extend the authority it has given to CINCFE yet further, the concurrence of the New Zealand Government would be required before this extension applied to New Zealand Forces'.[19]

Sir Varyl Begg described the CLARET security arrangements to Rear-Admiral Sir Peter Phipps, New Zealand's Chief of Defence Staff. He explained the 'restricted marking system under which all messages concerning these operations will be prefixed with a codeword. The codeword is "CLARET" and circulation of all messages bearing this prefix is restricted to a strictly limited number of officers in the Ministry of Defence [United Kingdom], at my headquarters and in Borneo.' Two weekly reports were to be passed to Phipps by the Head of the British Defence Liaison Staff in Wellington, one detailing CLARET operations carried out during the week, and the second assessing Indonesian reactions to these operations 'as revealed from special intelligence sources'.[20] The New Zealand High Commissioner in Kuala Lumpur, Hunter Wade, and the New Zealand Defence Liaison Officers attached to the High Commission were invited to attend the daily operational briefings for Begg and his service commanders in the War Room at Phoenix Park in Singapore. In New Zealand, details of CLARET operations were restricted to Phipps, the Director of Plans, the Secretary of the Chiefs of Staff Committee, and the Chief of General Staff. 'All the Claret reports are seen only by the first three and Chief of General Staff will be shown these only when they affect New Zealand units.' Outside this inner circle, only the Chairman of the Joint Intelligence

Staff Committee and 'a very small group' within the Department of External Affairs would even 'know that we possess this information'.[21]

## One Detachment, New Zealand Ranger Squadron, February to October 1965

In 1965 the New Zealand Special Air Service comprised a squadron organisation—the 1st New Zealand Ranger Squadron, New Zealand Special Air Service—and a training wing based at Papakura Camp.[22] Since being reformed in 1959, the New Zealand SAS had had little contact with 22 SAS Regiment. Its training and tactics was influenced by its involvement with United States Special Forces in Thailand in 1962. Under Major Mel Velvin, the squadron had introduced innovative training techniques to increase individual specialist skills. These included attaching troopers to the accident and emergency departments of Auckland hospitals to hone their first aid and medical skills in real-life crisis situations. Yet in many ways the squadron was searching for a role. Velvin's successor, Major Bill Meldrum, refocused on its traditional strengths of small-group, long-range patrolling, with an emphasis on the individual skills of bushcraft, navigation and shooting. Meldrum, who had served in Malaya as a platoon commander in Morrison's 1st Battalion, New Zealand Regiment, and as Adjutant in Pearce's battalion, typified the level of operational experience in the squadron. With his hands-on, larger-than-life personality, Meldrum gave the squadron something of 'a rude awakening'.[23] He believed that while individual skills within the squadron were of a high standard, the sense of teamwork essential for long-range patrolling was lacking. Meldrum's particular emphasis was on 'strengthening the quality of the non-commissioned officers'.[24] This was to prove critical to the initial success of the New Zealand SAS in Borneo. In January 1965 the New Zealand Special Air Service comprised some 60 personnel, of whom a core were highly experienced in jungle operations in South-East Asia. Sergeants Peter Rutledge, Danny Wilson and Ken Schimanski had cut their operational teeth with the battalions. So had the junior NCOs, among whom Len Wilson, Niwa Kawha, Tom Rautao, Johnno Johnston and others were outstanding trackers and scouts. They were the elite of the New Zealand Army, highly skilled in jungle operations and small-group patrolling, which they had learnt from men like Huia Woods. Having already served in Malaya, they viewed the SAS as another challenge. Dick Smith was one of the few who had not served overseas. A deer culler who was at home in the bush, Smith joined the Army in 1962 and was accepted for a selection course in 1963.

> It was a very rugged selection course. It was run by a guy called Shocker Shaw, and it was a hard course to pass. There were something like 50 or 60 on that course, there were 19 selected, and out of the 19 there were about eight that actually passed ... the three month SAS-type training that followed. That was harder than the selection course and would determine whether you got a red beret or not.[25]

The Borneo commitment came with little warning. Many of the squadron had only been back from parachute training at RAAF Base Williamtown, north of Newcastle, Australia, for about two weeks when they were warned about going to Borneo.[26] Providing a complete squadron was beyond New Zealand's resources, and even a 40-strong detachment required almost all the available and fit men, leaving the barest of skeletons in Papakura on which to build its replacement. Thirty of the 40 men selected had seen operational service in Malaya. 'They'd been with battalions and one or two of them had been up there twice ... [Meldrum's] main concern were those who hadn't been in that area before, the younger men like Heke, Ihaka and co.'[27] Only the detachment's Chief Clerk, Sergeant Bob Withers, and the SQMS, Staff Sergeant Ted Keene, remained from the original squadron that had served with 22 SAS Regiment in Malaya.[28] Meldrum was pleased with the quality of his troop commanders. 'We had Julian Baker, now he was pretty raw, but he had all the aplomb of a young Sandhurst graduate, and as gutsy as hell. Murray Winton who is an ace character ... The other one was Eru Manuera. Eru had great potential and I used to ride him to death ... but he learnt very quickly and he was a natural.'[29]

As Australia was also known to be considering sending a detachment, the New Zealand Defence Liaison Staff in Canberra was asked to establish whether a combined squadron would be acceptable. Meldrum crossed the Tasman for discussions, but although Australia was willing, the proposal foundered on British concerns that the combined squadron would be larger than the current British squadron and difficult to employ. This may have provided a convenient excuse for New Zealand not to pursue an Anzac linkage, as 22 SAS Regiment had expressed veiled disquiet at the proposal, and a preference for re-establishing the strong relationship with the New Zealanders that it had had in Malaya. Accordingly, it was decided that the New Zealanders would be employed within the existing structure of 22 SAS Regiment, first as part of a

British squadron and later as an independent detachment answerable to regimental headquarters.

Meldrum's 40-strong One Detachment, 1 NZ Ranger Squadron (Far East) flew out from Whenuapai on 25 February 1965 and landed in Singapore three days later. On their departure, the Minister of Defence sent the following message: 'As the Army specialist Paratroop Regiment you have been chosen to work with British and Australian units to help the people of that country [Malaysia] to resist attacks by Indonesian Guerrillas; this is the type of work you have been trained for and I know you will do it thoroughly and well.'[30] In Singapore the detachment came under the command of Colonel Leo Kermode's Headquarters NZ Force FARELF.

An incident in Singapore was to result in Meldrum's premature return to New Zealand. The British authorities, who wanted as little publicity as possible on the deployment of the New Zealand SAS to Borneo, had been embarrassed by Holyoake's public announcement. They were further discomfited by an article in the *New Zealand Weekly News* written by a Singapore-based New Zealand reporter, which stated that 'men of the British and Australian SAS groups have been probing at the Indonesians across the borders in Borneo for some time'. The implication was that Meldrum was the source.[31] Indeed, he had spoken to the reporter, apparently after clearing the interview with Kermode's headquarters.[32] While Meldrum was certain he had not mentioned cross-border operations, the publication of the article had irreparably damaged his credibility with 22 SAS Regiment. On his first visit to SAS Headquarters in Kuching, before he even knew about the article, Meldrum found he was not receiving briefings at the level he expected. 'Then of course I got called back to Singapore, and that probably explains why they weren't that open with me.'[33] Kermode recalled Meldrum from Borneo in late March, and recommended to Army General Staff that he be returned to New Zealand. This happened in early April, leaving Captain B. T. A. ('Punchy') Worsnop in command.[34] A Court of Inquiry in New Zealand concluded that while Meldrum had not breached security, he had acted irresponsibly and disregarded instructions by talking to the reporter.[35] Any service criticism of Meldrum was deliberately downplayed in the press.[36] Inevitably, the incident ended Meldrum's military career. It could also have had a devastating impact on the detachment just as it was about to start on operations. But as Trooper Dan Heke commented: 'We believed that we were professionals and we acted and behaved like professionals, so it didn't affect our work.'[37] This attitude was a tribute to the level of training and professional focus that the detachment had achieved under Meldrum's command.

This drama was still some weeks away when the New Zealand detachment flew to Labuan on 4 March 1965 and came under the command of 22 SAS Regiment.[38] They trained first at Tutong Camp, living alongside 1 Australian SAS Squadron; after the Australians moved out on 19 March, they shifted into Bolkiah Camp in Brunei Town for a fortnight. The New Zealanders had an uneasy relationship with the Australians, who seemed to lack the skills and discipline the New Zealanders took for granted and were seen as a 'bunch of cowboys'.[39] Contact between the two groups was to remain limited throughout Confrontation.

D Squadron, the current British SAS squadron in Borneo, provided an impressive four-man patrol under Sergeant G. J. ('Smudge') Smith to assist with training. Meldrum described Smith as 'the only Brit who I ever came across who was at one with nature'.[40] These British specialists were spread among Meldrum's three troops to advise on and critique their training. Little time was spent in camp; Meldrum got his men into the jungle as quickly as possible. Murray Winton, commanding 1 Troop, recalled that 'we trained, trained, trained. We trained to move at night. We did a lot of experimentation within the four-man patrols and got those sorted out, because when you're operating with four men there are some guys that get on the other guy's goat.'[41] The existing organisation of a headquarters and three troops, each of two patrols, was adjusted: the size of headquarters was reduced, and the detachment was reorganised into seven patrols, five of four men and two of five.[42] Meldrum's emphasis was on basic jungle techniques, and on live-firing, immediate-action drills to be used on patrols. The New Zealanders added 'some small adaptations and a few tricks that we ... learnt from 22 SAS' to their already well-established base of patrolling techniques.[43] In particular, they devised a drill for evacuating a wounded man under fire which became a standard procedure in 22 SAS.

> There was only four of you so if your lead scout gets hit, the idea was to say that 'I am hit', then your commander produced the covering fire and your signaller and your medic came up and pulled the guy out. And having pulled him out then the medic kept dragging him away and then you used fire and movement to disengage yourself ... there wasn't anything extraordinary about it except that we felt that every effort should be made to pull our wounded out and that we would not leave them behind.[44]

The regiment the New Zealanders joined was now very different from the one they had been part of in Malaya between 1955 and 1957. Then, the regiment was still finding its feet, and had not achieved the professionalism that was now its hallmark. In Malaya, the New Zealand Squadron had played an important part in establishing those standards; now it was the New Zealanders who had to lift their game and skills to match their British counterparts. On 3 April 1965 the detachment, now under the command of Major Worsnop, moved to Kuching in south-west Sarawak, where it came under the operational command of Major Roger Woodiwiss of D Squadron 22 SAS Regiment. The regiment's second-in-command, Major John Slim, was based at an SAS headquarters on Labuan—alongside that of the Director of Operations Borneo—that was headed by either himself or the Commanding Officer 22 SAS Regiment, Lieutenant-Colonel Mike Wingate-Gray. The number of units it controlled demonstrated the need for this headquarters. A Squadron had completed its third tour in Borneo, while D Squadron was on its third. Three independent parachute companies watched a sector of the border each, and both the New Zealanders and the Australians were soon to start operations.[45]

In Kuching, a typical bustling Asian town, the New Zealanders found themselves part of a uniquely SAS set-up. Headquarters personnel, including Worsnop, were located at D Squadron Headquarters in the 'Haunted House' on Fuchow Road; the majority of the squadron were billeted with D Squadron at Cloud Estate, a rented house, with the overflow living in the Palm Hotel. All the troop officers were accommodated in hotels, whose reception staff became used to seeing bedraggled, bearded, stinking individuals humping Bergen packs and equipment through the foyer, past startled guests, and claiming their room keys.

Brian Worsnop was a very different personality from Meldrum. 'Punchy was in a peculiar situation in that he went across as Bill Meldrum's administration officer and had conditioned himself for that particular role so he was absolutely divorced from operational issues. Given Bill's sudden departure, Punchy was thrust forward and I think for some considerable time underplayed his hand.' The integration of the New Zealand detachment into D Squadron allowed Worsnop to sit back and reassess his role, which he did very effectively. As Eru Manuera, who later in the tour became Operations Officer at Squadron Headquarters, observed, Worsnop showed 'steel' when this was needed.[46] Of the rest of the New Zealand headquarters staff, the Intelligence corporal and clerk worked with Worsnop in the Squadron Operations Room, while the vehicle mechanic was lent to the local brigade workshop and the storeman was used as a driver.

When they arrived in Kuching the New Zealanders were given their first and last general briefing on CLARET operations and Indonesian activity in Kalimantan. It was stressed that once across the border 'we were on our own. There were no arguments about it. We had to make up our own stories as to why we were there, whether we were lost, or whether we were a survey party ... We would be disowned and you had to fend for yourself.' Murray Winton recalled that as he was sitting in the briefing room, reading information on Indonesian positions covering the border, 'my knees started shaking ... but I looked at the others and they were all looking at the map as I was and I looked down to their knees, and you could just see the quivering of the jungle green trousers and you knew you weren't on your own.'[47]

The border area had originally been the responsibility of three brigades—West, Central and East—but increased pressures had seen West Brigade divided into West and Mid-West. Within each brigade area were a number of strongly protected jungle bases of company size that could be held by a third of the strength they could accommodate. Most of the infantry, based at these 'wild west' forts, patrolled and reconnoitred across the border into Kalimantan, and mounted ambushes against incursions identified by the SAS CLARET patrols. The SAS patrol screen had been effective in reducing attempts by IBT guerrillas to link up with the CCO, which had widespread support among the people of Sarawak.[48] The situation was now almost one of conventional warfare, as Indonesian regulars launched attacks against the string of rifle company bases along the border. The main areas of activity were the First and Second Divisions of Sarawak, opposite which the Indonesians concentrated most of their strength. However, the entire length of the border was open to carefully planned raids from Kalimantan. Keeping the many jungle trails that criss-crossed the border under surveillance was just one of the roles of the SAS.

It was in this climate that the New Zealanders began operational patrolling. Some changes were introduced when Major-General George Lea succeeded Walker as Director of Operations Borneo in March 1965. Lea was well known to New Zealanders, having been Commanding Officer 22 SAS Regiment between 1955 and 1957. While Lea agreed that the primary aim of CLARET operations was reconnaissance, he sanctioned offensive action in the last 48 hours of an operation, provided the target was 'soft' and complete success was possible.[49]

22 SAS were keen to get the New Zealanders into the jungle and see what they could do. The first three patrols crossed the border on separate CLARET operations on 10 April 1965. Lieutenant Murray Winton's four-man patrol was one of them.

> The normal procedure was that headquarters would ring you about two days beforehand and ask, 'Would you like to come up and have drinks?' You would ring your boys up and say 'It's on', and we would then go up and be briefed. Then you would be issued with all your equipment, ammunition, bits and pieces and so on, and you would do some rehearsals, just to get you back into thinking the way you should.[50]

The patrol commander and scout, and sometimes the entire patrol, would fly up to the border, reconnoitre the route, liaise with the battalion whose sector it was, arrange escorts to the border, and establish a rendezvous for their return. No patrol knew any other patrol's task. Once briefed, the members of the patrol lived in a cocoon, shielded from all other SAS activity. Detachment headquarters staff would not have dreamt of asking what operations were going on. Sergeant Bob Withers, the Chief Clerk, recalled: 'It was all played very close to the chest and everything was on a need-to-know basis.'[51]

It was the same on a patrol's return; only operational headquarters staff knew the bigger picture, and nothing leaked out. Men back from a mission would shower and change, then be called up for a detailed debrief, after which they hit the town. If they met up with another patrol group in a bar, nothing except the obvious was ever said. The extremely thorough debriefs involved all patrol members. Every aspect of what had been seen and heard was examined from all angles, and this thoroughness was reflected in the final reports. Johnno Johnston appreciated the atmosphere of relaxed professionalism.

> We used to go back to Cloud Estate, get a shower, get cleaned up, have something to eat. If you came out late afternoon, you could guarantee that you wouldn't be debriefed that day. Probably mid-morning next day with the whole patrol. The patrol commander would be debriefed ... everyone was involved. I always liked that system where the trooper has an input and he could have just as much say as the sergeant because he could have been in a position [on the patrol] where the sergeant wasn't.[52]

The first patrol was the one that everyone remembered. Dan Heke of Murray Winton's patrol recalled the 'apprehension and fear of going across the border'.[53] It was a journey into the unknown; once across an ill-defined line every man would be against them, with help a long way away. Even though the maximum limit of penetration into Kalimantan was 10,000 yards, reaching an objective took two or three times this distance to avoid an obvious approach route or populated areas. Each trooper carried 12 days' supplies in his Bergen pack and the pouches of his belt order. The latter comprised pouches containing ammunition, basic rations and water bottles, so that if a man had to drop his Bergen pack he would still be able to fight and survive. Patrols moved in a well-practised, pre-arranged order: scout first, then patrol commander, third man, and radio operator. There were standard procedures for rendezvous if patrols became separated, and immediate-action drills had been practised repeatedly until they became an automatic response, with four men working as one.

Most of the border area was a natural watershed of rugged mountains clad in primary jungle. Once the patrols descended into Kalimantan they moved through virgin jungle interspersed with areas of thick secondary growth around kampongs and ladangs (cultivated clearings with one or two shelters made from attap palms). It was beautiful country, but the SAS had little time to admire it. The objective was always at the extreme limit of the patrol's endurance, and the quicker they got there the longer they had to study it. In many ways their situation was similar to that of the communist MRLA guerrillas during the Emergency: they were the hunted, outnumbered and alone, aware that any sign of their passage would be reported, and followed up by Indonesian forces.

Their only ally was the jungle. Tracks were avoided; if one was encountered, the patrol would 'loop'—follow a semi-circular route that cut the track at irregular intervals in order to establish if there was any other movement along it. The patrol had to be at one with the jungle; the spacing between the four men was determined by the density of the vegetation. Photographs show that at times visibility could be measured in centimetres. Progress in such circumstances was made by barely perceptible, slow and deliberate movements that avoided the sharp crack of a twig or the rustle of a branch that might alert animals or other humans.

> Time of course was only urgent depending on the situation. It seems a bit odd to say it, but if you were being chased you ran. If you wanted to make up time you waited until it rained and then you could go very quickly, but normally you were travelling I suppose anything from 100 to 400 yards an hour. Now when you try and do that, you would think it's physically impossible, that's how slow you are

> going ... But when you're pushing through lallang, and cutting underneath the lallang so you don't disturb the top, time just keeps going.[54]

If their senses told them something was not quite right, the men just sat and listened to the jungle. 'The jungle told you if there was anything going on. When nothing happened, you moved on again.'[55] At night the patrol slept without sentries, the jungle itself standing guard; at first light, they moved on.

Winton's patrol established itself in this manner on the Sungai Bemban and waited for six days, carefully noting and reporting by radio all movement. From their concealed observation post in the jungle on the river's edge, they watched civilian-manned craft powered by outboard motors carry supplies and soldiers back and forth to Indonesian posts on the river. At the same time, two other New Zealand patrols searched the Telagus track at the headwaters of the Sungai Moekan. Corporal Len Wilson's patrol searched the headwaters themselves, while Second Lieutenant Julian Baker's five-man patrol looked for a suspected trade route from the headwaters of the Sungai Pedijan Merachi across the border west of Gunong Merachi. Each of the places they were seeking was a pinpoint in a vast jungle, a tiny camp near small settlements on the third largest island in the world. It was like looking for the proverbial needle in a haystack. Their maps were nearly blank sheets of paper showing only the major rivers and the question marks added by previous patrols.

These first patrols were followed by a further series in April and May, which looked for Indonesian supply routes opposite West Brigade in Kalimantan. On 19 April, Lieutenant Eru Manuera, with Corporal Niwa Kawha and Troopers Bob Passey and 'Snooks' Ririnui, went in to reconnoitre the Indonesian camp at Mangkau, a small kampong on the Sungai Sekajan.

> We got very close. We were on the near side of the bank and we could observe the movement on the far bank which was an Indonesian force of about platoon strength. We'd been told that Asians are pretty reserved so that when they bathe they cover their genitals. But not these guys. They were preening and they looked really fit and quite big. We were quite surprised. I don't know why because we'd never seen Indonesians before ... We made sure that we had a clear view of the sentries and maintained a log of the Indonesian soldiers that we saw there. We actually had to extract pretty quickly mainly because our radio became unserviceable and ... if we missed two consecutive calls then the base started to worry ... But we brought back sufficient information for the brigade headquarters to do whatever they wanted to do.[56]

On 27 May, A Squadron 22 SAS Regiment under Major Peter de la Billiere took over responsibility for SAS operations in West Brigade area from D Squadron, and assumed operational control of the New Zealand detachment. Peter de la Billiere had served in Malaya with 22 SAS Regiment alongside the New Zealand SAS Squadron, and the tenor of operations continued as it had under Woodiwiss.[57] But now that the New Zealanders had been tested on CLARET patrols, it was decided to blood them. Sergeant Danny Wilson, who had been one of the outstanding scouts in Morrison's battalion, took his four-man patrol across the border from West Brigade to kill any enemy found using the Sungai Sekajan. They went in for ten days from 6 May, and lay in ambush in thick jungle on the river bank watching civilians travelling in prahaus (canoes). No military movements were detected, and the patrol returned.[58] The lack of a sighting was as important as a sighting, because it identified routes that were not being used.

> A number of the patrols didn't have contacts, but contacts alone were not a sign of effectiveness. There were some patrols who had to abort a mission for reasons beyond their control ... We all had wins. When I say wins, they all achieved the primary objective [for] which they were sent. If they didn't achieve that, there were other gains that were made by going out across the border.[59]

Manuera had the first New Zealand contact when he took his patrol back to Mangkau. When they reached the Sungai Sekajan just on first light on 20 May, they found that their previous observation post on the river bank directly opposite the Indonesian camp had been cleared.

> So we had to revise our ambush plan and we took up position opposite the jetty where the soldiers bathed in the morning. As we were moving into position one of the soldiers was actually swimming. There was another one bathing. There were a couple of others within sight. I put myself beside Ririnui the Bren gunner and we'd already decided that he would initiate the ambush on my say-so and we hadn't even sunk into position when around the corner came two long boats. They passed us, went downstream and swung around and eased over towards the bank and at the same time as they were coming in, the soldiers were moving down from the camp and getting into these two boats. The first boat moved off as soon as it had taken aboard its load of four soldiers, coming up towards where we were hiding. It's a funny feeling actually. You realise that something is going to happen and you've got to make the decision on when to open fire. Whilst I knew that 'Snooks' Ririnui with the Bren was a good shot, I would have preferred to have been in a

> position where I could have got a better field of fire with it ... Anyway 'Snooks' started to whisper to me, 'Now? Now?' and I said, 'No, not yet'. The leading boat was coming closer, the crewman was accelerating. He was twisting the throttle and the boat was surging and the soldiers had their weapons cradled in their laps, and were holding onto both sides of the boat. They were just coming level with where I was and I said, 'OK!' and Snooks opened fire and almost simultaneously, it was so quick, the other two engaged targets.[60]

In seconds all four soldiers in the boat were shot and killed, either in the boat or in the water as they tried to swim to safety, and at least one of the Indonesians on the jetty was also killed. The two terrified civilian boatmen were unharmed, and after diving into the river were last seen clinging to their prahau as it drifted downstream.[61]

It was a chaotic couple of minutes. Manuera was surprised at how quickly the Indonesians responded to the ambush.

> We didn't see it but they had light mortar [in the camp] that was lobbing bombs back in the area where we'd occupied before, which led me to think that maybe our first recce position had been found. But after a while you think, 'Hell, those rounds are coming towards us and perhaps they know where we are' ... So we spun around and we took off. We had to clear the area very quickly. We automatically got into a drill where Bob Passey who was carrying the radio was in front, Ririnui with the Bren gun was next, myself and then Niwa Kawha ... We had a couple of quick stops just to make sure that there wasn't any close follow-up and then we moved on again because we were paralleling the river upstream. It didn't take us too long to realise that those two boats that came back to pick up soldiers had obviously already deposited some soldiers further upstream and we were hoping like hell that they were further up than where we had stashed our Bergen packs.[62]

That is just where they were, and as Passey 'came hurtling down' to a little stream and up the other side onto a small spur, shots were fired.

> [Passey's] first reaction was to pat himself to make sure he hadn't been hit, but at the same time he opened fire ... There was a lot of yelling and firing, and a lot of shooting. I think most of it was not aimed. We sort of jostled around and engaged in targets of opportunity, which I think is the phrase. One Indonesian, whom I presume was the platoon commander, obviously thought, 'Hell, I wonder if we were engaging our own people'. So he came up the track, and when he came into view I fired the Bren (which I had taken over carrying from Ririnui), which hit him. When he fell down there wasn't any coherent sequence. Niwa Kawha pulled out a

> grenade, and I said, 'No! Don't throw that fucking thing!' Anyway he did throw it, it hit a tree and bounced back to where we were. So we were distracted from whatever the Indonesians might be doing, taking cover from this goddamned grenade which was smoking. It's amazing how closely you can hug the earth—but it didn't go off.[63]

Manuera hastily extracted his patrol, leaving their packs still cached near the Indonesian group. 'Whereas before we were moving quickly, on this occasion we moved very quickly. At times we were actually abreast of each other, running to get away.'[64] Sporadic firing continued for the rest of the morning as the patrol returned to the border. The Indonesian casualties from the two contacts were assessed as six killed and three wounded.[65] Lieutenant Manuera received the Military Cross for this action, and Corporal Kawha was mentioned in despatches.

There was a further New Zealand contact on 23 May when Captain O'Conner, de la Billiere's second-in-command, leading the three members of Winton's patrol, ambushed a prahau on the Sungai Siglayan below a known KKO base. All six of the heavily armed soldiers in the boat were killed, while the civilian boatman was left unscathed. As the patrol pulled out, mortar fire was heard from the area of the camp as the Indonesians responded to the arrival of the boatman with his cargo of dead.[66]

In June 1965, Worsnop's detachment was withdrawn from operations and moved to Wellington Lines in Terendak Camp for two months of rest and retraining. It was a chance for the New Zealanders to improve their individual specialist skills where these were considered inferior to those of their SAS counterparts, as they were in first aid, language and communications. The New Zealanders now replaced their heavy Belgian-designed 7.62 mm self-loading rifles with lighter American AR-15 Colt Armalites. The latter was already 22 SAS Regiment's standard weapon in Borneo, as its 'lightness, robustness, increased "hitting" power and simplicity of maintenance' made it ideal for jungle operations.[67] In July everyone did a helicopter handler's course, followed by a ten-day exercise in the Tampin training area, which had been the 'Mountainous' operations area for the New Zealand squadron in 1957. It proved equally demanding as an exercise area, testing physical fitness and posing problems for communication and navigation.[68] On 31 July the detachment returned to East Malaysia.

In August and September 1965 the New Zealanders were employed under the operational control of West Brigade in the First Division of Sarawak. A combined British/New Zealand headquarters was set up at 'Pea Green Place' in Kuching, with New Zealanders filling a number of the appointments. Among them was Trooper Te Puni, who earned a Borneo-wide reputation for his cookhouse. Major Rod Dearing and Captain Neville Kidd, the advance party of the relieving Two Detachment, arrived in Kuching on 10 August and spent six days with the detachment before moving on to Labuan and Brunei. Captain David Ogilvy, the commander designate of Three Detachment, also visited the detachment.[69]

August was a busy month. Second Lieutenant Julian Baker took a patrol to locate a kampong at Segoeman which reportedly housed an Indonesian platoon. They had a difficult approach, skirting open cultivations and thick secondary growth. A kampong was found and watched for two days, but it seemed to be deserted. Baker withdrew to the border after mortar fire landed where his patrol had been the previous night, indicating that locals may have seen and reported them. At the same time, Sergeant Len Wilson led his patrol on a reconnaissance of a garrison on the Sungei Moekan. This took six days, and involved a difficult crossing of a river busy with civilian traffic, and then a careful approach around a large number of ladangs to the kampong on the eastern bank of the river. The relaxed garrison of ten to 15 Indonesian soldiers were camped in attap huts some distance from the local longhouse. At reveille on 12 August, as the Indonesians emerged sleepily from their huts, Wilson's group cut them down. Three soldiers were seen to fall, while the rest dived for cover and returned fire. After rapidly firing two magazines each, Wilson's patrol withdrew.[70]

This was one of nine New Zealand patrols mounted in August 1965.[71] Each patrol, of 12 days' planned duration, pushed the men to the limits of their endurance. Not everyone adapted well to this regime. Corporal Johnno Johnston, the scout in Sergeant Ken Schimanski's patrol, insisted that no noise reach him from the men behind. 'We had to get rid of a bloke out of the patrol ... He could become very noisy ... and these noises were coming past the patrol commander right up to me.'[72] It took patience to maintain a silent patrol day after day in the jungle. Individuals who proved unsuitable were rarely returned to New Zealand, but were employed around the detachment base or headquarters in Kuching. While there had been no New Zealand casualties, the rapid Indonesian response to sightings and incidents made everyone very aware of the danger once they crossed the border into Kalimantan. While the calibre of the Indonesian military varied a great deal, it was obvious that they 'were quite capable of tracking you down if you made mistakes ... These guys certainly were not afraid of the British and had no reason to be afraid of New Zealanders.'[73]

In late August, a combined operation of four patrols led by Lieutenant Murray Winton followed up information gained in recent patrolling by attempting to ambush Indonesians using the Sungai Sekajan north of Pesing. A larger group was needed because the objective was further inside Kalimantan. By now CLARET operations were selectively engaging targets located as far as twice the stated 10,000-yard maximum across the border, and the security risks in using a larger group were outweighed by their ability to carry more supplies and equipment. It took five hard days for Winton's group to get to the Sekajan; they then waited in ambush from 30 August to 1 September before withdrawing without any making any contact. Winton assessed that previous SAS activity had temporarily stopped Indonesians from using the river.[74] This in itself showed how effective CLARET operations had become in disrupting Indonesian patrolling and resupply, and forcing them to become increasingly defensive. Two patrols from 2 Troop, each boosted in numbers and carrying extra rations and equipment, followed up with a similar operation which aimed to get a patrol across the Sekajan. This had been attempted a number of times, without success. It was now the dry season, and river levels were lower. Sergeant Schimanski's six-man patrol would mount an ambush on the river to distract attention from the second patrol, which was to cross the river with Schimanski's assistance, report on enemy movement on the far bank, and find the Indonesian camp at Muroe.

The patrols spent two slow days moving through lallang, bamboo and secondary jungle to the river, their progress made particularly difficult by the local civilians using the tracks. A crossing point was reconnoitred on the third day, and Corporal Kawha's patrol crossed the river at first light on the fourth day, 14 September. Having located Muroe, the patrol watched the camp. Two members of the patrol crawled to within 20 yards of the perimeter to observe a relaxed garrison wearing white T-shirts and blue shorts react only slowly, and with much prompting from their NCOs, when firing was heard far downriver. The patrol then pulled back to the river north-west of Muroe and watched the river track for a further six days. The only movement seen was at 2 p.m. on 19 September, when a civilian hurried down the track towards Muroe. Two hours later a 21-strong patrol came from the Indonesian garrison at Muroe in response to a successful ambush by Schimanski's party at the river. They walked with weapons draped over their shoulders; only the first two soldiers carried their weapons at the alert.[75]

Schimanski's patrol had established an ambush some 200 yards upstream from the original crossing point. This covered a large clearing on the Muroe side, which they watched for six days. 'We would put the ambush in at first light and we would take it out at last light ... and we withdrew at last light back to where we had a firm base which was some 15 to 20 yards away.' In the heat of the afternoon, bamboo splits with a crack like a rifle shot; the first time this happened, Schimanski's party went on hair-trigger alert until the cause was identified. After five days of this, everyone was on edge. At mid-afternoon on 19 September, five Indonesian soldiers slowly emerged one by one from the jungle into the clearing on the other side of the river. Widely spaced and fully alert, they moved carefully through the clearing, scanning the jungle on the opposite bank. When all five were out in the open, Schimanski opened fire and everyone else joined in. In the seconds that followed, three Indonesians were shot, a wounded man crawled for cover, and the fifth soldier sheltered behind a fallen log. 'We couldn't get at him but he would not give up. He just kept firing shots ... so Ken [Schimanski] said, "Well, the arsehole can stay there", ... so we left this little fellow giving it heaps, and even as we departed that ambush he was still giving it heaps.'[76] His firing, and the machine-gun-like cracks of the bamboo, saw Schimanski's patrol abandon their Bergen packs, which were stashed in their night harbour area, and withdraw rapidly to the border, covering in one day's rapid march what had taken them five days on the way in.

At the same time, Winton's 1 Troop was mounting another troop-size operation. On 12 September, patrols led by Winton and Corporal Tom Rautao departed to seek an IBT training camp that was believed to exist in the Sekajan area. An attempt in August by A Squadron had been compromised by local people. It took three days to reach the area. Rautao's patrol then went south to watch the tracks along the Sungai Sekajan, while Winton spent four days looking for the camp. The sound of rifle and automatic fire from what was apparently a rifle range indicated its general location, but a surrounding ring of cultivated ladangs and the constant movement of local inhabitants prevented closer investigation. On 19 September, Winton's patrol was leaving the area, with Dan Heke as tail-end Charlie, when they ran into a patrol ahead of them on the track. There was a moment's frozen silence,

> then somebody on their side fired and then it was all on. We went through our withdrawal drills ... I was the last, being the medic. This guy had me [in his sights] but when he fired, nothing happened. The guy panicked and he moved. It wasn't till he moved that I saw him. We squeezed off some shots. He got away. I'm not sure whether I hit him or not, and then we just bugged out.[77]

It was the closest of calls, and at the first opportunity Heke radioed to base. Rautao's patrol monitored the call and believing that there was a casualty to evacuate, hurriedly rendezvoused with Winton's team, and the two moved back to the border together.

These troop-sized operations were the last mounted by the detachment. Each patrol had operated inside Kalimantan to the very limits of their physical ability. Johnno Johnston recalled:

> By the time you took your equipment, your ammunition and everything else you had to carry in, there wouldn't have been too much in the way of food ... it was pushed right to the limit. You never had a problem with water, but there was a big problem with the rations. The first two or three days [were] very hard because you were loaded but as each day went on, the load got lighter but you could not sit down all night and have a big meal. You could have plenty of water to drink but we used to live off these meat blocks and that was that.[78]

Worsnop's detachment ceased operations on 10 October 1965, and returned to New Zealand four days later. The men were exhausted, but after a troubled start the detachment had demonstrated a professionalism that made it a worthy successor to the New Zealand SAS Squadron in Malaya. It was now the task of Dearing's Two Detachment to build on what had been achieved.

## Two Detachment, August 1965 to February 1966

Major Rod Dearing's Two Detachment arrived in Singapore on 28 August 1965. Like its predecessor it came under the command of Headquarters NZ Army Force FARELF until it moved to Brunei on 2 September and passed to the command of 22 SAS Regiment. The detachment underwent a month's training at Tutong Camp, assisted by three members of Worsnop's detachment. Up-to-date information on operational techniques and drills had been incorporated in its training in New Zealand, and the period in Tutong polished and refined what had already been soundly established. A final ten-day exercise was 'as near as possible to a genuine operation', involving insertion by helicopter, individual patrol tasks over realistic distances, and shooting and immediate-action drills using live ammunition and grenades.[79]

Major Rod Dearing, a Sandhurst graduate, had joined the New Zealand Special Air Service after a tour as a platoon commander with Aitken's 2 New Zealand Regiment in Malaya. He went with the squadron as a troop commander to Thailand, and was recalled from his appointment as Adjutant Army Schools to command and train the second detachment.[80] Simply getting the numbers had been a Herculean task for Major John Mace, who succeeded Meldrum in command of the squadron in New Zealand. Mace had been one of the original SAS troop commanders in Malaya, and with David Ogilvy as his single troop commander had reformed the New Zealand Special Air Service in 1959. Now Mace returned, with the task of expanding the squadron to cope with the Borneo commitment. 'I went back in 1965. Bill Meldrum had gone off with Punchy Worsnop and we'd planned to bring a selection course [with] the normal 20 to 30 in number and then I think the difficulties of replacing the Detachment became apparent.' The selection course was opened up to National Service volunteers, and instead of the planned 20 to 30 'we had something like 120-odd come in. It was chaotic because we didn't have the manpower to expand in that fashion.'[81] Mace's concerns about some of those selected were overruled by Lieutenant-Colonel John Morris, Director of Infantry and SAS.

> There were at least two officers that in no way did I want. In the end we were ordered to take them. It was an order. If we were to man the subsequent detachments then we had to have folk in the SAS to do it ... and it was a commitment, which I don't believe we really had the capacity to meet, and I think as a result of that the quality of some of the subsequent detachments was not up to scratch.[82]

Dearing's detachment in the short term, and the New Zealand SAS in the longer term, had to live with the consequences.

New Zealand had made a commitment to maintain a half-squadron in Borneo, and planned to send a detachment every four months. To meet this commitment, the SAS in New Zealand had grown from 53 to 157 Regular Force personnel, and almost doubled its Territorial strength to 41, between February and October 1965.[83] By the time Two Detachment was committed to Borneo, the New Zealand Chief of General Staff, Major-General Walter McKinnon, was becoming increasingly concerned about the strain this expansion imposed on Army resources. Finding suitable officers was a particular problem. Colonel Jock Aitken, Commander 1 Infantry Brigade, of which 1 Ranger Squadron was a part, shared McKinnon and Mace's concerns. He believed that the squadron was being asked to do too much with far too few resources, and that this was placing enormous strain on its training and administration. It would be necessary for One Detachment personnel to return with the newly raised Three Detachment. With only one month for training in New Zealand before returning overseas, there would be no time for these men to relax and spend time with their families. Aitken, who had been a patrol commander with the Long Range Desert Group during the Second World War, considered that operational standards would inevitably suffer and casualties result if this pressure continued. Given the build-up in strength of British SAS squadrons and the creation of Gurkha, Parachute Regiment and Guards special patrol companies, he questioned whether the intended level of commitment was still necessary. Aitken recommended that New Zealand's contribution be reduced to an annual five-month tour by one detachment, which would spend four months at most on operations.[84]

In November 1965 McKinnon asked Lieutenant-General Sir Alan Jolly, Commander-in-Chief Far East Land Forces, if it would be possible to reduce New Zealand's commitment to two detachments a year from mid-1966.[85] Jolly discussed this with Lea, the Director of Borneo Operations, who proposed a number of options, including less frequent tours by half-squadrons and one full-squadron tour for four months each year.[86] In March 1966 Jolly told McKinnon that Lea had identified a need for there to be two squadrons in Borneo at any one time, and asked if New Zealand could provide a full squadron for a four-month tour 'not more than once a year, or less if you would find it more convenient'.[87] While this was the preferred option of Army General Staff, a shortage of suitable officers put it beyond New Zealand's capability.[88] McKinnon replied that the best New Zealand could do was two 40-strong detachments a year, each for six months including a four-month tour in Borneo.[89] This was discussed with the Commander-in-Chief Far East when the Minister of Defence and the Chief of Defence Staff, Lieutenant-General Thornton, visited Singapore. It was agreed that the New Zealand detachments would follow a six-monthly rotation, starting with Four Detachment in June 1966.[90]

Meanwhile, Dearing's detachment served in Borneo. While he unquestionably had many good people, it became obvious as the tour progressed that not all were of the necessary standard. This, and the resulting tensions within the command structure, detracted from the detachment's performance. However, this was also influenced by changes in the operational environment in Borneo. Since August 1965, at Lea's direction, cross-border CLARET operations had intensified; the SAS increasingly had the task of finding targets for the infantry battalions to attack. From the beginning, Dearing faced far greater competition in getting suitable tasks for his patrols, with operations 'very hard to get'.

> There were some very vigorous Brigadiers ... who were keen to make their mark and who safeguarded any prospect of good solid operational stuff for the battalions in their brigades ... I can recall John Slim, who was the SAS Commander on the spot, and myself talking over what prospects we had and what jobs might be available. We managed between us to think up one or two and these were mainly reconnaissance jobs. The opportunities for ambush were difficult to come by because the border brigadiers ... would earmark them for their own units.[91]

The detachment's move to Kuching on 6 October 1965 coincided with the departure of de la Billiere's A Squadron and the arrival of B Squadron under Major Terry Hardy. Whereas One Detachment had worked as an integral part of A and D Squadrons, Dearing's was to play an independent role. 'We sat in Kuching for a few days and it became obvious that there was a wider role for us to play along the Borneo frontier and not necessarily just in the First Division [of Sarawak].'[92] As a result, on 6 November the detachment moved its headquarters and base of operations from Kuching to Labuan, where it was accommodated and rationed with the 22 SAS regimental base and reported direct to Headquarters SAS Far East. October saw a coup and a counter-coup in Jakarta, and blood-letting began throughout Indonesia. The implications for Confrontation were unclear, and Two Detachment started operations in an atmosphere of uncertainty.

By late October all Dearing's patrols were committed to operations. The first to go out was 2 Troop under Captain Len Grant. Grant had joined the Army as a Regular Force Cadet in 1955, served as a section commander in Malaya with Morrison's battalion, and graduated from OCS Portsea as a Second Lieutenant in 1959. He passed an SAS selection course in 1960, and by October 1965 was one of the longest-serving officers in the unit.[93] His two patrols, led by Corporal Jim Barber and Sergeant Arthur Steele, went into Kalimantan on 19 October to support an ambush by B Company 2/10th Gurkha Rifles on the Kuala–Siding track, opposite West Brigade's area in the First Division of Sarawak. The New Zealand patrols were to position themselves on either side of the ambush site and alert the rifle company to any Indonesian movement into the area. It was an overly complex plan that was never put into effect. Movement into the area was hampered by the need to evacuate Gurkha medical casualties. Crossing the swiftly flowing Sungai Koemba, which was 30–40 yards wide, also proved a major undertaking. Steele's patrol secured the crossing point, and both patrols ferried the Gurkhas across by fixed rope. Grant and Barber's patrol moved with the Gurkhas. A strongly defended Indonesian camp was located, and the company commander had to be dissuaded from attacking it. As a compromise, an ambush was mounted on a well-used track leading towards the camp. Because the SAS and Gurkha communications systems turned out to be incompatible, the New Zealanders could not be used for early warning as planned; instead they were positioned on the flanks of the ambush.

At 9.30 a.m. on 27 October, a single Indonesian soldier was allowed to walk through the ambush unscathed. When he returned at 1.30 p.m. leading a party of 12 to 14 soldiers, the Gurkhas opened fire. The Indonesians responded with mortar fire that was aimed at nearby river-crossings as well as the ambush area. Fortunately this fell wide of the position where Steele's patrol had re-erected a hand rope across the river to assist the Gurkhas' return. Their extraction from the ambush was hurried and confused. Grant's group directed artillery fire while the Gurkhas withdrew. The New Zealanders ferried frightened Gurkhas across the swiftly flowing river. Grant recalled that 'The stark fear, not screams, but yells of desperation ... and the odd dropped weapon was something I had never really envisaged.' It was a messy, disorganised operation for which the Gurkha company commander wrote himself an undeserved citation. All the difficulties of infantry working with SAS were highlighted. Grant was well aware of the inherent pitfalls: 'We got out and it was very interesting but I would prefer to have done a lone SAS operation rather than work and to a degree nurse a Gurkha company commander along as we did.'[94] However, the New Zealanders were so keen to get out on CLARET operations that they would take on whatever was available.[95]

On 20 October, 1 Troop sent two patrols on a troop operation to establish the pattern of enemy movement along the Sungai Pijang opposite the Mid-West Brigade area, where there had been a series of contacts along the border. Things went wrong from the start when a man had to be evacuated from the border rendezvous point. The Sungai Pijang was found to be in flood, and another medical casualty forced the troop to regroup into two patrols under Captain Neville Kidd and Sergeant Jack Maskery. Kidd's patrol returned to the border with the casualty, while Maskery unsuccessfully searched for a point at which the river could be crossed before returning on 30 October.[96] Two 1 Troop patrols under Lieutenant Wilson and Sergeant Eric Ball also went in opposite Mid-West Brigade on 20 October to locate an Indonesian boat point and supply dump in the Sungai Melije area. After taking six days to reach the Sungai Melije, they moved upstream along it for four days without incident until they reached the border.[97] To cap a very busy first month, a five-man patrol under Staff Sergeant Ron Rowe went in on 27 October to observe the Sungai Bemban track, a major Indonesian supply route which was a favourite SAS target.[98] After taking three days to get into the area, the patrol pulled out on discovering indications that an Indonesian patrol had found their tracks.[99]

November saw the detachment operating from its new base in Labuan, conducting patrols from the First and Second Divisions of Sarawak and the Interior Residency of Sabah, and working in turn under the operational control of West, Mid-West and Central Brigades. Lieutenant Wilson took 1 Troop back in for its next operation on 6 November with two patrols, led by himself and Sergeant Eric Ball. Their tasks were to place psychological warfare leaflets in the Sungai Ketungau, establish the pattern of Indonesian movement on the river, and ambush any opportunity target found in the last 48 hours of the operation. On reaching the river, the troop released the leaflets downstream and established a lookout on the north bank. After five days Ball pulled back to the border with a sick man; Wilson continued watching the river before also coming out. In hindsight it was obvious that the operation was done the wrong way round. Releasing the leaflets simply announced the troop's presence to the Indonesians downstream, who promptly halted all river traffic. Indonesian movement was disrupted, but not in the manner intended.[100]

The next patrols, including the first from the Central Brigade area of Sabah, went out in late November. An ad hoc troop of three patrols commanded by the Squadron Sergeant-Major, WO2 Bruce Hill, left on 25 November to locate and ambush the supply route from Nantukidan to Panas along the Sungai Salilir, which ran roughly parallel to the border. This followed up a series of SAS attacks on the Sungai Salilir which had severely curtailed river traffic. A platoon of Gurkhas went in as escorts and remained to secure the crossing point. Hill's troop moved south, formed a firm base and sent out two patrols. On 2 December a reconnaissance patrol was seen by a group of Murut villagers who, when stopped and questioned, were found to have been scavenging iron and abandoned ammunition boxes from the Indonesian base at Labang, which they said was deserted. Having gained valuable information, but with secrecy compromised, Hill withdrew his patrols the following day.[101]

At the same time, Captain Neville Kidd took three patrols to the Sungai Sekajan, opposite the West Brigade area in the First Division of Sarawak. Two were to cross the river and locate a suspected camp, while the third remained on the river to monitor traffic. They took six days to reach the Sekajan. After a day spent watching the river, one patrol cached their Bergen packs, took five days' rations on their belts, and crossed the river. As they did so, a shot was fired from nearby; fearing discovery, all three patrols withdrew to the border.[102]

On 27 November, Wilson took his patrol back to the Sungai Ketungau, where on 2 December they were concealed on the river bank watching river traffic. Two prahaus went upstream in the morning, and an escort of soldiers was heard moving through the jungle on the far bank. At 1.55 p.m. both boats returned downstream. Just after the second boat passed out of sight, the patrol was fired at by unseen Indonesians on the far bank, hastening Wilson's withdrawal to the border.[103] Two New Zealand patrols had another go at the Sungai Ketungau on 13 December, with Steele leading No. 6 Patrol. 'We went in over a mountain feature and when we dropped down the other side the country was unbelievable. There were virtually cliffs in there and the only way down ... [was to] hang onto the tree and slide down ... this was how we progressed down to the valley floor.' Steele's party reached the river and established an ambush, setting out three Claymore anti-personnel mines which could be fired by remote control from the sentry post. The Claymores were disconnected at night,

> as we didn't want pigs or anything coming around ... and setting [them] off ... We reconnected them next morning and we were sitting there watching the river and the next thing this great explosion went off ... I knew it was a Claymore and I knew it wasn't obviously in our direction, but I immediately looked at the clips that we had and there was no one near them ... so I said, 'What the hell was that?' ... We all sort of froze and listened and there was no sound, no shots, no yelling, no nothing and we all said at the same time, 'It's a bloody Claymore that's gone off ... what are we going to do?' and I said, 'Grab the wires, pull them and we'll go and we'll leave the Claymores there' ... so we just pulled the wires and we packed up and took off.[104]

The Claymores had probably spontaneously detonated because of a build-up of static electricity. The New Zealand SAS had not had a good year on the Sungai Ketungau.[105]

The last patrols for 1965 were also dogged by difficulties. Kidd took a patrol to reconnoitre the north bank of the Sungai Semadja. On the way in, Trooper McMath twisted his knee badly and the mission was aborted.[106] Sergeant 'Bullet' Maskery's Christmas patrol was no luckier. It went in on 24 December to observe the Sungai Simangaris, but withdrew when one of the men developed an eye infection; returning on 30 December, it withdrew again because of wireless failure. On 15 January 1966 Maskery's patrol attempted the same task; this time Maskery sprained his knee and the patrol laid up for two days until he was able to limp back to the border. Staff Sergeant Rowe now took over, and the patrol reached the Sungai Simangaris in five days. However, thick tidal mangrove and palm swamp blocked their view of the river, and constant Indonesian patrolling forced Rowe to withdraw.[107]

Dearing's detachment had experienced an exhausting three months of intensive patrolling.

> We carried 200 rounds of ammunition with the majority on your belt order and at least one water bottle; the rest of the pouches were full with your magazines and then you had another pouch which contained your emergency kit which was what we considered could be seven days' rations. This would be one packet of mixed raisins and peanuts, maybe two oxo cubes ... a fish hook, razor blade, a bit of nylon and anything else you could sneak into a thing about the size of a matchbox ... On an average the belt order would weigh about 28 lb ... Your Bergen packs were rigged so that all you did was ... pull a strap and the Bergen fell off your back. We didn't wash. The only wash you had was if you crossed a stream and ... thought you had a chance you stuck your hands in the water and threw a bit on your face but you never worried about it otherwise. It was better to smell ... and after two or three weeks they reckoned we stunk to high heaven ... What we carried was our basics ... and that was it.[108]

The tension was always there once a patrol got off the helicopter and faced the long climb over the border range into Kalimantan. 'So you always used to have this big monstrous climb after about seven days out of the bush which really gets you going and gets your jungle legs.' After the first night out, the patrol would settle into a pattern. There was constant cross-checking to ensure that each member of the patrol knew where they were, the direction of movement, and the designated rendezvous point (RV) if they were separated during a contact. Four RVs were designated, with successive waiting times of 15 minutes, 30 minutes, 60 minutes, and three hours: 'so if you miss an RV you would always link up somewhere else. You always hope that nothing happens today, but by the second or third day you would start to wish that something would happen so that we can get out of there and go home quickly.'[109]

Many of the tasks were at the limit of the patrol's endurance in difficult country against a generally alert enemy. As Steele's scout, Corporal Kiriti Haami, observed: 'all the places they sent us to, there was not a thing'. Because the battalions reserved targets within two miles of the border for themselves, the SAS had 'to go further and further in and we did not have enough LPs [landing places for helicopter support] ... to get us further in'.[110] The SAS tasks were now the ones no one else wanted. The growing sense of frustration in the patrols resulted in increasingly tense relations between Dearing and his detachment which were exacerbated by the perceived ineffectiveness of the Squadron Sergeant-Major. While Two Detachment had its successes, Dearing was only too aware that the increasing number of aborted missions inevitably reflected on the New Zealanders.

> One had ... to show that we could do the job. Well, of course in operations something untoward always happens and the decision has to be made as to whether [it was] going to be worthwhile pushing on or whether ... [to] abort the mission and come back. Now that occurred very frequently. I think the chaps felt that they wouldn't mind pushing on and doing the job if they could see there were going to be results at the other end, but if you had a casualty or something wrong with ... [equipment] then it was probably better to be a bit prudent and pull out ... and of course I would have to go back to the Brigadier and report that the mission had been aborted, which didn't overly please them. It didn't please me either. In fact I can recall one Brigadier taking me to task ... but you just learned to live with those things.[111]

Major David Ogilvy and Three Detachment arrived in Labuan on 8 January 1966. Dearing placed Lieutenant Bill Wilson's patrol at their disposal to assist with training, initially at Labuan and then in the Tutong training area in Brunei. Meanwhile, Dearing's group continued to operate where needed. In January 1966 it conducted missions under the operational control of West, Central and East Brigades. The last mission was in the Central Brigade area. Captain Len Grant's troop of two patrols, with Ogilvy as an observer, went in on 24 January to establish the pattern of enemy movement along the Sungai Sembakung and then ambush a soft target during the last 48 hours. It was difficult going, and with many civilians working in the ladangs 'it took us some time to get in and it was hard yakka too, but we got there in the end ... and established an ambush ... It was a wide river, reasonably swift-flowing and just a bit of civilian traffic.' After three days, on 1 February, 'three military guys came up in a small canoe. In fact one end of our patrol could have nearly touched them ... because of the current flow, they were coming right in under the bank and the bank was only three feet or so high. We had a Claymore set up there. Luckily we heard the clank of the paddle.' The boat passed inches away and at midday came back downstream laden with grain. The three Indonesian soldiers were still aboard, 'so we gave them a nudge', and after killing all three pulled out.[112]

While this was Two Detachment's last task, some New Zealanders took part in a B Squadron operation which was the last carried out by the British SAS during Confrontation. In late January, intelligence indicated a possible Indonesian incursion from Sentas on the Sungai Sekajan, across the border from Tebedu in the First Division of Sarawak. Brigadier Cheyne agreed that Major Terry Hardy's B Squadron should mount a pre-emptive strike.[113] Hardy had three of his four troops available, and enlisted Sergeant Steele's four-man patrol and an Australian SAS patrol into Sergeant Dick Cooper's 6 Troop for the mission. They went in accompanied by Iban Cross-Border Scouts and a Royal Artillery forward observer, whose guns were registered on the longhouse at Sentas which could be seen from the border ridge. After a three-day approach march, B Squadron crossed the Sekajan after dark on 3 February, leaving a platoon of Argyll and Sutherland Highlanders to secure the crossing. Cooper's 6 Troop led the way, with Steele's group immediately behind the two scouts. Hardy planned to surround the kampong by night and attack it at dawn. The 'Two Huts' feature west of Kampong Sentas—thought to be a pepper farm—would have to be secured.

> There were two scouts, then us ... then [Hardy] ... and then the rest ... We crossed the river which was ... about 80 to 90 metres wide I suppose. It was fairly swift but it was only about chest height at the most ... we came onto this track ... It was 10 to 12 feet wide and you could have driven a car down it, no problem. It was a bit scary walking along this bloody great track on a moonlit night.[114]

Cooper's troop reached the base of the 'Two Huts' feature, where log steps provided access to a cluster of buildings. Low voices speaking Indonesian could be heard as Cooper directed his men up the steps. Steele was immediately behind the scouts. 'We were crawling up on our hands and knees because it was pretty light, and you could see it had been cleared, and my group had just about got to the top of the hill when all hell broke loose.' Instead of a pepper farm, the SAS found themselves inside an Indonesian position whose defenders responded immediately with small arms and then mortar fire. 'The bullets were flying in all directions and we were lying there on the ground and it was my first time under fire at night and it was quite comical in a way because I could hear these things buzzing past like bees ... It wasn't until later that I thought about it: they weren't bees, they were bloody bullets.'[115]

After SAS fire suppressed the Indonesian sentry position, rifle and machine-gun fire started coming from slit trenches inside the bashas, and from a neighbouring heavy machine-gun post. There was no option but to pull back. Steele looked after himself and his three men.

> I wasn't interested in anybody else. We got back down on the track and somebody behind us yelled out, 'Look out, grenade!' What had happened was that some fool (and I think it was the Squadron Commander) threw a bloody phosphorus grenade to try and light up the area and it had hit something and went rolling back down the hill. Well I grabbed the guy next to me and we jumped off the track. There was a straight drop of about six feet into the river, and we managed to grab the scrub as we went down and hung on. A couple of other guys had gone over the bank and into the river and we could hear them yelling. There was all hell breaking loose up top. There were phosphorus grenades going off. I got burnt on the finger by a bit of phosphorus which still flares up every now and again. Troopers Williams and Gordon both got quite badly burnt, mostly around the back of the neck and on the shoulders.[116]

The flare of the grenade, which was actually thrown by a British trooper, had revealed the SAS to the Indonesians. After becoming separated from the patrol, this man found himself alone among Indonesian soldiers who were following up the withdrawing SAS, but managed to slip away and find his own way back. 'Turning up four days later ... [was] a fantastic bit of work.'[117] Steele too was left behind when the squadron pulled back.

> We were about 20 metres behind the rest of them when they tore off down the track ... we came to this little stream which cut across the track into the main river, and I heard somebody up the front saying, 'Here they come, here they come', and I thought, 'Is he talking about us or somebody else?' I said, 'Hey, don't do anything, it's us, it's the Kiwis, Kiwis!' And out of the darkness this guy popped up and said, 'Shit you were lucky, we were just going to blow a Claymore.'[118]

Assisted by artillery fire, the squadron broke contact, crossed the Sekajan and withdrew to the border. Four men separated from the others in the fracas made their own way out. This was one occasion when the SAS bit off much more than they could chew; Steele later described it as 'the biggest kerfuffle I've been on in my life'. It was an inglorious finale to an outstanding performance by the British SAS in Borneo. 'Over the years when I've thought about it, I think it was the squadron wanting to go out on a blaze of glory. It had seen an opportunity, took it, went in, there was not enough planning, not enough thought given behind it all, no control over when it actually occurred. We were bloody lucky to get out.'[119]

Dearing's detachment withdrew from operations on 10 February 1966, flew to Singapore four days later, and returned to New Zealand on 20 February. Comparative success is always difficult to judge. Two Detachment operated independently in a totally different environment from that faced by One Detachment. Dearing had to compete for tasks, and so had little option but to accept missions at the extreme edge of even SAS patrols' operational endurance. Some were of questionable value, and many were aborted before completion. Whether this was due to bad luck or the unwillingness of patrols to complete missions they had little faith in, there was a feeling both within the detachment and in the wider headquarters that Two Detachment had not been as effective as its predecessor.

## Three Detachment, January to May 1966

Major David Ogilvy's Three Detachment returned to Labuan from Tutong, and after a few days' rest started looking for work. Ogilvy was one of the original New Zealand squadron who served with the SAS in Borneo.[120] As a sergeant and acting troop commander in Malaya, he developed a reputation for being hard but fair, never asking anything of his men that he would not do himself. His determination to get a job done was balanced by an empathy and understanding of limitations that was exemplified by his feat of endurance in saving Paddy Quested's life by carrying him down from 'Mountainous' in 1957. The newly commissioned Ogilvy did the hard graft in raising the first SAS troop in Papakura when the squadron was re-established in 1959, and also served a tour in Borneo as transport officer with Gurr's battalion in 1965. When named as Commander Three Detachment, he knew what he wanted from his troopers and moulded them accordingly. He managed to secure Captain Bob Burt as one of his troop commanders, despite the Director of Infantry's belief that he was too old. Burt described Ogilvy as a 'very strong man in every sense, morally, mentally, physically'. Ogilvy was equally well served in the make-up of his group, most of whom 'had already been twice, that is with the 2nd Battalion or the 1st Battalion, and they'd been to Thailand too. Borneo was their second operational tour so they were quite experienced.'[121] Burt had served in Malaya with 2 New Zealand Regiment. The two other troop commanders, Lieutenants Russ Martin and A. J. Wales, were both on their first operational tours.

Like Dearing before him, Ogilvy's first problem was finding tasks for his patrols. 'Regrettably the Second Detachment had a reputation, as I understood it, for not being able to finish their tasks and that was a real worry for us because David Ogilvy had to sell us to the infantry battalions along the border. He had to plead for operational opportunities. We got them, [and] after the first few ops we had no more problems getting tasks.'[122] Ogilvy found jobs for six of his seven patrols, and initially used his seventh in a liaison capacity. Like its predecessors, the detachment was under the command of 22 SAS Regiment and operated anywhere in Borneo that the SAS were needed. When B Squadron 22 SAS Regiment left in February 1966, it was not replaced. The Australian and New Zealand SAS, together with the independent patrol companies, now carried out the SAS role in Borneo.[123]

The first patrols went out at the end of February. Bob Burt took two patrols, one under his command, the other under Sergeant Danny Wilson. Escorted in by A Company 2 Royal Green Jackets, the patrols separated after crossing the Sungai Siglayan. Wilson spent five days searching fruitlessly for an enemy camp on the Sungai Simangaris which had eluded earlier patrols.[124] At the same time, Bob Burt's five-man patrol was hunting for a suspected camp between the Sungai Simoja and the Sungai Wason.[125] After a difficult crossing of the Simoja at midnight, they slowly patrolled the tidal estuaries between the two rivers in daytime. While lying up waiting to return across the Simoja, the men faced other dangers. The sentry, Trooper Ben Ngapo, pointed out a rather large crocodile, which eventually went back into the water and swam away. 'But I can tell you, when Ben and I swam [across the river] that night, it was a terrifying experience. The water was dead still, there were logs and rubbish floating on the water. Every one of them as far as I could see was a crocodile ... [but] it was the only way home, so we did it.'[126]

Discovering which Indonesian forward bases were still occupied became the detachment's task. In March 1966, Wales and Martin led their first CLARET patrols. Wales's group left from East Brigade's area in Sabah, while Martin's four-man group went in to find a suspected enemy camp on the west bank of the Sungai Siglayan.[127] Two deserted bases—one of company size and the other of battalion size—connected by a major track were located and reconnoitred by Martin's patrol, a task which took four days. On the fifth day, while reconnoitring an ambush site, the men heard conversation. There was no sign of any cut vegetation, and it was impossible to see anything through the thick matted undergrowth. Painstakingly slow and careful reconnaissance established that there were voices over an area of some 160 square yards, and the possibility that this was an Indonesian company base was confirmed by the sound of an FN rifle being cocked inside the perimeter. Artillery fire was requested but not granted, and the disappointed patrol departed.[128]

In late March, another attempt was made to locate the camp that was believed to be in the Simangaris area. Staff Sergeant McAndrew's patrol followed the swamp line towards the suspected location. On the 24th signal shots were heard, and late that afternoon a washing point was found. As McAndrew and his scout edged towards the camp, the talking and singing grew louder, but when a dog started barking they withdrew to the washing point. Five minutes later, four relaxed Indonesians—carrying towels, accompanied by a dog, and with only one weapon between them—came to within yards of the hidden pair. The man with the rifle went on sentry duty while the others washed and bathed. Only the dog sensed trouble; it advanced barking to Trooper Murray's hiding-place in the undergrowth. Finally one of the Indonesians decided to investigate. As he approached, he saw Murray and appeared to smile in recognition before being shot and killed. Murray shot two more men before pulling back. There was no immediate reaction from the stunned Indonesian position as the New Zealanders withdrew.[129]

In March 1966, after being informed of progress in the peace negotiations, Lea announced that while reconnaissance would continue, all offensive CLARET operations were to cease immediately. This forced the abandonment of a combined operation Ogilvy had arranged with the King's Own Scottish Borderers (KOSB), whose company at Long Jawi had been about to attack the major Indonesian camp and police post at Long Bawan. The KOSB wanted the SAS to knock out two of the three 12.7-mm heavy anti-aircraft machine-gun posts on the ridge overlooking the camp. For this task Ogilvy chose Bob Burt, who in turn selected Danny Wilson's and Johnno Johnston's patrols. Burt recalled: 'We were to hook around the town to the left, cross a river, go up through a cemetery onto a ridge where these two guns were, drop off Johnno Johnston's op group to take out one gun. My op group [was to] go further on round the back of the town and take out the other gun.' This demanded a simultaneous covert strike on both guns before the KOSB attacked the town at

8 a.m. Burt's patrols 'were to go in the night before, swim the river, go through the cemetery, take out these two guns quietly and get back across the river before it all started.' He was not exaggerating when he described this as 'quite a difficult operation'.[130] Indeed, it would have been by far the most sophisticated and difficult operation the New Zealand SAS had ever undertaken.

A great deal of planning went into how best to disable the guns. Burt's background in building construction led him to devise a screw-in bolt of 12.7 mm calibre that could be fitted into the barrel of the Indonesian machine guns. Once fitted, they could not be undone and the gun was disabled. The bolts were manufactured to Burt's specifications in the Gurkha Brigade's workshop in Brunei. Explosives were to be placed on each machine gun's bodycase, timed to explode simultaneously at 8 a.m. as the KOSB began their attack on the town. The timing devices were adapted from those used by the Indonesians in their sabotage raids in Malaysia.

> Basically it was just a little alarm clock and we drilled a hole through the glass, put a screw in it, took the minute hand off, left it so that when the hour hand got around to touch that screw it put an electric charge into the explosive ... we tried them out and they worked admirably ... So we carried three of these, one spare and one for each gun.
>
> We carried silenced Sten guns ... I carried the one for our group and Bill Lillicrap carried the one in Johnno's op group and we carried them because we had the need to take out a sentry quietly ... They were very effective. The first time we got them I fired one into the ground outside the window of the Officers' Mess and David Ogilvy who was leaning against the window never heard it.[131]

Burt's two patrols went in with the KOSB infantry company. 'Every man jack that you could get was there. Many of them unfit.' Half a day's march into Kalimantan the operation started to fall apart. A KOSB soldier accidentally set off a smoke grenade in his webbing, and this set fire to a bag of grenades he was carrying.

> Word came back, 'Get off the track'. They didn't tell us why, but we could see that a phosphorus grenade had gone up ahead of us ... Then the word came back that there was a bag of grenades burning just up the track and we would wait until it all went off and see what the reaction was around us and we might have to go home. My guys just lay there quietly waiting, but the wait went on and on and on. As it turned out, none of the grenades went off ... The Company Commander had just decided that perhaps we could move on, when he got a radio call saying that the attack was cancelled.[132]

Lea had just announced that all offensive CLARET operations were to cease immediately. Burt left an inconsolable KOSB company commander crying in the middle of the track and went back to brief his men. 'I said, "Well fellows, we've got to go home, it's all off." And do you know what they did? ... The tension just went out of them like that, and they burst out laughing.'[133]

CLARET reconnaissance operations continued as actively as before, and there was still the odd Indonesian incursion. On 1 April 1966, Johnston took his patrol across the border to the south of Batu Lintang company base in the Mid-West Brigade area to search the Sungai Ran for a suspected camp. After four days they found it on the south bank of the river. One member of the patrol wrote in a letter:

> Our camp watch was highly successful as we got right in and photographed the [Indonesians] and I must say that they are a pretty careless and unruly mob as they had no weapons at the wash-point and those in the camp itself seemed more impressed [sic] in Elvis Presley on their transisters [sic] than they were in the security of their camp. This of course made our job easier and I must say I was highly tempted to open up and spray the blokes at the wash-point as I was only 15 yards from them and could have got the lot with one burst and perhaps a grenade. However our job was purely a recce and nothing else and we were somewhat relieved to get in and out successfully.[134]

Getting 'in and out successfully' without being detected was the key to success for the SAS. Russ Martin went back to do a closer reconnaissance of the suspected company position he had found on the Sungai Siglayan. A firm base was established, and at mid-afternoon on 9 April Martin and his scout Fi Wanoa moved in on the camp. In the thick secondary growth, Wanoa and an Indonesian sentry spied each other simultaneously and fired. Every weapon on the perimeter immediately responded. It seems the SAS had been expected. Wanoa and Martin hugged the ground for cover while returning fire. Mortar bombs bursting on the likely escape routes forced the rest of the patrol to frantically dig shell-scrapes. It was only when the single 105-mm howitzer that was covering the operation from the border fired and silenced the mortar that the patrol was able to withdraw. Martin and Wanoa were separated while getting out. After failing to find the emergency rendezvous, Martin reached the Troop rendezvous at 10 a.m. the following day and met up with the two other members of his patrol and a platoon of C Company 2 Royal Green Jackets which had been sent in to assist. Meanwhile Wanoa, suspicious of Indonesian patrols, bypassed the rendezvous and reached the border two days after the contact. This was a time of enormous strain for Ogilvy and his headquarters. Bob Burt, now Operations Officer, remembered Ogilvy being 'in tears' when the two men were reported missing, and the enormous relief as first one and then the other returned.[135]

Martin's experience showed that the Indonesians were still dangerous if prodded. But there was growing confirmation that they were withdrawing from many of their border bases. These had to be checked in case they were reoccupied. Warrant Officer Midge Brown, who had replaced Bob Burt, carried out this task in the 'crocodile' country between the Simangaris and Wason rivers.[136] Corporal Jack Powley did the same on Sebatik Island, as did Fred Barclay from the Mid-West and Central Brigade areas.[137] It was the same all along the border. Some camps were still occupied, others deserted, but there were no further contacts. In May Lea ended all CLARET reconnaissance operations. The last such New Zealand operation was carried out by Powley on Sebatik Island. A camp surrounded by cultivations and occupied by about 30 Indonesian soldiers was located; but there were no trenches, no sentries, and indeed little military activity of any kind. After conducting a close reconnaissance for two and a half days, Powley withdrew his patrol.[138]

The highly professional performance of Ogilvy's Three Detachment was the culmination of the New Zealand SAS's service in Borneo. While Indonesian activity was not as intense as it had been during One Detachment's tour, Ogilvy built on the lessons that had been learned and benefited from the experience of the veterans he had inherited. Under his leadership, the detachment had confirmed the quality of the work of the New Zealand SAS on small-group, long-range cross-border patrol operations.

## Four Detachment, June to December 1966

Major David Moloney brought out Four Detachment in June 1966, after a training build-up similar to that of earlier detachments. Moloney had graduated from Duntroon in 1959 into the Royal New Zealand Engineers, and had passed an SAS selection course in 1965. Like Ogilvy, he was supported by SAS members with experience on previous tours. On his arrival it was obvious that the level of action was falling. In the last week of June, before training was completed, a patrol under Second Lieutenant George Field took over Operation ROSEWOOD from D Company 3 Battalion, The Parachute Regiment. This was an ongoing 'hearts and minds' operation in a part of the Central Brigade area of Sabah that had been largely unexplored before Confrontation. Field was soon joined by Sergeant Dave Heywood's patrol. Despite local reports, it was evident that there had been no Indonesians in the area for a long time. The SAS employed local Punan tribesmen to carry out patrols, paying them with food and supplies. The impact on the tribespeople of operations over the previous three years had been disastrous. Indiscriminate gifts of food and supplies had made the Punans totally dependent on the largesse of the security forces, as traditional food cultivation and gathering had been neglected. D Company and later the New Zealanders tried to wean them off this dependence, but they had had a 'taste of some of the luxuries of civilisation'. The most serious aspect of this contact was the impact of venereal disease on the tribe. No children had been born alive in the last three years. The women had all had miscarriages, and it appeared that the men were also infected. The elders of the tribe were very worried, but there was nothing the patrols could do. The 'hearts and minds' aspect of Operation ROSEWOOD seemed to be a belated attempt to repair some of the worst outcomes of the security force's presence, in the hope that the tribe might survive if it was left alone once again.[139]

The rest of Moloney's detachment became fully operational on 13 July. Six patrols were committed to operations during the month, while one carried out a further training exercise.[140] In late July, Captain David Slocombe's four-man patrol reconnoitred the rugged border area of 'The Gap', at the junction of Central and East Brigade, which had not been patrolled for some time. After a detailed brief by Richard Noone, the patrol covered the steep ridges and cliffs along the border, finding many signs of game and friendly tracks, but none of Indonesian activity.[141] Four New Zealand patrols were soon operating in The Gap, to the west of Slocombe's patrol, as part of Operation KITE, mounted in response to a suspected Indonesian incursion. Staff Sergeant Niwa Kawha reported that two Indonesian soldiers had been seen crossing a border landing place on 5 August. Footprints indicated that they had moved north-west, but heavy rain had washed out the tracks and made any follow-up difficult. Murray Winton's patrol tracked the prints without success, and it was thought that the Indonesians had turned back across the border into Kalimantan.[142]

During Operation KITE the New Zealanders were under the operational control of 2/6th Gurkha Rifles. It was not a happy marriage. Moloney believed his patrols were not being given the latitude to do their job properly, and told the Commanding Officer so.[143] The problems faced by the squadrons of 22

SAS Regiment that had been placed under the control of local battalions at the start of the Borneo campaign were now being repeated. However, training infantry battalions in the niceties of working with the SAS became irrelevant with the signing of the peace treaty between Indonesia and Malaysia on 12 August 1966. All SAS patrols returned to base and, apart from deploying in response to the odd alarm, stayed there until they were finally withdrawn from Borneo.

The Borneo deployment was the first and perhaps only time that the New Zealand SAS conducted truly SAS-type operations. Confrontation presented the New Zealand SAS with the classic challenge: to move deep inside enemy territory in four-man patrols and gain information without their presence being detected. Neither Malaya nor Vietnam offered the same challenges or made the same professional and physical demands on individuals as did the CLARET operations of 1965–66. Having played such a key role in establishing the professional standards of 22 SAS Regiment in 1955–57, the New Zealand SAS had been searching for a role since its reformation in 1959. This search was undertaken in total isolation from the professional developments occurring within the British SAS. The deployment to Thailand and the work of Meldrum and others had been just enough to keep the SAS concept alive in New Zealand until the deployment to Borneo in 1965. Confrontation made the men of the New Zealand SAS aware of how much they had to learn. Being attached to 22 SAS Regiment gave them the operational experience that allowed them to develop expertise in four-man jungle patrols. This specialist skill was subsequently maintained and refined. Equally important was the re-establishment of the relationship between the New Zealand SAS and 22 SAS Regiment. In the words of Murray Winton, 'we were back into the club'; the New Zealand SAS has remained a member of this 'club' ever since.[144]

# 10

# 'NO BETTER A SOLDIER'

*Infantry Operations, Borneo, 1965–66*

## First Battalion, Royal New Zealand Infantry Regiment in Borneo: The First Tour, June to October 1965

> This was a platoon commander's and company commander's little battle and as the Commanding Officer, you are basically an eavesdropper. What you have done is provide the training stimulus, but when the chips are down, they have got to go and do it themselves. In our case I always believed that our fellows did it very well, and were more than a match for the Indonesians.[1]
>
> Brigadier Bob Gurr, Commanding Officer
> 1RNZIR Borneo, 1965

Gurr's battalion was deployed to Borneo in May 1965.[2] After their experience on operations against Indonesian infiltrators in Johore, on the Malaysian mainland, the previous year, the New Zealanders were keen to have another go. Everyone in 1RNZIR saw a Borneo tour as a fitting climax to a busy two-year posting. This keenness was intensified by the knowledge that they would be relieving their arch-rivals, Lieutenant-Colonel 'Bunny' Burnett's 1/10th Gurkha Rifles, who had been deployed first to Labis and had claimed the lion's share of the action the previous September. Now the New Zealanders were once again following in their footsteps as part of Mid-West Brigade, which was taking responsibility for the Second Division of Sarawak.

Mid-West Brigade had been created on 17 January 1965 to control the two extra battalions, 1/10th Gurkha Rifles and 3RMR, which were being deployed to Sarawak in response to the build-up of Indonesian regular forces in Kalimantan. It was initially commanded by Headquarters 3 Commando

Brigade, which was replaced on 22 March by Headquarters 19th Infantry Brigade Group from the United Kingdom, commanded by Brigadier David W. Fraser.[3] The creation of Mid-West Brigade brought to four the number of brigade areas in Borneo. West Brigade, commanded by Headquarters 99 Gurkha Infantry Brigade under Brigadier W. W. Cheyne, had formerly covered the First, Second and Third Divisions of Sarawak, but was now confined to the First Division, where it faced the greatest concentration of Indonesian forces. The newly formed Mid-West Brigade's area was the Second and Third Divisions; Central Brigade covered the Fourth and Fifth Divisions, Brunei and the Interior Residency of Sabah; and East Brigade was responsible for the remaining residencies of Sabah, as well as West Coast, Sandakan and Tawau.[4]

Fraser's tasks were to keep his area 'free from Indonesian incursions' and 'aid the Civil Power to destroy any internal subversion'.[5] His two battalions and one armoured car squadron were supported by a single battery of guns, a troop of engineers and a number of logistic units.[6] The scarcity of roads severely limited his options. There was no natural link between Third Division, the catchment area of the Batang Rajang, and Second Division. A road ran from the capital, Kuching, in First Division, parallel to the range of hills that marked the border, to the police and administrative centre of Second Division, Simanggang. Another road, which linked the population centres of the lower Rajang with the small river ports of Sarikei and Binatang, did not continue either north-east to Sibu, the capital of Third Division, or south to Simanggang. A third isolated road served Fraser's headquarters at Sibu. The interior, mountainous and largely jungle-covered, was served only by four small airstrips. Most travel was on foot, by river, or by helicopter. Movement on foot was slow and laborious, limited to patrol pace. Movement by longboats was possible over much of the river system in the brigade area, but larger craft were limited to the Rajang in Third Division and as far as Lingga on the Batang Lupar in Second Division. Movement by helicopter, combined where possible with other means of transport, was the inevitable norm; resupplying the battalions was largely dependent on air-drops by parachute.

This was the context within which 1RNZIR assumed command in Second Division at midday on 5 June 1965.[7] Orders had been issued at the end of April for a move by sea and air through Singapore, with the advance party of Battalion Tactical Headquarters, Headquarters Company and Company Headquarters moving by Beverley transport aircraft and Bristol Freighter to Kuching on 18 May and then into the battalion's area by road. The rest were to follow by sea. The battalion had 669 personnel—39 officers, 52 warrant officers and senior NCOs, and 578 other ranks—and 35 vehicles, including ten 3-ton RL Bedfords, five 3-ton armoured trucks and two Ferret scout cars.

With the Borneo tour imminent, the quality of reinforcements was Gurr's principal concern. A 'trickle' system had been introduced, with individual reinforcements arriving from New Zealand and being posted to a company after acclimatisation training. The April 1965 report noted that one officer and 57 other ranks had completed their acclimatisation training during that month, but did not paint a positive picture. 'The standard of training of reinforcements arriving in theatre ... is becoming progressively worse. Many soldiers are physically unfit to a marked degree, their basic weapon handling is generally poor, and one man in the last April flight had never fired a Bren Light machine gun in six months service in the army.'[8] Gurr did not want these problems to affect the quality of reinforcements available to him. A rear party of 75 under Major Bill McCallum was left behind in Wellington Lines to carry out base administration and ensure a flow of trained reinforcements to the unit in Borneo.

The commitment of both the Australian and New Zealand battalions to Borneo during 1965 inevitably affected the ability of 28th Commonwealth Brigade to carry out its SEATO role. The New Zealand battalion could anticipate two five-month tours over two years, one of which would coincide with that of another battalion in the brigade. The New Zealand government made it clear that it did not want the Borneo commitment to impair the brigade's ability to carry out its primary role; it also did not want all three battalions in the brigade to be British if there was a SEATO emergency. It asked for a roulement of battalions to be arranged so that only one battalion from 28th Commonwealth Brigade was in Borneo at any one time. If this was not possible, it expected 'that arrangements would be made for priority withdrawal of 1RNZIR in [the] event of a SEATO call'.[9]

The 1RNZIR advance parties went by air on 1 May, followed by the battalion's vehicles and equipment on a Landing Craft, Tank on 26 May. The soldiers came by sea on MV *Auby*[10] in two sailings, each of two companies, arriving on 27 May and 9 June. One soldier remembered this as 'a very pleasant trip across. The sea was glassy smooth, nobody got seasick ... lying on the bunks below was too hot so most people sat up topside all the time.' During the three-day crossing, the sight of a submarine or the occasional escort vessel was the only reminder that they were not alone. The New Zealanders' only gripe was being served kippers—which usually ended up over the side—for every breakfast.[11] *Auby* sailed up the wide expanse of the Batang Lupar, and anchored at the river port of Lingga. From there the battalion travelled by assault craft to Simanggang, the site of Gurr's Battalion Headquarters. B and D Companies were the first lift, with B Company relieving C Company 1/10th Gurkha Rifles at Jambu and D Company relieving B Company 1/10th Gurkha Rifles at Sungai Tenggang on 27 May.[12] A and C Companies relieved the other Gurkha companies at Lubok Antu and Batu Lintang on 9 June.

Gurr, warned in February that New Zealand had approved a six-month tour of duty for the battalion, had planned and trained his men accordingly. Fraser had visited Terendak and briefed Gurr on his battalion's role. Gurr conducted a final rehearsal, Exercise TALISMAN, in which a rifle company defended a company base against probes and attacks by another rifle company representing an Indonesian force. The roles were then reversed.[13] In May, Gurr flew to Labuan with his operations team, which comprised Captain Owen Mann, the Intelligence Officer; Captain Lloyd Jones, the Support Company commander; and Captain Bryan Wells, the Signals Officer. At Labuan they met Major-General Peter Hunt, Commander Land Forces Borneo, and were briefed by his staff, before flying to Mid-West Brigade Headquarters at Sibu in the Third Division. 1RNZIR was to take over responsibility for Second Division, and undertake the tasks of 'surveillance of the frontier and the frontier area ... the prevention of enemy raids and penetration', including 'all necessary measures to deal with any Indonesian troops and irregulars who cross the Sarawak frontier', and the 'close defence of vulnerable points and garrisons ... particularly airfields and airstrips'.[14] Fraser emphasised the need to gain 'the confidence of the population, in order that information of enemy incursions, penetrations, may be freely passed'.[15] Supplies would be transported from a maintenance area at Kuching by 'sea, river and road'; only where none of these methods was possible would 1RNZIR be supplied by air; aircraft were critical to success, but always in short supply.[16]

Gurr's team spent three days visiting each of the company locations and being briefed in detail on the terrain and Indonesian activity. While the 1/10th Gurkha Rifles had had an active and successful tour, Gurr was concerned about the apparent vulnerability of the company bases, an impression that had been confirmed by an attack on the base of B Company 2nd Battalion, The Parachute Regiment, at Plaman Mapu in the First Division, on 27 April. This attack on the platoon garrison was skilfully mounted by a company of regular soldiers from the elite Parachute Commando Regiment (RPKAD) of the Indonesian Army; although it was unsuccessful, the fact that some soldiers got inside the perimeter revealed serious deficiencies in the defences.[17] Each of the New Zealand companies would operate with two of their three platoons on patrol at any one time, so it was essential that each base could be protected by a single platoon of 20–30. Gurr decided to change the site of his most isolated base, at Jambu, and improve the defences of the other three.

Gurr's principal task was to monitor and dominate 130 miles of mountainous, jungle-covered terrain which largely defined the border with Kalimantan. The Tinteng Kedang range, oriented east–west to the south of the company base at Jambu, linked with the Tinteng Ango Kara, to the south of Lubok Antu and Batu Lintang. The border then continued along the Klingkang Range, which ran as a steep escarpment 1,000–1,500 feet above the Kuching–Simanggang Road, south of the company base at Sungai Tenggang.

The bases were sited on important communication routes or adjacent to communities of the Iban people, of whom there were between 20,000 and 25,000 in the Second Division. They lived in groups of up to 200 in isolated longhouses in clearings, often separated from their neighbours by 10 or 20 miles of jungle-covered mountains. Iban traders visited the longhouses on foot or in canoes with outboard-motors. The Iban were at one with the jungle: they hunted for small game and birds, fished in the rivers and streams, and slashed and burnt small clearings to plant food crops and hill padi, which the jungle was allowed to reclaim after the harvest. They lived in the lowland jungle forests along the Batang Lupar, and in the steep dissected valleys of the Batang Ai and its tributaries. To the Iban, there was only the jungle, its rivers and its trails. This was the home of gods who dictated their lives, telling them when and where to hunt, and what areas to clear for padi and crops.[18] The Iban recognised no borders, only a way of life, and a wish to pursue it undisturbed by the implications of Malaysian federation or Sukarno's ambitions. They moved and traded freely on both sides of the border between Sarawak and in Kalimantan. The company bases were sited to monitor this pattern of movement: if the Iban could use the trails, so could Indonesian soldiers. The Iban knew who journeyed in their forests, and would support whichever authority allowed them to live as they had always done. Winning their support was one of Gurr's tasks, and central to his success would be the effectiveness of his company bases.

Jambu, the most eastern and isolated of the four bases, was sited near a group of longhouses on the Sungai Delak. Twenty-five miles to the south-west,

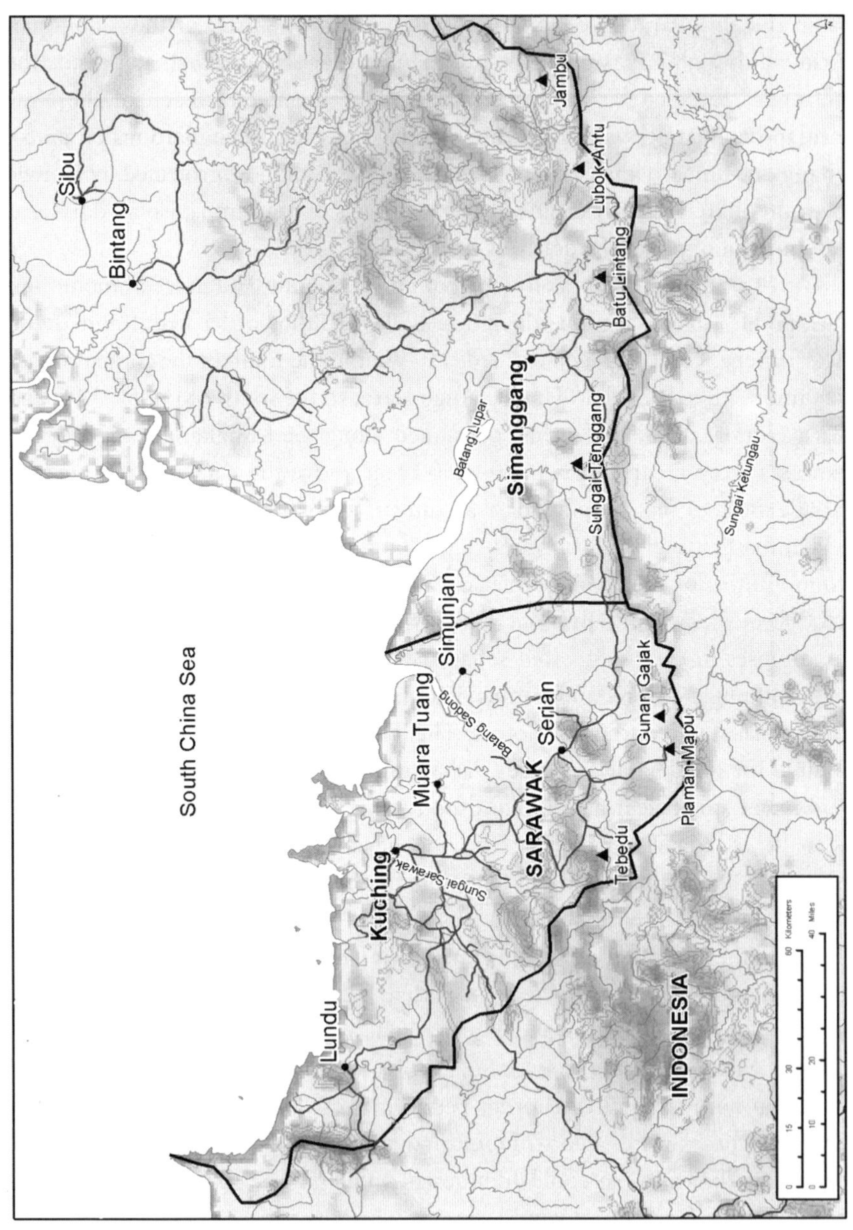


**Map 9** Western Sarawak, 1965

over a tangle of jungle-covered hills, was the almost equally isolated company base at Lubok Antu. Here a 'Beau Geste' police fort overlooked a small trading post and a number of longhouses on the banks of the Batang Ai, a major river which joined the Batang Lupar at Simanggang, a tortuous 50 miles downstream. At Lubok Antu, where jungle tracks converged, 'cross border traders exchanged lizard skins and other jungle produce for cash, or even outboard motor propeller shear springs, since this small community's link with the outside world was by river'.[19] Twenty-five miles further west, Batu Lintang was located in a border salient at the junction of the Klingkang Range and the Ango Kara Range. The salient was the nodal point of a myriad of tracks that crossed the jungle-covered hills to five longhouses, each set in its own clearing. Batu Lintang was connected to the outside world by a narrow dirt track which ran through a mixture of partly-milled jungle and crops to the road linking Simanggang with Engkilili, a small settlement 25 miles upstream from Simanggang on the Batang Ai. The westernmost base was at Sungai Tenggang, 30 miles further west on the road to Kuching. This was sited on a low ridge overlooking the road, about half a mile from the steep jungle-clad escarpment of the Klingkang Range which marked the border.

Gurr compared the requirements of each base with the capabilities of his company commanders. All four had been tested during the previous year's operations on the Peninsula. Knowing their strengths and weaknesses, Gurr positioned them accordingly.

> Up in Jambu, which was going to require all new works and was the most isolated from us all, I put Ian Burrows' B Company and into Lubok Antu I put Ian Thorpe's A Company ... which was a pretty isolated area as well. It also had a number of quite complex problems, particularly as there were a lot of border traders who used to try and come across from Kalimantan into Sarawak and there were quite a number of longhouses in the area. And then at Batu Lintang I put Bob Straight and his C Company. It was on a kidney-shaped, fairly easy defensible sort of base. It also had quite a number of longhouses. It had, I suppose, a number of vulnerabilities but it had the advantage of being also able to be reached by road as well as by helicopter. Down in Sungei Tenggan I put D Company under Stan McKeon and that was a rather interesting base in that it covered the road which ran almost below the escarpment along which the border ran and that escarpment was always a threat, not only to Sungei Tenggan itself but to anything coming along the road.[20]

Second Division had seen serious clashes with Indonesian regulars in the past. In March 1964 there had been a fight between a 40-strong platoon of the

328 Raider Battalion and A Company 2/10th Gurkha Rifles; in the same month, a 240-strong body made up of both regulars and irregulars had operated near Jambu.[21] Increased use of regulars was part of the rising tempo of operations that led to the Australian and New Zealand battalions being committed to Borneo. However, while there was a concentration of regular battalions of the Indonesian Army facing West Brigade in the First Division, the military threat facing 1RNZIR was based on the three battalions of V (Mandau) BRIMOB Brigade, a police mobile brigade deployed from the 20,000-strong paramilitary arm of the Indonesian National Police. The brigade operated under Army control, or at least within the labyrinthine command structure set up by the Indonesian Armed Forces (ABRI), which enabled the Army to limit Sukarno's attempts to 'increase the tempo of operations against Malaysia, something which many senior officers feared would provoke a heightened British response with which ABRI would be unable to contend'.[22] The New Zealanders' concern was with the nature of the Indonesian elements, what they were planning to do, and how effective they were. Brigade members wore Army uniforms and were issued with Army weapons, although these were often cast-offs and usually obsolete. Their communications equipment and transport were also dated. The brigade's role was primarily to handle internal security operations against the many low-level uprisings that occurred within Indonesia in the late 1950s and 1960s.[23] Like the New Zealanders opposite them, the brigade had only recently been deployed into the border area, and it was intent on establishing how its opponents were using the trails and guarding likely incursion routes into Sarawak.

The police mobile brigade was assessed as being less experienced than the Army battalions deployed against West Brigade; but initially at least it was prepared to probe and fight to establish the capabilities of its new opponents.

> We knew their bases that had been established because that had been passed to us by Bunny Burnett's 1/10th Gurkhas but we had to do a lot of work ourselves to find out a little bit more about them and what was in them. Buzz Burrows up at Jambu was confronting about a battalion's worth. Ian Thorpe probably had about the same. Opposite him at [Nangah] Badau there was really a battalion base with a company base off to the flank and they had that under pretty close surveillance through a big telescope right on the border. C Company, Bob Straight's company, [had] I suppose probably a couple of companies opposite him and well down on the other side of the escarpment about 5,000 or 6,000 yards in on the Indonesian side, there were two or three bases which were really in Stan McKeon's D Company

> area and I suppose they would each have been about a company strength. So there were a lot more Indonesians than there were Kiwis but they didn't have the logistic and air and communications support that we had.[24]

Gurr's headquarters was at Simanggang, 15 miles from the border on the banks of the Batang Lupar. Both the capital of the Second Division and its only centre of any size, Simanggang had a small jungle airstrip, and river traffic came up from Lingga, 30 miles downstream, which was the limit of navigation for small coastal trading vessels. Innumerable outboard-driven prahau brought jungle produce and game down the river from the small settlements of Engkilili and Lubok Antu, and the longhouses along its banks and those of its many tributaries. At Simanggang the verandahs of the colonial-style Residency building on the low hill above the town overlooked a cluster of shops, houses and markets where some 2,000 people—Iban, Malay, Chinese and Indian—lived and traded with the surrounding tribespeople. Despite Confrontation, Simanggang remained a bustling, colourful trading centre. Radios blaring Chinese and Malay music, the haggling and yelling of the traders, the distinctive smells of market produce and drains, combined to make it like thousands of similar centres throughout South-East Asia.[25]

The Resident—the first Iban to hold this position—was responsible to Kuching for the administration of the Second Division. He oversaw district officers situated in administrative posts such as Engkilili and Lubok Antu. A Police Field Force Company, made up of local Iban, was based in the town. At each longhouse in the division there were border scouts, local tribesmen placed on the company payroll to scout tracks and border crossing points. They were not soldiers, and did not wear uniforms or carry military weapons or equipment. Their role was to keep the company commander informed of what was happening in the longhouses, and of any movement of traders or others in the forests and on the rivers in the company's area. The best of these scouts provided invaluable information, but some simply invented stories to justify being paid. The military, police and border scout resources were co-ordinated by the Divisional Executive Committee in Simanggang. Gurr became the principal military adviser on this joint committee, which included the Resident as principal administrative officer, and senior police and local representatives.[26]

The main road from Kuching ended at Simanggang. Five miles to the south, a dirt vehicle track branched off towards Engkilili, a small settlement upriver on the Batang Ai which was the base for the armoured and scout cars of B

Squadron Queen's Dragoon Guards. This unit was responsible for route reconnaissance and convoy escort within the area, and was the brigade's 'counter-attack reserve in case of a major penetration in 2nd Division'.[27] Halfway along the track to Engkilili, an even worse seven-mile-long vehicle track branched off to the company base at Batu Lintang.

1RNZIR Headquarters was on the outskirts of Simanggang, about two miles from the small permanently guarded airstrip on which fixed-wing aircraft could land. It was grouped with Support Company—including both the Reconnaissance Platoon under the outstanding tracker, Second Lieutenant A. R. ('Albie') Kiwi, and the Anti-Tank Platoon under Lieutenant C. E. ('Ted') Brock—in a cluster of attap basha huts protected by barbed wire. Alongside was the helicopter pad for the three Whirlwind helicopters which, with their RAF crew and ground staff, were vital for communications and deploying men into the jungle. Later in the tour, the Whirlwinds were reinforced by two Sioux helicopters of 40 Commando Royal Marines Air Troop.[28] Despite their limited numbers and the scarcity of landing points, helicopter support was the key to success in this jungle war. It gave 1RNZIR the flexibility it needed to cope with its large operational area, allowing patrols to be deployed in ambush and as cut-offs, liaison to be carried out, and the sick and wounded evacuated. Gurr's headquarters was only a few minutes by helicopter from D Company at Sungai Tenggang and C Company at Batu Lintang, compared to an hour's drive by road. A Company at Lubok Antu was 15 minutes by helicopter, but half a day's boat journey from the roadhead at Engkilili. Jambu was a further ten minutes from Lubok Antu, instead of several hard days' march at patrol pace over steep jungle ranges. The large distances between company bases created problems for artillery support. 1RNZIR's direct support battery was B Battery Malaysian Artillery, which was relieved by C Battery on 1 August.[29] Contrary to conventional practice, individual 105-mm field guns were positioned in company bases to provide artillery support for patrols.

Gurr told his companies to get to know their respective areas at the same time as they improved the defences of their company bases. At Jambu, Major Buzz Burrows and B Company had to start from scratch. Gurr, concerned that this base could be fired on from the surrounding jungle-covered ridges, wanted it moved to higher ground above the Sungai Delak. This was done after a month's hard digging, 'with the help of a strong contingent of local Ibans who were very glad to get paid work'.[30] The employment of locally recruited labour allowed two of the company's platoons to be released to familiarise themselves with the border and the myriad of tracks that crossed it. Each platoon was away for up to 12 days at a time, followed by 12 days back at base. B Company took over a series of observation posts the Gurkhas had established on the border ridge, from which they could observe known Indonesian posts and longhouses where Indonesians were reportedly based. With the aid of powerful telescopes and binoculars, the routine of Indonesian activity was monitored closely. Initially, Burrows was also responsible for a platoon base at Nanga Mepi, on a hill overlooking a large longhouse on the Batang Ai. This was one of six bases that were close to the border and therefore vulnerable to Indonesian infiltration. As this additional task stretched B Company's resources to the limit, Gurr deployed his Anti-Tank Platoon under Lieutenant Ted Brock to man Nanga Mepi under Burrows' command. The platoon's 106-mm recoilless rifles were of little value in this setting, so the platoon worked as infantry.[31]

By the end of June, Jambu 'was completely underground, heavily wired and we believed defendable by a minimum of 22 personnel' manning 11 strong points connected by field telephones.[32] While Jambu's position was an extreme example, the difficulties of building defensive positions in the tropics were experienced at all the company bases. Unless trenches were drained, they filled up with rainwater. Trenches collapsed under the pressure of the run-off that raced down the cleared hillsides during each afternoon's torrential downpour unless they were revetted with sandbags or corrugated iron, supported by 2-metre-high iron pickets driven into the ground and tied with wire. It was reminiscent of the trenches on the Western Front in 1916–18. 'You really learn the realities of engineering and of getting rid of water, and no doubt our people did it in France a long time before us, and it's hard and damned difficult work with each trench and bunker needing a duckboard floor with pipes allowing a gravity run-out underneath.'[33] The men got used to living on duckboard that was fixed up to ten feet above the bottom of the trench; the sound of water flowing beneath them was an ever-present feature of their five-month tour.

The base was surrounded by heavy wire and panji defences (sharpened bamboo stakes set into pits as foot traps), and bunkers were sited so that machine guns covered all the likely approaches. 'Flares were erected in pairs all around the base and fired electrically ... They were sited to illuminate away from the base defences, generally on the other side of a tree. The flares were fired ... on a bring-up system every week, as the weather eroded them and rats tended to eat the wire.'[34] The Malaysian 105-mm howitzer and two mortars within the base had some 60 targets registered, but most of the company's area was out of range. Everything possible was done to make it difficult to approach the perimeter of bases undetected, and many 'infernal devices' were experimented with in addition to conventional mines and wiring. Corporal Clas Chamberlain, who was involved with the Assault Pioneer section attached to A Company, recalled that 'we had some 44-gallon drums filled with waste oil, each attached to an anti-personnel mine ... If that went bang it set off the fuel/oil mix ... we [also] had some dead-man booby traps, and if you tripped a stake or vine, a log would come swinging down across the track with sharpened stakes attached to it.'[35]

The men in the bases were never idle. They supervised Iban working parties who upgraded the defences or carried supplies up from drop zones on the river flats. The fact that Jambu was perched on a ridge overlooking the valley was 'great in terms of defence' but created resupply problems. Fresh water was pumped some 800 vertical feet up from the river, using two Alcon pumps and holding drums. 'We had tanks flown in which served not only as header tanks for gravity feed to the kitchen, showers and other taps throughout the base, but also at any time [we] always had five days' supply for the base should we have our supply cut off.'[36] Jambu was resupplied by a weekly air drop to the drop zone in the valley, where everything was unpacked and flown up by Whirlwinds to the helipad inside the base. This endless task kept the base platoon fully employed.

A soldier never had a bunk to call his own. During each platoon's time in base, soldiers could be 'hot-bunked'—allocated to different bunkers on the defensive perimeter. The meal system was arranged to suit the daily routine. With the exception of cooking arrangements for the Malaysian gun crew, who were Moslem, Burrows' company operated a central cookhouse.

> After stand-to in the morning there was a hot brew and a biscuit. A substantial cooked breakfast was at 0930, another brew at 1200 and dinner at 1700. This essentially two-meal day worked very well particularly as we were able to claim an extra day's ration for each of the many visitors who arrived on our daily helos [helicopters] too late for breakfast after the morning mist had lifted, and left too early for dinner in the evening.[37]

Rations included both fresh and tinned vegetables, and 'we dramatically improved the fresh meat situation after we sorted out a system of flying in live pigs and chickens underslung by helo. Two Ibans did our farming for us outside the base perimeter.'[38] As the rationing officer noted, this raised the standard of messing at Jambu appreciably, the animals being 'obtained from AH HENG the airdrop contractor, at Kuching prices'.[39] Burrows permitted two cans of beer per man per day while in base. 'This was not abused, and it was interesting to see how many elected not to drink at all.'[40]

For the local tribespeople, the bases were a source of lucrative employment. At Jambu, six Iban girls were employed full-time in a laundry for the soldiers, which was a 'great luxury'. In total, 120 Ibans were employed at the base, improving and repairing the defences, carrying in the supplies dropped by air, and undertaking a myriad of tasks that would otherwise have fallen to the New Zealand garrison. They all went home before last light, leaving the garrison to man the sentry posts until the workforce was allowed back in at 8 a.m. the next day.

The base was surrounded by a mile of wire, and Burrows 'wished it had been more'. Six Iban women were employed for a month hanging pairs of empty tins on the wire to give early warning of an intruder. Just as they finished, Major Trevor King, the Battalion Medical Officer, visited the base and 'told us the water which was gathering in the tins was a mosquito hazard. The women were then armed with tin openers and got an extra month's work putting holes in the tin bottoms to drain the water.' Rubbish removal was a major undertaking. 'Everything, particularly food tins, had to be bashed, burned and buried. A number of our labour force were employed on this full time and the quantity generated by a base of 160 men had to be seen to be believed.'[41]

Each base was different, positioned to suit the ground and the situation that each company commander found.[42] Major Ian Thorpe's A Company base at Lubok Antu was almost as isolated as Jambu. Built around the two-storey building that served as the local police post, it too had a single Malaysian-manned 105-mm field howitzer within the perimeter, and a dummy one at the other end of the post to give an impression of strength, plus two 81-mm mortars from the battalion's Mortar Platoon. Like the other bases it had its own helicopter landing pad, and was surrounded by a ring of underground bunkers whose firing loopholes covered the barbed wire entanglements and panji pits defending all the likely approaches to the base. Like the other company commanders, Thorpe also had signallers, cooks and medical orderlies attached from the battalion, as well as seven Iban policemen and a handful of border scouts who 'lived in'. Thorpe used the latter as escorts on the supply boat run up the Batang Ai from Engkilili, which took a full day. He was also fortunate in having an REME Staff Sergeant, 'Butch' Woodward, who spoke both Bahasa

Indonesian and Iban. Like Thorpe's company orderly, Private A. McKelvie, Woodward became an invaluable source of local information and intelligence.[43]

At Batu Lintang, Major Bob Straight's C Company solved the problems posed by the kidney-shaped feature which they dug themselves into. It too had a Malaysian 105-mm field howitzer and two of the battalion's mortars. Major Stan McKeon's D Company at Sungai Tenggang also undertook major defensive work, using the third of the company not out on patrols. Sungai Tenggang was within mortar range of the Klingkang Range and the border, and any enterprising Indonesian could make life in the base very difficult. The base 'badly needed overhead cover against mortar and grenade attack'.[44] McKeon had two mortars in his position, but not the single artillery pieces found in the other bases. The Saladin Armoured Cars of B Squadron, The Queen's Dragoon Guards at Engkilili, with their 90-mm cannon, were to respond to any need by D Company to bring direct fire onto the escarpment overlooking the camp. The defences of each base were worked on throughout the six months of the New Zealand tour: drainage always needed to be improved and rotting sandbags replaced, and refinements were always being added to the barbed wire and the panji pits surrounding each fort. As Ian Thorpe put it, all the bases continued to 'resound with two sources of pounding rhythm—Iban ladies belting dhobi (washing) and Iban diggers belting sandbags'.[45]

For six months, soldiers were either working to improve the base defences and doing sentry duty, or out on patrol. WO2 Howe James, who had been awarded the BEM for his patrol work as a platoon commander with 1 NZ Regiment in 1959, was Company Sergeant-Major of A Company and had charge of the Lubok Antu defences. Everything, including the bunkers and the communication trenches connecting them, was roofed over with corrugated iron, sandbags and earth thick enough to absorb the impact of a mortar round. 'We could move quickly and support any part of the perimeter at any time. We did many rehearsals and one of the first things a visitor would know, when he came into our base, was that he would be allocated a position within the defences and straight away was put through a rehearsal so that he knew what to do if the base came under fire while he was there.'[46] At night the bases were closed up tight until first light. Sometimes movies were shown, and many of the soldiers had shortwave radios. The base was home for the duration of the tour. 'It just went on ... and you got into the routine of things. We were well fed, you got cigarettes, and you were allowed a can of beer a night ... everyone just adjusted to it.'[47]

Gurr's priority was to establish effective radio communications between Battalion Headquarters, his company bases, and the extensive matrix of platoon-sized patrols extending over hundreds of square miles. The steep tree-covered ridges and valleys had restricted their predecessors, 1/10th Gurkhas, to a strict system of daily schedules using an uncertain HF radio link between Simanggang and the company bases. With the quality of signal strongly influenced by the constantly changing atmospheric and climatic conditions, HF communications 'required a lot of luck and dedication to make it work'. The man-packed A41 VHF patrol sets of each platoon were regarded as useless in these conditions unless positioned on high ground or very close to the company base.[48]

The Gurkhas' experience was almost universal among Commonwealth battalions in Borneo, but 1RNZIR's was different. Gurr was fortunate in the calibre of his Regimental Signals Officer, Captain Bryan Wells, and his 'mix of RNZ Signals mavericks and Infantry signallers'.[49] In training and operations on the Malay Peninsula, Wells and his innovative team had already gone some way towards overturning the common belief that VHF communications would not work in rugged bush-covered terrain. With Staff Sergeant D. MacIntosh and two RNZ Signals Sergeants, D. Vinton and W. T. Higginson, Wells refined the battalion's radio equipment requirements, using vehicle-carried VHF C42 sets at battalion and company headquarters, and A41 sets at platoon level, with HF C11 and A510 sets as back-up. By trial and error, Wells and his team realised 'early on that antenna height and intervisibility were key elements in obtaining good VHF radio communications'.[50] They experimented with using C42s as rebroadcast sets to guarantee line of sight over the worst country. Special antennae suited to the conditions were produced. Careful planning from maps was followed by helicopter reconnaissance of the radio path to confirm the site of each rebroadcast station. Gurr gave his Signal staff priority in helicopter hours, allowing the 1RNZIR Signal Platoon to achieve line of sight between each station and thus 24-hour voice radio communications.

When the battalion was deployed to Borneo, Gurr expected—and got—24-hour VHF voice communications with each company headquarters and every platoon. This cost Lieutenant-Colonel Bunny Burnett of 1/10th Gurkhas a case of Johnnie Walker Black Label whisky, as he had challenged Gurr on his signallers' ability to establish VHF voice communications between Simanggang and Jambu when the Gurkhas had had great difficulty establishing HF communications.[51] This system was a major New Zealand breakthrough in tactical communications in jungle warfare.[52] It gave Gurr an ability unrivalled in Borneo to know what was going on in what was essentially a company and platoon war.

> I had this extraordinarily good communications system and in fact Bryan Wells had built a radio link-up right alongside my bed so that any of my companies and platoons out on patrol could call in and the operator would stick it straight through to me at any time of the night. Wherever I went I had a communicator with me, and as soon as I got to a company or platoon base, there was absolutely no problem with communications, you could flick straight through to my headquarters or whoever I wanted to speak to. I spent a tremendous amount of my time moving between the bases and going out to see the patrols when they were somewhere within reasonable access of a jungle pad.[53]

Patrols went out as soon as each company took over its base from 1/10th Gurkhas. The New Zealanders had already seen 18 months' hard patrolling through every type of jungle country that could be found on the Malay Peninsula, from dry areas thick with bamboo on the Thai border to the fetid, leech-ridden mangrove swamps of southern Johore. Borneo presented its own challenges, from secondary jungle so thick that every cautious pace had to contend with spiked creeper or risked bamboo leaves crackling underfoot, to cathedral-like forests where the jungle canopy was 150 feet overhead and scattered secondary growth permitted easy and silent movement. Jungle held no fears for Gurr's New Zealanders, who were a hardened professional team with the experience and confidence to match their wits against the Indonesian enemy.

> We had our particular methods of doing it and, you know, a New Zealand infantryman isn't the same as an English infantryman and he's certainly not the same as a Gurkha, and we had developed our own particular jungle techniques. We'd learnt to move with a great silence in the jungle. We never used machetes; we used little saws to make our bashas ... We had our own ways of doing our ambushes and we had our own ways of doing our counter-ambush drills.[54]

This was a confidence born of hard training and operational experience. In Malaya and north Borneo, company commanders like Ian Thorpe and Buzz Burrows devised and tested the embryo triangular harbour drills and action on contact drills at section and platoon level. These drills became second nature to every soldier, conditioning his reactions when shots were fired or a hand-signal given. Jim Brown, one of the most successful platoon commanders of this tour in Borneo, recalled:

> We were simply conditioned that way and that's what we were trained to do and we got on with it ... I think there was also very much that excitement of the chase—the expectation. We went out hunting, not quite to the same degree as the search and destroy missions of Vietnam; but you went out looking for any movement from the other side across onto your side of the border.[55]

With the confidence of experience, the New Zealand patrols established platoon bases covering border trails. They familiarised themselves with the tracks across the border from the longhouses and centres of population that were likely targets for Indonesian raids. Helicopter pads were cut from the jungle at track junctions and on features to increase their ability to respond to sightings and cut off reported incursions. Observation posts were established on the border ridges.

> We had a huge telescope on a hill which we manned permanently and we would watch their movement from there ... We could tell when it was feeding time and when they were having the morning parades and the whole gambit of what they were doing. We could tell when they had an important visitor because you would see them all lined up. In that way any change in activity we could pretty well pin down at the time ... we then started to be able to anticipate what they would do.[56]

During June 1965, the New Zealand-manned observation posts noticed increasing Indonesian reconnaissance activity on the border opposite both Lubok Antu and Batu Lintang. On one occasion they saw an officer climb the border ridge and study the ground towards Batu Lintang. This may have been the Lieutenant-Colonel commanding V (Mandau) BRIMOB Brigade, whose presence strongly indicated that a major incursion into Second Division was being planned. Intelligence experts assessed that such a strike was likely to coincide with Indonesia's presence at the Second Afro-Asian Conference on 29 June, and the New Zealand bases prepared accordingly.[57]

A patrol of 10 Platoon D Company moving along the border ridge on 1 June had located two booby traps consisting of hand grenades attached to vines stretched across the track. They triggered the first booby trap, but it failed to explode because the striking arm had rusted onto the grenade. Only the alertness of the patrol's second scout prevented the second booby trap being triggered. Firing reported in the vicinity on 15–16 May had apparently been intended to draw security forces into the booby-trapped area. This was a salutary reminder of the Indonesians' willingness to contest control of the border. Similar booby traps had caused casualties to 3RAR on their first tour.

In March 1965 a 'jumping mine' had killed an Australian sergeant and an Iban tracker and wounded two soldiers, and two more soldiers had been killed in May.[58] Only the length of time the grenades had been exposed to moisture had saved the New Zealanders from similar casualties.

On the night of 8–9 June there were reports of an incursion across the border into C Company's area at Batu Lintang by a party of 20 Indonesians. C Company had a further scare on the night of 17–18 June when a Seismic Intrusion Detector sited beside one of the main tracks detected an 80-strong party approaching Batu Lintang from the south. The garrison stood to and manned bunkers until dawn. Patrols failed to find any tracks, and it was later suspected that foraging water buffalo had caused the vibrations.[59]

On 21 June, just on last light, 1RNZIR had its first contact with the Indonesians. Second Lieutenant Jim Brown's 3 Platoon A Company was waiting in ambush on a border track. 'We had a sentry out, a fellow by the name of Len Ormsby, and he gave the signal of enemy approaching ... There was absolute silence. The enemy lead scout came along. He had seen some disturbance in the undergrowth and he was leading right towards my sentry, and Ormsby really had no alternative but to shoot him.' A firefight broke out and the Indonesians withdrew. Brown remembered wondering during the total silence that followed, 'What the hell's out there? It's sort of like going and checking the fish trap afterwards.' Reluctant to send anyone else, Brown went forward. 'Just as I was about to move I heard this almighty groan, and "Help me".' The Indonesian scout whom Ormsby had shot was found badly wounded. 'He had a hole in the back of his shoulder that you could put your fist into. It really was nasty. So I filled him full of morphine and put him on a stretcher.' The platoon carried him out, 'and of course expecting an Indonesian company to come rushing down our bloody back, we were hot-footing it back to our company base where we were met by the base platoon and they took over the carrying because we were a little poked at the time'.[60] Coincidentally, the wounded man turned out to be a corporal of 3 Platoon A Company, II Battalion, V (Mandau) BRIMOB Brigade. Under interrogation, he said he was a member of a party of nine sent to check a track between Nangah Badau, his company base, and the border. When ambushed, he claimed, they were not aware that they had reached the border.[61]

On 30 June Lieutenant Brian Marshall and a small party from 1 Platoon A Company set out from the platoon's base to find a suitable position for a night ambush. They were reconnoitring the junction of two tracks just short of the border when, just after midday, Private Tahu Ashby, a sentry in the platoon position, saw three Indonesian soldiers moving towards him. He gave the silent alarm, and with the Indonesians only some 20 yards away the platoon hurriedly manned the perimeter. The movement alerted the Indonesians, who opened fire. Ashby fired almost simultaneously, wounding both leading scouts as a third disappeared into the undergrowth. Captain Harbin Singh of the Federation Artillery, the Forward Observation Officer with the platoon, immediately called in artillery fire from the 105-mm gun at Lubok Antu. A rifle section then searched and cleared the ambush area, locating and capturing the two wounded Indonesians.

Marshall and his party, caught on the wrong side of the firefight, moved to cut off the Indonesians' withdrawal. They stumbled into a clearing where a party of ten Indonesians were assembling a 60-mm mortar. Marshall's group opened fire, wounding three as the Indonesians hastily returned fire and took cover, dragging their wounded with them. Marshall's next concern was to rejoin his platoon. 'We spent the next quarter of an hour approaching our own platoon and in coming to terms with the dilemma of persuading our own troops we were "friendlies" and not the enemy.'[62] Singh directed artillery fire onto the enemy mortar position while Marshall took control of his platoon. One of the wounded Indonesians had died; the second said he was part of a party of 15 who were being followed by a larger party. Artillery fire was directed onto routes across the border this group was likely to take.

A helicopter was called in to evacuate the wounded man from the nearest landing point. Marshall's platoon then swept forward towards the border on either side of the track.

> As we progressed up the axis of the track one of our flank men spotted two Indonesians hiding under some lilies. I deployed troops around them, moved forward to disarm them shouting out in my best bazaar Malay not to shoot or they would be shot. They didn't seem to appreciate my language skills as one of them opened up with a Madsen sub machine gun and the other one threw a grenade at me. One of our machine gunners, Roy Kaaka from up Te Kao way, opened up, shouting they moved boss, they moved. I didn't know whether to laugh, or cry, but stood there looking at the grenade which hadn't gone off, while others seemed to be trying to dig a hole with their bare hands.[63]

With both Indonesians dead, Marshall's platoon cleared the track and then rapidly occupied a night ambush position, laying two Claymore mines. At 1 a.m., noises from the direction of the border alerted the platoon. Suddenly, intense firing broke out; machine-gun and automatic-rifle fire showered the prostrate platoon with foliage and branches as bursting mortar bombs added to the cacophony. Singh directed the Lubok Antu gun to the source of the firing, and its first rounds silenced the mortar. Anxious about the platoon's exposed position, Marshall decided to withdraw. In total darkness, the platoon packed up and moved out, firing the Claymores before they went. Travelling 'at night in the jungle is difficult to say the least. Anyway we did, and the main instrument to our success was 200 metres of good old Kiwi baling twine to which we roped everyone in the platoon at about five metres interval. Off we went in a blackness only coalminers or soldiers who have served in the jungle at night can appreciate.'[64]

Amazingly, they managed to withdraw without alerting the Indonesians to this fact. At 2.30 a.m. the Indonesians reopened intense fire with every calibre of weapon on the position they had abandoned. The Lubok Antu gun continued to fire, and the enemy withdrew before daylight. Lieutenant Albie Kiwi of the 1RNZIR Reconnaissance Platoon then 'climbed a huge tree in his solitary Observation Post in the hills overlooking us, and proceeded to direct artillery fire on the Indonesian company who were high tailing it back to their base. They had very unwisely switched on torches which gave away their location.'[65]

A follow-up next morning found evidence of some 40–60 personnel with 60-mm and 2-inch mortar fuse caps; trails of blood led across the border. Marshall's ambush had forestalled an Indonesian attack on Lubok Antu. Three Indonesians were known to have been killed; one seriously wounded man had been taken prisoner, and an unknown number wounded. Gurr was pleased, and Brigadier Fraser reported that Marshall's platoon 'showed a high standard of minor tactics, particularly in the follow-up action, a high standard of alertness by sentries and men giving covering fire, and above all, an excellent standard of shooting'.[66] The contact demonstrated the quality of Gurr's battalion at the start of its Borneo tour. Gurr recommended Marshall for a Military Cross for this action, and was disappointed when it came back as a Mentioned in Despatches.[67]

This contact triggered a burst of activity in A Company's area of the border. On 2 and 11 July, the Indonesians directed machine-gun and mortar fire across the border onto the tracks where the contact had occurred. In one case they were observed to be firing back across the border into Kalimantan. Thorpe concluded that rather than risk a contact and casualties, the group had advanced to the border, made a demonstration, and then gone home to report success.[68] On both occasions, the Indonesian firing ceased after New Zealand border posts brought down artillery fire from the Lubok Antu gun.[69]

During June, V (Mandau) BRIMOB Brigade kept two battalions and elements of its third battalion in forward bases close to the border.[70] The activity near Lubok Antu showed that the Indonesians were more than prepared to contest the border area. This may have been prompted by resentment that the New Zealand posts were actually in Indonesian territory. As Gurr noted, there was 'some doubt as to where the border runs in the area of this contact. There is a discrepancy of 400–600 yds between the old Dutch maps and the more recent British survey. It is possible that the Indonesians consider we are attempting to dominate 200–300 yds of their Territory. They may be right.'[71] Maps of the border area and Kalimantan were often simply sketches showing little more than the major rivers; patrols added information on the terrain as they went.[72]

Patrolling was concentrated on the valleys running off the border ridges, where the New Zealanders were likely to cut across any trails or signs left by an Indonesian incursion. 'You did that generally in a more difficult ground [because] their tracks were easier to pick and you were doing that sort of patrolling almost continuously.'[73] It was a demanding yet enormously satisfying time for the platoon commanders and their NCOs, as there was always the chance of a contact with the enemy.

In June 1RNZIR also started planning its first cross-border CLARET operations. Fraser now knew that he had an experienced and skilled battalion which had rapidly adjusted to the demands of operations in Borneo. It thus met Walker's stipulation in his 'Golden Rules' (see appendix 11) that:

> Only thoroughly seasoned and jungle-worthy troops under first class and experienced leadership are to be committed to these operations. Otherwise, there will be a military nonsense which could result in serious political and operational consequences. Brigade Commanders are at liberty to decide when units are worthy of this hallmark. As a guide, no battalion should be committed to cross border operations until they have spent at least four weeks getting to know their area.[74]

Although the Second Division border area was already well known to SAS CLARET patrols, Lea's increased latitude saw each of Gurr's companies plan one CLARET operation per month for the rest of the tour. There were 18 company-level operations in all, each usually involving at least two platoons.[75] Each CLARET operation was carried out in accordance with Walker's 'Golden Rules'.[76] Gurr cleared the concept of each operation with all three levels of command: Lea as Commander of Borneo Operations, Hunt as Commander

Land Operations, and Fraser at Mid-West Brigade. They 'asked all the questions as to what sort of artillery support we were going to provide, what the communications were going to be, how deep into Kalimantan it was going to be, whether it was going to be difficult to winch out casualties, and we had to satisfy a lot of things before we sent people off'.[77] Gurr had already laid down the ground rules for CLARET operations to his company commanders.

> There were several principles which I felt our battalion should observe. Any movement over the border should be capable of support from the field guns in the bases (in D Company's case they were supported by 90 mm guns in the two armoured cars at the base) plus a section of two 81 mm mortars we would lift on to, or just beyond the border. Any casualties we might sustain would be lifted or winched out by helicopter. To my mind one of the imperatives was to ensure a continuous wireless link with those carrying out the operation 'on the other side'. Whenever possible, I took a small Tactical HQ and some of our best operators to establish a link with those conducting the operation. This group, with a protective element of about six or eight, we normally positioned adjacent to the section of mortars which had been airlifted close by.[78]

Once the company commander had cleared the operation with him, Gurr left him to run the show, well aware that it was his war. However, Gurr would position either himself or Major Max Tebbutt, his second-in-command, at a point on the border where he would be in radio contact, and could respond with reinforcements if these were needed. 'You weren't crowding the fellow that was doing it and really I was just there more in support, and it gave me a sense of comfort even if it gave no sense of comfort to the company commander.'[79]

The battalion's first CLARET operation was mounted by B Company, which was based at Jambu under Major Buzz Burrows. Despite careful preparation and planning by Burrows, it assumed elements of a Monty Python sketch when the Indonesians decided to mount a simultaneous operation against the Jambu base. B Company's Operation BATTLE DRUM was an ambush on the Serit–Lawan track, which was used frequently by Indonesian patrols. Burrows' company of two platoons and a mortar section of two 3-inch mortars[80] took three days, starting on 3 July, to move by different routes to an assembly area at Bukit Perayung on the Sarawak side of the border. On the 6th they were joined by Gurr and a small Tactical Headquarters, who along with the mortar section established themselves on the border. Burrows' force crossed into Kalimantan at 4 p.m., and by first light the next morning it was in position to mount an ambush, covering some 400 yards of the track.

Meanwhile, on the Malaysian side of the border, elements of II Battalion, V (Mandau) BRIMOB Brigade were mounting an attack on Jambu itself.[81] On the evening of the 6th, four 60-mm mortar bombs landed 500 yards outside the perimeter. Burrows' 2IC, Captain Chris Wotton, was in charge of the garrison platoon.

> [Everyone] stood to as soon as the first rounds landed. Our own mortars had been airlifted to the border so were not available to us. We alerted our Malaysian gun crew, took sound bearings on the enemy and began firing defensive fire tasks at them. Some small arms fire was directed at us but it was inaccurate and ineffective. Our very reduced strength in Jambu inhibited our ability to send parties to ambush tracks leading to the border, but I sent a patrol under Ted Brock [from the platoon base at Nanga Mepi] to clear the high ground to the south of the base and to report the location of the enemy mortars. Although the patrol did not establish contact with the enemy party, they reported it to be of an estimated strength of thirty to forty which appeared to be withdrawing to their own side of the border. We had the approximate location of the CO's small Tac[tical] HQ but did not know it lay astride the enemy's withdrawal route. We got the impression the enemy had been ordered to mount an attack on Jambu and that having directed some ineffective fire against it, honour was satisfied and they got out of Sarawak in a hurry.[82]

It was ironic that after an—at best—half-hearted attack, the Indonesians' withdrawal route took them straight through Gurr's headquarters on the border. Gurr and his Support Company Commander, Captain Lloyd Jones, were both up a tree looking into Kalimantan where, half a mile away, one of Burrows' platoons was cautiously investigating an Indonesian camp in a clearing. Suddenly, 'just to the rear of our tree we heard a fusillade of shots in the vicinity of our Tac HQ and the mortars. We decided to get down and investigate, and were just about to do so when a crashing of foliage below us preceded the passage of thirty or forty enemy troops heading down the slope into their own territory. These were the Jambu visitors of the night before, on the way home.'[83]

It was fortunate that Gurr and Jones stayed treed, or the weak attack on Jambu could have become a major Indonesian success with the killing of the New Zealand Commanding Officer. The excitement did not end there. Shortly after, Gurr heard coming from Kalimantan 'the thump of enemy mortars followed by machine gun and small arms fire. We got busy on the radio, raised *Buzz*, and asked him what was happening. "We're fine" he assured me. "Who the hell is doing all the firing?"'[84] This remained a mystery. It may have been the returning Indonesians scaring one of their own posts, or a post reacting to suspected movement around its perimeter. Burrows remained in ambush on the Serit–Lawan track without incident until the 11th, when he withdrew back to the border before last light.[85] There were no casualties on either side, but the Indonesians had shown themselves to be still prepared to mount raids into Sarawak.

At the same time, Ian Thorpe's A Company at Lubok Antu was mounting its first cross-border CLARET operation, codenamed ANCHOR MATCH. This was an ambush on the track leading from Nangah Badau to the border, which the Indonesians had used in the fight with Marshall's platoon on 30 June/1 July. A Company had an observation post known as 'The Eye' on the border ridge looking down into the Indonesian camp at Nangah Badau, which they had been watching for some time. Deciding to 'blood' the company, Thorpe took them across the border into a fruit plantation and set up an ambush on the evening of 5 July.[86] An eight- to ten-strong Indonesian patrol usually came along the track at mid-morning, but no one appeared. Thorpe decided to remain in ambush for at least another day, but at 2.30 that afternoon a solitary Indonesian soldier wandered into the ambush area gathering jungle fruit. He had chosen the worst possible place in Kalimantan to do that. Neil Webb, a section commander in 3 Platoon, remembered that this 'one unfortunate ... got hit by a Claymore mine and kept on going, and got hit by a number of rifles on the way through. He was barely alive at the end and was dispatched by Punchy.'[87] After the firing stopped there was silence, followed by a hurried packing up and withdrawal. The New Zealanders were 'chased down the road by 81 mm mortars and 12.7 machine guns firing through the trees and we were moving quite quickly to get back over to our legal side of the border'.[88] Thorpe fired a mixture of smoke and high-explosive shells to mask his withdrawal and keep the Nangah Badau garrison in their trenches. While ANCHOR MATCH was less successful than Gurr had hoped, it was a start. It clearly unsettled the Indonesians at Badau, who retreated inside their perimeter and no longer mounted daily patrols or set up observation posts outside their main base for fear of a New Zealand ambush.[89]

In July, Stan McKeon's D Company mounted DEAN'S YARD from Sungai Tenggang and Bob Straight's C Company mounted CANDLE POD from Batu Lintang. Both were ambushes on major track complexes in Kalimantan, and both passed without incident.[90] The next major contact occurred during A Company's Operation ANGLE IRON in late July. This was intended to eliminate a small border checkpoint on the Perempang–Lubok Antu track, just outside the company-sized Indonesian base at Soependok. By the 28th,

A Company had crossed the border and was moving down a broad, gently sloping spur covered in knee-high grass towards a small bush-clad feature some 300 yards away. Worried by the open ground, Thorpe halted his rear platoon on a low ridge while his leading platoon, commanded by Lieutenant Jim Brown, made the final approach to the feature.

As they approached the trees, machine-gun and small arms fire raked them at close range. A 30-strong Indonesian platoon lining the edge of the forest yelled and fired at Brown's platoon as it spread out on the open slope in front of them.

> We were only ... 10 or 15 metres at the most from them. My forward section was in dead ground and really it was a question of grenades. We used grenades, whatever we had, phosphorus grenades, the bloody lot. Anything that goes bang, and anything to make them keep their head down. I used the 2-inch mortar in the same way. Anything to cause noise to take the initiative away from them while the rest of the Company behind us pulled back and got out of the way.[91]

Despite the intense fire, Private Jim Negri was the only casualty, with a bullet wound in the arm. Heedless of the shooting, the platoon medic rushed to help him, but as Negri could still walk Brown knew that the 'important thing there was to get to hell out of it ... I virtually had to push [the medic] out of the way and say "Hey, leave that for later"' as the platoon withdrew.[92]

Thorpe, who was immediately behind Brown's platoon, described the attack as being 'caught momentarily with our pants down'.

> It was both tactically and physically quite unlike my expectations. There was a great deal of shooting from the hill directly ahead, and of course we all went down into the grass which suddenly seemed no longer thigh high, but very close cropped. The volume would be about the same as you would get on a large rifle range when the instructor orders rapid fire with automatics ... There were other sounds coming from ahead of us too. To my astonishment there were shouts in English of 'Come and get it British'. At such times life becomes like a slow motion movie. I recall being intensely irritated that Indonesian intelligence should be so bad it could confuse a New Zealand infantry company with a British one.[93]

On the ridge behind Brown, Sergeant-Major Howe James' 1 Platoon had gone to ground, with 'sweat dripping off [our] noses, lying flat on our stomachs listening to "zip, zip" and "zing, zing" of bullets coming towards us'.[94] James raked the Indonesian position with fire to enable Brown's forward section to pull back. 'It could have been absolutely devastating. We were totally exposed on a forward slope. There was a hell of a lot of luck. That we actually inflicted a number of casualties on them was virtually unbelievable. My aim at the time was just to throw everything and any bloody thing at them, which gave them a shock and allowed us to get out of it.'[95] Using fire and movement by sections, A Company extricated itself as enemy mortar fire landed on its flanks. Artillery fire was called in from the Malaysian-manned gun at Lubok Antu, and the mortars ceased fire. It was all over in four minutes, the Indonesians having opened fire at 8.45 a.m., and the platoons being clear of the killing ground by 8.49. By 9.15 A Company was back in its previous night's harbour area.

The Indonesians had caught A Company totally by surprise. It seems that in response to the Badau ambush earlier in July, they had occupied by day a series of platoon strongpoints some 500–700 yards from each of their main company bases. They held all the advantages in their ambush of Thorpe's company, yet only one New Zealander was wounded, and the rapid response apparently caused a number of casualties. Indonesian mortar fire from Soependok was ineffective. By contrast, Iban cross-border traders reported that fire from New Zealand mortars and the Lubok Antu artillery gun had caused casualties at the border checkpoint that had been A Company's objective. When the firing started, the Indonesians at the checkpoint had left their trenches to see what was going on and two were killed by the first artillery shell.[96] Lieutenant Jim Brown was awarded the Military Cross for his bravery and leadership in this action. Private Tahu Ashby, who had already distinguished himself in the 1 Platoon contact of 30 June/1 July, had again showed his mastery of the Bren gun in suppressing one of the Indonesian machine guns during this action, for which he was awarded the Military Medal.[97]

ANGLE IRON highlighted the gulf between the inferior training and poor shooting skills of the Indonesian police brigade, and the immediate and aggressive reaction of the New Zealanders, instilled by ongoing training and rehearsals. It was this preparation that enabled Thorpe's Company to fight its way out of what should have been a disaster.[98] Brown himself had no doubts. 'Everybody reacted exactly how we had drilled [in section and platoon tactics] on the football field. It was instinctive because it had been drilled in ... it's those opening few seconds of an engagement that are the most critical.'[99] Had the ambush been mounted by a more professional and experienced Indonesian Army battalion, such as those deployed opposite West Brigade, the New Zealanders would probably not have escaped so easily. It was becoming increasingly apparent that V (Mandau) BRIMOB Brigade did not have the tactical skills of their New Zealand opponents. It was not that they lacked courage, but rather that they reacted first as policemen, instead of producing an instinctive military response. Consequently, they were too often caught at a disadvantage. 'Fundamentally they were policemen and the mistakes they made in the field and the sometimes incomprehensible initiatives they took stemmed from this fact.' For example, if the New Zealanders wanted to close a cross-border track, they did so with a 'clandestine ambush in the military style'.[100] By contrast, the Indonesian police brigade was more likely to have uniformed men standing on the track demanding that Iban traders produce their 'passports'. The stationing of the police brigade in the border area reflected the policy of the Indonesian High Command to limit the quality of the troops available for cross-border operations, thus ensuring that the British forces were not spurred into anything more than an acceptable level of aggression in this 'undeclared war'.[101]

On 21 July, McKeon's D Company at Sungai Tenggang mounted Operation DUGGAN'S ACRE to reconnoitre the Indonesian camp at Igit, and in particular to establish if it possessed an anti-aircraft machine gun. After an exhausting ascent from the foot of the Klingkang Range to the border track, the company faced an equally gut-wrenching climb on the Kalimantan side on the way back. The target was nearly four miles inside Kalimantan, and each man carried a heavy load of essential equipment. By the 23rd, two reconnaissance patrols had located the small camp with its cluster of attap huts. McKeon went forward to an elevated jungle-covered bank which offered both an observation point overlooking the camp across the river, and a suitable ambush position. Up to 11 soldiers could be seen in the camp, and on a low ridge behind it there appeared to be a heavy machine gun. It was all too tempting. McKeon positioned three Bren-gun teams immediately opposite the camp's main building, in front of which was a jetty. Just before 5 p.m. a number of the garrison gathered in front of this building while another man bathed in the river. All seemed very casual and relaxed.

The mood was shattered as the Brens opened fire and the riflemen joined in, raking the camp buildings with intense rifle and automatic fire at floor and bed level for two minutes. The Indonesians in front of the building and the man bathing in the river were hit. The surprise was complete, and it was 30 minutes before the shaken garrison replied with their heavy anti-aircraft machine gun, mortars and automatics. DUGGAN'S ACRE was a highly successful contact, but in terms of the 'Golden Rules' McKeon had stretched the definition of an 'ambush' to its limit. However, as Fraser noted, the company had opened fire on an enemy position from a static ambush position, so 'the definition will just fit'.[102] McKeon's company had at last been rewarded for some very hard patrolling.

By the time the garrison returned fire, McKeon's company was long gone, pushing themselves back up onto the Klingkang Range in a heart-pounding slog to avoid any pursuers. When one man collapsed with heat exhaustion, a stretcher was quickly built to carry him the last 2,000 feet up to the ridge. McKeon's company had to be the fittest in the battalion, as every patrol that went out faced the same back-breaking climb in intense heat and humidity. McKeon did everything he could to lighten the fighting load of his patrols, firmly believing that this was a vital factor in such difficult terrain. 'Ammunition and operational equipment remains standard, but food and clothing were reduced to bare essentials. As a result LMG men and radio operators carried about three quarters their normal load, and no rifleman had more than two thirds his normal four day patrol weight.'[103] The problem inspired continual experimentation throughout Borneo, as much of the equipment had been designed for a European war and was unsuitable for South-East Asian conditions. One of the major lessons of the Borneo campaign, the need to lighten the soldier's load had first been appreciated on the Somme in 1916, and has been the subject of review and experimentation in every war since.[104]

The battalion's record was not unblemished. Operation CHARGE ROYAL, an ambush on the Jaong–Mengering track mounted by Straight's C Company, almost ended in disaster. The plan was complex, and some slack sentries let what they thought was a civilian party through the ambush. They turned out to be armed Indonesian soldiers, who surprised the five-man observation post on the far side. Had it not been for poor Indonesian shooting and a tardy response from nearby camps, C Company could have been in trouble. In the event, two or three Indonesians were shot and the company withdrew into Sarawak. Gurr was not happy, noting that 'there should have been more positive action taken by the main ambush group'.[105] Straight was the weak link in Gurr's otherwise strong team of subordinate commanders, and Gurr ensured that over-complicated ambush plans were 'never used again'.[106] Burrows' B Company mounted another ambush on the Lawan–Serit track for four days in early August without making any sightings. It was evident that V (Mandau) Brigade was now very wary of ambushes and mounted few if any patrols between its bases.

Concurrent with the CLARET operations across the border, intensive patrolling continued within Sarawak. On 9–10 August there was a contact involving Lieutenant Bill Grassick's 2 Platoon, A Company. Unknown to Thorpe, his company commander, Grassick decided after last light to shift his night ambush position and moved his patrol down a moonlit track through thick fern and secondary jungle. Grassick was in the lead when he heard a noise and halted the patrol. Lance-Corporal Hakaraia and the Bren gunner, Private Peni, moved up alongside him. Voices, very low and indistinct, could be heard well to their left. The silhouettes of men moving down the track towards them appeared. When Grassick's party opened fire, two figures 'pitched forward and fell'; a third was hit and disappeared behind a tree. The remainder ran back up the track, the last man falling as he went out of sight. Further movement was then heard from the area of the original noise. Grassick placed his platoon in ambush but nothing more was seen. Despite the success of the contact, Grassick incurred his company commander's displeasure for risking a move by night from one ambush position to another; the success was also tempered by the discovery that an Iban trader who had been co-opted as a guide had been killed. Under the rules of engagement, civilian casualties were to be avoided at all costs. While the circumstances of a night ambush made assuring this impossible, the death of an Iban with links to the local community meant that relationships had to be rebuilt.[107]

This was the fifth incident in this area since 21 June, including three successful ambushes. It seemed that the Indonesians in the Soepenok–Perumbang area were still prepared to contest control of the border.[108] Along this part of the border, the Indonesians had the advantages of higher ground and the fact that A Company patrols had to operate in areas 'open and exposed to view and yet difficult and noisy to move through'.[109] The critical factor became the respective patrolling and tactical skills, in which the New Zealanders were superior.

The growing tensions within Malaysia, which culminated in the unexpected ejection of Singapore from the Federation on 9 August, had no discernible impact on the 'undeclared war' in Borneo. Gurr was injured at this time. Lieutenant-Colonel Brian Poananga, who was to take over command of 1RNZIR in November, was visiting the battalion, and as Gurr recalled:

> I had taken him round all the bases except Jambu, and we got down on to the landing pad there just after a solid monsoonal deluge. As we were walking round the perimeter of the base with Major 'Buzz' Burrows, I slipped and ran a very sharp bamboo panji clean through my midriff. This clumsy piece of footwork on my part had two results. One was a quick two day visit to the military hospital in Kuching where they patched me up and very reluctantly allowed me to return to Simanggang; the second was a rumour that Brian was so keen to get on active operations, he saw his chance and impaled me on a panji.[110]

CLARET operations into Kalimantan continued. The Indonesians had noticeably reduced their border patrolling, so Gurr's companies went in to find out what they were doing. McKeon's D Company conducted Operation DIAMOND LINE, which ventured some three miles across the border to reconnoitre a camp at Pangkalan Semawan. On 26 August, Lieutenant George Kereama's 12 Platoon moved in to mount an ambush on a track north of the camp. Sergeant 'Windy' McGee, perhaps the outstanding scout and tracker of this period, was acting as lead scout when he saw seven Indonesian soldiers approaching. McGee and the Bren gunner, Private T. M. Ingatu, held their fire until the Indonesians were ten yards away, and then killed or wounded all but one of the patrol. When D Company went in again on 28 August it found that A Company 1130 Battalion V (Mandau) BRIMOB Brigade had retreated into its main base and no longer patrolled to the border in the Semawan area.[111] Captain Merv West, Thorpe's second-in-command, took A Company in on Operation ANGUS BULL to see if the camp at Bunut was still occupied; it was. An Indonesian early warning post fired on an A Company patrol, which inflicted casualties on the Indonesians before withdrawing.[112] The New Zealanders increasingly dominated the first three miles of Kalimantan territory, with only III Battalion—facing Lubok Antu—showing any willingness to keep contesting the border tracks.[113]

Between 30 August and 2 September, Straight's C Company mounted Operation CARLTON TRAIL, in which Lieutenant Brett Bestic's platoon established that the security of the Indonesian camp at Mawang was pretty slack.[114] It was a tempting target, and in late September C Company conducted Operation COLD COMFORT against it. At first light on the 26th, two C Company platoons positioned on the camp's perimeter opened up Bren, machine-gun, 2-inch mortar, 3.5-inch anti-tank rocket launcher and 81-mm mortar fire. For ten minutes every building was riddled with fire. The rocket launcher team destroyed two buildings, including the company headquarters, and three Indonesian soldiers setting up a machine gun also received a direct hit. There was 'much noise, confusion and anguish heard' as C Company withdrew without casualties, while the Indonesians responded with fruitless mortar and machine-gun fire.[115] By October the New Zealanders had to seek out targets as the Indonesians had all but abandoned their border posts. D Company mounted Operation DARK HORSE to set up ambushes on the tracks along the Ketungau River near Kerebau and destroy a launch that was reported to be beached in the area. No launch was found, nor was there any sign of recent Indonesian activity.[116]

Perhaps the most outstanding incident involving any New Zealander in this campaign occurred in early September. Captain John Masters, RNZA, who was posted to 1RNZIR but seconded to 29th (Corunna) Battery of 4 Light Regiment, Royal Artillery for service in Borneo was reported missing after a CLARET operation with 2nd/2 Gurkhas. Masters was the forward observation officer in an ambush with Captain Christopher Bullock's Support Company when it was attacked by an Indonesian group of equal size. During the firefight that followed, Masters went to the aid of a badly wounded Gurkha Company Sergeant-Major. As the company withdrew under fire, the two men became separated from the rest. Masters stayed with the CSM, dragging and carrying him through the jungle towards the border for most of that day. The next day he tried to carry on, but after two hours was completely exhausted. Leaving the CSM with a weapon, food and water bottles, Masters set off to get help, 'belting off as fast as I could on my compass bearing'.[117] At 4 p.m. Masters turned up like a ghost at one of the gun positions on the border, and within an hour he was leading the Gurkha company back for the wounded man. They found him alive at 4 p.m. the next day, 54 hours after he was wounded. A helicopter was sent in and the CSM was winched out; Masters then returned to the border with the company. Masters received an immediate operational award of the Military Cross for this act of selfless bravery.[118] The 2nd/2 Gurkhas made him an honorary life member of the regiment, the greatest honour that can be bestowed on someone outside the battalion. As their Commanding Officer, Lieutenant-Colonel Nick Neill, said at the time: 'We will none of us forget what he did.'[119]

The abortive coup in Indonesia on 30 September/1 October 1965, which was to be ruthlessly and bloodily put down by the Indonesian Army over the subsequent months, had no impact on the New Zealanders' operations.[120] With the tour almost at an end, their last forays into Kalimantan were being planned. Operations BENT FIST and ANVIL HEAD were the farewell visits of B and A Companies respectively: B Company engaged the enemy posts at Amal and Serit with 81-mm mortar fire, and A Company subjected Nangah Badau to mortar and machine-gun fire for 30 minutes. In each case, the enemy responded promptly with mortar and machine-gun fire, but by then the New Zealanders were on their way back across the border.[121]

After the attack on Nangah Badau, the Indonesians shifted this camp further back into Kalimantan. This indicated how effectively 1RNZIR now dominated the area between the border and the Indonesian bases. Each company was operating, almost with impunity, up to the very perimeters of the Indonesian camps. V (Mandau) BRIMOB Brigade had started its tour aggressively, but it lacked the tactical skills of the best regular Indonesian infantry battalions. In five months, 1RNZIR had conducted intensive patrolling within Sarawak, mounted 18 CLARET cross-border operations into Kalimantan, and had 17 firefights, only two of which were initiated by the Indonesians. These contacts resulted in at least 33 Indonesian casualties, and probably many more. Only one New Zealander had been wounded. Even in the two contacts initiated by the Indonesians, the tactical skills of the New Zealanders had allowed them to extricate themselves.[122] To mount such an intense pattern of operations at such minimal cost took more than luck, and was more than simply a reflection of their dominance over their opponent. It indicated the level of professionalism at which Gurr's battalion performed during its tour in Borneo.

1RNZIR was replaced by the 1st Battalion of the Malaysian Rangers. MV *Auby* took half the battalion back to Singapore, and the remainder flew from Kuching to Malacca in RAF C130 Hercules transport aircraft. Gurr's component of 1RNZIR returned to New Zealand in November 1965, and was replaced by that of Lieutenant-Colonel B. M. Poananga. Gurr's battalion had been the first to serve under the title 1RNZIR. Another first was that a large number of its members stayed on to serve in Poananga's battalion. The strict divisions between battalion groups that had hitherto been a feature of the New Zealand experience had ended. It became the norm to serve a tour of duty in Malaysia under two commanding officers, with the unifying link being the battalion itself: 1RNZIR.

When 1RNZIR returned to Terendak, no one knew that this would be the first and last time a New Zealand battalion would conduct battalion-scale operations in contact with an enemy in South-East Asia.[123] At the time, it was anticipated that New Zealand infantry would one day serve in Vietnam. Brian Poananga expected that a light battalion would be committed to Vietnam, with a skeleton organisation remaining in Terendak, and his battalion's tour in Borneo was seen as a valuable shakedown for such a tour. Poananga was not to have that satisfaction, as 1RNZIR had no contacts with the Indonesians during its second tour. His hopes for Vietnam were also to be frustrated, as individual infantry companies from 1RNZIR were to operate there under Australian battalion command.

Gurr's experience was therefore the only test of New Zealand skills and capabilities at battalion level against other than an insurgent enemy. It was an impressive performance, despite their opponents' relative lack of skill. It was achieved not simply through the efforts of Gurr, his company and platoon commanders, NCOs and soldiers. Rather, it resulted from an accumulation of experience that had begun in 1952 with the first attachments of individual New Zealanders to the 1st Battalion Fiji Infantry Regiment, had been built upon and refined by the New Zealand Special Air Service Squadron and the 1st and 2nd Battalions, New Zealand Regiment under Morrison, Aitken and Pearce, and culminated in Gurr's 1RNZIR. Limited in time, obscured by the restrictions of CLARET security, and overshadowed by the war in Vietnam, these five months represent the peak of tactical and command achievement by New Zealand battalions in South-East Asia.

> I don't have any doubt at all in my mind that the platoons, companies and ... staff that I had performed very well, and justified an assessment that I had made about two and a half years earlier that we had a very good cross-section of New Zealand soldiers, that they were as good [as] and certainly better trained than many of the fellows I had served with in the Second World War. The military potential and quality of the individual was there, and as long as he was given the opportunity to have the training, the equipment and the encouragement, then there was no better a soldier.[124]

## 1RNZIR in Borneo: The Second Tour, May to October 1966

In May 1966, Lieutenant-Colonel Brian Poananga deployed 1RNZIR to Borneo on its second tour. For both him and his battalion, it was to be a frustrating five months. While the New Zealanders worked hard and demonstrated both the initiative and the skills of their predecessors, they were unable to gain any measure of their performance through contacts with the Indonesian forces opposing them in Kalimantan.

Poananga had been told that 1RNZIR would do a six-month tour from May to October 1966 as part of West Brigade, commanded by Brigadier W. W. Cheyne, whose Headquarters 99 Gurkha Infantry Brigade was responsible for the First Division of Sarawak. 1RNZIR was one of five battalions in West Brigade, the others being 42 Commando Royal Marines, 4RAR, 2/7th Gurkha Rifles, and 1RNZIR's old rivals, 1/10th Gurkha Rifles.[125] 1RNZIR replaced the 1st Battalion Durham Light Infantry (1DLI) in the area immediately west of Gurr's section of Second Division. This area had seen intense Indonesian activity in the past, and Poananga wrote to his Chief of General Staff, Major-General Walter McKinnon, anticipating a busy time for his battalion. 'You no doubt know that the opposing team have fielded one of their better XV's in our area and they have shown no reluctance to get on with the game so we are looking forward to the start of the first half.' He noted that the battalion 1RNZIR was replacing had had one man killed and five wounded in a recent action with the Indonesians.[126]

Brian Matauru Poananga was the first Maori officer to command a Regular New Zealand battalion, and his distinguished military career would culminate in his being the first Maori Chief of General Staff of the New Zealand Army from 1978 to 1981. Poananga had been one of the first New Zealand officers to graduate from the Royal Military College, Duntroon, after the Second World War. He saw operational service with a rifle company in 3RAR, on the Commonwealth Division staff in Korea, and as a company commander in Aitken's 2 NZ Regiment in Malaya. A reserved man, Poananga lacked the outward flourish of Pearce and Gurr, but he knew what he wanted, and subordinates who did not perform to his standards got short shrift. He was supported by an experienced group of company commanders, including Major Brian Worsnop (B Company), who had commanded the First New Zealand SAS Detachment in Borneo the previous year; Major John Mace (C Company), who had served as a troop commander with the original New Zealand SAS Squadron in Malaya, and had more recently commanded the 1 Ranger (SAS) Squadron in Papakura; and Major Roy Taylor (D Company), who had seen active service in Malaya with Morrison's 1 NZ Regiment. This range of experience was mirrored in the NCOs. For many of the soldiers this was their first tour to Malaysia, but they joined those remaining from Gurr's battalion who had already served in Borneo and had yet to complete their two years in theatre. Major Ian Thorpe also stayed on for six months to help the battalion train for service in Borneo.[127]

Poananga set about welding this talent into a team in the first months of 1966. He did so with Vietnam as the long-term goal, confident that 'by the time we go to BORNEO we will be in reasonable shape for that type of operation, which places less strain on the machine than does limited war and we will only reach this standard because of the quite extraordinary effort made by my staff and key chaps'. Poananga was well aware that, unlike Gurr, he did not have the luxury of 18 months' training and operational experience before going to Borneo. From the time his battalion arrived in Terendak, his goal was to get ready for the tour and the pressure was on. Despite concern that 'we may have pushed too hard', he described his battalion as being 'in first class order and looking forward to their tour of duty in BORNEO even if this enthusiasm is not shared by their families'.[128]

Poananga went to Borneo in March, visiting each of the 1DLI company bases. The battalion's headquarters was at Balai Ringin, 'a piece of bare flat ground beside the road to SIMANGGANG. The location has no tactical significance and is, I understand, ... where it is because the local police set up a road block on the site in the very early days of the emergency.' Poananga too would have his headquarters here, as well as Headquarters Company, some elements of Support Company, and C Company under Mace. The latter he intended 'to employ as a reserve to control the large unpopulated areas of our sector and on more exciting tasks as opportunities offer'.[129] Also located in Balai Ringin were the Headquarters of 7 Commando Battery and a single 105-mm howitzer providing artillery support, 'plus the usual collection of trackers and police field force'.[130]

Cheyne directed Poananga to 'keep your battalion area clear of the enemy'. One rifle company was to remain available to be the Brigade Reserve.

> You will do all you can to win and retain the goodwill and trust of the civilian population amongst whom you will be operating. Without this you will be operating in the dark. Every man in your Battalion must realise the operational necessity for doing all in his power to win the liking and respect of the civilians. Friendliness, helpfulness and first class soldierly bearing and discipline is required of the individual. Protection of them from enemy interference and assistance to them in an emergency is required of the Battalion as a whole.[131]

1DLI had only three infantry companies and two forward company bases, at Gunan Gajak and Plaman Mapu. Poananga decided to position two companies at Gunan Gajak. A Company, under Major Neil Schofield, the least experienced of his company commanders, would command the base and provide administrative support, giving Worsnop's B Company the freedom to mount operations. Taylor's D Company was to occupy Plaman Mapu, reinforced by an additional platoon made up primarily of members of Support Company's Anti-Tank Platoon. Two guns of 7 Commando Battery provided fire support at Gunan Gajak, and there was a single gun at Plaman Mapu.[132]

The companies were deployed from Terendak, and on 25 May 1RNZIR took over command of the battalion area from 1DLI. One incidental consequence was that it became the first unit in the New Zealand Army to adopt the stable belt as a dress distinction. This came about in an indirect manner. The battalion's second-in-command, Major Lin Smith, and the Intelligence Officer, Mike Woodard, were the first to join 1DLI, on 6 May. The fact that

Smith was a gunner and Woodard an Armoured Corps officer aroused some comment on the flexibility of the New Zealand Army's postings. When it was revealed that Smith had originally been commissioned in the Canterbury Regiment, which was allied to the Durham Light Infantry, the Commanding Officer 1DLI, Lieutenant-Colonel G. J. Maughan, presented him with a DLI stable belt to reinforce his infantry status. When Poananga arrived at Balai Ringin he took a liking to the belt, and it was decided that 1RNZIR would wear it. Unfortunately the belt available was too small for Poananga, so the RSM, WO1 Bill Morgan, wore it until a second belt was acquired. They alone wore this belt for the remainder of the tour, but now it is worn by all members of the Royal New Zealand Infantry Regiment.[133] It was a fitting gesture to mark the association between 1DLI, the successor to the 57th Regiment that had served in the New Zealand Wars, and 1RNZIR, which was made up of descendants of men who had fought on both sides.

In Borneo the battalion numbered about 650, which with attachments from outside the battalion grew to some 740 personnel. The forward companies were reorganised into two groups, each the size of five platoons. The A/B Company Group at Gunan Gajak numbered approximately 200, while the D Company Group was split between two locations, with 190 men in the main company base at Plaman Mapu and 50 in a platoon base at Pang Amo.[134] Poananga's headquarters at Balai Ringin numbered some 300 personnel, including his Headquarters Company, elements of Support Company, and Mace's C Company as battalion reserve. The company bases were similar to those that had been occupied by 1RNZIR the previous year. Major Roy Taylor recalled that at Plaman Mapu:

> There was a local Kampong at the bottom of the hill and we were perched on top of the hill ... and bristled like a hedgehog. It was a lone peak and an obvious company base. It was designed as a place to live and communicate, and a base for patrols to go out and protect the locals and to conduct cross-border operations. If anyone wanted to attack you they had to come up through four layers of barbed wire all with lights. There were airfield landing flares all backed onto corrugated iron so they reflected downwards so everyone back up the hill was in shadow, and anything coming up the hill was ablaze in light.[135]

Each base had to be capable of being defended by one-third of its garrison while the remainder were out patrolling. Poananga organised his defences to suit the 30 miles of jungle-clad frontier for which 1RNZIR was now responsible.

A female Chinese labourer at work near a Bristol Freighter of No. 41 Squadron, Changi, 1964.
*RNZAF Museum, DPR 5361*

A New Zealand soldier watches a Bristol Freighter of No. 41 Squadron dropping ammunition supplies, Borneo, 1965.
*RNZAF Museum, SEA PR.AF 227/5/4*

Aircrews of No. 14 Squadron at a briefing in Malaya, 1964.
*RNZAF Museum, DPR 5291*

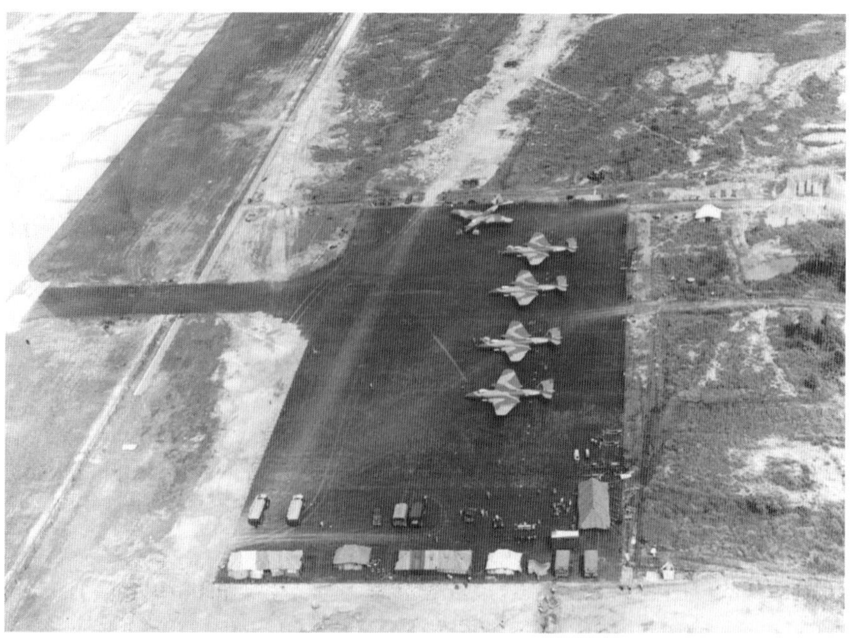

No. 14 Squadron Canberras in the dispersal area at Labuan, 1964.
*RNZAF Museum, DPR 5325*

Servicing a Canberra at Tengah, December 1964.
*RNZAF Museum, 14G34*

HMNZS *Otago* fires a gun salute to the flag of the Commander-in-Chief Far East Fleet on joining the Commonwealth Strategic Reserve in October 1964.
*Naval Museum, AAU 0569*

Members of *Otago*'s boarding party relax in mid-1966. Among this group enjoying the guitar playing of Neil Vercoe are Petty Officer Jim Lott (standing) and E. V. Newland (tattoo on upper arm).
*Naval Museum, AAU 0579*

An Indonesian trading vessel intercepted off Sabah by *Otago* in mid-1966 is searched for infiltrators.
*Naval Museum, AAU 0570*

RFA *Tidespring* refuels *Otago* and HMS *Eagle* in 1965.
*Naval Museum, AAU 0218*

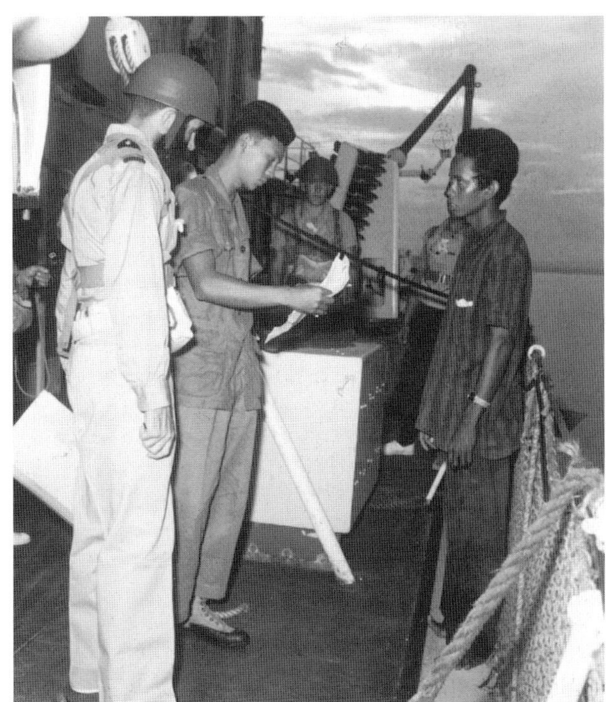

Lieutenant B. Commons oversees the checking of papers on *Otago*.
*Naval Museum, AAU 0572*

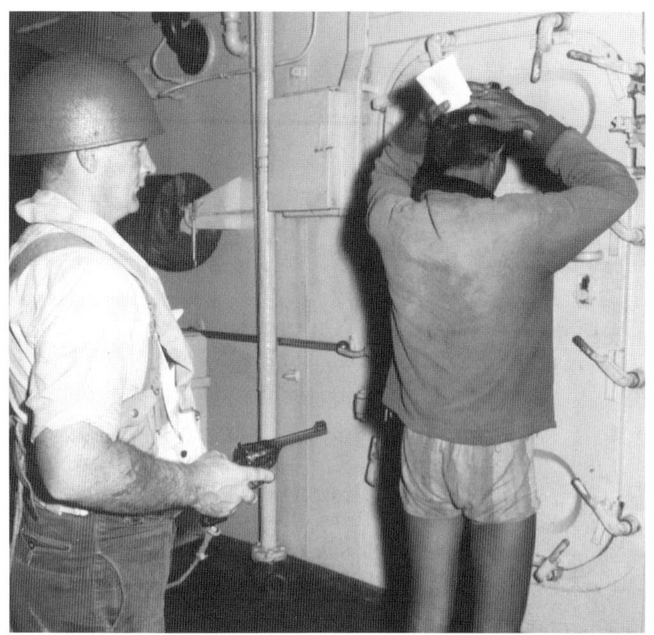

An Indonesian trader under guard on *Otago*.
*Naval Museum, AAU 0574*

An *Otago* seaman guards a group of traders.
*Naval Museum, AAU 0578*

HMNZS *Santon*, with kiwi insignia on its funnel.
*Naval Museum, ACY 0051*

Left to right: Petty Officer Electrician A. Wistrand, Petty Officer Seaman T. Bruce, Chief Engine Room Artificer A. Miller, Able Seaman Follitt-Powell and Leading Seaman M. Prouse pose with *Santon*'s forward 40 mm Bofor gun in 1965 or 1966.
*Naval Museum, AAU 0054*

One of the New Zealand minesweepers prepares to interrogate the crews of two small Indonesian trading vessels it has intercepted.
*Naval Museum, ACY 0041*

*Hickleton* steams upriver towards Kuching in June 1966.
*Naval Museum, ACY 0025*

Leading Seaman R. Wakefield prepares for action on *Hickleton*, 1966.
*Naval Museum, ACY 0019*

Able Seaman M. Liddell and 'Hickleberry Hound' on *Hickleton*, October 1965.
*Naval Museum, ACY 0016*

New Zealand SAS personnel in Borneo in 1965: Dick Smith, Pete Rutledge, and Kingi Ihaka.
*NZ SAS Museum*

An SAS camp area.
*NZ SAS Museum*

SAS troops on river patrol in Borneo.
*NZ SAS Museum*

SAS troops check their equipment.
*NZ SAS Museum*

Smoko break during a patrol.
*NZ SAS Museum*

Soldiers of Support Company wait to board MV *Auby* at Port Dickson, near Terendak, for the voyage to Sarawak in 1965.
*Chamberlain collection*

A 1RNZIR dog handler and an Iban tracker, near Simanggang, 1965.
*Chamberlain collection*

A Bren gunner from the Reconnaissance Platoon on patrol in bamboo in Sarawak.
*Chamberlain collection*

Off duty at a border observation post.
*QEII Army Memorial Museum*

Balai Ringin camp in 1966. The building in the foreground is the Battalion Headquarters.
*Chamberlain collection*

A and B Company base, Gunan Gajak, 1966.
*Chamberlain collection*

D Company's base at Plaman Mapu in 1966. The hilltop site was augmented by the clearance of vegetation and the construction of bunkers and barbed wire fences to make the base difficult to assault. The funnel-shaped device in the foreground is a urinal.
*Chamberlain collection*

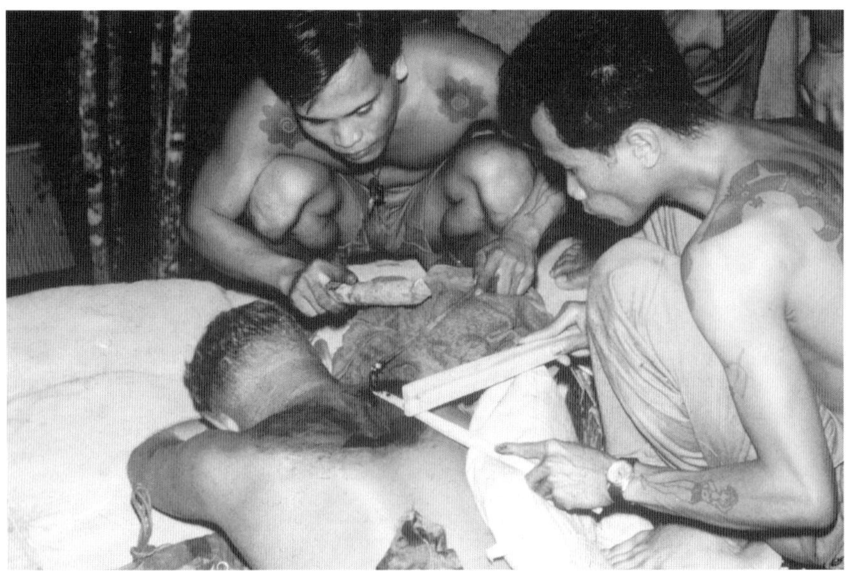

A 1RNZIR soldier is tattooed by Ibans using rudimentary equipment at a company base in Sarawak. The practice was stopped after several soldiers were unable to carry packs until their wounds healed.
*Chamberlain collection*

1RNZIR built this basketball court at the Balai Ringin school. They are playing a match against a local team just before the battalion's departure in September 1966.
*Chamberlain collection*

While this was a smaller area than Gurr's unit had covered it was still demanding, ranging from steep mountainous country near the Kalimantan border to more gently rolling land further inside Sarawak. All three forward bases received supplies solely from the air. There were drops every three days to Gunan Gajak and Plaman Mapu; the platoon at Pang Amo was supplied by helicopter from Plaman Mapu. Day-to-day helicopter support was provided by a solitary Whirlwind Mark X with two pilots, one crewman, and four ground crew, who were based with battalion headquarters at Balai Ringin.[136] Poananga was keen to experiment with the offensive use of troop-carrying helicopters, and with the co-operation of Steve Davies, the Air Liaison Officer at Balai Ringin, 1RNZIR made the maximum possible use of the limited resources available.[137]

During the first half of 1966, the Indonesians initiated a series of minor skirmishes along the whole border. Once the post-coup chaos settled down and the communists in Sumatra and Java were bloodily suppressed, the incursions increased.[138] Once the Bangkok peace talks began in early June, it was thought there would be no further overt action.[139] This proved not to be the case when the RPKAD mounted the MANJAR Operation, an incursion into First Division by two 15-strong groups. During a series of contacts by West Brigade units, 4RAR killed four Indonesians and wounded one on 15 June.[140] This was followed by a succession of contacts in which the infiltrators were either eliminated or withdrew into Kalimantan. In late July an Indonesian party of some 50 regulars and irregulars, led by Lieutenant Sumbi, moved towards Brunei Bay. By early September, after a prolonged hunt, all the party had surrendered or been captured, or were accounted for by local tribespeople. This was the last major operation in which British troops took part before their withdrawal was completed on 1 November. In early August, another mixed regular/irregular group attempted to reach the Brunei Bay area; it was contacted shortly after crossing the border and withdrew.[141]

Frustratingly for the New Zealanders, none of this action took place in their area. Although two battalions were known to be facing them across the border, the threat of a major incursion was declining rapidly. On 17 June all brigade units were ordered to cease artillery and mortar fire on or near the border unless it was needed to protect a patrol or base. A formal ceasefire between Indonesia and Malaysia seemed likely, but it was impossible to know when this would occur. Although Indonesian regular forces were unlikely to mount offensive operations, it seemed increasingly likely that small bands of Clandestine Communist Organisation and other dissaffected Sarawak elements would attempt to cross the border and establish contact with dissident groups among the Chinese population in the major centres.

This changing scenario led Poananga to alter the priorities of his patrols. 'Irregular groups passing through our area will be of much more use to us alive. Patrol commanders should therefore be briefed to capture rather than kill infiltrators, subject to the very clear proviso that if an attempt to capture hazards the lives of the Security Forces, fire will be opened in accordance with our rules of engagement.'[142] The insurgents would have to traverse 1RNZIR's area to get to the centres of population. Poananga wanted to let them come in rather than block their entry on the border, because

> Even with all our forces forward on the border there will be an infinite number of gaps. Further, if we do block an attempt at any particular point [the infiltrators] will be able to withdraw quickly and then infiltrate somewhere else. What we need therefore is depth to define his movement and provide a reasonable chance of effective follow up and reserve to do this. We must also clear all areas which could provide suitable places for the build up of enemy pockets.[143]

To give his battalion both time to react and enough space to locate and destroy any infiltration, Poananga established a screen, based on his border scouts, between the two forward company bases and the border. Behind this screen, platoons from the company bases patrolled in depth. Behind them was the C Company reserve at Balai Ringin. 1RNZIR also mounted a series of company operations to clear the likely enemy build-up areas.[144] The first (and as it turned out only) incident was unfortunate: a patrol sentry fired at and killed an armed uniformed man approaching him, who was later identified as a border scout.

Poananga had taken to heart Cheyne's directive to 'win and retain the goodwill and trust of the civilian population'.[145] As 1RNZIR got to know the area and gained the confidence of Special Branch and the border scouts, Poananga refined his surveillance plan. The border scouts remained his forward eyes and ears, but the areas behind them were covered by a network of small parties from the Battalion Reconnaissance Platoon, each with an Intelligence NCO attached. These were located in longhouses and kampongs on the most likely incursion routes, and were outstations on the Battalion Command radio net. Each rifle company had a platoon ready to respond to any reported sighting at two hours' notice.

On 1 July 'durbars' (meetings) of all the headmen and border scouts in the battalion area were held in turn at Gunan Gajak, Plaman Mapu and Pang Amo. Accompanied by Captain J. Welsh RA, the Border Scout Officer, and his interpreter, Poananga told the headmen that the Indonesian attempts to win Sarawak had been defeated and that the threat was now from 'dissatisfied local elements who are trying to overthrow the country from within. These are mainly Chinese who have been or are still across in Indonesia and at present trying to come back.' He sought the tribes' assistance in reporting any movement, and assured them that his battalion did not wish to interfere with their way of life and wanted to help them as much as possible. He acknowledged that his battalion had made mistakes and apologised for the fact that local tribesmen had been searched by New Zealand soldiers. His men had been 'over-zealous', and he had issued instructions to prevent this happening again. 'I want you to be assured that we trust you implicitly and I want you to trust us ... if we offend against your customs it will be because we are ignorant of them and I would be very grateful if you will help us to learn your customs. To this end I am sending some of my soldiers to live among you so that they can learn them better.'[146]

A four- or five-man patrol was positioned in each longhouse. Each was briefed in detail on the 'dos and don'ts' of longhouse life—from eating and accepting everything offered with the right hand to not staring at the bare breasts of the women, but rather 'treating them as an everyday occurrence'—and given advice on health and hygiene. The soldiers took guitars and in one case an accordion, and were told to participate in both work and play. 'It was a different culture and in the longhouse everything was communal on the front part of the longhouse and it was private for families behind each door. The size of the longhouse was known by how many doors it had. If you had a 10-door longhouse it wasn't very big. If you had a 50-door longhouse it was a large village.' Those fortunate enough to be in one of the longhouse groups glimpsed a totally different way of life.

> You would look up into the rafters and you'd see smoked heads ... One place where I went we were told that the heads there were Indonesians that had come across ... I was asked how Miss Victoria was, by one of the old men. He hadn't realised that she had died probably before he was born, but there was a photograph of Queen Victoria in that longhouse and that was the only royal photograph that was there, and so Miss Victoria was still alive.[147]

Daily medical clinics for the local people were held in the bases, and patrols in the kampongs gave first aid where practicable as well as advising on hygiene and animal husbandry. Corporal Neil Webb, who had served two years with Gurr and stayed on with Poananga, remembered the fascination of the longhouse environment: 'living as they do, eating as far as possible what they were eating, helping in the fields, and going bat hunting with them because bats were a great delicacy with them, and you would have to go out at night and catch these things in the huge caves that were there ... they were pretty good times'.[148] More tangible assistance was also given. The Battalion Assault Pioneers constructed a dam at Pa'on Gahat, a 33-door border kampong of Land Dyaks in the Serian District, which was a four-hour walk from the Serian–Simanggang road and not accessible by river in the dry season. Necessary material was flown in by four Belvedere helicopter lifts, and the work was completed in two weeks.[149] The extent of Poananga's 'Hearts and Minds' campaign fascinated Cheyne, who after a briefing by the duty officer 'shook his head and said, "Look, I've had 28 battalions under my command since I have been here, and I have never seen anything like this. Absolutely brilliant."'[150] So it was, but it also reflected the changing nature of operations—the likelihood of a major incursion was now slight. Perhaps this level of interaction was only possible because of the unique racial mix of the New Zealand battalion, who 'could do it because of the type of people that we were'.[151] A similar approach by a British or Australian battalion might not have worked.

In mid-July the Sarawak government made a surrender offer to anti-government elements which was to remain open for three months. The battalion conducted Operation HARAPAN, the distribution of leaflets describing the offer to all houses, kampongs and tracks within its area. Normal operations and defensive patrols continued. The forward companies still mounted surveillance and ambush patrols behind the border scouts' screen, and a series of operations cleared areas likely to be used by resistance groups. In July intelligence suggested that an Indonesian incursion was imminent; the battalion lived in hope, but nothing happened. There was Indonesian mortar and artillery fire on the border, but no ground action. Planning started for a CLARET operation involving Roy Taylor's D Company, but this stopped when Malaysia and Indonesia signed the Bangkok Agreement on 11 August.[152]

By 2 August Pang Amo had been demolished and evacuated, leaving the two forward company-group bases. Both soldiers and commanders found it hard to maintain their motivation 'when you had lost your rationale for being there'.[153] Light relief was provided by the visits of the Combined Services Entertainment Show and by meetings of the 'Balai Ringin Turf Club'. Soldiers were kept in touch with battalion gossip and New Zealand news through the battalion newspaper, *Morning Glory*. The 'Stop Press Column' featured daily incidents in the lives of the people of 'Zagreb', which was 'any town your memory takes you to. No more, no less.'[154]

With the signing of the Bangkok Agreement in Jakarta on 11 August 1966, Confrontation formally ended. Next day Major-General Dato Ibrahim became Director of Operations East Malaysia, and Major-General Lea, the former Director of Borneo Operations, became Commander, British Forces Borneo, under Ibrahim's operational direction. Headquarters West Brigade reverted to the title of Headquarters 99 Brigade, in anticipation of Malaysian forces assuming responsibility for operations in East Malaysia. It was now a local show; the Malaysians were keen to call the shots and see the Commonwealth forces leave Sarawak and Sabah as quickly as possible.[155] On 12 August, Headquarters 99 Brigade informed 1RNZIR that surveillance patrolling would continue on a limited basis. On the same day, 7 [Sphinx] Commando Light Battery RA, which had supported the battalion, ceased to be operational. The RAF Helicopter Detachment was withdrawn to Kuching, but continued to provide support to the battalion for the rest of August.[156]

The 'Interregnum' period until the Malaysian forces assumed command on 20 August was marked by daily changes in operational policy which led the New Zealanders to entitle that section of the battalion's August report 'The Grand Old Duke of York'. Company operations were planned, cancelled, reinstated, and cancelled again. There was a sense almost of desperation in the desire to contact the enemy before the battalion withdrew. They were hunting for 'will o' the wisps'. On 22 August the battalion, responding to sighting reports, placed an ambush on the border tracks north of Kampong Pa'on Gahat. When the ambush patrol sighted a possible enemy next morning, C Company, with elements of A/B Company, was deployed into the area. A six-platoon-strong cordon from Battalion Headquarters and Headquarters Company was inserted that night, and an intensive follow-up included the use of helicopters. Intensive searching found no one, and C Company was withdrawn on 25 August.

As arrangements for 8RMR to relieve 1RNZIR began, D Company prepared to return to Terendak. The men were kept busy with individual skills training, including rifleman, mortar handler, first aid, driver training, and junior NCO courses. Soldiers were sent on leave to Kuching, while all married personnel were rostered on duty to Terendak and their families for a week during their Borneo tour. As plans changed, there was constant pressure from the Malaysian forces to occupy areas well before the dates that had been given. Poananga's frustration shows in his reports. 'By their insistence on taking control of areas early the Malays did nothing to help implementation of the Commanding Officer's policy that they would be given every assistance.'[157]

As the base at Plaman Mapu was progressively demolished, the local people made good use of recycled corrugated iron, rough-sawn timber, spare clothing and jerry cans. On 1 September it was closed and D Company pulled out to Balai Ringin by helicopter. The next day they moved by road to Kuching, where they embarked for Singapore and Terendak. C Company left Balai Ringin on the 9th. A and B Companies withdrew from Gunan Gajak that day and the next, and at noon on the 10th the base was handed over to C Company 8RMR. By 11 September what remained of 1RNZIR in Borneo was concentrated at Balai Ringin. 'It was over-crowded. Bloody terrible. There were fights. Just straight-out boredom. As we said to each other, how did those poor guys get on in the Second World War? At least we were getting meals and they put movies on for us ... We were allowed to have two cans of beer a day ... It was bad, but as I say, Jesus we were lucky.'[158]

On 10 September, 1RNZIR received the last supply drop to the Commonwealth Forces in Borneo. Appropriately enough, it was delivered by Bristol Freighters of No. 41 Squadron RNZAF. With the supply drop came a 'Proclamation of Praise and Good-Wishes' to the 'Underprivileged Kiwis, Balai Ringin, Sarawak'. This read: 'This is officially our last drop in Borneo today and the last British aircraft to be detached in Kuching. Supply dropping aircraft that is. We are led to believe also that you are one of the last regiments to withdraw from this happy mosquito infested paradise, with the thought of where to next. On this momentous occasion good luck for the future and Kia Ora.'[159] At one minute after midnight on 10 September 1966, operational control passed to 8RMR, and 1RNZIR operations in Borneo ceased.

It had been a frustrating second tour for 1RNZIR. Poananga faced a very different situation from the one Gurr had encountered. In many ways, Poananga's response was broader than his predecessor's had been. Poananga demonstrated that he was a 'big picture' man, always thinking in battalion terms and looking for a battalion response to the tactical situation confronting him. His planning and tactics to deal with infiltration through his area showed him to be a lateral thinker who sought and applied answers outside the conventional framework. Cheyne, his brigade commander, recognised this strength in Poananga and thought his tactical response was 'brilliant' in the circumstances. Yet those circumstances also dictated that Poananga's battalion was never submitted to the acid test of combat.

Nonetheless, the New Zealanders of all three services had played a small but significant role in a unique campaign. In thanking all who had been involved, the Commander-in-Chief Far East, Air Chief Marshal John Grandy, observed that the campaign had been one of containment and non-escalation. Individuals' contributions had been characterised by 'fortitude, firmness and restraint', qualities which 'cannot be upheld in the field without discipline, complete interservice understanding and professional skills of the highest order'.[160] This was a fitting comment on the performance of the New Zealand armed forces during Confrontation.

## After Borneo, Vietnam

On 1 October 1966 1RNZIR left Balai Ringin, returning to West Malaysia on the faithful MV *Auby*. By the 7th the entire battalion was in Terendak. At a battalion parade, Lieutenant-Colonel Poananga publicly praised his troops for their performance in Borneo. Three days later he left for Vietnam to spend a fortnight visiting headquarters and units and being briefed on United States and Australian operations.[161] South Vietnam, which had been the focus for operational training since 1961, was the most likely next commitment for the battalion. Both Poananga and his second-in-command, Lin Smith, had anticipated this. 'We were aware from the time we arrived in Terendak that infantry would be going to Vietnam and we worked on a plan to get a "light battalion" into the Task Force in South Vietnam [while still] leaving enough in Terendak to placate the British and Malaysians.'[162]

New Zealand had committed a RNZE team to civic action tasks in South Vietnam in May 1964. In June 1965, Holyoake's government had taken the major step of committing combat forces by deploying 161 Battery, 16 Field Regiment RNZA to Bien Hoa in the III Military Region, in support of the First Battalion Royal Australian Regiment as part of 173 Airborne Brigade. The New Zealand battery became part of the 1st Australian Task Force based at Nui Dat in Phuoc Tuy province in 1966. An infantry commitment was the next logical escalation. This was made, but not in the form that Poananga and Smith hoped for.

Holyoake always recognised that New Zealand's military commitments were of little military significance in the context of the total commitment by the Commonwealth against Confrontation in Borneo or by the United States and its allies to South Vietnam. What was important for New Zealand was getting the maximum political and diplomatic value from the timing and nature of each commitment. With the traditional parsimony of National governments, additional resources were approved only when pressure from major partners became too great to resist. This had been Holland's approach to the initial commitment of an SAS squadron to the Commonwealth Strategic Reserve in 1955, and it was continued by Holyoake in his government's commitments to South Vietnam in 1964 and Borneo in 1965.

New Zealand's military opposition to Confrontation in Borneo was even more reluctant than its commitment to South Vietnam.[163] In 1965, New Zealand's defence priorities were the Commonwealth Strategic Reserve for SEATO contingency planning, followed by support for United States operations in Vietnam; Borneo was a distant third, a distraction that eventually had to be undertaken. Supporting the United States in Vietnam was more important than getting bogged down in what was clearly a British and Malaysian undertaking in Borneo. 1RNZIR's two five-month tours in 1965 and 1966 were timed to fit in with 1RNZIR's half-battalion changeovers every 12 months, and to ensure that 28th Commonwealth Brigade included at least one Australian or New Zealand battalion at all times. If there was a SEATO contingency that involved the deployment of 28th Commonwealth Brigade, it could not be made up entirely of British battalions.[164]

This focus changed after Confrontation ended.[165] A 'steady decline' in British military commitments east of Suez had been evident since the mid-1950s, and the financial burden imposed by Confrontation accelerated the British decision to withdraw. That decision was confirmed when Denis Healey, the British Secretary of State for Defence, visited Malaysia and Singapore in April 1967, and revealed that Britain intended to withdraw its forces east of Suez by the mid-1970s.[166] This shocked Holyoake, who had not expected the disengagement to be so sudden, or on such a scale. Despite intense New Zealand and Australian diplomacy, Britain's intentions did not change; indeed, a financial crisis in late 1967 saw the timing advanced, and all forces except those in Hong Kong were withdrawn by 1971.[167]

The British stance confirmed New Zealand's belief that its defence efforts should now focus on supporting the United States in South Vietnam. V (or

Victor) Company, an amalgam of Poananga's C and D Companies commanded by Major John Mace, was committed to South Vietnam in May 1967, and followed by W Company in December.[168] Initially part of separate Australian battalions, they were then grouped together in an Australian ANZAC Battalion, and together with a New Zealand SAS troop served in the 1st Australian Task Force. Army Air Corps and RNZAF helicopter pilots, RNZAF forward air controllers, and a 16-strong Services medical team, were also committed to South Vietnam.[169] The number of personnel peaked at 543 in November 1968, with inevitable consequences for New Zealand's obligations to the Commonwealth Strategic Reserve.[170] What was already available was simply stretched a little further, and redistributed to reflect the change in New Zealand's defence priorities.

In practice, New Zealand could neither effectively discharge its commitments to the Commonwealth Strategic Reserve, nor make a viable independent contribution in South Vietnam, where its presence was always dependent on the greater Australian effort. The infantry, artillery, SAS, medical and logistic attachments were never viable in themselves, but additions to the existing Australian commitment. They were proof that New Zealand was in Vietnam, but their presence caused administrative and command difficulties for both countries. The skills and professionalism displayed by the New Zealand units could not disguise the fact that their being there, rather than what they did, was their primary purpose. In terms of national identity and command, New Zealand's military commitment to South Vietnam abrogated everything the New Zealand Chiefs of Staff had striven for since the formation of the New Zealand Division in 1916. Its minor role, with no formed independent New Zealand units, was a foretaste of the pattern of New Zealand defence deployments for the rest of the twentieth century.

New Zealand's presence in peacekeeping operations has been a matter of filling individual appointments or attaching small elements to composite or other nations' units within a multinational force. This was the case with the commitments to Cambodia, Somalia and Bosnia-Herzegovina in the 1990s. The one exception has been Bougainville, but even there, New Zealand's leading role in establishing an initial presence was then surrendered to Australia. Finite resources impose realistic limitations. However, New Zealand has gained considerable recognition from such commitments. Its profile in peacekeeping operations belies its size and the scale of its defence forces; but this level of activity also disguises the reality of New Zealand's limited resources in both manpower and equipment, which are becoming less and less able to operate in situations of limited or major conflict. Doing much with little was a consistent theme of New Zealand's commitment to South-East Asia; it still applied at the end of the century in the commitment to peacekeeping operations, and will remain a constant in the years ahead. In hindsight, the miserly commitment of defence assets by Holland and Holyoake during the Cold War shaped New Zealand's approach to playing a meaningful role on the world stage into the next century.

The end of Confrontation and the shift in focus to Vietnam had significant implications for New Zealand's presence in Malaysia and Singapore. In 1965 New Zealand hastened to assure Malaysia that its initial commitment of 161 Battery to South Vietnam did not 'imply any weakening in our main military effort which would be continued to be directed towards the defence of Malaysia'.[171] The Malaysian government also had concerns about the staging of elements of V Force through Singapore en route to Vietnam.[172] This became an issue once the decision was made to commit a rifle company from 1RNZIR in Terendak to South Vietnam in 1967. 'We realise that to use the battalion at Terendak as the parent unit for a force engaged in operations in Vietnam could present certain difficulties for the Malaysians, but we would hope that the withdrawal of the company from the Commonwealth Strategic Reserve on departure from Malaysia would help them to feel absolved of responsibility.'[173] This did cause the Malaysians some qualms. The Deputy Prime Minister, Tun Abdul Razak, told the New Zealand High Commissioner that he could see 'great political difficulties for the Malaysian Government if it came out that each company, after fighting in Vietnam, would return to Malaysia'.[174] As it turned out, the Malaysian press showed little interest in the matter. Despite some muted opposition in Parliament and among government officials, Malaysia accepted the New Zealand and Australian reliance on facilities in Malaysia as a staging platform for their military operations in Vietnam, including the air support provided by No. 41 Squadron RNZAF from Changi.[175] The Singapore government was also concerned about New Zealand using Changi as a staging base in moving the rifle company to Vietnam. While Lee Kuan Yew agreed to its use, he was aware of the implication that 'we become a cog in the Vietnam machine'. Should circumstances change, his approval might have to be reconsidered.[176]

The New Zealand government assured the British authorities that there had been no weakening of its commitment to the Commonwealth Strategic Reserve, arguing that 'common objectives in South-East Asia would be better served if a company were temporarily detached from the Reserve and made available for service in what has now become an active operational theatre'. New Zealand's position was that while this would mean a temporary reduction in 1RNZIR's fighting strength, the battalion 'will also gain in operational efficiency through combat experience in Vietnam'.[177] The Commander-in-Chief Far East, General Sir Michael Carver, appreciated the reasons for New Zealand's decision. He believed there was no room for objection by the British military authorities because the Australian and New Zealand battalions had been deployed to Borneo from the Commonwealth Strategic Reserve during Confrontation.[178] Despite this, New Zealand's official approach to the British government over its decision was treated with a 'rather chilly formality' that was very different from the 'almost enthusiastic response' of the British military authorities in Singapore.[179]

The real impact of the decision on 1RNZIR and on its effectiveness within 28 Commonwealth Brigade was soon appreciated. Two of the battalion's four rifle companies had to be pooled to bring V Company and its supporting elements up to their strength of 182 in May 1967.[180] The commitment of W Company in December took another 150 men from the battalion, and meant that almost all its efforts were directed towards training and providing infantry reinforcements for South Vietnam. It was no longer an effective battalion, but rather a training depot. From mid-1967, the battalion's role in the Commonwealth Strategic Reserve had become a secondary if not somewhat academic consideration; it was to remain so until the Reserve was dissolved.

In April 1967, Tun Abdul Razak had discussions with New Zealand's Prime Minister and Cabinet in Wellington. Holyoake reaffirmed his government's intention

> to continue contributing New Zealand forces to the Commonwealth Strategic Reserve as long as the Malaysian Government wished it to do so. In our view the Reserve as well as providing an assurance to Malaysia played an essential role in the defence of the wider South East Asian area. What New Zealand itself could do ... was limited by the size of its resources. Australia and New Zealand together ... could not perform the military role which Britain had until now performed.[181]

Yet despite the rundown of British forces, both Australia and New Zealand resolved to remain in Malaysia/Singapore until at least the end of 1971.[182]

Australia's reluctance to commit itself to the cost of maintaining Terendak Camp saw 1RNZIR and an Australian battalion move to Singapore in 1970;

both governments committed themselves to keeping elements of all three services there beyond 1971.[183] In Britain, the election of a Conservative government in 1970 led to a change in policy, with a British battalion and brigade elements being retained in Singapore and 28 ANZUK Brigade being formed as part of the ANZUK Force in October 1971.[184] This commitment was made under the Five Power Defence Arrangements which replaced ANZAM, and which formally included Malaysia and Singapore for the first time. In the event of a threat to either Malaysia or Singapore, Australia, New Zealand and the United Kingdom would consult with both governments to decide what action—if any—should be taken.[185] The Australian decision to withdraw from the ANZUK Force by April 1975 led to the establishment on 31 January 1974 of New Zealand Force South East Asia. This Force included 1RNZIR, No. 41 Squadron RNZAF, and an assigned RNZN frigate, together with logistic and administrative units.[186] It remained in Singapore until 1989, occupying Dieppe Barracks, Kangaw Barracks, and what had previously been the Royal Naval Base at Sembawang. Apart from the Australian RAAF base at Butterworth in Malaysia, New Zealand was the only Commonwealth member to retain a substantial military presence in the area. Even after 1984, when the nuclear-free stance of David Lange's Labour administration made New Zealand an outcast in defence terms for both Britain and the United States, New Zealand Force South East Asia continued to provide port clearances for British and US naval ships berthing at the Stores Basin Sembawang, and to host exercises involving Australian, British, Malaysian and Singapore forces.[187] This was a surprisingly independent position for a country whose forward defence arrangements had always been marked by penny-pinching that could be attributed to its recurring foreign exchange crises.

# CONCLUSION

> For a very tiny country ... with a tin-pot little army, we really do extraordinary things.[1]
>
> Colonel David Moloney, former Commander 4 Detachment, 1 NZ Ranger Squadron FE

Colonel Moloney's comment applied to all three services during the years covered by this study. After the Second World War, New Zealand had no wish to become involved in defence and security issues in Asia. Its commitment of J Force to the British Commonwealth Occupation Forces in Japan was reluctant at best; and indeed, once it was committed, Prime Minister Peter Fraser's main concern was how soon it would be politically expedient to withdraw it. Despite New Zealand's fervent support for the United Nations, it had no illusion about the insecurities the organisation faced in the post-war world. It appreciated the realities of American power in the Pacific, but also recognised the United States' unwillingness to become entangled in security issues in the region. New Zealand's security was best guaranteed under British Commonwealth defence arrangements, and the New Zealand government sought and accepted British advice on such matters. The beginning of the Cold War saw New Zealand accept a commitment that Army and RNZAF expeditionary forces be deployed to the Middle East in the event of global war. Britain's priorities were Europe, the Middle East and Asia, in that order; of these, the Middle East was seen by the United States as primarily a British and Commonwealth responsibility. When Britain sought commitments from Australia, New Zealand and South Africa, New Zealand alone was unequivocal in promising assistance, in the form of an infantry division, an additional armoured brigade, and an RNZAF expeditionary force. Inevitably, the initial shape of the post-war New Zealand armed forces was determined by this commitment.

The Canberra Pact of 1944 had been a declaration of Australia and New Zealand's determination to have a say in shaping the post-war security arrangements in the South and South-West Pacific. At the time this angered both Britain and the United States, and influenced the role given to Australian and New Zealand forces in the final stages of the Pacific War. By 1948, however, an impoverished and militarily overstretched Britain, while anxious to divest itself of much of the burden of empire east of Suez, was keen to retain control over an economically important Malaya. As Britain had sought Commonwealth defence assistance in the Middle East, it also looked for similar help in South-East Asia. The outcome was the ANZAM arrangement, which in essence gave Australia and New Zealand the assurances they had been seeking under the Canberra Pact. It also gave Britain some assurance of Commonwealth support in the defence of Malaya. Yet the focus of New Zealand's concern was not Malaya, but the protection of trade routes to its markets in Britain and Europe. New Zealand saw its primary ANZAM role as providing naval forces and maritime air patrols for convoy protection. It certainly did not foresee any major ground commitment. New Zealand was determined to cordon itself off from the instability and uncertainties that inevitably resulted from the post-war emergence of Asian nationalism and the reluctant decolonisation by France and the Netherlands.

The communist victory in China in 1949 heightened New Zealand's concerns. Fraser responded to a British request for assistance in the defence of Hong Kong by committing A Flight No. 41 Squadron RNZAF and promising three RNZN frigates and four Mosquito fighter bombers. The three Dakota DC-3 transport aircraft of No. 41 Squadron were positioned at Changi, and the incoming National government agreed that they would be available to assist in 'anti-bandit operations in Malaya'. This was not a change in policy, signalling a greater commitment to Asia; rather it was an important gesture of support for Commonwealth defence, at a time when the situation in Europe and Asia convinced the Western powers that the Soviet Union and its ally in Asia, the People's Republic of China, were bent on world domination. The focus of New Zealand's global war commitment remained the Middle East, and despite the growing insurgency in Malaya, Britain did not want New Zealand distracted from that undertaking. It assured New Zealand that the security problem in Malaya was a 'side issue only', and that while any assistance would be welcome, preparations for global war should remain this country's primary concern.

New Zealand Army officers were attached to units in Malaya and Hong Kong in 1949 to gain regimental experience, rather than because of New Zealand's concern about the deteriorating situation in Malaya. Similarly, when New Zealand Army officers and NCOs assisted in raising, training, and manning critical appointments in 1FIR in Malaya between 1952 and 1956, New Zealand was simply meeting its responsibilities to the Fiji military forces.[2] The Army ensured that this commitment did not divert Regular officers and NCOs from the compulsory military training scheme which underpinned the potential provision of a third NZEF to the Middle East.

The Korean War saw the first major commitment of New Zealand resources to Asia, during a conflict that would involve some 6,000 New Zealanders on operations in and around Korea from 1950 to 1957. The principal outcome of this conflict was that the United States was drawn into Asia; it also coincided with the signing in 1951 of the ANZUS Treaty, which gave Australia and New Zealand the security guarantees they had sought from the United States since the end of the Second World War. Intended as a bulwark against a resurgent Japan, the Treaty countered both countries' concerns about an expansionist communist China and the deteriorating situation in Indo-China, Malaya and Indonesia; it also provided for 'bolting the back door' if Australia and New Zealand had to fulfil their commitments in the Middle East. The ANZUS Treaty did not establish the administration and machinery to plan and commit forces, as NATO had done in Europe; nonetheless, it gave Australia and New Zealand access to the highest levels of American policy-making, with the annual meeting of the ANZUS Council enabling regular discussions between their foreign ministers and the US Secretary of State. Britain, to its dismay, was excluded from ANZUS because the United States did not want to become involved in defending the vestiges of the British Empire in Asia—nor, it must be said, those of France, the Netherlands and Portugal. While there was some disquiet expressed in New Zealand at Britain's exclusion, the reality of ANZUS—the de facto extension of the Monroe Doctrine to include New Zealand and Australia—was too important to question.

The overstretching of its military resources, and the growing belief that Europe would be the only significant theatre in a nuclear war, saw a shift in Britain's strategic thinking on Commonwealth defence arrangements away from the Middle East. The Harding talks in Melbourne in 1953 recommended that Australia refocus its global war defence planning on Malaya. Perhaps mindful of New Zealand's prompt response in 1948, the British planners suggested that it split its commitment, with the land component going to the Middle East and the air and naval component to Malaya. Given that New Zealand had already deployed No. 14 Squadron RNZAF to Cyprus in September 1952, flying leased Vampire jets as part of the Middle East Air Force, this recommendation was met with the scepticism it deserved, and no action was taken.

By the mid-1950s, New Zealand had established a series of defence undertakings that gave it assurances of security in the Pacific. The ANZAM arrangement, which included Britain, provided the machinery for contingency planning in the ANZAM area, while ANZUS provided the comforting guarantee of American assistance in the event of a threat to New Zealand. The Manila Pact and the formation of SEATO in 1954 linked both Britain and the United States together with Australia and New Zealand in joint security arrangements in South-East Asia. For New Zealand, these agreements provided three overlapping comfort zones which together ensured British and American involvement in Pacific security.

While New Zealand remained committed to the Middle East in the event of a global war, the establishment of SEATO meant an inevitable shift in focus towards South-East Asia. The planning mechanism for this was provided by ANZAM, and at the Prime Ministers' Conference in London in 1955 New Zealand agreed to become part of a Commonwealth Far East Strategic Reserve that would involve the commitment of Regular ground, air and naval forces to Malaya and Singapore. This was a brave and significant step by Holland's government. The stationing of Regular forces overseas in peacetime irrevocably changed the nature and shape of New Zealand's armed forces. Since 1955, New Zealand has relied on Regular forces to meet its defence commitments.

Britain saw the Commonwealth Strategic Reserve as focused primarily on Malaya, whereas Australia and New Zealand saw it as having a wider SEATO role. Inevitably, the secondary role of counter-insurgency in Malaya preoccupied the Strategic Reserve, including the New Zealand ground and air forces, until the Emergency ended in 1960. Just as New Zealand's Middle East commitment had shaped its post-war defence forces, the commitment to the Commonwealth Strategic Reserve under the ANZAM arrangement saw an equally important shift in focus to Regular units providing the central core of the three services. The ANZAM and later the SEATO commitments envisaged a response from forces in being, and could not wait for the call-up of reserves. They required New Zealand to provide manned ships and Regular RNZAF squadrons, as well as trained and ready units of Regular Force soldiers. This shift reshaped the New Zealand armed forces, with Army Territorial Forces being allocated a secondary role for the first time in their history. This has been the situation ever since, with the Territorial Force becoming increasingly irrelevant to the Army's role.

New Zealand's armed forces played a small part in the closing stages of the Malayan Emergency, but while this provided valuable training in jungle warfare, it was always a secondary consideration. Malaya's independence in 1957, and its refusal to join SEATO, cast doubts on the long-term ability of the Commonwealth Strategic Reserve to function from Malayan bases in its primary SEATO role. However, the Suez Crisis of 1956 had confirmed Britain's decline as a world power, and neither Britain, Australia nor New Zealand envisaged fighting a limited war in Asia without American support. Despite British reservations about their commitments to SEATO, the agreement was central to New Zealand's defence strategy because it alone jointly committed Britain and the United States to the security of South-East Asia. To New Zealand eyes, the 'domino theory' was very real, and forward defence the only sensible policy. New Zealand was prepared to make commitments that it could not fulfil in order to ensure that Britain and the United States remained involved in South-East Asia.

In terms of military resources, New Zealand developed the art of promising to do—and indeed doing—much with little. This was particularly true during the Holyoake administration, from 1960 to 1972. Following the establishment of a SEATO Military Planning Office in Bangkok in 1957, a number of contingency plans were formulated which, by the 1960s, called for the commitment of contingency forces from member countries. In New Zealand, a series of balance of payments crises led to cutbacks and delays in defence spending which affected the country's ability to respond to its treaty commitments. This was rarely acknowledged by the government. Instead of being correspondingly reduced, New Zealand's defence commitments and undertakings actually increased. More was done with less. This is a persistent theme in New Zealand defence policy; one can argue that for the best part of 50 years the country got away with it.

The stationing of New Zealand forces in Malaya and Singapore led to the establishment of diplomatic representation, but was not at first matched by any corresponding growth in trade with Asia, or indeed in public interest in the region. The primary concern was New Zealand's security. In the eyes of the average New Zealander, the stationing of forces in Malaya and Singapore was part of the ongoing struggle against the communist menace, in which New Zealand had to do its bit. It was the insurance premium New Zealand had to pay in order to be part of the Western alliance and the British Commonwealth. On this point there was general consensus in both political parties, and little, if any, public debate.

## The Royal New Zealand Navy

The RNZN as an organisation traces its pedigree back to 1914, when the New Zealand Naval Forces (NZNF) were established. From 1926 the NZNF operated two cruisers, a minesweeper, a dockyard, shore establishments and four Volunteer Reserve units. The Royal New Zealand Navy was formalised in 1941. Its wartime reputation was built on the achievements of its cruisers, although the minesweeping flotilla and patrol craft also performed with distinction in the Pacific. By 1946 the raison d'être of the RNZN was for its cruisers to provide anti-aircraft defence to the aircraft carriers of the Royal Australian Navy in protecting convoys passing through the ANZAM area, supported in turn by the six RNZN anti-submarine frigates and a number of coastal craft. The Naval Board had investigated acquiring a light fleet aircraft carrier, but this proved to be beyond New Zealand's resources. Nonetheless, the post-war RNZN was well-equipped with comparatively modern vessels, and quite capable of fulfilling its ANZAM role.

The Achilles heel of the RNZN proved to be manpower. Heavily dependent on recruiting from the RN, it found it difficult to meet the manning requirements for ship deployments in Korean and South-East Asian waters of up to 15 months at a time. The RNZN has never been able to provide overseas accommodation for families, as became increasingly the norm for the Army and RNZAF during the 1950s. The Naval Board recognised that improved crewing could only be achieved by retaining personnel through improved conditions of service. Welfare, housing and administration all improved during the 1950s as the RNZN struggled to adjust to the changing expectations of New Zealand society. Young men were still attracted to the sea, but the RNZN faced a constant challenge to keep them in the service, particularly once they married.

In the 1950s it became increasingly clear that the RNZN could not afford to maintain cruisers as part of its fleet. Reluctantly, it saw its future as a small-ship, six-frigate Navy providing anti-submarine escorts as part of New Zealand's ANZAM commitment. This scenario was scuttled by Holland's decision to accept the cruiser *Royalist* instead of the two modern frigates he had been sent to purchase. The *Royalist* was too sophisticated and its complement of 600 too large for the RNZN to accommodate. While there is no question that *Royalist* became an effective part of the RNZN and made a significant contribution to the Far East Fleet, the long-term impact of its acquisition was disastrous. Staying with the cruiser standard effectively scuppered the Naval Board's plans for a six-frigate Navy. During his term as CDS, Rear-Admiral Phipps had to accept the financial reality that a four-frigate Navy was the largest New Zealand could afford. It was also a sensible minimum that allowed it to meet its obligations: one frigate could be on station with the Far East Fleet, one on duty in the Pacific and New Zealand waters, one in the dockyard undergoing a refit, and the fourth working up after a refit. Indeed, when one examines the manpower realities of the RNZN in the 1950s, the number of ships is deceptive. Despite having an inventory of two cruisers and six frigates, the Navy could effectively crew only the equivalent of four frigates. Manning the *Royalist* on its overseas deployments placed the RNZN under enormous strain, as crews had also to be provided for the frigate it replaced on station and the frigate that would replace it. The 'Reserve Fleet' concept fitted New Zealand's planning for a global war scenario, but by 1955 it was as outdated as the Reserve squadrons were for the RNZAF, or an embryo 3NZEF based on the Territorial Force was for the New Zealand Army. Four ships became the logical minimum fleet size for the RNZN. Although at times during the 1960s it made do with less, the cycle of refit, retraining and two ships on station meant that on these occasions the RNZN could not provide the speed of response or range of tasks that were expected of it.

By trial and error, the South-East Asian years saw the evolution of a uniquely New Zealand Navy and a uniquely New Zealand class of frigate. Geography dictated that the country's interests were best served by vessels able to withstand conditions in the most isolated and hazardous of seas. The sheer variety and complexity of tasks undertaken by the RNZN was another factor; these have ranged from individual deployments to providing disaster relief, servicing conferences on isolated islands, overseeing peace negotiations and picketing nuclear tests. All these actions in the national interest have been achieved by deploying New Zealand's naval assets. Some were carried out despite the unwillingness of other powers to support New Zealand's stance, or indeed their open opposition to it. The frigates of the RNZN have made independent action possible.

The frigate was also the minimum size of vessel that allowed New Zealand to work with the navies of other Pacific powers, principally Australia and the United States. Corvette-sized ships, large enough to handle rugged seas but less sophisticated than frigates, have sometimes been suggested as more appropriate for the RNZN. If all New Zealand wanted to do was police its coastal waters and not project its national interests into the Pacific, such a class of vessel would be adequate. It would give New Zealand similar capabilities to Iceland, but make no allowance for the country's isolation. It would have ruled out New Zealand's naval presence at the initial Bougainville negotiations, its stance against French nuclear testing, the RNZN's role in ANZAM, and its participation in the Commonwealth blockade during Confrontation, the multinational naval force in the Persian Gulf, or East Timor. Working in concert with allies or at a distance in an independent role demanded the sophistication, armament and protection of a frigate-class ship. A corvette class is a specialist luxury for navies big enough to afford both classes, or so small that of necessity they are totally reliant on their allies, whose interests become their own. Through hard and often bitter experience, for example over its anti-nuclear stance, the *Rainbow Warrior* sinking, and the Bougainville peace initiative, New Zealand has found that the national interests of seemingly like-minded nations with strong historical ties can differ dramatically. Expensive as it may be, a frigate-class vessel is the minimum size that can meet New Zealand's unique needs.

The RNZN played a small but significant operational role with the Far East Fleet during the Emergency, and a larger one during Confrontation. In war, ships must work in concert, and the professional skills of the RNZN were honed by the ongoing deployment of vessels to the Commonwealth Strategic Reserve under the ANZAM arrangement. The South-East Asian years were the testing time during the development of an independent and uniquely New Zealand Navy. The RNZN still faces the same problems: lack of finance, personnel, and the political will to pay for at least four frigate-class vessels.

These issues are unavoidable in a small nation of limited means which faces no immediate threat. Yet its role in South-East Asia also shows that one of the most immediate and effective ways of projecting New Zealand's presence overseas has been to use the ships of the RNZN.

## The Royal New Zealand Air Force

The RNZAF was also shaped by its South-East Asian experience. Of the three services, it had the greatest history of maintaining units overseas, through the stationing of No. 5 Squadron RNZAF at Lauthala Bay in Fiji, and the deployments of No. 14 Squadron to Japan as part of the British Commonwealth Occupation Forces, and then to Cyprus, flying leased Vampire fighter/ground-attack aircraft with the RAF Middle East Air Force from 1952 to 1955.

New Zealand's limited resources made the leasing of aircraft a sensible means of maintaining a state-of-the-art air combat capability. While the cost-effectiveness of providing offensive air support during the Emergency can be questioned, the RNZAF gained invaluable operational experience. With No. 14 Squadron flying leased Venom jet aircraft, and then No. 75 Squadron flying leased Canberra bombers as part of the Far East Air Force, skills in fighter/ground-attack and light-bomber interdictor roles were developed. Through repeatedly competing against similar squadrons from the Commonwealth and the USAF, they reached levels of efficiency that could not be achieved by squadrons based in New Zealand. This experience was complemented by the regular deployment of Sunderland flying boats of No. 5 Squadron RNZAF from Lauthala Bay, and the ongoing support provided to all three services by the long-range transport aircraft of No. 40 Squadron RNZAF. At an individual level, attachments to RAF Headquarters provided both operational and staff experience.

The B170 Bristol Freighters of No. 41 Squadron performed transport and aerial resupply functions during the Emergency and Confrontation. This transport capability was highly valued by New Zealand's allies because this niche was always difficult to fill. After the defence cuts of 1961, the RNZAF would have preferred to withdraw No. 41 Squadron rather than lose its combat presence. But as this would have left a serious gap in the air transport capability required for SEATO and ANZAM operations, the Bristol Freighters stayed on. The silver fern remained the ubiquitous symbol of New Zealand's presence in South-East Asia.

However, the 1961 Defence Review did lead to the withdrawal of No. 75 Squadron from Singapore. The RNZAF maintained its operational capability by regularly deploying to SEATO exercises the New Zealand-based Canberras of No. 14 Squadron. This was a second-best solution driven by financial stringency. Inevitably, operational effectiveness suffered. Air Vice-Marshal Morrison saw the outbreak of Confrontation in 1964 as a renewed opportunity to station a New Zealand strike squadron in Singapore on a long-term basis. His attempt was unsuccessful, and No. 14 Squadron was withdrawn in 1966. Operational capabilities continued to be maintained through individual attachments to the RAAF and USAF in Vietnam, and by ongoing deployments on SEATO exercises. After SEATO's demise in 1977, operational deployments continued under the Five Power Defence Arrangement which had replaced ANZAM in 1971. The long-term deployment of No. 2 Squadron RNZAF to Nowra in Australia, flying A-4 Skyhawks in a maritime strike role in support of the RAN which ended only in 2001, showed the importance of this ongoing arrangement, which enabled the squadron to maintain its operational skills at a higher level than would have been possible if it had been stationed in New Zealand.

New Zealand's purchase of the Canberra bombers was equivalent in some ways to the acquisition of the *Royalist*. The rapid evolution of jet aircraft during this period made it impossible for a small country to maintain a modern strike capability. This had been possible in the 1950s with leased Venom and Canberra aircraft, but Confrontation exposed the limitations of an air force with a single strike squadron. No one could doubt the professionalism of the RNZAF pilots and ground crews, but the stark reality was that the losses from one sortie against defended Indonesian targets could have removed New Zealand's strike capacity. This risk was demonstrated at the time by the accidental loss of one B12 Canberra.

During Confrontation, the RNZAF achieved the impossible with obsolete aircraft. Yet these years also saw the RNZAF revitalised by the introduction into service of the C-130H Hercules transport aircraft and the Bell 47G-3B1 Sioux helicopter in 1965, the UH-1D Iroquois helicopter and the Orion P-3B maritime patrol aircraft in 1966, and the A-4K Skyhawk fighter/ground-attack jet fighter in 1970. All remained in service at the end of the century. All but the last purchase was achieved by Air Vice-Marshal Morrison, who overcame the body-blow of the 1961 Defence Review and made the RNZAF into an effective modern service, not only by obtaining aircraft, but also by consolidating and reorganising the administrative structure into an Operations and Support Group.

## The New Zealand Army

Apart from the Bristol Freighters of No. 41 Squadron RNZAF, perhaps New Zealand's most valuable contribution to the Malayan Emergency was the role it played in the training of and initial provision of officers and NCOs to 1FIR in 1952. This unit played a significant part in the Emergency, and was the benchmark against which the performance of Commonwealth forces in Malaya was measured. This achievement was made possible by the efforts of the small cadre of New Zealanders who put it all together in the critical years when Tinker commanded the battalion. This experience with 1FIR provided the foundation for New Zealand's expertise in jungle warfare.

The Fijian involvement overlapped with the commitment of the first Regular units of the New Zealand Army to see active service overseas in peacetime, beginning in 1955 with the SAS Squadron. Its service with 22 SAS Regiment played an important if unrecognised role in the retention of the regiment within the organisation of the British Army. It also set a benchmark for SAS professionalism on jungle operations in Malaya. The blend of Maori and Pakeha within the squadron saw the New Zealanders excel in the tracking and patrolling skills essential to jungle warfare. They also excelled at 'winning the hearts and minds' of the indigenous tribespeople, something that was not part of the British squadrons' approach. These skills were complemented by careful selection, intensive training, and sound leadership. This combination remains the basis of the effectiveness of New Zealand soldiers.

The formation of a Regular brigade in 1958 broke with the past and committed New Zealand to deploying a professional Army as the first response to any SEATO contingency. The retreat from the Regular brigade concept and the reintroduction of National Service following the 1961 Defence Review merely stretched scarce Regular resources, rather than shifting the emphasis back to the Territorial Force, which increasingly became an anachronism. Constant changes in its organisation meant that it was never able to meet the demands made on it, and it came to exist more as a cost-saving measure than for any overseas service capability. It is true that by the late 1960s the Territorial Infantry Brigade Group and the Logistic Support Group were equipped and manned to meet New Zealand's potential SEATO commitments, but by the time these formations became effective the need had passed. All New Zealand was ever able to provide in the critical years was its single Regular battalion, with little in reserve.

Jungle operations during the Emergency from 1952 to 1960, followed by ongoing border operations from 1960 to 1964, honed the Army's jungle tactics and small-group leadership skills to a level unmatched by any similar Commonwealth or United States unit operating in South-East Asia at the time. This was due to the continuity of having a professional battalion in Malaya whose central core was a growing group of Regulars who knew the jungle and continued to improve their tactical skills. Instructors who first served with 1FIR returned to Malaya and passed on their skills within the battalions. They were joined by Regular soldiers who learned leadership and soldiering skills during the closing years of the Emergency. This period saw the transition from a New Zealand Army staffed by cadre instructors tailored to the needs of a citizen conscript army, to one staffed by NCOs who were adept both as instructors and as commanders practised in the leadership of sections and platoons. It was these men who thought through and formalised what they were actually doing in the jungle. They developed the shooting skills and techniques necessary in close-range jungle fighting, where the number of accurate shots in the first few seconds determined who would win the encounter. They developed the immediate-action drills of jungle fighting at section and platoon level, and honed and refined these drills until they became second nature.

This expertise was matched by the young Regular officers graduating from RMC Duntroon and OCS Portsea in Australia, RMA Sandhurst in the United Kingdom, and special commissioning courses in New Zealand. The Second World War background of the likes of Tinker, Low, Rennie, Morrison, Aitken, Pearce, Gurr and Voss complemented the abilities of the next generation, whose only operational experience was in South-East Asia. Burrows, Thorpe and others shaped and articulated the tactical drills and procedures that became the basis of New Zealand's patrolling and ambushing expertise in Malaya, Borneo and Vietnam. Officers from all corps learned their trade as platoon commanders with the battalions, returning as company commanders on later tours and seeing operational service.

These skills were matched by ongoing mobilisation practice and training for the SEATO role that involved all three services. The stationing of New Zealand's contribution to the Commonwealth Strategic Reserve in South-East

Asia allowed it to compare its standards with those of its Commonwealth and United States allies. The intense ongoing interchange and competition allowed units to reach a level of performance and skill that would not have been possible for New Zealand-based forces relying on occasional contact. It was a time of unparalleled professionalism in all three services.

Two figures, Weir and Thornton, dominated the Army in these years. Major-General (later Sir Stephen) Weir was CGS from 1955 to 1960, and was then appointed Chief Military Adviser to Nash's Labour government in New Zealand's first step towards the establishment of an integrated defence headquarters. Weir was the driving force in the commitment of Army units to South-East Asia. His aim of a comprehensive commitment from all arms and services to 28th Commonwealth Brigade group was frustrated by the 1961 Defence Review. Even so, he ensured that New Zealand's primary commitment was measured by what it had on the ground. Weir more than any other person influenced the nature of New Zealand's military presence in Asia. Major-General (later Lieutenant-General Sir Leonard) Thornton succeeded Weir as CGS and held this appointment until 1965. He then succeeded Rear-Admiral Sir Peter Phipps as Chief of Defence Staff, a position he retained until 1971. The Thornton years encompassed the critical period of SEATO planning, the Thailand commitments, Confrontation and Vietnam. As committed as Weir to South-East Asia, he found and juggled the resources needed to meet New Zealand's myriad commitments throughout the 1960s.

The change from the Territorial concept and the reduction in size of the armed forces did not mean a loss in skill at command and staff level. Phipps' appointment as the first Chief of Defence Force in 1963 was an important step in co-ordinating and integrating the three services. While it neither ended single-service competition for resources nor foreshadowed the full integration of defence staff, this streamlining of command and staff arrangements was essential for the armed forces of a small country. The commitment to the Commonwealth Strategic Reserve and the establishment of a SEATO Military Planning Office in Bangkok saw New Zealanders from all three services fill various appointments on the staffs and headquarters of both SEATO and the British Forces Far East. Headquarters New Zealand Army FARELF provided a national headquarters for the army component, and was paralleled during Confrontation by Headquarters RNZAF Malaysia under Wing-Commander Ewan Jamieson. Three New Zealanders commanded 28th Commonwealth Brigade: Brigadier R. B. Dawson from October 1962 to October 1964,

Brigadier R. M. Gurr from March 1969 to March 1971, and Brigadier M. R. Kennedy, who commanded 28 ANZUK Brigade from March 1973 until it was disbanded in January 1974.

New Zealand's commitments to the Commonwealth Strategic Reserve in 1955 had little real impact on the Emergency, which was in its closing stages. In terms of size of commitment, New Zealand was always a distant third behind Britain and Australia, a position that was often reflected in the belated inclusion of New Zealand in the discussion process. While the size of its force reflected the limitations New Zealand placed on its defence spending, in hindsight the country got good value for its money. This was Holyoake's achievement. The skill with which he sustained New Zealand's profile in South-East Asia throughout the 1960s with very limited and sparingly used resources was not negated by the breakdown in political and public consensus during the Vietnam conflict.

There was little domestic questioning of New Zealand's forward defence posture. The Cold War and the perceived threat of communist expansion in both Europe and Asia made New Zealand's stance not only understandable but inevitable in the context of the times. The threat from Japan during the Second World War had been too immediate and real for New Zealand not to take steps to ensure its post-war security in the Pacific. The Cold War continued this wartime perception, which began to fragment only when questioned by the post-war generation in the late 1960s, during New Zealand's involvement in Vietnam. Until then, those opposing New Zealand's military commitments to South-East Asia remained a small if sometimes vocal minority on the fringe of public awareness.[3]

New Zealanders took for granted their country's contribution of Regular military forces to the Commonwealth Far East Strategic Reserve. This was the logical consequence of the Iron Curtain in Europe and the establishment of communist power in China. Little distinction was made between J Force in Japan, K Force in Korea, and the overlapping commitments to Malaya, which flowed seamlessly into commitments to Thailand, Vietnam and Borneo. There was general agreement between the Labour and National parties on New Zealand's security needs and the validity of a forward defence posture. To the general public, the communist threat was real and New Zealand's response appropriate.

It was Peter Fraser's Labour administration that made the first commitment of Dakota aircraft and frigates to help protect Hong Kong against the communists in 1949. This stance was accepted and continued by Holland, Nash and Holyoake. All three were reluctant givers, but were conscious that a contribution had to be made. All three were happy to wait for the general public to believe it was time for New Zealand to act, before being seen to be prodded into making defence contributions to South-East Asia. This guaranteed the political and public consensus that was a feature of those years. New Zealand's commitment to South-East Asia rarely disturbed the tenor of affairs, featuring only occasionally in newsreels in the cinemas or in photographs and paragraphs in local newspapers. There was little in the way of public education as to why New Zealand was there, and why its contribution was so important. It was simply accepted. It was also seen as providing opportunities for New Zealand's young men to travel and see the world, and to build on the beneficial effects of compulsory military training.

All three services benefited from the contact with South-East Asia. Generations of leaders cut their operational teeth serving with New Zealand units and ships as part of the Commonwealth Strategic Reserve. The involvement made New Zealand more aware of Asia, and made New Zealanders adept at working with Commonwealth and SEATO forces. New Zealand was never big enough to do it alone; it could neither aspire to Australia's pretensions, nor match Australia's commitments. However, in both Malaya and Borneo, New Zealand was seen to make a national contribution and play a meaningful role. In individual terms—a ship, a squadron, a battalion—New Zealanders were seen to operate as well as the best of them, and often better. To be the best was always the aim, and that competitiveness remains an enduring New Zealand trait.

It is difficult to calculate how many New Zealanders and their families went to South-East Asia in these years. During the peaks of the commitment, from 1957 to 1962 and again in 1965–66, there were some 1,500 New Zealanders and their families from all three services in Malaya and Singapore at any one time. If one adds those who served until the withdrawal of the New Zealand Force South East Asia in 1989, it is clear that many thousands of New Zealanders experienced service life in South-East Asia.[4]

This contact was the most important feature of the New Zealand armed forces in these decades. The New Zealand armed forces did not have the same connection with South-East Asia as those of Australia, which had fought in Malaya and Borneo during the Second World War, with 20,000 becoming prisoners of the Japanese. The occupation force in Japan, the Korean War, and active service and garrison duties in Malaya and Singapore were New Zealand's first military contact with Asia, with the exception of a small RNZAF contribution during the Second World War. The young men and their families who came to Singapore and Malaya in the 1950s entered a strange and exotic world in which they were the outsiders. They returned home with goods, an appreciation of Asian food, and an awareness that much was lacking in the insular New Zealand society of the 1950s and early 1960s. Asia opened their eyes to a different world, and that experience stayed with them. A stubborn few, prepared to surmount the many deliberately placed administrative and legal hurdles, brought back Asian wives. These marriages were tested by the loneliness inevitably experienced by women living in bleak married quarters in a foreign land. Some of the marriages buckled under the strain, while others survived and prospered. These brave couples were the bow wave of New Zealand's growing cosmopolitan, multicultural society.

South-East Asia gave those who went there a better understanding and appreciation of what it meant to be a New Zealander: a person with a dogged determination to win, who with training became adept at fighting a jungle war which, by its very nature, was a war of fine detail. To be alert to the slightest of signs, the displacement of a leaf, the mere sense of another's presence, one needed to be in tune with and comfortable in that environment, as the New Zealanders proved to be. Most of all, it was the racial mix of Maori and Pakeha that enabled the New Zealanders to relate to the peoples of South-East Asia to a degree not matched by the largely Anglo-Saxon units of Australia and Great Britain. Major-General Keith Stewart insisted that the post-war New Zealand Army would have no exclusively Maori units. This was an important decision which shaped the character of the New Zealand Army. The permanent staff and Staff Corps had previously been Pakeha preserves; only the exigencies of wartime had broken down this racial exclusivity, and then only for the duration. The raising of a cadre of instructors in the 1950s, and more importantly the raising of battalions for ongoing service in Malaya, provided a conduit for Maori advancement that was not available anywhere else in New Zealand society. It was a career path open to talent, and a lack of formal education was no barrier. Maori excelled in the military world, and although educational requirements held them back from commissioned rank, they soon filled many of the NCO and warrant officer appointments. The proportion of Maori in the Army was significantly greater than their share of the New Zealand population as a whole.[5] The unstated and often unrecognised divide between Maori and Pakeha that was a feature of New Zealand society in this period was broken down in South-East Asia, where all three services reflected a unique racial amalgam.

South-East Asia gave many young New Zealanders the opportunity to 'find themselves'; after a one- or two-year tour they returned home and got on with their lives. Vietnam has overshadowed the importance of these years. There are a few books, one or two radio plays, some newsreel films in Archives New Zealand; but no paintings by commissioned war artists like those for the two world wars and Vietnam, only memories.[6] It is largely forgotten that New Zealand's first significant contact with Asia was military, and that diplomacy and trade then followed. Indeed, this contact helped make New Zealand society a more interesting and less insular place. The fruits of that 40-year association have extended far beyond the first contacts by the RNZN, RNZAF and 1 NZ SAS Squadron in the 1950s. The military link opened New Zealand to Asia. Our subsequent relationship with the continent, and indeed our view of the world, have been shaped by this association.

By the end of Confrontation in August 1966, the security that New Zealand had sought through its forward defence policy in South-East Asia was beginning to unravel. New Zealand faced a deteriorating strategic situation in the region. There were indications that Britain intended to reduce its commitments east of Suez, and that, should it remain, it expected a far greater contribution from New Zealand. At the same time, the United States was putting growing pressure on New Zealand to increase its combat commitment to South Vietnam. While the ending of Confrontation released the New Zealand forces in north Borneo, it was possible that contributions on a similar or greater scale would be required under its SEATO or ANZUS arrangements. The likelihood that New Zealand would be involved in major hostilities before 1970 had increased, but its armed forces still faced serious deficiencies in both equipment and the means to deploy them.[7] The RNZN had to borrow HMS *Blackpool* to maintain three front-line ships until the commissioning of HMNZS *Waikato* provided a workable minimum of four frigates. The capabilities of the RNZAF had been improved by the purchase of modern aircraft and helicopters, but there was an urgent need to replace its strike aircraft. 1RNZIR was back in Terendak and available to meet any immediate SEATO commitment, but it would take up to eight months to deploy the combat brigade and Logistic Support Group from New Zealand, and this force would not be fully equipped until 1968. It was amidst these uncertainties that New Zealand faced a growing commitment to South Vietnam.

# *Appendix 1*

## ROLL OF HONOUR, MALAYA AND BORNEO, 1949–66

### Royal New Zealand Air Force

| | | | |
|---|---|---|---|
| Flight Sergeant R. Fraser | died | No. 5 Sqn | 4 April 1956 |
| Squadron Leader A. S. Tie | aircraft accident | No. 41 Sqn | 10 December 1956 |
| Flying Officer W. A. Devescovi | aircraft accident | No. 41 Sqn | 10 December 1956 |
| Flying Officer D. E. Nelson | aircraft accident | No. 41 Sqn | 10 December 1956 |
| LAC J. A. R. Gudsell | died | No. 75 Sqn | 21 March 1959 |
| Sergeant W. Berry | died | No. 75 Sqn | 8 January 1961 |
| Flying Officer D. L. Finn | aircraft accident | No. 75 Sqn | 26 October 1961 |
| Flight Lieutenant J. W. Southgate | aircraft accident | No. 14 Sqn | 30 November 1964 |
| Flying Officer R. B. Thomson | aircraft accident | No. 14 Sqn | 30 November 1964 |
| LAC G. P. Ryder | accidentally killed | No. 14 Sqn | 25 June 1965 |

### New Zealand Army

| | | | |
|---|---|---|---|
| Second Lieutenant P. M. Hargest | accidentally killed | 1FIR | 19 December 1952 |
| Sergeant G. Nepia | accidentally killed | 1FIR | 18 November 1954 |
| Trooper A. R. Thomas | killed in action | NZ SAS Sqn | 2 May 1956 |
| Temp Corporal A. G. Buchanan | died on operations | NZ SAS Sqn | 11 May 1957 |
| Private T. U. Kawha | accidentally killed on operations | 1 NZ Regt | 23 February 1958 |
| Private B. J. Tuxworth | killed in action | 1 NZ Regt | 30 June 1958 |
| Private R. M. Breitmeyer | accidentally killed | 1 NZ Regt | 16 August 1958 |
| Temp Lance-Corporal P. Brown (also known as T. P. Iwihera) | killed in action | 1 NZ Regt | 22 August 1958 |
| Private G. W. Amas | died on operations | 2 NZ Regt | 31 March 1960 |

| | | | |
|---|---|---|---|
| Private T. F. Solia | drowned on operations | 2 NZ Regt | 10 December 1960 |
| Private B. H. Hay | accidentally killed | 2 NZ Regt | 25 March 1961 |
| Captain L. B. Shannon | died | 1 NZ Regt | 24 July 1962 |
| Private M. J. Dunn | accidentally killed | 1 NZ Regt | 10 September 1962 |
| Private N. L. Richards | accidentally killed | 1 NZ Regt | 30 January 1963 |
| Private O. T. Dawson | died | 1 RNZIR | 31 March 1964 |
| Private A. W. Monk | accidentally killed on operations | 1 RNZIR | 15 April 1964 |
| Sergeant I. L. King | died | 1 RNZIR | 18 August 1964 |
| Private T. J. Healey | accidentally killed | 1 RNZIR | 8 September 1964 |
| Sergeant R. E. Fry, RNZAMC | died | 1 RNZIR | 6 June 1965 |
| Sapper W. Toni, RNZE | accidentally drowned | 1 RNZIR | 26 January 1966 |
| Private P. W. Bonner | accidentally killed | 1 RNZIR | 2 February 1966 |
| Private R. Honatana | died | 1 RNZIR | 21 October 1966 |

## Royal New Zealand Navy

| | | | |
|---|---|---|---|
| Chief Radio Electrician J. L. Rogers | died | HMNZS *Royalist* | 3 June 1964 |

# *Appendix 2*

## HONOURS AND AWARDS, MALAYA AND BORNEO, 1949–66

## Royal New Zealand Air Force

### 'A' Flight, No. 41 Squadron, 1949–51

MEMBER OF THE ORDER OF THE BRITISH EMPIRE, MILITARY DIVISION (MBE)
Flight Lieutenant R. A. Manners

DISTINGUISHED FLYING CROSS (DFC)
Flight Lieutenant S. Mills

### Transport Operations Headquarters, Far East Air Force, 1955–60

OFFICER OF THE ORDER OF THE BRITISH EMPIRE (OBE)
Squadron Leader A. H. Harding, DFC
Squadron Leader R. F. Watson, AFC, mid

### No. 14 Squadron, 1955–58

DISTINGUISHED FLYING CROSS (DFC)
Squadron Leader A. F. Tucker, mid
Flight Lieutenant S. McIntyre

MENTIONED IN DESPATCHES (MID)
Flight Sergeant H. B. Dalton
Sergeant E. D. Waghorn
Sergeant K. V. G. Wolfendale

## No. 41 Squadron, 1955–62

MEMBER OF THE ORDER OF THE BRITISH EMPIRE, MILITARY DIVISION (MBE)
Flight Lieutenant W. F. R. Jackson

DISTINGUISHED FLYING CROSS (DFC)
Flight Lieutenant G. C. Bayliss

AIR FORCE CROSS (AFC)
Squadron Leader R. A. Manners, MBE
Squadron Leader O. D. Staple, DFC
Flying Officer B. G. Anderson

## No. 75 Squadron, 1958–62

MEMBER OF THE ORDER OF THE BRITISH EMPIRE (MBE)
Flight Lieutenant R. F. Ward

BAR TO THE AIR FORCE CROSS (AFC*)
Squadron Leader G. R. B. Highet, DFC, AFC

AIR FORCE CROSS (AFC)
Squadron Leader H. G. Moss
Flight Lieutenant P. Neville

BRITISH EMPIRE MEDAL (BEM)
Flight Sergeant J. E. Rasmussen

## 1 Fiji Infantry Regiment, 1952–56

COMPANION OF THE DISTINGUISHED SERVICE ORDER (DSO)
Lieutenant-Colonel H. J. G. Low, MC

OFFICER OF THE ORDER OF THE BRITISH EMPIRE, MILITARY DIVISION (OBE)
Lieutenant-Colonel R. A. Tinker, MC, MM

MEMBER OF THE ORDER OF THE BRITISH EMPIRE, MILITARY DIVISION (MBE)
Major W. A. Morgan, ED

MENTIONED IN DESPATCHES (MID)
Lieutenant-Colonel H. J. G. Low, MC
Major H. W. R. Peterson
Captain V. B. Brown
Captain A. T. A. Mataira
Warrant Officer I S. R. McGuinness
Warrant Officer II T. T. Babbington
Warrant Officer II R. A. Manning
Staff Sergeant S. A. Gilhooly
Sergeant R. T. Lowry

COMMANDER-IN-CHIEF FAR EAST LAND FORCES CERTIFICATE
Staff Sergeant C. G. O'Brien

## New Zealand Special Air Service Squadron, 1955–57

### British Awards

MILITARY CROSS (MC)
Major F. Rennie, MBE
Lieutenant I. H. Burrows

BRITISH EMPIRE MEDAL (BEM)
Trooper S. Watene

MENTIONED IN DESPATCHES (MID)
Major F. Rennie, MBE
Captain G. N. McL. Boswell
Lieutenant J. A. Mace
Lieutenant E. W. Yandall

### Malayan Awards

CONSPICUOUS GALLANTRY MEDAL (PINGAT KEBERANIAN CHEMERLANG)
Lieutenant I. H. Burrows, MC
Lieutenant E. W. Yandall

DISTINGUISHED CONDUCT MEDAL (PINGAT PEKERTI TERPILEN)
Trooper R. S. Hurle
Trooper G. C. Otene
Trooper R. P. Withers

## Malaya, 1957–61

### British Awards

OFFICER OF THE ORDER OF THE BRITISH EMPIRE (OBE)

| | |
|---|---|
| Lieutenant-Colonel W. R. K. Morrison, DSO | 1 NZ Regt |
| Lieutenant-Colonel D. J. Aitken | 2 NZ Regt |

MEMBER OF THE ORDER OF THE BRITISH EMPIRE (MBE)

| | |
|---|---|
| Major A. J. Voss, MC, MM | 1 NZ Regt |
| Major L. M. Wright | 2 NZ Regt |
| Major B. M. Poananga | 2 NZ Regt |
| Major F. A. Bishop | attached to HQ 17 Gurkha Division |
| Captain A. T. A. Maitaira | 1 NZ Regt |

MILITARY MEDAL (MM)

| | |
|---|---|
| Sergeant N. C. Jamieson | 1 NZ Regt |
| Corporal P. Dillon | 1 NZ Regt |

BRITISH EMPIRE MEDAL (BEM)

| | |
|---|---|
| Warrant Officer II T. T. Babbington | 1 NZ Regt |
| Sergeant H. James | 1 NZ Regt |
| Sergeant R. C. M. Brown | 2 NZ Regt |
| Sergeant D. I. McIntosh | 2 NZ Regt |
| Private Stuart | 2 NZ Regt |

MENTIONED IN DESPATCHES (MID)

| | |
|---|---|
| Lieutenant-Colonel W. R. K. Morrison, DSO, OBE | 1 NZ Regt |
| Major R. W. K. Ainge | 1 NZ Regt |
| Major B. Boyd, MBE | 1 NZ Regt |
| Lieutenant P. N. Anaru | 1 NZ Regt |
| Lieutenant K. M. Gordon | 1 NZ Regt |
| Lieutenant N. A. Wallace | 1 NZ Regt |
| Lieutenant A. R. Fraser | 2 NZ Regt |
| Lieutenant T. B. Butson | attached to King's Own Scottish Borderers |
| Warrant Officer II G. E. Butler | 1 NZ Regt |
| Warrant Officer II P. R. K. Carrington | 1 NZ Regt |
| Sergeant B. Hill | 1 NZ Regt |

| | |
|---|---|
| Sergeant D. W. J. Faulkner | 2 NZ Regt |
| Corporal R. H. Cassidy | 1 NZ Regt |
| Corporal N. L. Sinclair | 1 NZ Regt |
| Lance-Corporal W. Ferguson | 2 NZ Regt |
| Private H. Boyland | 1 NZ Regt |
| Private B. Nathan | 1 NZ Regt |

QUEEN'S COMMENDATION (QC)

| | |
|---|---|
| Private P. Brown | 2 NZ Regt |

COMMANDER-IN-CHIEF FAR EAST LAND FORCES CERTIFICATE

| | |
|---|---|
| Sergeant L. Hepi | 2 NZ Regt |
| Private W. T. P. Nathan | 2 NZ Regt |

### Malayan Awards

PERAK MERITORIOUS SERVICE MEDAL

| | |
|---|---|
| Captain A. T. A. Mataira, MBE | 1 NZ Regt |
| Lieutenant N. A. Wallace | 1 NZ Regt |

PERAK DISTINGUISHED CONDUCT MEDAL

| | |
|---|---|
| Private K. B. Chesterfield | 1 NZ Regt |

FEDERATION OF MALAYA GENERAL SERVICE MEDAL (PINGAT KHIDMAT BERBAKTI)

| | |
|---|---|
| Captain A. K. McKenzie | NZ Regt* |
| Captain C. J. Phillips | NZ Regt* |
| Warrant Officer II J. Davis | RNZ Sigs* |

*Awarded for service with the Federation of Malaya Police Field Force

## Confrontation, 1964–66

### British Awards

DISTINGUISHED SERVICE CROSS (DSC)

| | |
|---|---|
| Lieutenant-Commander P. N. Wright, RNZN | HMNZS *Hickleton* |

MILITARY CROSS (MC)

| | |
|---|---|
| Captain J. M. Masters, RNZA | attached to 4 Light Regt Royal Artillery |
| Lieutenant J. W. Brown, RNZIR | 1RNZIR |
| Lieutenant E. Manuera, RNZIR | 1 NZ Ranger Sqn (Far East) |

| AIR FORCE CROSS (AFC) | |
|---|---|
| Squadron Leader G. Wallingford, RNZAF | No. 14 Sqn |
| **DISTINGUISHED SERVICE MEDAL (DSM)** | |
| Able Seaman C. K. Taylor, RNZN | HMNZS *Hickleton* |
| **MILITARY MEDAL (MM)** | |
| Private T. Ashby, RNZIR | 1 RNZIR |
| **QUEEN'S COMMENDATION FOR BRAVERY (QC)** | |
| Private A. J. Smallridge, RNZIR | 1 RNZIR |
| **MENTIONED IN DESPATCHES (MID)** | |
| Lieutenant-Colonel B. M. Poananga, MBE | 1 RNZIR |
| Major R. I. Thorpe, RNZIR | 1 RNZIR |
| Captain D. R. McLeod, RNZAC | |
| Lieutenant B. J. Marshall, RNZIR | 1 RNZIR |
| Sergeant G. C. Faulkner, RNZIR | 1 RNZIR |
| Corporal W. A. McGee, RNZIR | 1 RNZIR |
| Sergeant N. Kawha, RNZIR | 1 NZ Ranger Sqn (Far East) |
| Corporal K. M. Schimanski, RNZIR | 1 NZ Ranger Sqn (Far East) |

## Malaysian Awards

**5TH DIVISION OF THE DISTINGUISHED ORDER OF PANGKUAN NEGARA (AHLI MANGKU NEGARA) (AMN)**

| Squadron Leader M. W. Hodge RNZAF | attached to Royal Malaysian Air Force |
|---|---|

**FEDERATION OF MALAYSIA BORNEO SERVICE MEDAL (PINGAT PERKHIDMANTON) (AM)**

Major I. W. Black, RNZEME
Lieutenant R. J. Hoskin, RNZIR

**MALAYSIA DAY MEDAL (PINGAT PERINGATUM)**

Major I. W. Black, RNZEME
Commander G. A. Lawrence, RNZN
Lieutenant-Commander C. J. Carl, RNZN
Lieutenant-Commander J. S. Day, RNZN

# *Appendix 3*

## UNIT AND FORMATION COMMANDERS, NEW ZEALAND ARMED FORCES, MALAYA AND BORNEO, 1949–66

### Royal New Zealand Air Force

#### RNZAF Headquarters Malaysia

| | |
|---|---|
| Wing Cdr D. E. Jamieson | Sep 1964 – Nov 1966 |

#### No. 14 Squadron

| | |
|---|---|
| Sqn Ldr N. H. Bright | May 1954 – Sep 1956 |
| Sqn Ldr A. F. Tucker, DFC | Sep 1956 – Jan 1959 |
| Sqn Ldr G. Wallingford | Jun 1964 – Dec 1966 |

#### A Flight, No. 41 (Transport) Squadron

| | |
|---|---|
| Flt Lt R. A. Manners | Sep 1949 – Mar 1950 |
| Flt Lt L. J. McLean | Mar–Aug 1950 |
| Flt Lt D. J. Phillips, DFC | Aug–Oct 1950 |
| Flt Lt S. Mills | Oct 1950 – Dec 1951 |

#### No. 41 Squadron

| | |
|---|---|
| Sqn Ldr R. A. Manners, MBE | Dec 1954 – Oct 1956 |
| Sqn Ldr A. S. Tie | Nov–Dec 1956 |
| Sqn Ldr G. H. S. Tosland, AFC | Jan 1957 – Aug 1959 |
| Sqn Ldr O. D. Staple, DFC | Sep 1959 |

| | |
|---|---|
| Sqn Ldr B. A. Wood, AFC | Dec 1961 |
| Sqn Ldr I. F. Garrett | Oct 1963 |
| Sqn Ldr I. A. Hutchins, AFC | Sep 1965 |

### No. 75 Squadron

| | |
|---|---|
| Sqn Ldr G. B. Highet, DFC, AFC | Jul 1958 – Dec 1960 |
| Sqn Ldr H. G. Moss | Jan 1961 – Apr 1962 |

## Royal New Zealand Navy

| | |
|---|---|
| Lt-Cdr L. G. Carr, DSC | HMNZS *Kaniere*, Jul 1953 – Mar 1954 (under operational command of Commander Far East Fleet from Feb 1954) |
| Lt-Cdr A. V. Kempthorne | HMNZS *Pukaki*, Sept 1953 – Sep 1954 |
| Lt-Cdr S. F. Mercer | HMNZS *Kaniere*, Jul 1954 – Jul 1955 |
| Lt-Cdr E. C. Thorne | HMNZS *Pukaki*, Apr 1955 – Apr 1956 (first deployment to Commonwealth Strategic Reserve) |
| Capt J. F. Whitfield, DSC, RN | HMNZS *Black Prince*, May–Jul 1955 |
| Lt-Cdr V. W. Were | HMNZS *Kaniere*, Feb 1956 – May 1957 |
| Capt G. D. Pound, DSC, RN | HMNZS *Royalist*, May 1957 – Jul 1958 |
| Lt-Cdr L. E. Hodge | HMNZS *Rotoiti*, Apr 1958 – Aug 1959 |
| Capt C. C. Stevens | HMNZS *Royalist*, Feb–Jun 1959 |
| Cdr W. R. Williams | HMNZS *Pukaki*, May 1959 – May 1960 |
| Lt-Cdr R. L. Harding | HMNZS *Rotoiti*, Apr 1960 – Mar 1961 |
| Capt H. D. Stevenson, RAN | HMNZS *Royalist*, Jan–Aug 1961 |
| Cdr P. L. Bardwell | HMNZS *Pukaki*, Jun 1961 – Jun 1962 |
| Cdr J. F. McKenzie | HMNZS *Otago*, Feb–Oct 1962 |
| Cdr N. D. Anderson | HMNZS *Taranaki*, Mar 1962 – Apr 1963 |
| Commodore J. O'C. Ross | HMNZS *Royalist*, Feb–Jul 1963 |
| Cdr E. C. Thorne | HMNZS *Otago*, Apr–Dec 1963 |
| Capt L. G. Carr, DSC | HMNZS *Taranaki*, Sep 1963 – Sep 1964 |
| Capt E. C. Thorne | HMNZS *Otago*, Jul–Dec 1964 |
| Cdr R. H. L. Humby | HMNZS *Otago*, Dec 1964 – May 1965 |
| Capt J. P. S. Vallant | HMNZS *Royalist*, Mar–Nov 1965 |
| Lt-Cdr M. N. Waymouth | HMNZS *Hickleton*, Apr 1965 – Jan 1966 |

| | |
|---|---|
| Lt-Cdr P. N. Wright | HMNZS *Hickleton*, Jan–Aug 1966 |
| Lt-Cdr D. G. Bamfield | HMNZS *Hickleton*, Aug 1966 |
| Lt L. J. Tempero | HMNZS *Santon*, Apr 1965 – Aug 1966 |
| Lt-Cdr G. W. Glyde | HMNZS *Santon*, Aug 1966 – Dec 1966 |
| Cdr K. M. Saull | HMNZS *Taranaki*, Aug 1965 – May 1966 |
| Cdr R. H. L. Humby | HMNZS *Otago*, Feb–Sep 1966 |
| Cdr J. I. Quinn | HMNZS *Blackpool*, Nov 1966 – May 1967 |

## Army

### 1FIR, 1951–56

| | |
|---|---|
| Lt-Col R. A. Tinker, OBE, MC, MM | Nov 1951 – May 1953 |
| Lt-Col E. T. T. Cakobau | Jun–Sep 1953 |
| Lt-Col H. J. G. Low, DSO, MC | Oct 1953 – Sep 1955 |
| Lt-Col P. Ganilau | Oct 1955 – May 1956 |

### HQ NZ Force FARELF

| | |
|---|---|
| Col G. P. Cade, DSO | Comd NZ Army Force FARELF, Sep 1957 – Feb 1960 |
| Col D. A. Caughley, MBE | Comd NZ Army Force FARELF, Feb 1960 – Jan 1964 |
| Col L. A. Kermode, OBE | Comd NZ Army Force FARELF, Jan 1964 – Jan 1966 |
| Col P. H. G. Hamilton, OBE, BSc, AOSM | Comd NZ Army Force FARELF, Jan 1966 – Dec 1968 |

### Commanders, 28 Commonwealth Brigade

| | |
|---|---|
| Brig P. N. M. Moore, DSO (two Bars), MC, BA | Sep 1955 – Jul 1958 |
| Brig H. J. Mogg, CBE, DSO (Bar) | Jul 1958 – Nov 1960 |
| Brig F. G. Hassett, DSO, MVO, OBE (Aust) | Nov 1960 – Oct 1962 |
| Brig R. B. Dawson, CB, DSO (NZ) | Oct 1962 – Oct 1964 |
| Brig T. D. R. McMeekin, OBE | Oct 1964 – Jan 1967 |

| | |
|---|---|
| Brig P. L. Tancred (Aust) | Jan 1967 – Mar 1969 |
| Brig R. M. Gurr, OBE, (NZ) | Mar 1969 – Mar 1971 |
| Brig M. J. H. Walsh, CB, DSO | Mar–Nov 1971 |

## Commanders 28 ANZUK Brigade

| | |
|---|---|
| Brig M. J. H. Walsh, CB, DSO | Nov 1971 – Mar 1973 |
| Brig M. R. Kennedy, MBE (NZ) | Mar 1973 – Jan 1974 |

## SAS

| | |
|---|---|
| Major F. Rennie, MBE, MC | 1 NZ Sqn, 22 SAS Regt, May 1955 – Nov 1957 |
| Major W. J. D. Meldrum | 1 Det, 1 NZ (SAS) Ranger Sqn, Feb–Apr 1965 |
| Major B. T. A. Worsnop | 1 Det, 1 NZ (SAS) Ranger Sqn, Apr–Oct 1965 |
| Major R. S. Dearing | 2 Det, 1 NZ (SAS) Ranger Sqn, Aug 1965 – Feb 1966 |
| Major D. L. Ogilvy | 3 Det, 1 NZ (SAS) Ranger Sqn, Jan–May 1966 |
| Major D. W. S. Moloney | 4 Det, 1 NZ (SAS) Ranger Sqn, Jun–Dec 1966 |

## Commanding Officers

| | |
|---|---|
| Lt-Col W. R. K. Morrison, DSO, OBE | 1 NZ Regt, Aug 1957 – Nov 1959 |
| Lt-Col D. J. Aitken, OBE | 2 NZ Regt, Nov 1959 – Nov 1961 |
| Lt-Col L. A. Pearce, MBE | 1 NZ Regt, Nov 1961 – Nov 1963 |
| Lt-Col R. M. Gurr, MBE | 1 NZ Regt, Nov 1963 – Apr 1964 |
| | 1RNZIR, May 1964 – Nov 1965 |
| Lt-Col B. M. Poananga, MBE | 1RNZIR, Nov 1965 – Nov 1967 |

# Appendix 4

## DIRECTIVES FOR NEW ZEALAND ELEMENTS OF THE COMMONWEALTH STRATEGIC RESERVE, 1956

SOURCE: JSO 32/34/4/2, 26 JUNE 1956

### DIRECTIVE FOR ROYAL NEW ZEALAND NAVY SHIPS ATTACHED TO THE COMMONWEALTH STRATEGIC RESERVE

1. Consequent on the establishment of the Commonwealth Strategic Reserve, the Naval Components of which form part of the British Far East Fleet, the New Zealand Government has approved the following conditions under which Her Majesty's New Zealand ships are placed under the operational command of the Commander-in-Chief, Far East Station.

a. British Commonwealth Strategic Reserve:

(i) Her Majesty's New Zealand ships allocated to the British Commonwealth Strategic Reserve may be employed in accordance with the conditions laid down in the ANZAM Directive to the Strategic Reserve.

(ii) With reference to paragraph 12 of the directive they may be used as are ships of the Royal Navy in the secondary role in Malaya for the prevention of infiltration by Communist agents or armed bands.

b. Ships Detached for Service Outside the Malayan Area:

(i) *Korean Operations.* Provision has been made in the Directive to the Strategic Reserve for a New Zealand frigate to be allocated for temporary duty in Korean waters in rotation with ships of the British Far East Fleet and the New Zealand Government desires that New

Zealand frigates should spend at least one period in Korean waters during their attachment.

(ii) *Formosa Patrol.* While allocated for duty in Korean waters New Zealand frigates on the Far East Station may be used as for Royal Navy ships for the Formosa Straits patrol.

(iii) *Protection of British Ships.* Her Majesty's New Zealand ships on the Far East Station may comply with the policy adopted by Royal Navy ships in the protection of British Merchant Shipping against intervention by Chinese Communist or Nationalist warships and aircraft, as laid down in Far East Station General Orders 252 (attached).

c. *Action in Event of Civil Disturbances.* While serving as part of the Strategic Reserve, HMNZ ships and personnel may, in the event of local disturbances, be employed to assist in the defence or protection of naval bases on the station, and may also participate in operations for the protection of the wives and families of personnel at such bases. New Zealand personnel may also be directed to take appropriate measures to safeguard their ships should these be threatened by civil disturbances. In all other cases, however, where the use of New Zealand naval personnel is requested to assist in the maintenance of law and order for any purpose outside the express terms of the Directive to the Strategic Reserve, the prior consent of the New Zealand authorities is to be sought, except in the circumstances of emergency envisaged in Section D below. Such consent should, where appropriate, be sought through the Commissioner for New Zealand in South East Asia; otherwise such consent is to be sought direct from New Zealand through the New Zealand Naval Board.

d. *Employment in Emergency.* Other than in the circumstances stated above, Her Majesty's New Zealand ships shall not be used for the conduct of any operations which may require the use of force until the whole circumstances have been laid before the New Zealand Government and its consent received; in cases of emergency, however, (other than civil disturbances, the procedure in respect of which is stated in Section C above) where time does not permit of the sanction of the New Zealand Government being obtained beforehand, New Zealand ships may be used for operations designed solely for the protection of British lives and property without reference to any higher authority. If possible, however, the sanction of the New Zealand Government shall always be obtained beforehand, and in cases where this is not practicable full information as to the action taken shall be furnished to the New Zealand Government as early as possible afterwards.

## DIRECTIVE FOR EMPLOYMENT OF THE NEW ZEALAND ARMY COMPONENT OF THE COMMONWEALTH STRATEGIC RESERVE

1. The New Zealand Army Component presently comprises:

   a. One Special Air Service squadron as part of the 22 United Kingdom Special Air Service Regiment.

   b. Personnel of the New Zealand Special Air Service employed on regimental duties in 22 United Kingdom Special Air Service Regiment and at Headquarters Malayan Command.

2. The New Zealand Army component will be under the command of the Commander-in-Chief, Far East Land Forces, who will delegate his responsibility in accordance with his command organization. The immediate superior commander of the New Zealand Special Air Service Squadron and New Zealand Special Air Service personnel employed on regimental duties will be the Officer Commanding 22 Special Air Service Regiment. The immediate superior commander of New Zealand Special Air Service personnel attached to Headquarters Malayan Command will be the officer at that headquarters authorized to exercise the powers of command of a Commanding Officer.

3. The general employment of the New Zealand Army component will be in accordance with the conditions laid down in the ANZAM Directive to the Strategic Reserve. Any operational restrictions which may be placed upon its employment will be notified separately. Under arrangements already made, the New Zealand Special Air Service Squadron and other Special Air Service personnel employed on regimental duties will continue to train and operate as an integral part of 22 Special Air Service Regiment, and in so doing, may be used on operations against Communist Terrorists.

4. In the event of local civil disturbances, members of the New Zealand Army component may be employed to assist in the defence or protection of the camp or accommodation facility at which they may be stationed; and may also participate in operations for the protection of the wives and families of personnel at such camp or accommodation facility, in accordance with existing arrangements. In all other cases, however, where the use of personnel of the New Zealand Army Component is requested to assist in the maintenance of law and order, the prior consent of the New Zealand Government is to be sought through the Commissioner for New Zealand in South East Asia.

5. The Officer Commanding the New Zealand Special Air Service Squadron will be responsible to the Officer Commanding 22 Special Air Service Regiment for

complying with orders and instructions pertaining to the command, employment, and administration of the Squadron except as may be separately advised on matters which are the concern of the New Zealand Army only, or as set out below.

6. Should circumstances arise in the operation or administration of the New Zealand Army component which, in the opinion of the Officer Commanding the New Zealand Special Air Service Squadron, affect the national interests of New Zealand, are contrary to the agreed policy for the employment of the New Zealand Army component, or adversely affect the well-being of New Zealand Special Air Service personnel or their families, he is to report the circumstances to higher authority in Far East Land Forces through the Officer Commanding 22 Special Air Service Regiment. If the action taken by the Far East Land Forces authorities is not, in the opinion of the Officer Commanding the New Zealand Special Air Service Squadron, sufficient to rectify the position, he is then to report direct to New Zealand Army Headquarters. Where this is done the Officer Commanding the New Zealand Special Air Service Squadron will keep the appropriate authorities in Far East Land Forces, and also the Commissioner for New Zealand in South East Asia, informed of his actions.

7. The Officer Commanding the New Zealand Special Air Service Squadron will observe the normal channels of communications provided within Far East Land Forces with the exceptions that:

a. On all administrative, personnel or other matters which are of concern to the New Zealand Army, only he may communicate with Army Headquarters direct with, in each case, copies of such correspondence being given to his Commanding Officer.

b. On matters affecting the National interests of New Zealand, the policy for the employment of the New Zealand Army component, or the welfare of New Zealand Army component personnel or their dependants, he may communicate with New Zealand Army Headquarters and with the Commissioner for New Zealand in South East Asia in accordance with paragraph 6 above.

DIRECTIVE TO OFFICER COMMANDING, NO. 14 SQUADRON, ROYAL NEW ZEALAND AIR FORCE

1. While serving in the Far East Air Force your unit will be under the command of the Commander-in-Chief, FEAF, who will delegate his responsibility in accordance with his command organization.

2. The general employment of the Squadron, which forms part of the Commonwealth Far East Strategic Reserve, will be in accordance with the conditions laid down in the Directive for the Strategic Reserve. You will be notified separately of any operational restrictions which may be placed upon employment of the Squadron. Under arrangements already made with the Commander-in-Chief, FEAF, No. 14 Squadron will continue to train and operate in a Day Fighter/Ground Attack role. In training for this role it may be used in operations against the Communist terrorists.

3. In the event of local civil disturbances, the personnel of the Squadron may be employed to assist in the defence or protection of the airfield at which it may be stationed, and may also participate in operations for the protection of the wives and families of personnel on the station, in accordance with existing arrangements. In all other cases, however, where the use of Squadron personnel is requested to assist in the maintenance of law and order, the prior consent of the New Zealand authorities is to be sought through the Commissioner for New Zealand in South East Asia.

4. You will be responsible to the Commander-in-Chief, FEAF for complying with orders and instructions pertaining to the command, employment and administration of your unit, except insofar as you may be separately advised on matters which are the concern of the Royal New Zealand Air Force only, or as are set out below.

5. Should circumstances arise in the operation or administration of your unit, which, in your opinion, affect the national interests of New Zealand, are contrary to the agreed policy for the employment of your unit, or adversely affect the well-being of the personnel under your command or their families, you are to report the circumstances to your higher authority in FEAF. If the action taken by the FEAF authorities is not, in your opinion, sufficient to rectify the position, you are then to report direct to RNZAF Headquarters. Where this is done the appropriate FEAF authorities and also the Commissioner for New Zealand in South East Asia are to be kept informed of your actions.

6. You will observe the normal channels of communication provided within FEAF with the exception that:

a. On all technical, administrative, personnel or other matters which are of concern to the RNZAF only, you may communicate with RNZAF Headquarters direct with, in each case, copies of such correspondence being given to your Commanding Officer.

b. On matters affecting the national interests of New Zealand, the policy for the unit, or the welfare of RNZAF personnel under your command or their dependants, you may communicate with RNZAF Headquarters and with the Commissioner for New Zealand in South East Asia in accordance with paragraph 5 above.

## DIRECTIVE TO OFFICER COMMANDING, NO. 41 SQUADRON, ROYAL NEW ZEALAND AIR FORCE

1. While serving in the Far East Air Force your unit will be under the command of the Commander-in-Chief, FEAF, who will delegate his responsibility in accordance with his command organization.

2. The general employment of the Squadron, which forms part of the Commonwealth Far East Strategic Reserve, will be in accordance with the conditions laid down in the Directive for the Strategic Reserve. You will be notified separately of any operational restrictions which may be placed upon employment of the Squadron. Under arrangements already made with the Commander-in-Chief, FEAF, No. 41 Squadron will continue to train and operate in a medium range transport role. In training for this role it may be used in operations against Communist terrorists.

3. In the event of local civil disturbances, the personnel of the Squadron may be employed to assist in the defence or protection of the airfield at which it may be stationed, and may also participate in operations for the protection of the wives and families of personnel on the station, in accordance with existing arrangements. In all other cases, however, where the use of Squadron personnel is requested to assist in the maintenance of law and order, the prior consent of the New Zealand authorities is to be sought through the Commissioner for New Zealand in South East Asia.

4. You will be responsible to the Commander-in-Chief, FEAF for complying with orders and instructions pertaining to the command, employment and administration of your unit, except insofar as you may be separately advised on matters which are the concern of the Royal New Zealand Air Force only, or as are set out below.

5. Should circumstances arise in the operation or administration of your unit, which, in your opinion, affect the national interests of New Zealand, are contrary to the agreed policy for the employment of your unit, or adversely affect the well-being of the personnel under your command or their families, you are to report the circumstances to your higher authority in FEAF. If the action taken by the FEAF authorities is not, in your opinion, sufficient to rectify the position, you are then to report direct to RNZAF Headquarters. Where this is done the appropriate FEAF authorities and also the Commissioner for New Zealand in South East Asia are to be kept informed of your actions.

6. You will observe the normal channels of communication provided within FEAF with the exception that:

a. On all technical, administrative, personnel or other matters which are of concern to the RNZAF only, you may communicate with RNZAF Headquarters direct with, in each case, copies of such correspondence being given to your Commanding Officer.

b. On matters affecting the national interests of New Zealand, the policy for the unit, or the welfare of RNZAF personnel under your command or their dependants, you may communicate with RNZAF Headquarters and with the Commissioner for New Zealand in South East Asia in accordance with paragraph 5 above.

# Appendix 5

## SOME NOTES ON N[EW] Z[EALAND] SQ[UADRO]N TECHNIQUES [1957]

SOURCE: RENNIE PAPERS, NZ SAS GROUP ARCHIVES

SOME NOTES ON NZ SQN TECHNIQUES

These should be read in conjunction with the ATOM pamphlet. [HQ Malaya, *The Conduct of Anti-Terrorist Operations in Malaya*, Kuala Lumpur, 1952]

### Introduction

1. The drills cover the following only:

   a. Ptl grouping.

   b. Ptl size.

   c. Ptl weapons.

   d. Balance of weapons.

   e. Tac order of weapons.

   f. Scouting.

   g. Obstacle crossing.

   h. Halts.

   i. IA Drills.

NB: The drills for ambushing have not been dealt with because of probable difference in techniques prompted by differences in nos. involved and terrain.

## Ptl Grouping

2. A ptl, regardless of size, should always be divided into 3 gps known as:

   a. Recce gp (R).

   b. Bren gp (B).

   c. Rfl gp (RFL).

3. Whether the Bren gp has a Bren in it or not, it will always be known as such. In this way hand sigs can always be used to deploy any ptl of 3 or more men.

4. Except in special circumstances, a ptl should never be more than 9 men – 3 gps. When there are more, in cases like a pl or tp move the body should be divided into 2 or more ptls with a gap of anything up to 30 yds but ideally about 10 yds between ptls. In this way each ptl can set its own pace and avoid the inevitable and tiring 'concertina' effect.

## Ptl Size

5. The best ptl size is 6 men – 2 in each gp.

6. Except for a security ptl close to or around the base, a ptl must always be considered a fighting ptl.

## Ptl Weapons

7. A ptl should always have a Bren gun or GMC and until 30 FN amn tracer becomes available, the Bren is the better of the two:

   a. Tracer amn enables a gunner firing from the hip to get on tgt in minimum time.

   b. Another man in the ptl who cannot see the CT can get a line from the tracer to put some fire in the area.

   c. Tracer should be loaded the first 4 rds tracer and 1 in 4 thereafter.

   d. The GMC has the advantage that its mags and amn are interchangeable with the FN rfl.

8. The FN rfl is an excellent weapon:

   a. Hard hitting power.

   b. Semi-automatic fire.

   c. Easily kept clean.

9. The Owen or Pachett SMG:

   a. Short barrel.

   b. High rate automatic fire.

   c. Light wgt (the Pachett much the lighter of the two).

10. Shot Gun (pump action):

   a. Excellent at close range.

   b. Light wgt.

   c. Night ambs.

11. No. 5 rfl and Carbine should not be considered if the FN rfl is available.

## Balance of Weapons

12. A good balance of weapons in any form is:

   1 Bren to 2 SMGs to 3 FN rfls.

## Tac Order of Weapons in a Ptl

13. The order of weapons must always vary according to:

   a. The type of terrain or bush being encountered at the time.

   b. A scout changeover.

   c. Whether a tracker is working in front.

14. When the going is hard and (or) visibility short, a good weapon order would be:

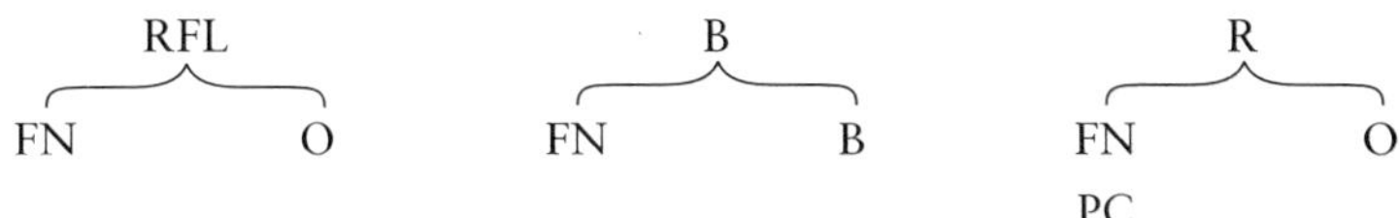


a. This gives the obvious advantage of an Owen in front.

b. A hard hitting easily aimed weapon at No. 2 (ptl comd).

c. The Bren which is the ptl fire power next to the ptl comd.

d. In a camp attack:

(i) A Bren gp of a Bren and FN.

(ii) An aslt gp of O, FN, O, FN.

15. Where the going is easier and visibility much of the time more than 20 yds (e.g. a good ridge track) a good ptl order would be:

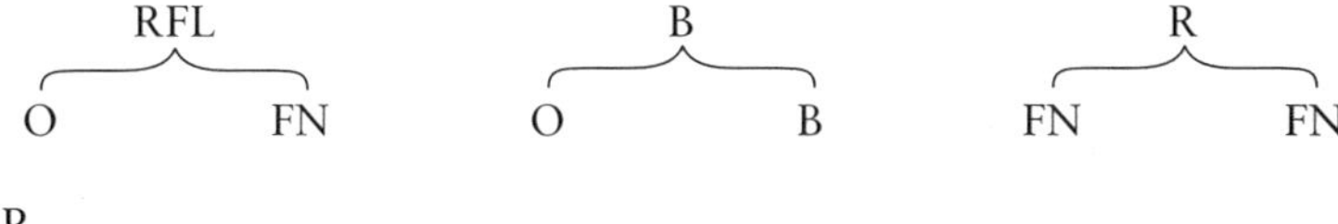


OR

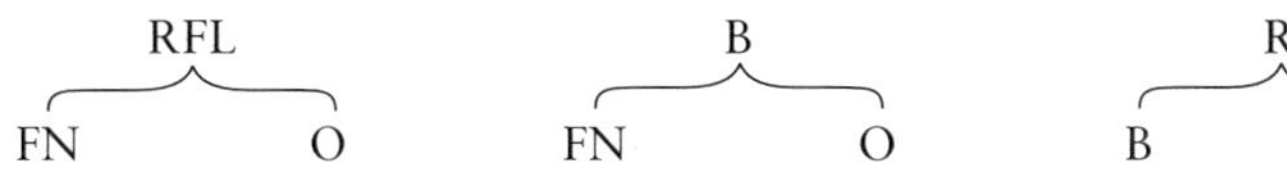


16. In exceptional cases where the going is very good, visibility long and there is little danger of CTs ambushing from a flank (e.g. a long down-hill ridge track), a good order would be:

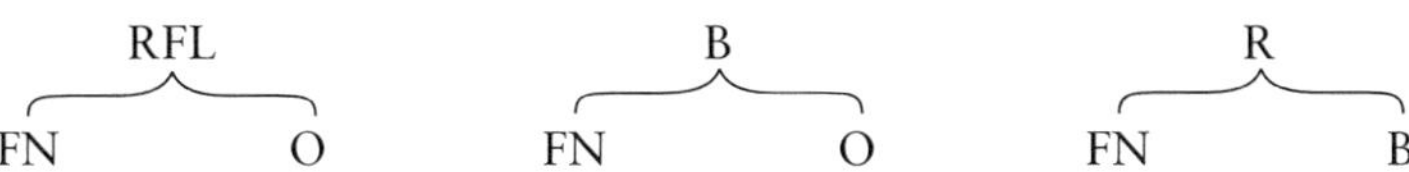

17. When a tracker is working, you have the exceptional case where:

a. A ptl comd can be No. 3.

b. The No. 1 (tracker) is ridden by his coverer (No. 2) who covers from one side to avoid bunching if possible and if not just moves very close behind the No. 1.

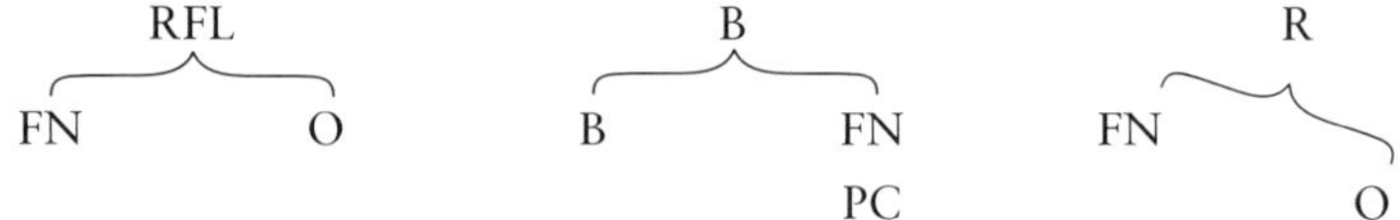


## Scouting

18. A leading scout should be a reliable, experienced man with a good jungle knowledge.

19. As there is a terrific strain on him all the time, he should be changed to a posn towards the rear of the ptl every 2 hrs at least.

20. At all times he is responsible for watching in the direction the ptl is moving.

21. If he spots a sign on or to one side of the track, he should either:

a. Signal the No. 2 through to watch the front; or

b. Keeping his eyes to the front, indicate the sign to the No. 2 and let him investigate it.

22. During any halts over 10 mins he should be brought back into the bdy of the ptl to rest while someone else (ideally the Bren) is put in front.

23. He should never move fwd until he is satisfied to the best of his knowledge the area is clear, or until someone is adequately covering him (in the case of an obstacle).

24. When crossing an obstacle he should move quickly to make a difficult tgt until he is in good cover on the far side.

25. The ptl speed is governed by the ptl comd and a scout, with experience, can keep himself the correct distance from the ptl comd at No. 2. He must imagine himself a pair of eyes and a weapon on a leash.

26. If in doubt as to direction, he should pause and without looking around be redirected by the ptl comd.

## Obstacle Crossing

27. Large Obstacles – e.g. ladangs, rivers, clearings, etc:

   a. On reaching the obstacle, the ptl comd should place his Bren gp to cover the move across by Recce and Rfl gps.

   b. The Recce gp will move through one man at a time. The Rlf gp cover the rear.

   c. The Rfl gp go through while the Recce gp cover the front.

   d. The Bren gp go through covered by the Rfl gp on the other side, bump the back of the Recce gp and the ptl moves on.

NB. There should never be more than one man on the obstacle at a time. The crossing should be quick to make as poor a tgt as possible.

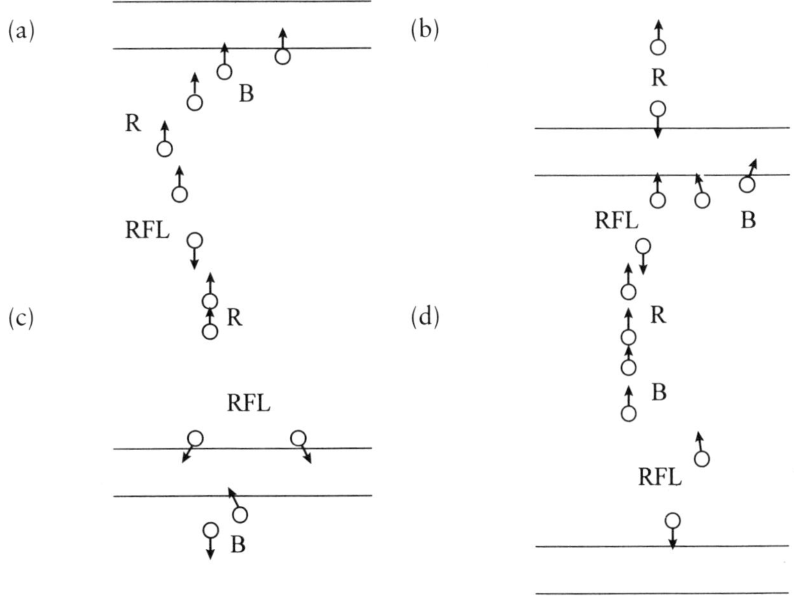

28. Small Obstacles – e.g. small stream, log, etc.

a. The No. 1 Scout will pause until he is satisfied the obstacle is clear while the ptl will keep moving fwd until the No. 2 bumps the back of No. 1.

b. The No. 1 then quickly crosses covered by the No. 2 during which time the ptl continues fwd and the No. 3 should have bumped the back of No. 2.

c. The No. 2 then crosses covered by No. 3, etc, etc.

d. Except in the case of No. 1 who will always watch fwd the successive ptl numbers having just crossed the obstacle, will cover the following man across.

NB. Each man must cross the obstacle quickly.

## Ptl Halts

29. The important thing to remember is that the ptl must at all times be in good condition to react to any situation. In other words the men must be just as capable of shooting accurately and assaulting at the top of a 6000 ft mt as they were at the bottom.

30. A ptl will halt for the following reasons:

a. *Listening halt.* Should occur at least every 10 mins and more when the ground is dry or more noisy. The ptl will remain standing and only move on when satisfied no one else is moving in the area.

b. *5 min spell.* Should occur at least every half hour and more if the ptl condition indicates it.

c. *Smoke.* Only when the ptl comd is satisfied the area is clear.

d. *Midday brew.* As in para c.

e. *Overnight halt.*

31. Every halt irrespective of reason should be a temporary ambush posn. Points to remember in siting are:

a. High ground.

b. Good fds of fire at front and rear of ptl. The front being usually the more likely, time permitting, the Bren gp should be brought up.

c. Each man must be able to quickly contact the man either side of him.

d. All round observation.

e. Smokers get away from any shafts of sunlight.

IMMEDIATE ACTION DRILLS (6 MAN PTL)

## Head on

32. If the CT is met head on the leading scout will immediately lift his weapon to the shoulder (wherever possible) and fire. Time permitting he should go down on one knee:

a. To give a steadier aim.

b. To give the No. 2 a clear line. As soon as possible the No. 1 or No. 2 must yell 'CT front!'

33. The Bren gp will swing to the right and the rfl gp to the left, but still maintaining contact with the Recce gp. If this is not possible due to the terrain or bush, they will swing their weapons off 45 degs in those directions and let go a burst or few rds until the ptl charges.

CT

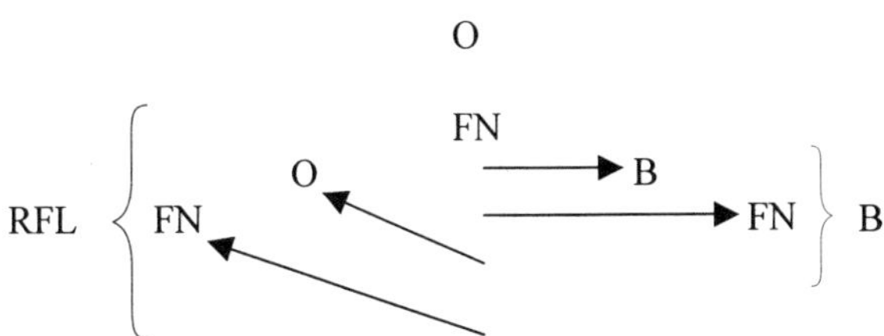


34. The ptl will immediately charge and the Bren and Rfl gps, if not already to right and left, will get there now.

35. The essential thing is to stay in one gp at this stage.

36. The object of the Recce gp is to keep the CT in sight and run him down. It may be necessary to leave the Bren gp guarding wounded or dead CTs and continue a follow-up with the remainder.

37. The RV is the point of contact.

38. When a member of the ptl is wounded, he will never be left on his own and as soon as possible the man nearest him will go to his aid..

CT AMBUSH

1st Case

39. When a ptl is ambushed, every man will bring maximum fire to bear in the direction of the CT whether he can see a tgt or not. Simultaneously the ptl will charge the CT firing from the hip as they run right through the ambush posns and reorg on the other side.

40. By this time the ptl have regained the initiative and the next move is over to the ptl comd except where wounded may have been left on the track in which case the ptl must get back to them as fast as possible.

41. The reorg over, it is important to get to the CT base as soon as possible as there may be other CTs there and at least a lot of kit. The track from their ambush to their base should not be difficult to pick up.

42. The important thing is that when the CT open up, on no account to move off the track away from their fire as that is exactly what they plan you to do and are bound to have land mines, grenades, sharpened bamboo, spikes, etc.

2nd Case

43. If any of the ptl are pinned down and are unable to get fwd, they will go to ground and return the fire. The first man to realise he is free to move will take control by yelling, 'FOLLOW ME!' and do an immediate semi-circular flanking attack.

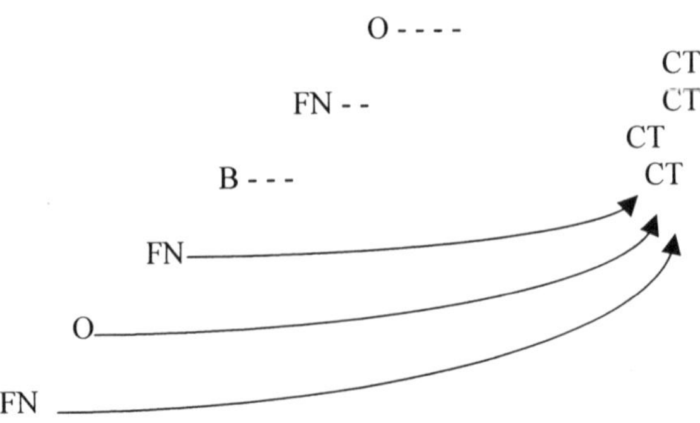

## Attacking a CT Camp

44. It will seldom be possible to get a good view of a CT camp but the ptl comd must do his best, without unduly jeopardising the ptl's chance of surprise, to indicate the general area for the Bren gp whose ideal posn is one from where they can fire on the CT camp in enfilade.

45. While the Bren gp is getting in posn, the Aslt gp (Recce and Rlf gps) led by the ptl comd move into a posn which ideally:

- a. Is at right angles to the Bren fire.
- b. Is not an uphill aslt.
- c. Is not on the CT water point side of the camp to lessen the danger of having a CT behind you washing or using a latrine.
- d. Is not on any of the tracks in or out of the camp.

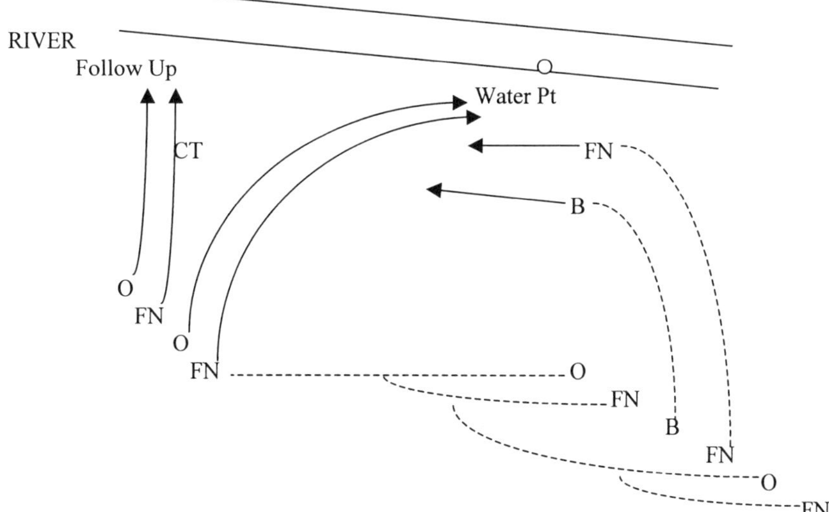


46. The initiative at this stage is over to the Bren gp comd who, having given the aslt gp enough time to get into posn, will open fire with a complete mag at any CTs seen or just through their bashas.

47. The aslt gp hold their fire for the initial 2 or 3 secs. Failing any of the CT running towards them, they will charge through the camp in a straight line firing from the hip as they go. Then, under the direction of the ptl comd, they will probably split, checking water and washing points or on a follow-up if necessary.

48. The Bren gp keep their fire ahead of the Aslt gp, change mags and move in immediately behind the Aslt gp.

a. They will ensure there is no further worry from any CTs alive in the camp.

b. Reorg in the camp.

Date Oct 57

I H BURROWS
LT
NZ SAS Sqn

# *Appendix 6*

## THE REQUIREMENTS OF INDIVIDUAL TRAINING TO MEET THE CONDITIONS OF A LIMITED SCALE WAR IN CLOSE COUNTRY

SOURCE: RENNIE PAPERS, NZ SAS GROUP ARCHIVES

Mental Attitude

1. There is always doubt or fear of the unknown. The town-bred soldier enters a completely different world when he enters the jungle. By giving him trg and experience in these conditions, this problem can be overcome. The soldier must be taught that his approach to the mass of undergrowth is all important. The jungle can be his greatest assistant if he learns to use its conditions, his greatest enemy if he doesn't.

Jungle Craft

2. The soldier must be taught to:

   a. Track and to read signs.

   b. To observe in depth – look beyond the immediate foliage.

   c. To live happily under the trees and how to survive if necessary.

   d. Listen to birds, monkeys and other animals and learn their reactions to the presence of man.

   e. Use the jungle wherever possible to decrease the articles carried by the soldier.

Tactics

3. All ranks must study tactics for drills covering:

a. The laying of ambushes up to coy level.

b. Infiltration, how to do it and to defeat it.

c. IAs for:

(i) Caught in ambush.

(ii) Laying on an immediate ambush.

(iii) Head on contact.

(iv) Attack on en posts.

(v) Snatch raids.

d. The all important weapon pit, its siting, drainage and how to live in it.

e. How to improve F of F by thinning out and by trimming undergrowth from thigh hgt down, so that from outside it is not obvious.

f. Warning devices and comns between wpn pits.

Weapon Trg

4. a. All ranks must be masters of all pl wpns.

b. Emphasis must be placed on the extreme value of the single well aimed snap shot.

c. Continual practice at snap shooting at short ranges on the open range and on jungle lanes.

d. Annual range practices should incl greater emphasis on these aspects rather than on the open range.

e. Annual classification should incl TOET.

f. Shooting should be from all posns.

Movement

5. Practice of movement both day and ni carrying all eqpt by:

   a. AC, MT and trains, embussing, debussing.

   b. Emplaning, deplaning and scrambling from hcptrs.

   c. Route march on jungle tracks in moonlight when possible.

Ptls

6. a. Fighting, recce and standing, up to 14 days in duration.

   b. Actions while tracking.

   c. Orders of march of pers and of wpns and IAs.

Map Reading

7. a. Map reading of all ranks especially offrs and NCOs must be of the highest order.

   b. All ranks must be able to use simple maps such as form-line maps or aerial photos with simple grid superimposed.

   c. All ranks must be able to 'navigate' ascertaining their posns by time, distance, bearing as for 'dead reckoning'.

Handling of Local Peoples

8. Local peoples will often form the only sources of info. All ranks must:

   a. Be taught how to handle Eastern peoples such as Chinese, Malays, Indians, Aborigines, etc.

   b. Know elements of Chinese and Malay languages.

Comns Trg

9. a. Aerials, erection and how to obtain best results must be known by all.

   b. All should be able to set up and use a set on RT, one in 4 should be able to send and receive morse at 6 wpm.

Fitness and Youth

10. a. Tps should be of 20–30 years of age.

b. Offrs not more than:

CO 40 )
Coy Comd 34 ) All must be fit for these ages.
Pl Comd 27 )

c. Fitness standards required for basic trg should be maint within every unit at all times.

Sp Wpns and Fire

11. a. Units are responsible for their own local def – Sp units must do more on this aspect than previously.

b. Because of terrain aspects, Inf units will not be able to place the same reliance on the availability of sp fire as in the past. Emphasis must be upon own small arms with a little sp from own 3-inch Mors.

c. Sp fire ranging will have to be by the 'creep onto tgt' method – all ranks must have a basic knowledge, Cpls and above must have a thorough grounding.

First Aid and Hygiene

12. a. There must be pl level med ords. Own soldiers trg to the extent of handling fevers, stomach disorders, elementary stitching, GSW treatment.

b. Transfusions must be possible at coy level.

c. Med aid at RAP must be greater than under basic conditions.

d. Trg in hygiene both personal and camp must be so ingrained as to be automatic.

DZ/LZ

13. a. All rank instr in explosives – selected pers to attend adv courses.

b. Selection, clearing and operation of DZ/LZ by day and ni, will be necessary. Pl Comds must have an adv knowledge.

Sup

14. a. Standard block indents should be evolved and used in trg.

b. Simple sup indent codes must be tried.

c. Colns by porter, animal, trolley, air, MT, etc. methods will be used and pers must have experience of organising these tasks.

Rations

15. a. Individual 24 hr ration packs must be obtained and used in trg.

b. Pers must be trg to use them and to make the most of the ration.

c. A form of heating for cooking is required. The 'tommy cooker' is good.

Clothing and Eqpt

16. a. Bare necessity clothing scales should be evolved now.

b. Clothing to meet these requirements should be available in this country to eqpt pers prior to embarkation.

c. Eqpt must be aval for trg in NZ.

11 Jul 1958

I H Burrows
Lt
School of Infantry

# Appendix 7

## ESTABLISHMENT: A NEW ZEALAND INFANTRY BATTALION (NEW ZEALAND ARMY FORCE FAR EAST LAND FORCES)

SOURCE: WA-M 2/1/1

## A NEW ZEALAND INFANTRY BATTALION (NEW ZEALAND ARMY FORCE FAR EAST LAND FORCES) SPECIAL ESTABLISHMENT

### (i) PERSONNEL

| Detail | Battalion Headquarters | Headquarter Company | | | | | | | Four Rifle Companies (Each) | | | Total, a NZ Infantry Battalion, NZ Army Force FARELF |
|---|---|---|---|---|---|---|---|---|---|---|---|---|
| | | Headquarters | Signal Platoon | Administrative Platoon | Mortar Platoon | Machine-Gun Platoon | Assault Pioneer Section | Total, Headquarter Company | Headquarters | Three Platoons (Each) | Total, a Rifle Company | |
| Officer Commanding (lieutenant-colonel) | 1 | - | - | - | - | - | - | - | - | - | - | 1 |
| Second-in-command (major) | 1 | - | - | - | - | - | - | - | - | - | - | 1 |
| Majors | - | 1 | - | - | - | - | - | 1 | 1 | - | 1 | 5 |
| Adjutant (captain) | 1 | - | - | - | - | - | - | - | - | - | - | 1 |
| Captains | - | 1 | 1 | 1 | 1 | 1 | - | 5 | 1 | - | 1 | 9 |
| Subalterns | 1 | - | 1 | - | - | - | - | 1 | - | 1 | 3 | 14 |
| Quarter-masters (1 captain, 1 captain/subaltern) | - | - | - | 2 | - | - | - | 2 | - | - | - | 2 |
| Total, officers | 4 | 2 | 2 | 3 | 1 | 1 | - | 9 | 2 | 1 | 5 | 33 |

| Detail | Battalion Headquarters | Headquarter Company | | | | | | | Four Rifle Companies (Each) | | | Total, a NZ Infantry Battalion, NZ Army Force FARELF |
|---|---|---|---|---|---|---|---|---|---|---|---|---|
| | | Headquarters | Signal Platoon | Administrative Platoon | Mortar Platoon | Machine-Gun Platoon | Assault Pioneer Section | Total, Headquarter Company | Headquarters | Three Platoons (Each) | Total, a Rifle Company | |
| Regimental sergeant-major | 1 | - | - | - | - | - | - | - | - | - | - | 1 |
| Regimental quarter-master-sergeant | - | - | - | 1 | - | - | - | 1 | - | - | - | 1 |
| Company sergeant-majors | - | 1 | - | - | - | - | - | 1 | 1 | - | 1 | 5 |
| Drill and weapon training instructor | 1 | - | - | - | - | - | - | - | - | - | - | 1 |
| Total, warrant officers | 2 | 1 | - | 1 | - | - | - | 2 | 1 | - | 1 | 8 |
| Company quarter-master-sergeants | - | 1 | - | - | - | - | - | 1 | 1 | - | 1 | 5 |
| Cook | - | - | - | 1 | - | - | - | 1 | - | - | - | 1 |
| Drum/bugle major | - | - | - | 1 | - | - | - | 1 | - | - | - | 1 |
| Intelligence NCO | 1 | - | - | - | - | - | - | - | - | - | - | 1 |
| Medical NCO | 1 | - | - | - | - | - | - | - | - | - | - | 1 |
| Officers mess steward | - | - | - | 1 | - | - | - | 1 | - | - | - | 1 |
| Orderly room sergeant | 1 | - | - | - | - | - | - | - | - | - | - | 1 |
| Pioneer NCO | - | - | - | - | - | - | 1 | 1 | - | - | - | 1 |
| Regimental police NCO | 1 | - | - | - | - | - | - | - | - | - | - | 1 |
| Sergeants | - | - | - | - | 4 | 4 | - | 8 | - | 1 | 3 | 20 |
| Signal NCOs | - | - | 2 | - | - | - | - | 2 | - | - | - | 2 |
| Storeman (technical) | - | - | - | 1 | - | - | - | 1 | - | - | - | 1 |
| Transport NCO | - | - | - | 1 | - | - | - | 1 | - | - | - | 1 |
| Total, staff-sergeants and sergeants | 4 | 1 | 2 | 5 | 4 | 4 | 1 | 17 | 1 | 1 | 4 | 37 |
| Corporals | 5 | - | 6 | 9 | 5 | 6 | 1 | 27 | - | 3 | 9 | 68 |
| Privates (includes 56 lance-corporals | 27 | 4 | 44 | 48 | 23 | 21 | 9 | 149 | 5 | 31 | 98 | 568 |
| Total, rank and file | 32 | 4 | 50 | 57 | 28 | 27 | 10 | 176 | 5 | 34 | 107 | 636 |
| Total, other ranks | 38 | 6 | 52 | 63 | 32 | 31 | 11 | 195 | 7 | 35 | 112 | 681 |
| Total, all ranks | 42 | 8 | 54 | 66 | 33 | 32 | 11 | 204 | 9 | 36 | 117 | 714 |

| Detail | Battalion Headquarters | Headquarter Company | | | | | | | Four Rifle Companies (Each) | | | Total, a NZ Infantry Battalion, NZ Army Force FARELF |
|---|---|---|---|---|---|---|---|---|---|---|---|---|
| | | Headquarters | Signal Platoon | Administrative Platoon | Mortar Platoon | Machine-Gun Platoon | Assault Pioneer Section | Total, Headquarter Company | Headquarters | Three Platoons (Each) | Total, a Rifle Company | |
| Attached – | | | | | | | | | | | | |
| RNZAMC – | | | | | | | | | | | | |
| Medical officer (major or captain | 1 | - | - | - | - | - | - | - | - | - | - | 1 |
| Nursing orderlies – | | | | | | | | | | | | |
| Sergeant | 1 | - | - | - | - | - | - | - | - | - | - | 1 |
| Corporals | 5 | - | - | - | - | | - | - | - | - | - | 5 |
| RNZAOC – | | | | | | | | | | | | |
| Shoemaker (corporal) | - | - | - | 1 | - | - | - | 1 | - | - | - | 1 |
| Tailor (corporal) | - | - | - | 1 | - | - | - | 1 | - | - | - | 1 |
| RNZEME – | | | | | | | | | | | | |
| Vehicle mechanic (includes 1 sergeant and 1 corporal) | 1 | - | - | 2 | 1 | 1 | - | 4 | - | - | - | 5 |
| Armourers (includes 1 corporal) | - | - | - | 2 | - | - | - | 2 | - | - | - | 2 |
| RNZDC – | | | | | | | | | | | | |
| Dental officer (captain or subaltern) | - | - | - | 1 | - | - | - | 1 | - | - | - | 1 |
| Dental assistant (includes 1 sergeant) | - | - | - | 1 | - | - | - | 1 | - | - | - | 1 |
| Dental mechanic | - | - | - | 1 | - | - | - | 1 | - | - | - | 1 |
| RNZ ChD – | | | | | | | | | | | | |
| Chaplain 3rd class | 1 | - | - | - | - | - | - | - | | - | - | 1 |
| NZAPC – | | | | | | | | | | | | |
| Paymaster (major or captain) | 1 | - | - | - | - | - | - | - | - | - | - | 1 |
| Clerks (includes 1 sergeant) | 2 | - | - | - | - | - | - | - | - | - | - | 2 |
| Public Relations – | | | | | | | | | | | | |
| Public relations officer and force photographer (captain or subaltern) | 1 | - | - | - | - | - | - | - | - | - | - | 1 |
| YMCA secretary | 1 | - | - | - | - | - | | | - | - | - | 1 |
| Total, attached | 14 | - | - | 9 | 1 | 1 | - | 11 | - | - | - | 25 |
| Total, a NZ infantry battalion, NZ Army Force FARELF | 56 | 8 | 54 | 75 | 34 | 33 | 11 | 215 | 9 | 36 | 117 | 739 |

## (ii) DISTRIBUTION OF RANK AND FILE BY TRADES AND DUTIES

| Detail | Battalion Headquarters | Headquarter Company | | | | | | | Four Rifle Companies (Each) | | | Total, a NZ Infantry Battalion, NZ Army Force FARELF |
|---|---|---|---|---|---|---|---|---|---|---|---|---|
| | | Headquarters | Signal Platoon | Administrative Platoon | Mortar Platoon | Machine-Gun Platoon | Assault Pioneer Section | Total, Headquarter Company | Headquarters | Three Platoons (Each) | Total, a Rifle Company | |
| TRADESMEN – | | | | | | | | | | | | |
| Clerks, general duties (includes 1 corporal) | 2 | 1 | - | 3 | - | - | - | 4 | 1 | - | 1 | 10 |
| Cooks for – | | | | | | | | | | | | |
| Officers mess (includes 1 lance-corporal | - | - | - | 3 | - | - | - | 3 | - | - | - | 3 |
| Other ranks mess (includes 4 corporals) | - | - | - | 12 | - | - | - | 12 | - | - | - | 12 |
| Drivers (includes 3 corporals) | 2 | - | 3 | 8 | 5 | 7 | 1 | 24 | 1 | - | 1 | 30 |
| Driver batmen | 6 | 2 | 2 | 4 | - | - | - | 8 | 1 | - | 1 | 18 |
| Equipment repairer | - | - | - | 1 | - | - | - | 1 | - | - | - | 1 |
| Pioneers – | | | | | | | | | | | | |
| Bricklayer | - | - | - | 1 | - | - | - | 1 | - | - | - | 1 |
| Carpenters (includes 1 corporal) | - | - | - | 4 | - | - | - | 4 | - | - | - | 4 |
| Plumber | - | - | - | 1 | - | - | - | 1 | - | - | - | 1 |
| Electrician | - | - | - | 1 | - | - | - | 1 | - | - | - | 1 |
| Storemen (technical) | - | - | - | 2 | - | - | - | 2 | - | - | - | 2 |
| Total, tradesmen | 10 | 3 | 5 | 40 | 5 | 7 | 1 | 61 | 3 | - | 3 | 83 |
| NON TRADESMEN – | | | | | | | | | | | | |
| Assault pioneers (includes 1 corporal) | - | - | - | - | - | - | 9 | 9 | - | - | - | 9 |
| Batman/orderlies | 1 | - | - | - | 1 | 1 | | 2 | 1 | 1 | 4 | 19 |
| Bandsmen (includes 1 corporal) | - | - | - | 7 | - | - | - | 7 | - | - | - | 7 |
| Hygiene dutymen (includes 1 corporal) | - | - | - | 6 | - | - | - | 6 | - | - | - | 6 |
| Intelligence section | 2 | - | - | - | - | - | - | - | - | - | - | 2 |
| LMG and riflemen – | | | | | | | | | | | | |
| Corporals | - | - | - | - | - | - | - | - | - | 3 | 9 | 36 |
| Privates | - | - | - | - | | - | - | - | - | 27 | 81 | 324 |
| Mortarmen – | | | | | | | | | | | | |
| 4.2/3-inch mortars (includes 5 corporals) | - | - | - | - | 21 | - | - | 21 | - | - | - | 21 |
| 2-inch mortars | - | - | - | - | - | - | - | - | - | 3 | 9 | 36 |

| Detail | Battalion Headquarters | Headquarter Company | | | | | | | Four Rifle Companies (Each) | | | Total, a NZ Infantry Battalion, NZ Army Force FARELF |
|---|---|---|---|---|---|---|---|---|---|---|---|---|
| | | Headquarters | Signal Platoon | Administrative Platoon | Mortar Platoon | Machine-Gun Platoon | Assault Pioneer Section | Total, Headquarter Company | Headquarters | Three Platoons (Each) | Total, a Rifle Company | |
| NON TRADESMEN – cntd | | | | | | | | | | | | |
| MMG numbers (includes 6 corporals) | - | - | - | - | - | 15 | - | 15 | - | - | - | 15 |
| Orderlies for – | | | | | | | | | | | | |
| Motor-cycle | - | - | 2 | - | - | - | - | 2 | - | - | - | 2 |
| Postal (lance-corporal) | - | - | - | 1 | - | - | - | 1 | - | - | - | 1 |
| Orderlies | - | - | 2 | - | - | - | - | 2 | - | - | - | 2 |
| Rangetakers | - | - | - | - | - | 3 | - | 3 | - | - | - | 3 |
| Ration NCO (corporal) | - | - | - | 1 | - | - | - | 1 | - | - | - | 1 |
| Regimental police (includes 1 corporal) | 4 | - | - | - | - | - | - | - | - | - | - | 4 |
| Signallers (includes 5 corporals) | - | - | 40 | - | - | - | - | 40 | - | - | - | 40 |
| Storemen | - | 1 | 1 | 2 | 1 | 1 | - | 6 | 1 | - | 1 | 10 |
| Stretcher bearers (includes 1 corporal) | 15 | - | - | - | - | - | - | - | - | - | - | 15 |
| Total, non tradesmen | 22 | 1 | 45 | 17 | 23 | 20 | 9 | 115 | 2 | 34 | 104 | 553 |

## (iii) TRANSPORT

| Detail | Battalion Headquarters | Headquarters | Signal Platoon | Administrative Platoon | Mortar Platoon | Machine-Gun Platoon | Assault Pioneer Section | Total, Headquarter Company | Headquarters | Three Platoons (Each) | Total, a Rifle Company | Total, a NZ Infantry Battalion, NZ Army Force FARELF |
|---|---|---|---|---|---|---|---|---|---|---|---|---|
| Motor-cycles | 2 | - | 2 | 1 | - | - | - | 3 | - | - | - | 5 |
| Car, 4 seater, saloon | 1 | - | - | - | - | - | - | - | - | - | - | 1 |
| Trucks – | | | | | | | | | | | | |
| ¼-ton, GS | 5 | 1 | 3 | 1 | 1 | 7 | - | 13 | 1 | - | 1 | 22 |
| 1-ton, GS – | | | | | | | | | | | | |
| Cargo | - | - | - | - | 4 | - | - | 4 | 1 | - | 1 | 8 |
| Wireless/FFW | - | - | 1 | - | - | - | - | 1 | - | - | - | 1 |
| Water | - | - | - | 2 | - | - | - | 2 | - | - | - | 2 |
| 3-ton, GS – | | | | | | | | | | | | |
| Cargo | 3 | 1 | 1 | 10 | 1 | 1 | 1 | 15 | 1 | - | 1 | 22 |
| Cargo with winch | - | - | - | 1 | - | - | - | 1 | - | - | - | 1 |
| Trailers – | | | | | | | | | | | | |
| ½-ton, cargo | 4 | 1 | 3 | 1 | 1 | 7 | - | 13 | 1 | - | 1 | 21 |
| ½-ton, water | - | - | - | 3 | - | - | - | 3 | - | - | - | 3 |
| ¾-ton, dental | - | - | - | 1 | - | - | - | 1 | - | - | - | 1 |
| 1-ton, cargo | 3 | 1 | 1 | 8 | 3 | - | 1 | 14 | 1 | - | 1 | 21 |

## (iv) WEAPONS

| Detail | Battalion Headquarters | Headquarter Company | | | | | | | Four Rifle Companies (Each) | | | Total, a NZ Infantry Battalion, NZ Army Force FARELF |
|---|---|---|---|---|---|---|---|---|---|---|---|---|
| | | Headquarters | Signal Platoon | Administrative Platoon | Mortar Platoon | Machine-Gun Platoon | Assault Pioneer Section | Total, Headquarter Company | Headquarters | Three Platoons (Each) | Total, a Rifle Company | |
| LMGs .303-inch | 5 | - | 3 | 3 | 3 | 3 | 1 | 13 | 4 | 3 | 13 | 70 |
| Mortars – | | | | | | | | | | | | |
| 4.2-inch | - | - | - | - | 2 | - | - | 2 | - | - | - | 2 |
| 3-inch | - | - | - | - | 4 | - | - | 4 | - | - | - | 4 |
| 2-inch | - | - | - | - | - | - | - | - | 1 | 1 | 4 | 16 |
| Rocket launchers 3.5-inch | 1 | - | - | 3 | 3 | 3 | - | 9 | - | 1 | 3 | 22 |
| MMGs .303-inch | - | - | - | - | - | 6 | - | 6 | - | - | - | 6 |
| Guns, anti-tank, 120-mm BAT | - | - | - | - | - | - | - | - | - | - | - | 2 |

## (v) WIRELESS SETS

| | | | | | | | | | | | | |
|---|---|---|---|---|---|---|---|---|---|---|---|---|
| WS No 62 | 3 | 2 | 4 | - | 1 | 1 | - | 8 | 1 | - | 1 | 15 |
| WS No 68 | - | - | 1 | - | 9 | 4 | - | 14 | - | - | - | 14 |
| WS No A510 | - | - | 8 | - | - | - | - | 8 | 2 | 1 | 5 | 28 |

# Appendix 8

## STATISTICS OF 1 NEW ZEALAND REGIMENT, 1957

SOURCE: WA-M 1/1

### 1 NZ REGT STATISTICS – BREAKDOWN

| | *Bn HQ* | *HQ Coy* | *A Coy* | *B Coy* | *C Coy* | *D Coy* |
|---|---|---|---|---|---|---|
| Number of Maori | 4 | 24 | 42 | 55 | 26 | 12 |
| Average Age | 26 | 24.8 | 24.3 | 24 | 24.5 | 25 |
| *Previous Overseas Service* | | | | | | |
| Second World War | 4 | 15 | 10 | 4 | 8 | 5 |
| Korea | 5 | 37 | 11 | 24 | 27 | 21 |
| Malaya | 1 | 3 | – | – | – | 1 |
| Passed through CMT | 19 | 107 | 82 | 82 | 83 | 65 |
| Average Weight | 12st | 11st 10lb | 12st 5lb | 11st 5lb | 12st | 11st |
| Average Height | 5ft 9in | 5ft 7½in | 5ft 8½in | 5ft 9¼in | 5ft 7½in | 5ft 8in |
| Number Married | 12 | 32 | 13 | 10 | 12 | 13 |
| Long Service Regulars | 12 | 28 | 9 | 11 | 9 | 10 |

# *Appendix 9*

## ORGANISATION AND STRENGTH: 28 COMMONWEALTH INFANTRY BRIGADE GROUP (WEF MARCH 1963)

SOURCE: AD 31/2/3 PT 2

**ORGANISATION AND STRENGTH: 28 COMMONWEALTH INFANTRY BRIGADE GROUP (WEF MARCH 1963)**

| *Serial* | *Unit* | *UK* | *Aust* | *NZ* | *Total* |
|---|---|---|---|---|---|
| 1. | Headquarters | 34 | 27 | 2 | 63 |
| 2. | Defence and Employment Platoon | 14 | 8 | - | 22 |
| 3. | Field Regiment RA | 397 | 154 | - | 551 |
| 4. | 11 Indep Field Sqn RE | 236 | 55 | - | 291 |
| 5. | Infantry Battalion UK | 763 | - | - | 763 |
| 6. | Infantry Battalion AUST | - | 737 | - | 737 |
| 7. | Infantry Battalion NZ | - | - | 702 | 702 |
| 8. | 7 Recon Flight AAC | 38 | 2 | 2 | 42 |
| 9. | 208 Commonwealth Signal Squadron | 69 | 42 | - | 111 |
| 10. | 368 Postal Unit RE | 12 | 1 | - | 13 |
| 11. | 28 Commonwealth Provost Unit | 6 | 24 | 6 | 36 |
| 12. | 28 Commonwealth Ordnance Field Park | 42 | 14 | - | 56 |
| 13. | 16 Commonwealth Field Ambulance | 132 | 27 | - | 159 |
| 14. | 32 Army Dental Unit RAADC | - | 11 | - | 11 |
| 15. | 28 Commonwealth Brigade Group Light Aid Detachment | - | 14 | - | 14 |
| 16. | Light Aid Detachment (Field Regiment) | 23 | 5 | - | 28 |
| 17. | 3 Company RASC | 241 | 2 | - | 243 |
| 18. | 2 Infantry Workshop (REME) | 133 | - | - | 133 |
| Total | | 2140 | 1123 | 712 | 3975 |

# Appendix 10

## AUTHORITY FOR THE USE OF THE COMMONWEALTH FORCES IN MALAYSIA

| Serial No | Nature of Operations | Authority | | | References |
|---|---|---|---|---|---|
| | | United Kingdom | Australia | New Zealand | |
| 1. | SEATO Plans Commonwealth Strategic Reserve Primary Role | Chiefs of Staff (1) | Australian Government through High Commissioner and ANZAM DC (1) | New Zealand Government through High Commissioner and ANZAM DC (1) | (1) COS 235/64 (Directive for British Commonwealth Strategic Reserve) |
| 2. | Land Operations against infiltrators from Indonesia into Malaya and Singapore (Commonwealth Strategic Reserve Secondary Role) (2) | CINCFE (2)(3) | Australian Government through High Commissioner (2) | New Zealand Government through High Commissioner (2) | (2) Following the request of the Malaysian Government<br>(3) COS 251/64 (Supplementary Directive) |
| 3. | Air Defence of Malaya and Singapore:<br>a. Rules of Engagement (basic)<br>b. ADIZ<br>c. Addendum to Rules of Engagement | <br><br>CINCFE (4)<br>CINCFE (7)<br>CINCFE (7) | <br><br>CINCFE (5)<br>CINCFE (6)<br>CINCFE (6) | <br><br>CINCFE (8)<br>CINCFE (8)<br>CINCFE (8) | (4) COS 318/63<br>(5) AUST 96/ AUSTSEC 5<br>(6) Canberra to CRO 1007 of 19 Sept<br>(7) COSSEA 206<br>(8) Wellington CRO 374 of 18 Sept |
| 4. | Sea operations against infiltrators into Malaya and Singapore (9) | CINCFE (9)(10) | Australian Government through High Commissioner (9) | New Zealand Government through High Commissioner (9) | (9) Following the request of the Malaysian Government<br>(10) COS 251/64 (Supplementary Directive) |

| Serial No | Nature of Operations | Authority | | | References |
|---|---|---|---|---|---|
| | | United Kingdom | Australia | New Zealand | |
| 5. | Operations against CT on the Thai/ Malay Border (Commonwealth Strategic Reserve Second Role) | CINCFE (11)(12) | CINCFE (11)(12) | CINCFE (11)(12) | (11) Following the request of the Malaysian Government<br>(12) COS 86/64 (Supplementary Directive) agreed by ANZAM DC |
| 6. | Employment of Australian LAA Battery | | CINCFE but unit only to be used in the defence of Butterworth | | |
| 7. | Plan SHALSTONE | British High Commissioner (13)(14) | Australian Government through High Commissioner (13)(15) | New Zealand Government through High Commissioner (13)(16) | (13) Following the request of the Malaysian Government<br>(14) CRO to KL 2302 of 17 Sep<br>(15) Canberra to CRO 980 of 13 Sep Canberra to CRO 1010 of 19 Sep<br>(16) Wellington to CRO 360 of 14 Sep Wellington to CRO 376 of 20 Sep |
| 8. | Plan ADDINGTON | British High Commissioner (17) | CINCFE having received authority for Serial 7 above (17) | CINCFE having received authority for Serial 7 above (18) | (17) References as for Serial 7 above |
| 9. | Plan ALTHORPE | Chiefs of Staff (18) | Australian Government through the Chiefs of Staff (18) | New Zealand Government through the Chiefs of Staff (18) | (18) COS 63/64 |
| 10. | Air Defence of Borneo:<br>a. Rules of Engagement<br>b. Hot Pursuit | CINCFE (19)<br>Chiefs of Staff | Not to be used | No fighters available | (19) COSSEA 42 |
| 11. | Employment of RAAF and RNZAF Transport Aircraft in Borneo | | CINCFE | CINCFE | |

| Serial No | Nature of Operations | Authority | | | References |
|---|---|---|---|---|---|
| | | United Kingdom | Australia | New Zealand | |
| 12. | Employment of Australian Engineer unit in Borneo | | CINCFE, but unit only to be employed on engineer construction tasks (20) | | (20) COS 232/64 |
| 13. | Employment of naval ships in Borneo waters:<br>a. CMS<br>b. Frigate at Tawau | a. CINCFE<br>b. CINCFE | a. CINCFE (21)<br>b. CINCFE (22) | a. CINCFE<br>b. CINCFE (23) | (21) CINCFE 2956/124/6<br>(22) ACNB Signal of 280710Z AUG<br>(23) NZNB of 240443Z SEP 64 |
| 14. | Operations against Indonesian Border Terrorists in Borneo | CINCFE (24) | CINCFE | CINCFE (25) | (24) COS 279/63<br>(25) Ext Affairs 16 Feb 65 NZ Army 15/15 Vol 1 |
| 15. | Operations against CCO | CINCFE (26) | Not to be used | Not to be used | (26) Following the request of the Malaysian Government |
| 16. | Assistance in Preservation of Public Order in Borneo:<br>a. Non Active<br>b. Active | CINCFE (27)<br>British High Commissioner in KL (27) | Not to be used<br>Not to be used | Not to be used<br>Not to be used | (27) Following the request of the Malaysian Government |
| 17. | Assistance in the Preservation of Public Order in Singapore Categories 1–4 | British High Commissioner in KL (28) | Not to be used | Not to be used | (28) Following the request of the Malaysian Government |

# *Appendix 11*

## THE GOLDEN RULES

[Extracts from the file, 'New Zealand Operations in Borneo, 1965–1966', held by the Directorate of Defence Intelligence, but subsequently destroyed]

DBO 4/53 HQ Dir of Borneo Operations LABUAN, dated 1 March 1965.

CROSS BORDER OPERATIONS, THE GOLDEN RULES

Cross border operations first authorised on 11 May 64. Defined:

a. fire in self-defence,
b. cutting-off operations,
c. offensive patrol operations to a depth of 10,000 yards.

Of these, only fire in self-defence is currently authorised. The maintenance by SAS squadrons of the cross border surveillance screen continues as heretofore.

Aim:

a. the prosecution of a successful defence by:
   [1] maintaining contact with the enemy;
   [2] offensive patrolling;
   [3] probing weak spots;
   [4] mounting strictly disruptive raids, where these were likely to yield a good dividend.
b. the protection of patrol bases close to the border.
c. the obtaining of early warning of the number and direction of incursions, thus enabling Commanders to deploy their forces accordingly and also to enable reinforcements to be anticipated.
d. the buying of time.
e. the regaining of the initiative along the border.
f. the restoration of confidence among the local peoples, thus safeguarding a valuable source of information.

Though currently in suspense, the Golden Rules at Annex B have been evolved to define precisely the freedom of action enjoyed until 28th February, and the conditions imposed upon us. They are the product of months of patient negotiation. They are NOT intended to serve as the basis for discussion.

W C Walker
Major General
Director of Borneo Operations:

Distribution included:
Comd West Bde
Comd Mid-West Bde
Comd Central Bde
Comd East Bde
CO 22 SAS Regt

Annex B to DBO 4/53, dated 1 March 65 [Incorporating Amdt No. 1, issued 4 May 1965]

OFFENSIVE PATROL OPERATIONS, THE GOLDEN RULES

1. The National Defence Council and British Ministers have agreed upon the necessity for a more active defence in East Malaysia, and have authorised offensive patrol operations across the border to a depth of 10,000 yards.
2. Any targets within this area may be attacked, subject to the following conditions:

> a. Attacks will not normally exceed one company group in strength, and must therefore be within the capacity of one full company to ensure success.
> b. Offensive air support will NOT be planned into these operations, but may be authorised by the Commander Air Forces Borneo in an extreme emergency ... if NO other means of relief is possible.
> c. Casualty evacuation provision may be made in the tactical plan. If approved at Command may be delegated to Brigade Commanders.
> d. Photographic reconnaissance to cover any operations may be requested.
> e. Artillery and mortars may be used in direct support of an operation provided that fire is controlled by direct observation. Limited to
>
> > [1] defensive fire;
> > [2] to cover withdrawal in a 'tight corner' situation;
> > [3] one or two rounds to trigger-off an induced ambush in certain pre-planned circumstances.

The softening-up of a target is not permissible.
g. *Civilians.* All precautions must continue to be taken to minimise civilian casualties.
h. *Preparations.* Operations of this nature are NOT lightly to be undertaken. They call for:
[1] Careful and thorough reconnaissance of targets before troops are committed.

'Only thoroughly seasoned and jungle-worthy troops under first class and experienced leadership are to be committed to these operations. Otherwise, there will be a military nonsense which could result in serious political and operational consequences. Brigade Commanders are at liberty to decide when units are worthy of this hallmark. As a guide, no battalion should be committed to cross border operations until they have spent at least four weeks getting to know their area.'
3. *Ground Reconnaissance.* A pre-requisite. Brigade Commanders [have] a reasonably free hand to authorise subject to strict observation of Golden Rules. Careful control and coordination, seasoned teams minimise security risk.
4. *Control of offensive patrol operations.* The political factor demands that the control of these operations be exercised at the highest level, namely at Headquarters Director of Borneo Operations. COMLANBOR has power of veto, sent to both HQ at same time, COMLANBOR in consultation with COMANVBOR and COMAIRBOR will approve tactical plan and cover story.
6. *Security.* All cross border operations are still to be deniable in the sense that we are to deny that we ever crossed the border. Therefore, the importance of keeping such operations secret cannot be over emphasised. Perhaps the most serious consequence from our point of view is that, if they become too widely known, or known to the Press and Her Majesty's Government is embarrassed, it may lead to their being stopped. Therefore the 'need to know' principle is to be very strictly applied.
7. *Cover Story.* Each tactical plan ... will include a cover story in order that we shall be prepared to project the operation as credibly deniable should questions be asked, or accusations made.
9. *Reports.* Factual reports including diagrams.

Annex C to DBO 4/53, dated 1 March 1965

SECURITY THE GOLDEN RULES

Individual codewords for specific operations.
Communications and papers channelled through one Control Officer on each HQ.
'In no circumstances will any attributable document be issued below the level of a brigade headquarters which suggests that we ever intended deliberately to cross the border.' Two packs relating to a specific operation, original at bde, duplicate for CO concerned, not to be taken forward of Bn HQ.

Ops maps of cross border operations never to be displayed.
'Press are NOT to be provided with facilities to visit forward areas where cross border operations are in progress.'
In event of capture all ranks 'are to deny having deliberately crossed the border'.

Annex D to DBO 4/53, dated 1 March 65

PUBLIC RELATIONS ASPECTS OF CROSS BORDER OPERATIONS THE GOLDEN RULES

'All cross border operations are still to be deniable in the sense that we are to deny that we ever crossed the border. It follows that nothing should be volunteered to the Press or other information media, either about specific operations or about any other change in policy involved. Indeed, it is of the highest importance that maximum security be adhered to throughout by all concerned ...'

# Notes

## 1 A 'Side Issue Only', 1949–55

1 Sergeant J. T. Johnston, RNZIR, interview, 14 Oct 1992.

2 See James Cowan, *The Maoris in the Great War,* Maori Regimental Committee, Whitcombe & Tombs, Wellington, 1926; Christopher Pugsley, *Te Hokowhitu A Tu: The New Zealand Maori Pioneer Battalion in the First World War*, Reed, Auckland, 1995; J. F. Cody, *28 (Maori) Battalion*, War History Branch, Department of Internal Affairs, Wellington, 1956; Wira Gardiner, *Te Mura O Te Ahi: The Story of the Maori Battalion*, Reed, Auckland, 1992.

3 'Maori Battalion—Territorial Force', Major-General K. L. Stewart, CGS, to Min of Defence, 18 Oct 1949, initialled and approved 7 Dec 1949. Opposition recorded in 'Maori Bn 3 NZEF', Comd NMD to Army HQ, 25 Oct 1949, and 'Maori Battalion Territorial Proposal Opposed', *Auckland Star*, 24 Oct 1949, AD 1, 209/3/170. See also 'Training: Maoris: Policy', AD 1, 210/1/103.

4 Minister of Defence to General Secretary, NZ Returned Services Association, 6 Nov 1952, supported by Memo CGS to Min of Defence, 30 Oct 1952, AD 1, 209/3/170.

5 Minister of Defence to Mr M. Steemson, 18 Aug 1961, and 'Maori Battalion: Vanguard or Rearguard?', An Address by Secretary of Defence (J. K. Hunn) at the Annual Reunion of the Maori Battalion Association, Gisborne, 28 Mar 1964, AD 1, 209/3/170.

6 Educational standards seem to have been the principal reason for there being so few Maori of commissioned rank in the three services. There was no apparent policy discriminating against Maori joining the armed forces. In 1951 the RNZAF initiated reports from Maori Welfare Officers of the Department of Maori Affairs on Maori applicants, 'to assist Recruiting Officers in their efforts to preclude undesirable applicants from being accepted for service'. This policy, which was cancelled in 1969, was begun after Maori members of the RNZAF at Te Rapa remained absent without

leave when visiting local marae. See correspondence, 'Recruiting: Maori in RNZAF: General Instructions', Air 1, 33/20/4. The file also contains the case of Charles Barton, a man of Maori blood who trained as a pilot with the Canterbury Aviation School in 1917. The New Zealand government sought a ruling on whether candidates of Maori blood could be admitted for commissions in the Royal Flying Corps. The War Office approved this, on condition that candidates were considered suitable for commissions in the NZEF. The War Office subsequently requested that 'their educational standard should be higher than that for the European candidate'. At the start of the Second World War, Maori were accepted for entry into the RNZAF and clearance was sought from the Air Ministry, which replied that it would 'gladly accept good type of Maori for aircraft crews if up to educational standard', with the proviso that the Ministry relied on New Zealand to select applicants carefully.

7 Ritchie Ovendale, *British Defence Policy Since 1945*, Manchester University Press, Manchester, 1994, pp. 60–1.

8 Ritchie Ovendale, *The English-Speaking Alliance: Britain, the United States, the Dominions and the Cold War 1945–1951*, George Allen & Unwin, London, 1985, pp. 118–42.

9 For the evolution of post-war defence policy, see Ian McGibbon, *New Zealand and the Korean War, Vol. 1, Politics and Diplomacy*, Oxford University Press, Auckland, 1992, pp. 26–33, 284–300; W. David McIntyre, *Background to the Anzus Pact*, Macmillan, London/Canterbury University Press, Christchurch/St Martin's Press, New York, 1995, pp. 3–14, 119–222.

10 Berendsen to McIntosh, 25 Aug 1949, in Ian McGibbon (ed.), *Undiplomatic Dialogue: Letters Between Carl Berendsen & Alister McIntosh 1943–1952*, Auckland University Press, Auckland, 1993, p. 181. See also McGibbon, *New Zealand and the Korean War, Vol. 1*, pp. 26–33. The Military Training Act 1949 made every British male subject resident in New Zealand liable to be called up for service on reaching the age of 18 years. The training obligation included 14 weeks' full-time training in a training camp, three years' part-time service, consisting of 14 days' in-camp training and six days' out-of-camp training, and six years' Army Reserve liability with no training obligations. *New Zealand Official Yearbook*, 1950, p. 199.

11 'Report on the Composition of the Armed Forces of New Zealand', COS (47), 12 Feb 1947; 'New Zealand's Contribution to Commonwealth Defence Arrangements', JPC (49) 1, 3 Feb 1949, JSO 2/1/1 pt 1.

12 McIntyre, *Background to the Anzus Pact*, pp. 138–40.

13 Holland's government grudgingly agreed to compulsory military training proceeding on 13 March 1950. See notes by CGS to Cabinet Committee, Examination of Defence Plan and Compulsory Military Training Scheme—1950, and Record of Ministerial Committee Meetings with COS, 10 and 16 Mar 1950, JSO 2/1/1 pt 1. But it was not until June 1950, and the visit of Field Marshal Sir William Slim, Chief of Imperial General Staff, for discussions with the government and the New Zealand Chiefs of Staff, that Holland said 'he regarded the undertaking previously given by Mr Fraser to send expeditionary land and air forces to the Middle East as an obligation on

New Zealand's part'. COS (50) M.7, 23 Jun 1950, JSO 1/4/3 pt 2. See McGibbon, *New Zealand and the Korean War, Vol. 1*, pp. 30–1; McIntyre, *Background to the Anzus Pact*, pp. 205–9.

14 'At present for the first time ever in peace, the New Zealand services have been given a guide as to their tasks in war. This guidance had been based on the best possible advice, and he [Stewart] suggested therefore that the plan should stand if for no other reason than it was the best basis on which to organise and train the services.' COS Minutes of Meeting with National Cabinet Defence Committee, 16 Mar 1950, JSO 2/1/1 pt 1; McGibbon, *New Zealand and the Korean War, Vol. I*, pp. 29–31. See also McIntosh to Berendsen, 6 Mar 1950: 'Mr Holland has developed an anti-Service hate ... and it is quite clear that the present Government will not—or, as they will put it, cannot—fulfil commitments we have made to the United Kingdom', McGibbon (ed.), *Undiplomatic Dialogue*, p. 216; Corner to McIntosh, 11 Dec 1952, and McIntosh to Corner, 9 Jan 1953, in Ian McGibbon (ed.), *Unofficial Channels: Letters Between Alister McIntosh and Foss Shanahan, George Laking and Frank Corner, 1946–1966*, Victoria University Press, Wellington, 1999, pp. 109, 117; Ovendale, *British Defence Policy Since 1945*, pp. 69–71.

15 'Holland, Sir Sidney George (1893–1961)', in A. H. McLintock (ed.), *An Encyclopaedia of New Zealand*, vol. 2, Government Printer, Wellington, 1966, pp. 107–8; Keith Sinclair, *Walter Nash*, Auckland University Press, Auckland, 1976, p. 280. For comments on Major-General Sir Keith Stewart, see Lieutenant-General Sir Leonard Thornton, interviews, Mar–Apr 1992. For character sketches of Peter Fraser and Sidney Holland, see McIntyre, *Background to the Anzus Pact*, pp. 4–7.

16 McGibbon, *New Zealand and the Korean War, Vol. 1*, p. 286.

17 Economic and social development was always a higher priority, and in 1961 New Zealand committed 1.9% of its gross domestic product to defence, compared with the United Kingdom (6.5%), Canada (4.6%), and the United States (9.8%). These figures convert to US$30.2 per capita in New Zealand, US$93.6 in the United Kingdom, US$91.5 in Canada, and US$293 in the United States. Wing-Commander Ian MacFarling, 'New Zealand and the Vietnam Conflict', *Australian Defence Force Journal*, no. 79, Nov/Dec 1989, pp. 8–19, citing Trevor R. Reese, *Australia, New Zealand and the United States 1941–1968*, Oxford University Press, London, 1968, p. 278.

18 'The position in Malaya would continue to be a long term problem and any help that could be given by New Zealand would be most acceptable. On the other hand he wished to emphasize that Malaya was a "side issue only" and that no plans should be entered into in regard to it which would interfere with the all important problem of the defence of the Middle East.' Air Chief Marshal Sir Hugh Saunders during his visit to New Zealand and briefing of Cabinet in June 1950. [TS] Cabinet, Note of a Discussion with Air Chief Marshal Sir Hugh Saunders on Tuesday, 6 Jun 1950, Annex to CM.[50] 32, Air 227/20/1A. See Ovendale, *The English-Speaking Alliance*, pp. 118–42, 144–84; *British Defence Policy Since 1945*, pp. 78–9.

19 Ovendale, *British Defence Policy Since 1945*, pp. 67–8.

20 Sec to Min of Defence, 'NZ Defence Policy', 1 May 1953, JSO 3/1/1. ANZAM remained in the shadows for most of its existence. The nature of the arrangement was discussed between 1946 and 1948, ANZAM began sometime between 1948 and 1953. On its development see R. M. Mullins, 'ANZAM', unpublished typescript, Ministry of Foreign Affairs, 1971. See also A. & R. Burnett, *The Australia and New Zealand Nexus*, Australian and New Zealand Institutes of International Affairs, Canberra, pp. 77–8; McGibbon, *New Zealand and the Korean War, Vol. 1*, pp. 32–3, 284–300, including map on p. 288; McIntyre, *Background to the Anzus Pact*, pp. 210–22; David McIntyre, 'The Road to Vietnam', in Malcolm McKinnon (ed.), *The American Connection*, Allen & Unwin/Port Nicholson Press, Wellington, 1988, pp. 141–7. For Australian perspectives see David Lee, 'Australia and Allied Strategy in the Far East, 1952–1957', *Journal of Strategic Studies*, vol. 16, no. 4, Dec 1993, pp. 511–38, and Alan Watt, *The Evolution of Australian Foreign Policy 1938–1965*, Cambridge University Press, London, 1967, pp. 163–80.

21 'While there was no suggestion that New Zealand should provide forces for the external defence of Malaya, because, in war, the direction of the defence of Malaya would be of concern to the ANZAM Chiefs of Staff, it was reasonable that the New Zealand Chiefs of Staff should be represented by an observer, at least.' COS (51) M.1, 18 Jan 1951, JSO 1/4/3 pt 3.

22 See, for example: McIntyre, *Background to the Anzus Pact;* Malcolm McKinnon, *Independence and Foreign Policy: New Zealand in the World Since 1935*, Auckland University Press, Auckland, 1993; John Hammond Moore, *The American Alliance: Australia, New Zealand and the United States: 1940–1970*, Cassell, North Melbourne, 1970; Trevor R. Reese, *Australia, New Zealand and the United States 1941–1968*, Oxford University Press, London, 1968, pp. 84–149; Ann Trotter, *New Zealand and Japan 1945–1952: The Occupation and the Peace Treaty*, Athlone Press, London, 1990; Thomas-Durrell Young, *Australia, New Zealand, and the United States Security Relations, 1951–1986*, Westview Press, Boulder, Colorado, 1992.

23 Ovendale, *British Defence Policy Since 1945*, pp. 90–4.

24 A. & R. Burnett, *The Australia and New Zealand Nexus*, pp. 77–9.

25 New Zealand gave the French forces in Indo-China 30,000 .303 No. 1 Mk3 and 3* rifles, 750 .30 M1919 A 4 Browning machine guns, 500 Smith & Wesson and Webley .455 revolvers, and 10,000 rounds of 40 mm Shot Armour Piercing ammunition, and also offered war surplus 40 mm Bofors anti-aircraft guns and 155 mm field howitzers, which were refused. See Major-General Gentry, 5 Nov 1953, Army 257/1/19G, and accompanying translations. Copies provided by Alexander J. Zervoudakis. For the Five-Power Staff Agency, see McIntyre, *Background to the Anzus Pact*, pp. 357–9, 366.

26 Chatham House Study Group, *Collective Defence in South East Asia*, Oxford University Press, London, 1956; Mark Pearson, *Paper Tiger: New Zealand's Part in SEATO 1954–1977*, New Zealand Institute of International Affairs, Wellington, 1989. See also Ministry of Foreign Affairs, *New Zealand Foreign Policy Statements*

*and Documents 1943–1957*, Government Printer, Wellington, 1972, pp. 362–74; McIntyre, *Background to the Anzus Pact*; McKinnon, *Independence and Foreign Policy*.

27 See McGibbon, *New Zealand and the Korean War, Vol. 1*; and *Vol. 2, Combat Operations*, Oxford University Press, Auckland, 1996.

28 COS (52) M.5, 16 May 1952, COS (52) M.7, 17 Jul 1952, JSO 1/4/3 pt 3. For the evolution of this policy see Corner to McIntosh, 12 Jun 1952, in McGibbon (ed.), *Unofficial Channels*, pp. 101–3.

29 COS (53) M.21, 23 Oct 1953, and M.22, 27 Oct 1953, JSO 1/4/3.

30 For these discussions (known as the Harding Talks), see COS (53) M.27, 21 Dec 1953, and COS (54) M.2, 3 and 4, dated 4, 9 and 16 Feb 1954, JSO 1/4/3 pt 5, formerly JSO 1/3/3 pt 5. Air Vice-Marshal D. V. Carnegie RAF, Chief of Air Staff from January 1951 to February 1954, was replaced by Air Vice-Marshal W. H. Merton RAF, who served until June 1956. See Geoffrey Bentley & Maurice Conly, *Portrait of an Air Force: The Royal New Zealand Air Force 1937–1987*, Grantham House, Wellington, 1987, Appendix C, p. 190.

31 'New Zealand Global War Commitments', Report by Chiefs of Staff, Annex to COS (54) M.4, 16 Feb 1954, JSO 1/4/3 pt 5, formerly JSO 1/3/3 pt 5. Statement by Rt Hon. S. G. Holland, 18 Jan 1955, in Ministry of Foreign Affairs, *New Zealand Foreign Policy Statements and Documents 1943–1957*, pp. 374–7. For an insight into the shift in focus from the Middle East to South-East Asia, see Corner to McIntosh, 13 Jul 1953, and McIntosh to Corner, 11 Aug 1954 and 22 Oct 1954, in McGibbon (ed.), *Unofficial Channels*, pp. 133–45, 172, 176.

32 'It could be argued that the United Kingdom authorities had been somewhat disingenuous over their approach to New Zealand on a changed global war deployment': COS (54) M.49, 26 Nov 1954 and subsequent meetings, 'Defence Policy', JSO 1/4/3 pt 6, formerly JSO 1/3/3 pt 6.

33 In September 1954, in response to a comment by Pat Booth, a Press Gallery journalist for the *Auckland Star*, that the reduction of Kayforce might lead to Australia and New Zealand playing a bigger part in the fight against communism in Malaya, the Minister of Defence, T. L. Macdonald, replied that it was an indigenous movement and a matter for the Malayan government and the Colonial Office: 'New Zealand troops would not be allocated to that area unless, firstly, there was a widening of this country's political commitments in South East Asia and, secondly, that an invitation was received from the Malayan Government and the British Colonial Office.' T. L. Macdonald to P. Booth, 24 Sep 1954, AD 1, 281/1/146. For British efforts to 'get the Australians and New Zealanders firmly committed to the defence of Malaya', see 339, CO 1030/67, no. 13, 15 Nov 1954, and 340, CO 1030/67, no. 12, 13 Dec 1954, A. J. Stockwell (ed.), *Malaya, Part III, The Alliance Route to Independence 1953–1957*, British Documents on the End of Empire, Her Majesty's Stationery Office, London, 1995, pp. 79–82.

34 See A. D. McIntosh's comments to the Chiefs of Staff: 'The Middle East commitment had a certain advantage in that, as framed at present, it gave us room for

manoeuvre. On the other hand a commitment for the Far East was much more binding. Once New Zealand forces became involved in the Far East he could not see them being withdrawn. Therefore this gave additional point to the need for the Government to be quite aware of the implications of accepting such a deployment plan. The great value of having a commitment was [that] it encouraged the Government to carry out a positive defence programme. Apart from that a strong case could be made for not having a firm war time commitment—we could thus retain flexibility and deploy to the dictates of the strategic situation at the time.' COS (54) M.43, 4 Nov 1954, 'ANZAM Planning', JSO 1/4/3 pt 6, formerly JSO 1/3/3 pt 6. The New Zealand Force South East Asia withdrew from its base in Singapore in 1989, leaving only a small residual planning element for the conduct of exercises under the 1971 Five Power Defence Arrangements.

35 'At the request of the United Kingdom Government, the New Zealand Government have agreed to provide one Dakota transport flight to assist and afford relief to the United Kingdom Air Force in Hong Kong.' Air Department Operations Order 9/1949, 2 Sep 1949, No. 41 Sqn RNZAF Unit History, 15 Aug 1944 – Dec 1949, ABFK 7232/6. See Peter Fraser, 18 Aug 1949, *NZPD*, vol. 286, p. 1381, reprinted in Ministry of Foreign Affairs, *New Zealand Foreign Policy Statements and Documents 1943–1957*, pp. 196–7.

36 Lieutenants G. N. McL. Boswell, RNZAC, N. E. McLeod, NZ Regt, J. McL. Ross, RNZA, G. R. Tomline, RNZA, were seconded to Far East Land Forces with effect from 29 July 1949. NZ Military Forces, *Appointments, Promotions, Transfers, etc.* List no. 296, 18 Aug 1949, held at Defence Library. Also Captain Graham Boswell, interview, and written notes provided by Brigadier R. I. Thorpe, 6 Apr 1999.

37 See 'Post War Policy, RNZAF', pts 1 & 2, Air 1, 1/1/35, 'Expansion of RNZAF from 1948', Air 1, 1/1/84.

38 Bentley & Conly, *Portrait of an Air Force*, pp. 112–14.

39 Group Captain R. J. Cohen, RNZAF, serving on exchange as Senior Air Staff Officer at No. 46 Group, RAF, drafted the operational plan for the airlift and controlled the movement of all British and United States aircraft into Berlin. He was awarded the CBE and the US Legion of Merit for this work. Bentley & Conly, *Portrait of an Air Force*, pp. 115–17. See '41 Transport Squadron', Air 1, 1/1/41 pts 1 & 2.

40 6 Sep 1949, No. 41 Squadron RNZAF Unit History, 15 Aug 1944 – Dec 1949, ABFK 7232/6. See also 'Organisation Transport Squadron, No. 41', Air 1, 1/1/41 pt 1.

41 The RNZAF still had the ranks of Cadet Aircrew; Aircrew 1–4, equivalent to Flight Sergeant, Sergeant and Corporal-Pilot; and Master Aircrew, equivalent to Warrant Officer. With the exception of Cadet Aircrew, these ranks had been adopted from the RAF, which had soon stopped using them. Wing-Commander R. A. Manners, interview, 27 May 1992; D. Duxbury, letter and comments on draft, 11 Nov 1999.

42 The word 'jungle' is a colonialist term derived from the Hindi and Marathi words for desert or dry land. It came to mean 'forest' by reference to the British medieval land law concept of 'wastes and forests', i.e. uncultivated land. When applied in the tropics it meant any wild tract of land containing wild animals. It also acquired the

connotation of a disorganised, tangled mass of growth, a place of mystery and confusion. The word now evokes a struggle for survival, as in the 'law of the jungle' applied to the business world, schools, cities, etc. In the 1950s and 1960s, however, it was the term commonly used to describe tropical rainforest, and it is used here in this context. W. David McIntyre, notes to author.

43 C. A. Fisher, *South-East Asia: A Social, Economic and Political Geography*, Methuen, London, 1964, table 84, p. 634. In 1952 the population was 5,337,000, of whom 2,631,000 were Malays, 2,044,000 Chinese, and 586,000 Indian or Pakistani. See Royal Air Force, *The Malayan Emergency 1948–1960*, Ministry of Defence, London, 1970, p. xv. In 1947, 372,000 Chinese had automatic citizenship rights. Richard Stubbs, *Hearts and Minds in Guerrilla Warfare: The Malayan Emergency 1948–1960*, Oxford University Press, New York, 1989, pp. 30 (fn 48), 40. For useful concise histories of Malaya, see Nicholas Tarling, *Southeast Asia: Past and Present*, F. W. Cheshire, Melbourne, 1966, pp. 178–88, 286–95; and T. N. Harper, *The End of Empire and the Making of Malaya*, Cambridge University Press, Cambridge, 1999.

44 Harper, *The End of Empire*, pp. 94–148.

45 'Orang Asli', meaning 'original person', was a semi-offensive term used to describe the aboriginal tribes inhabiting the Central Highlands of Malaya. See John D. Leary, *Violence and the Dream People: The Orang Asli in the Malayan Emergency 1948–1960*, Ohio University Centre for International Studies, Athens, Ohio, 1995; Richard Noone, *Rape of the Dream People*, Hutchinson, London, 1972; Tom Stacey, *The Hostile Sun*, Gerald Duckworth, London, 1953; John Slimming, *Temiar Jungle*, Travel Book Club, London, 1958.

46 F. Spencer Chapman, *The Jungle is Neutral*, Chatto & Windus, London, 1949, is the classic account of service with Force 136 and contact with the Chinese communists of the Malayan People's Anti-Japanese Army in the jungles of Malaya during the Japanese occupation. See Paul H. Kratoska, *The Japanese Occupation of Malaya 1941–1945*, Allen & Unwin, St Leonards, 1998. See also Chin Kee Onn, *Ma-Rai-Ee*, Australasian Publishing Company, Sydney, 1952, a novel based on the experiences of Malayan Chinese under Japanese occupation.

47 In 1947 Malaya was the world's foremost producer of rubber, which earned it US$120 million. 'In 1948 the USA imported 727,000 tons of rubber, of which 371,000 tons came from Malaya, and 158,000 tons of tin, of which 155,000 tons were Malayan produced ... This trade increased during the Korean War boom, with Malaya's dollar surplus being US$170m (1948), $160m (1949), $271m (1950) and $350m (1952).' A. J. Stockwell, 'British Imperial Policy and Decolonization in Malaya, 1942–1952', *Journal of Imperial and Commonwealth History,* Oct 1984, pp. 68–87.

48 J. B. Perry Robinson, *Transformation in Malaya*, Secker & Warburg, London, 1956, pp. 14–70, is still one of the best overviews of this period in Malaya. See also Kratoska, *The Japanese Occupation of Malaya,* pp. 306–61.

49 Albert Lau, *The Malayan Union Controversy 1942–1948*, South-East Asian Historical Monographs, Oxford University Press, Singapore, 1991. See also Stubbs, *Hearts and Minds in Guerrilla Warfare*, pp. 22–32.

50 See Richard Clutterbuck, *The Long Long War: The Emergency in Malaya 1948–1960*, Cassell, London, 1967, Appendix A, pp. 184–8; also Richard Clutterbuck, *Conflict and Violence in Singapore and Malaysia 1945–1983*, Graham Brash, Singapore, 1984; Anthony Short, *The Communist Insurrection in Malaya*, Frederick Muller, London, 1975.

51 Royal Air Force, *The Malayan Emergency*, p. 3.

52 Clutterbuck, *The Long Long War*, pp. 13–35; Stubbs, *Hearts and Minds in Guerrilla Warfare*, pp. 54–62. For an assessment of Chin Peng, see Clutterbuck, *The Long Long War*, pp. 17, 136–7.

53 Stockwell, 'The Origins of the Malayan Emergency', pp. 66–88. See also Clutterbuck, *Conflict and Violence*; Short, *The Communist Insurrection in Malaya*; and Thomas R. Mockaitis, *British Counterinsurgency, 1919–1960*, Macmillan, in association with King's College, London, 1990.

54 For a very detailed summary, see Peter Dennis & Jeffrey Grey, *Emergency and Confrontation*, Allen & Unwin in association with the Australian War Memorial, Sydney, 1996. See also Nicholas Tarling, *Britain, Southeast Asia and the Onset of the Cold War 1945–1950*, Cambridge University Press, Cambridge, 1998, pp. 309–13.

55 Rhoderick Dhu Renick Jnr, 'The Emergency Regulations of Malaya: Causes and Effect', *Journal of Southeast Asian History*, vol. 6, no. 2, Sep 1965, pp. 1–5.

56 Richard Allen, *Malaysia: Prospect and Retrospect: The Impact and Aftermath of Colonial Rule*, Oxford University Press, London, 1968, p. 92.

57 Royal Air Force, *The Malayan Emergency*, p. 3.

58 Tarling, *Britain, Southeast Asia and the Onset of the Cold War*, pp. 309–13.

59 Quoted in R. Stubbs, *Hearts and Minds in Guerrilla Warfare*, Oxford University Press, Singapore, 1989, p. 75.

60 Clutterbuck, *The Long Long War*, p. 186. See also Clutterbuck, *Conflict and Violence*; Richard Jackson, *The Malayan Emergency*, Routledge, London, 1991; Mockaitis, *British Counterinsurgency*.

61 See Royal Air Force, *The Malayan Emergency*, pp. 75–122. See also Air Chief Marshal Sir David Lee, *Eastward: A History of the Royal Air Force in the Far East 1945–1972*, Ministry of Defence, Air Historical Branch (RAF), Her Majesty's Stationery Office, London, 1984, pp. 93–106, 131–58.

62 Royal Air Force, *The Malayan Emergency*, p. 88.

63 Manners, interview. See also J. F. Baragwanath, NZPA Correspondent, 'Air Force Dakota's Courier Service to Hongkong', *Auckland Star*, 3 Jul 1950.

64 22 Dec 1949, No. 41 Squadron RNZAF Unit History, 15 Aug 1944 – Dec 1949, ABFK 7232/6. The term 'bandits' was used to identify the communists as criminals. However, the Chinese in Malaya were well aware that both the Kuomintang (Nationalist Chinese) and the Japanese had also described the communists as 'bandits'—and both had failed to defeat them. In 1950, at the start of the Korean War, the term was dropped in favour of 'Communist Terrorists' (CTs); this expression too had a propaganda element to it, and in this study the term 'guerrilla' is used instead. See Lucian W. Pye, *Lessons from the Malayan Struggle Against Communism*, Center

for International Studies, Massachusetts Institute of Technology, Cambridge, Mass., 1957, pp. 35–7.

65 'Air Force Duty in Malaya', *NZ Herald*, 10 Apr 1950.

66 Royal Air Force, *The Malayan Emergency*, pp. 77–8.

67 'Target—A Jungle Clearing', *Wings*, May 1950, pp. 5, 17. Also Manners, interview.

68 'Target—A Jungle Clearing'; Manners, interview.

69 Lee, *Eastward*, p. 133.

70 Royal Air Force, *The Malayan Emergency*, p. 77. A. H. Peterson, G. C. Reinhardt & E. E. Conger, *Symposium on the Role of Airpower in Counterinsurgency and Unconventional Warfare: The Malayan Emergency*, Rand Corporation, Santa Monica, Calif., 1963, p. 33.

71 Manners, interview.

72 *Flight*, 30 Nov 1951, p. 706.

73 Royal Air Force, *The Malayan Emergency*, p. 81.

74 Dennis & Grey, *Emergency and Confrontation*, pp. 25–33; Royal Air Force, *The Malayan Emergency*, p. 81.

75 See Appendix C for list of Officers Commanding A Flight No. 41 (Transport) Squadron RNZAF, 1949–51.

76 Bentley & Conly, *Portrait of an Air Force*, pp. 127–31.

77 Mar–May 1951, No. 41 Squadron RNZAF Unit History, Jan 1950 – Dec 1952, ABFK 7232/6.

78 [TS and Pers] Slessor to Nevill, 3 Apr 50, CAS Guard File, Air 227/20/1A. This was reinforced by the visit of Air Chief Marshal Sir Hugh Saunders for discussions in New Zealand. [TS] Cabinet, Note of a Discussion with Air Chief Marshal Sir Hugh Saunders on Tuesday, 6 Jun 1950, Annex to CM.[50] 32, Air 227/20/1A.

79 Dennis & Grey, *Emergency and Confrontation*, p. 30.

80 [TS] Defence Council Meeting, DC [51] M.6, 7 Jun 1957, JSO 41/6/4, pt 1. 'R.N.Z.A.F. Planes to Return from Malaya', undated clipping, *NZ Herald*, Sep 51, No. 41 Sqn RNZAF Unit History, Jan 1950 – Dec 1952, ABFK 7232/6.

81 [S] 'R.N.Z.A.F. Squadrons Overseas', Air Department memo for Minister of Defence, 18 Sep 1953, Air 227/9/4.

82 'Extract from the Minutes of Meeting of the Executive Council of 19 October 1951', SF. A8/122, Fiji Archives, Suva. In 1948, with the resumption of Territorial training at the wish of the Council of Chiefs, discussions started with British authorities on the employment of a Fijian battalion overseas, after an address to the King expressed the willingness of Fijians to 'offer our services against Your Majesty's foes'. *Journal of the Legislative Council Fiji*, Council Paper no. 48, Council of Chiefs, Report on the Proceedings of the Council of Chiefs held at Draiba, Suva, on 22 June 1948 and following days. It seems that sending a battalion to a number of theatres, including Palestine, was discussed and rejected until in 1951, after 'considerable negotiation between the United Kingdom, the Federation of Malaya and Fiji, the decision to employ a Battalion of the Fiji Infantry Regiment in Malaya was agreed in principle'. Comd FMF Report to NZ COS, Jul–Oct 1951, dated 13 Nov 1951, JSO 35/6/3/1.

83 The New Zealand Army Act 1950, which provided for 'the Constitution, Administration, Organization, and Discipline of the New Zealand Army', came into effect on 1 November 1950.
84 *New Zealand Official Yeabook*, 1951–52, p. 208.
85 McGibbon, *New Zealand and the Korean War, Vol. 1*, pp. 86–101.
86 Extract on UKSLS/S.4245, 1 Oct 1953, Army S.23/1. The discussions that led to this agreement are summarised in 'Aide Memoire, Background to Fiji Examination', undated, and also 'Draft—Paper on Fiji Defence', undated, Army S.23/1.
87 Military Forces of New Zealand, Annual Report, *AJHR*, 1949, H-19, p. 2.
88 Lieutenant-Colonel V. B. Brown, interview, 21 Nov 1991.
89 Brown, interview.
90 WO1 T. T. ('Sonny') Babbington, interview, 12 Mar 1992.
91 'Fiji', COS (51) M.13, 4 Dec 1951, JSO 1/4/3 pt 3, formerly JSO 1/3/3 pt 3.
92 For details of Fijian forces in the Pacific during the Second World War, see Lieutenant R. A. Howlett, *The History of the Fiji Military Forces 1939–1945*, Historical Committee, Crown Agents for the Colonies, London, 1948; Colin R. Larson, *Pacific Commandos*, A. H. & A. W. Reed, Wellington, 1946; Oliver A. Gillespie, *The Pacific*, War History Branch, Department of Internal Affairs, Wellington, 1952.
93 'Officers—1FIR' (Army 238/3/16/MS), 7 Nov 1952, A. T. A. Mataira file, Base Records.
94 Lieutenant-Colonel A. T. A. Mataira, interview, 12 Dec 1991.
95 There was the same reluctance to send Regular officers and NCOs to Kayforce as to 1FIR, and this policy change affected both operational deployments. 'Regular OR—Active Service Overseas' (Army 243/1/12/MS), 29 Nov 1951, Major R. A. Manning file, Base Records. See also McGibbon, *New Zealand and the Korean War, Vol. 2*, pp. 47–8.
96 Major R. A. Manning, interview, 17 Feb 1992.
97 'Establishment—War Fiji Infantry Battalion (Far East)', AD 1, 228/5/34, lists 755 in the battalion, a further 29 attachments, and a Fiji-based component of 28.
98 This led to the temporary removal of all New Zealand officers from company appointments. 1FIR War Diary, Fiji Military Forces Archives, Queen Elizabeth Barracks, Suva. See also Henniker to Governor, 22 Sep 1952, F8/232/1, Fiji Archives; and Comd FMF Report, May–Jul 1952, dated 26 Aug 1952, JSO 35/6/3/1.
99 Manning, interview.
100 Major J. R. M. Barker, interview, 17 Feb 1992; Manning, interview.
101 Barker, interview.
102 Clutterbuck, *Conflict and Violence*, p. 186.
103 Dhu Renick Jnr, 'The Emergency Regulations of Malaya'; Kernial Singh, 'The Saga of the Malayan Squatter', *Journal of Southeast Asian History*, vol. 5, no. 1, Mar 1964, pp. 143–53.
104 Stubbs, *Hearts and Minds in Guerrilla Warfare*, pp. 100–7; Coates, *Suppressing Insurgency*, pp. 86–94.
105 Clutterbuck, *The Long Long War*, p. 58.

106 Quoted in Robinson, *Transformation in Malaya*, p. 165.
107 Federation of Malaya, *Annual Report 1952*, HMSO, London, p. 4.
108 Clutterbuck, *Conflict and Violence*, pp. 175–8. See also Clutterbuck, *The Long Long War*, pp. 60–4.
109 Clutterbuck, *Conflict and Violence*, pp. 178–80.
110 Robinson, *Transformation in Malaya*, pp. 116–70.
111 Clutterbuck, *Conflict and Violence*, pp. 186–94.
112 For CO from GOC, 1 Nov 1952, 1FIR War Diary, FMF Archives.
113 Templer said as much, according to 1FIR veterans of the time. However, the account in John Cloake, *Templer, Tiger of Malaya*, Harrap, London, 1985, p. 244, may be the basis for this conclusion.
114 Cloake, *Templer*, pp. 242–3.
115 1FIR War Diary, Nov 1952, FMF Archives.
116 Brown, interview.
117 The British authorities, as they were wont to do with any Commonwealth battalion, treated 1FIR as just another British battalion. In particular they ignored one of the stipulations laid down when 1FIR was committed to Malaya: that it not be brigaded with battalions of the King's African Rifles. This arose from Fijian concern after incidents between Fijians and Africans at the Victory Parade in London in 1946. In September 1952 it was initially proposed to brigade 1FIR as part of 1 Malay Brigade, which included two battalions of the King's African Rifles. Tinker objected, and informed Pleasants in Fiji. Malaya Command tried to bluster the decision through, and it was only when they realised that the Fijians were serious and might withdraw the battalion from Malaya that they grudgingly backed down. Tinker became the focus of their ire, and the failure to award him a DSO for his services in Malaya was attributed by his subordinates to his stand on this issue. See HQ FMF 21/1, 7 Dec 1951, referred to in DEFENCE SUVA to HQ MALAYA KL, Info GHQ FARELF MALAYA 0141, 30 Sep 1952, and the subsequent signals on SF 8/122/7, Fiji Archives.
118 Comd FMF to NZCOS, Report 1 Jul 1953 – 30 Oct 1953, dated 19 Nov 1953, JSO 35/6/3/1.
119 Mataira, interview. The description of Lieutenant Mataira's reception by armoured train is given by Manning, interview.
120 Brigadier R. I. Thorpe, interview, 19 Nov 1991. See McGibbon, *New Zealand and the Korean War, Vol. 2*, pp. 400, 412.
121 Major C. G. O'Brien, interview, 22 Nov 1991.
122 John Coates, *Suppressing Insurgency: An Analysis of the Emergency in Malaya, 1948–1954*, Westview Press, Boulder, Colorado, 1992, pp. 166–7, 178. See also M. C. A. Henniker, *Red Shadow over Malaya*, William Blackwood, Edinburgh, 1955.
123 Thorpe, interview.
124 Comd FMF to COS, Report 1 Jan – 30 Jun 1955, dated 27 Aug 1955, JSO 35/6/3/1.
125 Thorpe, interview.
126 Thorpe, interview.

127 1FIR War Diary, Nov 1953, FMF Archives.

128 1FIR War Diary, Jul 1954, FMF Archives.

129 The payroll, but not the money, was recovered from an empty MRLA camp in March 1955. 1FIR War Diary, FMF Archives. See also H. W. R. Petersen Papers, which include the B Company 1FIR War Diaries and Reports 1952–56, 89-074, Alexander Turnbull Library.

130 Comd FMF to COS, Report 1 Jan–30 Jun 1955, dated 27 Aug 1955, JSO 35/6/3/1.

131 Thorpe, interview.

132 Thorpe, interview.

133 Captain J. Webster, interview, 22 Nov 1991.

134 See J. Bryant Haigh & Alan J. Polaschek, *New Zealand and the Distinguished Service Order*, authors, Christchurch, 1993, p. 149.

135 Thorpe, interview. See also H. W. R. Petersen Papers, ATL; and 'Reports Operations 1FIR Malaya', AD 1, 239/4/77.

136 See chapter 3 for a description of Operation KINGLY PILE, which led to the death of Goh Peng Tuan. 1FIR had 210 'eliminations' during its operations in Malaya, including three captures, 'plus one surrender and one baby liberated'. 1FIR War Diary, FMF Archives.

137 Interview with Templer, cited in Coates, *Suppressing Insurgency*, p. 166. See also Short, *The Communist Insurrection,* p. 369.

138 John Masters, *Bugles and a Tiger*, Michael Joseph, London, 1956.

139 This number (40) cannot be verified as many of the relevant New Zealand Army files have been destroyed. The following officers are known to have served with 1FIR: R. A. Tinker, H. J. G. Low, B. T. Poananga, W. A. Morgan, P. A. M. Brant, H. W. R. Petersen, S. R. McKeon, H. M. McDonald, R. B. Lockett, V. B. Brown, R. G. Williams, G. Beaton, W. K. King, D. J. Stellin, A. T. A. Mataira, R. I. Thorpe, G. P. Brown, R. I. Launder, G. A. Hyde, J. P. Brosnahan, R. A. Miles, P. M. Hargest, H. McM. H. Salmon, J. W. R. Murphy, P. J. Burtt, J. B. Webster, E. V. Braggins, J. R. M. Barker, G. M. L. Whyte. Warrant officers and NCOs include T. T. Babbington, C. G. O'Brien, R. A. Manning, S. Gilhooly, L. Marceau, Samuels, Martin, C. M. Kennedy, McDonnell and G. Nepia. Brigadier R. I. Thorpe, notes to author, 6 Apr 1999.

140 Thorpe, interview.

## 2 Finding their Way: Naval Duties, 1949–62

1 Chief Petty Officer Fire Control 1st Class J. L. C. Carter, interview, 16 Jan 1998, RNZN Museum.

2 'Report on the Composition of the Armed Forces of New Zealand', COS (47), 12 Feb 1947, JSO 2/1/1 pt 1.

3 *Hawea* (formerly HMS *Loch Eck*) was launched 25 April 1944, completed 7 November 1944. *Kaniere* (formerly HMS *Loch Achray*) was launched 7 July 1944, completed 1 February 1945. *Pukaki* (formerly HMRCNS *Loch Achanalt*) was

launched 25 January 1944, completed 1 February 1945, and involved in the sinking of U1006 on 5 June 1945. *Taupo* (formerly HMS *Loch Shin*) was launched 23 February 1944, completed 10 October 1944. *Rotoiti* (formerly HMS *Loch Katrine*) was launched 21 August 1944, completed 29 December 1944. *Tutira* (formerly HMS *Loch Morlich*) was launched 25 January 1944, completed 2 August 1944. Information on all six ships is taken from R. V. B. Blackman (ed.), *Jane's Fighting Ships 1950–51*, David & Charles Reprints, Newton Abbot, 1975, p. 102.

4 Rear-Admiral E. C. Thorne, interview, 1992, RNZN Museum, p. 90.

5 Commander A. V. Kempthorne, interview, Sep 1990, RNZN Museum, p. 13.

6 Thorne, interview, p. 90.

7 *New Zealand Official Yearbook, 1950*, p. 196.

8 Ian McGibbon, *New Zealand and the Korean War, Vol. 2, Combat Operations*, Oxford University Press, Auckland, 1996, pp. 11–12. See also Grant Howard & Colin Wynn, *Portrait of the Royal New Zealand Navy*, Grantham House, Wellington, 1991; Grant Howard, *The Navy in New Zealand*, A. H. & A. W. Reed, Wellington, 1981.

9 For details on the mutinies or strikes, see 'Discipline—Mutiny and Unrest in HMNZS Philomel following new pay code, 1947', N 1, 13/21/10. See also McGibbon, *New Zealand and the Korean War, Vol. 2*, p. 12, and Royal New Zealand Navy, Annual Reports for the 1950s and 1960s, *AJHR*, H-5.

10 Carter, interview.

11 COS (51) 4, 12 Mar 1951, JSO 1/4/3 pt 3.

12 'New Zealand's Contribution to Commonwealth Defence Arrangements', JPC (49) 1, 3 Feb 1949, JSO 2/1/1 pt 1.

13 'New Zealand's Defence Policy' (JSO 3/1/1), 1 May 1953, JSO 2/1/1 pt 2.

14 COS (54) 52, 9 Dec 1954, JSO 1/4/3 pt 6.

15 'Hong Kong' (PM 300/3/1), 18 Aug 1949, N 1, 6/1/31 pt 1.

16 'Loan of Frigates to Far East' (Navy 8/11/24), 26 Sep 1949, N 1, 6/1/31 pt 1.

17 'New Zealand Naval Assistance at Hong Kong', Memo for Minister of Defence, 10 Aug 1950, N 1, 6/1/31 pt 1.

18 Royal New Zealand Navy, Annual Report, *AJHR*, 1954, H-5, p. 3.

19 F. A. Ballance to Admiral the Hon. Sir Guy Russell, 23 Jun 52, N 1, 6/1/31 pt 2.

20 COS [52] M.13, 10 Sept 1952, JSO 1/4/3.

21 Reports of Proceedings, 'HMNZS *Pukaki*—Service in the Far East 1953–54', 15 Oct 1954, N 1, 140/30/6/A. See also 'Loan of Frigates and Cruisers to Far East Station', N 1, 6/1/31 pt 3.

22 Thorne, interview, p. 112.

23 'Review of Defence Policy and Programme', JPC (54) 32 (Revised), 5 Jan 1955, JSO 2/1/1 pt 2.

24 Thorne, interview, p. 113.

25 Reports of Proceedings, 'HMNZS *Pukaki*—Service in the Far East 1953–54', 15 Oct 1954, N 1, 140/30/6/A. See also 'Loan of Frigates and Cruisers to Far East Station', N 1, 6/1/31 pt 3.

26 Reports of Proceedings, 'HMNZS *Pukaki*—Service in the Far East 1953–54', 15 Oct 1954, N 1, 140/30/6/A. See also 'Loan of Frigates and Cruisers to Far East Station', N 1, 6/1/31 pt 3.
27 Rear-Admiral C. J. Steward, interview, Jun 1992, RNZN Museum, p. 51.
28 Steward, interview, p. 53.
29 Steward, interview, p. 54.
30 Steward, interview, p. 55.
31 Captain G. D. Pound, interview, Jun 1991, RNZN Museum.
32 Steward, interview, p. 58.
33 Lieutenant-Commander P. Y. Dennerly to author, 11 Mar 1999.
34 In 1951 Cabinet approved a naval housing programme for the construction of 509 housing units, of which 457 were to be built in Auckland. See 'Housing Accommodation: Naval Housing at Auckland', N 1, 25/7/11, pts 1 & 2. A Naval Housing and Welfare Officer was appointed in 1955, and the 88-unit Ngataringa Road naval housing block was constructed on the North Shore. See Royal New Zealand Navy, Annual Report, *AJHR*, H-5, 1955; 1956, pp. 16, 18.
35 'Review of Defence Policy and Programme', COS (55) 1, 7 Jan 1955, JSO 2/1/1 pt 2.
36 'Review of Defence Policy and Programme', COS (55) 1, 7 Jan 1955, p. 5, JSO 2/1/1 pt 2.
37 Jeffrey Grey, *Up Top: The Royal Australian Navy and Southeast Asian Conflicts 1955–1972*, Allen & Unwin, St Leonards, 1998, p. 26.
38 After Malaya's independence in 1957 the BDCC(FE) was augmented by the High Commissioners for Australia and New Zealand, and in November 1962 the powers and functions of the BDCC(FE) were replaced by a single Commander-in-Chief for the Far East. Grey, *Up Top*, p. 26.
39 The British contribution was reduced to two destroyers or frigates by 1962, and even before the Strategic Reserve became fully operational the RN considered reducing its commitment from four to three vessels and secured agreement that RN ships undergoing refits in the Singapore Dockyard would be included within the RN commitment. Grey, *Up Top*, p. 27.
40 Defence Council, 'Note of Proceedings of Council of Defence on Friday 11 February 1955', JSO 2/1/1 pt 2.
41 Malcolm Templeton, *Ties of Blood and Empire*, Auckland University Press, Auckland, 1994, pp. 123–5. One can take issue with Templeton (p. 125) in his criticism of *Royalist* being an anti-aircraft cruiser designed to protect aircraft carriers. All New Zealand's post-war cruisers were acquired with this role in mind, and with the task of protecting the Australian aircraft carriers which would be part of the ANZAM naval task force. See also Corner to McIntosh, 5 Jul 1955; McIntosh to Corner, 15 Jul 1955, in Ian McGibbon (ed.), *Unofficial Channels: Letters Between Alister McIntosh and Foss Shanahan, George Laking and Frank Corner, 1946–1966*, Victoria University Press, Wellington, 1999, pp. 185–8.

42 HMNZS *Bellona* had been in reserve since December 1952 and was commissioned in September 1955, under command of Captain P. Phipps DSC, to return to England for the commissioning of *Royalist*. *Bellona* was paid off from the RNZN on 17 April 1956 and broken up in 1959. See RNZN Museum Notes on HMNZS *Bellona* and HMNZS *Royalist; HMNZS Royalist, Second Commission, April 1957–July 1958* (ship's magazine), Cathay Press, Hong Kong; Templeton, *Ties of Blood and Empire,* pp. 123–5.
43 Templeton, *Ties of Blood and Empire,* p. 124.
44 'Review of Defence Policy', Navy, Annex I to COS (57) 15, JSO 2/1/1 pt 2.
45 COS (56) M.50, JSO 1/4/3.
46 'HMNZS *Royalist*—Attachment to the British Far East Fleet', Def Secretariat, 28 Mar 1957, JSO 41/6/1.
47 Pound, interview, p. 6.
48 Pound, interview, p. 6. See undated letter to Minister of Defence from Mrs M. Cotton: 'Our opinion is that 15 months is a long time for any ship to be away in peace time when there is no need for it.' 'Loan of Frigates and Cruisers to Far East Station', N 1, 6/1/31 pt 5.
49 Pound, interview, p. 8.
50 Letter of Proceeding, HMNZS *Royalist*, 5 Sep 1957, N 1, 18/36/75Y.
51 Carter, interview.
52 Carter, interview.
53 Letter of Proceeding, HMNZS *Royalist*, 5 Sep 1957, N 1, 18/36/75Y.
54 Letter of Proceeding, HMNZS *Royalist*, 10 Mar 1958, N 1, 18/36/75Y. See also 'Royalist to Admiralty', 200444Z Feb 1958, 'Loan of Frigates and Cruisers to Far East Station', N 1, 6/1/31 pt 5.
55 Letter of Proceeding, HMNZS *Royalist*, 6 Jun 1958, N 1, 18/36/75Y.
56 Pound, interview, p. 3.
57 Rear-Admiral K. M. Saull, interview, Oct 1993, RNZN Museum, p. 42.
58 Royal New Zealand Navy, Annual Report, *AJHR*, 1957, H-5, p. 6.
59 Thorne, interview, p. 128. Royal New Zealand Navy, Annual Report, *AJHR*, 1957, H-5, p. 6. Many of the modifications that New Zealand achieved in this design were then adopted by the Royal Navy.
60 Michael Burgess, *Ships of the Royal New Zealand Navy*, Southern Press, Wellington, 1979, pp. 16–17; Howard & Wynn, *Portrait of the Royal New Zealand Navy*, p. 105; Howard, *The Navy in New Zealand*, p. 91; 'Weapons—Type 12 Frigates', ABFK, W4010, 69/1/4 pts 1 & 2.
61 Rear-Admiral K. M. Saull, correspondence with author, Oct 1999.
62 Saull, correspondence.
63 HMNZS *Pukaki* was fitted with an operations room in the late 1950s. Lieutenant-Commander P. Y. Dennerly to author, 11 Mar 1999.
64 Thorne, interview.
65 Carter, interview.
66 Howard & Wynn, *Portrait of the Royal New Zealand Navy*, p. 107.

67 Thorne, interview.

68 RNZN Deployments to Malaya, 1948–60: HMNZS *Pukaki*, Sep 1953 – Sep 1954; Apr 1955 – Apr 1956; May 1959 – May 1960; HMNZS *Kaniere,* Jul 1954 – Jul 1955, Feb 1956 – May 1957; HMNZS *Rotoiti,* Apr 1958 – Aug 1959, Apr 1960 – Mar 1961; HMNZS *Black Prince*, May–Jul 1955; HMNZS *Royalist*, May 1957 – Jul 1958, Feb–Jun 1959. (Source: JOZWEL to NZMLO SINGAPORE, 020410Z Jun 1960, JSO 20/4/1.) See also 'Loan of Frigates and Cruisers to Far East Station', N 1, 6/1/31 pts 1–5.

69 See Personnel Manning files, ABFK W4010: *Royalist* (66/10/2); Lochs (66/10/3); Whitbys (66/10/4).

## 3 Flying the Silver Fern: Air Force Operations, 1955–62

1 Extracts from a statement by the Right Honourable S. G. Holland, London, 8 Feb 1955, Ministry of Foreign Affairs, *New Zealand Foreign Policy Statements and Documents, 1943–1957*, Government Printer, Wellington, 1972, p. 382.

2 The RNZAF global war commitment to the Middle East was the immediate deployment of three squadrons RNZAF, followed by two further squadrons two months later. In 1955 the Chief of Air Staff assessed that the RNZAF could provide for any Cold War situation in peacetime using the resources of the fighter/ground attack squadron in Cyprus, one medium-range transport flight of Bristol Freighter aircraft, and the detachment of flying boats stationed at Lauthala Bay in Fiji. 'Review of Defence Policy and Programme', COS [55] M.1, 7 Jan 1955, JSO 1/4/3.

3 The four fighter squadrons of the Territorial Air Force had their Mustangs withdrawn from service in 1955, and flying training during the year was undertaken in Harvard aircraft. Grading on Vampire jet aircraft was carried out at annual camps. The fifth Territorial squadron was No. 6 (Flying Boat) Squadron at Hobsonville, which had been a mix of Regular and Territorial, and became completely Territorial in 1955. Annual Report, Air Department, *AJHR*, 1956, H-37, p. 4.

4 This move back to British aircraft from its wartime inventory of United States-manufactured aircraft was a deliberate decision of the post-war committee which planned the structure of the RNZAF. David Duxbury, Ross Ewing & Ross MacPherson, *Aircraft of the Royal New Zealand Air Force*, Heinemann, Auckland, 1987, pp. 14–15.

5 G. Bentley, *RNZAF: A Short History*, A. H. & A. W. Reed, Wellington, 1969, pp. 154–64; Geoffrey Bentley & Maurice Conly, *Portrait of an Air Force: The Royal New Zealand Air Force 1937–1987*, Grantham House, Wellington, 1987, pp. 125–6.

6 No. 41 Squadron RNZAF, Unit History, May 1958, ABFK 7232/6.

7 *NZ Herald,* 12 May 1955, No. 41 Squadron RNZAF, Unit History, Jan 1953 – Dec 1957, ABFK 7232/6.

8 *Auckland Star*, 11 May 1955, No. 41 Squadron RNZAF, Unit History, Jan 1953 – Dec 1957, ABFK 7232/6.

9 'Directive to Officer Commanding, No. 14 Squadron Royal New Zealand Air Force', 'Directive to Officer Commanding, No. 41 Squadron Royal New Zealand Air Force', 26 Jun 1956, JSO 34/4/2. See Appendix 4.

10 *Federation of Malaya Annual Report 1955*, Government Printer, Kuala Lumpur, 1956, pp. 422–37.

11 Richard Clutterbuck, *The Long Long War: The Emergency in Malaya 1948–1960*, Cassell, London, 1967, p. 113.

12 *Federation of Malaya Annual Report 1955*, pp. 422–37.

13 On the deployment of the four Bristol Freighters with No. 41 Squadron to Singapore, the remaining Freighters in New Zealand were redesignated the Transport Support Unit. The four long-range Hastings aircraft had been formed into No. 40 (Transport) Squadron RNZAF in December 1954. Annual Report, Air Department, *AJHR*, 1955, H-37, pp. 4–5; No. 41 Squadron RNZAF, Unit History, Jan 1953 – Dec 1957, ABFK 7232/6; Duxbury, Ewing & MacPherson, *Aircraft of the RNZAF*, p. 15.

14 The Bristol Type 170B, Mark 31/31E had two 1980-horsepower Bristol Hercules 734 engines. It had a take-off weight of 44,000 lb and a cargo space of 85 cubic yards. Carrying cargo, it had a maximum range of 820 miles. There was provision for a crew of three: a pilot, co-pilot, and a radio operator behind the co-pilot. Leonard Bridgman (ed.), *Jane's All the World's Aircraft 1955–1956*, Jane's, London, 1956, pp. 60–1. The RNZAF's model had Hercules 735 engines and was crewed by a pilot, navigator and signaller. Seating was far less than the maximum of 44. Notes on draft by David Duxbury.

15 'The RNZAF, in conjunction with the Soil Conservation and Rivers Control Council, has been charged by the Government with the task of investigating and developing aerial top dressing in New Zealand.' Air Department, Administrative Instruction No. 7/1949, 'Research and Development Flight—Formation, No. 41 Squadron', Air 1, 1/1/41. Bentley & Conly, *Portrait of an Air Force*, pp. 121–2. Annual Report, Air Department, *AJHR*, 1950, H-37, p. 6. The top-dressing role was quickly downplayed by the CAS of the time, despite successful trials of the aerial top-dressing of farmland in the Wairarapa. 'Bristol Freighter proves its worth as a topdresser', *Auckland Star*, 5 Apr 1954. See also 'Bristol Freighters Fly with the Royal New Zealand Air Force', *Imperial Review*, Feb 1952, pp. 22–3.

16 The twelve aircraft were numbered NZ5901–NZ5912. Personal communication, Squadron Leader Paul Harrison, RNZAF. Some 200 Freighters had been manufactured by 1955, and military versions had been purchased by the Royal Australian Air Force, Royal Canadian Air Force, Royal Pakistan Air Force, Royal Iraqi Air Force, and the Burma Air Force, in addition to the RNZAF. Bridgman (ed.), *Jane's All the World's Aircraft 1955–1956*, pp. 60–1. See also 'Bristol Freighter: Policy', Air 1, W2330, 20/43/1.

17 Wing Commander Ron Manners, interview, 27 May 1992.

18 20 May 1955, No. 41 Squadron RNZAF, Unit History, Jan 1953 – Dec 1957, ABFK 7232/6.

19 Manners, interview.

20 The Vickers Type 651 Valetta was a twin-engine aircraft designed to act as a 'troop transport, freighter, ambulance, glider-tug, or paratroop carrier'. It was a derivative of the Vickers Viking airliner. L. Bridgman (ed.), *Jane's All the World's Aircraft 1952–53*, Sampson Low, London, 1953, pp. 86–7. See also Air Chief Marshal Sir David Lee, *Eastward: A History of the Royal Air Force in the Far East 1945–1972*, Ministry of Defence, Air Historical Branch (RAF), HMSO, London, 1984, p. 125; Royal Air Force, *The Malayan Emergency 1948–1960*, Ministry of Defence, London, 1970, p. 82.

21 Manners, interview.

22 Squadron Leader G. Tosland to AVM C. E. Kay, 26 Mar 1957, Air 1, 26/1/20 pt 2.

23 6 Jun 1955, No. 41 Squadron RNZAF, Unit History, Jan 1953 – Dec 1957, ABFK 7232/6.

24 5 Jul 1955, No. 41 Squadron RNZAF, Unit History, Jan 1953 – Dec 1957, ABFK 7232/6.

25 J. P. Cross, *Jungle Warfare: Experiences and Encounters*, Arms & Armour Press, London, 1989, p. 137.

26 13 Mar 1956, No. 41 Squadron RNZAF, Unit History, Jan 1953 – Dec 1957, ABFK 7232/6.

27 Manners, interview.

28 Lee, *Eastward*, p. 140; A. H. Peterson, G. C. Reinhardt & E. E. Conger (eds), *Symposium on the Role of Airpower in Counterinsurgency and Unconventional Warfare: The Malayan Emergency*, RAND Corporation, Santa Monica, California, 1963, pp. 26–35.

29 *NZ Herald,* 29 Jun 1955, No. 41 Squadron RNZAF, Unit History, Jan 1953 – Dec 1957, ABFK 7232/6.

30 See 'Report on a Visit to the Forces in Singapore–Malaya, Sunday 16th July – Sunday 13th August, 1961 by Senior Chaplain, The Rt Rev. F. O. Hulme-Moir' and similar reports, 'Visits and Inspections by Staff Officers and RNZAF Chaplains to FEAF', Air 1, W2330, 19/4/46.

31 Malcolm McNaught, written reminiscences, 29 Jul 1999.

32 Air Commodore I. G. Morrison to Right Rev. F. O. Hulme-Moir, 18 Sep 1961, Air 1, W2330, 19/4/46.

33 For observations on the importance of food and morale, see 'Policy Committee—Defence', W. Wood to H. Pickering, 9 Nov 1964, Air 1, W2330, 20/49/1 pt 2.

34 McNaught, written reminiscences, 24 Jul 1999.

35 McNaught, written reminiscences, 20 Jul 1999.

36 Shanahan to Kay, 5 Feb 1957, Air 227/20/5.

37 28 Nov 1956, No. 41 Squadron RNZAF Unit History, Jan 1953 – Dec 1957, ABFK 7232/6.

38 Manners, interview. See NZ SAS operations at Fort Brooke in Chapter 4, and infantry operations in Chapter 5. See No. 41 Squadron RNZAF Unit History, Jan 1953 – Dec 1957, ABFK 7232/6, and Bentley & Conly, *Portrait of an Air Force*, p. 140.

39 Kay to Shanahan, 18 Jan 1957, Air 227/20/5.
40 Colonel Richard L. Clutterbuck, quoted in Peterson, Reinhardt & Conger (eds), *Symposium*, p. 28.
41 *Federation of Malaya Annual Report 1955*, pp. 422–37.
42 Kay to Shanahan, 18 Jan 1957, Air 227/20/5.
43 Royal Air Force, *The Malayan Emergency 1948–1960*, p. 167.
44 Mar 1957, No. 41 Squadron RNZAF Unit History, Jan 1953 – Dec 1957, ABFK 7232/6.
45 See chapters 4 and 5.
46 Major-General K. M. Gordon, interview, 27 Apr 1992.
47 'Air Drops over Wild Jungle Country', *NZ Herald*, 3 Apr 1957, Air 1, 26/1/20 pt 2.
48 No. 41 Squadron RNZAF, Unit History, Mar 1958, ABFK 7232/6. For a complete summary of No. 41 Squadron's experience with Bristol Freighters see Ross Dunlop, 'Antipodean Uglies of the East', *Wings*, Oct 1977, pp. 9–13.
49 No. 41 Squadron RNZAF, Unit History, Mar 1958, ABFK 7232/6.
50 No. 41 Squadron RNZAF, Unit History, Apr 1958, ABFK 7232/6.
51 No. 41 Squadron RNZAF, Unit History, Nov 1958, ABFK 7232/6.
52 No. 41 Squadron RNZAF, Unit History, Jan 1959, ABFK 7232/6.
53 No. 41 Squadron RNZAF, Unit History, Jan 1959, ABFK 7232/6.
54 No. 41 Squadron RNZAF, Unit History, Sep 1959, ABFK 7232/6.
55 No. 41 Squadron RNZAF, Unit History, May–Jun 1960, ABFK 7232/6.
56 No. 41 Squadron RNZAF, Unit History, Oct 1960, ABFK 7232/6.
57 No. 41 Squadron RNZAF, Unit History, Dec 1960, ABFK 7232/6.
58 No. 41 Squadron RNZAF, Unit History, May–Dec 1962, ABFK 7232/6.
59 Bentley & Conly, *Portrait of an Air Force*, pp. 149–50; Mathew Wright, *Kiwi Air Power: The History of the RNZAF*, Reed, Auckland, 1998, p. 142. See Minute No. 73/1964, CAS, 'AMP Staff: Briefing for Far East Visit', 'Visits and Inspections: Chief of Air Staff, Visits to FEAF', Air 1, W2330, 19/8/21.
60 Kay to Shanahan, 23 Jul 1956, Air 227/20/5.
61 Shanahan to Kay, 5 Feb 1957, Air 227/20/5.
62 Kay to Shanahan, 27 Feb 1957, Air 227/20/5.
63 After 26 years continuous service, the Bristol Freighters were retired and No. 41 Squadron was disbanded on 6 December 1977. Bentley & Conly, *Portrait of an Air Force*, p. 165.
64 The 'Marker' was an Army Auster spotter aircraft used to mark the target. The call sign was always the pilot's first name. Air Commodore Stuart McIntyre, interview, 23 Feb 1993.
65 McIntyre, interview, and correspondence with author, 30 Sep 1999.
66 No. 14 [Fighter] Squadron RNZAF, Unit History Sheet, May 1955, Air 149/2.
67 McIntyre, interview.
68 'Financial Arrangements—No. 14 Squadron', Various papers in Air 227/9/4.
69 Air Commodore Nelson Bright, interview, 9 Jun 1993. 'Directive to Officer Commanding, No. 14 Squadron Royal New Zealand Air Force', 'Directive to Officer

Commanding, No. 41 Squadron Royal New Zealand Air Force', JSO 32/34/4/2, 26 Jun 1956, 'Directive to the Commonwealth Strategic Reserve', COS (55) 35, 28 Oct 1955, Air 226/7/3. The first two directives are reproduced in appendix 4. See also 'No. 14 Squadron', Air 1, 1/1/60.

70 Norman Franks, *Forever Strong: The Story of 75 Squadron RNZAF 1916–1990*, Random Century, London, 1991, p. 166.

71 Bentley & Conly, *Portrait of an Air Force*, p. 141.

72 No. 1 Squadron RAAF was the only Lincoln bomber squadron under the operational command of the FEAF. However, between 1950 and 1955 six UK-based RAF squadrons equipped with Lincolns were temporarily attached to the FEAF for 'firedog' operations. Royal Air Force, *The Malayan Emergency 1948–1960*, pp. 62–72, Annex M. See also Lee, *Eastward*, pp. 150–1.

73 Lee, *Eastward*, pp. 150–1; Peterson, Reinhardt & Conger (eds), *Symposium*, pp. 79–83.

74 Bright, interview.

75 McIntyre, interview.

76 L. Bridgman (ed.), *Jane's All the World's Aircraft 1953–54*, Jane's, London, 1955, pp. 61–2.

77 Bright, interview.

78 No. 14 [Fighter] Squadron RNZAF, Unit History Sheet, May 1955, Air 149/2; Wright, *Kiwi Air Power*, p. 134.

79 McIntyre, interview. See also Bentley & Conly, *Portrait of an Air Force*, p. 141.

80 Bright, interview.

81 No. 14 [Fighter] Squadron RNZAF Unit History Sheet, May 1955, Air 149/2.

82 Bright, interview.

83 Group Captain Geoff Wallingford, interview, 18 Feb 1993.

84 McIntyre, interview.

85 McIntyre, interview.

86 McIntyre, interview, and correspondence with author. In July 1957 Flying Officer Hubbard ejected at 5,000 ft after ending up in an inverted spin from which he could not recover. No. 14 [Fighter] Squadron RNZAF, Unit History Sheet, Jul 1957, Air 149/2.

87 No. 14 [Fighter] Squadron RNZAF, Unit History Sheet, Jul 1955, Air 149/2. See also No. 14 Squadron, RNZAF, Annual Report for the Year Ending 31st March 1958, Appendix to No. 14 [Fighter] Squadron RNZAF, Unit History Sheet, Mar 1958, Air 149/2.

88 No. 14 [Fighter] Squadron RNZAF, Unit History Sheet, Dec 1955, Air 149/2.

89 Joe Keegan, interview, 24 Feb 1993.

90 Keegan, interview.

91 McNaught, reminiscences, 24 Jul 1999; Keegan, interview.

92 McNaught, reminiscences, 24 Jul 1999.

93 Keegan, interview.

94 Royal Air Force, *The Malayan Emergency 1948–1960*, p. 68.
95 No. 14 [Fighter] Squadron RNZAF, Unit History Sheet, Jan 1956, Air 149/2.
96 McIntyre, interview.
97 Royal Air Force, *The Malayan Emergency 1948–1960*, p. 69.
98 No. 14 [Fighter] Squadron RNZAF, Unit History Sheet, Feb 1956, Air 149/2.
99 Special Branch assessed that the bodies of eight others might have been completely disintegrated by the force of the explosions. Royal Air Force, *The Malayan Emergency 1948–1960*, p. 69.
100 Brigadier Ian Thorpe, interview, 19 Nov 1991.
101 Royal Air Force, *The Malayan Emergency 1948–1960*, p. 69.
102 No. 14 [Fighter] Squadron RNZAF, Unit History Sheet, Jun 1956, Air 149/2. See Wright, *Kiwi Air Power*, p. 136.
103 No. 14 [Fighter] Squadron RNZAF, Unit History Sheet, Oct 1956, Air 149/2.
104 McIntyre, interview, and correspondence with author.
105 McNaught, reminiscences, 24 Jul 1999.
106 Group Captain A. F. Tucker, interview, 26 Feb 1993. See also Franks, *Forever Strong*, p. 166.
107 Tucker, interview.
108 McNaught, reminiscences, 29 Jul 1999.
109 Keegan, interview.
110 No. 14 [Fighter] Squadron RNZAF, Unit History Sheet, Jan 1956, Air 149/2.
111 McIntyre, interview.
112 McIntyre, interview.
113 Tucker, interview.
114 Appendix A to No. 14 [Fighter] Squadron RNZAF, Unit History Sheet, Apr 1957, Air 149/2. Air Commodore Mike Palmer, interview, 11 Jun 1993.
115 Bentley & Conly, *Portrait of an Air Force*, p. 142. See also Wright, *Kiwi Air Power*, pp. 135–6. Notes on draft by David Duxbury.
116 Appendix A to No. 14 [Fighter] Squadron RNZAF, Unit History Sheet, May 1957, Air 149/2.
117 Royal Air Force, *The Malayan Emergency 1948–1960*, p. 70.
118 It was thought that the continued harassing strikes were a factor in the break-up and surrender of the platoon in September–October 1957. No. 14 [Fighter] Squadron RNZAF, Unit History Sheet, Jul 1957, Air 149/2.
119 An agreement was concluded between the United Kingdom and the Federation of Malaya on the defence arrangements. Her Majesty's Government, *Arrangements for the Employment of Overseas Commonwealth Forces in Emergency Operations in Malaya after Independence*, HMSO, London, 1957, JSO 31/2/11.
120 Lee, *Eastward*, p. 149.
121 No. 14 [Fighter] Squadron RNZAF, Unit History Sheet, Jan 1958, Air 149/2.
122 No. 14 [Fighter] Squadron RNZAF, Unit History Sheet, Mar 1958, Air 149/2.
123 Palmer, interview.

124 14 Squadron C905/1/ORG, No. 14 Squadron RNZAF, RAF Tengah, Annual Report for the Year Ending 31st March 1958, Appendix to No. 14 [Fighter] Squadron RNZAF, Unit History Sheet, Mar 1958, Air 149/2.

125 14 Squadron C905/1/ORG, No. 14 Squadron RNZAF, RAF Tengah, Annual Report for the Year Ending 31st March 1958, Appendix to No. 14 [Fighter] Squadron RNZAF, Unit History Sheet, Mar 1958, Air 149/2.

126 Nos 3 and 77 (Fighter) Squadrons, RAAF. Royal Air Force, *The Malayan Emergency 1948–1960*, Annex M.

127 'The Introduction of Canberra Aircraft into Service', transcript of address given by CO RNZAF Ohakea at Station Commanders' Conference 1960, Air 1, W2330, 20/49/1 pt 1.

128 COS (52) 4, 28 Mar 1952, JSO1/4/3 pt 3.

129 No. 14 [Fighter] Squadron RNZAF, Unit History Sheet, May 1958, Air 149/2.

130 Wallingford, interview.

131 Air Commodore Harold Moss, interview, 9 Jun 1993.

132 There was no formal agreement setting out the financial charges that would be made; rather, the Air Ministry set out a list of principles upon which these would be assessed, and this was accepted in an exchange of letters. This arrangement had operated satisfactorily since No. 14 Squadron first deployed to Cyprus, and had been modified to meet changes in aircraft and location. The RNZAF policy of using RAF facilities and services in preference to making independent arrangements was felt to be 'in accordance with the spirit of integration of RNZAF Squadrons with the RAF'. All the charges levied 'have been accepted as fair and reasonable'; while the New Zealand government met its share of the operating and maintenance expenses for the stations at which the RNZAF squadrons were based, there was no commitment to meeting any of the capital costs of facilities and runways. 'Financial arrangements with Air Ministry for the Provision of Supplies and Services for RNZAF Squadrons deployed with Far East Air Force, Singapore [as at May 1960]', Air 227/9/4.

133 No. 2 Squadron RAAF, flying Canberra B2s, replaced the Lincolns of No. 1 Squadron RAAF in 1958; they were were based at RAAF Butterworth Air Base. See Lee, *Eastward*, p. 151; Bentley & Conly, *Portrait of an Air Force*, p. 143; Wright, *Kiwi Air Power*, pp. 141–3.

134 Air Vice Marshal Pat Neville, interview, 11 Jun 1993.

135 Neville, interview.

136 No. 75 Squadron, 'Summary of Aircraft History from Arrival at RAF Tengah until 31st December 1958', Air 1, W2330, 20/49/1 pt 1.

137 Air Commodore Ian Gillard, interview, 10 Jun 1993.

138 No. 75 Squadron RNZAF, Unit History, Sep 1958, Air 167/2.

139 Gillard, interview.

140 Neville, interview. See also Paul Harrison with Brian Lockstone & Andy Anderson, *The Golden Age of New Zealand Flying Boats*, Random House, Auckland, 1997, pp. 241–7; for the intricacies of bombing from a Sunderland MR5, see pp. 247–8, 257.

141 Neville, interview.

142 Royal Air Force, *The Malayan Emergency 1948–1960*, pp. 48–9, 71.
143 Gillard, interview.
144 Gillard, interview. Also Moss, interview; Bentley & Conly, *Portrait of an Air Force*, p. 145.
145 Review of Defence Policy, *AJHR*, 1961, A-19, p. 3.
146 'Defence Review', Minister of External Affairs, Wellington to HCNZ London, No. 1662, 25 Aug 1961, JSO 2/1/1 pt 5.
147 Review of Defence Policy, *AJHR*, 1961, A-19; correspondence on JSO 2/1/1 pt 5.
148 Moss, interview. See correspondence, 'Welfare: RNZAF Personnel Malaya', Air 1, 30/1/10.
149 Moss and his Squadron had been given previous warning of the withdrawal when the Chief of Air Staff, Air Vice-Marshal M. F. Calder, visited in August 1961 en route to the United Kingdom. No. 75 Squadron, Unit History, Aug and Sep 1961, Air 167/1, Micro 3446.
150 No. 75 Squadron, Unit History, Oct 1961, Air 167/1, Micro 3446.
151 No. 75 Squadron, Unit History, Oct 1961, Air 167/1, Micro 3446.
152 'Implications of Withdrawing No. 41 Squadron from Singapore, COS (61) 37, 17 Jul 1961, JSO 2/1/1 pt 5.

## 4 Setting the Standard: The SAS, 1955–57

1 Rennie noted that the fourth line was sometimes changed to 'He will lead us to disaster'. Frank Rennie, *Regular Soldier*, Endeavour Press, Auckland, 1986, p. 144.
2 Minister's notation, 21 Apr 1955, to 'SAS Squadron', Gentry to Minister of Defence (S.45/11/6/G), 22 Mar 1955, AD 1, 209/3/210. See also Matter for Decision by Army Board, 'Formation of NZ Special Air Service (Malaya)', 13 Apr 55, AD 1, 209/3/210. A formal alliance between the New Zealand Special Air Service and the Special Air Service Regiment was approved by the Queen on 15 June 1965; AD 1, 238/15/42.
3 'Formation of and Recruiting for Special Air Service Squadron' (S.45/11/6/A2), 22 Mar 1955, AD 1, 209/3/210.
4 Perhaps the only other claimant, but in very different circumstances, is No. 1 Platoon of A Company, New Zealand Regular Force, which embarked on HMS *Leander* on 30 August 1939 for Fanning Island as guard for the cable station, four days before the declaration of war on 3 September. Robin Kay, *Chronology: New Zealand in the War 1939–1946*, Historical Branch, Department of Internal Affairs, Wellington, 1968, p. 1. See also C. Pugsley, L. Barber, B. Mikaere, N. Prickett & R. Young, *Scars on the Heart: Two Centuries of New Zealand at War*, David Bateman, Auckland, 1996, p. 218.
5 Commonwealth Conference Matters, COS (55) M.10, 8 Mar 1955, JSO 1/4/3 pt 7.
6 'SAS Squadron', Army Secretary to Minister of Defence, 3 Oct 1955, AD 1, 209/3/210.
7 Holland announced this commitment to Parliament on 24 March 1955. See 'SAS Squadron', Army Secretary to Minister of Defence, 3 Oct 1955, AD 1, 209/3/210.

8 See chapters 1 and 10.

9 Robert Jackson, *The Malayan Emergency*, Routledge, London, 1991, p. 53.

10 Dir of Ops to GHQ FARELF for transmission through COS FE to COS UK with comments (DOO/PERS/302), 23 Jul 1954, Air 23/8556.

11 J. D. Leary, *Violence and the Dream People: The Orang Asli in the Malayan Emergency, 1948–1960*, Ohio University Centre for International Studies, Southeast Asia Series no. 95, Athens, Ohio, 1995; C. N. M. Blair, *Guerilla Warfare*, Ministry of Defence, London, 1957, pp. 170–2; Charles Allen, *The Savage Wars of Peace*, Futura, London, 1990, pp. 47–8.

12 'There were 22 infantry battalions in Malaya, divided between seven brigades: the 1st and 2nd Federal Infantry, the 18th Independent Infantry, the 26th, 63rd and 99th Gurkha Infantry and the 28th Commonwealth Infantry.' Jackson, *The Malayan Emergency*, p. 54. See also Richard Clutterbuck, *The Long Long War: The Emergency in Malaya 1948–1960*, Cassell, London, 1967, pp. 151–2; E. D. Smith, *Counter-Insurgency Operations: 1. Malaya and Borneo*, Ian Allen, London, 1985, pp. 25–30; Richard Noone, *Rape of the Dream People*, Hutchinson, London, 1972, pp. 178–9.

13 Dir of Ops to GHQ FARELF (DOO/PERS/302), 23 Jul 1954, Air 23/8556.

14 Dir of Ops to GHQ FARELF (DOO/PERS/302), 23 Jul 1954, Air 23/8556.

15 'Independent SAS Squadron', Gentry to Minister of Defence (S.45/11/6/CGS), 11 Mar 1955, AD 1, 209/3/210.

16 'SAS Squadron', Gentry to Minister of Defence (S.45/11/6/G), 22 Mar 1955, AD 1, 209/3/210. An Independent Squadron of the Parachute Regiment under Major Dudley Coventry was also attached to 22 SAS Regiment in 1956. Jackson, *The Malayan Emergency*, p. 57.

17 Her Majesty's Government, *Arrangements for the Employment of Overseas Commonwealth Forces in Emergency Operations in Malaya after Independence*, 1957, HMSO, London, JSO 31/2/11. See Richard Allen, *Malaysia: Prospect and Retrospect*, Oxford University Press, London, 1968, pp. 107–9.

18 The Australian authorities had had difficulty establishing this distinction when 2nd Battalion Royal Australian Regiment (2RAR) joined 28 Commonwealth Infantry Brigade in 1955. See 413, DEFE 7/501, no. 4, 7 May 1956, in A. J. Stockwell (ed.), *Malaya, Part III: The Alliance Route to Independence 1953–1957*, British Documents on the End of Empire, HMSO, London, 1995, pp. 280–2; Peter Edwards with Gregory Pemberton, *Crises and Commitments: The Politics and Diplomacy of Australia's Involvement in Southeast Asian Conflicts 1945–1965*, Allen & Unwin in association with the Australian War Memorial, Sydney, 1992, pp. 174–8, and also Hamish Eaton, *Something Extra: 28 Commonwealth Brigade, 1951–1974*, Portland Press, Bishop Auckland, 1993.

19 Colonel F. Rennie, interview, 8 Mar 1992.

20 Lieutenant-Colonel J. A. Dixon, interview, 4 Oct 1991.

21 Major G. Brighouse, interview, 3 Oct 1991.

22 Brigadier W. H. B. Bull, DGMS to SALO NZ [UK] and AG, 16 Mar 1955, quoting Pozner RAMC, 'Parachutists', *Journal of the RAMC*, vol. 86, no. 5, May 1946.

Enlistment criteria were laid down in 'Formation of and Recruiting for Special Air Service Squadron' (Army S45/11/6/A2), 22 Mar 1955, AD 1, 209/3/210.

23 'SAS Squadron', Army Secretary to Minister of Defence, 3 Oct 1955, AD 1, 209/3/210.

24 WOI Ross Cameron, interview, 25 Feb 1992.

25 Rennie Unit Diary, Jun 1955, NZ SAS Group Archives.

26 Dixon, interview.

27 Captain D. Mackintosh, interview, 26 Sep 1991.

28 Rennie Unit Diary, Jun 1955.

29 Mackintosh, interview.

30 Captain Noel O'Dwyer, interview, Oct 1991.

31 Dixon, interview.

32 Cameron, interview.

33 Major B. P. Martin, interview, Sep 1991.

34 Brighouse, interview.

35 Rennie Unit Diary, 26 Jul 1955.

36 Brigadier I. H. Burrows, interview, 3 Oct 1991.

37 O'Dwyer, interview.

38 O'Dwyer, interview.

39 'Some Notes for Discussion with Comd SAS Sqn', Notes passed to OC NZ SAS Sqn by GSO2 Plans AGS after visit by CGS in Nov 1955, NZ SAS Group Archives.

40 'Notes on Standards of Training—New Zealand SAS Squadron', by Major C. H. Mercer, 2IC, 22 SAS Regt, Appendix B to Op Report No. 2 NZ Special Air Service Sqn, Jan 1956, NZ SAS Group Archives. Lieutenant-Colonel G. Lea, CO 22 SAS Regiment, reported to NZ Army Headquarters and the NZ Commissioner to South East Asia that the general appearance of the NZ Squadron on its arrival was 'most impressive'; the Commander of the Far East Parachute School regarded the New Zealanders as 'the best he has ever handled' and the personal contribution to the success of each course made by Major Rennie and his two troop commanders as 'magnificent'. Personal Comments by Lt-Col. G. Lea to NZ Squadron Operational Report no. 1, 16 Dec 1955, Rennie Papers, NZ SAS Group Archives.

41 Mackintosh, interview. Two New Zealanders failed to qualify and were returned to New Zealand. 'General Report NZSAS in Malaya', 7 Dec 1957, NZ SAS Group Archives.

42 William Seymour, *British Special Forces*, Sidgwick & Jackson, London, 1985, p. 270.

43 This merged with the Artists Rifles, so its official title was 21 SAS (Artists) TA. It included many veterans who had served in the SAS during the Second World War and was commanded by one of them.

44 Barbara Cole, *The Elite: The Story of the Rhodesian Special Air Service*, Three Knights, Transkei, 1984, pp. 5–13; Seymour, *British Special Forces*, p. 275.

45 Seymour, *British Special Forces*, p. 271.

46 Seymour, *British Special Forces*, p. 275.

47 Lieutenant-Colonel John Woodhouse, interview, 11 Aug 1992.

48 Captain Graham Boswell, notes to author, 3 May 1996.

49 Woodhouse, interview. Woodhouse was the only officer who had served previously with 22 SAS in Malaya, before returning to the United Kingdom in 1952. He established the current selection process for the SAS, which ensured that the regiment at last received reinforcements of an appropriate calibre. See Allen, *The Savage Wars of Peace*, pp. 49–65; Rennie, *Regular Soldier*, pp. 166–7.

50 'Notes at Random on NZ SAS Sqn Ops in Malaya', Rennie Papers, NZ SAS Group Archives.

51 Mackintosh, interview.

52 Rennie, *Regular Soldier*, pp. 169–72.

53 Rennie, interview.

54 Lieutenant-General Sir John Mace, interview, 4 Nov 1991.

55 'Notes on Standards of Training—New Zealand SAS Squadron', by Major C. H. Mercer, 2IC, 22 SAS Regt, Appendix B to Op Report No. 2 NZ Special Air Service Sqn, Jan 1956, NZ SAS Group Archives. See also 'Reports SAS Squadron', AD 1, 239/4/87.

56 See NZ SAS Sqn, General Report NZ SAS in Malaya, 7 Dec 1957, NZ SAS Group Archives. See also 'Reports SAS Squadron', AD 1, 239/4/87.

57 Mackintosh, interview.

58 Mrs Fran Martin, interview, 24 Oct 1992.

59 NZ SAS Sqn, General Report NZ SAS in Malaya, 7 Dec 1957, NZ SAS Group Archives. See also 'Reports SAS Squadron', AD 1, 239/4/87.

60 Mrs Fran Martin, interview. See 'Some Notes Which May Assist Housewives Coming to Malaya', by Mrs Rennie, n.d., Rennie Papers, NZ SAS Group Archives.

61 Rennie adjusted his squadron organisation to produce five troops, each 19 strong. See NZ SAS Sqn, 'NZ Sqn Org wef 10 Jan 56', Annex B, Jan 1956, NZ SAS Group Archives.

62 Martin, interview. A similar view was held by Sergeant David Ogilvy, who commanded 1 Troop when Lieutenant Vail was appointed Operations Officer at Headquarters 22 SAS Regiment. Lieutenant-Colonel David Ogilvy, interview, 5 May 1992.

63 Lieutenant Neville Wallace had been appointed reserve troop commander during the raising and training of the NZ SAS Squadron in Waiouru, with the intention that he be called to Malaya should an additional officer be needed. See Colonel N. J. Wallace, interview, 12 Mar 1992. Rennie wrote to the Military Secretary expressing doubts about Wallace's physical fitness to handle the demands of patrolling and suggesting four names as likely replacements. Rennie to Lieutenant-Colonel J. D. McKercher, Military Secretary, 19 Jul 1956, Rennie Papers, NZ SAS Group Archives. Williams was not one of the four, and he has no idea why he was chosen. Colonel L. G. Williams, interview, 18 Feb 1992.

64 'Report on Ops By NZ Sqn 22 SAS Regiment in Fort Brooke Area Between 2 Apr–11 Jun 56', 28 Jun 1956, NZ SAS Group Archives. See also 'Reports SAS Squadron', AD 1, 239/4/87.

65 Rennie, *Regular Soldier*, p. 180.

66 Leary, *Violence and the Dream People*, pp. 99–100, 108–17.

67 Noone, *Rape of the Dream People*, pp. 17–45.
68 J. Slimming, *Temiar Jungle*, Travel Book Club, London, 1958, pp. 3–4; Noone, *Rape of the Dream People*, pp. 6–7.
69 Leary, *Violence and the Dream People*, pp. 117–33; T. N. Harper, *The End of Empire and the Making of Malaya*, Cambridge University Press, Cambridge, 1999, pp. 267–73. Also Mr J. J. West, interview, 7 Aug 1992, and papers in his possession: 'Memorandum by Lieutenant-Colonel J. M. Calvert, DSO, RE, Police Increment of proposed Special Force "The Malayan Scouts"'; and draft appreciation, 'Perak Aborigines in the Emergency', Ipoh, 19 Oct 1953.
70 'Asal' (or 'Asli'), the Malay term for 'origin' or 'original people', was used by the MRLA in preference to the more derogatory term 'Sakai' ('slave'), which was used by the authorities and security forces. Leary, *Violence and the Dream People*, p. 1, fn 1; Noone, *Rape of the Dream People*, p. 5; Rennie, *Regular Soldier*, p. 180. See also West, interview and papers.
71 Leary, *Violence and the Dream People*, pp. 101–8; Slimming, *Temiar Jungle*, p. 5.
72 Mackintosh, interview.
73 Noone, *Rape of the Dream People*, p. 38.
74 Dixon, interview.
75 Mackintosh, interview.
76 Mackintosh, interview.
77 Ogilvy, interview; Rennie Unit Diary, 9 Apr 1956.
78 1 Troop, Report on Contact 9 Apr 56, 13 Jun 56, attached to 'Report on Ops by NZ Sqn 22 SAS Regiment in Fort Brooke Area Between 2 Apr–11 Jun 56', NZ SAS Group Archives. See also 'Reports SAS Squadron', AD 1, 239/4/87.
79 Department of Aborigines, 'Operation Uda', Appendix A to 'Report on Ops by NZ Sqn 22 SAS Regiment in Fort Brooke Area Between 2 Apr–11 Jun 56', NZ SAS Group Archives. See also 'Reports SAS Squadron', AD 1, 239/4/87.
80 Burrows, interview.
81 Burrows, interview; I. H. Burrows, letter to his father, Brigadier J. T. Burrows, 4 May 1956; Letter to John D. Leary, 29 Aug 1988, Burrows Papers, held privately.
82 Burrows, interview.
83 Brigadier I. H. Burrows, Notes, 'Steve Watene, BEM, Eulogy at Internment of Ashes, Dargaville, 18 May 96', Burrows Papers.
84 See chapter 5.
85 Burrows, interview.
86 Burrows, interview. See also 3 Troop NZ Sqn Contact 27 Apr 1956, Appendix E to 'Report on Ops by NZ Sqn 22 SAS Regiment in Fort Brooke Area Between 2 Apr–11 Jun 56', NZ SAS Group Archives; I. H. Burrows, letter to his father, Brigader J. T. Burrows, 4 May 1956, Burrows Papers, and correspondence with author, 13 Jan 1999; Hugh Fraser, 'Happiness is Knowing One's Place', copy in author's possession.
87 Rennie Unit Diary, 29 Apr 1956. The difficulty of carrying two-day-old bodies through the jungle to a clearing and then helicoptering them out can be appreciated. Burrows, interview.

88 Rennie Unit Diary, 27 Apr 1956.
89 Cameron, interview.
90 Cameron, interview.
91 2 Troop Incident Report 3 May 1956, Appendix A to NZ SAS War Diary, Apr–May 1956, NZ SAS Group Archives. (This more formal diary was kept when the squadron was not on operations, as opposed to the detailed and almost personal notes that Rennie kept in a series of notebooks, identified as 'Rennie Unit Diary', which also form part of the NZ SAS Group Archives.) Mace, interview; Cameron, interview.
92 Rennie Unit Diary, 3 May 1956. See Lea's comments, 16 May 1956, Appendix B to NZ SAS War Diary, Apr–May 1956. See also 'Reports SAS Squadron', AD 1, 239/4/87.
93 Cameron, interview.
94 Brighouse, interview.
95 Rennie, 'Notes at Random on NZ SAS Sqn Ops in Malaya', Rennie Papers, NZ SAS Group Archives.
96 Rennie Unit Diary, 4 May, 14 May 1956.
97 Rennie Unit Diary, 21 May 1956.
98 Burrows, interview.
99 Burrows, interview. Rennie Unit Diary, 21 May 1956; 3 Troop Contact 26 May 56, Appendix G to 'Report on Ops by NZ Sqn 22 SAS Regiment in Fort Brooke Area Between 2 Apr–11 Jun 56', NZ SAS Group Archives. See also 'Reports SAS Squadron', AD 1, 239/4/87.
100 'Report on Ops by NZ Sqn 22 SAS Regiment in Fort Brooke Area Between 2 Apr–11 Jun 56', NZ SAS Group Archives. See also 'Reports SAS Squadron', AD 1, 239/4/87.
101 Appendix C to 'Report on Ops by NZ Sqn 22 SAS Regiment in Fort Brooke Area Between 2 Apr–11 Jun 56', NZ SAS Group Archives. See also 'Reports SAS Squadron', AD 1, 239/4/87. Rennie recommended the resettlement of the aborigines to Lea and the Brigade Commander on 29 May 1956. See Rennie Unit Diary, 29 May 1956. For the impact of this on the aboriginal groups, see Leary, *Violence and the Dream People*.
102 22 SAS 315/G [S], CO to AHQ Wellington on NZ SAS Sqn Report No. 4 of 4 Jul 1956. See also 'Reports SAS Squadron', AD 1, 239/4/87.
103 Burrows, interview.
104 Mackintosh, interview.
105 Captain Graham Boswell, interview, 30 Sep 1991.
106 Rennie, interview. Also Burrows and Mace, interviews.
107 Burrows, Mace and Rennie, interviews. See Allen, *The Savage Wars of Peace*, pp. 59–62.
108 Rennie, interview.
109 Woodhouse, interview. See Allen, *The Savage Wars of Peace*, pp. 60–2.
110 Woodhouse, interview.
111 NZ SAS War Diary, 22 Jul 1956.

112 As part of its Commonwealth Strategic Reserve role, the New Zealand squadron was included in the ANZAM planning for the defence of Malaya against a Chinese communist attack. Operation HERMES envisaged Malaya being defended at the southern end of the Kra Isthmus in southern Thailand, known as the 'Songkhla position'. The forces involved included 17 Gurkha Infantry Division, 28 Commonwealth Independent Infantry Brigade, and the New Zealand Army and Air Force elements. The NZ Squadron and another squadron of 22 (SAS) Regiment were designated as the airborne force which would seize the airfield and port of Songkhla and be reinforced by the flying in of an infantry rifle company. The RNZAF Venoms would provide air defence and the Bristol Freighters transport support to the forward units. The concentration of the force was to be disguised as a normal Emergency operation against communist terrorists in north Malaya. This operation was never practised in Thai territory. [TS] Operation 'HERMES' Draft Outline Plan BDCC [FE][56]1, 22 May 1956, Air 204/22/1.

113 NZ SAS War Diary, 14–20 Jul 1956. Sergeant Ray Delves had an unlucky run during his tour with the NZ SAS Squadron. On Friday 13 September 1957 he was slightly injured when his patrol ran into an unmanned Type A (Grenade) ambush. Two other New Zealanders and one aboriginal were also slightly wounded. See Rennie Unit Diary, 13 Sep 1957.

114 'Op Directive for Entry NZ SAS Sqn into Op GABES SOUTH on 27 July 56', 22 SAS Regt, 19 Jul 1956, Appendix A to 'Report on Op GABES SOUTH—Fort Brooke Area—NZ Sqn 27 Jul–28 Oct 56', Oct 1956, NZ SAS Group Archives. See also 'Reports SAS Squadron', AD 1, 239/4/87.

115 'Report on Op GABES SOUTH—Fort Brooke Area—NZ Sqn 27 Jul–28 Oct 56', Oct 1956, NZ SAS Group Archives. See also 'Reports SAS Squadron', AD 1, 239/4/87; Mace, interview.

116 'Report by 2 Lt Yandall, CT Camp Attack S/Paldar 28 Jul 56', Appendix B to 'Report on Op GABES SOUTH—Fort Brooke Area—NZ Sqn 27 Jul–28 Oct 56', Oct 1956, NZ SAS Group Archives. See also 'Reports SAS Squadron', AD 1, 239/4/87.

117 Mace, interview.

118 Mackintosh, interview.

119 Lieutenant Earle Yandall, interview, 4 Oct 1991.

120 Mackintosh, interview.

121 Yandall, interview.

122 NZ SAS War Diary, 28 Jul 1956; 'Report by 2 Lt Yandall, CT Camp Attack S/Paldar 28 Jul 56', Appendix B to 'Report on OP GABES SOUTH—Fort Brooke Area—NZ Sqn 27 Jul–28 Oct 56', NZ SAS Group Archives. See also 'Reports SAS Squadron', AD 1, 239/4/87.

123 Dixon, interview.

124 Rennie Unit Diary, Boswell entry, 31 Jul 1956.

125 Harper, *The End of Empire*, pp. 149–68.

126 Much depended on the calibre of the liaison officers working with the SAS. In this instance the New Zealanders were fortunate that the Perolak aboriginals trusted Mat

Yunus, the liaison officer attached to Mace's troop. See 'Liaison with Abos', in 'Report on Op GABES SOUTH—Fort Brooke Area—NZ Sqn 27 Jul–28 Oct 56', NZ SAS Group Archives. See also 'Reports SAS Squadron', AD 1, 239/4/87.

127 Rennie Unit Diary, Boswell entry, 7 Aug 1956.

128 'Report on Op GABES SOUTH—Fort Brooke Area—NZ Sqn 27 Jul–28 Oct 56', NZ SAS Group Archives. See also 'Reports SAS Squadron', AD 1, 239/4/87.

129 Mace, interview. 'Capture of Abehlum', Appendix C to 'Report on Op GABES SOUTH—Fort Brooke Area—NZ Sqn 27 Jul–28 Oct 56', NZ SAS Group Archives. See also 'Reports SAS Squadron', AD 1, 239/4/87.

130 See Leary, *Violence and the Dream People*; Harper, *The End of Empire*, pp. 267–73.

131 Mace, interview; Burrows, interview; Rennie Unit Diary, 6–7 Oct 1956. See also 'Reports SAS Squadron', AD 1, 239/4/87.

132 Burrows, interview.

133 Burrows, interview.

134 Burrows, interview.

135 'Report on Op GABES SOUTH—Fort Brooke Area—NZ Sqn 27 Jul–28 Oct 56', NZ SAS Group Archives. See also 'Reports SAS Squadron', AD 1, 239/4/87.

136 Mackintosh, interview.

137 'NZ SAS Sqn Report No. 5', 22 SAS Regt, 19 Nov 1956 to Army HQ, Wellington, NZ SAS Group Archives. See also 'Reports SAS Squadron', AD 1, 239/4/87.

138 John Mace's 2 Troop remained on operations in the Fort Selim area of Perak until mid-March 1957, coming in turn under the operational command of A, D and B Squadrons of 22 (SAS) Regiment.

139 Tony Geraghty, *Who Dares Wins: The Special Air Service, 1950 to the Gulf War*, Little, Brown & Co, London, 1980, pp. 343–51.

140 'General Report NZSAS in Malaya', NZ SAS Sqn, 7 Dec 1957, NZ SAS Group Archives. See also 'Reports SAS Squadron', AD 1, 239/4/87.

141 [TS] Shanahan to Minister of External Affairs, 9 Aug 1956, Air 204/22/1.

142 NZ SAS War Diary, Dec 1957.

143 West, interview.

144 NZ SAS War Diary, Dec 1957.

145 Rennie Unit Diary, 21 Dec 1956.

146 'Report on Op LATIMER SOUTH—MOUNTAINOUS Area 18 Dec 56–15 Mar 57', NZ Sqn 22 SAS Regt, 30 Mar 57, NZ SAS Group Archives. See also 'Reports SAS Squadron', AD 1, 239/4/87.

147 Li Hak Chi's wife survived this contact and two others before surrendering on 12 September 1957. Major Ray Hurle, interview, 15 May 1992.

148 Hurle, interview; Contact Statement by L/Cpl Hurle, HQ Troop NZ Sqn, 22 SAS Regt, Appendix B to 'Report on Op LATIMER SOUTH—MOUNTAINOUS Area 18 Dec 56–15 Mar 57', NZ Sqn 22 SAS Regt, 30 Mar 57, NZ SAS Group Archives. See also 'Reports SAS Squadron', AD 1, 239/4/87.

149 Appendix B to 'Report on Op LATIMER SOUTH—MOUNTAINOUS Area 18 Dec 56–15 Mar 57'. See also 'Reports SAS Squadron', AD 1, 239/4/87.

150 Contact Statement, Appendix D to 'Report on Op LATIMER SOUTH—MOUNTAINOUS Area 18 Dec 56–15 Mar 57'. See also 'Reports SAS Squadron', AD 1, 239/4/87.

151 Colonel R. L. Clutterbuck, 'The SEP–Guerrilla Intelligence Source', *Military Review*, Oct 1962, pp. 13–21.

152 Rennie Unit Diary, 8–11 Feb 1957.

153 Appendix D to 'Report on Op LATIMER SOUTH—MOUNTAINOUS Area 18 Dec 56–15 Mar 57'. See also 'Reports SAS Squadron', AD 1, 239/4/87.

154 During their two years on operations, the New Zealanders had numerous close calls, usually with other security force patrols. In the Fort Brooke operations, Rennie complained about unnotified intrusions by both other squadrons of 22 (SAS) Regt and the Gurkhas, who passed through New Zealand ambushes. See Rennie, *Regular Soldier*, pp. 193, 195. There had also been a near incident between two aboriginals and a 4 Troop patrol in 'Mountainous'. 'Report on Op LATIMER SOUTH—MOUNTAINOUS Area 18 Dec 56–15 Mar 57'. See also 'Reports SAS Squadron', AD 1, 239/4/87.

155 'Report on Op LATIMER SOUTH—MOUNTAINOUS Area 18 Dec 56–15 Mar 57'. See also 'Reports SAS Squadron', AD 1, 239/4/87.

156 'Report on Op LATIMER SOUTH—MOUNTAINOUS Area 18 Dec 56–15 Mar 57'. See also 'Reports SAS Squadron', AD 1, 239/4/87.

157 Proposal for the future deployment of the NZ Sqn of 22 SAS Regt in MOUNTAINOUS District, Appendix A to SS SAS Regt letter 315/g/1 [S], 27 Feb 57, NZ SAS Group Archives.

158 Proposal for the future deployment of the NZ Sqn of 22 SAS Regt in MOUNTAINOUS District, Appendix A to SS SAS Regt letter 315/g/1 [S], 27 Feb 57, NZ SAS Group Archives. The patrol sequence was 1, 2 and 3 Troops from 8 to 14 April, followed by 4 and 5 Troops and the Tracker Team from 15 to 21 April. Report on Phase II—NZ Sqn Ops—MOUNTAINOUS DIST 29 Apr–17 Jul 57, NZ SAS Group Archives. See also 'Reports SAS Squadron', AD 1, 239/4/87.

159 Colonel L. G. Williams, interview, 18 Feb 1992.

160 Major R. P. Withers, interview, 9 Jun 1993.

161 Report by Patrol Commander on contact at GR284191 on 19 April 1957. Appendix B to Report on Phase II—NZ Sqn Ops—MOUNTAINOUS DIST 29 Apr–17 Jul 57. Rennie Unit Diary, 19 Apr 1957. See also 'Reports SAS Squadron', AD 1, 239/4/87.

162 Withers, interview.

163 Appendix A to Report on Phase II—NZ Sqn Ops—MOUNTAINOUS DIST 29 Apr–17 Jul 57. See also 'Reports SAS Squadron', AD 1, 239/4/87.

164 Yandall, interview. Report on Contact, Appendix C to Report on Phase II—NZ Sqn Ops—MOUNTAINOUS DIST 29 Apr–17 Jul 57. See also 'Reports SAS Squadron', AD 1, 239/4/87.

165 Rennie Unit Diary, 12 Jul 1957.

166 NZ Sqn Op Report Phase III—MOUNTAINOUS District, 2 Aug–1 Nov 57. See also 'Reports SAS Squadron', AD 1, 239/4/87.

167 For this operation each patrol was equipped with the Australian-designed and -manufactured A510 set, giving the New Zealanders a communications flexibility they had previously lacked.

168 Captain Graham Boswell, notes to author, 3 May 1996.

169 Rennie Unit Diary, 28 May 1957.

170 'The Government therefore proposes that a fully equipped regular infantry battalion be made available to the Commonwealth Strategic Reserve as soon as possible. This will replace our present contribution, a Special Air Service Squadron, which is due to be withdrawn in November 1957. The contribution of a battalion was first requested by the United Kingdom in 1955, but was not then feasible because of our effort in Korea. The withdrawal of the remaining New Zealand forces from Korea now makes it possible to agree to the renewed United Kingdom request. The Government of the Federation of Malaya has welcomed this proposal.' 'Review of Defence Policy', 12 Jun 1957, in Ministry of Foreign Affairs, *New Zealand Foreign Policy, Statements and Documents, 1943–1957*, Government Printer, Wellington, 1972, pp. 474–5.

171 Bill Edwards, interview, 16 Apr 1992.

172 'Li Hak Chi Kill: NZ SAS, Burrows' Account', Burrows Papers.

173 'Contact—19 Aug 57', Appendix C to NZ Sqn Op Report Phase III—MOUNTAINOUS District, 2 Aug–1 Nov 57. See also 'Reports SAS Squadron', AD 1, 239/4/87; Burrows, interview; Rennie Unit Diary.

174 Edwards, interview. 'Li Hak Chi Kill: NZ SAS, Burrows' Account', Burrows Papers.

175 'Li Hak Chi Kill: NZ SAS, Burrows' Account'. See also Rennie, Edwards, interviews. During the debriefing, Edwards 'looked across at Huia and he went white. It was that close.' Edwards, interview.

176 Rennie Unit Diary, 24 Aug 1957.

177 Rennie, interview.

178 This was Ah Tam, who had become separated from the rest of his group and surrendered shortly afterwards. Major Ray Hurle, correspondence with author re Incident 27 Aug 1957. Rennie Unit Diary, 27 Aug 1957. NZ Sqn Op Report Phase III—MOUNTAINOUS District, 2 Aug–1 Nov 57. See also 'Reports SAS Squadron', AD 1, 239/4/87.

179 Appendix E to NZ Sqn Op Report Phase III—MOUNTAINOUS District, 2 Aug–1 Nov 57.

180 Edwards, interview.

181 On interrogation they revealed that one of Li Hak Chi's section commanders, Li Chun, had been killed by artillery fire in July 1957, when likely campsites were shelled by 48 Federation Regiment in support of the New Zealanders' operations in the Sungei Batu Hampar area. It was one of the rare occasions that any of the thousands of rounds fired to harass the guerrillas was known to have had an effect. Li Chun had been the Bren gunner in the 'Mountainous' group, and after his death the weapon was buried 'because no one could operate it'! NZ Sqn Op Report Phase III—MOUNTAINOUS District, 2 Aug–1 Nov 57; Rennie Unit Diary, 20 Sep 1957.

182 1 Troop Op Report—Negri Sembilan 24 Sep–3 Oct 57, NZ SAS Group Archives.
183 NZ Sqn Op Report Phase III—MOUNTAINOUS District, 2 Aug–1 Nov 57. See also 'Reports SAS Squadron', AD 1, 239/4/87.
184 Edwards, interview.
185 'General Report NZ SAS in Malaya', 7 Dec 1957, NZ SAS Group Archives. See also 'Reports SAS Squadron', AD 1, 239/4/87.
186 NZ Sqn Op Report Phase III—MOUNTAINOUS District, 2 Aug–1 Nov 57. See also 'Reports SAS Squadron', AD 1, 239/4/87.
187 Brigadier G. R. Turner-Cain, 1 Federation Infantry Brigade to Lt Col G. Lea, 8 Nov 1957, Rennie Papers, NZ SAS Group Archives.
188 Lea to Army Headquarters Wellington, NZ SAS Sqn Report No. 8, 19 Nov 1957, NZ SAS Group Archives.
189 Jackson, *The Malayan Emergency*, pp. 57–60.
190 There was one non-battle fatality: Corporal A. G. Buchanan, NZ SAS, died from a heart attack whilst on patrol on 11 May 1957. 'General Report NZ SAS in Malaya', 7 Dec 1957, NZ SAS Group Archives. See also 'Reports SAS Squadron', AD 1, 239/4/87.
191 Lea to Army Headquarters Wellington, NZ SAS Sqn Report No. 8, 19 Nov 1957, NZ SAS Group Archives. See also 'Reports SAS Squadron', AD 1, 239/4/87.
192 Woodhouse to Rennie, 9 Oct 1957, Rennie Papers, NZ SAS Group Archives.
193 'Notes at Random on NZ SAS Sqn Ops in Malaya', Rennie Papers.
194 Lt I. H. Burrows, 'Some Notes on NZ Sqn Techniques', Oct 1957, Rennie Papers.
195 O'Dwyer, interview.
196 Major-General C. E. Weir to Rennie, 5 Nov 1957, Rennie Papers.

## 5 Fighting a Jungle War: Infantry Operations, 1957–59

1 Major-General K. M. Gordon, interview, 7 Apr 1992. While Gordon joined 1 NZ Regt in 1958, his description rings true for the original battalion that sailed to Malaya in 1957.
2 The commitment was approved in principle by Cabinet on 17 June 1957. 'New Zealand Contribution to Commonwealth Strategic Reserve CM (57) 23', AD 1, 209/3/128. The 1st Battalion New Zealand Regiment in Malaya was combined with a small New Zealand Force headquarters in Singapore and named New Zealand Army Force FARELF (Far East Land Forces), with a total strength of 750. See 'Far East 1 NZ Regt Strength Returns', AD 1, 228/7/36. Its evolution into the 1960s can be traced through 'NZ Army Force FARELF: Organisation and Formation', AD 1, 209/3/218, pts 1–5, and 'Re-organisation of the NZ Army', AD 1, 209/1/125, pts 1–2.
3 Brigadier W. R. K. Morrison, series of interviews beginning 11 Feb 1991. Lieutenant-General Sir Leonard Thornton, who was Adjutant-General at this time, said there was a deliberate attempt to give command experience to those who had shown talent during the Second World War but for various reasons had not held unit command.

Morrison had been badly wounded in 1943. Lieutenant-General Sir Leonard W. Thornton, interview, 8 Oct 1991.

4 'GHQ Far East Land Forces Directive No. 1 to HQ Malaya Command For the Army Component of the British Commonwealth Far East Strategic Reserve' (COS (56) M.47), Air 226/7/3. In 1958 Brigade Headquarters was established in Taiping as part of 17 Gurkha Division, which had assumed command of the British Commonwealth forces in Malaya when Headquarters Malaya Command closed on Malaya's independence.

5 A. & R. Burnett, *The Australia and New Zealand Nexus*, Australian and New Zealand Institutes of International Affairs, Canberra, 1978, p. 79. See also Alastair Buchan, 'Commonwealth Military Relations', in W. B. Hamilton, K. Robinson, & C. D. W. Goodwin (eds), *A Decade of the Commonwealth, 1955–1964*, Duke University Commonwealth Studies Center, Duke University Press, Durham, North Carolina, 1966, p. 199.

6 The text of the 1957 and 1963 agreements, together with the details of the exchange of letters dated 24 March and 21 April 1959, are given in 'Documents Concerning New Zealand Forces Serving in Malaysia', *AJHR*, 1963, A–27.

7 Malcolm McKinnon, *Independence and Foreign Policy: New Zealand in the World Since 1935*, Auckland University Press, Auckland, 1993, pp. 140–4. See also Keith Sinclair, *Walter Nash*, Auckland University Press, Auckland, 1976, pp. 304–36.

8 Thornton, interview.

9 For Weir's views, see Corner to McIntosh, 12 Mar 1956, in Ian McGibbon (ed.), *Unofficial Channels: Letters between Alister McIntosh and Foss Shanahan, George Laking and Frank Corner, 1946–1966*, Victoria University Press, Wellington, 1999, pp. 200–2.

10 Thornton, interview. For Weir's involvement, see Chief of Staff Meetings, 1955–61, JSO 2/1/1.

11 McKinnon, *Independence and Foreign Policy*, pp. 140–4.

12 Morrison, interviews.

13 Major I. F. Forsythe, interview, 18 Feb 1992.

14 Morrison, interviews.

15 Mataira believed he was selected as company commander because of the initial intention to form a Maori company. Lieutenant-Colonel A. T. A. Mataira, MBE, interview, 12 Dec 1991. There is no mention of this in any of the correspondence relating to the recruitment of the battalion. 'Formation of and Recruiting for NZ Army Force in Commonwealth Strategic Reserve, FARELF' (Army 209/3/218/A2), 14 Jun 1957, AD–W6, W2566, 42/13 pt 2. Brigadier Morrison has stated that he was not aware of any such suggestion and would not have been happy with a separate Maori company. Morrison, notes on draft chapters, 19 Apr 1993.

16 'Formation of and Recruiting for NZ Army Force in Commonwealth Strategic Reserve, FARELF', AD–W6, W2566, 42/13 pt 2.

17 WO1 Peter Rutledge, interview, 27 Oct 1992.

18 Major W. J. Meldrum, interview, 9 Mar 1992.

19 1 NZ Regt Statistics Breakdown, 1 NZ Regt War Diary, WA–M 1/1. There were 163 Maori in the battalion: Bn HQ (4), HQ Coy (24), A Coy (42), B Coy (55), C Coy (26), and D Coy (12). This statistical analysis is drawn from attestation forms and is the only one compiled for the battalions that deployed to Malaya. The average age of battalion personnel was 24.7 years; the average weight was between 11 stone 5 lb and 12 stone; the average height was 5 ft 8 in; 438 had been trained under the CMT scheme, 105 had served in Korea, 46 had Second World War service, and 5 had previous service in Malaya; 92 were married; 79 were long-service Regulars.

20 *New Zealand Official Yearbook*, 1958, pp. 31, 55.

21 J. V. T. B. [Baker], 'Population', in A. H. McLintock (ed.), *An Encyclopaedia of New Zealand*, vol. 2, Government Printer, Wellington, 1966, p. 824; *New Zealand Official Yearbook*, 1968, p. 60. Author's personal observations, 1970–71.

22 On my own first posting as a newly commissioned officer to a National Service platoon at Burnham Military Camp in 1970, three of my four Regular Force NCOs were Maori; and when I was posted to a 1RNZIR rifle company in Singapore in 1971, the CSM, CQMS and all three platoon sergeants in A Company were Maori. While this was not typical of every company, it reflected the significant proportion of Maori in the battalion.

23 Rutledge, interview.

24 1 Oct 1957, 1 NZ Regt War Diary, Oct 1957, WA–M 1/1/5.

25 14 Oct 1957, 1 NZ Regt War Diary, Oct 1957, WA–M 1/1/5.

26 Rutledge, interview.

27 Author's discussions with Lieutenant-General Sir Leonard Thornton, who was Adjutant-General at this time; Morrison, interviews.

28 'Long Service Regulars—Service in FARELF' (Army 243/1/98/MS), 26 Jul 1957, AD–W6, W2566, 42/13 pt 2.

29 'NZ Army Force: Term of Service Overseas and Allocation of Married Quarters' (Army 209/3/218/A), 12 Sep 1957, AD–W6, W2566, 42/13 pt 2.

30 Morrison's reaction as quoted by Lieutenant-Colonel N. A. Wallace, interview, 12 Mar 1992.

31 Mrs Florence Hall, interview, 28 Apr 1993.

32 G. McKay to author, 29 Nov 1998.

33 Mrs Pru Meldrum, interview, 6 Apr 1993.

34 Mrs Doreen Cooke, interview, 7 Apr 1993.

35 In May 1958 the Minister of Defence directed that no family with more than two children would be moved to Malaya without his specific approval. This ruling softened as the tour progressed, and in 2 NZ Regt priority was given to the families of long-serving Regular soldiers. Army Board Minute, 'Families in Malaya', 10 Dec 1958, AD 1, 209/3/218.

36 28 Dec 1957, 1 NZ Regt War Diary, 31 Jul 1957–3 Mar 1958, WA–M 1/1/1.

37 WO2 W. J. White, 1 NZ Regt, 'Journey to & Early Days in Malaya: Extracts from Letters Home', 1 RNZIR Museum.

38 11 Feb 1958, 1 NZ Regt War Diary, 31 Jul 1957–3 Mar 1958, WA–M 1/1/1.

39 31 Dec 1957, 1 NZ Regt War Diary, 31 Jul 1957–3 Mar 1958, WA–M 1/1/1; Report by Commander NZ Army Force FARELF for period 1–31 Dec 1957, WA–M 1/1/7.

40 WO1 Alan Polaschek, interview, 19 Feb 1992. Also G. McKay to author, 29 Nov 1998. For a background to the rationing system in the battalion, see Julia Millen, *Salute to Service: A History of the Royal New Zealand Corps of Transport and its Predecessors 1860–1996,* Victoria University Press, Wellington, 1997, pp. 371–7.

41 Colonel I. Launder, interview, 11 Dec 1991.

42 Brigadier R. T. V. Taylor, interview, 1 Jun 1992.

43 1 NZ Regt Monthly Report 1–30 Apr 1958, WA–M 1/1/10.

44 An interim directive was issued to Cade which was later confirmed. 'Directive to the Commander, New Zealand Army Force, FARELF', Army S.31/2/11.

45 (Army 209/3/218/G) 21 Sep 1959, JSO 142/3/2.

46 The detailed administrative history of New Zealand Army Force FARELF is contained in 'Reports—Activities of NZ Army Force—FARELF', AD 1, 239/4/96, pts 1–4.

47 C. E. Brock, *The Diplomat in Uniform: A History of the First Battalion Royal New Zealand Infantry Regiment*, 1RNZIR, Singapore, 1971. See also P. Dennis & J. Grey, *Emergency and Confrontation*, Allen & Unwin in association with the Australian War Memorial, Sydney, 1996, pp. 133–49; H. B. Eaton, *Something Extra: 28 Commonwealth Brigade, 1951–1974*, Durham, 1993, pp. 178–207.

48 Former Brigade-Major Colin East, quoted in Eaton, *Something Extra,* pp. 193–4.

49 Morrison, interviews.

50 23 Feb 1958, 1 NZ Regt War Diary, 31 Jul 1957–3 Mar 1958, WA–M 1/1/1.

51 WO2 White, 'Journey to & Early Days in Malaya'. See also Laurie Barber & Cliff Lord, *Swift and Sure: A History of the Royal New Zealand Corps of Signals and Army Signalling in New Zealand*, New Zealand Signals, Auckland, 1996, p. 168.

52 Rutledge, interview.

53 WO2 White, 'Journey to & Early Days in Malaya'.

54 WO2 White, 'Journey to & Early Days in Malaya'.

55 Yuen Yuet Leng, 'Operation Ginger', manuscript extracts in author's possession, provided by Leon Comber; Dennis & Grey, *Emergency and Confrontation*, p. 136.

56 Comds Narrative 28 COMWEL Bde, 1 Jan–31 Dec 1958, WO 305/1863.

57 'The Emergency in Federation of Malaya' (9/C/5/1), Commissioner for New Zealand in South East Asia to Secretary of External Affairs, 10 Jun 1958, JSO 142/1/1. See also Yuen Yuet Leng, 'Operation Ginger', pp. 82–3, 86–7.

58 For an excellent study of the winning of the intelligence war, see Riley Sutherland, *Antiguerrilla Intelligence in Malaya 1948–1960*, RAND Corporation, Santa Monica, California, 1964.

59 Paper from the Director of Operations: Emergency Policy after September 1957 (DOPS.S1/1), Jul 1957, WA–M 2/1/3.

60 R. Clutterbuck, *Conflict and Violence in Singapore and Malaysia 1945–1983*, Singapore, 1984, p. 256. See also R. Clutterbuck, *The Long Long War: The Emergency in Malaya 1948–1960*, Cassell, London, 1967, pp. 16–17, 35.

61 Clutterbuck, *Conflict and Violence,* p. 256.

62 WO2 White, 'Journey to & Early Days in Malaya'.
63 Major G. Hornbrook, interview, 5 Jun 1992.
64 Captain N. C. Jamieson, interview, 13 Feb 1992.
65 Hornbrook, interview.
66 Contact Report 2 Platoon A Company, 20 Mar 1958, WA–M 2/1/4.
67 Contact Report 7 Platoon C Company, 231730 GH Mar [1958], WA–M 2/1/4.
68 Contact Report 4 Platoon B Company, 18 Apr 1958, WA–M 2/1/4.
69 Lieutenant-Colonel N. A. Wallace, manuscript; Wallace, interview. See Leong Chi Woh, *Scorpio: The Communist Eraser*, Lao Bai & Tang Publishing House, Taiwan, 1996, pp. 81–92.
70 Colonel R. L. Clutterbuck, 'The SEP–Guerrilla Intelligence Source', *Military Review*, Oct 1962, pp. 13–21.
71 Major Bruce Hill, interview, 16 Jun 1993.
72 Rutledge, interview.
73 Contact Report 6 Platoon B Company, 4 Jun 1958, WA–M 2/1/4.
74 Yuen Yuet Leng, 'Operation Ginger', pp. 98–9. See also Major W. J. D. Meldrum, notes to author.
75 Detailed in 'Previous SF Treatment of Abos', in Lt W. J. Meldrum, Report on 6 Pl Op in Jak–Cheor–Legap Area, Oct–Nov 1958, Meldrum Papers; see also T. N. Harper, *The End of Empire and the Making of Malaya*, Cambridge University Press, Cambridge, 1999, pp. 267–73.
76 Report from Sergeant Jamieson R. C., 'Karawat', WA–M 2/1/4. Also Bruce Jamieson, interview, 27 Apr 1993.
77 Leong Chi Woh, *Scorpio*, pp. 81–92.
78 Report on Contact, 3 Jun 1958, WA–M 2/1/4.
79 D Company Contact Report, 030830 Jun 1958, WA–M 2/1/4; 1 NZ Regt War Diary, Jun 1958, WA–M 1/1/12.
80 Monthly Operation Report, Jun 1958, 1 NZ Regt, WA–M 2/1/5.
81 Contact Report 12 Platoon D Company, 061200 GH Aug 1958, WA–M 2/1/4.
82 Monthly Operation Report, Jun 1958, 1 NZ Regt, WA–M 2/1/5.
83 Sg Siput and Ipoh District Combined Pol/Mil Operational and Intelligence Summary, No. 26, 28 Jun 1958, White Papers, 1 RNZIR; Monthly Operation Report Jun 1958, 1 NZ Regt, WA–M 2/1/5.
84 Yuen Yuet Leng, 'Operation Ginger', pp. 98–100.
85 Monthly Operation Report, Sep 1958, 1 NZ Regt, WA–M 2/1/5.
86 Wallace, interview and manuscript.
87 Hornbrook, interview.
88 Jamieson, interview. Private B. Nathan was Mentioned in Despatches for this work. See Leong Chi Woh, *Scorpio*, pp. 81–92.
89 Hornbrook, interview; also Jamieson, interview.
90 Jamieson, interview. Compare these procedures with those outlined in Sutherland, *Army Operations in Malaya*.
91 Incident Report 5 Platoon, B Company, 121530 GH, WA–M 2/1/4.

92 Report on CT Contact B Company, 30 Jun 1958, Major A. N. King—OC B Coy, 1 NZ Regt, WA–M 2/1/4.

93 This philosophy developed after the success in February 1956 of Operation KINGLY PILE, which killed 14 guerrillas. Air strikes against camps that were known to be occupied and could be accurately located were to be given priority. See Royal Air Force, *The Malayan Emergency 1948–1960*, Ministry of Defence, London, 1970, p. 69. See chapter 3.

94 Report on CT Contact B Company, 30 Jun 1958, WA–M 2/1/4. See Brock, *The Diplomat in Uniform*, ch. 2, p. 4; also marginal notes by Lieutenant-Colonel M. J. Hall, RNZIR, on his copy.

95 Contacts and Incidents 30 Jun 1958, B Company, WA–M 2/1/4. Corporal Pat Dillon was awarded the Military Medal for his leadership in this action.

96 Report on CT Contact B Company, 30 Jun 1958, WA–M 2/1/4; Brock, *The Diplomat in Uniform*, ch. 2, p. 4.

97 Brock, *The Diplomat in Uniform*, ch. 2, p. 4. See also Yuen Yuet Leng, 'Operation Ginger', pp. 99–100.

98 Taylor, interview.

99 Brock, *The Diplomat in Uniform*, ch. 2, p. 5.

100 Brock, *The Diplomat in Uniform*, ch. 2, p. 6.

101 'Tracking Organization—1 NZ Regt' (NZT/1), 26 Apr 1958, White Papers, 1RNZIR Museum.

102 Lt H. Woods, quoted in Brock, *The Diplomat in Uniform*, ch. 2, p. 6.

103 Jamieson, interview.

104 Contact Report and Sketch of Ambush 1 Jul 1958, WA–M 2/1/4; Brock, *The Diplomat in Uniform*, ch. 2, p. 4, and marginal notes by Lieutenant-Colonel M. J. Hall, RNZIR.

105 Yuen Yuet Leng, 'Operation Ginger', pp. 107–8.

106 Sg Siput and Ipoh District Combined Pol/Mil Operational and Intelligence Summary, no. 28, 12 Jul 1958, White Papers, 1RNZIR Museum.

107 Contact Report 1 NZ Regt, 8 Platoon, 1035 hrs, 28 Jul 1958, WA–M 2/1/4.

108 Op Report–Jul 1958, 1 NZ Regt, WA–M 2/1/5; 1 NZ Regt War Diary, Jul 1958, WA–M 1/1/13.

109 Yuen Yuet Leng, 'Operation Ginger'.

110 'Company Statistics: Jungle Bashing', HQ A Company, 28 Jul 1958, White Papers, 1RNZIR Museum.

111 Report on Welfare and Padre's Activities, Annex D to Monthly Report Jul 1958, WA–M 2/1/5.

112 Report on Housing, Annex F to Monthly Report 1–31 Aug 1958, WA–M 2/1/5. On 12 November 1958 there were 72 wives and 107 children in Malaya. Army Secretary to Minister of Defence, 'New Zealand Army Personnel and Families in Malaya', 12 Nov 1958, AD 1, 228/7/36.

113 WO2 White, 'Journey to & Early Days in Malaya'.

114 WO2 White, 'Journey to & Early Days in Malaya'.

115 Mrs Anne Morrison, interview, 13 May 1991.
116 Morrison, interview.
117 Colonel O. E. Mann, interview, 8 Apr 1992.
118 Wallace, interview.
119 Mrs Pru Meldrum, interview, 6 Apr 1993.
120 Mrs Anne Morrison, interview, 6 May 1991.
121 WO2 White, 'Journey to & Early Days in Malaya'.
122 Private R. M. Breitmeyer, who died on 16 August 1958, is buried in the Kamunting Road Christian Cemetery, Taiping, Perak, together with other New Zealand soldiers who died between 1958 and 1961 while serving with 1 NZ Regt and 2 NZ Regt, Far East Command. *1948–1971 The Dead of the British Commonwealth West Malaysia* FARELF, Singapore, 1971, pp. 89, 95. See appendix 1.
123 'Daily and Overnight Leave Policy', 1 NZ Regt, 10 Mar 1958, White Papers, 1RNZIR Museum.
124 Cheam Yeom Toon, interview, Aug 1992.
125 M. Dattaya, interview, Aug 1992.
126 First Battalion The New Zealand Regiment Routine Orders No. 3/59, 21 Jan 1959, 1RNZIR Museum.
127 'Brief for the CSM A Coy 2 NZ Regt', White Papers, 1RNZIR Museum.
128 1 NZ Regt War Diary, Jul 58, WA–M 1/1/13.
129 Meldrum, interview.
130 Welfare and OD Padre's Activities, Annex E to 1 NZ Regt Monthly Report 1–31 Mar 1959, WA–M 1/1/21.
131 Meldrum, interview; Forsythe, interview.
132 Morrison, interviews.
133 Report by Comd NZ Army Force FARELF for Month ended 30 Apr 1959, WA–M 1/1/22. See also correspondence 'Unsatisfactory Soldiers Return to NZ', AD 1, 243/1/104.
134 Wallace, interview.
135 Morrison, interviews.
136 Eaton, *Something Extra,* p. 194.
137 1 NZ Regt Monthly Report 1–31 Aug 1958, WA–M 2/1/5.
138 1 NZ Regt Monthly Report 1–30 Jun 1958, WA–M 2/1/5.
139 Discussions on draft with Lieutenant-Colonel A. T. A. Mataira, Jan 1999.
140 Lieutenant-Colonel B. P. Wells, interview, 11 Jun 1992.
141 Rutledge, interview.
142 Director of Emergency Operations, Malaya, Instruction on the Senoi Pra'ak (DOPS 4/4), 7 Mar 1958, WA–M 2/1/2.
143 Brief Description of Contact—VE131065 22 Aug 1958. Also 1 NZ Regt Weekly Intelligence Summary No. 2 from 1800 hrs 27 Dec to 1800 hrs 3 Jan 1959, WA–M 2/1/4.
144 Contact Report 10 Platoon, D Company, 210800 Aug 1958, WA–M 2/1/4.
145 HQ Tracking Team 1 NZ Regt Report, 16 Sep 1958, WA–M 2/1/4.

146 Taylor, interview. Braybrooke has been the Labour MP for Napier since 1981.
147 Brock, *The Diplomat in Uniform*, ch. 2, p. 5.
148 Information Services Perak Monthly Report—Oct 1958, WA–M 2/1/3.
149 Rutledge, interview; Hill, interview.
150 Information Services Perak Monthly Report—Oct 1958. The discrepancy between the nine surrenders to 1 NZ Regt listed in the Perak Monthly Report for October and the 13 featured in the 1 NZ Regt contact reports occurred because some were later classified as 'seeking government protection'.
151 Rutledge, interview.
152 1 NZ Regt Monthly Report 1–31 Mar 1959, WA–M 1/1/21.
153 1 NZ Regt Weekly Intelligence Summary No. 2 From 1800 hrs 27 Dec to 1800 hrs 3 Jan 1959, WA–M 2/1/4. The rough treatment of aboriginals continued the approach of British squadrons seen in 1956–57 by the NZ SAS Squadron. See chapter 4.
154 Lieutenant-General D. S. McIver, interview, 9 Jun 1992.
155 Wells, interview.
156 Mann, interview.
157 Wells, interview; also Gordon, interview. See chapter 3. For the work of the battalion signallers, see Barber & Lord, *Swift and Sure*, pp. 165–75.
158 1 NZ Regt Monthly Report 1–28 Feb 1959, WA–M 1/1/20.
159 F. Burdett, correspondence with author and notes on draft; Morrison, interviews; Brock, *The Diplomat in Uniform*, ch. 2, p. 5, and marginal notes by Lieutenant-Colonel M. J. Hall, RNZIR.
160 C Company 1 NZ Regt, Notes on C Company Tasks Op JAYA 15–30 Jun 1959, WA–M 2/1/4.
161 Lieutenant-Colonel P. G. Hotop, interview, 31 Mar 1992.
162 Mataira, interview, and discussions on draft with author, Apr 1999.
163 Morrison, interviews.
164 Organisation of 17 Gurkha Division, Air Portability, Annex B to Monthly Report Commander NZ Army Force, 1–31 May 1958, WA–M 1/1/11.
165 These were the eight nominated dog-handlers who were attached to 1 NZ Regt before attending a dog-handlers' course at the Jungle Warfare School at Kota Tinggi.
166 Rutledge, interview; 'Court of Inquiry—Death of Pte Kumpang Anak Tinngi', AD 1, 222/7/249.
167 'Congratulation For The First Battalion', unidentified newspaper cutting, Brigadier W. R. K. Morrison scrapbook.
168 Mann, interview.
169 This provided the legal basis for the stationing of Commonwealth forces in Malaya. 'Extracts from the White Paper on Malayan Defence', London & Kuala Lumpur, 19 Sep 1957, pp. 12–13, in Ministry of Foreign Affairs, *New Zealand Foreign Policy Statements and Documents 1943–57*, Wellington, 1972, pp. 484–6. N. Mansergh, *Documents and Speeches on Commonwealth Affairs 1951–1962*, Oxford University Press, London, 1963, pp. 570–3. See also Ian McGibbon, 'Forward Defence: The Southeast Asian Commitment', in Malcolm McKinnon (ed.), *New Zealand in World*

*Affairs, Volume II: 1957–1972*, New Zealand Institute of International Affairs, Wellington, 1991, p. 22.

170 Gordon, interview.

## 6 Interlude: SEATO Commitments, 1960–64

1 'Order of the Day by Brigadier H. J. Mogg CBE, DSO', 2 NZ Regt Sobraon Camp Routine Order No. 175/60, 8 Nov 1960, Commander's Diary, 2 NZ Regt, WA–M 1/2/11.

2 Brigadier D. J. Aitken, interview, 27 Oct 1992.

3 Major-General R. G. Williams, interview, 10 Apr 1992.

4 WO1 Rex Harris, interview, 2 Jun 1992.

5 Aitken, interview.

6 Williams, interview.

7 Compulsory military training ceased with the end of the 27th intake on 15 July 1958. 'Review of Defence Policy Reorganization of the New Zealand Army' (Army 281/1/134/ Plans and Mob), AD–W6, W2566, 39/75 pt 1. See also Ian McGibbon, 'Forward Defence: The Southeast Asian Commitment', in Malcolm McKinnon (ed.), *New Zealand in World Affairs, Volume II: 1957–1972*, New Zealand Institute of International Affairs, Wellington, 1991, pp. 14–22.

8 'Review of Defence Policy Reorganization of the New Zealand Army' (Army 281/1/134/ Plans and Mob), AD–W6, W2566, 39/75 pt 1.

9 A 'combat team' was a battalion-sized unit with its supporting arms, such as an artillery battery, engineer troop, and transport elements. In current terminology, such an organisation is a 'battle group'.

10 Brigade Headquarters was established at Linton. The artillery regiment, 16 Field Regiment RNZA, together with its headquarters and headquarters battery, was at Papakura; of the two regular batteries, 161 Battery was at Papakura and 163 Battery at Waiouru. Of the infantry, 2 NZ Regt at Papakura was rostered to replace 1 NZ Regt, which would return from Malaya to Burnham, while 3 NZ Regt would be at Waiouru. 'Reorganisation: NZ Army Accommodation Plan' (Army 203/1/110/Q(Q)), 18 Aug 1958, AD–W6, W2566, 39/75 pt 1.

11 Lieutenant-General Sir John Mace, interview, 4 Nov 1991; Lieutenant-Colonel D. Ogilvy, interview, 5 May 1992.

12 Colonel H. J. G. Low, DSO, MC, who had commanded 1FIR in Malaya in 1953–55, and district recruiting officers were appointed to stimulate the recruiting of Regular and Territorial Force personnel. In the first 12 months, 1,656 recruits were enlisted into the Regular Force, against a target figure of 1,500, raising the Regular Force by 1,112 after attrition; 7,248 volunteers were recruited into the Territorial Force, against a target of 7,000, giving a net strength of 6,543. Personal Copy, Statement by Director of Recruiting Colonel H. J. G. Low, DSO, MC, ED, Report on Recruiting for Period Ending 31 Mar 1960, AD–W6, W2566, 40/4 pt 2.

13 Williams, interview.

14 Aitken, interview.
15 Harris, interview.
16 Notes Bde Comd's O Gp held at the Perak SWEC, Ipoh, Tues 12 Jan 1960, WO 305/1864. See also P. Dennis & J. Grey, *Emergency and Confrontation*, Allen & Unwin in association with the Australian War Memorial, Sydney, 1996, pp. 150–7.
17 28 COMWEL Bde Directive No. 1/60, 7 Mar 1960, WO 305/1866.
18 Commander's Diary, 2 NZ Regt, Jan 1960, WA–M 1/2/1.
19 Also spelled 'Keringcheng' and in many other ways in the reports and logs in Commander's Diary, 2 NZ Regt, WA–M 1/2/1. The group leaders of 12th Regiment ASAL were identified as: DCM Ah Soo Chye, BCM Tet Meuw, BCM Hing Ho, and BCM Lo Sai. 28 COMWEL Bde, Ops 68, OO No. 15 [Op BAMBOO], 6 Jan 1960, WO 305/1864.
20 1 NZ Weekly Intelligence Summary No. 4 from 1800 hrs 10 Jan to 1800 hrs 17 Jan 1959, White Papers, 1 RNZIR Museum.
21 Notes Bde Comd's O Gp held at the Perak SWEC, Ipoh, Tues 5 Jan 1960 and 19 Jan 1960, WO 305/1864.
22 Commander's Diary, 2 NZ Regt, Jan 1960, WA–M 1/2/1.
23 Lieutenant-Colonel R. Dearing, interview, 3 Jun 1992.
24 'Assessment of Information on Kerinching', D Coy, Fort Kemar, 28 Feb 1960, Commander's Diary, 2 NZ Regt, Mar 1960, WA–M 1/2/3.
25 Dearing, interview. See also 28 COMWEL BDE Narrative, Feb 1960, WO 305/1865.
26 SB, Perak Weekly Intelligence Summary No. 9/60, WO 305/1866.
27 SB, Perak Weekly Intelligence Summary No. 10/60, WO 305/1866.
28 Routine Order No. 38/60, 15 Mar 1960, Commander's Diary, 2 NZ Regt, Mar 1960, WA–M 1/2/3.
29 Aitken, interview.
30 Dearing, interview.
31 2 NZ Regt Sobraon Camp Routine Order No. 126/60, 12 Aug 1960, Commander's Diary, 2 NZ Regt, Aug 1960, WA–M 1/2/8. The MCP continued the struggle from its bases in Thailand, and peace was not formalised until 2 December 1989, when the survivors of the 1948 leadership, Chin Peng, Rashid Maidin and Abdullah C. D., signed separate agreements with the Malaysian and Thai governments in Haad Yai, southern Thailand. T. N. Harper, *The End of Empire and the Making of Malaya*, Cambridge University Press, Cambridge, 1999, p. 150.
32 JOZWEL from Dyson, MLO 69, 27 Apr 1960, Air 226/7/13.
33 'Malaya: End of Emergency Legislation', ABHS 950, W4627, 253/3/5/5 pt 2.
34 'Border Security Council Directive No. 1' (DOPS 6/1), Director of Border Security Staff, Air 226/7/13. These revisions were included in the directives to the GOC Overseas Commonwealth Land Forces and the AOC Overseas Commonwealth Air Forces in Malaya, which were then approved by the ANZAM Defence Committee.
35 'Termination of the Malayan Emergency' (1/3/10), Dyson to Secretary COS Committee, 5 May 1960, and correspondence, ABHS 950, W4627, 253/3/5/5 pt 2, Air 226/7/13.

36 'Anti-Terrorist Operations in Malaya and Thailand' (1/3/10), Dyson to Secretary COS Committee, 30 May 1960, Air 226/7/13.

37 The Malayan government enacted legislation empowering it to combat subversion and enabling both the Commonwealth and Federation forces to continue operations against the guerrillas. This legislation included the Constitution Amendment Act, which provided for detention for periods of up to two years on the order of the Minister; the Visiting Forces Act 1960; the Malayan Internal Security Act 1960; and the Emergency Regulations (Indemnity) Act. The last created a border security area on the Thai border in which the government would be able to impose regulations similar to the existing Emergency Regulations. The legislation was examined by the New Zealand authorities, in consultation with Australia and the United Kingdom, who were satisfied that it provided the appropriate legal protection for their servicemen in Malaya. 'Malaya: End of Emergency Legislation', ABHS 950, W4627, 253/3/5/5 pt 2.

38 In April 1960 it was estimated that there were 492 MRLA members in Thailand and 117 [i.e. the total was 609] still active in Malaya. Dennis & Grey, *Emergency and Confrontation*, p. 150.

39 'Anti-Terrorist Operations: Federation of Malaya' (1/3/10), Dyson to Patterson, 24 & 30 Mar 1960, Air 226/7/13.

40 Williams, interview.

41 Harris, interview.

42 Harris, interview.

43 Commander's Diary, 2 NZ Regt, Dec 1960, WA–M 1/2/12.

44 There were 240 privately owned motor vehicles in 2 NZ Regt. 'N.Z. Soldiers in Malaya are Top Owners of Cars', *Auckland Star*, clipping, n.d., NZ Army Department, 2nd Battalion NZ Regt, Scrapbook, Photographic Archive, ATL.

45 Annex C to Commander's Diary, 2 NZ Regt, May 1960, WA–M 1/2/5.

46 'Company Commanders' Conference 27/28 April 60', Annex A, Commander's Diary, 2 NZ Regt, May 1960, WA–M 1/2/5.

47 Dearing, interview.

48 RMO's Monthly Report, Jun 1960, Commander's Diary, 2 NZ Regt, Jul 1960, WA–M 1/2/7.

49 See 'Report on a Visit to the Forces in Singapore–Malaya: Sunday 16th July–Sunday 13th August, 1961 by Senior Chaplain, The Rt Rev. F. O. Hulme-Moir', and similar reports, 'Visits and Inspections by Staff Officers and RNZAF Chaplains to FEAF', Air 1, W2330, 19/4/46.

50 See appendices to the unit war diaries, e.g. Welfare and OD Padre's Activities, Annex E to 1 NZ Regt Monthly Report 1–31 Mar 1959, WA–M 1/1/21. Also 'Report on a Visit to the Forces in Singapore–Malaya', and similar reports, 'Visits and Inspections by Staff Officers and RNZAF Chaplains to FEAF', Air 1, W2330, 19/4/46.

51 See 'Report on a Visit to the Forces in Singapore–Malaya' and similar reports, 'Visits and Inspections by Staff Officers and RNZAF Chaplains to FEAF', Air 1, W2330, 19/4/46. Author's discussions with former 1RNZIR padres, including Professor

Laurie Barber, University of Waikato; also awareness of procedures during tour as platoon commander with 1RNZIR in Singapore, 1971–73.

52 'Returning Troops Yearn For Malaya', *NZ Herald*, 6 Nov 1961.

53 Major-General L. A. Pearce, interview, 9 Mar 1992. By direction of the New Zealand Army Board, all members of the New Zealand Army Force FARELF and New Zealand personnel serving with British units in Malaya ceased to be on active service from midnight 15 November 1963. 'Active Service—Malaya and Singapore' (Army 222/1/30/A1), 3 Dec 1963, AD–W6, W2566, 42/13 pt 3. The New Zealand General Service Medal was subsequently awarded for operations conducted between 1960 and 1963.

54 '2 New Zealand Regiment Training Directive No. 2 Nov 60–Sep 61', 18 Nov 1960, Commander's Diary, 2 NZ Regt, Nov 1960, WA–M 1/2/11.

55 While this dilution of the role that had originally been contemplated disappointed both McIntosh and Weir, it was seen as a step towards better co-ordination of the three services. McIntosh had been concerned for some time about the nature of New Zealand's defence planning. In 1958 he wrote to Walter Nash: 'It has always seemed to me that a small country like New Zealand would have a better chance than most in integrating its defence forces. Having decided on the nature of the threats and the role that New Zealand can fulfil, it might be better for us to contribute towards the common pool some composite force rather than three separate elements—Navy, Air, Army.' McIntosh to PM, 6 Jun 1958 (PM 156/1/22/1), PM 81/20/4. The experiment ended in October 1961 when Weir was appointed Ambassador to Thailand, but he had had a major influence in shaping the 1961 Defence Review, which also commented on the lack of progress towards the integration of the armed services. In 1963, Rear-Admiral P. Phipps became New Zealand's first Chief of Defence Staff.

56 Leszek Buszynski, *Seato: The Failure of an Alliance Strategy*, Singapore University Press, Singapore, 1983, pp. 49–50.

57 'New Zealand's Defence Relations with the United Kingdom, Australia and the United States', Brief for Prime Minister: Mr Macmillan's Visit, Dept of External Affairs, Jan 1958, JSO 3/1/5; McGibbon, 'Forward Defence', p. 24.

58 'New Zealand's Defence Relations with the United Kingdom, Australia and the United States', JSO 3/1/5.

59 G. Wyn Rees, *Anglo-American Approaches to Alliance Security, 1955–60*, Macmillan Press in association with the Mountbatten Centre for International Studies, University of Southampton, Southampton, 1996, pp. 121–5.

60 'Memorandum on New Zealand Defence Policy for use at New Zealand–United States Defence Talks, Washington, D.C., 3 October 1957', JSO 3/1/5.

61 ANZUS was seen as being 'in many ways far more important on political grounds than on considerations of security guarantees or military alliances. The ANZUS relationship which Australia and New Zealand enjoyed with the United States has with the course of time developed into a specially intimate and close form of cooperation. The annual meeting of the Council of Ministers, for example, provides us with an

unequalled forum for the frankest possible discussion of common problems with the Americans. The special relationship with the Americans is also reflected in the growing extent of consultation which Australia and New Zealand share with the Americans on general political issues.' 'New Zealand's Defence Relations with the United Kingdom, Australia and the United States', Brief for Prime Minister: Mr Macmillan's Visit, Dept of External Affairs, Jan 1958, JSO 3/1/5.

62 'New Zealand's Defence Relations with the United Kingdom, Australia and the United States', Brief for Prime Minister: Mr Macmillan's Visit, Dept of External Affairs, Jan 1958, JSO 3/1/5.

63 Keith Sinclair, *Walter Nash*, Auckland University Press, Auckland, 1976, pp. 320–7; Malcolm McKinnon, *Independence and Foreign Policy: New Zealand in the World Since 1935*, Auckland University Press, Auckland, 1993, pp. 140–4.

64 'Federation-Based Commonwealth Forces and SEATO Activities', NZ Commissioner Singapore to Minister of External Affairs, no. 85, 25 Apr 1959, Air 226/7/13; McGibbon, 'Forward Defence', pp. 24–6.

65 Brief for Prime Minister, 'Malayan PM's Visit to NZ January 1960, Possible Use in Laos of Commonwealth Forces Stationed in Malaya'. Malaya later indicated that the commitment of forces in Malaya would be acceptable under United Nations, but not SEATO, auspices. PM notes, PMs' Conference, London, May 1960, 'The Commonwealth Reserve and its Role in SEATO Activities', 28 Mar 1960, ABHS 950, W4627, 253/3/3/8 pt 1.

66 'Participation in SEATO Exercises by Commonwealth Forces in Malaya', MEA to All Stations from PM, 22 Feb 1960, ABHS 950, W4627, 253/3/3/8 pt 1.

67 'Federation-Based Commonwealth Forces and SEATO Activities', NZ Commissioner Singapore to Minister of External Affairs No. 85, 25 Apr 1959, Air 226/7/13.

68 'Commonwealth Forces in Malaya—Participation in SEATO Exercises', Minister of External Affairs to NZ Commissioner Singapore, no. 126, 30 Apr 1959, Air 226/7/13. See also McKinnon, *Independence and Foreign Policy*, pp. 152–4.

69 'Laos', JSO 145/2/1, 145/2/2.

70 'Laos', Message from SOS CRO to PM, 26 Mar 1961, ABHS 950, W4627, 253/3/3/8 pt 1.

71 'Laos', JSO 145/2/1, 145/2/2.

72 'Laos', Minister of External Affairs to NZ HC London, no. 801, 1 May 1961 (PM 120/15/2), ABHS 950, W4627, 253/3/3/8 pt 1.

73 The GOC 17 Gurkha Division, Major-General J. A. R. Robertson, CB, CBE, DSO, was succeeded in February 1961 by Major-General W. C. Walker, CBE, DSO. Commander's Diary, 2 NZ Regt, Feb 1961, WA–M 1/2/14.

74 'The Concept of ANZAM Plan No. 1 (BUCKRAM)', Defence Brief, PM's Conference, London, May 1960, JSO 43/3/3.

75 'Federation Based Commonwealth Forces: Repercussions of Recent Precautionary Moves initiated by C-In-C FARELF' (NZHC 6/D/S/5/16), 12 May 1961, W4627, 253/3/3/8 pt 1.

76 M. Templeton to Scott, 25 May 1961, W4627, 253/3/3/8 pt 1. While there was some basis for complaint, New Zealand's tardiness in issuing national directives had also contributed to this litany of omissions. National directives were issued in 1962.

77 Aitken, interview.

78 H. B. Eaton, *Something Extra: 28 Commonwealth Brigade, 1951–1974*, Pentland Press, Bishop Auckland, 1993, p. 230.

79 Williams, interview.

80 'An important factor in the review has been the need to limit governmental expenditure in the present economic situation ... defence plans calling for a steeply ascending scale of expenditure in the next few years cannot prudently be accepted. To keep defence expenditure within reasonable bounds, certain measures of retrenchment and deferment of certain proposals for re-equipment have proved necessary.' Review of Defence Policy, *AJHR*, 1961, A-19, pp. 3–9.

81 Review of Defence Policy, *AJHR*, 1961, A-19, p. 7. See chapters 2 and 3.

82 'Part-time service will consist of 20 days training a year, including 14 days in camp and six days out-of-camp training.' Review of Defence Policy, *AJHR*, 1961, A-19, p. 13; *New Zealand Official Yearbook*, 1962, pp. 272–3.

83 The United Kingdom was unhappy with these reductions, but not audibly. HC Canberra to Minister of External Affairs, no. 453, 17 Aug 1961, JSO 2/1/1/5.

84 For Holyoake's attitude to defence issues, see McIntosh to Laking, 25 Feb 1965, in Ian McGibbon (ed.), *Unofficial Channels: Letters between Alister McIntosh and Foss Shanahan, George Laking and Frank Corner, 1946–1966*, Victoria University Press, Wellington, 1999, pp. 320–2.

85 'Posting Policy: 2 NZ Regt' (Army 263/3/7), 19 Dec 1962; 'Recruiting Policy and Enlistment Procedure 2 NZ Regt' (Army 209/3/218/DPA), 1 Mar 1963; 'Posting Policy: 2 NZ Regt' (Army 209/3/218/DPA), 19 Apr 1963, AD–W6, W2566, 42/13 pt 3; Lieutenant-Colonel M. J. Hall, marginal notes to C. E. Brock, *The Diplomat in Uniform: A History of the First Battalion Royal New Zealand Infantry Regiment*, RNZIR.

86 Brigadier R. I. Thorpe to author, 6 Apr 1999. Burns' approach was: 'If someone came up with something we would have a go with it.' Bernard B. Falls' works on the Indo-China war became prescribed reading and a correspondence was started with the author. Brigadier John Burns, interview, 12 Apr 1999.

87 Burns, interview.

88 Pearce, interview.

89 The Japanese had removed the railway running through Malacca during the Second World War and used the material to construct the Thailand railway.

90 'Malacca Cantonment', Mr Macmillan's visit, Summary Brief, Dept of External Affairs, 22 Jan 1958, Army S.31/2/1.

91 'Cantonment for the Commonwealth Strategic Reserve in Malaya', Secretary of External Affairs to Prime Minister, 8 Feb 1958, Army S.31/2/1.

92 The post-Emergency deployment of Commonwealth forces was originally examined at General Templer's direction; he had considered Malacca the most suitable location

for a British regular brigade serving as a permanent British garrison in Malaya. 'Bukit Terendak' GHQ FARELF (FE42812 Q Wks), 16 Mar 1956, Army 31/2/1.

93 Singapore was ruled out as a site for the Commonwealth Brigade because of the lack of training areas and the risk of the brigade becoming involved in internal security duties, which would be unacceptable to Australia and New Zealand. 'Malacca Cantonment', Acting Commissioner to Secretary of External Affairs, 7 Aug 1958, Air 226/7/13.

94 'Memorandum on the Arrangements agreed for the Sharing of Capital Costs of Malacca Cantonment' (JSO 142/2/2/5), 5 Aug 1958; 'Malacca Cantonment', Minister of External Affairs to NZHC Canberra, no. 143, 15 May 1959, both on Air 226/7/13.

95 'Malacca Cantonment', Draft Cabinet Memo, and accompanying correspondence, Army 31/2/1.

96 'Capital Costs of Terendak Camp, Malacca', Deputy Secretary of Defence to Secretary of External Affairs (Def 3/5/8), 13 Sep 1967, Army S.31/2/1.

97 'Malacca Cantonment to be Known as "Fort George"', High Commissioner Kuala Lumpur to Secretary of External Affairs (JSO 142/3/5), 26 Aug 1960, Air 226/7/13.

98 Correspondence on Air 226/7/13.

99 Pearce, interview.

100 Pearce, interview.

101 Major W. J. Meldrum, interview, 9 Mar 1992.

102 '1 NZ Regt Comd's Diary: Move to Malaya', no. 511, Army Non-File Material, HQ NZ Defence Force. See also 'Malaya Battalion airlift will set record for N.Z.', *Auckland Star*, 31 Oct 1961.

103 Pearce, interview.

104 Lieutenant-Colonel J. W. Brown, interview, 9 Mar 1993.

105 Brown, interview.

106 Meldrum, interview.

107 Mrs Pru Meldrum, interview, 6 Apr 1993.

108 Hall, marginal notes on Brock, *The Diplomat in Uniform*, RNZIR.

109 Mrs Pru Meldrum, interview.

110 Mrs Pru Meldrum, interview.

111 Eaton, *Something Extra*, p. 238.

112 Brown, interview.

113 Meldrum, interview.

114 Correspondence with Major W. J. Meldrum; discussions with Major R. A. Manning, MBE. This is specifically referred to by Major-General Walter Walker in his signal thanking Pearce for his battalion's performance during its tour. COMBRITBOR to 1 NZ Regt of 280300Z, Major-General L. A. Pearce Papers.

115 'Employment of 1st Battalion NZ Regiment on Border Security Operations in Malaya' (S.31/2/11/ Plans and Army S.15/2/SD), 27 May 1963, Army S.15/2/3.

116 In 1963, 31 Medium Radio Sub Troop, made up entirely of Regular Signal Corps personnel, was formed at Addington as the New Zealand component of 249 Signal Squadron, the Commonwealth Strategic Reserve Signal Squadron, with which it

would deploy on mobilisation. L. Barber & C. Lord, *Swift and Sure: A History of the Royal New Zealand Corps of Signals and Army Signalling in New Zealand*, New Zealand Signals Incorporated, Auckland, 1996, p. 170.

117 '1 NZ Regt Comd's Diary: SEATO Ex 1963', no. 507, Army Non-File Material, HQ NZ Defence Force.

118 '1 NZ Regt Comd's Diary: Malaya/Thailand Border Operations 1962', no. 506, Army Non-File Material, HQ NZ Defence Force.

119 Brown, interview.

120 Pearce, interview.

121 Elements of the battalion were in Thailand on the SEATO exercise, 'DHANA RAJATA'.

122 'Border Security Operations—1 NZ Regt—OP MAGNUS' (NZF/4046/G), 12 Sep 1963, Army 15/2/3.

123 Meldrum, interview.

124 COMBRITBOR to 1 NZ Regt of 280300Z, Major-General L. A. Pearce Papers; Major J. M. Spiers, interview, 4 Jun 1992. For background to this period, see Tom Pocock, *Fighting General: The Public and Private Campaigns of General Sir Walter Walker*, Collins, London, 1973, pp. 127–42. See also Dennis & Grey, *Emergency and Confrontation;* P. H. F. Webb, 'Revolt in Brunei and the Formation of an Ad Hoc Joint Force Headquarters', *Journal of the Royal Signals Institution*, 1965, pp. 176–82.

125 Spiers, interview.

126 Wing Commander O. D. Staples, DFC, AFC, the previous OC 41 Squadron, was appointed New Zealand Military Representative to Joint Task Force 116 in Thailand and attached to 41 Squadron while working at Joint Force Headquarters at Khorat. When Staples flew back to New Zealand with the SAS on 16 September 1962, the post of New Zealand Representative to JTF116 was taken over by Squadron Leader B. A. Wood, OC 41 Squadron RNZAF.

127 'Having once made a useful gesture of support for Thailand and for SEATO we are naturally concerned at the prospect of New Zealand forces—especially ground troops—remaining in Thailand for a long period. The fact that we and others have been prepared promptly to despatch forces to Thailand is probably more important than their actual role or the length of time they stay. If we could decently withdraw the whole contribution within six months (this would of course depend very largely on developments within Laos) we should be greatly relieved. If we could do no more than withdraw the SAS and "run down" the Bristol detachment we should be pleased enough. Our fear is that if a regular "SEATO force" were established it would become a great deal more difficult to withdraw or run [down] our contribution ... It suits us better therefore to have New Zealand forces in Thailand on the current basis, even though this may cause some difficulties for national commanders and Thai authorities and some confusion in the minds of press and public.' Minister of External Affairs to London 1196, Washington 310 and Canberra 321, 3 Jun 1962, 1100 hrs, and JOZWEL 164 to NZMAR Bangkok and NZ Rep Korat of 050345Z Jun 1962, Army S.15/11 pt 1.

128 No. 41 Squadron RNZAF Unit History, Jun 1962, Air Staff RNZAF.

129 No. 41 Squadron RNZAF Unit History, Oct 1962, Air Staff RNZAF.

130 W. D. Baker, *Dare to Win: The Story of the New Zealand Special Air Service*, Lothian, Port Melbourne, 1987, pp. 68–72.

131 General Report Det 1[NZ] SAS Squadron [Thailand], 17 May–20 Sep 1962, Army S.15/11.

132 'Forces in Thailand', Secretary of External Affairs to Prime Minister, 3 Aug 1962, Army S.15/11.

133 General Report Det 1[NZ] SAS Squadron [Thailand], 17 May–20 Sep 62, Army S.15/11.

134 'Improvement of Logistic Facilities in Thailand', JAPC [63]3, Army S.33/7/14/1.

135 CM [62]52, JSO 1/4/3.

136 'Improvement of Logistic Facilities in Thailand', JAPC [63]3, Army S.33/7/14/1. For the troubled history of the Mukdahan airfield project, see Army S.33/7/14/1 and JSO 40/9/1.

137 'RNZE Road Construction Project in Thailand' [Feeder Roads Project], Mounting Instruction (Army S.33/7/14/2 SD [Ops and Mob]), 22 Oct 1965, and following material on MOD 23/3/2.

138 CGS to Minister of Defence, 'Reorganisation of the Army', 27 Aug 1963, AD 1, 209/1/25.

139 'Army Readiness for War' (Army S.11/3/1/CGS), 2 Nov 1962, JSO 4/5/1. The Chiefs of Staff contrasted New Zealand's situation unfavourably with that of Australia, which under a three-year defence programme appeared to be effectively reshaping its defence forces. They requested a similar programme for New Zealand, and an increase in defence spending from the £30 million ceiling recommended by Treasury to £33 million. 'New Zealand Forces, Readiness For War', JSO 4/5/1.

140 On 25 March 1963 Cabinet approved in principle the reorganisation of the Army into a combat force, a logistic support force, a combat reserve and a static support force. The implementation of this scheme was approved on 17 June. This was to be achieved within the ceilings of 6,250 Regulars and 10,000 Territorials; 750 Regulars were stationed in Malaya and a further 400 within Battalion Depot. The 5,950-strong Combat Brigade was made up of 875 Regulars and 5,075 Territorials, while the Logistic Support Force comprised 1,175 Regulars and 2,075 Territorials. CGS to Minister of Defence, 'Reorganisation of the Army', 27 Aug 1963, AD 1, 209/1/25. 'Survey of the Present Effectiveness and Immediate Equipment Requirements of the Three Armed Services of New Zealand' (COS (63)7), 1 Feb 1963, JSO 4/5/1, indicates that half the equipment had been purchased. Treasury gave the proportion as two-thirds in 'Survey of New Zealand Armed Forces', (T.42/255/91(S)), 26 Feb 1963, JSO 4/5/110. See also 'SEATO Planning Studies, Plans for the Defence of South East Asia Against an Attack by Vietminh and Chinese Forces', JSO 40/11/9; Mark Pearson, *Paper Tiger: New Zealand's Part in SEATO 1954–1977*, New Zealand Institute of International Affairs, Wellington, 1989, pp. 66–7; McGibbon, 'Forward Defence', pp. 24–6.

141 Gurr notes that the introduction of this system of continuous relief was 'a cause of some friction' between himself and the Adjutant-General's Branch. Brigadier R. M. Gurr, marginal notes on author's draft. See also 'Manning—NZ Battalion FARELF Continuous Relief' (Army 208/3/218/DPA), 21 Aug 1963, AD–W6, W2566, 42/13 pt 3; 'Re-organisation NZ Army 1963–1964', AD 1, 209/1/25. In this period the battalion strength was approximately 700, with 50 on HQ NZ Army Force FARELF. See 'Far East 1 NZ Regt Strength Returns', AD 1, 228/7/36.

142 'Active Service—Malaya and Singapore' (Army 222/1/30/A1), 3 Dec 1963, AD–W6, W2566, 42/13 pt 3.

143 Gurr, marginal notes on author's draft.

144 Sir Peter Phipps was not promoted to Vice-Admiral until the month of his retirement from the post of CDS, June 1965.

145 CDS to Minister of Defence (S.34/9), 21 Jan 1964, Army 15/2 vol. 3.

## 7 Confronting Intruders: Infantry Operations, Malay Peninsula, 1964

1 Kuala Lumpur to Wellington 370, 4 Sep 1964, Army S.15/2 pt 3.

2 M. Leifer, *Indonesia's Foreign Policy*, Royal Institute of International Affairs, Allen & Unwin, London, 1983, pp. 75–110. See also R. C. de Iongh, 'West Irian Confrontation', in T. K. Tan (ed.), *Sukarno's Guided Indonesia*, Jacaranda, Brisbane, 1967, pp. 101–13. J. M. van der Kroef, 'Communism and the Guerrilla War in Sarawak', *The World Today*, Feb 1964, pp. 50–60.

3 The most authoritative and in-depth analysis of this period is J. A. C. Mackie, *Konfrontasi: The Indonesian–Malaysia Dispute 1963–1966*, Oxford University Press, Kuala Lumpur, 1974. The only omission is details of Commonwealth CLARET cross-border operations, which were not known to the author at the time of publication. They were covered in Mackie, *Low-Level Military Incursions: Lessons of the Indonesia–Malaysia 'Confrontation' Episode, 1963–66*, Working Paper no. 105, Strategic and Defence Studies Centre, Australian National University, Canberra, 1986. For the evolution and details of CLARET operations, see Moreen Dee, 'Deniable or Undeniable: An Australian View of the Policy and Strategy of Cross-border Operations in North Borneo, 1963–1966', MDS dissertation, University of New England, 1999; T. Pocock, *Fighting General: The Public and Private Campaigns of General Sir Walter Walker*, Collins, London, 1973; P. Dennis & J. Grey, *Emergency and Confrontation*, Allen & Unwin in association with the Australian War Memorial, Sydney, 1996, pp. 214–17, 239–62; and 'Joint Report on the Borneo Campaign CINCFE 9/67', 10 Nov 1966, pp. 35–8, copy issued by Malaysian Armed Forces Staff College, Winton Papers.

4 Garry Woodard, 'Best Practice in Australia's Foreign Policy: "Konfrontasi" (1963–66)', *Australian Journal of Political Science*, vol. 33, no. 1, Mar 1998, pp. 85–99. Australia had consulted the United States (on 7 June, 8 July & 14 October 1963) about the applicability of the ANZUS treaty in the event of an attack on Australian troops stationed in Malaysia. The United States confirmed that it would

act, and at the 14 October meeting Australia promised to consult the United States before 'stationing armed forces in Sarawak or Sabah'. Record of Understanding Kennedy/Barwick, 17 Oct 1963 (PMD 1963/6587), CRS A1209/80, Australian Archives. New Zealand was critical of these discussions, both because it was not consulted at the time and because it feared the United States might attempt to exercise some kind of veto on the despatch of forces to Borneo. NZ High Commissioner (Shepherd) to Barwick, 12 Dec 1963 (DEA 270/1/1 pt 2), CRS A1838/3, Australian Archives. New Zealand took no action to formally associate itself with this understanding. I am grateful to Moreen Dee for making available this material from her own research in the Australian Archives. See also Moreen Dee, 'The Applicability of ANZUS to Confrontation: An Australian View', MDS dissertation, University of New England, 1998.

5 Holyoake to Sir Alec Douglas-Home, 19 Dec 1963, JSO 156/2/1 pt 3.

6 CM [64]12, JSO 152/2/3, pt 3. New Zealand, as always, offered obsolete equipment that was surplus to its requirements. As a result, some of the equipment, and some of the training, was not required. The Cabinet-imposed ceiling of £300,000 ended up being underspent.

7 Commonwealth defence in South-East Asia in the light of Confrontation was discussed at a meeting of the ANZAM Defence Committee on 3 October 1963; it was noted 'that possible Australian and New Zealand force contributions to operations in Sabah and Sarawak would be likely to be limited, as far as possible, to those serving with the British Commonwealth Far East Strategic Reserve'. 'Malaysia—Defence Planning in the Context of Indonesian Confrontation', CGS to Comd NEWZARM, 26 Mar 1964, Army S.15/2 pt 3.

8 On 27 January 1964 Holyoake's Cabinet agreed to the commitment of 1RNZIR to operations on the Thai border. CM [64]3, JPS(64)32, 'New Zealand Battalion Operations on Thai/Malay Border: New Zealand Military Assistance to counter infiltration from Indonesia', dated 22 Apr 1964, Army S.15/2 pt 3.

9 Problems of over-commitment applied equally to Australian and British units in 28th Commonwealth Brigade. The Engineers, including the Australian component, were engaged in airfield construction at Mukdahan in Thailand, while the British battalion was committed to a tour in Borneo as part of the normal rotation of British battalions in Malaysia. CDS to Minister of Defence (s.34/9), 21 Jan 1964, Army S.15/2 pt 3.

10 CDS to Minister of Defence (s.34/9), 21 Jan 1964, Army S.15/2 pt 3.

11 Kuala Lumpur to Wellington 221, JSO 156/2/1 pt 4.

12 A Company was acting as enemy to 1 King's Own Yorkshire Light Regiment, the British battalion in 28th Commonwealth Brigade, prior to its deployment to Borneo. Robert Gurr, *Voices from a Border War*, self-published, Melbourne, 1995, p. 24.

13 Gurr, *Voices from a Border War*, pp. 25–6. Also Brigadier R. M. Gurr, interview, 13–14 Jan 1993.

14 Brigadier R. I. Thorpe, discussions with author, Apr 1999.

15 'Border Security Operations: 1RNZIR Post Activity Report 6 Apr–15 May 64', Comd NEWZARM to Army (NZF/4046/G), 6 Jun 1964, Army S.15/2 pt 3.

16 Kuala Lumpur to Wellington 271, 10 Jul 1964, Army S.15/2 pt 3.
17 Kuala Lumpur to Wellington 183, Army S.15/2 pt 3.
18 National Defence Council Directive no. 1, 'Control of Operations', Kuala Lumpur, 13 May 1965, MOD 3/5/12 pt 1.
19 The use of Australian forces such as 3RAR with 28th Commonwealth Brigade would be approved only for specific operations, rather than 'as the need demanded'. Dennis & Grey, *Emergency and Confrontation*, p. 226. See also Moreen Dee, 'Not Ahead of Need: Australian Policy and the Decision to Commit Australian Combat Forces to North Borneo 1963–1965', MDS dissertation, University of New England, 1998.
20 'Deployment of New Zealand Battalion on Counter Infiltration Operations', Holloway, NZDLO Malaysia to Secretary COS (273/3/4), 9 Sep 1964, Army S.15/2 pt 3.
21 'External 359 to Tainui', Army S.15/2 pt 3.
22 'Deployment of New Zealand Battalion on Counter Infiltration Operations', Holloway to Secretary COS (273/3/4), 9 Sep 1964, Army S.15/2 pt 3. This was passed to the Director Plans and Operations at Far East Command [Phoenix Park] at 9.30 p.m. on 3 September 1964.
23 'Deployment of New Zealand Battalion on Counter Infiltration Operations'.
24 The counter-infiltration operations presented C-in-C FE and GOC FARELF with a problem: the only reserve available to meet counter-infiltration tasks was two newly arrived British battalions which were not yet fit for jungle operations 'except in dire emergency'. Singapore to Wellington 329, 24 Sep 1964, Army S.34/9/3 pt 2.
25 Kuala Lumpur to Wellington 366, 4 Sep 1964, Army S.15/2 pt 3.
26 Statement by New Zealand Prime Minister on 'Malaysia', 8 Sep 1964, Army S.34/9/3 pt 2.
27 Although individual members of the Territorial Force have been deployed on peace-keeping assignments with the United Nations.
28 1 RNZIR, 'Post Activity Report Anti Indonesian Infiltration Operations, 5 Sep–30 Oct 1964', 20 Nov 1964, ABFK, W3788, box 26.
29 Colonel O. E. Mann, interviews, commencing 8 Apr 1992.
30 Marginal notes by CGS on 'Deployment of New Zealand Battalion on Counter Infiltration Operations', Holloway to Secretary COS (273/3/4), 9 Sep 1964, Army S.15/2 pt 3.
31 Gurr, interview.
32 Major M. W. Clark, 'Indonesian "Confrontation" Operations of a Malaysian Brigade July–October 1964', *Journal of the Royal Electrical and Mechanical Engineers*, vol. 8, no. 1, Feb 1965, pp. 67–74.
33 Indonesian leaders' proclamation of Indonesia's independence on 17 August 1945 was rejected by the Netherlands, which eventually transferred sovereignty in 1949. Ide Anak Agung Gde Agung, *Twenty Years Indonesian Foreign Policy 1945–1965*, Mouton, The Hague/Paris, 1973, pp. 17–18.
34 The strength of each group was: Benut, 36 Indonesians and 9 Malaysian Chinese; Pontian, 19 Indonesians, 9 Malaysian Chinese, 5 Malays; Kukup, 21 Indonesians, 9

Malaysian Chinese. 1RNZIR, 'Post Activity Report Anti Indonesian Infiltration Operations, 5 Sep–30 Oct 1964', 20 Nov 1964, ABFK, W3788, box 26.

35 In the Pontian group only four Malaysian Chinese were unaccounted for, and in the Kukup group only four Indonesians. Intelligence later established that the four Indonesians escaped by sea to the Riau Islands and then returned to Indonesia. 1RNZIF, 'Post Activity Report Anti Indonesian Infiltration Operations, 5 Sep–30 Oct 1964', 20 Nov 1964, ABFK, W3788 box 26.

36 Clark, 'Indonesian "Confrontation" Operations of a Malaysian Brigade', p. 72.

37 Gurr, interview.

38 Brigadier I. H. Burrows, 'Confrontation 1RNZIR Operations 1965', 1RNZIR Museum.

39 Brigadier I. H. Burrows, interviews from Oct 1991.

40 Brigadier R. M. Gurr, draft narrative for *Voices from a Border War*, p. 3–3. The same impression is gained from Gurr, *Voices from a Border War*, p. 47. Also Gurr, interview.

41 FE 5603 Ops, 'Notes on a Visit to 1/10 GR and 1RNZIR 6 September 1964', Army S.15/2 pt 3.

42 Gurr, draft narrative for *Voices from a Border War,* p. 3–3; Gurr, *Voices from a Border War*, p. 51; also Gurr, interview.

43 Grey concludes: 'Probably four, and certainly three C130s took off but at least one appears to have crashed en route.' Dennis & Grey, *Emergency and Confrontation*, pp. 224–5.

44 J. P. Craw, 'Indonesian Military Incursions into West Malaysia and Singapore between August 1964 and 30th September 1965', *Royal United Services Institute Journal*, vol. 111, May 1966, pp. 203–18.

45 1RNZIR, 'Post Activity Report Anti Indonesian Infiltration Operations, 5 Sep–30 Oct 1964', 20 Nov 1964, ABFK, W3788, box 26. Clark, 'Indonesian "Confrontation" Operations of a Malaysian Brigade', p. 72; Craw, 'Indonesian Military Incursions into West Malaysia and Singapore', pp. 213–15.

46 Gurr, draft narrative for *Voices from a Border War*, p. 3–5; Gurr, *Voices from a Border War*, p. 55; also Gurr, interview.

47 1RNZIR, 'Post Activity Report Anti Indonesian Infiltration Operations, 5 Sep–30 Oct 1964', 20 Nov 1964, ABFK, W3788, box 26.

48 Gurr, draft narrative for *Voices from a Border War,* p. 3–5; Gurr, *Voices from a Border War*, p. 55; also Gurr, interview.

49 Mann, interviews.

50 Brigadier I. H. Burrows, quoted in Gurr, draft narrative for *Voices from a Border War*, p. 3–4.

51 Burrows, interviews.

52 Gurr, draft narrative for *Voices from a Border War,* p. 3–6; also Gurr, interview.

53 Gurr, *Voices from a Border War*, p. 59; also Gurr, interview.

54 This had been a company base for 1FIR during the Emergency. It was to be used again in the 1980s as the control headquarters of New Zealand Force Southeast Asia during its annual month-long counter-insurgency exercise PEMBURU RUSA.

55 1RNZIR, 'Post Activity Report Anti Indonesian Infiltration Operations, 5 Sep–30 Oct 1964', 20 Nov 1964, ABFK, W3788, box 26.
56 Brigadier I. H. Burrows to author, 13 Jan 1999.
57 Mann, interviews.
58 Gurr, interview.
59 This meant that the New Zealanders would not be available to deploy for border operations on Operation MAGNUS from 15 October as originally planned. 3RAR, which had not yet been cleared for operations against Indonesian infiltration, extended its tour to enable the New Zealanders to continue counter-infiltration tasks. Singapore to Wellington 329, 24 Sep 1964, Army S.34/9/3 pt 2.
60 Lieutenant-Colonel Max Ritchie, interview, 1992; correspondence with author.
61 Gurr, *Voices from a Border War*, p. 62.
62 1RNZIR, 'Post Activity Report Anti Indonesian Infiltration Operations, 5 Sep–30 Oct 1964', 20 Nov 1964, ABFK, W3788 box 26.
63 Gurr, draft narrative for *Voices from a Border War*, p. 3–8; Gurr, *Voices from a Border War*, p. 64; Gurr, interview.
64 Burrows, 'Confrontation 1RNZIR Operations 1965'; also Burrows, interviews.
65 Gurr, draft narrative for *Voices from a Border War*, p. 3–8; Gurr, interview.
66 Burrows, interviews.
67 Ritchie, interview, and correspondence with author.
68 Burrows, 'Confrontation 1RNZIR Operations 1965'; Burrows, interviews.
69 Ritchie, interview, and correspondence with author. See Gurr, *Voices from a Border War*, pp. 64–7.
70 Ritchie, interview, and correspondence with author. See Gurr, *Voices from a Border War*, pp. 64–7.
71 Burrows, 'Confrontation 1RNZIR Operations 1965'.
72 WO1 Rex Harris, interview, 2 Jun 1992.
73 Gurr, *Voices from a Border War*, p. 68; Gurr, interview.
74 All but one of the incursions on this scale that were attempted after the Kesang landing were intercepted at sea. On 17 March 1965, 44 personnel landed in south-east Johore; all were killed or captured, at a cost of ten killed and six wounded among the Malaysian and Commonwealth Forces. HQ FARELF, 'Claim for a Clasp for the General Service Medal to Cover Operations in West Malaysia', 3 May 1965, AD 95/14/1. Craw, 'Indonesian Military Incursions into West Malaysia and Singapore', pp. 208–19.
75 Burrows, quoted in Gurr, *Voices from a Border War*, p. 70; also Burrows, interviews.
76 For the background to this request, see Grey's account of McMeekin's role in enabling Australian participation in Dennis & Grey, *Emergency and Confrontation*, pp. 226–7.
77 Gurr, draft narrative for *Voices from a Border War*, p. 3–14; Gurr, interview.
78 Burrows, quoted in Gurr, *Voices from a Border War*, p. 72; also Burrows, interviews.
79 'Record of Visit of Army Commander and GSO1 Ops to Operation FLOWER Friday 30 October 1964', Army S.34/9/3 pt 2.

80 Burrows, quoted in Gurr, *Voices from a Border War*, p. 72; also Burrows, interviews.
81 Gurr, draft narrative for *Voices from a Border War*, p. 3–15; Gurr, interview.
82 Ritchie, interview, and correspondence with author.
83 Burrows, quoted in Gurr, *Voices from a Border War*, pp. 72–3; also Burrows, interviews.
84 Craw, 'Indonesian Military Incursions into West Malaysia and Singapore', p. 219.
85 These figures are based on Craw's.
86 Gurr, interview.

## 8 'A Real Job to Do': Air and Naval Operations, 1962–66

1 No. 41 Sqn Weekly Report, 2 Mar 1967, Air 227/20/5.
2 Colonel R. Pearce, interview, 13 Nov 1992.
3 Major J. S. Riggall, 'RCT Light Aircraft Operations in Borneo', *Royal Corps of Transport Review*, 1966, pp. 11–12.
4 Pearce, interview. See also Lieutenant-Colonel P. E. Collins RA, 'The Front Was Everywhere', *Royal United Services Institute Journal*, May 1962, pp. 143–8; Riggall, 'RCT Light Aircraft Operations in Borneo'; Wing Commander D. L. Eley, 'Helicopters in Malaysia', *Royal Air Force Quarterly*, 1966, pp. 5–10.
5 RNZAF HQ Malaysia Report, Nos 74 and 95, Air 227/20/5.
6 Jamieson to Gill (HQM.1/AIR), 14 Nov 1964, Air 227/20/10.
7 RNZAF HQ Malaysia Report No. 32, Air 227/20/5.
8 RNZAF HQ Malaysia Report No. 35, Air 227/20/5.
9 The Commander RAF Kuching equated Bristols to Valettas, which were limited to dropping 400-lb loads, so that one ton of supplies required six runs over the drop zone. When air drops were carried out close to the border, it was preferable to do as few runs as possible to avoid Indonesian anti-aircraft fire. It was here that the Argosy came into its own, because it could drop one-ton loads from its rear-facing doors and do the work of two Bristols or Valettas. Only five Army Despatchers were required, rather than the ten needed for two aircraft. (41:S.1/3/Air), 1 Jun 1965, Air 227/20/5. The UK Minister of Defence [Air], Lord Shackleton, visited RAF Kuching on 11 June 1966 and was introduced to Squadron Leader Hutchins, OC 41 Squadron. Told the squadron flew Bristol Freighters, he commented that he did not know that aircraft.
10 Jamieson to Gill [DCAS] (2/6/Air), 11 Aug 1965, Air 227/20/10. For the organisation of the Air Forces Borneo, see Section 7—Air Forces Borneo, 'Joint Report on the Borneo Campaign', CINCFE 9/67, Revised Copy, 27 Jan 1967. Air Chief Marshal Sir David Lee, *Eastward: A History of the Royal Air Force in the Far East 1945–1972*, Ministry of Defence, Air Historical Branch (RAF), HMSO, London, 1984, pp. 192–232.
11 Jamieson to Gill [DCAS] (2/6/Air), 11 Aug 1965, Air 227/20/10.
12 Squadron Leader R. I. F. Garrett succeeded Squadron Leader Wood in October 1963, and was in turn succeeded by Squadron Leader I. A. Hutchins in September 1965.

G. Bentley & M. Conly, *Portrait of an Air Force: The Royal New Zealand Air Force 1937–1987*, Grantham House, Wellington, 1987, p. 150.

13 RNZAF HQ Malaysia Report No. 41, Air 227/20/5.
14 No. 41 Sqn Weekly Report, 15 Feb 1967, Air 227/20/5.
15 RNZAF HQ Malaysia Report No. 50, Air 227/20/5.
16 Jamieson to Gill [DCAS] (2/6/Air), 11 Aug 1965, Air 227/20/10.
17 RNZAF HQ Malaysia Report No. 43, Air 227/20/5.
18 RNZAF HQ Malaysia Report No. 60, Air 227/20/5.
19 RNZAF HQ Malaysia Report No. 57, Air 227/20/5.
20 RNZAF HQ Malaysia Report No. 46, Air 227/20/5.
21 Lieutenant-Colonel P. de L. Bainbridge RCT, 'Air Despatch Operations in the Far East', *Royal Corps of Transport Review*, Apr 1967, p. 17.
22 RNZAF HQ Malaysia Report No. 55, Air 227/20/5.
23 RNZAF HQ Malaysia Report No. 46, Air 227/20/5.
24 RNZAF HQ Malaysia Report No. 47, Air 227/20/5.
25 RNZAF HQ Malaysia Report No. 49, Air 227/20/5.
26 RNZAF HQ Malaysia Report No. 51, Air 227/20/5. See Bentley & Conly, *Portrait of an Air Force*, p. 150.
27 RNZAF HQ Malaysia Report No. 76, Air 227/20/5.
28 RNZAF HQ Malaysia Report Nos 74 and 82, Air 227/20/5.
29 RNZAF HQ Malaysia Report No. 47, Air 227/20/5.
30 RNZAF HQ Malaysia Report No. 66, Air 227/20/5.
31 RNZAF HQ Malaysia Report No. 68, Air 227/20/5.
32 RNZAF HQ Malaysia Report No. 85, Air 227/20/5.
33 RNZAF HQ Malaysia Report No. 91, Air 227/20/5.
34 Neville, interview.
35 Group Captain Geoff Wallingford, notes on *Portrait of an Air Force*. See also M. Wright, *Kiwi Air Power: The History of the RNZAF*, Reed, Auckland, 1998, pp. 144–5.
36 Group Captain Geoff Wallingford, interview, 18 Feb 1993.
37 Group Captain Del de Lorenzo, interview, 10 Mar 1993.
38 Air Vice-Marshal John Hosie, interview, 8 Mar 1993. Hosie was the first Chief of Air Staff in the RNZAF to rise to this rank from boy entrant.
39 Wing Commander Eric McPherson, interview, 10 Mar 1993.
40 Wellington to All Posts (A2), 16 Sep 1964, Air 206/2/4 pt 3.
41 In its SEATO role, No. 14 Squadron RNZAF was required to be able to deploy at 48 hours' notice and operate immediately on arrival in South-East Asia. This was practised in the Vanguard series of routine deployment exercises. Two deployments were made in 1962, and in his planning for 1963 Air Vice-Marshal I. G. Morrison, Chief of Air Staff, requested approval in principle for four deployment exercises to South-East Asia each year. Three Vanguard exercises were approved for 1963; the first was combined with the major SEATO exercise Dhanarajata, but the other two were not held, one because the changeover of the New Zealand Infantry Battalion

in November 1963 fully utilised all RNZAF air transport, and the other because the planned FEAF exercise was cancelled because of RAF commitments in Borneo. In April 1964 Vanguard V was held in combination with the SEATO exercise Air Boon Choo. Vanguard VI was planned as a routine training deployment for four aircraft and crews in October 1964. CAS to Minister of Defence, 4 Mar 1964, Air 206/2/4, 250/5/6, 250/6/7.

42 CM (64)36, Air 206/2/4 pt 3. See Ian McGibbon, 'Forward Defence: The Southeast Asian Commitment', in Malcolm McKinnon (ed.), *New Zealand in World Affairs, Volume II: 1957–1972*, New Zealand Institute of International Affairs, Wellington, 1991, p. 23.

43 P. Dennis & J. Grey, *Emergency and Confrontation*, Allen & Unwin in association with the Australian War Memorial, Sydney, 1996, pp. 194–6. Plan ALTHORPE was a modification of Plan ADDINGTON, which envisaged a rapid response to an overt Indonesian attack by, in part, a light bomber force of 30 Canberras: 16 RAF, eight RAAF and six RNZAF. The Canberra force needed to be readily available in the theatre. AF/W930/64 ACAS [Ops] to VCAS, 16 Jun 1965, ID9/625/1 AHB [RAF]. See also Moreen Dee, 'Not Ahead of Need: Australian Policy and the Decision to Commit Australian Combat Forces to North Borneo 1963–1965', MDS dissertation, University of New England, 1998.

44 Wallingford, interview.

45 De Lorenzo, interview.

46 Wallingford, interview; de Lorenzo, interview.

47 Wallingford, notes on *Portrait of an Air Force*.

48 'Report on Visit of No. 14 Squadron Crew to Clark A.F.B. and Tan Son Nhut Airport Saigon', Air 206/2/4 pt 3.

49 Air Commodore Stuart McIntyre, interview, 23 Feb 1993; Air Commodore Mike Palmer, interview, 11 Jun 1993. See also Wright, *Kiwi Air Power*, pp. 142–5.

50 The distinct differences in layout between the different marks of Canberra suited the needs of each country. The B2 (and the B6) had bubble canopies with side-by-side seats and a third seat behind the pilot. It was flown by the RAF with a crew of three (one pilot and two navigators), while the RNZAF manned it with a crew of two (a pilot and a navigator). The Australians flew the B20 (a modification of the B2, also with a bubble canopy). De Lorenzo, interview.

51 The underneath of the aircraft was painted dark blue-grey. Wallingford, interview; written comments on author's draft, 31 Mar 1999.

52 Wallingford, interview; written comments on author's draft, 31 Mar 1999.

53 Wallingford, interview.

54 'Provocation by R.N. Alleged', *Press*, 18 Sep 1964.

55 Wallingford, interview.

56 De Lorenzo, interview.

57 Hosie, interview.

58 RNZAF Malaysia Weekly Report No. 5, Air 227/20/5.

59 RNZAF Headquarters Malaysia, Air 1, 1/1/179.

60 RNZAF HQ Malaysia to RNZAF HQ Wellington, 220305Z Sep 1964, Air 206/2/4 pt 3.
61 Air Marshal Sir Ewan Jamieson, interview, 10 Jun 1993.
62 RNZAF Wellington to RNZAF HQ Malaysia, A647 and A648/Sept 2364, Air 206/2/4 pt 3; Wellington to Singapore 441, 29 Sep 1964, Army S.34/9/3 pt 2.
63 Jamieson, interview.
64 RNZAF HQ Wellington to RNZAF HQ Malaysia, A473/Oct 1264, Air 206/2/4 pt 3.
65 Wright, *Kiwi Air Power*, p. 148.
66 No. 14 Squadron Deployment, CAS Minute No. 478/1964 (file 206/2/4) to CDS, CNS, CGS, and Sec Def, 11 Nov 1964, Army S.34/9/3 pt 2, Air 206/2/4 pt 3. Wellington to Singapore 468, 8 Oct 1964, Air 206/2/4 pt 3.
67 Wellington to Singapore 481, 16 Oct 1964, Singapore to Wellington 373, Lendrum, DHC Singapore to Secretary of External Affairs (408/5/9), 10 Nov 1964, enclosing Begg to Lendrum, 7 Nov 1964, Army S.34/9/3 pt 2. In November, after the Labuan affair, Morrison agreed to the squadron being used in Malaya on operations within the parameters set by the National Directive, and gave permission for Jamieson to 'press with Air Commander for as much operational employment as you can get and as opportunity offers'. That was to prove difficult. While the ANZAM directives clearly permitted the squadron to be employed on operations on the Malay/Thai border, subject to prior notice to the New Zealand government, Wellington made it clear to Jamieson that it did not want No. 14 Squadron to be involved in such operations. JOZWEL to JOZSING draft, Air 206/2/4 pt 3; RNZAF HQ to RNZAF HQ Malaysia [A478/Nov 0464], Air 206/2/4. Flight Lieutenant B. E. Gilliver, who was attached to 224 Group RAF from HQ RNZAF Malaysia, was dispatched to provide air liaison with 4 Royal Malay Regiment after a landing by 29 infiltrators at Pontian was reported in December 1964. By the afternoon of Christmas Day, three Indonesians had been killed and 11 captured. It seemed that the rest of the group had gone to ground in the Pontian swamps, and the commanding officer of 4 Royal Malay requested an air strike to keep the Indonesian party moving and lower their morale. On Boxing Day Gilliver acted as Forward Air Controller to a strike by four Hunter fighters armed with three-inch rockets and 30 mm cannon, and one RAF Canberra bomber armed with 72 two-inch rockets. Gilliver's involvement in this action was the only active combat seen by HQRNZAF and 14 Squadron RNZAF during the Borneo Confrontation. RNZAF Malaysia Weekly Report No. 14, Air 227/20/5. See also Lee, *Eastward*, pp. 212–16.
68 Lee, *Eastward*, pp. 193–4.
69 RNZAF HQ Malaysia to RNZAF HQ Wellington, 020435Z Oct 1964, Air 206/2/4 pt 3.
70 Singapore to Wellington 380, 27 Oct 1964, Air 206/2/4 pt 3.
71 FEAFOC to HQ 224 Gp, 240924Z, Appendix B to RNZAF Malaysia Weekly Report No. 6, Air 227/20/5.
72 'No. 14 Squadron RNZAF Deployment to RAF Labuan 28 October to 4 November 1964', Appendix A to RNZAF Malaysia Weekly Report No. 7, Air 227/20/5.
73 CAS to Minister of Defence covering draft signals of 2 Nov 1964, Air 206/2/4 pt 3.

74 Wellington to Singapore 509, 2 Nov 1964, Air 206/2/4 pt 3.
75 Wellington to Singapore 509, 2 Nov 1964, Army S.34/9/3 pt 2.
76 'No. 14 Squadron RNZAF Deployment to RAF Labuan 28 October to 4 November 1964', Appendix A to RNZAF Malaysia Weekly Report No. 7, Air 227/20/5.
77 RNZAF HQ Malaysia to RNZAF HQ Wellington, 030206Z Nov 1964, Air 206/2/4 pt 3.
78 McIntosh to PM, 15 Dec 1964, Air 206/2/4 pt 3.
79 RNZAF HQ Wellington to RNZAF HQ Malaysia, Personal for Jamieson, A877/Nov 0164, Air 206/2/4 pt 3.
80 Kuala Lumpur to Wellington 482, 2 Nov 1964, Army S.34/9/3 pt 2.
81 Singapore to Wellington 396, 5 Nov 1964, Air 206/2/4 pt 3.
82 CDS to Minister of Defence (JSO 156/2/9), 20 Nov 1964. RNZAFHQ WN to Station List, RNZAFHQ Malaysia, A483/Nov 2564, Air 206/2/4 pt 3. In giving permission to extend the deployment to March 1965, Holyoake also agreed that the detachment should be reviewed by February. Air Commodore Gill, the Deputy Chief of Air Staff, visited Malaysia and Singapore in December, authorised to 'discuss at military level without commitment the transition of present deployment into permanent deployment with married personnel accompanied'. RNZAFHQ WN to RNZAFHQ Malaysia, A491/Dec 0164, Air 206/2/4 pt 3. After discussing this with the Air Commander FEAF and his senior staff, Gill reported to Morrison that the deployment would be welcomed on the same basis as that of No. 41 Squadron RNZAF. It was anticipated that RNZAF HQ Malaysia would continue in existence, and that five RNZAF officers would be integrated into the staffs of FEAF. RNZAF HQ Malaysia to RNZAF HQ Wellington A230/Dec 1164, Air 206/2/4 pt 3.
83 McIntosh to PM (PM 253/3/5/3), 24 Nov 1964, Air 206/2/4 pt 3.
84 14 Squadron Personnel Requirement Policy—Brief for CAS, Air 206/2/4 pt 3.
85 CAS Minute No. 21/1965, 3 Feb 1965, Air 206/2/4 pt 3.
86 Minute to Air Board 223/19/23, Air 206/2/4 pt 3.
87 CM 5/8/27, to RNZAF HQ Malaysia and all Stations, A49/Mar 1565, Air 206/2/4 pt 3. Cabinet agreed (CM 65/8/27) that 'indefinite' deployment in fact meant deployment until April 1967. RNZAF Malaysia to RNZAF HQ WN, 180741Z Mar 1965, Air 221/2/7 pt 1.
88 Minister of Defence to Prime Minister, draft, 11 Jun 1965, Air 206/2/4 pt 3.
89 Secretary of External Affairs to Prime Minister, 11 Jun 1965, Air 221/2/7.
90 The pilot, Flying Officer R. B. Thomson, and the navigator, Flight Lieutenant J. W. Southgate, were killed in the crash. Their bodies were not recovered.
91 RNZAF HQ WN to RNZAF HQ Malaysia, CAS to DCAS, A17 Dec 0864, Air 206/2/4 pt 3. The possibility of hiring a USAF Martin B57, a Canberra variant, was also explored without success, and discussions began on the hire of a fighter/bomber replacement from the United States as 'a gap-filler, to keep our national flag flying in offensive air'. CAS to Agar, A999 Feb 0365; NZJSM Washington to RNZAFHQ Wellington, for CAS from Agar, A976 Feb 0565; RNZAFHQ Wellington to NZJSM Washington, A879 060930Z Feb 1965, Air 206/2/4 pt 3.

92 Secretary of External Affairs to Prime Minister, 9 Dec 1964, JSO 152/2/3 pt 4.
93 'Planning by Services Not Geared For an Emergency', *Press*, 21 Sep 1964.
94 RNZAF Malaysia Weekly Report No. 28, Air 227/20/5.
95 RNZAF Malaysia Weekly Report No. 44, Air 227/20/5.
96 Group Captain Geoff Wallingford to author, 31 Mar 1999.
97 CAS to Minister of Defence, through Secretary of Defence File, 7 Mar 1966, Air 206/2/4 pt 4.
98 A/Sec Def to CAS (Def 23/2/2), 21 Mar 1966, Air 206/2/4 pt 4. Thornton, who was visiting South-East Asia with the Minister of Defence, supported the continued deployment of No. 14 Squadron but was apprehensive that the 'submission seeking firm Government endorsement may have exactly the opposite effect especially if additional overseas expenditure involved'. The apparent lull in Confrontation would also not help. 'I would not object to current RNZAF proposal going forward but unless climate has changed since my departure I strongly advise against it.' CDS to Secretary of Defence, JOZSING 99, Kuala Lumpur to Wellington 241, Air 206/2/4 vol. 4. See also 'Withdrawal of No. 14 Squadron from Singapore, 1966, Air 1, 1/1/196.
99 Neville, interview.
100 Captain C. J. Carl, RNZN, interview, DLA 0102, RNZN Museum, Auckland.
101 Holyoake to Sir Alec Douglas-Home, 19 Dec 1963, JSO 156/2/1 pt 3. HMNZS *Otago* alternated with HMNZS *Taranaki* on duty with the Far East Fleet between 1962 and 1966, with the exception of the deployment of HMNZS *Royalist* from June to November 1965. *Otago*'s deployments were: Feb–Oct 1962, Apr–Dec 1963, Jul 1964–May 1965. See Lieutenant-Commander Peter Dennerly, letter to author, 24 Mar 1999, and Ship's Logs: *Taranaki*, 1961–65, N 113; *Otago*, 1961–68, N 112. See also Reports Of Proceedings: HMNZS *Otago*, 1961–68, ABFK W4010, 72/3/19 pts 1 & 2; HMNZS *Taranaki*, 1961–66, ABFK W4010, 72/3/20; HMNZS *Royalist*, 1959–66, ABFK W4010, 72/3/1; and Minutes of Naval Board Meetings 1960–1964, ABFK W4010, 68/3/9. The most detailed account from a parallel Australian perspective is Jeffrey Grey, *Up Top: The Royal Australian Navy and Southeast Asian Conflicts 1955–1972*, Allen & Unwin, Sydney, 1988, pp. 42–70.
102 'KD' stands for 'Kepal Di Rajah' ('Ship of the Rajah').
103 External Affairs Wellington to All Stations, 26 Jul 1963, MOD 3/5/1 vol. 2. See also 'Secondment to Malaysian Armed Forces', ABFK W4010, 66/2/68, pts 1 & 2.
104 Carl, interview.
105 Carl, interview.
106 Carl, interview.
107 Carl, interview.
108 Carl, interview. For details of Jaguar-class (BT) patrol boats, see R. V. B. Blackman (ed.), *Jane's Fighting Ships 1965–66*, Sampson Low, Marston & Co., Great Missenden, Buckinghamshire, 1966, p. 131.
109 Carl, interview. See also Grey, *Up Top*, pp. 54–9, and 'Gisborne', 'Naval Operations in the Malacca and Singapore Straits 1964–66', *Naval Review*, vol. 55, no. 1, Jan 1967, pp. 43–6.

110 This restriction was relaxed following the separation of Singapore from Malaysia in August 1965, after which trade with merchant ships anchored outside Malaysian and Singaporean territorial waters was permitted. See 'The Barter Trade', Annex C to 'Naval Operations in the Malacca and Singapore Straits 1964–1966', N 1132/2.

111 The Naval Operations Plan for Borneo, known as 'Whiskey Galore', was modified by experience. This is detailed in 'Lessons Learned in Borneo', Naval Force Headquarters to Commander Far East Fleet, 19 Sep 1966, N 1132/1.

112 NZNB to CINCFE, 240443Z Sep 1964, JSO 156/2/1 pt 5.

113 For an example, see Report of Proceedings, HMNZS *Taranaki*, 3 Jan 1966, ABFK W4010, 72/3/20. See also Operations: Movements of HMNZ Ships—HMNZS *Taranaki*, 1962–1967, ABFK W4010, 62/1/29, pts 2 & 3.

114 Annex A (p. 2) to Commander Naval Forces Borneo's letter 2/1, 19 Sep 1966, 1132/1. See also Reports of Proceedings, HMNZS *Taranaki*, pt 1, 1961–1965, ABFK W4010, 72/3/20.

115 See Incident Reports from Ships Patrolling in Defence of Western Malaysian Seaboard (MALPOS II—Part II), N 1132/5.

116 Rear-Admiral K. M. Saull, CB, RNZN, interview, Oct 1993, DLA 117, RNZN Museum, Auckland.

117 'Naval Operations in the Malacca and Singapore Straits 1964–1966', N 1132/2.

118 Rear-Admiral E. C. Thorne, RNZN, interview, DLA 0101, RNZN Museum, Auckland. For details of *Otago*'s activities in this period under Thorne and his successor (from December 1964) Commander R. H. L. Humby, RNZN, see Reports of Proceedings, HMNZS *Otago*, ABFK W4010, 72/3/19, pts 1 & 2. See also Operations: Movements of HMNZ Ships: HMNZS *Otago*, 1962–1968, ABFK W4010, 62/1/28, pts 1–3.

119 Saull, interview. See also Report of Proceedings, HMNZS *Taranaki*, Feb 1966, ABFK W4010, 72/3/20, pt 1.

120 Saull, interview.

121 HMNZS *Royalist*, Report of Proceedings, 1 Jul 1965 to 28 Sep 1965, RNZN Museum, Auckland. See also HMNZS *Royalist*, Ship's Log, Jan–Dec 1965, N 109/25.

122 HMNZS *Royalist*—Report of Proceedings, 3 May to 30 Jun 1965, RNZN Museum, Auckland. See also HMNZS *Royalist*, Ship's Log, Jan–Dec 1965, N 109/25; Report of Proceedings, HMNZS *Taranaki*, 14 May 1964, ABFK W4010, 72/3/20 pt 1.

123 HMNZS *Otago*—Report of Proceedings 1–31 Jul 1966, ABFK W4010, 72/3/19 pt 2.

124 HMNZS *Royalist*—Report of Proceedings, 1 Jul 1965 to 28 Sep 1965, RNZN Museum, Auckland. See also HMNZS *Royalist*, Ship's Log, Jan–Dec 1965, N 109/25; Operations: Movements of HMNZ Ships—HMNZS *Royalist*, ABFK W4010, 62/1/1 pts 1–5; Reports of Proceedings—HMNZS *Royalist*, 1959–1966, ABFK W4010, 72/3/1.

125 Chief Petty Officer J. R. Rees RNZN, interview, 16 Jan 1998, RNZN Museum, Auckland.

126 See RNZN LO to Dep Sec Navy, 12 Mar 1965, enclosing 'RNZN Offer to man two RN CMS on the Far East Station', 12 Mar 1965, and correspondence on 'Personnel Manning—Crews for Coastal Minesweepers and Base Support Party Singapore', ABFK W4010, 66/10/74.

127 M. Burgess, *Ships of the Royal New Zealand Navy*, Southern Press, Wellington, 1979, p. 27.

128 Commander M. N. Waymouth RNZN, interview, Mar 1997, DLA 0153, RNZN Museum, Auckland.

129 NZNB to COMAUCK etc., 050425Z Feb 1965, and following correspondence, ABFK W4010, 66/10/74.

130 Lieutenant P. M. Robertshaw's Report, 20 Apr 1965, and following correspondence, ABFK W4010, 66/10/74.

131 Waymouth, interview. See also Reports of Proceedings, HMNZS *Hickleton*, ABFK W4010, 72/3/21.

132 Dep Sec Navy to CO HMNZS *Philomel* etc., 'RNZNVR Officers for Duty in Coastal Mine Sweepers on Far East Station', 17 Mar 1965, ABFK W4010, 66/10/74.

133 Lieutenant-Commander G. C. Wright, interview, Feb 1994, DLA 0085, RNZN Museum, Auckland.

134 Wright, interview. See also Reports of Proceedings, HMNZS *Santon*, ABFK W4010, 72/3/21.

135 Wright, interview. See also Reports of Proceedings, HMNZS *Santon*, ABFK W4010, 72/3/21.

136 Wright, interview. See also Reports of Proceedings, HMNZS *Santon*, ABFK W4010, 72/3/21.

137 Report of Proceedings, HMNZS *Hickleton*, 1–31 Dec 1965, ABFK W4010, 72/3/21.

138 Wright, interview. See also Reports of Proceedings, HMNZS *Santon*, ABFK W4010, 72/3/21.

139 Wright, interview. See also Reports of Proceedings, HMNZS *Santon*, ABFK, W4010, 72/3/21.

140 Warrant Officer T. A. Bruce RNZN, interview, DLA 0161, RNZN Museum, Auckland.

141 Report of Proceedings, HMNZS *Hickleton*, 1–31 May 1966, ABFK W4010, 72/3/21.

142 The 'Borneo' clasp and General Service Medal 1962 were awarded to officers and ratings who served in East Malaysia and the waters surrounding them for 30 days or more, not necessarily continuously. 'Honours and Awards', Army 95/14/1.

143 Bruce, interview.

144 Report of Proceedings, HMNZS *Hickleton*, 1–30 June 1966, ABFK W4010, 72/3/21. See also Grant Howard & Colin Wynn, *Portrait of the Royal New Zealand Navy*, Grantham House, Wellington, 1991, p. 110. This action is the subject of a painting by Colin Wynn entitled 'HMNZS *Hickleton* in action off Horsburgh Light, 28 June 1966', RNZN Collection.

145 'Lessons Learned in Borneo', Naval Force Headquarters to Commander Far East Fleet, 19 Sep 1966, N 1132/1.

146 Quoted in detailed comments on draft by Lieutenant-Commander P. Y. Dennerly to author, 11 Mar 1999.

147 Peter Phipps, quoted in G. Howard, *The Navy in New Zealand*, A. H. & A. W. Reed, Wellington, 1981, p. 93.

148 'HMNZS *Royalist:* Breakdown of Main Propulsion Machinery', 1965, ABFK W4010, 68/6/24, pt 1.

149 'Hire of Royal Navy Ship', Matter for Naval Board Consideration, prepared by CNS on 11 Aug 1965, Naval Board Papers 1964–1965, N 1133/1. See also Ministry of Defence, Annual Report, *AJHR*, 1966, H-4, pp. 12–13.

150 Burgess, *Ships of the Royal New Zealand Navy*, pp. 18–19. Howard & Wynn, *Portrait of the Royal New Zealand Navy*, pp. 110–13.

## 9 'The Codeword is "CLARET"': The SAS, Borneo, 1965–66

1 Wellington to Kuala Lumpur 450, 7 Sep 1964, Army S.34/9/3 pt 2.

2 Tom Pocock, *Fighting General: The Public & Private Campaigns of General Sir Walter Walker*, Collins, London, 1973, pp. 196–8; Peter Dennis & Jeffrey Grey, *Emergency and Confrontation: Australian Military Operations in Malaya and Borneo 1950–1966*, Allen & Unwin in association with the Australian War Memorial, Sydney, 1996, pp. 197–217; D. M. Horner, 'The Australian Army and Indonesia's Confrontation with Malaysia', *Australian Outlook*, vol. 43, no. 1, Apr 1989, pp. 61–76.

3 Joint Report on the Borneo Campaign, 10 Nov 1966, CINCFE 9/67, pp. 9–15 (copy issued by Malaysian Armed Forces Staff College, Winton Papers). See also C. M. A. R. Roberts, 'Operations in Borneo', *British Army Review*, 1964, pp. 27–30; E. D. Smith, 'The Confrontation in Borneo: Part I', *Army Quarterly*, Oct 1975, pp. 479–83; 'The Confrontation in Borneo: Part II', *Army Quarterly*, Jan 1976, pp. 30–6; 'The Undeclared War: Indonesian Confrontation with Malaysia', *War in Peace*, no. 41, pp. 813–15.

4 Lieutenant-Colonel A. S. Harvey, 'Random Reflections of an Infantry Battalion Commander on the Indonesian Border', *The Infantryman*, no. 81, Nov 1965, pp. 47–51.

5 Douglas-Home to Menzies, 28 Apr 1964, PMD 64/6040 pt 2, CRS A1209/80, NAA, quoted in Moreen Dee, 'Deniable or Undeniable: An Australian View of the Policy and Strategy of Cross-border Operations in North Borneo, 1963–1966', MDS dissertation, University of New England, p. 11.

6 The most detailed account of the evolution of CLARET operations is Moreen Dee, 'Deniable or Undeniable'. See also Dennis & Grey, *Emergency and Confrontation*; E. D. Smith, *Counter-Insurgency Operations: 1. Malaya and Borneo*, Ian Allen, London, 1985; Thomas R. Mockaitis, *British Counterinsurgency in the Post-imperial Era*, Manchester University Press, Manchester, 1995, pp. 14–43.

7 Director of Borneo Operations Instruction no. 10: Command, Roles and Employment of the Special Air Service Regiment in Borneo, HQ British Forces Borneo, 10 Jan 1964, MOD 3/5/12.

8 DBO 4/53 HQ Director of Borneo Operations LABUAN, 1 Mar 1965, sent under covering letter, Begg to Phipps (CINCFE 1578/2160/2), 13 Mar 1965, 'New Zealand Operations in Borneo 1965–1966' [TS], DDI HQ NZ Defence Force. See appendix 11.

9 'Security: The Golden Rules', Annex C to DBO 4/53, 1 Mar 1965, 'New Zealand Operations in Borneo. 1965–1966' [TS], DDI HQ NZ Defence Force.

10 'Public Relations Aspects of Cross Border Operations: The Golden Rules', Annex D to DBO 4/53, 1 Mar 1965, 'New Zealand Operations in Borneo 1965–1966' [TS], DDI HQ NZ Defence Force.

11 Joint Report on the Borneo Campaign, 10 Nov 1966, CINCFE 9/67, copy issued by Malaysian Armed Forces Staff College, Winton Papers.

12 Military Measures to Counter Indonesian Confrontation, CINCFE 118/64, Annex to COS 321/64, 30 Dec 1964, JSO 152/2/3 pt 5. See also Dennis & Grey, *Emergency and Confrontation*, pp. 214–17, 239–62; Pocock, *Fighting General*, pp. 196–8.

13 Military Measures to Counter Indonesian Confrontation, CINCFE 118/64.

14 External Affairs Wellington to Kuala Lumpur and Canberra, 'Malaysia: New Zealand Defence Assistance', no. 65, 27 Jan 1965, Army 15/15 pt 1.

15 External Affairs Wellington to Kuala Lumpur and Canberra, 'Malaysia: New Zealand Defence Assistance'.

16 Major-General H. A. Lascelles, CBE, DSO, HQ FARELF to Colonel L. A. Kermode, Commander NZ Army FARELF, 1 Feb 1965, Army 15/15 pt 1.

17 NZ Army Singapore to AGS Wellington 3055/Comd, For CGS of 040210Z Feb 1965, Army 15/15 pt 1.

18 'Further New Zealand Defence Aid: Statement by Prime Minister, 5 February 1965', *External Affairs Review*, vol. 15, no. 2, Feb 1965, in Peter Boyce, *Malaysia and Singapore in International Diplomacy: Documents and Commentaries*, Sydney University Press, Sydney, 1968, pp. 211–13. Folios 2715, 2720 in d/COS 48/c/18 pt 21, MOD. Ian McGibbon, 'Forward Defence: The Southeast Asian Commitment', in Malcolm McKinnon (ed.), *New Zealand in World Affairs, Volume II: 1957–1972*, New Zealand Institute of International Affairs, Wellington, 1991, p. 29.

19 Extracts of Signal from External Affairs NZ handed to Comd NZ Army FARELF by Lt-Col Holloway, 1415 hrs 16 Feb 1965, Army 15/15 pt 1. The distance was later extended to 20,000 yards for selected operations. David Horner, *Phantoms of the Jungle: A History of the Australian Special Air Service*, Allen & Unwin, Sydney, 1989, p. 101.

20 Begg to Phipps (CINCFE 1578/2160/2), 13 Mar 1965, 'New Zealand Operations in Borneo 1965–1966' [TS], DDI HQ NZ Defence Force. For an overview of intelligence-gathering during Confrontation, see Dennis & Grey, *Emergency and Confrontation*, pp. 247–51.

21 Phipps to Begg, 14 Apr 1965, 'New Zealand Operations in Borneo 1965–1966' [TS], DDI HQ NZ Defence Force.

22 The New Zealand Special Air Service Squadron became the 1st Ranger Squadron, New Zealand Special Air Service in 1963 to commemorate the centenary of the formation of the Taranaki Bush Rangers and the Forest Rangers, who served in the

New Zealand Wars. Chosen by the Officer Commanding, Major M. N. Velvin, the new name was strongly disliked by squadron members because it suggested they were no longer SAS but were akin to Ranger units in the United States. Lieutenant-Colonel L. G. Grant, interview, 24 Oct 1992. See W. D. Baker, *Dare to Win: The Story of the New Zealand Special Air Service*, Lothian, Port Melbourne, 1987, p. 73.

23 WO2 J. T. Johnston, interview, 14 Oct 1992.

24 Major W. J. Meldrum, interview, 21 Oct 1992.

25 WO2 Dick Smith, interview, 6 Nov 1992.

26 Smith, interview.

27 Meldrum, interview.

28 Major R. P. Withers, interview, 6 May 1993. Major Ray Hurle, in correspondence with the author, named the original squadron members who served with the SAS detachments in Borneo as: 1 Det, Sergeant R. C. Withers and Staff Sergeant E. E. Keene; 2 Det, none; 3 Det, Major David Ogilvy and Staff Sergeant F. Ayres, SQMS; 4 Det, Staff Sergeant E. E. Keene, SQMS.

29 Meldrum, interview.

30 Message from Minister of Defence, PR 25/2/2, NZ SAS Group Archives.

31 'Jungle War can be Grim', *NZ Weekly News*, 24 Mar 1965, p. 3.

32 This was later disputed by the staff officer concerned, who admitted receiving the telephone call but said he did not consider it a request for clearance. Army S.34/9/1.

33 Meldrum, interview.

34 Monthly Report: Apr 1965, Det 1NZ Ranger Sqn (Far East), 10 May 1965, NZ SAS Group Archives.

35 The reporter, Lee Martin, insisted that Meldrum was not the source of his information, and it seems that it was possible to pick up rumours of what 22 SAS Regiment was doing from gossip around RAF Changi Air Base. Army S.34/9/1. Nonetheless, by talking to the reporter Meldrum had opened himself to censure by an Army hierarchy that viewed any contact with the press with suspicion, particularly as he had already been criticised for an interview he had given in Auckland on SAS training. Meldrum, interview.

36 'In light of recent publicity Major Meldrum was brought back to New Zealand in order that inquiries might be made into the source of this publicity and to see whether there had been breaches of either discipline or security. His posting to S.A.S. detachment was intended to be a short one and plans made earlier for him made it convenient to return [him] to New Zealand.' 'S.A.S. major's army career is assured', *Auckland Star*, 1 Jun 1965.

37 Dan Heke, interview, 10 Nov 1992; also Johnston, interview.

38 For all matters except administration, which remained the responsibility of Kermode's headquarters in Singapore.

39 Meldrum, interview, and correspondence; also Withers, interview. For Australian SAS operations see Horner, *Phantoms of the Jungle*, and Dennis & Grey, *Emergency and Confrontation*, pp. 300–8.

40 Meldrum, interview.
41 Lieutenant-Colonel S. J. M. Winton, interview, 22 Oct 1992.
42 Monthly Report: 4–31 Mar 1965, Det 1NZ Ranger Sqn (Far East), 12 Apr 1965, NZ SAS Group Archives. Appendices include the detailed training programme, and the revised organisation and manning of the three troops.
43 Meldrum, interview.
44 Winton, interview.
45 Peter Dickens, *SAS Secret War in South East Asia* (originally titled *SAS: The Jungle Frontier*), Greenhill Books, London/Presidio Press, California, 1991, p. 157.
46 Lieutenant-Colonel E. I. Manuera, interview, 23 Sep 1992.
47 Winton, interview.
48 For details of guerrilla organisation, see J. A. C. Mackie, *Konfrontasi: The Indonesian-Malaysia Dispute 1963–1966*, Oxford University Press, Kuala Lumpur, 1974, pp. 64–5, 215–16, 301–2. See also Dennis & Grey, *Emergency and Confrontation*; Pocock, *Fighting General*.
49 For an assessment of Lea's performance, see Dennis & Grey, *Emergency and Confrontation*, pp. 242–3.
50 Winton, interview.
51 Withers, interview.
52 Johnston, interview; also Manuera, interview.
53 Heke, interview.
54 Winton, interview.
55 Winton, interview.
56 Manuera, interview.
57 Dickens, *SAS Secret War in South East Asia*, pp. 181–209. See also Peter de la Billiere, *Looking for Trouble: An Autobiography from SAS to the Gulf*, Harper Collins, London, 1994.
58 A Sqn 22 SAS Ops/90/62, 29 May 1965, MOD.
59 Manuera, interview.
60 Manuera, interview.
61 Manuera, interview.
62 Manuera, interview.
63 Manuera, interview.
64 Manuera, interview.
65 D Sqn 22 SAS Ops/90/61, 23 May 1965, MOD. See also Harold James & Denis Sheil-Small, *The Undeclared War: The Story of the Indonesian Confrontation, 1962–1966*, Leo Cooper, London, 1971, p. 165.
66 HQ SAS Far East, Ops/90/a/5 Patrol Report Op UNION, 29 May 1965, MOD.
67 Det 1NZ Ranger Sqn [FE] 2.2, 10 May 1965, NZ SAS Group Archives.
68 Det 1NZ Ranger Sqn [FE] 2.1, 8 Aug 1965, NZ SAS Group Archives.
69 Det 1NZ Ranger Sqn [FE] S/6, 14 Sep 1965, NZ SAS Group Archives.
70 Det 1NZ Ranger Sqn [FE] OPS/90/88, 19 Aug 1965, NZ SAS Group Archives.

71 See patrol details as follows: Det 1NZ Ranger Sqn [FE] OPS/90/89, 20 Aug 1965; Det 1NZ Ranger Sqn [FE] OPS/90/90, 21 Aug 1965; Det 1NZ Ranger Sqn [FE] OPS/90/92, 24 Aug 1965; Det 1NZ Ranger Sqn [FE] OPS/90/96, 7 Sep 1965; Det 1NZ Ranger Sqn [FE] OPS/90/95, 7 Sep 1965, Box 463/4/5, MOD. For the last two reports, see also nos 729 and 731, Army Non File Material, HQ NZ Defence Forces.
72 Johnston, interview.
73 Lieutenant-Colonel Ian ('Tanky') Smith, 22 SAS, interview, 30 Jul 1992. See Dennis & Grey, *Emergency and Confrontation*, pp. 204–14; 'Joint Report on the Borneo Campaign', 10 Nov 1966, CINCFE 9/67 (copy issued by Malaysian Armed Forces Staff College, Winton Papers); Australian Military Forces, *The Indonesian Army*, 1966, no. 898, Army Non-File Material, HQ NZ Defence Forces.
74 Det 1NZ Ranger Sqn [FE] OPS/90/96, 7 Sep 1965; OPS/90/98, 12 Sep 1965, Box 463/4/5, MOD.
75 Det 1NZ Ranger Sqn [FE] OPS/90/103, 10 Oct 1965, Box 463/4/5, MOD.
76 Johnston, interview; Det 1NZ Ranger Sqn [FE] OPS/90/100, 21 Sep 1965, Box 463/4/5, MOD.
77 Heke, interview; Det 1NZ Ranger Sqn [FE] OPS/90/101, 2 Oct 1965, Box 463/4/5, MOD.
78 Johnston, interview.
79 Monthly Report: 2–30 Sep 1965, 2 Det 1NZ Ranger Sqn (Far East), 12 Oct 1965, NZ SAS Group Archives.
80 Lieutenant-Colonel R. S. Dearing, interview, 22 Oct 1992.
81 Lieutenant-General Sir John Mace, interview, 4 Nov 1992.
82 Mace, interview.
83 Lt-Col J. Morris, D Inf and SAS, memo 'SAS' to CGS, 27 Oct 1965, Army 15/15 pt 1.
84 1 Inf Bde Gp to OC NMD 91.24, '1 Ranger Sqn NZSAS – Establishment', 22 Oct 1965, Army 15/15 pt 1.
85 McKinnon to Lt-Gen Sir Alan Jolly, Commander-in-Chief HQ FARELF, DO/CGS, 22 Nov 1965, Army 15/15 pt 1. For background, see CGS to DCGS, 26 Oct 1965, Army 15/15 pt 1.
86 Jolly to McKinnon, Comd 10/12, 10 Dec 1965, Army 15/15 pt 1.
87 Jolly to McKinnon, Comd 10/12, 7 Mar 1966, Army 15/15 pt 1.
88 This would require an increase in the regular strength of NZ SAS to 125 personnel and the establishment of a training and base element separate from 1 Ranger Squadron. DSAS to DCGS, 26 Jan 1966; SD to DCGS, 15 Feb 1966, Army 15/15 pt 1.
89 New Zealand Army Headquarters Far East believed this would be unacceptable to the British authorities. While a full squadron could be fitted into 22 SAS Regiment's roulement programme, the limited size and capability of the New Zealand detachment would make it awkward to accommodate. It would also have to be additional to the two-squadron level required by Lea, and therefore difficult to employ. Col P. H. G. Hamilton, Comd NZSARM FARELF to McKinnon (NZEF/DO/1580/Comd), 22 Mar 1966, Army 15/15 pt 1.

90 Lascelles to McKinnon (MGGS 12/3), 6 Apr 1966, Army 15/15 pt 1.
91 Dearing, interview.
92 Dearing, interview.
93 Grant, interview.
94 Grant, interview; also WO2 Arthur Steele, interview, 27 Oct 1992.
95 Det 1NZ Ranger Sqn [FE] OPS/90/108, 8 Nov 1965, Box 463/4/53, MOD; Grant, interview; Steele, interview.
96 Det 1NZ Ranger Sqn [FE] OPS/90/MW2, 12 Nov 1965, Box 463/4/53, MOD.
97 Det 1NZ Ranger Sqn [FE] OPS/90/MW1, 12 Nov 1965, Box 463/4/53, MOD.
98 See Dickens, *SAS Secret War in South East Asia*, pp. 144–5, 158, 188–93, 203–6, 213–16.
99 Det 1NZ Ranger Sqn [FE] OPS/90/110, 12 Nov 1965, Box 463/4/53, MOD.
100 Det 1NZ Ranger Sqn [FE] OPS/90/MW3, 24 Nov 1965, Box 463/4/53, MOD.
101 Det 1NZ Ranger Sqn [FE] OPS/90/CENT/40, 12 Dec 1965, Box 463/4/53, MOD.
102 Det 1NZ Ranger Sqn [FE] OPS/90/113, 12 Dec 1965, Box 463/4/53, MOD.
103 Det 1NZ Ranger Sqn [FE] OPS/90/MW4, 31 Dec 1965, Box 463/4/53, MOD.
104 Steele, interview.
105 Det 1NZ Ranger Sqn [FE] OPS/90/MW5, 31 Dec 1965, Box 463/4/53, MOD.
106 Det 1NZ Ranger Sqn [FE] OPS/90/EAST/1, 31 Dec 1965, Box 463/4/53, MOD.
107 Det 1NZ Ranger Sqn [FE] OPS/90/EAST/3, 9 Feb 1966, Box 463/4/53, MOD.
108 Steele, interview.
109 WO1 Kiriti Haami, interview, 16 Nov 1992.
110 Haami, interview.
111 Dearing, interview.
112 Grant, interview; Det 1NZ Ranger Sqn [FE] OPS/90/CENT/41, 12 Feb 1966, Box 463/4/53, MOD.
113 For a detailed account of this operation see Dickens, *SAS Secret War in South East Asia*, pp. 218–26.
114 Steele, interview.
115 Steele, interview.
116 Steele, interview; also Haami, interview.
117 Steele, interview. See Dickens, *SAS Secret War in South East Asia*, pp. 218–26.
118 Steele, interview.
119 Steele, interview; also Haami, interview.
120 Staff Sergeant Bob Withers served as Chief Clerk with One Detachment.
121 Lieutenant-Colonel H. R. Burt, interview, 24 Oct 1992.
122 Burt, interview; also Colonel D. W. S. Moloney, interview, 8 Oct 1992.
123 D Squadron 22 SAS Regt deployed to Borneo in July 1966, but had not commenced operations when peace was declared on 11 August. Dickens, *SAS Secret War in South East Asia*, pp. 227–9. For the Australian operations, see Dennis & Grey, *Emergency and Confrontation*, pp. 263–308, and Horner, *SAS, Phantoms of the Jungle*, which devotes seven chapters to Australian SAS CLARET operations.
124 Det 1NZ Ranger Sqn [FE] OPS/90/EAST/5, 22 Mar 1966, Box 463/4/53, MOD.

125 Det 1NZ Ranger Sqn [FE] OPS/90/EAST/6, 24 Mar 1966, Box 463/4/53, MOD.
126 Burt, interview.
127 Det 1NZ Ranger Sqn [FE] OPS/90/EAST/10, Apr 1966; Det 1NZ Ranger Sqn [FE] OPS/90/EAST/7, 31 Mar 1966; Det 1NZ Ranger Sqn [FE] OPS/90/EAST/8, Apr 1966, Box 463/4/53, MOD.
128 Det 1NZ Ranger Sqn [FE] OPS/90/EAST/8, Apr 1966, Box 463/4/53, MOD.
129 Det 1NZ Ranger Sqn [FE] OPS/90/EAST/9, Apr 1966, Box 463/4/53, MOD.
130 Burt, interview.
131 Burt, interview.
132 Burt, interview.
133 Burt, interview; also Johnston, interview, for his account of this operation. No operational report was located.
134 When this letter was found on a bed in the barracks at Labuan, its author was immediately returned to New Zealand. CLARET's security has been tightly maintained: only when assured that I had clearance to do so would members of the NZ SAS detachments agree to talk about their involvement. Army 15/15 pt 1. The operational report is Det 1NZ Ranger Sqn [FE] OPS/90/MIDWEST/6, 15 Apr 1966, Box 463/4/53, MOD.
135 Burt, interview. Det 1NZ Ranger Sqn [FE] OPS/90/EAST/11, 26 Apr 1966, Box 463/4/53, MOD.
136 Det 1NZ Ranger Sqn [FE] OPS/90/EAST/12, 6 May 1966, Box 463/4/53, MOD.
137 Det 1NZ Ranger Sqn [FE] OPS/90/EAST/13, 17 May 1966, Box 463/4/53, MOD.
138 Det 1NZ Ranger Sqn [FE] OPS/90/EAST/14, 6 Jun 1966, Box 463/4/53, MOD.
139 Det 1NZ Ranger Sqn [FE] A/7, 1 Oct 1966, Army S.15/15/1; also Moloney, interview.
140 The major problem facing the detachment was the theatre-wide shortage of serviceable Bergen packs, which prevented the full number of patrols being committed. Det 1NZ Ranger Sqn [FE] B/4, 1 Aug 1966, NZ SAS Group Archives.
141 Det 1NZ Ranger Sqn [FE], Patrol Report The Gap, Aug 1966, Army S.15/15/1; also David Slocombe, interview, 4 Jun 1992.
142 Det 1NZ Ranger Sqn [FE] OPS/10/66/1, 20 Aug 1966, Army S.15/15/1; Winton, interview.
143 Moloney, interview.
144 Winton, interview.

## 10 'No Better a Soldier': Infantry Operations, Borneo, 1965–66

1 Brigadier R. M. Gurr, interview, 13 & 14 Jan 1993.
2 The author is grateful to Brigadier R. M. Gurr for permitting me to read his draft narratives, later self-published as Robert Gurr, *Voices from a Border War*, Melbourne, 1995, and for a series of interviews which were taped. I am also appreciative of access to HQ 19 Inf Bde Gp files held by the Ministry of Defence, United Kingdom. This chapter is largely based on these sources, as the 1RNZIR Unit War Diaries for this period could not be located in HQNZ Defence Force Registry, Archives New

Zealand, or the 1RNZIR Museum. This appears to be a genuine misplacement, unlike the deliberate action of the Registrar AGS who, apparently to save space, destroyed a large number of historically priceless files on the NZ Army's involvement in Korea and South-East Asia. For parallel British accounts, see Brigadier E. N. W. Bramell, 'Reflections on Borneo', *The Infantryman*, no. 83, Nov 1967, pp. 13–24, and E. D. Smith, *Malaya and Borneo: Counter-Insurgency Operations: 1*, Ian Allen, London, 1985.

3 1RNZIR served under Brigader D. W. Fraser's 19th Infantry Brigade Group Headquarters and not Headquarters 5th Infantry Brigade Group, as is stated in Peter Dennis & Jeffrey Grey, *Emergency and Confrontation*, Allen & Unwin in association with the Australian War Memorial, Sydney, 1996, p. 243.

4 See Annex E to Joint Report on the Borneo Campaign, 10 Nov 1966, CINCFE 9/67, copy issued by Malaysian Armed Forces Staff College, Winton Papers.

5 17 Div 102/4 Ops, Directive for Brigadier D. W. Fraser OBE, by Commander Land Force Borneo, 19 Mar 1965, Folio 3 to WO 305/1560.

6 HQ 19 Inf Bde Gp and Logistic Units' Report on Emergency Tour of Borneo, 5 Nov 1965, WO 305/1560.

7 Commander's Diary, 19 Inf Bde Gp, Annex H, Encl 5, WO 305/1562.

8 Training Officer's Report Apr 1965, 1RNZIR Monthly Report Apr 1965, 17.3, 7 May 1965, ABFK W3788, Box 26.

9 '28 CW Brigade: Planning Level Comments', JOZWEL to JOZSING, JOZWEL 164 of 140630Z Apr 1965. Also 'Policy for Using Units of 28 Commonwealth Brigade on Periodic Tours in Borneo in Relation to their SEATO Role', NZ DLO Singapore to Secretary Chief of Staff Committee, and Secretary of External Affairs, 408/5/1, 28 Apr 1965; Draft for CGS, 'Deployment 28 Commonwealth Brigade in a SEATO Role: Brief for Discussions with Brigade Commander', 26 Apr 1965, all on Army 31/2/3.

10 MV *Auby* was a small coastal vessel of 1,732 tons, speed 10 knots, chartered from the Straits Steamship Company. After modification it could accommodate 385 soldiers and their personal equipment 'in comparative comfort'. The sailing time from Singapore to Kuching was two days. 'Lessons Learned from Borneo Operations', G Operational Requirements & Analysis, HQ FARELF, Report 1/69, pp. 79–80, AD 14.

11 WO1 H. E. Chamberlain, interview, 15 Mar 1993.

12 Commander's Diary, 19 Inf Bde Gp, WO 305/1562.

13 Exercise Talisman Exercise Instructions, 1RNZIR Monthly Report Apr 1965, ABFK W3788, Box 26.

14 Midwest Bde Op Directive DWF/1, Mar 1965, WO 305/1560; Midwest Bde Op Directive DWF/4, 1 Jun 1965, WO 305/1560.

15 This was stated to be 'essential for tactical success', and the 'direct concern of military forces'. Action to build up confidence in the Federation, while generally more a matter for 'political and administrative action' than a 'direct concern' of the military, was recognised as being of 'fundamental long term importance'. Minutes of Comd Midwest Brigade Conference on Operations held at Sibu on 31 Mar 1965, dated 3 Apr 1965, WO 305/1560.

16 HQ Midwest Bde Administrative Instruction 4/65, dated 27 May 1965, and 2240/1 A/MWB, Administration, 13 May 1965, WO 305/1562.

17 Gurr erroneously locates this attack at Balai Ringin; see *Voices from a Border War*, p. 80. Also Gurr, interview; Dennis & Grey, *Emergency and Confrontation,* p. 256; and the bland unattributed account, 'Jungle Patrol 2nd Battalion The Parachute Regiment in Borneo', *The Infantryman*, no. 81, Nov 1965, pp. 73–5. Major R. I. Thorpe's A Company helped provide tactical training in jungle warfare to the Second Battalion The Parachute Regiment at the Jungle Warfare School at Kota Tinggi immediately before the battalion's deployment on operations to Borneo. Thorpe was unimpressed by the almost arrogantly confident approach to jungle warfare taken by 2 Para's command element, a perception validated by events at Plaman Mapu. Brigadier R. I. Thorpe, correspondence and discussions with author, Apr 1999.

18 See Derek Freeman, *Report on the Iban*, Athlone Press, London, 1970.

19 Brigadier R. I. Thorpe, quoted in Gurr, *Voices from a Border War*, p. 95.

20 Gurr, interview.

21 Lieutenant-Colonel J. A. I. Fillingham, 'Operations in Sarawak', *British Army Review*, 1965, pp. 13–19. Both incidents seem to have grown in the telling in General Sir William Jackson, *Withdrawal from Empire*, Batsford, London, 1986, pp. 202–3.

22 The complexity and the political and military implications of the Indonesian command structure are explained in detail by Jeffrey Grey in Dennis & Grey, *Emergency and Confrontation,* pp. 204–17. See also Harold Crouch, *The Army and Politics in Indonesia,* Cornell University Press, Ithaca/London, 1978, pp. 55–62, 69–75.

23 Australian Military Forces, *The Indonesian Army*, Army Headquarters, Canberra, 1966, Confidential, pp. 68–70, HQ NZDF.

24 Gurr, interview.

25 For a description of a typical Borneo town, see the portrayal of Sibu in Richard Holworthy, 'Keeping the Borneo Peace—1964', *The Infantryman*, no. 80, Oct 1964, pp. 24–31.

26 Commander's Diary Narrative, HQ 19 Inf Bde Gp, WO 305/1560.

27 Midwest Bde Op Directive DWF/1, Mar 1965; Midwest Bde Op Directive DWF/4, 1 Jun 1965, WO 305/1560.

28 Captain C. E. Brock, *The Diplomat in Uniform: A History of the First Battalion Royal New Zealand Infantry Regiment*, Singapore, 1971, p. 7-1.

29 Brock, *The Diplomat in Uniform*, p. C-1.

30 Brigadier I. H. Burrows, quoted in Gurr, *Voices from a Border War*, p. 97.

31 Gurr, interview; Burrows, interview.

32 Brigadier I. H. Burrows, 'Confrontation 1RNZIR Operations 1965', 1RNZIR Museum. See also Burrows' account in Gurr, *Voices from a Border War*, pp. 97–101; also interview with author, 12 Mar 1992.

33 Burrows, interview.

34 Burrows, 'Confrontation 1RNZIR Operations 1965'. See also Gurr, *Voices from a Border War*, pp. 97–101; Burrows, interview.

35 Chamberlain, interview.

36 Burrows, 'Confrontation 1RNZIR Operations 1965'.
37 Burrows, 'Confrontation 1RNZIR Operations 1965'. See also Gurr, *Voices from a Border War*, pp. 97–101; Burrows, interview.
38 Burrows, 'Confrontation 1RNZIR Operations 1965'. See also Gurr, *Voices from a Border War*, pp. 97–101; Burrows, interview.
39 'Rationing Officer's Report', Annex E to 1RNZIR 17.2, 15 Sep 1965, Burrows Papers.
40 Burrows, 'Confrontation 1RNZIR Operations 1965'. See also Gurr, *Voices from a Border War*, pp. 97–101; Burrows, interview.
41 Burrows, 'Confrontation 1RNZIR Operations 1965'. See also Gurr, *Voices from a Border War*, pp. 97–101; Burrows, interview.
42 These procedures had been discussed and outlined during 1RNZIR's training and preparation before deployment. See 'Company and Platoon Bases' under 'Unit Tactical Doctrine', 14 Apr 1965, 1RNZIR Monthly Report, Apr 1965, 1RNZIR Museum. See also 1 NZ Regt Comd's Diary and 1RNZIR Comd's Diary, Jul 1964–May 1965, nos 508 & 509, Non File Material Army, HQ NZ Defence Force. 'Lessons Learned from Borneo Operations', G Operational Requirements & Analysis, HQ FARELF, Report No. 1/69, pp. 1–8, AD 14.
43 Brigadier R. I. Thorpe, quoted in Gurr, *Voices from a Border War*, pp. 95–6.
44 Lieutenant-Colonel S. R. McKeon, quoted in Gurr, *Voices from a Border War*, p. 92.
45 Thorpe, quoted in Gurr, *Voices from a Border War*, p. 96.
46 Major H. James, interview, 14 Jun 1993.
47 Lieutenant-Colonel James W. Brown, interview, 9 Mar 1993.
48 Lt-Col A. S. Harvey, MC, 'Random Reflections of an Infantry Battalion Commander on the Indonesian Border', *The Infantryman*, no. 81, Nov 1965, pp. 47–51.
49 Lieutenant-Colonel Bryan Wells, RNZ Signals, 'The Breaking of the High Frequency (HF) Paradigm', cited in Laurie Barber & Cliff Lord, *Swift and Sure: A History of the Royal New Zealand Corps of Signals and Army Signalling in New Zealand*, New Zealand Signals Incorporated, Auckland, 1996, pp. 165–80. Also Lieutenant-Colonel B. P. Wells, interview, 11 Jun 1992.
50 Wells, 'The Breaking of the High Frequency (HF) Paradigm'. Also Wells, interview; 'Lessons Learned from Borneo Operations', G Operational Requirements & Analysis, HQ FARELF, Report no. 1/69, pp. 37–45, AD 14.
51 Wells, 'The Breaking of the High Frequency (HF) Paradigm'; also Gurr, Mann and Wells, interviews.
52 This was acknowledged by Fraser in his final report: 'The best solution in 2nd Division was found to be a VHF battalion command net with SR C42 links up to 35 miles long.' Equally, 'some success was achieved in 2nd Division using the SR A41 as a patrol set. The set worked reliably 10–15 thousand yards to the company base.' HQ 19 Inf Bde Gp and Logistic Units' Report on Emergency Tour of Borneo, 5 Nov 1965, WO 305/1560. See 'Lessons Learned from Borneo Operations', G Operational Requirements & Analysis, HQ FARELF, Report No. 1/69, AD 14. Also Barber & Lord, *Swift and Sure*, pp. 165–80.
53 Gurr, interview. See Gurr, *Voices from a Border War*, pp. 27, 105.

54 Gurr, interview.
55 Brown, interview.
56 Brown, interview.
57 DOBOPS Weekly Assessment of the Threat to East Malaysia and Brunei and Summary of Enemy Activities during the period 12–19 Jun 1965, Borneo Box 6, MOD.
58 Dennis & Grey, *Emergency and Confrontation*, pp. 266–8, Appendix D.
59 DOBOPS Weekly Assessment, 12–19 Jun 1965, Borneo Box 6, MOD.
60 Brown, interview.
61 DOBOPS Weekly Assessment, 19–26 Jun 1965, Borneo Box 6, MOD.
62 Lieutenant-Colonel Brian J. Marshall, quoted in Gurr, *Voices from a Border War*, p. 112.
63 Marshall, quoted in Gurr, *Voices from a Border War*, p. 112.
64 Marshall, quoted in Gurr, *Voices from a Border War*, p. 113.
65 Marshall, quoted in Gurr, *Voices from a Border War*, pp. 113–14.
66 1950/3/G/MWB Engagement Reports, 9 Jul 1965, WO 305/1564. See also Commander's Diary 19 Inf Bde Gp, July 1965, WO 305/1564.
67 Gurr, interview. New Zealand had agreed to a British proposal that a joint scale of operational awards cover the Australian, British, Gurkha and New Zealand troops in the Borneo territories, as well as naval and air force units. Calculated on a six-monthly basis corresponding to the duration of the standard operational tour, it allowed for one gallantry and one distinguished service award for every 350 personnel, and one Mentioned in Despatches for every 200. See correspondence, 'Honours and Awards', Army 95/14.
68 Discussions with Brigadier R. I. Thorpe on author's draft, Apr 1999.
69 Weekly Intelligence Summary No. 24, ending 14 Jul 1965, WO 305/1564.
70 CINCFE Report 5/66, and DOBOPS Weekly Assessment, 3–10 Jul 1965, Borneo Box 6, MOD.
71 1950/3/G/MWB Engagement Reports, 9 Jul 1965, WO 305/1564.
72 Brown, interview.
73 Burrows, interview.
74 Annex B to DBO 4/53, 1 Mar 1965 (incorporating Amdt No. 1, issued 4 May 1965). OFFENSIVE PATROL OPERATIONS THE GOLDEN RULES, New Zealand Operations in Borneo, 1965–1966. [TS], DDI HQ NZ Defence Force.
75 Brigadier I. H. Burrows wrote: 'As a Coy Comd I was permitted one border operation a month against Indonesians. For these I had to submit a plan one month in advance and have it approved at Operational HQ in Labuan. I never had a plan questioned and we used our full quota.' Burrows, 'Confrontation 1RNZIR Operations 1965'. Also Burrows, interview.
76 DBO 4/53 HQ Director of Borneo Operations LABUAN, 1 Mar 1965, sent under covering letter, Admiral Sir Varyl Begg, KCB, DSO, DSC, to Rear-Admiral Sir Peter Phipps, KBE, DSC, VRD, RNZN, CDS. Commander in Chief Far East CINCFE 1578/2160/2, 13 Mar 1965, 'New Zealand Operations in Borneo, 1965–1966'. [TS], DDI HQ NZ Defence Force. See Appendix 11.

77 Gurr, interview. See Gurr, *Voices from a Border War*, pp. 119–33.

78 Gurr, *Voices from a Border War*, p. 115; also Gurr, interview.

79 Gurr, interview.

80 1RNZIR's Mortar Platoon was deployed to Borneo with 3-inch mortars, which were replaced by 81mm mortars while they were there. Lieutenant J. W. Brown was later one of the first to undergo a formal training course on the new mortar: 'It was interesting that whilst we were making it work, some of the methods that we were using were totally wrong; but it doesn't matter, we never killed any of our own people on the thing.' Brown, interview.

81 II Battalion, V (Mandau) BRIMOB Brigade, which had been relatively inactive, had apparently been gingered into action by its brigade headquarters, and as it had been reinforced by a Raider Company further incursions into the New Zealand sector were thought likely. Weekly Intelligence Summary No. 24, ending 14 Jul 1965, WO 305/1564.

82 Lieutenant-Colonel C. G. Wotton, quoted in Gurr, *Voices from a Border War*, pp. 115–16.

83 Gurr, *Voices from a Border War*, p. 120.

84 Gurr, *Voices from a Border War*, p. 120. See also Burrows, 'Confrontation 1RNZIR Operations 1965', and Burrows, interview.

85 Annex A to MW/FS/14, 16 Jul 1965, WO 305/1569.

86 WO1 Neil Webb, interview, 16 Mar 1994.

87 Webb, interview; MW/FS/14 Op ANCHOR MATCH, 16 Jul 1965, WO 305/1569.

88 Webb, interview.

89 MW/FS/14 Op ANCHOR MATCH, 16 Jul 1965, WO 305/1569.

90 MW/FS/14, 22 Jul 1965, WO 305/1569.

91 Brown, interview.

92 Brown, interview.

93 Brigadier R. I. Thorpe, quoted in Gurr, *Voices from a Border War*, pp. 124–5. A detailed account of the contact from the company commander's perspective appears on pp. 122–8.

94 James, interview.

95 Brown, interview.

96 Thorpe, quoted in Gurr, *Voices from a Border War*, p. 127.

97 See the citations to both awards, quoted in Gurr, *Voices from a Border War*, pp. 153–5, 166. Gurr records Lieutenant James Wairata Brown, RNZIR, awarded Military Cross; Private Tahu Ashby, RNZIR, awarded Military Medal, *London Gazette*, 24 May 1966, p. 6112.

98 Annex A to MW/FS/14, Aug 1965, WO 305/1569.

99 Brown, interview.

100 Brigadier R. I. Thorpe, notes on draft, Apr 1999.

101 During 1964–65, army leaders deliberately obstructed the Confrontation policy. They starved the Kalimantan Combat Command of properly equipped army troops,

limiting such forces to units of the air force, navy and police, as well as 'volunteers'. Crouch, *The Army and Politics in Indonesia*, p. 73.

102 Annex A to MW/FS/14, Aug 1965, WO 305/1569.

103 Annex A to MW/FS/14, Aug 1965, WO 305/1569.

104 'Joint Report on the Borneo Campaign', CINCEFE 9/67, 10 Nov 1966, pp. 35–8, copy issued by Malaysian Armed Forces Staff College, Winton Papers. 'The Jungle Patrol: A Study of the Load Carried by the Unit and the Individual Soldier', FARELF G (OR & A) Branch Report 3/65, Aug 1965, AD 14. See also Dennis & Grey, *Emergency and Confrontation*, pp. 260–2.

105 MW/FS/16, 12 Aug 1965, WO 305/1569.

106 Gurr, *Voices from a Border War*, p. 130.

107 Thorpe, notes for author.

108 There were also interruptions of the A Company radio net by Indonesian stations, including during this contact: 'You fools, you must give up your base at Lubok Antu. Don't listen to Tunku Abdul Rahman. We have your net. You fools, go back to Lubok Antu or we'll get you.' This made everyone aware that the Indonesians were monitoring the battalion's communications, and highlighted the need for radio security. DOBOPS Weekly Assessment, 21–28 Aug 1965, Borneo Box 6, MOD. See also Barber & Lord, *Swift and Sure*, pp. 165–80.

109 1950/3 G/MWB, 17 Aug 1965, WO 305/1565.

110 Gurr, *Voices from a Border War*, p. 131.

111 MW/FS/18, 4 Sep 1965, WO 305/1569.

112 MW/FS/14, 10 Sep 1965, WO 305/1569.

113 Weekly Intelligence Summary No. 31, ending 1 Sep 1965, 1400/2/2 G/MWB, dated 2 Sep 1965, WO 305/1566.

114 Brigadier B. Bestic, interview, 2 Jun 1992.

115 MW/FS/16, 5 Oct 1965, WO 305/1569.

116 MWB/FS/18, 14 Oct 1965, WO 305/1569.

117 Gurr, *Voices from a Border War*, pp. 134–9, 152–3. This operation is described in Christopher Bullock, *Journeys Hazardous: Gurkha Clandestine Operations Borneo 1965*, Square One Publications, Worcester, 1994, pp. 76–122.

118 Gurr, *Voices from a Border War*, pp. 139, 152–3.

119 Harold James & Denis Sheil-Small, *A Pride of Gurkhas: The 2nd King Edward VII's Own Goorkhas 1948–1971*, Leo Cooper, London, 1975, pp. 200–6.

120 See Grey's excellent summary in Dennis & Grey, *Emergency and Confrontation*, pp. 282–4.

121 There was one further unofficial incursion in the battalion area before 1RNZIR handed over to 1 RENJER. At 3 a.m. on 14 October, Deputy Superintendent R. Graver, GM, with a two-platoon group from B Company Police Field Force (PFF), mounted an unauthorised attack on a dug-in Indonesian post at Nanggan Anggan, two miles across the border. During the attack, Graver was mortally wounded when he climbed onto the roof of a bunker and fired into an adjacent hut, calling on its

occupants to surrender. The PFF assault group withdrew under fire, dragging Graver for some 500 yards until it was confirmed that he was dead. They then left his body and withdrew to the border. It seems that Graver, who was intensely unhappy at the abrupt end of his relationship with a local woman, intended to mount an attack from the moment he set out on patrol. CSC 422/20, 14 Oct 1965, Special Report Police Field Force Contact 2nd Division—14 Oct 1965, WO 305/1569.

122 The casualties inflicted on the enemy in East Malaysia between 1 January 1965 and 26 March 1966, when offensive CLARET operations ceased, totalled 144 killed and 92 wounded. From 30 January 1965, when undeniable CLARET operations were authorised, 502 known casualties were inflicted inside Kalimantan. During these operations there were 116 contacts; in 93 of them, casualties were inflicted on the Indonesian forces without loss. In the remaining 23 contacts, Commonwealth forces lost 10 killed, 33 wounded, and three missing believed killed. Dennis & Grey, *Emergency and Confrontation*, p. 281.

123 Ironically, the next time a battalion-size New Zealand group was deployed it was to East Timor in September 1999, as part of a multinational force sent in response to the Indonesian Army's inability (or unwillingness) to control pro-Indonesian militia reprisals after an overwhelming vote for independence from Indonesia.

124 Gurr, interview.

125 For details of 4RAR's tour, see Dennis & Grey, *Emergency and Confrontation*, pp. 282–99.

126 Poananga to McKinnon, 10 Mar 1966, Army 15/2 pt 3.

127 Thorpe, notes on draft.

128 Poananga to McKinnon, 10 Mar 1966, Army 15/2 pt 3.

129 This required Cheyne's West Brigade Headquarters to arrange for the building of accommodation and ablutions for an additional company at Balai Ringin. The cost of £6,500 was charged to the New Zealand government. The submission to the Minister of Finance wryly noted that it was 'not practicable to insist that 1RNZIR goes only to areas where full accommodation exists', and that 'efforts are being made to ensure that other New Zealand expenditure in Borneo is kept as low as possible'. Minute to Minister of Finance (T.42/255/20/4), 20 Apr 1966, and attached papers, 'Works Expenditure on Behalf 1RNZIR in Borneo', Army 15/2 pt 3.

130 Poananga to McKinnon, 10 Mar 1966, Army 15/2 pt 3.

131 15701 Personal Directive from Commander West Brigade [99 Gurkha Inf Bde] to Lt-Col B. M. Poananga, MBE, Comd 1 RNZIR, 3 May 1966, Commander's Diary 99 Gurkha Inf Bde, May 1966, Army 15/2 pt 3.

132 Poananga to McKinnon, 10 Mar 1966, Army 15/2 pt 3.

133 Notes by Brigadier J. L. Smith. See Major P. J. Fry (ed.), *The First Battalion Royal New Zealand Infantry Regiment Journal, 25th Anniversary Commemorative Edition*, Dieppe Barracks, Singapore, 1982, p. 26.

134 This was taken over from 1/10th GR in an inter-battalion boundary adjustment on 17 June 1966.

135 Brigadier R. T. V. Taylor, interview, 1 Jun 1992.

136 Poananga was concerned about having only one helicopter as 'the workhorse for moving men and fragile stores between Bn HQ and the forward bases'. He explored the possibility of attaching two Sioux Light Helicopters, which would be 'invaluable for recces, casualty evacuation, liaison and the passage of sensitive documents', from 3 Battlefield Support Squadron RNZAF in New Zealand, but this was not approved. Army 15/2 pt 3.

137 A film shows a Belvedere, an RN Wessex, a Whirlwind and a Scout on the pad at Balai Ringin at the same time. Brigadier J. L. Smith, notes.

138 For an assessment of the abortive coup and its origins, see Crouch, *The Army and Politics in Indonesia*; J. Hughes, *The End of Sukarno: A Coup that Misfired: A Purge that Ran Wild*, Angus & Robertson, London, 1968; and Oey Hong Lee, 'Sukarno and the Pseudo-Coup of 1965: Ten Years Later', *Journal of Southeast Asian Studies*, vol. 7, no. 1, Mar 1976, pp. 119–35. There is an increasingly strong belief that the coup was started by disgruntled groups within the Indonesian armed forces, rather than being a plot by the Indonesian Communist Party, which became the scapegoat.

139 DOBOPS Weekly Assessment, 4–10 Jun 1966, Borneo Box 6, MOD.

140 DOBOPS Weekly Assessment, 11–17 Jun 1966, Borneo Box 6, MOD. See also Dennis & Grey, *Emergency and Confrontation*, pp. 292–5.

141 Joint Report on the Borneo Campaign, 10 Nov 1966, CINCFE 9/67, copy issued by Malaysian Armed Forces Staff College, Winton Papers.

142 1RNZIR 'Planning Directive June 1966' (G/OPS/1), 12 Jun 1966, WA-M 1/1/29.

143 'Brief for Visiting VIPs on 1RNZIR Role', WA-M 1/1/29.

144 1RNZIR 'Planning Directive June 1966' (G/OPS/1), 12 Jun 1966, WA-M 1/1/29.

145 1RNZIR 'Planning Directive II', 19 Jun 1966, WA-M 1/1/29.

146 1RNZIR Commander's Diary, 'Durbar – 1 Jul 1966', WA-M 1/1/30.

147 Chamberlain, interview.

148 Webb, interview.

149 Extract from *Sarawak Tribune*, 19 Sep 1966. See summary of Hearts and Minds effort on Op Picture File for Op Hudson, Army S.31/2/6 pt 3.

150 Brown, interview. See Brigadier Sir Bernard Fergusson's account of his visit to 1RNZIR in *Travel Warrant*, quoted in Fry (ed.), *The First Battalion Royal New Zealand Infantry Regiment Journal, 25th Anniversary Commemorative Edition*, pp. 90–1.

151 Brown, interview.

152 Taylor, interview.

153 Taylor, interview.

154 The Final Issue, *Morning Glory*, WA-M 1/1/33.

155 'Plan for Withdrawal of British, Australian and New Zealand Forces from East Malaysia', CDS to Minister of Defence, MOD 3/5/1, 22 Sep 1966, and other correspondence on MOD 3/5/1 pt 1. 'National Operations Committee', Lt-Col A. W. Fitchett, NZ ADLO, NZ High Commission Kuala Lumpur, to Secretary, Chiefs of Staff Committee (127/10/3), 16 Aug 1965, and correspondence on MOD 3/5/12.

156 Between May and the end of August, the RAF Detachment moved 3,724 personnel and 557,191 lb of freight through Balai Ringin.

157 1RNZIR Monthly Report: Sep 1966, 16.4, dated 15 Oct 1966, WA-M 1/1/34.

158 Pte R. W. Wallace, interview, 1RNZIR Tape, RNZAF Museum, Christchurch.

159 WA-M 1/1/33.

160 'Personal message from the Commander in Chief to all ranks of Far East Command', 160345Z Aug 1966, MOD 3/5/1.

161 1RNZIR Commander's Diary, Oct 1966, WA-M 1/1/34.

162 Notes by Brigadier J. L. Smith.

163 I. C. McGibbon, 'New Zealand's Involvement in the Vietnamese War 1960–1965', MS, Ministry of Defence, Wellington, 1974. Wing-Commander Ian MacFarling, RAAF, 'Facts and Figures on the Deployment of New Zealand Troops in South Vietnam 1964–1972', Annex A to 'New Zealand and the Vietnam Conflict', *Defence Force Journal,* no. 79, Nov/Dec 1989.

164 28 CW Bde Planning Commitments, No. 164, JOZWEL to SOZSING, 140630Z Apr 1965, Army 31/2/3. Also 'Policy for Using Units of 28 Commonwealth Brigade on Periodic Tours in Borneo in Relation to their SEATO Role', Lt-Col Holloway, DLA Singapore, to Secretary Chiefs of Staff Committee and Secretary of External Affairs (408/5/1), 28 Apr 1965, Army 31/2/3.

165 'Post Confrontation Level of New Zealand Forces in Malaysia/Singapore', COS (66)68, 24 Aug 1966 and correspondence, MOD 3/5/1.

166 Ritchie Ovendale, *British Defence Policy Since 1945*, Manchester University Press, Manchester, 1994, pp. 131–57. Derek McDougall, 'The Wilson Government and the British Defence Commitment in Malaysia-Singapore', *Journal of Southeast Asian Studies*, vol. 4, no. 2, Sep 1973, pp. 229–40.

167 *New Zealand External Affairs Review*, vol. 17, Jul 1967, pp. 24–5; Ian McGibbon, 'Forward Defence: The Southeast Asian Commitment', in Malcolm McKinnon (ed.), *New Zealand in World Affairs, Volume II: 1957–1972*, New Zealand Institute of International Affairs, Wellington, 1991, p. 32; Alan & Robin Burnett, *The Australia and New Zealand Nexus*, Australian Institute of International Affairs/New Zealand Institute of International Affairs, Canberra, 1978, pp. 80–1.

168 'Planning Inf Coy', no. 231, Non File Material Army, HQ NZ Defence Force. V Company was commanded by Major J. A. Mace; Taylor, interview. 'A Report on the Chief of General Staff's Exercise 1972', in I. C. McGibbon (ed.), *The New Zealand Army in Vietnam*, Army General Staff, Wellington, 1973, states that V Company was deployed in April 1967; but it arrived in South Vietnam on 8 May. See Brock, *The Diplomat in Uniform*, p. 10.

169 McGibbon, 'Forward Defence', p. 31. See also McGibbon (ed.), *The New Zealand Army in Vietnam*, pp. 22-8; McGibbon, 'New Zealand's Involvement in the Vietnamese War'; Geoffrey Bentley & Maurice Conly, *Portrait of an Air Force*, Grantham House, Wellington, 1987, pp. 157–60; Matthew Wright, *Kiwi Air Power: The History of the RNZAF*, Reed, Auckland, 1998, pp. 146–7.

170 MacFarling, 'Facts and Figures on the Deployment of New Zealand Troops in South Vietnam', p. 93.
171 R. H. Wade, NZHC, to Dato Ghazali bin Shafie, Secretary of External Affairs, Kuala Lumpur, 9 Jun 1965, KL 103/6/3, NZ High Commission, Kuala Lumpur.
172 Kuala Lumpur to Wellington 406, 16 Jul 1965, KL 103/6/3.
173 Wellington to Kuala Lumpur 169, 21 Feb 1967, KL 103/6/3.
174 Kuala Lumpur to Wellington 160, 28 Feb 1967, KL 103/6/3.
175 NZHC Kuala Lumpur to Secretary of External Affairs, 17 Mar 1963, KL 103/6/3.
176 Singapore to Wellington 115, 6 Mar 1967, KL 103/6/3.
177 Wellington to London 700, Canberra 222, 21 Feb 1967, KL 103/6/3.
178 Singapore to Wellington 82, 22 Feb 1967, KL 103/6/3.
179 NZHC London to Secretary of External Affairs, 7 Apr 1967, KL 103/6/3.
180 Taylor, interview.
181 Malaysia: Visit of Tun Razak to New Zealand, filed 26 Apr 1967, KL 102/1/1.
182 McGibbon, 'Forward Defence', pp. 33–6.
183 See 'Outline Plan re Rundown/Total Withdrawal of British Forces from Malaysia/ Singapore and Brunei', and various planning papers, nos 64–88, Army Non File Material, HQ NZ Defence Force. See also Keith Jackson, '"Because it's there...": A Consideration of the Decision to Commit New Zealand Troops to Malaysia Beyond 1971', *Journal of Southeast Asian Studies*, vol. 2, Mar 1971, pp. 22–31.
184 H. B. Eaton, *Something Extra: 28 Commonwealth Brigade, 1951–1974*, Durham, 1993, pp. 298–9.
185 McGibbon, 'Forward Defence', pp. 34–5. Jim Rolfe, *New Zealand's Security: Alliances and Other Military Relationships*, CSS Working Paper 10/97, Centre for Strategic Studies, Wellington, 1997, p. 14.
186 'History of New Zealand Force South East Asia', MS, May 1980, pp. 1–13. Copy in author's possession.
187 The author was SO1 Operations, HQ NZ Force SEA in 1986–87.

## 11 The New Zealand Armed Forces in South-East Asia, 1949–66

1 Colonel D. W. S. Moloney, interview, 8 Oct 1992.
2 COS (51)M.13, 4 Dec 1951, JSO 1/4/3/3.
3 Elsie Locke, *Peace People: A History of Peace Activities in New Zealand*, Hazard Press, Christchurch, 1992, pp. 151–7.
4 Former WO1 H. E. Chamberlain of Wellington is compiling a nominal roll of all servicemen who served in Korea, Malaya, Borneo and Vietnam. An incomplete list of individual Army postings can be found on 'HQ NZ Army Force FARELF – RF Personnel Selected', AD 1, 243/1/98, pts 2, 3.
5 See Ian McGibbon, *New Zealand and the Korean War, Vol. 2, Combat Operations*, Oxford University Press, Auckland, 1996, pp. 46, 366, 383.

6 A visit to Malaya by the former war artist Peter McIntyre to paint a series for all three services was approved in 1961, but apparently never made. 'Visit – Peter McIntyre to NZ Forces in Malaya', AD 1, 242/7/150.

7 'New Zealand's Defence Effort in Asia and the Pacific', under cover of NZ HC London to Secretary of External Affairs, 30 Jun 1965, JSO 3/1/5.

# *Bibliography*

## Unpublished sources—official

### Australia

AUSTRALIAN ARCHIVES, MITCHELL, ACT

Department of Defence: CRS A1945 Department of Defence, correspondence files, classified, 1957–66.

Department of Foreign Affairs and Trade: CRS A1838 Department of External Affairs, correspondence files, 1948–60.

Department of Prime Minister and Cabinet: CRS A4940 Cabinet files, Menzies and Holt ministries, 1949–67.

### Fiji

FIJI ARCHIVES, SUVA

SF. A8 1FIR Malaya, 1952–56.

FIJI MILITARY FORCES ARCHIVES, QUEEN ELIZABETH BARRACKS, SUVA

1FIR War Diary.

### Malaysia

NEW ZEALAND HIGH COMMISSION, KUALA LUMPUR

KL 102 Units.

KL 103 Assistance to Vietnam.

## New Zealand


ALEXANDER TURNBULL LIBRARY, WELLINGTON

H. W. R. Petersen Papers (including B Company 1FIR War Diaries and Reports 1952–56), 89-074.

ARCHIVES NEW ZEALAND, HEAD OFFICE, WELLINGTON

*Air Department (Air)*

Air 1 Registered Subject Files, 1935–70.

Air 149 No. 14 (F) Squadron RNZAF Unit History, 1942–68.

Air 167 No. 75 (NZ) Squadron RNZAF Unit History, 1916–19, 1937–70.

*Army Department (AD)*

AD 1 Inwards Letters and Registered Files.

AD-W6 Central Military District, Registered Subject Files.

*Navy Department (N)*

N 1 Registered Subject Files, 1913–55.

N 2 Registered Secret Subject Files, 1925–49.

N 109 HMNZS *Royalist*, Ships Records, 1959–66.

N 112 HMNZS *Otago*, Ships Records, 1961–68.

N 113 HMNZS *Taranaki*, Ships Records, 1961–65.

*Headquarters New Zealand Defence Force (ABFK)*

Series 7232 RNZAF Unit Histories, 1944–95.

Accession W3788 1RNZIR War Diaries.

Accession W4010 Registered Subject Files: subseries 62 Operations: Movements of HMNZ Ships; subseries 66 Personnel; subseries 68/3/- Minutes of Naval Board Meetings, 1960–64; subseries 72/3/- Reports of Proceedings, HMNZ Ships.

*Ministry of External Relations and Trade/Ministry of Foreign Affairs and Trade, Head Office (ABHS)*

Series 950, Accession W4627; subseries 153 Conferences; subseries 253 Malaysia; subseries 420 Malaysia; subseries 434 Defence of Southeast Asia; subseries 438 Southeast Asia.

*Nash Papers (NASH)*

*War Archives (WA)*

WA–M Malayan Emergency.

MINISTRY OF FOREIGN AFFAIRS AND TRADE, WELLINGTON

PM 87 NZ Forces Overseas.

PM 156 Defence.

PM 120 SEATO Military Aspects.

Baker, T. C., 'New Zealand Involvement in Vietnam, 1961–1966', unpublished narrative, 1971.

Mullins, R. M., 'ANZAM', unpublished typescript, 1971.

NEW ZEALAND DEFENCE FORCE HEADQUARTERS, WELLINGTON

*Air Department*

Air 202 Liaison Letters; Air 204 Committees; Air 206 Training Operational; Air 213 Aircraft; Air 221 Operations; Air 223 Plans; Air 226 Commonwealth Defence; Air 227 Organisation; Air 250 SEATO Planning (non file material).

*Army Department*

Army 14 Manuals; Army 15 New Zealand Forces Overseas; Army 23 Commonwealth Defence, Fiji; Army 31 New Zealand Force Southeast Asia; Army 33 SEATO Planning; Army 34/9 Aid to Malaysia; Army 34/12 Defence of Southeast Asia; Army 95 Visits to NZ and Overseas (including Honours and Awards; non file material).

*Joint Services Organisation*

JSO 1 Defence Organisation in New Zealand; JSO 2 New Zealand Defence Policy; JSO 4 New Zealand Forces; JSO 15 Administration; JSO 17 Defence Policy RNZN; JSO 18 Defence Policy RNZAF; JSO 24 SEATO; JSO 25 Defence of the Pacific; JSO 26 Commonwealth Defence; JSO 29 Higher Military Direction and Command; JSO 31 Plans; JSO 33 SEATO Exercises; JSO 34 Regional Defence; JSO 35 Overseas Liaison; JSO 41 ANZAM; JSO 42 Regional Defence; JSO 43 Commonwealth Defence; JSO 140 Southeast Asia; JSO 142 Malaya; JSO 152.

*Ministry of Defence*

MOD 3 Commonwealth Defence; MOD 5 ANZAM; MOD 22 Operations and Planning (non file material).

McGibbon, I. C., 'New Zealand's Involvement in the Vietnamese War 1960–1965', 1974.

*Directorate of Defence Intelligence*

New Zealand Operations in Borneo, 1965–66.

*Navy*

Non file material.

*Base records*

Personal files.

NZ SAS GROUP ARCHIVES, HOBSONVILLE

1 NZ SAS Squadron Unit Diaries, and Major Frank Rennie, Correspondence 1955–57, Rennie Papers.

Papers and Monthly Reports, Detachments, 1 NZ Ranger Squadron (Far East), 1965–66.

**1RNZIR MUSEUM, LINTON CAMP**

1NZ Regt, 2NZ Regt and 1RNZIR Unit War Diaries.

Burrows, Brigadier I. H., 'Confrontation 1RNZIR Operations 1965'.

White, WO2 W. J., 1NZ Regt 1957–59, 'Journey to & Early Days In Malaya, Extracts from Letters Home', and papers.

### United Kingdom

Most of the official United Kingdom records used in this history had not been reviewed for selection and transfer to the Public Record Office, London, or been given Public Record Office reference numbers, when seen by the author. They have therefore been cited with their original references. The main PRO classes consulted were:

DEFE 4 Chiefs of Staff Committee, Minutes of Meetings, 1947– .

DEFE 5 Chiefs of Staff Committee, Memoranda, 1947– .

DEFE 6 Chiefs of Staff Committee, Joint Planning Staff Reports, 1947– .

DEFE 11 Chiefs of Staff Committee, Registered Files, 1946– .

WO 32 Registered Files.

WO 291 Military Operation Research, 1941– .

WO 305 Unit Historical Records and Reports (Commanders' Diaries).

## Unpublished sources—unofficial

### Personal papers and correspondence

Boswell, Captain G., RNZAC, correspondence with author.

Burdett, Mr F., correspondence with author and notes on draft.

Burrows, Brigadier I. H., letters 1 NZ SAS Squadron 1955–57, 'Li Hak Chi Kill: NZ SAS, Burrows' Account', Steve Watene, BEM, Eulogy at Interment of Ashes, Dargaville, 18 May 1996, and correspondence with author.

Cameron, WO1 Ross, letters and diaries, 1NZ SAS Squadron, 1955–57.

Chamberlain, WO1 H. E., notes on drafts, correspondence, and 1RNZIR photos, Malaysia and Borneo 1964–66.

Comber, Mr Leon, extracts from Yuen Yuet Leng, 'Operation Ginger' manuscript, and correspondence with author.

Dennerly, Lieutenant-Commander P. Y., RNZN, notes on drafts and correspondence with author.

Dickens, Dr David, papers and correspondence with author.

Fairfax, Lieutenant-Commander D., notes on drafts.

Fraser, Trooper Hugh, 'Happiness is Knowing One's Place', unpublished memoir and photo collection, 1 NZ SAS Squadron, 1955–57.

Grover, Mr Ray, comments on drafts and correspondence with author.

Gurr, Brigadier R. M., draft of *Voices from a Border War*, notes on drafts and correspondence with author.

Hall, Lieutenant-Colonel M. J., RNZIR, personal copy of Major C. E. Brock, *The Diplomat in Uniform: A History of the First Battalion Royal New Zealand Infantry Regiment* (with marginal notes), platoon notebook, and correspondence with author.

Harrison, Squadron Leader Paul, RNZAF, correspondence with author.

Hurle, Major R. S., RNZIR, diaries, notes and maps, 1 NZ SAS Squadron 1955–57, notes on drafts and correspondence with author.

Jansen, Mr M. M., research material for MA thesis, 'The New Zealand Army in Malay(si)a and Singapore 1955–1967'.

McIntyre, Air Commodore Stuart, correspondence with author and notes on draft.

McIvor, Lieutenant-General D. S., correspondence with author and notes on draft.

McKay, Captain G. M., correspondence with author.

McKeon, Lieutenant-Colonel S. R., letter to Brigadier I. H. Burrows re draft.

McNaught, Malcolm, written reminiscences of No. 14 Squadron RNZAF, Tengah, 1955–56.

Mann, Dr Robert, notes on drafts and correspondence with author.

Manuera, Lieutenant-Colonel E. I., RNZIR, correspondence with author.

Mataira, Lieutenant-Colonel A. T. A., RNZIR, correspondence on drafts with author.

Meldrum, Major W. J., RNZIR, 'No. 6 Platoon (Quiz Kids) Jungle Drills', B Coy, 1 NZ Regt, February 1958, patrol reports, 1NZ Regt 1957–59, notes on drafts and correspondence with author.

Morrison, Brigadier W. R. K., personal scrapbook and notes on drafts.

O'Dwyer, Captain Noel, scrapbook, 1NZ SAS Squadron, 1955–57.

Ogilvy, Lieutenant-Colonel David, correspondence with author.

Pearce, Major-General L. A., papers.

Pearce, Colonel R., letters, diaries, pilot's log book and maps, Malaysia and North Borneo, No. 656 Squadron RAAC, 1964–65.

Rolfe, Dr James, notes on draft and correspondence with author.

Saull, Rear-Admiral K. Michael, correspondence with author.

Smith, Brigadier J. L., Exercise GEDGLEY papers and notes on drafts.

Thorpe, Brigadier R. I., notes on drafts and correspondence with author.

Wade, Mr R. Hunter, correspondence with author.

Wallace, Lieutenant-Colonel N. A., RNZIR, manuscript on 1NZ Regt intelligence operations, 1957–59.

Wallingford, Group Captain Geoff, RNZAF, notes on RNZAF history, notes on draft and correspondence with author.

Webster, Captain J., correspondence with author.

Wells, Lieutenant-Colonel Bryan, 'The Breaking of the High Frequency (HF) Paradigm', manuscript.

West, Mr J. J., 'Memorandum by Lieutenant-Colonel J. M. Calvert, DSO, RE, Police Increment of proposed Special Force "The Malayan Scouts"', and draft appreciation, 'Perak Aborigines in the Emergency', Ipoh, 19 October 1953.

Winton, Lieutenant-Colonel M. J., 'Joint Report on the Borneo Campaign', 10 November 1966, CINCFE 9/67 (copy issued by Malaysian Armed Forces Staff College).

## Interviews

### AUSTRALIAN WAR MEMORIAL, CANBERRA

Harvey, Colonel J., interview.

### AUTHOR

Note: The master copies of these interviews are deposited in the Oral History Centre, National Library of New Zealand, Wellington.

Ackland, Lieutenant J., FMF, 23 November 1991.
Aitken, Brigadier D. J., 27 October 1992.
Aldridge, Colonel T. A., 3 June 1992.
Babbington, WO1 T. T., 12 March 1992.
Barclay, WO1 F. D., 17 June 1993.
Barker, Major J. R. M., RNZIR, 17 February 1992.
Bestic, Brigadier B., 2 June 1992.
Boswell, Captain Graham, RNZAC, 30 September 1991.
Brighouse, Major G., RNZIR, 3 October 1991.
Bright, Air Commodore Nelson, RNZAF, 9 June 1993.
Brown, Lieutenant-Colonel J. W., RNZIR, 9 March 1993.
Brown, Lieutenant-Colonel V. B., RNZA, 21 November 1991.
Burns, Brigadier John, 12 April 1999.
Burrows, Brigadier I. H., 3 October 1991, and subsequent interviews and discussions.
Burt, Lieutenant-Colonel H. R., RNZIR, 24 October 1992.
Cameron, WO1 Ross, RNZAMC, 25 February 1992.
Chamberlain, WO1 H. E., RNZE, 15 March 1993.
Cheam Yeom Toon, August 1992.
Cooke, Mrs Doreen, 7 April 1993.
Cooper, Captain Bill RNZIR, 9 November 1992.
Dattaya, Mr M., August 1992.
Dearing, Lieutenant-Colonel R. S., RNZIR, 3 June 1992.
de Lorenzo, Group Captain D., RNZAF, 10 March 1993.
Devlin, Lieutenant-Colonel Martin, RNZIR, 23 March 1994.
Dixon, Lieutenant-Colonel J. A., RNZIR, 4 October 1991.
Edwards, Mr Bill, NZ SAS, 16 April 1992.
Edwards, Major Oliver, FMF, 30 November 1991.

Forsythe, Major I. F., RNZIR, 18 February 1992.
Gentry, Major-General Sir William, series of interviews, February 1991.
Gillard, Air Commodore I. A., RNZAF, 10 June 1993.
Gordon, Major-General K. M., 27 April 1992.
Grant, Lieutenant-Colonel L. G., RNZIR, 24 October 1992.
Gurr, Brigadier R. M., 13, 14 January 1993.
Haami, WO1 Kiriti, RNZIR, 16 November 1992.
Hall, Mrs Florence, 28 April 1993.
Hall, Lieutenant-Colonel M. J., RNZIR, 29 April 1993.
Harris, WO1 Rex, RNZIR, 2 June 1992.
Heke, Mr Dan, RNZIR, 10 November 1992.
Hill, Major Bruce, RNZIR, 16 June 1993.
Hornbrook, Major G., RNZIR, 5 June 1992.
Hosie, Air Vice-Marshal John, RNZAF, 8 March 1993.
Hotop, Lieutenant-Colonel P. G., RNZIR, 31 March 1992.
Hurle, Major R. S., RNZIR, 15 May 1992, and subsequent discussions.
Jacobs, Sergeant H. S., RNZIR, 21 January 1994.
James, Major H., RNZIR, 14 June 1993.
Jameson, Captain N. C., RNZAC, 13 February 1992.
Jamieson, Lieutenant Bruce, NZ Regt, 27 April 1993.
Jamieson, Air Marshal Sir Ewan, RNZAF, 10 June 1993.
Johnston, WO2 J. T., RNZIR, 14 October 1992.
Keegan, Mr J., RNZAF, 24 February 1993.
Keelan, Captain A. P., FMF, 22 November 1991.
Launder, Colonel I., 11 December 1991.
Low, Colonel H. J. G., 23 November 1991.
McIntyre, Air Commodore Stuart, RNZAF, 23 February 1993.
McIvor, Lieutenant-General D. S., 9 June 1992.
Mackintosh, Captain D., RNZIR, 26 September 1991.
McPherson, Wing Commander Eric, RNZAF, 10 March 1993.
Mace, Lieutenant-General Sir John, 4 November 1991, and subsequent interviews.
Mann, Colonel O. E., 8 April 1992, and subsequent interviews.
Manners, Wing Commander R. A., RNZAF, 27 May 1992.
Manning, Major R. A., RNZIR, 17 February 1992.
Manuera, Lieutenant-Colonel E. I., RNZIR, 23 September 1992, and subsequent interviews.
Martin, Major B. P., RNZIR, September 1991.
Martin, Mrs Fran, 24 October 1992.
Mataira, Lieutenant-Colonel A. T. A., 12 December 1991, and subsequent interviews and discussions.
Mate, Lieutenant-Colonel George, FMF, 28 November 1991.
Meldrum, Mrs Pru, 6 April 1993.
Meldrum, Major W. J., RNZIR, 9 March 1992.

Mogg, General Sir John, 10 August 1992.
Moloney, Colonel D. W. S., 8 October 1992.
Morrison, Mrs Anne, 13 May 1991.
Morrison, Brigadier W. R. K., series of interviews beginning 11 February 1991.
Moss, Air Commodore Harold, RNZAF, 9 June 1993.
Nasilivata, Lieutenant-Colonel Levi, FMF, 29 November 1991.
Neville, Air Vice-Marshal Pat, RNZAF, 11 June 1993.
O'Brien, Major C. G., RNZIR, 22 November 1991.
O'Dwyer, Captain Noel RNZAC, October 1991.
Ogilvy, Lieutenant-Colonel David, RNZIR, 5 May 1992.
Palmer, Air Commodore Michael, RNZAF, 11 June 1993.
Pearce, Major-General L. A., 9 March 1992.
Pearce, Colonel R., 13 November 1992.
Polaschek, WO1 Alan, RNZIR, 19 February 1992.
Quested, Major T. A., RNZAC, 1 October 1991.
Rennie, Colonel F., 8 March 1992.
Ritchie, Lieutenant-Colonel Max, RNZIR, 1992.
Rutledge, WO1 Peter, RNZIR, 27 October 1992.
Sands, Sergeant John ('Paddy'), NZ Regt, 25 October 1992.
Shattky, Major Gray, RNZIR, 28 October 1992.
Slim, Colonel the Viscount John, 30 July 1992.
Slocombe, Captain David, RNZIR, 4 June 1992.
Smith, Lieutenant-Colonel D. S., RNZCT, 25 January 1994.
Smith, WO2 Dick, RNZIR, 6 November 1992.
Smith, Lieutenant-Colonel Ian ('Tanky'), SAS, 30 July 1992.
Smith, Brigadier J. L., 1992.
Spiers, Major J. M., RNZIR, 4 June 1992.
Steele, WO2 Arthur, RNZIR, 27 October 1992.
Takala, Major Jack, FMF, 29 November 1991.
Taylor, Brigadier R. T. V., 1 June 1992.
Thornton, Lieutenant-General Sir Leonard, series of interviews, March and April 1992.
Thorpe, Brigadier R. I., 19 November 1991.
Tucker, Group Captain A. F., RNZAF, 26 February 1993.
Wait, Mr R. J. C., 8 August 1992.
Wallace, Lieutenant-Colonel N. A., RNZIR, 12 March 1992.
Wallingford, Group Captain Geoff, RNZAF, 18 February 1993.
Webb, WO1 Neil, RNZIR, 16 March 1994.
Webster, Captain J., RNZIR, 22 November 1991.
Wells, Lieutenant-Colonel B. P., RNZ Sig, 11 June 1992.
West, Mr J. J., 7 August 1992.
Williams, Colonel L. G., 18 February 1992.
Williams, Major-General R. G., 10 April 1992.
Wilson, WO2 Danny, RNZIR, 14 June 1993.

Winton, Lieutenant-Colonel S. J. M., RNZIR, 22 October 1992.
Withers, Mrs Joyce, 6 May 1993.
Withers, Major R. P., RNZIR, 9 June 1993.
Woodhouse, Lieutenant-Colonel J. W., 11 August 1992.
Yandall, Lieutenant Earle, 4 October 1991.

IMPERIAL WAR MUSEUM, LONDON
West, Mr J. J., interviews.

ROYAL NEW ZEALAND AIR FORCE MUSEUM, CHRISTCHURCH
Smith, Squadron Leader K. B., RNZAF.
Wallace, Mr R., 1RNZIR.
Westgate, Mr Errol, NZ Regt.

ROYAL NEW ZEALAND NAVAL MUSEUM, AUCKLAND
Bruce, Warrant Officer T. A., RNZN, DLA 0161.
Carl, Captain C. J., RNZN, DLA 0102.
Carter, Chief Petty Officer Fire Control 1st Class J. L. C., RNZN, 16 January 1998.
Kempthorne, Commander A. V., OBE, September 1990.
Pound, Captain G. D., CBE, DSC, RN, June 1991.
Rees, Chief Petty Officer Seaman J. R., RNZN, 16 January 1998.
Saull, Rear-Admiral K. M., CB, RNZN, October 1993, DLA 117.
Steward, Rear-Admiral C. J., CB, RNZN, June 1992.
Thorne, Rear-Admiral E. C., RNZN, DLA 0101.
Wright, Lieutenant-Commander G. C., February 1994, DLA 0085.

## Published sources—official

### Allied Geographical Section, South West Pacific Area

SPECIAL REPORTS
*No. 79, S. W. Borneo*, 24 July 1945.
*No. 81, Kuching (Sarawak, Borneo)*, 28 August 1945.

TERRAIN STUDIES
*No. 89, Sarawak and Brunei, Vol. 1: Text and Maps, Vol. 2: Photographs*, 25 September 1944.
*No. 90, North Borneo*, 15 November 1944.
*No. 109, S. E. Borneo*, 15 January 1945.

### Australia

Australian Military Forces, *The Indonesian Army*, Army Headquarters, Canberra, 1966.

## Fiji

*Fiji Royal Gazette,* Government Press, Suva, 1952–56.

## Malaya/Malaysia

Federation of Malaya, *Federation of Malaya Annual Report,* Government Printer, Kuala Lumpur, 1949–55.

HQ Malaya, *The Conduct of Anti-Terrorist Operations in Malaya*, Kuala Lumpur, 1952.

Malaysia, Department of Information, *Indonesian Involvement in Eastern Malaysia*, Kuala Lumpur, n.d.

## New Zealand

*Appendix to the Journals of the House of Representatives*: A-19 Review of Defence Policy, 1961; H-4 Ministry of Defence, Annual Report, 1964–67; H-5 Royal New Zealand Navy, Annual Report, 1948–63; H-19 Military Forces of New Zealand, Annual Report, 1949; H-37 Air Department, Annual Report, 1949–63.

New Zealand Army, Annual Report, 1950–63.

*Documents on New Zealand External Relations*, Department of Internal Affairs, Wellington: *Vol. I: The Australian–New Zealand Agreement*, 1972; *Vol. II: The Surrender and Occupation of Japan*, 1982; *Vol. III: The ANZUS Pact and the Treaty of Peace with Japan*, 1985.

Ministry of Defence (I. C. McGibbon, ed.), *The New Zealand Army in Vietnam 1964–1972: A Report on the Chief of the General Staff's Exercise 1972*, Army General Staff, Wellington, 1973.

Ministry of Foreign Affairs, *New Zealand Foreign Policy, Statements and Documents, 1943–1957*, Government Printer, Wellington, 1972.

New Zealand Army, *New Zealand Army Quarterly Liaison Letters*, Government Printer, Wellington, 1950–67.

New Zealand Military Forces, *Appointments, Promotions, Transfers, etc.*, Government Printer, Wellington, 1949.

*New Zealand Official Yearbook*, 1947–68.

*New Zealand Parliamentary Debates*, 1949–67.

*Statutes of New Zealand 1908–1957*, Volume II, 1960.

## United Kingdom

Blair, C. N. M., *Guerilla Warfare*, Ministry of Defence, London, 1957.

Far East Command, *1948–1971 The Dead of the British Commonwealth West Malaysia*, FARELF, Singapore, 1971.

Her Majesty's Government, *Arrangements for the Employment of Overseas Commonwealth Forces in Emergency Operations in Malaya after Independence*, HMSO, London, September 1957.

Mansergh, N., *Documents and Speeches on British Commonwealth Affairs 1931–1952*, Oxford University Press, London, 1953.

——*Documents and Speeches on Commonwealth Affairs 1951–1962*, Oxford University Press, London, 1963.

Royal Air Force, *Air Support*, Air Ministry, London, 1955.

——*The Malayan Emergency 1948–1960*, Ministry of Defence, London, June 1970. Later published as M. R. Postgate, *Operation Firedog: Air Support in the Malayan Emergency 1948–1960*, HMSO, London, 1992.

Stockwell, A. J. (ed.), *Malaya, Part III: The Alliance Route to Independence 1953–1957*, British Documents on the End of Empire, HMSO, London, 1995.

War Office, Military Training Pamphlet No. 52, *Warfare in the Far East*, December 1944.

## Published sources—general

### Newspapers and periodicals

*Auckland Star*, 1949–66; *Dominion* (Wellington), 1949–66; *Evening Post* (Wellington), 1949–66; *New Zealand Herald* (Auckland), 1949–66; *Otago Daily Times* (Dunedin), 1949–66; *Press* (Christchurch), 1949–66; *Weekly News/New Zealand Weekly News*, 1949–66.

*Keesing's Contemporary Archives*, Keesing's Publications, Bristol, 1949–66.

### Books and pamphlets

Allen, C., *The Savage Wars of Peace*, Futura, London, 1990.

Allen, R., *Malaysia: Prospect and Retrospect*, Oxford University Press, London, 1968.

Anak Agung Gde Agung, Ide, *Twenty Years Indonesian Foreign Policy 1945–1965*, Mouton, The Hague/Paris, 1973.

Andrew, H., *Who Won the Malayan Emergency?*, Graham Brash, Singapore, 1995.

Asprey, R. B., *War in the Shadows*, Little, Brown & Co., London, 1994.

Bailey, M., *Aspects of the Australian Army Intelligence System during Confrontation and Vietnam*, Working Paper No. 22, Australian Defence Studies Centre, Australian Defence Force Academy, Canberra, 1994.

Baker, W. D., *Dare to Win: The Story of the New Zealand Special Air Service*, Lothian, Port Melbourne, 1987.

Bannister, C., *An Inch of Bravery: 3RAR in the Malayan Emergency 1957–59*, Directorate of Army Public Affairs, Sydney, 1994.

Barber, L., & C. Lord, *Swift and Sure: A History of the Royal New Zealand Corps of Signals and Army Signalling in New Zealand*, New Zealand Signals Incorporated, Auckland, 1996.

Barber, N., *The War of the Running Dogs*, Collins, London, 1971.

Barker, E., *The British Between the Superpowers, 1945–1950*, Macmillan, London, 1983.

Barnett, C., *The Collapse of British Power*, Eyre Methuen, London, 1972.

Bartlett, Vernon, *Report from Malaya*, Derek Verschoyle, London, 1954.

Bentley, G., *RNZAF: A Short History*, A. H. & A. W. Reed, Wellington, 1969.

Bentley, G., & M. Conly, *Portrait of an Air Force: The Royal New Zealand Air Force 1937–1987*, Grantham House, Wellington, 1987.

Blackman, R. V. B. (ed.), *Jane's Fighting Ships 1965–66*, Sampson Low, Marston & Co., Great Missenden, Bucks, 1966.

——*Jane's Fighting Ships 1950–51*, David & Charles Reprints, Newton Abbot, 1975.

Bloodworth, Dennis, *An Eye for the Dragon*, Secker & Warburg, London, 1970.

Boyce, Peter, *Malaysia and Singapore in International Diplomacy: Documents and Commentaries*, Sydney University Press, Sydney, 1968.

Brackman, A. C., *Southeast Asia's Second Front*, Pall Mall Press, London, 1966.

Bridge, C. (ed.), *Munich to Vietnam*, Melbourne University Press, Melbourne, 1991.

Bridgman, L. (ed.), *Jane's All the World's Aircraft 1952–53*, Sampson Low, London, 1953.

——*Jane's All the World's Aircraft 1954–55*, Jane's, London, 1955.

——*Jane's All the World's Aircraft 1955–1956*, Jane's, London, 1956.

Brock, C. E., *The Diplomat in Uniform: A History of the First Battalion Royal New Zealand Infantry Regiment*, 1RNZIR, Singapore, 1971.

Brown, B., *New Zealand Foreign Policy in Retrospect*, New Zealand Institute of International Affairs, Wellington, 1970.

Buchanan, I., *Singapore in Southeast Asia*, G. Bell & Sons, London, 1972.

Buchanan, K., *Out of Asia*, Sydney University Press, Sydney, 1968.

Bullock, Christopher, *Journeys Hazardous: Gurkha Clandestine Operations Borneo 1965*, Square One Publications, Worcester, 1994.

Burgess, A., *The Long Day Wanes: A Malayan Trilogy*, W. W. Norton, New York, 1964.

Burgess, M., *Ships of the Royal New Zealand Navy*, Southern Press, Wellington, 1979.

Burnett, A., & R. Burnett, *The Australia and New Zealand Nexus*, Australian Institute of International Affairs/New Zealand Institute of International Affairs, Canberra, 1978.

Buszynski, L., *Seato: The Failure of an Alliance Strategy*, Singapore University Press, Singapore, 1983.

Cable, J., *The Political Influence of Naval Force in History*, Macmillan, Basingstoke, 1998.

Campbell, A., *Jungle Green*, George Allen & Unwin, London, 1953.

——*Guerillas: A History and Analysis*, Arthur Barker, London, 1967.

Catley, B., & Dugis Vinsensio, *Australian Indonesian Relations Since 1945*, Ashgate, Sydney, 1998.

Chamberlain, H. E., *Service Lives Remembered: The Meritorious Service Medal in New Zealand and its Recipients 1895–1994*, self-published, Wellington, 1995.

Chapman, F. Spencer, *The Jungle is Neutral*, Chatto & Windus, London, 1949.

Chatham House Study Group, *Collective Defence in South East Asia*, Oxford University Press, London, 1956.

Cloake, J., *Riot and Revolution in Singapore and Malaya 1945–1963*, Faber & Faber, London, 1973.

——*Conflict and Violence in Singapore and Malaysia 1945–1983*, Singapore University Press, Singapore, 1984.

——*Templer, Tiger of Malaya*, Harrap, London, 1985.

Clutterbuck, R., *The Long Long War: The Emergency in Malaya 1948–1960*, Cassell, London, 1967.

Coates, J., *Suppressing Insurgency: An Analysis of the Emergency in Malaya, 1948–1954*, Westview Press, Boulder, Colorado, 1992.

Cody, J. F., *28 (Maori) Battalion*, Department of Internal Affairs, Wellington, 1956.

Cole, Barbara, *The Elite: The Story of the Rhodesian Special Air Service*, Three Knights, Transkei, 1984.

Coulthardt-Clark, C., *The RAAF in Vietnam: Australian Air Involvement in the Vietnam War 1962–1975*, Allen & Unwin in association with the Australian War Memorial, Sydney, 1995.

Cowan, J., *The Maoris in the Great War*, Maori Regimental Committee, Whitcombe & Tombs, Wellington, 1926.

Crawford, O., *The Door Marked Malaya*, Rupert Hart-Davis, London, 1958.

Crockett, A., *Green Beret, Red Star*, Eyre & Spottiswoode, London, 1954.

Cross, J. P., *Conflict in the Shadows: The Nature and Politics of Guerrilla Warfare*, Constable, London, 1964.

——*Jungle Warfare: Experience and Encounters*, Arms & Armour Press, London, 1989.

Crouch, H., *The Army and Politics in Indonesia*, Cornell University Press, Ithaca/London, 1978.

Darby, P., *British Defence Policy East of Suez 1947–1968*, Oxford University Press, London, 1973.

de la Billiere, Peter, *Looking for Trouble: An Autobiography from SAS to the Gulf*, Harper Collins, London, 1994.

Dennis, P., & J. Grey, *Emergency and Confrontation*, Allen & Unwin in association with the Australian War Memorial, Sydney, 1996.

——*The Second Fifty Years: The Australian Army 1947–1997*, Australian Defence Force Academy, Canberra, 1997.

Dennis, P., J. Grey, E. Morris & R. Prior, with J. Connor, *The Oxford Companion to Australian Military History*, Oxford University Press, Melbourne, 1995.

Dickens, P., *SAS Secret War in South East Asia* (originally titled *SAS: The Jungle Frontier*), Greenhill Books, London/Presidio Press, Novato, California, 1991.

Dobby, E. H. G., *Southeast Asia*, University of London Press, London, 1960.

Duxbury, D., R. Ewing & R. MacPherson, *Aircraft of the Royal New Zealand Air Force*, Heinemann, Auckland, 1987.

Eaton, H. B., *Something Extra: 28 Commonwealth Brigade, 1951–1974*, Pentland Press, Bishop Auckland, 1993.

Edwards, P., with G. Pemberton, *Crises and Commitments: The Politics and Diplomacy of Australia's Involvement in Southeast Asian Conflicts 1945–1965*, Allen & Unwin in association with the Australian War Memorial, Sydney, 1992.

Feuchtwanger, E. J. (ed.), *Perspectives upon British Defence Policy 1945–1970*, University of Southampton, Southampton, 1978.

Fisher, C. A., *South-East Asia: A Social, Economic and Political Geography*, Methuen & Co., London, 1964.

Franks, N., *Forever Strong: The Story of 75 Squadron RNZAF, 1916–1990*, Random Century, Auckland, 1991.

Freeman, D., *Report on the Iban*, Athlone Press, London, 1970.

Fry, P. J. (ed.), *The First Battalion Royal New Zealand Infantry Regiment Journal, 25th Anniversary Commemorative Edition*, 1RNZIR, Singapore, 1982.

Gaddis, J. L., *Strategies of Containment: A Critical Appreciation of Postwar American National Security Policy*, Oxford University Press, New York, 1982.

Gardiner, W., *Te Mura O Te Ahi: The Story of the Maori Battalion*, Reed, Auckland, 1992.

Geraghty, T., *Who Dares Wins: The Special Air Service, 1950 to the Gulf War*, Little, Brown & Co., London, 1992. Also, earlier edition, *Who Dares Wins: The Story of the Special Air Service 1950–1980*, Arms & Armour Press, London, 1980.

Gillespie, O. A., *The Pacific*, Department of Internal Affairs, Wellington, 1952.

Gordon, B. K., *New Zealand Becomes a Pacific Power*, University of Chicago Press, Chicago, 1960.

Grant, B., *Indonesia*, Melbourne University Press, Melbourne, 1996.

Grey, J., *A Military History of Australia*, Cambridge University Press, Melbourne, 1990.

——*Up Top: The Royal Australian Navy and Southeast Asian Conflicts 1955–1972*, Allen & Unwin, Sydney, 1998.

Gurr, R., *Voices from a Border War*, self-published, Melbourne, 1995.

Haigh, J. Bryant, *Men of Faith and Courage: The Official History of the New Zealand Chaplains Department*, Word Publishers, Auckland, 1983.

Haigh, J. Bryant, & Alan J. Polaschek, *New Zealand and the Distinguished Service Order*, self-published, Christchurch, 1993.

Hamilton, W. B., K. Robinson & C. D. W. Goodwin, *A Decade of Commonwealth, 1955–1964*, Duke University Press, Durham, NC, 1966.

Hanrahan, G. Z., *The Communist Struggle in Malaya*, University of Malaya Press, Kuala Lumpur, 1979.

Harper, T. N., *The End of Empire and the Making of Malaya*, Cambridge University Press, Cambridge, 1999.

Harrison, P., with B. Lockstone & A. Anderson, *The Golden Age of New Zealand Flying Boats*, Random House, Auckland, 1997.

Henniker, M. C. A., *Red Shadow over Malaya*, William Blackwood, Edinburgh, 1955.

Hindley, D., *The Communist Party of Indonesia 1951–1963*, University of California Press, Berkeley/Los Angeles, 1966.

*HMNZS Bellona*, RNZN Museum, Auckland, n.d.

*HMNZS Royalist*, RNZN Museum, Auckland, n.d.

*HMNZS Royalist, Second Commission, April 1957–July 1958*, Cathay Press, Hong Kong, n.d.

Hoe, A., & E. Morris, *Re-enter the SAS: The Special Air Service and the Malayan Emergency*, Leo Cooper, London, 1994.

Holman, D., *Noone of the Ulu*, Heinemann, London, 1958.

Holyoake, K., *A Defence Policy For New Zealand*, New Zealand Institute of International Affairs, Wellington, 1969.

Horner, D., *Phantoms of the Jungle: A History of the Australian Special Air Service*, Allen & Unwin, Sydney, 1989.

Horner, D. (ed.), *Duty First: The Royal Australian Regiment in Peace and War*, Allen & Unwin, Sydney, 1990.

Howard, G., *The Navy in New Zealand*, A. H. & A. W. Reed, Wellington, 1981.

Howard, G., & C. Wynn, *Portrait of the Royal New Zealand Navy*, Grantham House, Wellington, 1991.

Howlett, Lieutenant R. A., *The History of the Fiji Military Forces 1939–1945*, Crown Agents for the Colonies, London, 1948.

Hughes, J., *The End of Sukarno: A Coup that Misfired: A Purge that Ran Wild*, Angus & Robertson, London, 1968.

Jackson, D. G. M., *The Road to Malaysia*, Hawthorn Press, Melbourne, 1963.

Jackson, R., *The Malayan Emergency*, Routledge, London, 1991.

Jackson, General Sir William, *Withdrawal from Empire*, Batsford, London, 1986.

James, H., & D. Sheil-Small, *The Undeclared War: The Story of the Indonesian Confrontation 1962–1966*, Leo Cooper, London, 1971.

——*A Pride of Gurkhas: The 2nd King Edward VII's Own Goorkhas 1948–1971*, Leo Cooper, London, 1975.

Jones, H. P., *Indonesia: The Possible Dream*, Hoover Institute Press, New York, 1971.

Kennaway, R., *New Zealand Foreign Policy, 1951–1971*, Hicks Smith, Wellington, 1972.

Kirk, N., *New Zealand and its Neighbours*, New Zealand Institute of International Affairs, Wellington, 1971.

Kratoska, P. H., *The Japanese Occupation of Malaya 1941–1945*, Allen & Unwin, Sydney, 1998.

Laqueur, Walter, *Guerrilla: A Historical and Critical Study*, Weidenfeld & Nicolson, London, 1977.

Larkin, T. C. (ed.), *New Zealand's External Relations*, New Zealand Institute of Public Administration, Wellington, 1962.

Larson, C. R., *Pacific Commandos*, A. H. & A. W. Reed, Wellington, 1946.

Lau, Albert, *The Malayan Union Controversy 1942–1948*, Oxford University Press, Singapore, 1991.

Leary, J. D., *Violence and the Dream People: The Orang Asli in the Malayan Emergency 1948–1960*, Ohio University Center for International Studies, Athens, Ohio, 1995.

Lee, Air Chief Marshal Sir David, *Eastward: A History of the Royal Air Force in the Far East 1945–1972*, Ministry of Defence, Air Historical Branch (RAF), Her Majesty's Stationery Office, London, 1984.

Legge, J. D., *Sukarno: A Political Biography*, Allen & Unwin, Sydney, 1984.

Leifer, M., *Indonesia's Foreign Policy*, Royal Institute of International Affairs/Allen & Unwin, London, 1983.

Leong Chi Woh, *Scorpio: The Communist Eraser*, Lao Bai & Tang Publishing House, Taiwan, 1996.

Locke, E., *Peace People: A History of Peace Activities in New Zealand*, Hazard Press, Christchurch, 1992.

Lowe, D., *Menzies and the 'Great World Struggle': Australia's Cold War 1948–1954*, University of New South Wales Press, Sydney, 1999.

McGibbon, I., *New Zealand and the Korean War, Vol. 1: Politics and Diplomacy*, Oxford University Press, Auckland, 1992.

——*New Zealand and the Korean War, Vol. II: Combat Operations*, Oxford University Press, Auckland, 1996.

McGibbon, I. (ed.), *Undiplomatic Dialogue: Letters Between Carl Berendsen & Alister McIntosh 1943–1952*, Auckland University Press, Auckland, 1993.

——(ed.), *Unofficial Channels: Letters Between Alister McIntosh and Foss Shanahan, George Laking and Frank Corner, 1946–1966*, Victoria University Press, Wellington, 1999.

McIntosh, Sir Alister (ed.), *New Zealand in World Affairs*, Vol. 1, New Zealand Institute of International Affairs, Wellington, 1977.

McIntyre, W. David, *Britain, New Zealand and the Security of South-East Asia in the 1970s*, New Zealand Institute of International Affairs, Wellington, 1969.

——*The Significance of the Commonwealth, 1965–90*, Canterbury University Press, Christchurch, 1991.

——*Background to the Anzus Pact: Policy-making, Strategy and Diplomacy, 1945–55*, Macmillan, London/Canterbury University Press, Christchurch/St Martin's Press, New York, 1995.

McIntyre, W. David, & W. J. Gardner, *Speeches and Documents on New Zealand History*, Oxford University Press, London, 1971.

Mackay, D., *The Malayan Emergency 1948–1960: The Domino That Stood*, Brassey's, London, 1997.

Mackie, J. A. C., *Konfrontasi: The Indonesia–Malaysia Dispute 1963–1966*, Oxford University Press, Kuala Lumpur, 1974.

——*Low-level Military Incursions: Lessons of the Indonesia-Malaysia 'Confrontation' Episode, 1963–66*, Working Paper No. 105, Strategic and Defence Studies Centre, Australian National University, Canberra, 1986.

McKinnon, M., *Independence and Foreign Policy: New Zealand in the World Since 1935*, Auckland University Press, Auckland, 1993.

McKinnon, M. (ed.), *The American Connection*, Allen & Unwin/Port Nicholson Press, Wellington, 1988.

——(ed.), *New Zealand in World Affairs, Volume II: 1957–1972*, New Zealand Institute of International Affairs, Wellington, 1991.

McLane, C. B., *Soviet Strategies in Southeast Asia: An Exploration of Eastern Policy under Lenin and Stalin*, Princeton University Press, Princeton, 1966.

McLintock, A. H. (ed.), *An Encyclopaedia of New Zealand*, 3 vols, Government Printer, Wellington, 1966.

McNeill, I., *To Long Tan: The Australian Army and the Vietnam War 1950–1966*, Allen & Unwin in association with the Australian War Memorial, Sydney, 1993.

Marshall, Sir John, *Evolution and Foreign Policy: The Struggle for Existence*, New Zealand Institute of International Affairs, Wellington, 1975.

Masters, John, *Bugles and a Tiger*, Michael Joseph, London, 1956.

Miers, Richard, *Shoot to Kill*, Faber & Faber, London, 1959.

Millen, J., *Survey of Commonwealth Affairs: Problems of Expansion and Attrition 1953–1969*, Royal Institute of International Affairs/Oxford University Press, London, 1974.

——*Salute to Service: A History of the Royal New Zealand Corps of Transport and its Predecessors 1860–1996*, Victoria University Press, Wellington, 1997.

Miller, J. D. B., *The Commonwealth in the World*, Gerald Duckworth, London, 1965.

——*Britain and the Old Dominions*, Chatto & Windus, London, 1966.

Mockaitis, T. R., *British Counterinsurgency, 1919–1960*, Macmillan in association with King's College, London, 1990.

——*British Counterinsurgency in the Post-imperial Era*, Manchester University Press, Manchester, 1995.

Moore, J. E. (ed.), *Jane's Fighting Ships 1976–77*, Jane's, London, 1977.

Moore, J. Hammond, *The American Alliance: Australia, New Zealand and the United States: 1940–1970*, Cassell, North Melbourne, 1970.

Moran, J. W. G., *Spearhead in Malaya*, Peter Davies, London, 1959.

——*The Camp Across the River*, Peter Davies, London, 1961.

Nasution, A. H., *Fundamentals of Guerilla Warfare*, Indonesian Army Information Service, Jakarta, 1953.

New Zealand Institute of International Affairs, *New Zealand Foreign Policy with Special Reference to Southeast Asia*, Wellington, 1968.

——*The Commonwealth: Its Past, Present and Future*, Wellington, 1972.

——*New Zealand Foreign Policy: Occasional Papers 1973–74*, Wellington, 1975.

Noone, R., *Rape of the Dream People*, Hutchinson, London, 1972.

O'Keefe, B., *Medicine at War: Medical Aspects of Australia's Involvement in Southeast Asian Conflicts 1952–1972*, Allen & Unwin in association with the Australian War Memorial, Sydney, 1994.

O'Neill, R., *Australia in the Korean War 1950–1953*, Vols 1 & 2, Australian War Memorial/Australian Government Publishing Service, Canberra, 1981 & 1985.

Ongkili, J. P., *Nation-building in Malaysia 1964–1974*, Oxford University Press, Singapore .

——*The Borneo Response to Malaysia 1961–1963*, Donald Moore Press, Singapore, 1967.

Onn, C. K., *Ma-Rai-Ee*, Australasian Publishing Company, Sydney, 1952.

——*Malaya Upside Down*, Federal, Kuala Lumpur, 1977.

Ovendale, R., *The English-speaking Alliance: Britain, the United States, the Dominions and the Cold War 1945–1951*, George Allen & Unwin, London, 1985.

——*British Defence Policy Since 1945*, Manchester University Press, Manchester, 1994.

Page, M., *KAR: A History of the King's African Rifles*, Leo Cooper, London, 1998.

Pearson, M., *Paper Tiger: New Zealand's Part in SEATO 1954–1977*, New Zealand Institute of International Affairs, Wellington, 1989.

Peterson, A. H., G. C. Reinhardt & E. E. Conger (eds), *Symposium on the Role of Airpower in Counterinsurgency and Unconventional Warfare: The Malayan Emergency*, RAND Corporation, Santa Monica, 1963.

Pocock, T., *Fighting General: The Public and Private Campaigns of General Sir Walter Walker*, Collins, London, 1973.

Polomka, P., *Indonesia since Sukarno*, Penguin, Ringwood, Victoria, 1971.

Postgate, M. R., *Operation Firedog: Air Support in the Malayan Emergency 1948–1960*, HMSO, London, 1992.

Pugsley, C., *Te Hokowhitu A Tu: The New Zealand Maori Pioneer Battalion in the First World War*, Reed, Auckland, 1995.

——*Gallipoli: The New Zealand Story*, Reed, Auckland, 1998 edn.

Pugsley, C., L. Barber, B. Mikaere, N. Prickett & R. Young, *Scars on the Heart: Two Centuries of New Zealand at War*, David Bateman, Auckland, 1996.

Purcell, V., *The Chinese in Malaya*, Oxford University Press, London, 1948.

——*The Chinese in Modern Malaya*, Donald Moore, Singapore, 1960.

Pye, L. W., *Lessons from the Malayan Struggle Against Communism*, Center for International Studies, Massachusetts Institute of Technology, Cambridge, Mass., 1957.

Rees, G. W., *Anglo-American Approaches to Alliance Security, 1955–60*, Macmillan Press in association with the Mountbatten Centre for International Studies, University of Southampton, Southampton, 1996.

Reese, T. R., *Australia, New Zealand and the United States 1941–1968*, Oxford University Press, London, 1968.

Rennie, F., *Regular Soldier*, Endeavour Press, Auckland, 1990.

Robinson, A., *Australia and New Zealand: The Search for New Security Policies*, New Zealand Institute of International Affairs, Wellington, 1970.

Robinson, J. B. Perry, *Transformation in Malaya*, Secker & Warburg, London, 1956.

Rolfe, J., *New Zealand's Security: Alliances and Other Military Relationships*, CSS Working Paper 10/97, Centre for Strategic Studies, Wellington, 1997.

——*The Armed Forces of New Zealand*, Allen & Unwin, Sydney, 1999.

Rowling, W. E., *New Zealand in an Interdependent World*, New Zealand Institute of International Affairs, Wellington, 1975.

Ryan, N. J., *The Making of Modern Malaysia: A History from Earliest Times to 1966*, Oxford University Press, Kuala Lumpur, 1967.

Sanderson, Richard, *Looking for a Needle*, Vantage Press, New York, 1994.

Seymour, W., *British Special Forces*, Sidgwick & Jackson, London, 1985.

Shaplin, R., *Time out of Hand: Revolution and Reaction in Southeast Asia*, Andre Deutsch, London, 1969.

Short, A., *The Communist Insurrection in Malaya*, Frederick Muller, London, 1975.

Siaw, L. K. L., *Chinese Society in Rural Malaysia*, Institute of Southeast Asian Studies/ Oxford University Press, Kuala Lumpur, 1983.

Sinclair, K., *Walter Nash*, Auckland University Press/Oxford University Press, Auckland, 1976.

——*A Destiny Apart: New Zealand's Search for National Identity*, Allen & Unwin, Wellington, 1986.

Slimming, J., *Temiar Jungle*, Travel Book Club, London, 1958.

Smith, E. D., *Counter Insurgency Operations: 1. Malaya and Borneo*, Ian Allen, London, 1985.

——*Wars Bring Scars*, R. J. Leach & Co., Ditton, 1993.

Smith, T. E., *The Background to Malaysia*, Oxford University Press, Oxford, 1963.

Stacey, T., *The Hostile Sun: A Malayan Journey*, Gerald Duckworth, London, 1953.

Stenson, M., *New Zealand and the Malay World*, New Zealand Institute of International Affairs, Wellington, 1970.

Stenson, M. R., *Industrial Conflict in Malaya: Prelude to the Communist Revolt of 1948*, Oxford University Press, London, 1970.

——*Stability or Social Justice in Southeast Asia: Alternatives for New Zealand*, New Zealand Institute of International Affairs, Wellington, 1974.

Stubbs, R., *Hearts and Minds in Guerrilla Warfare: The Malayan Emergency 1948–1960*, Oxford University Press, New York, 1989.

Study Group, *New Zealand Foreign Policy with Special Reference to Southeast Asia*, New Zealand Institute of International Affairs, Wellington, 1968.

Sutherland, R., *Antiguerrilla Intelligence in Malaya 1948–1960*, RAND Corporation, Santa Monica, 1964.

——*Army Operations in Malaya, 1947–1960*, RAND Corporation, Santa Monica, 1964.

——*Organizing Counterinsurgency in Malaya 1947–1960*, RAND Corporation, Santa Monica, 1964.
——*Winning the Hearts and Minds of the People: Malaya, 1948–1960*, RAND Corporation, Santa Monica, 1964.
Tan, T. K., *Sukarno's Guided Indonesia*, Jacaranda Press, Brisbane, 1967.
Tarling, N., *Southeast Asia: Past and Present*, F. W. Cheshire, Melbourne, 1966.
——*Britain, Southeast Asia and the Onset of the Cold War 1945–1950*, Cambridge University Press, Cambridge, 1998.
Templeton, M., *Ties of Blood and Empire: New Zealand's Involvement in Middle East Defence and the Suez Crisis, 1947–57*, Auckland University Press, Auckland, 1994.
Thakur, Ramesh, *In Defence of New Zealand: Foreign Policy Choices in the Nuclear Age*, Westview Press, Boulder/London, 1986.
Thomas, M., & C. Lord, *New Zealand Army Distinguishing Patches 1911–1991*, self-published, Wellington, 1995.
Thompson, Sir Robert, *Defeating Communist Insurgency*, Chatto & Windus, London, 1966.
——*No Exit from Vietnam*, D. McKay, New York, 1970.
——*Revolutionary War in World Strategy 1945–1969*, Taplinger, New York, 1970.
——*Peace is Not at Hand*, Chatto & Windus, London, 1974.
Thompson, Sir Robert (ed.), *War in Peace: An Analysis of Warfare Since 1945*, Orbis, London, 1981.
Trotter, A., *New Zealand and Japan 1945–1952: The Occupation and the Peace Treaty*, Athlone Press, London, 1990.
Turnbull, C. M., *A History of Malaysia, Singapore and Brunei*, Allen & Unwin, Sydney, 1989.
Watt, A., *The Evolution of Australian Foreign Policy 1938–1965*, Cambridge University Press, London, 1967.
Williams-Hunt, P. D. R., *An Introduction to the Malayan Aborigines*, Government Press, Kuala Lumpur, 1952.
Wood, G. A. (ed.), *Ministers and Members in the New Zealand Parliament*, Tarkwode Press, Dunedin, 1987.
Wright, M., *Kiwi Air Power: The History of the RNZAF*, Reed, Auckland, 1998.
Wyn, Humphrey, *Forged in War: A History of the Royal Air Force Transport Command 1943–1967*, Stationery Office, London, 1996.
Young, T.-D., *Australian, New Zealand, and the United States Security Relations, 1951–1986*, Westview Press, Boulder, 1992.

## Articles and chapters

Anderson, W. F., 'Engineers in the Emergency in Malaya, 1954/56', *Royal Engineers Journal*, 1956, pp. 330–42.

Archer, T. R. C., 'Medical Problems of the Operational Infantry Soldier in Malaya', *Journal of the Royal Army Medical Corps*, vol. 104, no. 1, January 1958, pp. 1–13.

Bainbridge, P. de L., 'Air Despatch Operations in the Far East', *Royal Corps of Transport Review*, April 1967, pp. 9–22.

Banyard, P. J., 'With Silence and Stealth: British Tactics During Confrontation', *War in Peace*, no. 41, n.d., pp. 818–19.

Barclay, G. St J., 'In the Sticky Fly Paper: The United States, Australia and Indonesia, 1959–1964', *Naval War College Review*, vol. 34, no. 4, July/August 1981, pp. 67–80.

Bluett, D., 'Medical Arrangements in Malaya During the Emergency 1948–49', *Journal of the Royal Army Medical Corps*, 1950, pp. 14–27.

B. N. R., 'The Campaign in Malaya: Tactics of Jungle Fighting', *The World Today*, 1949, pp. 477–86.

Bramell, E. N. W., 'Reflections on Borneo', *The Infantryman*, no. 83, November 1967, pp. 13–24.

Brown, Lt.-Col. H. P., & Major A. W. Blackmore, 'Road Transport Operations in Borneo', *Review of the RCT*, 1966, pp. 32–8.

Brown, V. B., 'Helicopter Rescue Work in Malaya', *New Zealand Army Journal*, vol. 1, no. 2, 1 August 1954, pp. 34–8.

Buszynski, L., 'SEATO: Why It Survived Until 1977 and Why It Was Abolished', *Journal of Southeast Asian Studies*, vol. 12, no. 2, September 1981, pp. 287–96.

Carver, J. H., 'Field Engineering with Gurkha Sappers in Malaya', *Royal Engineers Journal*, 1956, pp. 246–54.

Catley, R., 'Malaysia: The Lost Battle for Merger', *Australian Outlook*, vol. 21, no. 1, April 1967.

Clark, K. H., 'Some Account of an Operation in the Malayan Jungle', *Journal of the Royal Army Medical Corps*, 1950, pp. 307–15.

Clark, M. W., 'Indonesian "Confrontation" Operations of a Malaysian Brigade July–October 1964', *Journal of the Royal Electrical and Mechanical Engineers*, vol. 8, no. 1, February 1965, pp. 67–74.

Clifton, G. H., 'The Army of New Zealand', *New Zealand Junior Encyclopaedia*, Ruskin Group, Wellington, 1963, pp. 876–91.

Clutterbuck, R. L., 'The SEP: Guerrilla Intelligence Source', *Military Review*, October 1962, pp. 13–21.

——'Communist Defeat in Malaya', *Journal of the Royal Artillery*, March 1964, pp. 55–66.

Collins, Lt.-Col. P. E., 'The Front Was Everywhere', *Royal United Services Institute Journal*, May 1962, pp. 143–9.

Craw, J. P., 'Indonesian Military Incursions into West Malaysia and Singapore between August 1964 and 30th September 1965', *Royal United Services Institute Journal*, May 1966, pp. 203–19.

Crawford, J., '"A Political H-Bomb": New Zealand and the British Thermonuclear Weapon Tests of 1957–1958', *Journal of Imperial and Commonwealth History*, vol. 26, no. 1, January 1998, pp. 127–50.

Danaher, S. J., 'Brunei Revolt: The Australian Involvement', *Sabretache*, vol. 32, no. 2, April/June 1991, pp. 30–5.

Dougherty, J. E., 'The Guerrilla War in Malaya', *US Naval Institute Proceedings*, September 1958, pp. 41–9.

Dunlop, R., 'Antipodean Uglies of the East', *Wings*, October 1977, pp. 9–13.

Eley, D. L., 'Helicopters in Malaysia', *Royal Air Force Quarterly*, 1966, pp. 5–10.

Ferry, Major J. P., 'Full Employment: Eight Weeks as a Battery Commander in Sarawak', *Journal of the Royal Artillery*, 1965, pp. 21–9.

Fillingham, Lt.-Col. J. A. I., 'Operations in Sarawak', *British Army Review*, 1965, pp. 13–19.

Ford, P. W., 'Operation White Christmas', *The Oak Tree: The Cheshire Regiment*, 1957, pp. 197–209.

Forster, M. O., 'A Long-range Jungle Operation in Malaya: 1951', *Journal of the Royal Army Medical Corps*, 1951, pp. 328–39.

Foxley-Norris, C. N., 'Air Aspects of Operations against "Confrontation"', *Brassey's Annual*, 1967, pp. 281–91.

Garland, R. S., 'Operations in Malaya', *Australian Army Journal*, 1959, pp. 25–31.

'Gisborne', 'Naval Operations in the Malacca and Singapore Straits 1964–1966', *Naval Review*, vol. 55, no. 1, January 1967.

Godfrey, F. A., 'Brunei in Revolt', *War in Peace*, no. 41, n.d., pp. 809–12.

Grey, J., 'Confrontation: Then and Now', *Sydney Papers*, vol. 8, no. 3, Winter 1996, pp. 113–20.

Hadfield, J., & A. J. Heber, 'Experiences in a Field Surgical Team Working in Pahang State, Malaya (January–July 1950)', *Journal of the Royal Army Medical Corps*, vol. 96, no. 6, June 1951, pp. 339–44.

Harvey, A. S., 'Random Reflections of an Infantry Battalion Commander on the Indonesian Border', *The Infantryman*, no. 81, November 1965, pp. 47–51.

Heelis, B. D., 'REME in Borneo 1965–1966', *Journal of the REME*, 1967, pp. 64–9.

Heelis, J. E., 'Operations of a Gurkha Battalion in Borneo', *The Infantryman*, no. 79, October 1963, pp. 53–6.

Holworthy, R., 'Keeping the Borneo Peace: 1964', *The Infantryman*, no. 80, October 1964, pp. 24–31.

Horner, D. M., 'The Australian Army and Indonesia's Confrontation with Malaysia', *Australian Outlook*, vol. 43, no. 1, April 1989, pp. 61–76.

Jackson, Keith, '"Because it's there…": A Consideration of the Decision to Commit New Zealand Troops to Malaysia beyond 1971', *Journal of Southeast Asian Studies*, vol. 2, March 1971, pp. 22–31.

'Jungle Patrol: 2nd Battalion The Parachute Regiment in Borneo', *The Infantryman*, no. 81, November 1965, pp. 73–5.

Lee, D., 'Australia and Allied Strategy in the Far East, 1952–1957', *Journal of Strategic Studies*, vol. 16, no. 4, December 1993, pp. 511–38.

——'The Origins of Menzies Government's Policy on Indonesia's Confrontation of Malaysia', in F. Cain (ed.), *Menzies in War and Peace*, Allen & Unwin in association with the Australian Defence Studies Centre, Sydney, 1997, ch. 5.

Lyons, R., 'Borneo Reflections', *Journal of the Royal Artillery*, vol. 93, no. 2, September 1966, pp. 105–13.

McDougall, D., 'The Evolution of Australia's Defence Policy in Relation to Malaysia-Singapore, 1964–1971', *Journal of Southeast Asian Studies*, vol. 3, no. 1, March 1972, pp. 97–110.

——'The Wilson Government and the British Defence Commitment in Malaysia–Singapore', *Journal of Southeast Asian Studies*, vol. 4, no. 2, September 1973, pp. 229–40.

——'The Malayan Emergency and Confrontation', in C. Bridge (ed.), *Munich to Vietnam: Australia's Relations with Britain and the United States since the 1930s*, Melbourne University Press, Melbourne, 1991, ch. 8.

MacFarling, I., 'New Zealand and the Vietnam Conflict', *Australian Defence Force Journal*, no. 79, November/December 1989, pp. 8–19.

McKinnon, M., '"Equality of Sacrifice": Anglo-New Zealand Relations and the War Economy, 1939–1945', *Journal of Imperial and Commonwealth History*, vol. 12, no. 3, May 1984.

McLean, D., 'New Zealand's Future Defence Role in Southeast Asia', in T. Wesley-Smith (ed.), *New Zealand and its Southeast Asian Neighbours*, New Zealand Institute of International Affairs, Wellington, 1980, pp. 28–33.

McLean, David, 'Anzus Origins: A Reassessment', *Australian Historical Studies*, vol. 24, no. 94, April 1990, pp. 64–82.

Maconochie, C., 'A National Serviceman in Malaya', *Army Quarterly*, vol. 63, no. 1, October 1951, pp. 43–9.

Man, P. H., 'Operation "Nassau"', *Royal Hampshire Regiment Journal*, November 1955, pp. 165–8.

Moulton, J. L., 'The Indonesian Confrontation', *USNI Naval Review*, 1969, pp. 144–71.

Mullins, R. M., 'New Zealand's Defence Policy', *New Zealand Foreign Affairs Review*, vol. 22, no. 7, July 1972.

Odling, W., 'A Problem in Logistics', *Royal United Services Institute Journal*, July 1972, pp. 63–6.

Oey Hong Lee, 'Sukarno and the Pseudo-Coup of 1965: Ten Years Later', *Journal of Southeast Asian Studies*, vol. 7, no. 1, March 1976, pp. 119–35.

Officers, S. T. Directorate, GHQ, FARELF, 'R. A. S. C. Water Transport in the Borneo Operations', *Royal Army Service Corps Review*, 1965, pp. 18–22.

Properjohn, T. J., 'The Attitude of the Indonesian Army to Indonesia's Three Overseas Campaigns', *Defence Force Journal*, no. 48, September/October 1984, pp. 23–35.

Pugsley, C., 'Your Target: Jakarta', *New Zealand Defence Quarterly*, no. 14, Spring 1996, pp. 12–14.

Queen's Royal Irish Hussars, *The Crossbelts: The Journal of the Queen's Royal Irish Hussars, Borneo Supplement*, 1963, pp. 259–74.

Quinn, D., 'Artillery Operations in Borneo', *Army Journal*, no. 243, August 1969, pp. 3–6.

'REME in the Field: Malaya', *REME Magazine*, November 1958, pp. 280–2.

Renick, R. D., Jnr, 'The Emergency Regulations of Malaya: Causes and Effect', *Journal of Southeast Asian History*, vol. 6, no. 2, September 1965, pp. 1–39.

Rickets, R. A. S., 'Borneo 1966', *Royal Engineers Journal*, 1967, pp. 132–63.

Riggall, J. S., 'RCT Light Aircraft Operations in Borneo', *Royal Corps of Transport Review*, 1966, pp. 8–19.

Ritchie, G. N., 'Airstrip Construction in Borneo 1963–66', *Royal Engineers Journal*, 1966, pp. 216–29.

Ritchie, G. N., & D. H. Bowen, 'The Gurkha Engineers in Borneo 1962 to 1964', *Royal Engineers Journal*, 1966, pp. 138–44.

Roberts, C. M. A. R., 'Operations in Borneo', *British Army Review*, 1964, pp. 27–30.

Royal United Services Institute of New South Wales, 'Proceedings of Seminar "Konfrontasi", 12 April 1994', *United Service*, vol. 48, no. 1, Summer 1994.

Sandhu, K. S., 'The Saga of the Malayan Squatter', *Journal of Southeast Asian History*, vol. 5, no. 1, March 1964, pp. 143–77.

Scott, R. W., & R. B. Stalbow, 'The Health of the Guards Brigade in Malaya', *Journal of the Royal Army Medical Corps*, 1950, pp. 196–9.

Slater, K. R. C., 'Air Operations in Malaya', *Royal United Services Institute Journal*, 1958, pp. 379–87.

Smith, E. D., 'The Confrontation in Borneo, Part I', *Army Quarterly*, October 1975, pp. 479–83.

——'The Confrontation in Borneo, Part II', *Army Quarterly*, January 1976, pp. 30–6.

——'The Undeclared War: Indonesian Confrontation with Malaysia', *War in Peace*, no. 41, n.d., pp. 813–15.

Sodhy, Pamela, 'Malaysian–American Relations during Indonesia's Confrontation against Malaysia, 1963–66', *Journal of Southeast Asian Studies*, vol. 19, no. 1, March 1988, pp. 111–36.

Stewart-Cox, A. G. E., '"Operation Tiger" Conducted by 99 Gurkha Infantry Bde in South Johore 1958', *British Army Review*, no. 9, September 1959, pp. 31–9.

Stockwell, A. J., 'British Imperial Policy and Decolonization in Malaya, 1942–1952', *Journal of Imperial and Commonwealth History*, October 1984, pp. 68–87.

——'A Widespread and Long-concocted Plot to Overthrow Government in Malaya? The Origins of the Malayan Emergency', *Journal of Imperial and Commonwealth History*, vol. 21, no. 3, September 1993, pp. 66–88.

——'Malaysia: The Making of a Neo-Colony?', *Journal of Imperial and Commonwealth History*, vol. 26, no. 2, May 1998.

Streeton, A. B., 'On Active Service in Malaya, 1962', *Australian Army Journal*, no. 165, February 1963, pp. 10–20.

'Target: A Jungle Clearing', *Wings*, May 1950, pp. 5, 17.

Templeton, H., 'New Zealand and Southeast Asia', in T. Wesley-Smith (ed.), *New Zealand and its Southeast Asian Neighbours*, New Zealand Institute of International Affairs, Wellington, 1980, pp. 23–7.

Thakur, R., 'The Elusive Essence of Size: Australia, New Zealand, and Small States in International Relations', in R. Higgot & J. L. Richardson (eds), *International Relations: Global and Australian Perspectives on an Evolving Discipline*, Australian National University, Canberra, 1991.

Thompson, Captain A. L., 'Provost in Sarawak', *Royal Military Police Journal*, Third Quarter 1965, pp. 69–71.

Tilman, R. O., 'The Non-lessons of the Malayan Emergency', *Military Review*, December 1966, pp. 62–71.

van der Kroef, J. M., 'Communism and the Guerrilla War in Sarawak', *The World Today*, February 1964, pp. 50–60.

Walker, W., 'How Borneo was Won: The Untold Story of an Asian Victory', *The Round Table*, no. 233, January 1969, pp. 9–20.

Watt, A., 'The Australian Commitment to Malaysia', *World Review*, vol. 3, no. 2, July 1964, pp. 3–12.

Webb, P. H. F., 'Revolt in Brunei and the Formation of an Ad Hoc Joint Force Headquarters', *Journal of the Royal Signals Institution*, 1965, pp. 176–82.

Weller, J., 'British Weapons and Tactics in Malaysia', *Military Review*, November 1966, pp. 17–24.

Wheatley, P. R., 'Research on Missile Wounds: The Borneo Operations January 1963–June 1965', *Journal of the RAMC*, 1967, pp. 18–26.

'Whirlwinds Over Borneo', *Officer*, no. 16, Autumn 1965, pp. 18–22.

Woodard, G., 'Best Practice in Australia's Foreign Policy: "Konfrontasi" (1963–66)', *Australian Journal of Political Science*, March 1998, vol. 33, no. 1, pp. 85–100.

## Theses

Dee, M., 'The Applicability of ANZUS to Confrontation: An Australian View', MDS dissertation, University of New England, 1998.

——'Deniable or Undeniable: An Australian View of the Policy and Strategy of Cross-border Operations in North Borneo, 1963–1966', MDS dissertation, University of New England, 1999.

Filer, D. J., 'The New Zealand Armed Services: Their Development in Relationship to Defence Policy 1946–1972', MA thesis, University of Canterbury, 1972.

Jansen, M. M., 'The New Zealand Army in Malay(si)a and Singapore 1955–1967', MA thesis, University of Auckland, 1990.

## Radio

'"Evil Willie": The Story of a Soldier in Malaysia', Radio New Zealand, 27 April 1998.

## Film

All the following films were made by the National Film Unit and are held at Archives New Zealand, Wellington.

'14 Squadron for Cyprus', *Pictorial Parade*, no. 1, B&W, 35mm.
'A Ship Sails Home' [HMNZS *Otago*], Eastmancolour, 35mm, 17 mins.
'Air Force Day', *Pictorial Parade*, no. 33, B&W, 35mm.
'Air Force Day 1964', *Pictorial Parade*, no. 150, B&W, 35mm.
'Fiji Battalion Comes Home', Eastmancolour, 35mm, 22½ mins.
'Fijian Soldiers for Malaya', B&W, 35mm, 6½ mins.
'Final Parade', *Pictorial Parade*, no. 147, B&W, 35mm.
'High Commissioner Visits NZ Regiment', *Pictorial Parade*, no. 101, B&W, 35mm.
'HMNZS *Bellona*', *Pictorial Parade*, no. 4, B&W, 35mm.
'Jungle Patrol by SAS Squadron', *Pictorial Parade*, no. 54, B&W, 35mm.
'Kampong New Zealand', *Pictorial Parade*, no. 135, B&W, 35mm.
'Leave in Malaya', *Pictorial Parade*, no. 59, B&W, 35mm.
'Little Malaya', *Pictorial Parade*, no. 83, B&W, 35mm.
'Malaya Force', *Pictorial Parade*, no. 71, B&W, 35mm.
'Malayan Airlift', *Pictorial Parade*, no. 121, B&W, 35mm, 10½ mins.
'Naval Exercises', *Pictorial Parade*, no. 35, B&W, 35mm.
'Naval Force 75', B&W, 35mm, 10½ mins.
'New Cruiser' [HMNZS *Royalist*], *Pictorial Parade*, no. 53, B&W, 35mm.
'New Jets for Air Force' [Canberra Bombers], *Pictorial Parade*, no. 95, B&W, 35mm.
'New Zealand Paratroopers', *Pictorial Parade*, no. 131, B&W, 35mm.
'NZ Helps Malaya', *Pictorial Parade*, no. 103, B&W, 35mm.
'Regular Force Training', *Pictorial Parade*, no. 46, B&W, 35mm.
'RNZAF in Fiji', B&W, 35mm, 11 mins.
'*Royalist*'s Family Day', *Pictorial Parade*, no. 64, B&W, 35mm.
'Salute to the SAS', *Pictorial Parade*, no. 41, B&W, 35mm.
'SAS in Malaya', *Pictorial Parade*, no. 50, B&W, 35mm, 13½ mins.
'Sea-minded Airmen', *New Zealand Mirror*, no. 18, B&W, 35mm.
'SEATO Meets', *Pictorial Parade*, no. 87, B&W, 35mm.
'South-East Asia is our Neighbour', B&W, 35mm, 14 mins.
'The Eventful Years' [RNZAF], B&W, 35mm, 21 mins.
'The New Army', *Pictorial Parade*, no. 96, B&W, 35mm, 9 mins.
'Twenty-one Today' [RNZAF], *Pictorial Parade*, no. 74, B&W, 35mm.

# Index